THE DIRECTORY OF GRANT MAKING TRUSTS

FOCUS SERIES

Children and Youth

1ST EDITION

EDITOR
ELINOR DENMAN

© 1996 Charities Aid Foundation

Published by the
Charities Aid Foundation
Kings Hill
West Malling
Kent ME19 4TA

Telephone
+44 (0)1732 520000

Web address
http://www.charitynet.org

E-mail address
cafpubs@CAF.
charitynet.org

Database management
and typesetting
BPC Whitefriars Ltd

Design
Eugenie Dodd Typographics

Printed and bound
in Great Britain by
Bell & Bain Ltd, Glasgow

A catalogue record for this book is available from the British Library.

ISBN 1-85934-017-2

All rights reserved; no part of this work may be reproduced in any form, by mimeograph or any other means, without permission in writing from the publisher.

No responsibility for loss occasioned to any person acting or refraining from action as a result of the material in this publication can be accepted by the Charities Aid Foundation.

Contents

Introduction — v

About this directory — vi
Criteria for inclusion — vi
Structure and content — vii

How to use the directory — ix

INDEX A
Fields of interest — 3

INDEX B
Trusts by field of interest — 7

INDEX C
Trusts by beneficial area — 27

INDEX D
Alphabetical register of grant making charitable trusts — 39

Introduction

Grant making trusts are a major source of funding that is available to the voluntary sector in the UK and overseas. The figures published by CAF in the 1996 edition of *Dimensions of the Voluntary Sector* indicate that the top 500 trusts had an income of £865 million and made grants of £705 million.

Many of the major grant making trusts are household names. Others are less well known. Yet the vast majority, large and small, are open to funding applications for a wide range of projects and activities which reflect their charitable purposes.

CAF published the first edition of *The Directory of Grant Making Trusts* in 1968. Since that time the title has gained a pre-eminent reputation among grant seekers as the definitive guide to UK grant making trusts and their funding priorities. Today it is hard to imagine the difficulties which must have been encountered in trying to obtain funds from trusts before the directory threw a spotlight on to their existence and provided a mechanism by which fundraisers could identify the trusts most likely to be in sympathy with their needs.

Predictably, some trusts continue to be unhappy at the loss of their anonymity. Nor are established beneficiaries always eager to share information on a rich vein of financial support into which they have tapped for years and about which they may have come to feel distinctly proprietorial. Over a period of time, however, it has become accepted that the directory provides a significant bridge between grant makers and grant seekers and has helped to make the workload of both types of organisation less onerous.

The Directory of Grant Making Trusts Focus Series has been developed in reponse to demand from our readers. Many have expressed the view that while the main edition of the directory is extremely useful to larger organisations and reference libraries, smaller local bodies with a specialist interest could benefit from a publication containing a shorter, more focused selection of trusts.

Consequently, it is hoped that this book will provide grant seekers working in the field of children and youth with clear and accurate information on the trusts most likely to be interested in funding their work.

Unlike the main directory the *Focus Series* includes data on sample grants made by trusts. This section has been introduced in order to give fundraisers an indication of how closely a trust's grant making activities relate to its funding priorities.

About this directory

Criteria for inclusion

The details of trusts registered under the law of England and Wales which appear in this directory are recorded on the public register at the Charity Commission and are consequently available for publication. As there is no register open to the public in Scotland, the publishers have relied on direct contact with the Scottish trusts listed in order to obtain the latest information.

The trusts included in this book are largely those listed under the classification Children and Youth (220–234) in the 1995–96 edition of *The Directory of Grant Making Trusts*.

Prior to publication, every trust listed was asked to check the information appearing in its entry and to amend the text in such a way that it would reflect its grant making policy in the support of causes associated with children and young people. It should be noted that the trusts listed do not necessarily give exclusively to this area of charitable activity. In order to underline this point, certain trusts have chosen to retain information in their entry on other causes which are of interest to them.

In responding to our approach, some trusts indicated that they did not wish to be included in this publication. While the editor has reviewed each case individually, in general she has only excluded those trusts which:

a have been wound up;

b are not open to unsolicited applications in any circumstances;

c advised that they had been wrongly classified and/or had changed their policy since the publication of the 1995–96 edition of the directory and consequently did not fund causes supporting children and young people.

Where it has been judged, on the basis of the information available, that a speculative application could be successful, either currently or at some future date, trusts' details have been included.

The core data appearing in this book have either been checked by the trust concerned or verified at the Charity Commission within an established timeframe.

Structure and content

In order to enable grant seekers to identify as accurately as possible trusts which are likely to be sympathetic to their cause, this directory is driven by a series of indices.

INDEX A FIELDS OF INTEREST

This section lists the 15 fields of interest against which trusts supporting causes associated with children and youth have been asked to indicate their funding priorities.

INDEX B TRUSTS BY FIELD OF INTEREST

This index lists the names of all the trusts appearing in the directory against the fields of interest which they have indicated they might be willing to support. Where a trust has stated that it will consider grant applications for children and youth causes generally but has a specific interest in a particular area (eg youth organisations) then the trust will be listed under **Children and youth – general** as well as **Youth organisations (eg Guides, Scouts, YWCA etc)**. Where a trust has been included in the directory despite not responding to CAF's approach, its listing has been determined on the basis of information held at the Charity Commission.

INDEX C TRUSTS BY BENEFICIAL AREA

In this section trusts are listed under the geographical areas for which they have expressed a funding preference, as indicated under the heading **Beneficial area** in their entry in Index D. The geographical regions have been divided according to county council boundaries with the exception of large urban areas such as Birmingham, which we have listed separately. We have not included the titles of the new unitary authorities which, we are advised, are still in a state of transition. Those trusts which have not expressed a funding preference under the heading **Beneficial area** have not been included in this index. Where a trust has stated that it will consider grant applications from a large geographical area (eg the whole of the UK) but prefers to concentrate its work in a particular region or county (eg Cornwall) then the trust is listed under both headings (eg UK and Cornwall).

INDEX D ALPHABETICAL REGISTER OF GRANT MAKING CHARITABLE TRUSTS

This section contains the core data about the individual trusts held on the CAF database. Trusts are listed in alphabetical order. A complete entry should contain the fields which are listed overleaf; an explanation of the content of some of the fields is given in italics.

Trust name	
Objects	*The legal charitable purposes of the trust required for registration at the Charity Commission.*
Policy of Trustees	*The main and/or specialist areas of interest of the trust in more detail.*
Type of grant	*The style of expenditure the trust will support, eg recurrent, capital, running costs. Where possible, the average size of grants awarded is also indicated.*
Type of beneficiary	*The types of project or organisation most likely to succeed with an application.*
Restrictions	*The types of project/cause to which Trustees will not make grants.*
Beneficial area	*The geographical areas where the trust prefers to direct its funding.*
Sample grants	*Examples of recent grants made by the trust. Where possible, both the recipient and the amount are recorded.*
Finances	*The most up-to-date details of the trust's income, assets and grants made for which details are available.*
Trustees	
Submission of applications	*The trust's rules for the submission of funding requests and practice in responding to applications. Where guidelines are available, this is indicated.*
Correspondent	*The name and address of the person (or firm) to whom correspondence relating to the activities of the trust should be directed.*
Classification	*The fields of interest of the trust (see above).*
Charity Commission number	
Established	*The year of the trust's foundation.*

How to use the directory

This directory is designed to enable fundraisers to navigate their way round the information in four easy steps.

STEP 1

Turn to Index A. In order to identify the trusts most likely to respond favourably to a funding application you must decide which of the fields of interest corresponds most closely to the area of work for which you are seeking support.

STEP 2

Turn to Index B and find the list of trusts appearing under your selected field of interest. Also look at those trusts listed under **Children and youth – general**.

Where trusts have not themselves indicated that they are interested in funding charitable activity in the relevant field of interest, the publishers may have included them in the listing on the basis that their records at the Charity Commission suggest that they might be open to an application in the area of activity.

STEP 3

If your project is of benefit to a particular geographical area turn to Index C. Start by looking at those trusts listed under the area most local to your requirements (eg Kent) then, look at those trusts listed under the broader heading (eg South East England) finally look at those trusts listed under the broad heading UK. If your project is to be of benefit overseas then look at those trusts listed under this heading. Then check whether any of the trusts listed in Index B have a particular commitment to supporting activity in your chosen area.

STEP 4

Turn to Index D – the main register. The trusts in this index are listed in alphabetical order.

Look up the entries for the trusts identified via steps 2 and 3 and study their details carefully, paying particular attention to the policy of the trustees and the restrictions listed.

If you feel that there is a good match between your needs and the funding objectives of the trust identified, you could decide to make an application for support. However, you should avoid applying on the off-chance. Trusts are inundated with ill-directed appeals, and haphazard applications waste postage and time.

INDEX A

Fields of interest

This section lists the 15 fields of interest against which the trusts appearing in this directory have indicated their funding priorities.

Fields of interest
Children and youth – general
Adoption/fostering
Advancement in life
Adventure centres and playgrounds
Centres, clubs and institutes
Community groups
Day centres and nurseries
Development of character
Counselling (inc helplines)
Holidays
Homes and hostels
Special needs housing
Special classes
Youth organisations (eg Guides, Scouts, YWCA etc)
Children and violence (inc abuse)

INDEX B

Trusts by field of interest

This index lists all the trusts appearing in this directory under the fields of interest which they have indicated they might be willing to support.

Children

■ Children and youth – general

Keith & Freda Abraham Charitable Trust
Access 4 Trust
The John and Florence Adamson Charitable Trust
Green and Lilian F M Ainsworth and Family Benevolent Fund
The Alchemy Foundation
Alexandra Rose Day
Allied Dunbar Foundation
Sir John and Lady Amory's Charitable Trust
The Prince Andrew Charitable Trust
J C W Anstey Charitable Settlement
The Armstrong Trust
The Arnold Foundation
The Ashby Charitable Trust
The Ashcroft Charitable Trust
The Lord Ashdown Charitable Settlement
The Norman C Ashton Foundation
The Dorothy Askew Trust

The BBC Children in Need Appeal
BCH 1971 Charitable Trust
The Bacta Charitable Trust
The Nancy Balfour Trust
The Baring Foundation
The Barleycorn Trust
The Elaine Barratt Charitable Trust
The Paul Bassham Charitable Trust
The Batchworth Trust
The Philip Baxendale Charitable Trust
The Beaverbrook Foundation
The Heather Beckwith Charitable Settlement
The Sylvia Bell Charity
Benham Charitable Settlement
Rowan Bentall Charity Trust
Berkshire Community Trust
The Bewley Charitable Trust
The Bingham Trust
The Hubert Blake Charitable Trust
The Blanchminster Trust
The M Bourne Charitable Trust

C T Bowring (Charities Fund) Ltd
The Brand Trust
The Bridon Group Charitable Trust
Joseph Brough Charitable Trust
Peter Brough Trust
The Jack Brunton Charitable Trust
Buckets and Spades Charitable Trust
Buckingham Trust
Burges Salmon Charitable Trust
The Reg Burns Foundation
Lucilla Butler's Trust
The Buttle Trust

J & L A Cadbury Charitable Trust
Richard Cadbury Charitable Trust
William Adlington Cadbury Charitable Trust
The Edward & Dorothy Cadbury Trust (1928)
The Cadell-Samworth Foundation
CAF
The Campden Charities
The Cardy Beaver Foundation
The Carr-Ellison Charitable Trust
Sir John Cass's Foundation
The Challice Trust
Chapman Charitable Trust
Chapman Foundation
The Charterhouse Charitable Trust
The Chase Charity
Child Growth Foundation
The Chrimes Family Charitable Trust
Christabella Charitable Trust
Church Urban Fund
The City of London School Charitable Trust
City Parochial Foundation
J Anthony Clark Charitable Trust
Cleveland Community Foundation
The Clifford Charity Oxford
Lord Clinton's Charitable Trust
The Collier Charitable Trust
The Norman Collinson Charitable Trust
The Construction Industry Trust for Youth

Cooper Charitable Trust
Cooper Charitable Trust
J Reginald Corah Foundation Fund
The Cotton Trust
The Coulthurst Trust
The Augustine Courtauld Trust
The Coutts Charitable Trust
Cripplegate Foundation
Cripps Foundation
Crossfield Charitable Fund
The Wallace Curzon Charitable Trust
Cystic Fibrosis Trust

The DLM Charitable Trust
DM Charitable Trust
The Damont Charitable Trust
Baron Davenport's Charity Trust
The Sarah D'Avigdor Goldsmid Charitable Trust
Lily & Henry Davis Charitable Foundation
Wilfrid Bruce Davis Charitable Trust
The De Clermont Charitable Company Limited
Edmund De Rothschild Charitable Trust
The Leopold De Rothschild Charitable Trust
The Emma de Yong Charitable Trust
Nicholas De Yong's Charitable Trust 1984
The Delfont Foundation
Delmar Charitable Trust
The Denby Charitable Foundation
Denby Charitable Trust
J N Derbyshire Trust
The Duke of Devonshire's Charitable Trust
The Dibs Charitable Trust
Dinam Charity
Elsie Doidge Fund
The Dolphin Charitable Trust
The D'Oyly Carte Charitable Trust
Drapers' Charitable Fund
The Dulverton Trust

E D B Memorial Charitable Trust
The Earley Charity
Richard Early's Charitable Settlement

7

Children

Earwicker Trust
Sir John Eastwood Foundation
Ebenezer Trust
The Gilbert Edgar Trust
The Edinburgh Medical Missionary Society – Hawthornbrae Trust
E V Elias Charitable Settlement
The Maud Elkington Charitable Trust
The Ellbridge Trust
The John Ellerman Foundation
The Vernon N Ely Charitable Trust
Enkalon Foundation

The FR 1978 Charitable Trust
The Esmee Fairbairn Charitable Trust
Walter Farthing (Trust) Limited
The John Feeney Charitable Bequest
Ferguson Benevolent Fund Limited
The Fidelity UK Foundation
Fishmongers' Company's Charitable Trust
The Fitton Trust
The Ian Fleming Charitable Trust
Roy Fletcher Trust
Ford of Britain Trust
The Russell and Mary Foreman 1980 Charitable Trust
The Fortune Trust
The Gordon Fraser Charitable Trust
Joseph Strong Frazer Trust
A J Freeman Charitable Trust
Charles S French Charitable Trust
The Freshgate Trust Foundation
The Friends of the Clergy Corporation
Frognal Trust

Angela Gallagher Memorial Fund
The Gannochy Trust
J Paul Getty Jr General Charitable Trust
The Gibbins Trust
The G C Gibson Charitable Trust
The Simon Gibson Charitable Trust
The Hon Mr & Mrs Clive Gibson's Charity Trust

The Hon H M T Gibson's Charity Trust
The Hon P N Gibson's Charity Trust
The John Gilpin Trust
Glebe Charitable Trust
The Penelope Gluckstein Charitable Settlement
The Glyn Charitable Trust
The Isaac Goldberg Charity Trust
The Goldsmiths' Company's Charities
The S & F Goodman Trust
The Gough Charitable Trust
The Mrs D M Graham Charity
The Grand Metropolitan Charitable Trust
Grange Farm Centre Trust
J G Graves Charitable Trust
The Gordon Gray Trust
Greater Bristol Foundation
The Charles Green Foundation
The D W Greenwood Charitable Settlement
The Gresham Charitable Trust
Grocers' Charity
The Guardian Royal Exchange Charitable Trust
Gwynedd County Council Welsh Church Fund

Hampton Fuel Allotment Charity
Handicapped Children's Aid Committee
The Philip & Pauline Harris Charitable Trust
The Harris Charity
Haslemere Estates Charitable Trust
The Howard Hatton Charitable Trust
The Hawthorne Charitable Trust
Haymills Charitable Trust
The Hayward Foundation
Heath Charitable Trust
The Hedley Foundation
J R Henderson's Settlement
The Hertfordshire Community Trust
Joseph and Mary Hiley Trust
Lady Hind Trust
Mrs F E Hinton Charitable Trust
The Hobson Charitable Trust
The Dorothy Holmes Charitable Trust

The Homfray Trust
The Charity of Joseph Hopkins
The Horne Foundation
The Charles Hughesdon Foundation
The Patrick Mitchell Hunter Fund
David Hyman Charitable Trust

The International Nickel Donations Fund
The Inverforth Charitable Trust
Isle of Dogs Community Foundation

J and A Charitable Trust
The Yvette and Hermione Jacobson Charitable Trust
The James Trust
John Jarrold Trust Ltd
The Jenour Foundation
Jewish Child's Day
The Nicholas Joels Charitable Trust
The Joicey Trust
Edward Cecil Jones Settlement
The Anton Jurgens Charitable Trust

C M Keyser Charitable Trust
The Lorna King Charitable Trust
The King's Fund
Richard Kirkman Charitable Trust
Kleinwort Benson Charitable Trust
The Sir Cyril Kleinwort Charitable Settlement
Sir James Knott Trust
The Heinz & Anna Kroch Foundation

Beatrice Laing Trust
Laing's Charitable Trust
Lalonde Charitable Trust
Bryan Lancaster's Trust
The Lankelly Foundation
Laspen Trust
Kathleen Laurence's Trust
The Lavender Trust
The Leach Fourteenth Trust
The League of the Helping Hand
Joseph Levy Charitable Foundation
Lewis Family Charitable Trust
The Lewis Family Charitable Trust

Children

The John Spedan Lewis Foundation
The Fred Linford Charitable Trust
Lloyds Bank Charitable Trust
Lloyd's Charities Trust
London Law Trust
The London Taxi Drivers' Fund for Underprivileged Children
The Low & Bonar Charitable Fund
Lower Hall Charitable Trust
The Vanessa Lowndes Charitable Trust
The Lubricators Charitable Trust
The Luke Trust
John Lyon's Charity

The B V MacAndrew Trust
The E M MacAndrew Trust
Macfarlane Walker Trust
MacGregor's Bequest
The MacRobert Trusts
Man of the People Fund
The Manchester Guardian Society Charitable Trust
R W Mann Trustees Limited
The Margaret Foundation
The Erich Markus Charitable Foundation
The Sir George Martin Trust
The Catherine Martineau Charitable Trust
The Nancie Massey Charitable Trust
Matthews Wrightson Charity Trust
The Amela and Jack Maxwell Foundation
The Ivona Mays-Smith Charitable Trust
The James Frederick and Ethel Anne Measures Charity
Mercers' Charitable Foundation
The Metropolitan Hospital-Sunday Fund
Mickel Fund
Frederick Milburn Charitable Trust
Millfield House Foundation
The Millichope Foundation
The Peter Minet Trust
Victor Mishcon Trust
The Montagu Family Charitable Trust
The Peter Morrison Charitable Foundation

Mount 'A' Charitable Trust
Mount 'B' Charitable Trust

The Neighbourly Charitable Trust
New Court Charitable Trust
Newby Trust Ltd
Newcastle Children's Mission & Institute
The Newman Charitable Trust
Normanby Charitable Trust
Northcott Charitable Trust
The Northumberland Village Homes Trust
The Norton Foundation

William Older's School Charity
Oldham Foundation
K A Oppenheim Charitable Settlement
Ormiston Trust

The PDC Trust
PF Charitable Trust
PJD Charitable Trust
The Constance Paterson Charitable Foundation
Arthur James Paterson Charitable Trust
Pedmore Sporting Club Trust Fund
The Philip & Judith Petley Charitable Trust
The Phillips Family Charitable Trust
Pike Charity Settlement
Dr L H A Pilkington's Charitable Trust
The John Pitman Charitable Trust
The Sir Richard Carew Pole 1973 Charitable Trust
The Portrack Charitable Trust
The Primrose Trust
The Pye Christian Trust
The Pye Foundation
Pyke Charity Trust

Racal Charitable Trust
Radley Charitable Trust
ZVM Rangoonwala Foundation
The Eleanor Rathbone Charitable Trust
The Ravensdale Trust
The Rayne Foundation
The Rayne Trust
The Albert Reckitt Charitable Trust

The Rhondda Cynon Taff Welsh Church Acts Fund
Richmond Parish Lands Charity
The F A Riley-Smith Charitable Trust
The Rivendell Trust
The Cheshire Robbins Trust
Sir Edward Robinson Charitable Trust
Rokeby Charitable Trust
The Ross Charitable Trust
The Rothley Trust
The Rowan Charitable Trust
The Christopher Rowbotham Charitable Trust
J B Rubens Foundation
The Frank and Enid Rubens Highgate Trust

The Alan & Babette Sainsbury Charitable Fund
The Sainsbury Charitable Fund Ltd
St Hilda's Trust
Save & Prosper Educational Trust
Save & Prosper Foundation
Henry James Sayer Charity
The R H Scholes Charitable Trust
The Schuster Charitable Trust
The Scott Bader Commonwealth Ltd
The Scouloudi Foundation
Sears Foundation
The Securicor Charitable Trust
The Sheldon Trust
Colonel J D Sherwood Charitable Trust
Silvester Charitable Gift Trust
Singer Foundation
Skinners' Company Lady Neville Charity
The John Slater Foundation
Slater Trust Limited
The N Smith Charitable Settlement
E H Smith Charitable Trust
The Harold Smith Charitable Trust
Henry Smith (Estates Charities)
The Stanley Smith General Charitable Trust
The Albert & Florence Smith Memorial Trust
The Snowball Trust
The Sobell Foundation

Adoption/fostering

South Yorkshire Community Foundation
Southdown Trust
The Eric F Sparkes Charitable Trust
The Spencer Hart Charitable Trust
Sport Aid 88 Trust
Stanley Foundation Limited
The June Stevens Foundation
The Leonard Laity Stoate Charitable Trust
F C Stokes Trust
Eric Stonehouse Trust Ltd
The Samuel Storey Family Charitable Trust
David James Streeter Charitable Settlement
The Summerfield Charitable Trust
The Late Misses A N Summer's and I May's Charitable Settlement
Sir John Sumner's Trust Section 'A'
The Bernard Sunley Charitable Foundation
Adrienne & Leslie Sussman Charitable Trust
The Charles Sykes Trust
The Stella Symons Charitable Trust

TSB Foundation for England and Wales
A R Taylor Charitable Trust
The Margaret Thatcher Charitable Trust
Tollemache (Buckminster) Charitable Trust
The Torquay Charities
The Fred Towler Charity Trust
Mrs S H Troughton's Charity Trust
The Truemark Trust
Trust for London
The Sir Mark and Lady Turner Charitable Settlement
The Douglas Turner Charitable Trust
G J W Turner Trust
The 29th May 1961 Charity

The Vec Acorn Trust
Queen Victoria & Johnson Memorial Trust

The Charity of Thomas Wade & Others
The Princess of Wales' Charities Trust
Robert & Felicity Waley-Cohen Charitable Trust
The Francis Wallis Charitable Trust
John Watson's Trust
William Webster Charitable Trust
The Wedge
The Weinstock Fund
The James Weir Foundation
The Barbara Welby Trust
The Weldon UK Charitable Trust
Westminster Amalgamated Charity
Anne Duchess of Westminster's Charity
Garfield Weston Foundation
The Hon Mrs R G A Whetherly's Charitable Trust
Mr Frederick Wills 1961 Charitable Trust
Major Michael Thomas Wills 1961 Charitable Trust
P J H Wills 1962 Charitable Trust
The H D H Wills 1965 Charitable Trust
Wiltshire Community Foundation
The Harold Hyam Wingate Foundation
Mrs Wingfield's Charitable Trust
Hyman Winstone Foundation
The Wolfe Family's Charitable Trust
The Women Caring Trust
Woodlands Trust
The Woolmen's Company Charitable Trust
John William Wright Deceased Trust

The Yorkshire Bank Charitable Trust

■ Adoption/fostering

Access 4 Trust
The Adint Charitable Trust
Athlone Trust
The Rt Hon Herbert, Baron Austin of Longbridge Will Trust

C T Bowring (Charities Fund) Ltd
The Bridon Group Charitable Trust
The Buttle Trust

William Adlington Cadbury Charitable Trust
City Parochial Foundation
Lord Clinton's Charitable Trust

The De Clermont Charitable Company Limited
J N Derbyshire Trust

Sir John Eastwood Foundation
The John Ellerman Foundation

The Fitton Trust
Ford of Britain Trust

J Paul Getty Jr General Charitable Trust
The Gibbins Trust
The G C Gibson Charitable Trust
The Simon Gibson Charitable Trust
The Gunnell Charitable Trust

The Hayward Foundation
Homelands Charitable Trust

Edward Cecil Jones Settlement

The Allen Lane Foundation
The William Leech Charity
Lilley Benevolent Trust
Lloyd's Charities Trust
The Low & Bonar Charitable Fund
The Vanessa Lowndes Charitable Trust

Mercers' Charitable Foundation
The Peter Minet Trust

The Norman Family Charitable Trust
The Northumberland Village Homes Trust

The David Pickford Charitable Foundation

The Schuster Charitable Trust
The Leslie Smith Foundation
The Sobell Foundation
The Spencer Hart Charitable Trust

Trusts by field of interest

Advancement

TSB Foundation for Scotland
The Douglas Turner Charitable Trust
The 29th May 1961 Charity
Tyne & Wear Foundation
The Wates Foundation
The Weinstock Fund

■ Advancement in life

Access 4 Trust
The Alper Charitable Trust
Ambika Paul Foundation
The Dorothy Askew Trust
Lawrence Atwell's Charity (Skinner's Company)
The Percy Bilton Charity
The Herbert And Peter Blagrave Charitable Trust
C T Bowring (Charities Fund) Ltd
British Humane Association
The Edward & Dorothy Cadbury Trust (1928)
The Ellis Campbell Charitable Foundation
The Campden Charities
Sir John Cass's Foundation
The Chandaria Foundation
Charity Projects
The Chase Charity
Cherry Tree Foundation
City Parochial Foundation
Cleveland Community Foundation
The Clifford Charity Oxford
Lord Clinton's Charitable Trust
The Coutts Charitable Trust
Cripplegate Foundation
DM Charitable Trust
Dacorum Community Trust
The De Clermont Charitable Company Limited
De La Rue Charitable Trust
J N Derbyshire Trust
The Esmee Fairbairn Charitable Trust
The Fitton Trust
The Fleurus Trust
Friarsgate Trust
The Friends of the Clergy Corporation

The Gatsby Charitable Foundation
The Gibbins Trust
The Simon Gibson Charitable Trust
The Everard and Mina Goodman Charitable Foundation
The Grand Metropolitan Charitable Trust
Grocers' Charity
The Guardian Royal Exchange Charitable Trust
The Charles Hayward Trust
The Highland Children's Trust
The Edward Hornby Charitable Trust
Jewish Child's Day
Sheila Kay Fund
Laing's Charitable Trust
The Lawlor Foundation
The Lester Trust Fund
Joseph Levy Charitable Foundation
The John Spedan Lewis Foundation
The Lister Charitable Trust
Lloyd's Charities Trust
London Law Trust
The Low & Bonar Charitable Fund
The Mackintosh Foundation
R W Mann Trustees Limited
The Betty Martin Charity
The Material World Charitable Foundation Limited
The Robert McAlpine Foundation
The McKenna & Co Foundation
The Anthony and Elizabeth Mellows Charitable Settlement
The Mental Health Foundation
Frederick Milburn Charitable Trust
The Morgan Crucible Company Charitable Trust
The Munro Charitable Trust
The Norman Family Charitable Trust
The Northumberland Village Homes Trust
The Norton Foundation

William Older's School Charity
The John Phillimore Charitable Trust
The Pilgrim Trust
Racal Charitable Trust
The Rank Xerox Trust
Reeve's Foundation
The Harry James Riddleston Charity of Leicester
The Cheshire Robbins Trust
The Rowley Trust
St Katharine & Shadwell Trust
The Basil Samuel Charitable Trust
Peter Samuel Charitable Trust
Save & Prosper Educational Trust
The R H Scholes Charitable Trust
The Scouloudi Foundation
The Seedfield Trust
The Sheldon Trust
The Harold Smith Charitable Trust
The Leslie Smith Foundation
The Summerfield Charitable Trust
TSB Foundation for England and Wales
TSB Foundation for Scotland
Mrs S H Troughton's Charity Trust
The Douglas Turner Charitable Trust
The 29th May 1961 Charity
Tyne & Wear Foundation
Bernard Van Leer Foundation UK Trust
The Vec Acorn Trust
The Charity of Thomas Wade & Others
The Wakeham Trust
The Francis Wallis Charitable Trust
John Wates Charitable Trust
The Wates Foundation
John Watson's Trust
William Webster Charitable Trust
Sydney Dean Whitehead's Charitable Trust
Major Michael Thomas Wills 1961 Charitable Trust

Adventure

The Connolly Thomas Wilson Foundation

Young Explorers' Trust

■ Adventure centres and playgrounds

AGF Charitable Trust
Green and Lilian F M Ainsworth and Family Benevolent Fund
Alexandra Rose Day
The Ashcroft Charitable Trust
The Ian Askew Charitable Trust

The Barbour Trust
The Beaverbrook Foundation
Berkshire Community Trust
The Bewley Charitable Trust
The Herbert And Peter Blagrave Charitable Trust
C T Bowring (Charities Fund) Ltd
The Brand Trust
The J & M Britton Charitable Trust
The Charles Brotherton Trust
Joseph Brough Charitable Trust

William Adlington Cadbury Charitable Trust
The Edward & Dorothy Cadbury Trust (1928)
The Campden Charities
Sir John Cass's Foundation
Chapman Foundation
City Parochial Foundation
Cleveland Community Foundation
Lord Clinton's Charitable Trust
Cobb Charity
Cripplegate Foundation

The De Clermont Charitable Company Limited
J N Derbyshire Trust
The Duke of Devonshire's Charitable Trust

The Earley Charity
The Gilbert and Eileen Edgar Foundation
The Gilbert Edgar Trust
The Maud Elkington Charitable Trust
Elmgrant Trust
The Eveson Charitable Trust

The Esmee Fairbairn Charitable Trust
The Fitton Trust
The Joyce Fletcher Charitable Trust
Ford of Britain Trust
Charles Henry Foyle Trust
The Freshgate Trust Foundation
Frognal Trust

The General Charity Fund
The Gibbins Trust
The Simon Gibson Charitable Trust
The John Gilpin Trust
The Penelope Gluckstein Charitable Settlement
The Isaac Goldberg Charity Trust
The Good Neighbours Trust
Greater Bristol Foundation
Constance Green Foundation

Hampstead Wells and Campden Trust
The Charles Hayward Trust
The Charity of Joseph Hopkins
The Hornsey Parochial Charities
William Hunt's Trust

John Jarrold Trust Ltd
Jewish Child's Day
The Joicey Trust

Sir James Knott Trust

Laing's Charitable Trust
The Allen Lane Foundation
Laspen Trust
Lloyd's Charities Trust
The London Taxi Drivers' Fund for Underprivileged Children
The Lord's Taverners
The Low & Bonar Charitable Fund

Macdonald-Buchanan Charitable Trust
A N McKechnie Foundation
The James Frederick and Ethel Anne Measures Charity
The Violet Melchett Children's Trust
Mickel Fund
Middlesex County Rugby Football Union Memorial Fund
The Peter Minet Trust
The Moores Family Charity Foundation

The Needham Cooper Charitable Trust
Newby Trust Ltd
The Norman Family Charitable Trust
The Northumberland Village Homes Trust
The Norton Foundation

The Oakdale Trust
William Older's School Charity
Oldham Foundation

Pedmore Sporting Club Trust Fund
Carew Pole Charitable Trust
The Provincial Trust for Kendal

The Ravenscroft Foundation
The Rind Foundation

Peter Samuel Charitable Trust
Save & Prosper Educational Trust
The Francis C Scott Charitable Trust
The Frieda Scott Charitable Trust
The Scouloudi Foundation
The Securicor Charitable Trust
Bassil Shippam Trust
The Skelton Bounty
The Leslie Smith Foundation
The Sobell Foundation
The Summerfield Charitable Trust

TSB Foundation for Scotland
Mrs S H Troughton's Charity Trust
The Truemark Trust
The 29th May 1961 Charity
Tyne & Wear Foundation

The Charity of Thomas Wade & Others
The Wakeham Trust
Thomas Wall Trust
The Wates Foundation
John Watson's Trust
William Webster Charitable Trust
The Wedge
Major Michael Thomas Wills 1961 Charitable Trust
The Women Caring Trust
Woodlands Trust
The Woodward Charitable Trust

Trusts by field of interest

The Worshipful Company of Glass Sellers' Charity Trust

■ **Centres, clubs and institutes**

AGF Charitable Trust
The Adint Charitable Trust
Green and Lilian F M Ainsworth and Family Benevolent Fund
The Arts Council of Wales
The Ian Askew Charitable Trust
The Dorothy Askew Trust
The Astor Foundation
The Rt Hon Herbert, Baron Austin of Longbridge Will Trust

The Barbour Trust
The Sylvia Bell Charity
Berkshire Community Trust
The Bewley Charitable Trust
The Percy Bilton Charity
Isabel Blackman Foundation
The Herbert And Peter Blagrave Charitable Trust
The Boltons Trust
C T Bowring (Charities Fund) Ltd
The Bridon Group Charitable Trust
R E Brook Charitable Settlement
The Charles Brotherton Trust
Joseph Brough Charitable Trust
The J H Burn Charity Trust
The Burton Breweries Charitable Trust
Lucilla Butler's Trust

Edward Cadbury Charitable Trust
J & L A Cadbury Charitable Trust
William Adlington Cadbury Charitable Trust
The Edward & Dorothy Cadbury Trust (1928)
The Campden Charities
Carnegie Dunfermline Trust
The Carr-Ellison Charitable Trust
Sir John Cass's Foundation
Chapman Foundation
City Parochial Foundation
Clark Foundation II
The Thomas Edward Clarke Trust

Cleveland Community Foundation
The Clifford Charity Oxford
Lord Clinton's Charitable Trust
J Reginald Corah Foundation Fund
Sir Kenneth Cork Charitable Trust
The Augustine Courtauld Trust
The Coutts Charitable Trust
Cripplegate Foundation
The Violet & Milo Cripps Charitable Trust
Cripps Foundation
The Harry Crook Charitable Trust

Dacorum Community Trust
The Sir Peter Daniell Charitable Trust
The De Clermont Charitable Company Limited
The Leopold De Rothschild Charitable Trust
J N Derbyshire Trust
R M Douglas Charitable Trust
The Duveen Trust

The Earley Charity
Sir John Eastwood Foundation
The Gilbert and Eileen Edgar Foundation
The Maud Elkington Charitable Trust
Elmgrant Trust

The Esmee Fairbairn Charitable Trust
The A M Fenton Trust
Ferguson Benevolent Fund Limited
The Fitton Trust
The Joyce Fletcher Charitable Trust
Ford of Britain Trust
The Four Lanes Trust
Sydney E Franklin Deceased's New Second Charity
Charles S French Charitable Trust
The Freshgate Trust Foundation
Frognal Trust

The General Charity Fund
The Gibbins Trust
The G C Gibson Charitable Trust
The Simon Gibson Charitable Trust

The Hon H M T Gibson's Charity Trust
The Hon P N Gibson's Charity Trust
The John Gilpin Trust
The Good Neighbours Trust
Greater Bristol Foundation
Grocers' Charity
The Guardian Royal Exchange Charitable Trust

The Hadrian Trust
Hampstead Wells and Campden Trust
Haslemere Estates Charitable Trust
The Hawthorne Charitable Trust
Hedgcock Bequest
Lady Hind Trust
Homelands Charitable Trust
The Charity of Joseph Hopkins
The Horne Foundation
The Hornsey Parochial Charities
The Thomas Hudson Benevolent Trust
The Hull & East Riding Charitable Trust

J and A Charitable Trust
The Jarman Charitable Trust
John Jarrold Trust Ltd
Jewish Child's Day
The Joicey Trust
The Anton Jurgens Charitable Trust

The Nancy Kenyon Charitable Trust
Kleinwort Benson Charitable Trust
The Sir Cyril Kleinwort Charitable Settlement
Sir James Knott Trust

Laing's Charitable Trust
Langdale Trust
The Langtree Trust
Laspen Trust
The Lawlor Foundation
The Julian Layton Charity Trust
The William Leech Charity
Lord Leverhulme's Charitable Trust
Joseph Levy Charitable Foundation
Lloyd's Charities Trust
The London Taxi Drivers' Fund for Underprivileged Children

13

Community

Trusts by field of interest

The Low & Bonar Charitable Fund
The Vanessa Lowndes Charitable Trust
Macdonald-Buchanan Charitable Trust
MacGregor's Bequest
The Manchester Guardian Society Charitable Trust
R W Mann Trustees Limited
A N McKechnie Foundation
The James Frederick and Ethel Anne Measures Charity
Mickel Fund
Middlesex County Rugby Football Union Memorial Fund
Frederick Milburn Charitable Trust
The Millichope Foundation
The Peter Minet Trust
Victor Mishcon Trust
The Moores Family Charity Foundation
Mount 'A' Charitable Trust
Mount 'B' Charitable Trust
The Needham Cooper Charitable Trust
New Court Charitable Trust
Newcastle Children's Mission & Institute
The Educational Foundation of Alderman John Norman
The Norman Family Charitable Trust
The Northumberland Village Homes Trust
The Norton Foundation
Norwich Church of England Young Men's Society
The Oak Trust
Oldham Foundation
The Owen Family Trust
The PDC Trust
The Harry Payne Trust
Pedmore Sporting Club Trust Fund
Pettit Charitable Trust
Dr L H A Pilkington's Charitable Trust
S H and E C Priestman Trust
The Provincial Trust for Kendal
The Pye Foundation
Mr and Mrs J A Pye's No 1 Charitable Settlement

The Eleanor Rathbone Charitable Trust
The Ravenscroft Foundation
Roger Raymond Charitable Trust No 2
The Rayne Trust
The Ridgmount Foundation
The J C Robinson Trust No 3
Rosca Trust
The Rowan Charitable Trust
The Christopher Rowbotham Charitable Trust
St Katharine & Shadwell Trust
Peter Samuel Charitable Trust
Save & Prosper Educational Trust
The R H Scholes Charitable Trust
The Francis C Scott Charitable Trust
The Storrow Scott Charitable Will Trust
The Scouloudi Foundation
Sears Foundation
The Securicor Charitable Trust
Colonel J D Sherwood Charitable Trust
Bassil Shippam Trust
Singer Foundation
The Skelton Bounty
The N Smith Charitable Settlement
The Harold Smith Charitable Trust
The Albert & Florence Smith Memorial Trust
The Sobell Foundation
W F Southall Trust
The Eric F Sparkes Charitable Trust
Stanley Foundation Limited
The Star Foundation Trust
Sulgrave Charitable Trust
The Summerfield Charitable Trust
The Bernard Sunley Charitable Foundation
The Charles Sykes Trust
TSB Foundation for England and Wales
TSB Foundation for Scotland
A R Taylor Charitable Trust
Mrs S H Troughton's Charity Trust
The Truemark Trust

The Sir Mark and Lady Turner Charitable Settlement
The Douglas Turner Charitable Trust
The 29th May 1961 Charity
Tyne & Wear Foundation
The Vec Acorn Trust
The Charity of Thomas Wade & Others
The A F Wallace Charity Trust
The Francis Wallis Charitable Trust
The Ward Blenkinsop Trust
The Wates Foundation
John Watson's Trust
The Weavers' Company Benevolent Fund
William Webster Charitable Trust
The Weinstock Fund
The James Weir Foundation
Anne Duchess of Westminster's Charity
Whitaker Charitable Trust
Major Michael Thomas Wills 1961 Charitable Trust
The H D H Wills 1965 Charitable Trust
The Wolfe Family's Charitable Trust
Edwin Woodhouse Charitable Trust
Woodlands Trust
The Worshipful Company of Glass Sellers' Charity Trust

■ Community groups

The AHJ Charitable Trust
Abel Charitable Trust
Green and Lilian F M Ainsworth and Family Benevolent Fund
Allied Dunbar Staff Charity Fund
The Armstrong Trust
The Arts Council of Wales
The Barbour Trust
Berkshire Community Trust
The Bewley Charitable Trust
The Billmeir Charitable Trust
The Percy Bilton Charity
Isabel Blackman Foundation
C T Bowring (Charities Fund) Ltd

Trusts by field of interest

Community

- The J & M Britton Charitable Trust
- Joseph Brough Charitable Trust
- The Burton Breweries Charitable Trust
- J J & M Burton Charitable Trust

- Edward Cadbury Charitable Trust
- J & L A Cadbury Charitable Trust
- William Adlington Cadbury Charitable Trust
- The Edward & Dorothy Cadbury Trust (1928)
- The Campden Charities
- Chapman Foundation
- Charity Projects
- The Chase Charity
- The Chrimes Family Charitable Trust
- Church Urban Fund
- City Parochial Foundation
- Clark Foundation II
- Cleveland Community Foundation
- The Clifford Charity Oxford
- Cripplegate Foundation
- The Harry Crook Charitable Trust

- Dacorum Community Trust
- The De Clermont Charitable Company Limited
- J N Derbyshire Trust
- R M Douglas Charitable Trust
- The Duveen Trust

- The Earley Charity
- Sir John Eastwood Foundation
- The Gilbert and Eileen Edgar Foundation
- Elmgrant Trust

- The Esmee Fairbairn Charitable Trust
- The Joyce Fletcher Charitable Trust
- Ford of Britain Trust
- The Freshgate Trust Foundation
- The Patrick Frost Foundation

- The General Charity Fund
- J Paul Getty Jr General Charitable Trust
- The Gibbins Trust
- The Simon Gibson Charitable Trust

- The John Gilpin Trust
- Greater Bristol Foundation

- The Hadrian Trust
- Hampstead Wells and Campden Trust
- The Kenneth Hargreaves Trust
- R J Harris Charitable Settlement
- The Hayward Foundation
- The Hertfordshire Community Trust
- Gay & Peter Hartley's Hillards Charitable Trust
- The Charity of Joseph Hopkins
- The Hornsey Parochial Charities

- The Ireland Fund of Great Britain
- Isle of Dogs Community Foundation

- The James Trust
- John Jarrold Trust Ltd
- The Jenour Foundation
- Jewish Child's Day
- The Joicey Trust
- The Anton Jurgens Charitable Trust

- Beatrice Laing Trust
- Laing's Charitable Trust
- The Allen Lane Foundation
- The Lankelly Foundation
- The Lawlor Foundation
- The William Leech Charity
- Lord Leverhulme's Charitable Trust
- The London Taxi Drivers' Fund for Underprivileged Children

- The MacRobert Trusts
- R W Mann Trustees Limited
- The Leonard Matchan Fund Limited
- The Peter Minet Trust
- The Moores Family Charity Foundation
- The Morgan Crucible Company Charitable Trust
- Mount 'A' Charitable Trust

- The Educational Foundation of Alderman John Norman
- The Northumberland Village Homes Trust
- The Norton Foundation
- Norwich Church of England Young Men's Society

- The Oakdale Trust
- Oldham Foundation

- The Harry Payne Trust
- The Pye Foundation

- ZVM Rangoonwala Foundation
- Richmond Parish Lands Charity
- The J C Robinson Trust No 3

- The Sainsbury Charitable Fund Ltd
- St Hilda's Trust
- St Katharine & Shadwell Trust
- Peter Samuel Charitable Trust
- Save & Prosper Educational Trust
- Save & Prosper Foundation
- The Frieda Scott Charitable Trust
- Second Ferndale Trust
- The Sheldon Trust
- The Skelton Bounty
- The John Slater Foundation
- The Sobell Foundation
- South Yorkshire Community Foundation
- W F Southall Trust
- The Eric F Sparkes Charitable Trust
- The Leonard Laity Stoate Charitable Trust
- The Samuel Storey Family Charitable Trust
- The Summerfield Charitable Trust
- The Charles Sykes Trust

- TSB Foundation for England and Wales
- TSB Foundation for Scotland
- Tesco Charity Trust
- The Sir Mark and Lady Turner Charitable Settlement
- The Douglas Turner Charitable Trust
- The 29th May 1961 Charity
- Tyne & Wear Foundation

- Bernard Van Leer Foundation UK Trust
- The Vec Acorn Trust
- Queen Victoria & Johnson Memorial Trust

- The Charity of Thomas Wade & Others
- The Wakeham Trust
- The Francis Wallis Charitable Trust

Day centres

The Wates Foundation
William Webster Charitable Trust
The Wedge
The Weinstock Fund
Wiltshire Community Foundation
The Women Caring Trust

■ Day centres and nurseries

Green and Lilian F M Ainsworth and Family Benevolent Fund
Alexandra Rose Day
The Hon M L Astor's 1969 Charity
The Barbour Trust
Eleanor Barton Trust
Berkshire Community Trust
The Bewley Charitable Trust
The Oliver Borthwick Memorial Trust
C T Bowring (Charities Fund) Ltd
Joseph Brough Charitable Trust
William Adlington Cadbury Charitable Trust
The Edward & Dorothy Cadbury Trust (1928)
The Campden Charities
Church Urban Fund
City Parochial Foundation
Clark Foundation II
Cleveland Community Foundation
Lord Clinton's Charitable Trust
Cobb Charity
The Timothy Colman Charitable Trust
Cripplegate Foundation
J N Derbyshire Trust
The Earley Charity
The Joyce Fletcher Charitable Trust
Ford of Britain Trust
Charles Henry Foyle Trust
The Freshgate Trust Foundation
GNC Trust
The Gibbins Trust
The Simon Gibson Charitable Trust

The Hon H M T Gibson's Charity Trust
The Hon P N Gibson's Charity Trust
The Isaac Goldberg Charity Trust
The Hadrian Trust
Hampstead Wells and Campden Trust
Hedgcock Bequest
The Hertfordshire Community Trust
The Hoover Foundation
The Charity of Joseph Hopkins
Isle of Dogs Community Foundation
John James Bristol Foundation
The Jarman Charitable Trust
John Jarrold Trust Ltd
The Jenour Foundation
Jewish Child's Day
The Joicey Trust
The Anton Jurgens Charitable Trust
Sir James Knott Trust
The Allen Lane Foundation
Langdale Trust
The Langtree Trust
Laspen Trust
Lloyd's Charities Trust
The London Taxi Drivers' Fund for Underprivileged Children
The Low & Bonar Charitable Fund
The Vanessa Lowndes Charitable Trust
R W Mann Trustees Limited
The Violet Melchett Children's Trust
The Peter Minet Trust
The Moores Family Charity Foundation
Newby Trust Ltd
The Norman Family Charitable Trust
The Northumberland Village Homes Trust
The Norton Foundation
Norwich Church of England Young Men's Society
William Older's School Charity
Oldham Foundation

The Harry Payne Trust
The Ravenscroft Foundation
The J C Robinson Trust No 3
Save & Prosper Educational Trust
The Frieda Scott Charitable Trust
Sears Foundation
The Sylvia and Colin Shepherd Charitable Trust
The Skelton Bounty
The Sobell Foundation
The Leonard Laity Stoate Charitable Trust
The Summerfield Charitable Trust
TSB Foundation for England and Wales
TSB Foundation for Scotland
Mrs S H Troughton's Charity Trust
The Sir Mark and Lady Turner Charitable Settlement
The 29th May 1961 Charity
Tyne & Wear Foundation
The Charity of Thomas Wade & Others
The Weinstock Fund
The Women Caring Trust
The Yapp Education and Research Trust

■ Development of character

Ambika Paul Foundation
The Armstrong Trust
The Astor Foundation
The Hon M L Astor's 1969 Charity
The Rt Hon Herbert, Baron Austin of Longbridge Will Trust
The Barbour Trust
The Batchworth Trust
The Beaverbrook Foundation
The Gerald Bentall Charitable Trust
Berkshire Community Trust
The Bewley Charitable Trust
The Percy Bilton Charity
The Herbert And Peter Blagrave Charitable Trust
C T Bowring (Charities Fund) Ltd

Development

- The Bridon Group Charitable Trust
- R E Brook Charitable Settlement
- The Charles Brotherton Trust
- The Jack Brunton Charitable Trust
- J & L A Cadbury Charitable Trust
- William Adlington Cadbury Charitable Trust
- The Edward & Dorothy Cadbury Trust (1928)
- The Ellis Campbell Charitable Foundation
- The Campden Charities
- The Carr-Ellison Charitable Trust
- The Chase Charity
- The Chetwode Foundation
- The John & Celia Bonham Christie Charitable Trust
- City Parochial Foundation
- Cleveland Community Foundation
- The Clifford Charity Oxford
- Cobb Charity
- The Ernest Cook Trust
- J Reginald Corah Foundation Fund
- The Coutts Charitable Trust
- Crossfield Charitable Fund
- The De Clermont Charitable Company Limited
- De La Rue Charitable Trust
- The Leopold De Rothschild Charitable Trust
- Denby Charitable Trust
- J N Derbyshire Trust
- The Esmee Fairbairn Charitable Trust
- Ford of Britain Trust
- Jill Franklin Trust
- Charles S French Charitable Trust
- The Freshgate Trust Foundation
- The Friends of the Clergy Corporation
- Angela Gallagher Memorial Fund
- The Gatsby Charitable Foundation
- J Paul Getty Jr General Charitable Trust
- The Gibbins Trust
- The Simon Gibson Charitable Trust
- The Grand Metropolitan Charitable Trust
- Greater Bristol Foundation
- The D W Greenwood Charitable Settlement
- The Guardian Royal Exchange Charitable Trust
- The Hadrian Trust
- The Kenneth Hargreaves Trust
- The Philip & Pauline Harris Charitable Trust
- The Hayward Foundation
- The Charles Hayward Trust
- The Hertfordshire Community Trust
- The Edward Hornby Charitable Trust
- The Inverforth Charitable Trust
- John Jarrold Trust Ltd
- The Anton Jurgens Charitable Trust
- Sir James Knott Trust
- The Kirby Laing Foundation
- The Maurice Laing Foundation
- Laing's Charitable Trust
- The Lankelly Foundation
- Laspen Trust
- The Lawlor Foundation
- Raymond and Blanche Lawson Charitable Trust
- The John Spedan Lewis Foundation
- The Lister Charitable Trust
- Lloyd's Charities Trust
- London Law Trust
- The London Taxi Drivers' Fund for Underprivileged Children
- The Low & Bonar Charitable Fund
- The Vanessa Lowndes Charitable Trust
- Macdonald-Buchanan Charitable Trust
- The Mackintosh Foundation
- Macpherson Memorial Trust
- R W Mann Trustees Limited
- The Sir George Martin Trust
- Matthews Wrightson Charity Trust
- The Millichope Foundation
- The Moores Family Charity Foundation
- The Morgan Crucible Company Charitable Trust
- The Munro Charitable Trust
- New Court Charitable Trust
- The Educational Foundation of Alderman John Norman
- The Norman Family Charitable Trust
- The Northumberland Village Homes Trust
- The Norton Foundation
- Oldham Foundation
- The PDC Trust
- Pike Charity Settlement
- The Pilgrim Trust
- Dr L H A Pilkington's Charitable Trust
- The John Pitman Charitable Trust
- Carew Pole Charitable Trust
- The Project Charitable Trust
- The Provincial Trust for Kendal
- Reeve's Foundation
- The Cheshire Robbins Trust
- Roedean School Mission Fund
- The Christopher Rowbotham Charitable Trust
- J B Rubens Foundation
- St Katharine & Shadwell Trust
- Save & Prosper Educational Trust
- Save & Prosper Foundation
- The R H Scholes Charitable Trust
- The Scouloudi Foundation
- Sears Foundation
- The Securicor Charitable Trust
- The Seedfield Trust
- Thomas Stanley Shipman Charitable Trust
- The N Smith Charitable Settlement
- The Harold Smith Charitable Trust
- Southdown Trust
- The Summerfield Charitable Trust
- Swale Charity Trust
- TSB Foundation for England and Wales
- TSB Foundation for Scotland
- Mrs S H Troughton's Charity Trust

Counselling

Trusts by field of interest

The Douglas Turner Charitable Trust
The R D Turner Charitable Trust
The 29th May 1961 Charity

The Vec Acorn Trust
The Charity of Thomas Wade & Others
The Francis Wallis Charitable Trust
Warbeck Fund Limited
May Watkinson Charity Trust
The Weinstock Fund
The Barbara Welby Trust
The Connolly Thomas Wilson Foundation
The Woolmen's Company Charitable Trust
The Worshipful Company of Blacksmiths Charitable Trust

Young Explorers' Trust

■ Counselling (inc helplines)

AGF Charitable Trust
The Artemis Charitable Trust
The Hon M L Astor's 1969 Charity

The Barbour Trust
Berkshire Community Trust
The Bewley Charitable Trust
C T Bowring (Charities Fund) Ltd
Joseph Brough Charitable Trust

The Edward & Dorothy Cadbury Trust (1928)
The Chase Charity
City Parochial Foundation
Cleveland Community Foundation
The Clifford Charity Oxford
Sir Kenneth Cork Charitable Trust
The Cotton Trust
Cripplegate Foundation

Dacorum Community Trust
The De Clermont Charitable Company Limited
J N Derbyshire Trust
The George Drexler Foundation

The Gilbert and Eileen Edgar Foundation
The Gilbert Edgar Trust
Eling Trust
The John Ellerman Foundation
Elmgrant Trust

Fishmongers' Company's Charitable Trust
The Joyce Fletcher Charitable Trust
Ford of Britain Trust
Charles Henry Foyle Trust
The Freshgate Trust Foundation
Frognal Trust

J Paul Getty Jr General Charitable Trust
The Simon Gibson Charitable Trust
The Gibbins Trust
Naomi & Jeffrey Greenwood Charitable Trust
The Gunter Charitable Trust

The Hadrian Trust
The Hawthorne Charitable Trust
Bill & May Hodgson Charitable Trust

Jewish Child's Day
The Joicey Trust

The KC Charitable Trust
Sheila Kay Fund
The King's Fund
Sir James Knott Trust

Laing's Charitable Trust
The Allen Lane Foundation
Lilley Benevolent Trust
Lloyd's Charities Trust

R W Mann Trustees Limited
The Marchday Charitable Fund
A N McKechnie Foundation
The Robert McKenzie Trust
The Mental Health Foundation
The Peter Minet Trust
The Moores Family Charity Foundation
The Morgan Crucible Company Charitable Trust
S C and M E Morland's Charitable Trust
Arthur Morphy Memorial Fund

The Needham Cooper Charitable Trust
The Northumberland Village Homes Trust
The Norton Foundation
The Gerald Palmer Trust
The Harry Payne Trust

The Rank Xerox Trust
The Cheshire Robbins Trust
J B Rubens Foundation

St Hilda's Trust
The Basil Samuel Charitable Trust
The Malcolm Sargent Cancer Fund for Children
Save & Prosper Educational Trust
The Francis C Scott Charitable Trust
The Frieda Scott Charitable Trust
The Leslie Smith Foundation
The Sobell Foundation
The Summerfield Charitable Trust
The Charles Sykes Trust

TSB Foundation for England and Wales
TSB Foundation for Scotland
Alfred Tankel Charitable Trust
The Thorpe Charity Trust
The Truemark Trust
The 29th May 1961 Charity
Tyne & Wear Foundation

The Wakeham Trust
The Francis Wallis Charitable Trust
The Wates Foundation
John Watson's Trust
The Weavers' Company Benevolent Fund
The Harold Hyam Wingate Foundation
The Woodward Charitable Trust

■ Holidays

AGF Charitable Trust
Alexandra Rose Day
The Ashcroft Charitable Trust
The Lord Ashdown Charitable Settlement
The Norman C Ashton Foundation

Holidays

- The Dorothy Askew Trust
- The Hon M L Astor's 1969 Charity
- The Barbour Trust
- The Bewley Charitable Trust
- The Cyril W Black Charitable Trust
- The Herbert And Peter Blagrave Charitable Trust
- Brighton & Hove Charitable Youth Trust
- R E Brook Charitable Settlement
- J & L A Cadbury Charitable Trust
- William Adlington Cadbury Charitable Trust
- The Edward & Dorothy Cadbury Trust (1928)
- The Campden Charities
- Chapman Foundation
- City Parochial Foundation
- The Cotton Trust
- Cripplegate Foundation
- The Thomas Curtis Charitable Trust
- Dacorum Community Trust
- Baron Davenport's Charity Trust
- The De Clermont Charitable Company Limited
- De La Rue Charitable Trust
- The Leopold De Rothschild Charitable Trust
- J N Derbyshire Trust
- R M Douglas Charitable Trust
- E D B Memorial Charitable Trust
- The Earley Charity
- Sir John Eastwood Foundation
- The Gilbert Edgar Trust
- The Edinburgh Medical Missionary Society – Hawthornbrae Trust
- The Maud Elkington Charitable Trust
- Elmgrant Trust
- The Eveson Charitable Trust
- The Farne Trust
- Ferguson Benevolent Fund Limited
- The Fitton Trust
- The Joyce Fletcher Charitable Trust
- Ford of Britain Trust
- The Russell and Mary Foreman 1980 Charitable Trust
- Charles Henry Foyle Trust
- The Freshgate Trust Foundation
- The Friends of the Clergy Corporation
- The Gibbins Trust
- The Simon Gibson Charitable Trust
- The John Gilpin Trust
- The Penelope Gluckstein Charitable Settlement
- The Isaac Goldberg Charity Trust
- The Good Neighbours Trust
- Constance Green Foundation
- The D W Greenwood Charitable Settlement
- Grocers' Charity
- E F & M G Hall Charitable Trust
- Hampstead Wells and Campden Trust
- The Highland Children's Trust
- Homelands Charitable Trust
- The Charity of Joseph Hopkins
- The Thomas Hudson Benevolent Trust
- David Hyman Charitable Trust
- Jewish Child's Day
- Kleinwort Benson Charitable Trust
- Laing's Charitable Trust
- Langdale Trust
- The Langtree Trust
- The Lankelly Foundation
- Laspen Trust
- Liverpool Children's Welfare Trust
- The Vanessa Lowndes Charitable Trust
- R W Mann Trustees Limited
- Matthews Wrightson Charity Trust
- Anthony Mayhew Charitable Trust
- A N McKechnie Foundation
- The James Frederick and Ethel Anne Measures Charity
- The Peter Minet Trust
- The Moores Family Charity Foundation
- The Morgan Crucible Company Charitable Trust
- Mount 'A' Charitable Trust
- Mount 'B' Charitable Trust
- The Munro Charitable Trust
- Newby Trust Ltd
- Normanby Charitable Trust
- The Northumberland Village Homes Trust
- The Norton Foundation
- Ogilvie Charities
- William Older's School Charity
- Oldham Foundation
- The PDC Trust
- R J Paul's Charitable Trust
- The Harry Payne Trust
- Pedmore Sporting Club Trust Fund
- The John Pitman Charitable Trust
- The Eleanor Rathbone Charitable Trust
- The Ravenscroft Foundation
- The Rayne Trust
- The River Trust
- Roedean School Mission Fund
- The Christopher Rowbotham Charitable Trust
- The R H Scholes Charitable Trust
- The Francis C Scott Charitable Trust
- The Frieda Scott Charitable Trust
- The Securicor Charitable Trust
- The Skelton Bounty
- The Harold Smith Charitable Trust
- The Leslie Smith Foundation
- The Sobell Foundation
- The Spurgin Charitable Trust
- The Charles Sykes Trust
- The Stella Symons Charitable Trust
- TSB Foundation for Scotland
- The Thorpe Charity Trust
- The Truemark Trust
- The 29th May 1961 Charity
- The Charity of Thomas Wade & Others
- The Wakeham Trust
- Thomas Wall Trust
- The Francis Wallis Charitable Trust
- Warbeck Fund Limited

Homes

The Ward Blenkinsop Trust
The Wates Foundation
John Watson's Trust
William Webster Charitable Trust
The Weinstock Fund
The James Weir Foundation
The Barbara Welby Trust
Whitaker Charitable Trust
Whitehall Charitable Foundation Limited
Major Michael Thomas Wills 1961 Charitable Trust
The Wolfe Family's Charitable Trust
The Women Caring Trust
The Worshipful Company of Glass Sellers' Charity Trust
The Worshipful Company of Shipwrights Charitable Fund

■ Homes and hostels

AGF Charitable Trust
Abel Charitable Trust
Green and Lilian F M Ainsworth and Family Benevolent Fund
Sir John and Lady Amory's Charitable Trust
The Princess Anne's Charities
J C W Anstey Charitable Settlement
The Ashcroft Charitable Trust
The Norman C Ashton Foundation
The Rt Hon Herbert, Baron Austin of Longbridge Will Trust
Charles and Edith Aveling Bounty
The Avon Trust
The Bamford Charitable Trust
The Barbour Trust
The Richard Baxendale Charitable Trust
The Gerald Bentall Charitable Trust
Rowan Bentall Charity Trust
The Bewley Charitable Trust
The Birmingham Amenities and Welfare Trust
The Herbert And Peter Blagrave Charitable Trust
C T Bowring (Charities Fund) Ltd
The Brand Trust
The Bridon Group Charitable Trust

R E Brook Charitable Settlement
The Charles Brotherton Trust
The Burden Trust
William Adlington Cadbury Charitable Trust
The Chase Charity
The John & Celia Bonham Christie Charitable Trust
The City and Metropolitan Welfare Charity
Cleveland Community Foundation
The Clifford Charity Oxford
Ruth and Charles Corman Charitable Trust
The Augustine Courtauld Trust
The Harry Crook Charitable Trust
Crossfield Charitable Fund
D A Curry's Charitable Trust
Baron Davenport's Charity Trust
J Davies Charities Limited
J N Derbyshire Trust
The Duke of Devonshire's Charitable Trust
The Albert Dicken Charitable Trust
Elsie Doidge Fund
The Dolphin Charitable Trust
R M Douglas Charitable Trust
Richard Early's Charitable Settlement
Sir John Eastwood Foundation
Ebenezer Trust
The Gilbert and Eileen Edgar Foundation
The Gilbert Edgar Trust
Emmandjay Charitable Trust
The Eveson Charitable Trust
The Esmee Fairbairn Charitable Trust
Lord Faringdon Second Charitable Trust
The Farne Trust
Fishmongers' Company's Charitable Trust
The Fitton Trust
The Joyce Fletcher Charitable Trust
The Gerald Fogel Charitable Trust
Fourth Settlement Charity
Charles S French Charitable Trust

The Freshgate Trust Foundation
Frognal Trust
J Paul Getty Jr General Charitable Trust
The Gibbins Trust
The G C Gibson Charitable Trust
The Simon Gibson Charitable Trust
The John Gilpin Trust
The Penelope Gluckstein Charitable Settlement
The D W Greenwood Charitable Settlement
Grocers' Charity
The Guardian Royal Exchange Charitable Trust
HACT
Handicapped Children's Aid Committee
Haslemere Estates Charitable Trust
The Hawthorne Charitable Trust
The Charles Hayward Trust
The C B and A B Holinsworth Fund of Help
Homelands Charitable Trust
The Hoover Foundation
The Charity of Joseph Hopkins
The Patrick Mitchell Hunter Fund
William Hunt's Trust
David Hyman Charitable Trust
The Jarman Charitable Trust
Jewish Child's Day
Edward Cecil Jones Settlement
Kleinwort Benson Charitable Trust
The Sir Cyril Kleinwort Charitable Settlement
Sir James Knott Trust
Beatrice Laing Trust
Laing's Charitable Trust
Laspen Trust
Raymond and Blanche Lawson Charitable Trust
The Alfred Leadbeater Trust
The William Leech Charity
Lewis Family Charitable Trust
The Enid Linder Foundation
Lloyd's Charities Trust
The London Taxi Drivers' Fund for Underprivileged Children

Trusts by field of interest

Special

The Low & Bonar Charitable Fund
Lower Hall Charitable Trust
The Vanessa Lowndes Charitable Trust

MKR Charitable Trust
The Mackintosh Foundation
Leslie & Lilian Manning Trust
The Marchday Charitable Fund
Matthews Wrightson Charity Trust
Anthony Mayhew Charitable Trust
Mickel Fund
Frederick Milburn Charitable Trust
The Millichope Foundation
The Peter Minet Trust
Victor Mishcon Trust
Arthur Morphy Memorial Fund

Natwest Staff Samaritan Fund
The Needham Cooper Charitable Trust
Newcastle Children's Mission & Institute
The Norman Family Charitable Trust
The Northumberland Village Homes Trust
The Norton Foundation

PB Charitable Trust
Pedmore Sporting Club Trust Fund
Pettit Charitable Trust
Pike Charity Settlement
Dr L H A Pilkington's Charitable Trust
The Provincial Trust for Kendal
The Pye Foundation
Mr and Mrs J A Pye's No 1 Charitable Settlement

Raeth Charity
Roger Raymond Charitable Trust No 2
The Rayne Trust
The John Rayner Charitable Trust
Joseph Rowntree Foundation

The SMB Trust
St Hilda's Trust
Peter Samuel Charitable Trust
Henry James Sayer Charity
The Francis C Scott Charitable Trust

The Securicor Charitable Trust
Thomas Stanley Shipman Charitable Trust
Bassil Shippam Trust
The Leslie Smith Foundation
The Stanley Smith General Charitable Trust
The Albert & Florence Smith Memorial Trust
The Sydney Smith Trust
The Sobell Foundation
W F Southall Trust
The Eric F Sparkes Charitable Trust
Eric Stonehouse Trust Ltd
The Summerfield Charitable Trust
The Charles Sykes Trust
TSB Foundation for Scotland
The 29th May 1961 Charity

The A F Wallace Charity Trust
The Francis Wallis Charitable Trust
The Ward Blenkinsop Trust
The Wates Foundation
William Webster Charitable Trust
The Weinstock Fund
The James Weir Foundation
The Hon Mrs R G A Whetherly's Charitable Trust
Whitehall Charitable Foundation Limited
Major Michael Thomas Wills 1961 Charitable Trust
Wiltshire Community Foundation
Mrs Wingfield's Charitable Trust
The Wolfe Family's Charitable Trust
Woodlands Trust
The Woodroffe Benton Foundation
The Worshipful Company of Founders Charities
The Yapp Welfare Trust

■ **Special needs housing**

AGF Charitable Trust
Green and Lilian F M Ainsworth and Family Benevolent Fund
The Ian Askew Charitable Trust

The Barbour Trust
The Bewley Charitable Trust
The Birmingham Amenities and Welfare Trust
The Herbert And Peter Blagrave Charitable Trust
The Oliver Borthwick Memorial Trust
The Charles Brotherton Trust

William Adlington Cadbury Charitable Trust
The Campden Charities
Clergy Orphan Corporation
Cleveland Community Foundation
The Clifford Charity Oxford
The Cotton Trust
The Thomas Curtis Charitable Trust

Baron Davenport's Charity Trust
J N Derbyshire Trust

The Earley Charity
Eling Trust
Emmandjay Charitable Trust
The Eveson Charitable Trust
The Esmee Fairbairn Charitable Trust
Ford of Britain Trust

The Gibbins Trust
The G C Gibson Charitable Trust
The Simon Gibson Charitable Trust
Greater Bristol Foundation
Grocers' Charity

HACT
The Hadrian Trust
Handicapped Children's Aid Committee
The Hayward Foundation

Jewish Child's Day
The Joicey Trust

Beatrice Laing Trust
Laing's Charitable Trust
The Lankelly Foundation
The League of the Helping Hand
The William Leech Charity
Lloyd's Charities Trust
The Low & Bonar Charitable Fund

Special

The Peter Minet Trust
Arthur Morphy Memorial Fund
The Northumberland Village Homes Trust
The Norton Foundation
The Gerald Palmer Trust
The Harry Payne Trust
The Rank Xerox Trust
Joseph Rowntree Foundation
St Hilda's Trust
The Francis C Scott Charitable Trust
The Sobell Foundation
Eric Stonehouse Trust Ltd
The Summerfield Charitable Trust
TSB Foundation for Scotland
Tyne & Wear Foundation
The Wates Foundation
The Will Charitable Trust
Woodlands Trust
The Worshipful Company of Founders Charities

■ Special classes

Green and Lilian F M Ainsworth and Family Benevolent Fund
Paul Balint Charitable Trust
The Bewley Charitable Trust
The Brand Trust
The Campden Charities
Charipot Trust
The Chase Charity
The Clifford Charity Oxford
The Peter Courtauld Charitable Trust
J N Derbyshire Trust
The Ellbridge Trust
The Esmee Fairbairn Charitable Trust
The Farne Trust
The Fitton Trust
The Gibbins Trust
The Simon Gibson Charitable Trust
Greater Bristol Foundation

Hampton Fuel Allotment Charity
The Hayward Foundation
Isle of Dogs Community Foundation
Jewish Child's Day
Beatrice Laing Trust
Laing's Charitable Trust
The William Leech Charity
The John Spedan Lewis Foundation
The Low & Bonar Charitable Fund
The Northumberland Village Homes Trust
Norwich Church of England Young Men's Society
William Older's School Charity
St Katharine & Shadwell Trust
The Francis C Scott Charitable Trust
The Charles Sykes Trust
TSB Foundation for Scotland
The Douglas Turner Charitable Trust
John Watson's Trust
The Connolly Thomas Wilson Foundation

■ Youth organisations (eg Guides, Scouts, YWCA etc)

Kate Adams Charitable Trust
Green and Lilian F M Ainsworth and Family Benevolent Fund
Alexandra Rose Day
Sir John and Lady Amory's Charitable Trust
The Armstrong Trust
The Ashby Charitable Trust
The Ian Askew Charitable Trust
The Rt Hon Herbert, Baron Austin of Longbridge Will Trust
Charles and Edith Aveling Bounty
The Bacta Charitable Trust
The Barbour Trust
John Bell Charitable Trust
The Sylvia Bell Charity

Hervey Benham Charitable Trust
Rowan Bentall Charity Trust
Berkshire Community Trust
The Bewley Charitable Trust
The Birchwood Trust
The Cyril W Black Charitable Trust
Isabel Blackman Foundation
The Herbert And Peter Blagrave Charitable Trust
C T Bowring (Charities Fund) Ltd
The Bridon Group Charitable Trust
Brighton & Hove Charitable Youth Trust
The J & M Britton Charitable Trust
The Brocton Trust
The Charles Brotherton Trust
Burges Salmon Charitable Trust
The J H Burn Charity Trust
The Burton Breweries Charitable Trust
Edward Cadbury Charitable Trust
J & L A Cadbury Charitable Trust
William Adlington Cadbury Charitable Trust
The Edward & Dorothy Cadbury Trust (1928)
The Campden Charities
The Carr-Ellison Charitable Trust
Sir John Cass's Foundation
Chapman Foundation
Charity Projects
The Charterhouse Charitable Trust
City Parochial Foundation
Clark Foundation II
The Thomas Edward Clarke Trust
Cleveland Community Foundation
The Clifford Charity Oxford
Lord Clinton's Charitable Trust
The Timothy Colman Charitable Trust
The Ernest Cook Trust
J Reginald Corah Foundation Fund
The Augustine Courtauld Trust
The Coutts Charitable Trust
Cripplegate Foundation

Trusts by field of interest **Youth**

Cripps Foundation
The Harry Crook Charitable Trust
Crossfield Charitable Fund

The DLM Charitable Trust
Dacorum Community Trust
Baron Davenport's Charity Trust
Lily & Henry Davis Charitable Foundation
The De Clermont Charitable Company Limited
The Leopold De Rothschild Charitable Trust
Delmar Charitable Trust
J N Derbyshire Trust
The Duke of Devonshire's Charitable Trust
R M Douglas Charitable Trust
The Dulverton Trust

The Earley Charity
Richard Early's Charitable Settlement
Sir John Eastwood Foundation
The Gilbert and Eileen Edgar Foundation
The Maud Elkington Charitable Trust
The John Ellerman Foundation
The Vernon N Ely Charitable Trust
Emmandjay Charitable Trust
The Everard Foundation
The Eveson Charitable Trust

The Esmee Fairbairn Charitable Trust
Lord Faringdon Charitable Trust
The Farne Trust
The Thomas Farr Charitable Trust
Walter Farthing (Trust) Limited
The John Feeney Charitable Bequest
Fishmongers' Company's Charitable Trust
The Fitton Trust
Ford of Britain Trust
The Four Lanes Trust
Charles Henry Foyle Trust
Charles S French Charitable Trust
The Freshgate Trust Foundation
Friarsgate Trust
Fritillary Trust

GNC Trust
The General Charity Fund
The Gibbins Trust
The G C Gibson Charitable Trust
The Simon Gibson Charitable Trust
The Hon Mr & Mrs Clive Gibson's Charity Trust
The Hon H M T Gibson's Charity Trust
The John Gilpin Trust
The E W Gladstone Charitable Trust
The Goodman Trust
The Grand Metropolitan Charitable Trust
Constance Green Foundation
The D W Greenwood Charitable Settlement
The Guardian Royal Exchange Charitable Trust
The Gunnell Charitable Trust

The Hadrian Trust
The Hame Trust
R J Harris Charitable Settlement
Harrisons & Crosfield Charitable Fund
Haslemere Estates Charitable Trust
The Hawthorne Charitable Trust
Hedgcock Bequest
J R Henderson's Settlement
The Hoover Foundation
The Charity of Joseph Hopkins
The Hornsey Parochial Charities
The Thomas Hudson Benevolent Trust
The Hull & East Riding Charitable Trust
The Patrick Mitchell Hunter Fund

The Ireland Fund of Great Britain
Isle of Dogs Community Foundation

The Jarman Charitable Trust
John Jarrold Trust Ltd
The Jenour Foundation
Edward Cecil Jones Settlement
The Anton Jurgens Charitable Trust

The Kirby & West Charitable Trust
Kleinwort Benson Charitable Trust
The Sir Cyril Kleinwort Charitable Settlement
Sir James Knott Trust

The Kirby Laing Foundation
The Maurice Laing Foundation
Laing's Charitable Trust
Langdale Trust
Laspen Trust
The William Leech Charity
Lord Leverhulme's Charitable Trust
The London Taxi Drivers' Fund for Underprivileged Children
The Low & Bonar Charitable Fund

R W Mann Trustees Limited
Leslie & Lilian Manning Trust
Matthews Wrightson Charity Trust
Anthony Mayhew Charitable Trust
The James Frederick and Ethel Anne Measures Charity
K S Mehta Charitable Trust
Mickel Fund
Frederick Milburn Charitable Trust
The Millichope Foundation
The Peter Minet Trust
Victor Mishcon Trust
The George A Moore Foundation
Mount 'A' Charitable Trust
Mount 'B' Charitable Trust
Gweneth Moxon Charitable Trust

The Needham Cooper Charitable Trust
Newcastle Children's Mission & Institute
The Newman Charitable Trust
Nichol-Young Foundation
Normanby Charitable Trust
The Northumberland Village Homes Trust
The Norton Foundation
Norwich Church of England Young Men's Society

Children

The Oakdale Trust
William Older's School Charity
Oldham Foundation
The Owen Family Trust
PF Charitable Trust
R J Paul's Charitable Trust
The Harry Payne Trust
Pedmore Sporting Club Trust Fund
Pettit Charitable Trust
The David Pickford Charitable Foundation
Dr L H A Pilkington's Charitable Trust
The Sir Richard Carew Pole 1973 Charitable Trust
The Ronald & Kathleen Pryor Charity
The Pye Foundation
Mr and Mrs J A Pye's No 1 Charitable Settlement
The Eleanor Rathbone Charitable Trust
The Ravenscroft Foundation
Roger Raymond Charitable Trust No 2
Rokeby Charitable Trust
The Christopher Rowbotham Charitable Trust
The SMB Trust
Peter Samuel Charitable Trust
Save & Prosper Educational Trust
Save & Prosper Foundation
The Schuster Charitable Trust
The Frieda Scott Charitable Trust
The Storrow Scott Charitable Will Trust
The Seahorse Charitable Trust
Sears Foundation
The Securicor Charitable Trust
Leslie Sell Charitable Trust
Colonel J D Sherwood Charitable Trust
Thomas Stanley Shipman Charitable Trust
Bassil Shippam Trust
Singer Foundation
The Skelton Bounty
Edward Skinner Charitable Trust
The John Slater Foundation
The Harold Smith Charitable Trust

The Albert & Florence Smith Memorial Trust
The Sobell Foundation
W F Southall Trust
The Leonard Laity Stoate Charitable Trust
The Bernard Sunley Charitable Foundation
The Charles Sykes Trust
TSB Foundation for England and Wales
TSB Foundation for Scotland
A P Taylor Fund
Mrs R P Tindall's Charitable Trust
Mrs S H Troughton's Charity Trust
The Douglas Turner Charitable Trust
The R D Turner Charitable Trust
The Edwin Henry Tutty Charitable Trust
The 29th May 1961 Charity
The Vec Acorn Trust
The Charity of Thomas Wade & Others
The Cynthia Walker Charitable Trust
Thomas Wall Trust
The A F Wallace Charity Trust
The Ward Blenkinsop Trust
The Wates Foundation
William Webster Charitable Trust
Whitaker Charitable Trust
Dame Violet Wills Charitable Trust
Woodlands Trust
The Woodroffe Benton Foundation
The Worshipful Company of Founders Charities

■ Children and violence (inc abuse)

Green and Lilian F M Ainsworth and Family Benevolent Fund
Allied Dunbar Staff Charity Fund
The Bewley Charitable Trust
The Herbert And Peter Blagrave Charitable Trust
The Clifford Charity Oxford
J N Derbyshire Trust
The George Drexler Foundation
The Gilbert and Eileen Edgar Foundation
The John Ellerman Foundation
Elmgrant Trust
Fishmongers' Company's Charitable Trust
The Joyce Fletcher Charitable Trust
The Russell and Mary Foreman 1980 Charitable Trust
The Gibbins Trust
The Simon Gibson Charitable Trust
The Hon Mr & Mrs Clive Gibson's Charity Trust
The Guardian Royal Exchange Charitable Trust
The Jenour Foundation
Jewish Child's Day
The Joicey Trust
Laing's Charitable Trust
The Allen Lane Foundation
The William Leech Charity
Lilley Benevolent Trust
The Margaret Foundation
Matthews Wrightson Charity Trust
The Mental Health Foundation
Newby Trust Ltd
The Newman Charitable Trust
The Norton Foundation
The Rank Xerox Trust
The Skelton Bounty
The Sobell Foundation
TSB Foundation for Scotland
The Wates Foundation

INDEX C

Trusts by beneficial area

This index lists the trusts appearing in this directory under the geographical areas for which they have expressed a funding preference. They appear under the following area headings.

UK
England
London and Greater London
South East England
South West England and Channel Islands
East Anglia
East Midlands
West Midlands
North East England
North West England
Yorkshire and Humberside
Scotland
North Scotland
South Scotland
Northern Ireland
Wales
North Wales
South Wales
Overseas

UK

Keith & Freda Abraham Charitable Trust
The Alchemy Foundation
Alexandra Rose Day
Ambika Paul Foundation
The Prince Andrew Charitable Trust
The Artemis Charitable Trust
The Ashby Charitable Trust
The Astor Foundation
The Rt Hon Herbert, Baron Austin of Longbridge Will Trust
The Avon Trust
The BBC Children in Need Appeal
The Bacta Charitable Trust
The Baring Foundation
The Barleycorn Trust
Eleanor Barton Trust
The Paul Bassham Charitable Trust
The Beaverbrook Foundation
The Heather Beckwith Charitable Settlement
The Sylvia Bell Charity
The Percy Bilton Charity
The Hubert Blake Charitable Trust
The Oliver Borthwick Memorial Trust
The M Bourne Charitable Trust
The Bridon Group Charitable Trust
British Humane Association
The J & M Britton Charitable Trust
Buckingham Trust
The Reg Burns Foundation
The Buttle Trust
Edward Cadbury Charitable Trust
Richard Cadbury Charitable Trust
William Adlington Cadbury Charitable Trust
The Edward & Dorothy Cadbury Trust (1928)
CAF
The Carr-Ellison Charitable Trust
Chapman Charitable Trust
Chapman Foundation
Charity Projects
The Charterhouse Charitable Trust
The Chase Charity
Cherry Tree Foundation
Child Growth Foundation
The City and Metropolitan Welfare Charity
The Clifford Charity Oxford
The Ernest Cook Trust
Cooper Charitable Trust
The Cotton Trust
The Wallace Curzon Charitable Trust
Cystic Fibrosis Trust
Lily & Henry Davis Charitable Foundation
The De Clermont Charitable Company Limited
The Emma de Yong Charitable Trust
Nicholas De Yong's Charitable Trust 1984
The Denby Charitable Foundation
Denby Charitable Trust
The Dibs Charitable Trust
R M Douglas Charitable Trust
The D'Oyly Carte Charitable Trust
Drapers' Charitable Fund
The Dulverton Trust
The Gilbert and Eileen Edgar Foundation
The Gilbert Edgar Trust
The Ellbridge Trust
The John Ellerman Foundation
The FR 1978 Charitable Trust
The Esmee Fairbairn Charitable Trust
The Farne Trust
Fishmongers' Company's Charitable Trust
The Fitton Trust
The Joyce Fletcher Charitable Trust
The Russell and Mary Foreman 1980 Charitable Trust
Jill Franklin Trust
The Friends of the Clergy Corporation
Frognal Trust
Angela Gallagher Memorial Fund
The Gatsby Charitable Foundation
J Paul Getty Jr General Charitable Trust
The Simon Gibson Charitable Trust
The Hon P N Gibson's Charity Trust
The E W Gladstone Charitable Trust
Glebe Charitable Trust
The Isaac Goldberg Charity Trust
The Goldsmiths' Company's Charities
The Good Neighbours Trust
The Grand Metropolitan Charitable Trust
The Charles Green Foundation
Constance Green Foundation
The Gresham Charitable Trust
Grocers' Charity
The Guardian Royal Exchange Charitable Trust
The Gunnell Charitable Trust
HACT
The Hame Trust
Harrisons & Crosfield Charitable Fund
The Hawthorne Charitable Trust
The Hayward Foundation
The Charles Hayward Trust
The Hedley Foundation
Joseph and Mary Hiley Trust
Mrs F E Hinton Charitable Trust
The Dorothy Holmes Charitable Trust
The Hoover Foundation
The Thomas Hudson Benevolent Trust
David Hyman Charitable Trust
The Inverforth Charitable Trust
The Ireland Fund of Great Britain
J and A Charitable Trust
The James Trust
Kleinwort Benson Charitable Trust
The Heinz & Anna Kroch Foundation
The Kirby Laing Foundation
The Maurice Laing Foundation
Beatrice Laing Trust
Laing's Charitable Trust
The Allen Lane Foundation
Langdale Trust
The Lankelly Foundation
Laspen Trust
Kathleen Laurence's Trust
The Lawlor Foundation
Raymond and Blanche Lawson Charitable Trust
The Leach Fourteenth Trust

England

Trusts by beneficial area

The League of the Helping Hand
Joseph Levy Charitable Foundation
The John Spedan Lewis Foundation
The Enid Linder Foundation
The Lister Charitable Trust
Lloyd's Charities Trust
London Law Trust
The Low & Bonar Charitable Fund
The E M MacAndrew Trust
The Mackintosh Foundation
Macpherson Memorial Trust
Man of the People Fund
Leslie & Lilian Manning Trust
The Margaret Foundation
The Sir George Martin Trust
The Leonard Matchan Fund Limited
Matthews Wrightson Charity Trust
The Robert McAlpine Foundation
A N McKechnie Foundation
The Mental Health Foundation
Mickel Fund
Middlesex County Rugby Football Union Memorial Fund
The Millichope Foundation
The Moores Family Charity Foundation
Mount 'A' Charitable Trust
Mount 'B' Charitable Trust
The Munro Charitable Trust
New Court Charitable Trust
Newby Trust Ltd
Nichol-Young Foundation
The Northumberland Village Homes Trust
The Oakdale Trust
Ogilvie Charities
The Owen Family Trust
The PDC Trust
The Constance Paterson Charitable Foundation
Arthur James Paterson Charitable Trust
The John Phillimore Charitable Trust
The Pilgrim Trust
Dr L H A Pilkington's Charitable Trust
The Sir Richard Carew Pole 1973 Charitable Trust
Carew Pole Charitable Trust

The Ronald & Kathleen Pryor Charity
The Pye Christian Trust
Pyke Charity Trust
Racal Charitable Trust
Radley Charitable Trust
ZVM Rangoonwala Foundation
The Rank Xerox Trust
The Eleanor Rathbone Charitable Trust
Roger Raymond Charitable Trust No 2
The John Rayner Charitable Trust
The Ridgmount Foundation
The F A Riley-Smith Charitable Trust
The Rivendell Trust
Joseph Rowntree Foundation
The Frank and Enid Rubens Highgate Trust
The Sainsbury Charitable Fund Ltd
The Malcolm Sargent Cancer Fund for Children
Save & Prosper Educational Trust
Save & Prosper Foundation
The Scott Bader Commonwealth Ltd
The Scouloudi Foundation
The Seahorse Charitable Trust
Sears Foundation
The Securicor Charitable Trust
The Seedfield Trust
Leslie Sell Charitable Trust
The Sheldon Trust
Singer Foundation
Edward Skinner Charitable Trust
Skinners' Company Lady Neville Charity
The Harold Smith Charitable Trust
Henry Smith (Estates Charities)
The Leslie Smith Foundation
The Sobell Foundation
Southdown Trust
Eric Stonehouse Trust Ltd
David James Streeter Charitable Settlement
The Summerfield Charitable Trust
Sir John Sumner's Trust Section 'A'
The Bernard Sunley Charitable Foundation

Adrienne & Leslie Sussman Charitable Trust
The Charles Sykes Trust
The Stella Symons Charitable Trust
A R Taylor Charitable Trust
The Margaret Thatcher Charitable Trust
The Thorpe Charity Trust
Tollemache (Buckminster) Charitable Trust
Mrs S H Troughton's Charity Trust
The Truemark Trust
The Sir Mark and Lady Turner Charitable Settlement
G J W Turner Trust
The 29th May 1961 Charity
Bernard Van Leer Foundation UK Trust
The Wakeham Trust
Thomas Wall Trust
The Ward Blenkinsop Trust
The Weavers' Company Benevolent Fund
The James Weir Foundation
Garfield Weston Foundation
Major Michael Thomas Wills 1961 Charitable Trust
The H D H Wills 1965 Charitable Trust
The Harold Hyam Wingate Foundation
Mrs Wingfield's Charitable Trust
The Wolfe Family's Charitable Trust
The Woodroffe Benton Foundation
The Woodward Charitable Trust
The Worshipful Company of Founders Charities
The Worshipful Company of Shipwrights Charitable Fund
The Yapp Education and Research Trust
The Yapp Welfare Trust
Young Explorers' Trust

■ England

Access 4 Trust
Paul Balint Charitable Trust
Benham Charitable Settlement
Charity Projects
Church Urban Fund

Trusts by beneficial area

South East England

The City of London School Charitable Trust
The Coutts Charitable Trust
Joseph Strong Frazer Trust
The Gibbins Trust
The Kenneth Hargreaves Trust
Lady Hind Trust
Lloyds Bank Charitable Trust
The Ivona Mays-Smith Charitable Trust
Natwest Staff Samaritan Fund
Oldham Foundation
The R H Scholes Charitable Trust
The Schuster Charitable Trust
The Leonard Laity Stoate Charitable Trust
TSB Foundation for England and Wales
The Cynthia Walker Charitable Trust
The Wates Foundation
The Barbara Welby Trust

■ London and Greater London

Abel Charitable Trust
The Baring Foundation
The Gerald Bentall Charitable Trust
Buckets and Spades Charitable Trust
The Campden Charities
Sir John Cass's Foundation
The Charterhouse Charitable Trust
Christabella Charitable Trust
City Parochial Foundation
Sir Kenneth Cork Charitable Trust
The Coutts Charitable Trust
Cripplegate Foundation
De La Rue Charitable Trust
Delmar Charitable Trust
Drapers' Charitable Fund
E D B Memorial Charitable Trust
Ebenezer Trust
The Vernon N Ely Charitable Trust
The Fidelity UK Foundation
Fishmongers' Company's Charitable Trust
The Fleurus Trust
The Gerald Fogel Charitable Trust

Ford of Britain Trust
Charles S French Charitable Trust
The Hon Mr & Mrs Clive Gibson's Charity Trust
The Goldsmiths' Company's Charities
Hampstead Wells and Campden Trust
Hampton Fuel Allotment Charity
Haslemere Estates Charitable Trust
Haymills Charitable Trust
The Hoover Foundation
The Hornsey Parochial Charities
Isle of Dogs Community Foundation
The King's Fund
The Lester Trust Fund
The London Taxi Drivers' Fund for Underprivileged Children
John Lyon's Charity
The Violet Melchett Children's Trust
The Metropolitan Hospital-Sunday Fund
The Peter Minet Trust
The Morgan Crucible Company Charitable Trust
Arthur Morphy Memorial Fund
The Munro Charitable Trust
Ogilvie Charities
Reeve's Foundation
Richmond Parish Lands Charity
Roedean School Mission Fund
St Katharine & Shadwell Trust
The Schuster Charitable Trust
Silvester Charitable Gift Trust
Sulgrave Charitable Trust
A P Taylor Fund
Trust for London
The Sir Mark and Lady Turner Charitable Settlement
The Francis Wallis Charitable Trust
John Wates Charitable Trust
The Weavers' Company Benevolent Fund
Woodlands Trust
The Woolmen's Company Charitable Trust
The Worshipful Company of Blacksmiths Charitable Trust
The Yorkshire Bank Charitable Trust

■ South East England

Abel Charitable Trust
J C W Anstey Charitable Settlement
The Gerald Bentall Charitable Trust
Rowan Bentall Charity Trust
Buckets and Spades Charitable Trust
Delmar Charitable Trust
E D B Memorial Charitable Trust
The Fleurus Trust
Raymond and Blanche Lawson Charitable Trust
The Catherine Martineau Charitable Trust
The Morgan Crucible Company Charitable Trust
The John Pitman Charitable Trust
Alfred Tankel Charitable Trust
The Francis Wallis Charitable Trust
John Wates Charitable Trust

Bedfordshire
De La Rue Charitable Trust
Haymills Charitable Trust
The Luke Trust
The Neighbourly Charitable Trust
The Yorkshire Bank Charitable Trust

Berkshire
Berkshire Community Trust
The Herbert And Peter Blagrave Charitable Trust
Eling Trust
Fritillary Trust
Haymills Charitable Trust
J R Henderson's Settlement
The Gerald Palmer Trust
Peter Samuel Charitable Trust

Buckinghamshire
The Ernest Cook Trust
The Cotton Trust
The Thomas Curtis Charitable Trust
Haymills Charitable Trust
The Yorkshire Bank Charitable Trust

East Sussex
The Ian Askew Charitable Trust
The Dorothy Askew Trust

South West England and Channel Islands

Trusts by beneficial area

Brighton & Hove Charitable Youth Trust
The Gibbins Trust
Hedgcock Bequest
Lilley Benevolent Trust
The B V MacAndrew Trust
Anthony Mayhew Charitable Trust
The River Trust
Sir Edward Robinson Charitable Trust
The J C Robinson Trust No 3
Roedean School Mission Fund

Essex
Hervey Benham Charitable Trust
Christabella Charitable Trust
The Augustine Courtauld Trust
DM Charitable Trust
Ebenezer Trust
Walter Farthing (Trust) Limited
The Fleurus Trust
Ford of Britain Trust
Charles S French Charitable Trust
Grange Farm Centre Trust
Haymills Charitable Trust
Heath Charitable Trust
Edward Cecil Jones Settlement
Ogilvie Charities
Rosca Trust
Colonel J D Sherwood Charitable Trust
The Albert & Florence Smith Memorial Trust
The Francis Wallis Charitable Trust

Hampshire and Isle of Wight
The Herbert And Peter Blagrave Charitable Trust
The Ellis Campbell Charitable Foundation
The Wallace Curzon Charitable Trust
De La Rue Charitable Trust
Ford of Britain Trust
The Four Lanes Trust
GNC Trust
Richard Kirkman Charitable Trust
The John Phillimore Charitable Trust
The Cheshire Robbins Trust
Peter Samuel Charitable Trust

A R Taylor Charitable Trust
The Vec Acorn Trust
The Francis Wallis Charitable Trust
Whitehall Charitable Foundation Limited

Hertfordshire
The Cotton Trust
DM Charitable Trust
Dacorum Community Trust
The Fleurus Trust
Haymills Charitable Trust
The Yorkshire Bank Charitable Trust

Kent
The Birchwood Trust
Isabel Blackman Foundation
The Sarah D'Avigdor Goldsmid Charitable Trust
The Fidelity UK Foundation
The John Phillimore Charitable Trust
Raeth Charity
Second Ferndale Trust
Swale Charity Trust

Oxfordshire
Cooper Charitable Trust
Richard Early's Charitable Settlement
Haymills Charitable Trust
The Schuster Charitable Trust
The Yorkshire Bank Charitable Trust

Surrey
The Billmeir Charitable Trust
The Challice Trust
The Vernon N Ely Charitable Trust
The Fidelity UK Foundation
The Lavender Trust
Arthur Morphy Memorial Fund
The Francis Wallis Charitable Trust

West Sussex
The Ian Askew Charitable Trust
The Dorothy Askew Trust
Brighton & Hove Charitable Youth Trust
Friarsgate Trust
The Gibbins Trust
Lilley Benevolent Trust
The B V MacAndrew Trust

The Betty Martin Charity
Anthony Mayhew Charitable Trust
The Munro Charitable Trust
William Older's School Charity
Raeth Charity
The River Trust
The J C Robinson Trust No 3
Roedean School Mission Fund
Bassil Shippam Trust

■ South West England and Channel Islands
The Arnold Foundation
The Gerald Bentall Charitable Trust
Clark Foundation II
The Wallace Curzon Charitable Trust
Alfred Tankel Charitable Trust

Avon
The Armstrong Trust
The J & M Britton Charitable Trust
Burges Salmon Charitable Trust
The Harry Crook Charitable Trust
The Wallace Curzon Charitable Trust
The Joyce Fletcher Charitable Trust
Greater Bristol Foundation
R J Harris Charitable Settlement
John James Bristol Foundation
Lalonde Charitable Trust
The Needham Cooper Charitable Trust
Oldham Foundation
Raeth Charity
The J C Robinson Trust No 3
The Leonard Laity Stoate Charitable Trust

Channel Islands (Jersey and Guernsey)
Ferguson Benevolent Fund Limited

Cornwall and Scilly Isles
BCH 1971 Charitable Trust
The Blanchminster Trust
The Wallace Curzon Charitable Trust

Trusts by beneficial area **East Midlands**

Wilfrid Bruce Davis Charitable Trust
GNC Trust
The Norman Family Charitable Trust
Oldham Foundation
The Sir Richard Carew Pole 1973 Charitable Trust
Carew Pole Charitable Trust
The Leonard Laity Stoate Charitable Trust

Devon
Keith & Freda Abraham Charitable Trust
Sir John and Lady Amory's Charitable Trust
BCH 1971 Charitable Trust
Lord Clinton's Charitable Trust
The Wallace Curzon Charitable Trust
Elsie Doidge Fund
The Joyce Fletcher Charitable Trust
The Howard Hatton Charitable Trust
The Norman Family Charitable Trust
Northcott Charitable Trust
Oldham Foundation
Pike Charity Settlement
The Sir Richard Carew Pole 1973 Charitable Trust
Carew Pole Charitable Trust
Sir Edward Robinson Charitable Trust
The Leonard Laity Stoate Charitable Trust
The Torquay Charities

Dorset
The Armstrong Trust
The Ernest Cook Trust
The Wallace Curzon Charitable Trust
Haymills Charitable Trust
The Dorothy Holmes Charitable Trust
Oldham Foundation
The Cheshire Robbins Trust
Sir Edward Robinson Charitable Trust
The Leonard Laity Stoate Charitable Trust
Mrs R P Tindall's Charitable Trust

Gloucestershire
The Armstrong Trust
Richard Cadbury Charitable Trust
The Ernest Cook Trust
R J Harris Charitable Settlement
Haymills Charitable Trust
The Sir Cyril Kleinwort Charitable Settlement
The Langtree Trust
The Needham Cooper Charitable Trust
Oldham Foundation
Raeth Charity
The J C Robinson Trust No 3
The Ross Charitable Trust
The June Stevens Foundation
The Summerfield Charitable Trust
Mr Frederick Wills 1961 Charitable Trust
P J H Wills 1962 Charitable Trust

Somerset
Clark Foundation II
The Wallace Curzon Charitable Trust
The Joyce Fletcher Charitable Trust
R J Harris Charitable Settlement
The Needham Cooper Charitable Trust
The Norman Family Charitable Trust
Oldham Foundation
The Leonard Laity Stoate Charitable Trust

Wiltshire
Allied Dunbar Staff Charity Fund
The Herbert And Peter Blagrave Charitable Trust
The Wallace Curzon Charitable Trust
The Joyce Fletcher Charitable Trust
R J Harris Charitable Settlement
Haymills Charitable Trust
Oldham Foundation
The Leslie Smith Foundation
Mrs R P Tindall's Charitable Trust
Wiltshire Community Foundation

■ **East Anglia**
The Alper Charitable Trust
Charles S French Charitable Trust
Haymills Charitable Trust
John Jarrold Trust Ltd
The Catherine Martineau Charitable Trust
Nichol-Young Foundation
Ormiston Trust
R J Paul's Charitable Trust
Radley Charitable Trust
The Leslie Smith Foundation
The Yorkshire Bank Charitable Trust

Cambridgeshire
The Fleurus Trust
The Gordon Fraser Charitable Trust
The Pye Foundation

Norfolk
The Paul Bassham Charitable Trust
The Timothy Colman Charitable Trust
The Fleurus Trust
The Goodman Trust
The Educational Foundation of Alderman John Norman
Norwich Church of England Young Men's Society
Sir Edward Robinson Charitable Trust

Suffolk
The Fleurus Trust
The Gordon Fraser Charitable Trust
The John Gilpin Trust
Nichol-Young Foundation
Ogilvie Charities
R J Paul's Charitable Trust
Sir Edward Robinson Charitable Trust

■ **East Midlands**
The Cadell-Samworth Foundation
The Everard Foundation
GNC Trust
The Lorna King Charitable Trust
The Sheldon Trust
The Yorkshire Bank Charitable Trust

West Midlands

Trusts by beneficial area

Leicestershire
The Chetwode Foundation
The Ernest Cook Trust
J Reginald Corah Foundation Fund
The Cotton Trust
The Maud Elkington Charitable Trust
The Everard Foundation
Gay & Peter Hartley's Hillards Charitable Trust
The Kirby & West Charitable Trust
The Harry James Riddleston Charity of Leicester
Thomas Stanley Shipman Charitable Trust

Lincolnshire
Gay & Peter Hartley's Hillards Charitable Trust
May Watkinson Charity Trust
John William Wright Deceased Trust

Northamptonshire
The Elaine Barratt Charitable Trust
Benham Charitable Settlement
Cripps Foundation
The Maud Elkington Charitable Trust
Gay & Peter Hartley's Hillards Charitable Trust
The Horne Foundation
The Connolly Thomas Wilson Foundation

Nottinghamshire
Kate Adams Charitable Trust
The Sylvia Bell Charity
The Chetwode Foundation
The Thomas Edward Clarke Trust
J N Derbyshire Trust
Sir John Eastwood Foundation
The Thomas Farr Charitable Trust
Gay & Peter Hartley's Hillards Charitable Trust

■ West Midlands
The Rt Hon Herbert, Baron Austin of Longbridge Will Trust
The Bewley Charitable Trust
The Brocton Trust
Edward Cadbury Charitable Trust
J & L A Cadbury Charitable Trust
William Adlington Cadbury Charitable Trust
The Edward & Dorothy Cadbury Trust (1928)
The Cadell-Samworth Foundation
The Eveson Charitable Trust
GNC Trust
The Mrs D M Graham Charity
MKR Charitable Trust
The James Frederick and Ethel Anne Measures Charity
The Owen Family Trust
Pedmore Sporting Club Trust Fund
The Sheldon Trust
F C Stokes Trust
Sir John Sumner's Trust Section 'A'
G J W Turner Trust
The 29th May 1961 Charity
Woodlands Trust
The Yorkshire Bank Charitable Trust

Birmingham
The Rt Hon Herbert, Baron Austin of Longbridge Will Trust
The Birmingham Amenities and Welfare Trust
The Charles Brotherton Trust
Richard Cadbury Charitable Trust
The John Feeney Charitable Bequest
Charles Henry Foyle Trust
Gay & Peter Hartley's Hillards Charitable Trust
The C B and A B Holinsworth Fund of Help
The Charity of Joseph Hopkins
The Jarman Charitable Trust
The Alfred Leadbeater Trust
The Millichope Foundation
The Harry Payne Trust
Pedmore Sporting Club Trust Fund
Henry James Sayer Charity
The R D Turner Charitable Trust

Coventry
Richard Cadbury Charitable Trust
The Jarman Charitable Trust
The Millichope Foundation
The Harry Payne Trust
The 29th May 1961 Charity

Dudley
The Jarman Charitable Trust
The Millichope Foundation
The Harry Payne Trust
Pedmore Sporting Club Trust Fund

Herefordshire and Worcestershire
Richard Cadbury Charitable Trust
Charles Henry Foyle Trust
The Howard Hatton Charitable Trust
The Hawthorne Charitable Trust
The Millichope Foundation
The Morgan Crucible Company Charitable Trust
Pedmore Sporting Club Trust Fund

Sandwell
The Jarman Charitable Trust
The Millichope Foundation
The Harry Payne Trust
Pedmore Sporting Club Trust Fund

Shropshire
Roy Fletcher Trust
The Howard Hatton Charitable Trust
The Millichope Foundation

Solihull
The Jarman Charitable Trust
The Harry Payne Trust
Pedmore Sporting Club Trust Fund

Staffordshire
The Bamford Charitable Trust
The Burton Breweries Charitable Trust
R M Douglas Charitable Trust
The Fred Linford Charitable Trust
Pedmore Sporting Club Trust Fund
The Rowley Trust

Sutton Coldfield
The Jarman Charitable Trust
The Millichope Foundation
The Harry Payne Trust

Trusts by beneficial area

North West England

Pedmore Sporting Club Trust Fund

Walsall
The Jarman Charitable Trust
The Millichope Foundation
The Harry Payne Trust
Pedmore Sporting Club Trust Fund

Warwickshire
Ford of Britain Trust
The Harry Payne Trust
Rokeby Charitable Trust
The Snowball Trust
The 29th May 1961 Charity

Wolverhampton
Lower Hall Charitable Trust
The Millichope Foundation
The Harry Payne Trust
Pedmore Sporting Club Trust Fund

■ North East England
The Barbour Trust
The Baring Foundation
John Bell Charitable Trust
The Carr-Ellison Charitable Trust
De La Rue Charitable Trust
The Albert Dicken Charitable Trust
The Hadrian Trust
The William Leech Charity
Leslie & Lilian Manning Trust
The Christopher Rowbotham Charitable Trust
The Sylvia and Colin Shepherd Charitable Trust
The Wates Foundation
William Webster Charitable Trust
The Yorkshire Bank Charitable Trust

Cleveland
Joseph Brough Charitable Trust
Cleveland Community Foundation

Durham
John Bell Charitable Trust
Joseph Brough Charitable Trust
The Gordon Fraser Charitable Trust
Sir James Knott Trust

The William Leech Charity
R W Mann Trustees Limited

Northumberland
John Bell Charitable Trust
Joseph Brough Charitable Trust
The Carr-Ellison Charitable Trust
The Joicey Trust
Sir James Knott Trust
The William Leech Charity
R W Mann Trustees Limited
Frederick Milburn Charitable Trust
St Hilda's Trust
The Storrow Scott Charitable Will Trust
Tyne & Wear Foundation

Tyne and Wear
John Bell Charitable Trust
Joseph Brough Charitable Trust
The Carr-Ellison Charitable Trust
Chapman Foundation
Bill & May Hodgson Charitable Trust
The Joicey Trust
Sir James Knott Trust
The William Leech Charity
R W Mann Trustees Limited
Frederick Milburn Charitable Trust
Millfield House Foundation
Newcastle Children's Mission & Institute
The Ravenscroft Foundation
The Storrow Scott Charitable Will Trust
Tyne & Wear Foundation

■ North West England
Green and Lilian F M Ainsworth and Family Benevolent Fund
Ferguson Benevolent Fund Limited
The Christopher Rowbotham Charitable Trust
The Yorkshire Bank Charitable Trust

Cheshire
Lord Leverhulme's Charitable Trust
Oldham Foundation

Cumbria
The John Gilpin Trust
The Provincial Trust for Kendal
The Francis C Scott Charitable Trust
The Frieda Scott Charitable Trust
The Skelton Bounty
Slater Trust Limited

Derbyshire
The Bamford Charitable Trust
The Bingham Trust
The Chetwode Foundation
Oldham Foundation
The Woodroffe Benton Foundation

Greater Manchester
A J Freeman Charitable Trust
The Manchester Guardian Society Charitable Trust
Oldham Foundation
The Skelton Bounty
Sydney Dean Whitehead's Charitable Trust

Lancashire
The General Charity Fund
The Harris Charity
Gay & Peter Hartley's Hillards Charitable Trust
The Hoover Foundation
Oldham Foundation
The Pye Christian Trust
The Francis C Scott Charitable Trust
The Skelton Bounty
The John Slater Foundation
Sydney Dean Whitehead's Charitable Trust

Merseyside
Charles and Edith Aveling Bounty
The Baring Foundation
The Charles Brotherton Trust
The Chrimes Family Charitable Trust
Ford of Britain Trust
The General Charity Fund
The John Gilpin Trust
Sheila Kay Fund
Laspen Trust
Liverpool Children's Welfare Trust

Yorkshire and Humberside

Trusts by beneficial area

The Moores Family Charity Foundation
The Morgan Crucible Company Charitable Trust
The Eleanor Rathbone Charitable Trust
The Ravensdale Trust
The John Rayner Charitable Trust
The Skelton Bounty
The Ward Blenkinsop Trust
The Wates Foundation
The Wedge

■ Yorkshire and Humberside

The Bridon Group Charitable Trust
The Jack Brunton Charitable Trust
The Gordon Fraser Charitable Trust
The D W Greenwood Charitable Settlement
Joseph and Mary Hiley Trust
The Sir George Martin Trust
Normanby Charitable Trust
Oldham Foundation
The F A Riley-Smith Charitable Trust
William Webster Charitable Trust
The Yorkshire Bank Charitable Trust

Humberside, East Riding

Gay & Peter Hartley's Hillards Charitable Trust
The Thomas Hudson Benevolent Trust
The Hull & East Riding Charitable Trust
S H and E C Priestman Trust
The Sydney Smith Trust
May Watkinson Charity Trust

North Yorkshire

The Charles Brotherton Trust
Lucilla Butler's Trust
The Norman Collinson Charitable Trust
The Coulthurst Trust
The A M Fenton Trust
Constance Green Foundation
Joseph and Mary Hiley Trust
The George A Moore Foundation

Normanby Charitable Trust
The John Rayner Charitable Trust
The F A Riley-Smith Charitable Trust
The Sylvia and Colin Shepherd Charitable Trust
The Cynthia Walker Charitable Trust
Whitehall Charitable Foundation Limited

South Yorkshire

The Coulthurst Trust
The Freshgate Trust Foundation
J G Graves Charitable Trust
Gay & Peter Hartley's Hillards Charitable Trust
The Ronald & Kathleen Pryor Charity
The John Rayner Charitable Trust
South Yorkshire Community Foundation
Queen Victoria & Johnson Memorial Trust
The Cynthia Walker Charitable Trust

West Yorkshire

The Norman C Ashton Foundation
The Charles Brotherton Trust
The Coulthurst Trust
Emmandjay Charitable Trust
Constance Green Foundation
Joseph and Mary Hiley Trust
Gay & Peter Hartley's Hillards Charitable Trust
The George A Moore Foundation
The Morgan Crucible Company Charitable Trust
The John Rayner Charitable Trust
The F A Riley-Smith Charitable Trust
The Sylvia and Colin Shepherd Charitable Trust
The Charity of Thomas Wade & Others
The Cynthia Walker Charitable Trust
Edwin Woodhouse Charitable Trust

■ Scotland

Charity Projects
The Gordon Fraser Charitable Trust
The Gannochy Trust
The Gough Charitable Trust
The Kenneth Hargreaves Trust
The KC Charitable Trust
The MacRobert Trusts
Natwest Staff Samaritan Fund
The Spurgin Charitable Trust
TSB Foundation for Scotland
John Watson's Trust
The Barbara Welby Trust

■ North Scotland

Grampian

The E W Gladstone Charitable Trust
The Howard Hatton Charitable Trust
The Patrick Mitchell Hunter Fund

Highland

Mr Frederick Wills 1961 Charitable Trust

■ South Scotland

Fife

Carnegie Dunfermline Trust
De La Rue Charitable Trust

Lothian

The Edinburgh Medical Missionary Society – Hawthornbrae Trust
The KC Charitable Trust
The Nancie Massey Charitable Trust

Strathclyde

Peter Brough Trust
The Chrimes Family Charitable Trust
The Hoover Foundation
MacGregor's Bequest
Mickel Fund
The James Weir Foundation

Tayside

The Ellis Campbell Charitable Foundation

Trusts by beneficial area **Overseas**

■ Northern Ireland

Charity Projects
Enkalon Foundation
The Gordon Fraser Charitable Trust
The Hon P N Gibson's Charity Trust
The Ireland Fund of Great Britain
Laspen Trust
The Wates Foundation
The Women Caring Trust

Antrim
Ford of Britain Trust

Armagh
Ford of Britain Trust

Down
Ford of Britain Trust

■ Wales

The Arts Council of Wales
Charity Projects
Dinam Charity
Joseph Strong Frazer Trust
The Gibbins Trust
The Kenneth Hargreaves Trust
Lady Hind Trust
Lloyds Bank Charitable Trust
The Ivona Mays-Smith Charitable Trust
Natwest Staff Samaritan Fund
The Oakdale Trust
The Owen Family Trust
The Leonard Laity Stoate Charitable Trust
TSB Foundation for England and Wales
The Barbara Welby Trust

■ North Wales

The Chrimes Family Charitable Trust
Laspen Trust

Clwyd
The Chrimes Family Charitable Trust
The E W Gladstone Charitable Trust

Gwynedd
Gwynedd County Council Welsh Church Fund

■ South Wales

The Hoover Foundation
The Morgan Crucible Company Charitable Trust

Gwent
Ford of Britain Trust

Mid Glamorgan
Ford of Britain Trust
The Rhondda Cynon Taff Welsh Church Acts Fund

South Glamorgan
Ford of Britain Trust

West Glamorgan
Ford of Britain Trust

■ Overseas

Access 4 Trust
The Alchemy Foundation
Allied Dunbar Staff Charity Fund
The Princess Anne's Charities
The Baring Foundation
The Beaverbrook Foundation
The Hubert Blake Charitable Trust
The M Bourne Charitable Trust
British Humane Association
Edward Cadbury Charitable Trust
William Adlington Cadbury Charitable Trust
The Edward & Dorothy Cadbury Trust (1928)
CAF
Charity Projects
The City of London School Charitable Trust
Cooper Charitable Trust
The Wallace Curzon Charitable Trust
De La Rue Charitable Trust
The Emma de Yong Charitable Trust
Nicholas De Yong's Charitable Trust 1984
The Dulverton Trust
The Gilbert and Eileen Edgar Foundation
The Farne Trust
Ferguson Benevolent Fund Limited
The Russell and Mary Foreman 1980 Charitable Trust

Jill Franklin Trust
The Friends of the Clergy Corporation
Angela Gallagher Memorial Fund
The Gatsby Charitable Foundation
The Charles Green Foundation
The Ireland Fund of Great Britain
The James Trust
Beatrice Laing Trust
Langdale Trust
The Enid Linder Foundation
Lloyd's Charities Trust
The Vanessa Lowndes Charitable Trust
The Mackintosh Foundation
Mount 'A' Charitable Trust
Mount 'B' Charitable Trust
The Northumberland Village Homes Trust
The PDC Trust
Dr L H A Pilkington's Charitable Trust
The Project Charitable Trust
The Pye Christian Trust
Radley Charitable Trust
The F A Riley-Smith Charitable Trust
The Rivendell Trust
The Rowan Charitable Trust
The Securicor Charitable Trust
The Seedfield Trust
Singer Foundation
Edward Skinner Charitable Trust
Eric Stonehouse Trust Ltd
The Bernard Sunley Charitable Foundation
Adrienne & Leslie Sussman Charitable Trust
The Charles Sykes Trust
The Stella Symons Charitable Trust
The Margaret Thatcher Charitable Trust
The Thorpe Charity Trust
G J W Turner Trust
Bernard Van Leer Foundation UK Trust
The Wakeham Trust
The Barbara Welby Trust
The Harold Hyam Wingate Foundation
The Woodward Charitable Trust

INDEX D

Alphabetical register of grant making charitable trusts

This index lists the individual entries for the trusts appearing in this directory in alphabetical order.

■ AGF Charitable Trust (formerly NEM Charitable Trust)

OBJECTS General charitable purposes

POLICY OF TRUSTEES Support for local initiatives, particularly where AGF Insurance Group staff or pensioners involved in fund raising

TYPE OF GRANT Single donations

TYPE OF BENEFICIARY a) Pensioners of AGF Insurance Group in need of assistance b) Various charitable institutions and other bodies or persons with charitable objectives

BENEFICIAL AREA Mostly in areas surrounding AGF Group offices

FINANCES
- Year 1993
- Grants £4,857
- Income £14,926
- Assets £50,384

TRUSTEES J-P Paumier, A Dean, R Neal, S Taylor, P Saunders

SUBMISSION OF APPLICATIONS Applications received during a quarter normally accumulated and reviewed at the subsequent meeting of the Trustees

CORRESPONDENT Ms A Wilson, AGF House, 41 Botolph Lane, London EC3R 8DL

CLASSIFICATIONS
- Adventure centres and playgrounds
- Centres, clubs and institutes
- Counselling (inc helplines)
- Holidays
- Homes and hostels
- Special needs housing

C.C. NO 327671   **ESTABLISHED** 1988

■ The AHJ Charitable Trust

OBJECTS General charitable purposes

POLICY OF TRUSTEES General charitable trusts, the arts, and youth work

TYPE OF GRANT Both recurrent and one-off

TYPE OF BENEFICIARY Arts, youth work and occasionally the aged

RESTRICTIONS No grants to individuals

FINANCES
- Year 1993
- Grants £2,295
- Income £3,000
- Assets £54,673

TRUSTEES R R Jessel, P J Willoughby, J W R Lindsey, J M Bogaardt

SUBMISSION OF APPLICATIONS Written applications only will be considered by the Trustees

CORRESPONDENT c/o Poole & Co, Dolphin House, 21 Hendford, Yeovil, Somerset BA20 1TP

CLASSIFICATIONS
- Community groups

C.C. NO 279452   **ESTABLISHED** 1980

■ Abel Charitable Trust

OBJECTS General charitable purposes

POLICY OF TRUSTEES Orientating to resolve rather than alleviate problems

TYPE OF BENEFICIARY Mainly emergent charities aiming to make the individual more self sufficient and treating the person as a whole and not a malfunctioning part

RESTRICTIONS Registered charities only. Applications from individuals, including students, are ineligible. Funds will not be given for building projects or to reduce extant deficits, or for vehicles, or for work with the elderly. No grants made in response to general appeals from large, National organisations

BENEFICIAL AREA London and South East

SAMPLE GRANTS £1,500 to the Homeless Network for cost of newsletter for single homeless people
£1,350 to Oasis Children's Venture for senior swings and equipment for nature garden
£1,100 to the Drugs and Alcohol Foundation for drug and alcohol education programme
£1,000 to North Lambeth Day Centre for purchase of equipment for training and education programme
£1,000 to the Housing Services Agency for Resettlement Welfare Fund for single homeless people

FINANCES
- Year 1994
- Grants £25,162
- Income £18,675
- Assets £580,960

TRUSTEES The Rev Canon I Smith-Cameron, The Rev Canon M Baddeley, The Rev A R C Arbuthnot

CORRESPONDENT The Rev D J Abel, Balcombe Mill, Mill Lane, Balcombe, Haywards Heath, West Sussex RH19 1DS

CLASSIFICATIONS
- Community groups
- Homes and hostels

C.C. NO 288421   **ESTABLISHED** 1983

■ Keith & Freda Abraham Charitable Trust

OBJECTS General charitable purposes

POLICY OF TRUSTEES To make donations to national charities but only assist local charities and projects which benefit North Devon

TYPE OF GRANT Various

TYPE OF BENEFICIARY National charities, North Devon based charities and projects

RESTRICTIONS The Trust does not support charitable causes outside North Devon, other than those of a national or international nature. No grants are made to individuals

BENEFICIAL AREA National charities, but North Devon based local causes only

FINANCES
- Year 1994
- Grants £7,225
- Income £13,471
- Assets £266,041

TRUSTEES K N Abraham, Mrs F Abraham, H J Purnell, C D Squire, C T Mill

SUBMISSION OF APPLICATIONS To correspondent. Grants usually made in December

---

Does the trust you have chosen match your needs? Haphazard applications waste postage and time

Access

CORRESPONDENT R J Stanbury, Barrow Bartlett & Stanbury, 30 Bear Street, Barnstaple, Devon EX32 7DD

CLASSIFICATIONS
- Children and youth – general

C.C. NO 288672   **ESTABLISHED** 1983

■ Access 4 Trust

OBJECTS General charitable purposes

POLICY OF TRUSTEES Trustees focus their grant-giving primarily towards deprived children and needy, women's organisations and adoption

TYPE OF GRANT Single donations

TYPE OF BENEFICIARY Institutions and registered charities

RESTRICTIONS Not individuals

BENEFICIAL AREA England

SAMPLE GRANTS £70,000 to Womankind Worldwide
£10,000 to Post Adoption Centre
£3,000 to After Adoption Centre
£1,800 to Tower Hamlets Deaf Youth Club

FINANCES
- Year 1995
- Grants £146,026
- Income £62,535
- Assets £588,490

TRUSTEES Miss S M Wates, J R F Lulham

CORRESPONDENT C W Sudlow, 16a St James Street, London SW1A 1ER

CLASSIFICATIONS
- Children and youth – general
- Adoption/fostering
- Advancement in life

C.C. NO 267017   **ESTABLISHED** 1973

■ Kate Adams Charitable Trust

OBJECTS Relief of poverty and advancement of education of individuals; Methodist Missionary Society or associated and similar objects; general charitable purposes

POLICY OF TRUSTEES The Trustees are willing to consider any request for financial assistance. The tendency in recent years has been to support medical students, people in dire need, and causes in and around Nottingham which the Trustees feel are deserving

BENEFICIAL AREA Mainly Nottingham

FINANCES
- Year 1994
- Grants £1,500
- Income £2,526
- Assets £28,324

TRUSTEES B R Hartley, P H Jenkins

CORRESPONDENT Browne Jacobson, Solicitors, 44 Castle Gate, Nottingham NG1 7BJ

CLASSIFICATIONS
- Youth organisations (eg Guides, Scouts, YWCA etc)

C.C. NO 249914   **ESTABLISHED** 1964

■ The John and Florence Adamson Charitable Trust

OBJECTS General charitable purposes

POLICY OF TRUSTEES Funds distributed to charities in which donors are interested

RESTRICTIONS Only applications by registered charities can be considered

BENEFICIAL AREA North East England

FINANCES
- Year 1994
- Grants £6,650
- Income £8,373

TRUSTEES Mrs M C Sharp, J R Adamson, Mrs D Oglethorpe, N Sherlock

CORRESPONDENT Mrs M C Sharp, Secretary, The John & Florence Adamson Charitable Trust, PO Box No 68, Head Post Office, Morpeth, Northumberland NE61 1LR

CLASSIFICATIONS
- Children and youth – general

C.C. NO 305956   **ESTABLISHED** 1965

■ The Adint Charitable Trust

OBJECTS General charitable purposes

POLICY OF TRUSTEES Grants to registered charities only

TYPE OF BENEFICIARY Registered charities only

RESTRICTIONS Grants may be made to registered charities only. No applications from individuals can be entertained under any circumstances

FINANCES
- Year 1993
- Grants £318,781
- Income £418,489
- Assets £5,135,033

TRUSTEES Mrs M Edwards, A E Edwards, A A Davis, Mrs D Jeffery, D R Oram

CORRESPONDENT A A Davis, Stoy Hayward, 8 Baker Street, London W1M 1DA

CLASSIFICATIONS
- Adoption/fostering
- Centres, clubs and institutes

C.C. NO 265290   **ESTABLISHED** 1973

■ Green and Lilian F M Ainsworth and Family Benevolent Fund

OBJECTS General charitable purposes. Specific project preferred

POLICY OF TRUSTEES The Trustees have a comprehensive list of charitable objects from whom they select each year. Other applicants are made secondary to these preferred charities

TYPE OF BENEFICIARY The young, the elderly and the handicapped preferred

RESTRICTIONS Payments to registered charities only considered. The Trustees do not sponsor individuals but preference for secondary awards is given to charities whose work is in the North West of England

BENEFICIAL AREA North West of England

FINANCES
- **Year** 1995
- **Grants** £1,000
- **Income** £19,512
- **Assets** £255,065

TRUSTEES The Royal Bank of Scotland plc

CORRESPONDENT The Royal Bank of Scotland plc, Preston Trustee Office, Guildhall House, Guildhall Street, Preston, Lancs PR1 3NU

CLASSIFICATIONS
- Children and youth – general
- Adventure centres and playgrounds
- Centres, clubs and institutes
- Community groups
- Day centres and nurseries
- Homes and hostels
- Special needs housing
- Special classes
- Youth organisations (eg Guides, Scouts, YWCA etc)
- Children and violence (inc abuse)

C.C. NO 267577 **ESTABLISHED** 1974

■ The Alchemy Foundation (formerly the Starlight Foundation)

OBJECTS General charitable purposes

POLICY OF TRUSTEES The Trustees favour in particular: (a) Any charities involved in promoting the material, mental and spiritual welfare of – (i) Persons suffering from mental or physical illness or disability and in particular babies and children so suffering. (ii) Persons suffering from the effects of famine. (b) Any charity benefiting children. (c) The Orpheus Trust

BENEFICIAL AREA UK and international

FINANCES
- **Year** 1994
- **Grants** £523,374
- **Income** £998,568

TRUSTEES R H Z S Stilgoe, Mrs A Stilgoe, Rev D Reeves, Dr M Smith, Esther Rantzen, A Armitage, A Murison

CORRESPONDENT R H Z S Stilgoe, Trevereux Manor, Limpsfield Chart, Oxted, Surrey RH8 0TL

CLASSIFICATIONS
- Children and youth – general

C.C. NO 292500 **ESTABLISHED** 1985

■ Alexandra Rose Day

OBJECTS To provide a 'Voice' and fundraising opportunities for 'people caring' charities in UK

POLICY OF TRUSTEES Grants to registered charities only who come under the umbrella of Alexandra Rose Day

TYPE OF GRANT Grants in region of £300–£500 each

BENEFICIAL AREA UK

SAMPLE GRANTS Supply of hobby kits to children's hospices
The Pace Centre, Aylesbury, Bucks
Whizz Kidz, London
Buxton Sea Cadets, Derbyshire
Gingerbread Creche, Clwyd, Wales

FINANCES
- **Year** 1995
- **Grants** £251,461
- **Income** £495,787
- **Assets** £269,449

TRUSTEES The Council

PUBLICATIONS Newsletter

CORRESPONDENT Mrs Gillian Greenwood, National Director, Alexandra Rose Day, 2A Ferry Road, Barnes, London SW13 9RX

CLASSIFICATIONS
- Children and youth – general
- Adventure centres and playgrounds
- Day centres and nurseries
- Holidays
- Youth organisations (eg Guides, Scouts, YWCA etc)

C.C. NO 211535 **ESTABLISHED** 1912

■ Allied Dunbar Foundation

OBJECTS General charitable purposes

POLICY OF TRUSTEES The charities to be supported each year are chosen in advance, following an annual theme

TYPE OF GRANT For tangible projects with visible end results. (Capital/revenue split 75/25%) – one-off (not recurrent)

TYPE OF BENEFICIARY National and local charities

RESTRICTIONS Restricted to social welfare. Applications are not invited from charities. The Trustees make their own enquiries, following suggestions put forward by the sales force and IFA divisions of the Company

FINANCES
- **Year** 1995
- **Grants** £933,000
- **Income** £964,000

TRUSTEES P Smith, G Greener, S Leitch, K Baldwin

PUBLICATIONS Annual Report

SUBMISSION OF APPLICATIONS On request from the Trustees when annual theme has been agreed. Application form is essential

CORRESPONDENT Mrs Hilary Hares, Allied Dunbar Foundation, Allied Dunbar Centre, Swindon, Wiltshire SN1 1EL

CLASSIFICATIONS
- Children and youth – general

C.C. NO 266983 **ESTABLISHED** 1981

■ Allied Dunbar Staff Charity Fund

OBJECTS General charitable purposes

POLICY OF TRUSTEES The Fund supports a variety of social welfare projects in the staff travel to work area (Wiltshire mainly) and, in addition, commits around 15% of its income to overseas charities

TYPE OF GRANT Capital and revenue balanced between one-off and three-year funding

TYPE OF BENEFICIARY Voluntary organisations, community groups, local charities

RESTRICTIONS No grants given to religious organisations, schools (except special) or to individuals

BENEFICIAL AREA Swindon and surrounding rural area; developing overseas countries

SAMPLE GRANTS £12,000 pa x three years to fund salary of project worker to co-ordinate special needs children into mainstream rural out-of-school activities
£7,200 to fund costs of session workers for

Alper

photography/crafts mobile project for 12–15 age group in remote village areas
£5,000 pa x three years to a Swindon secondary school to part-fund school counsellor post

FINANCES
- **Year** 1995
- **Grants** £381,000

TRUSTEES P Smith, A P Leitch, K Baldwin, G Greener

PUBLICATIONS Annual Report

NOTES Guidelines are available outlining the policy areas and criteria

SUBMISSION OF APPLICATIONS Applications dealt with at regular meetings of Fund Committee

CORRESPONDENT Jennie Shearer, Community Affairs, Allied Dunbar Staff Charity Fund, Allied Dunbar Centre, Swindon, Wiltshire SN1 1EL

CLASSIFICATIONS
- Community groups
- Children and violence (inc abuse)

C.C. NO 266983 **ESTABLISHED** 1975

■ The Alper Charitable Trust

OBJECTS General charitable purposes

POLICY OF TRUSTEES Grants are generally limited to help young musicians and some support for other arts

TYPE OF BENEFICIARY (a) Individual loans for musical courses (but not dancing) will continue to be made. The Trust will also consider making interest-free loans to enable young musicians to purchase instruments. (b) Grants for other charitable purposes will be limited to charities whose activities lie within the areas of the South Cambridgeshire District, the East Cambridgeshire District, West Suffolk and the Saffron Walden area

RESTRICTIONS See Policy of Trustees and Type of Beneficiary

BENEFICIAL AREA Preference towards East Anglian applicants

FINANCES
- **Year** 1994
- **Grants** £7,422
- **Income** £20,648
- **Assets** £191,104

TRUSTEES S Alper, Mrs I D Alper, T Yardley, J Horwood-Smart

CORRESPONDENT S Alper, Chilford Hall, Linton, Cambridgeshire

CLASSIFICATIONS
- Advancement in life

C.C. NO 272104 **ESTABLISHED** 1976

■ Ambika Paul Foundation (formerly Ambika Charitable Foundation)

OBJECTS General charitable purposes

POLICY OF TRUSTEES To support educational institutions and projects

TYPE OF GRANT Direct cash donations, deeds of covenant. Lump sum payments

TYPE OF BENEFICIARY Large organisations, registered charities, colleges, universities

RESTRICTIONS Only available to children and young people's registered charities. Will not fund individuals or DSS requests. Will not pay individuals' salaries/running costs. Applications from individuals, including students, mainly ineligible. Funding for scholarships made direct to colleges/universities, not to individuals. No expeditions

BENEFICIAL AREA UK

SAMPLE GRANTS £4,000 to Hull University for scholarships

FINANCES
- **Year** 1995
- **Grants** £798,362
- **Income** £470,984

TRUSTEES S Paul, Mrs A Paul, Mrs A Punn

PUBLICATIONS Annual Report

SUBMISSION OF APPLICATIONS In writing to the Trustees at above address. Acknowledgements sent if sae enclosed

CORRESPONDENT S Paul, Caparo House, 103 Baker Street, London W1M 1FD

CLASSIFICATIONS
- Advancement in life
- Development of character

C.C. NO 276127 **ESTABLISHED** 1978

■ Sir John and Lady Amory's Charitable Trust (formerly Sir John Heathcoat Amory Trust)

OBJECTS General charitable purposes

POLICY OF TRUSTEES Local charities

TYPE OF BENEFICIARY Local organisations plus a few National ones

RESTRICTIONS New applications are restricted

BENEFICIAL AREA Mostly Devon

FINANCES
- **Year** 1994
- **Grants** £30,575
- **Income** £34,048
- **Assets** £629,980

TRUSTEES Joyce, Lady Heathcoat Amory, Sir John Palmer, Sir Ian Heathcoat Amory, Lady Palmer

CORRESPONDENT Sir John Palmer, Messrs Bevan Ashford, Solicitors, Gotham House, Tiverton, Devon EX16 6LT

CLASSIFICATIONS
- Children and youth – general
- Homes and hostels
- Youth organisations (eg Guides, Scouts, YWCA etc)

C.C. NO 203970 **ESTABLISHED** 1961

■ The Prince Andrew Charitable Trust

OBJECTS General charitable purposes

POLICY OF TRUSTEES Contributions to those organisations with which the Duke of York has a particular link or interest — research into the alleviation of blindness and deafness, scientific and practical assistance for disabled, brain-damaged or socially disadvantaged children, participation of the disabled into sporting activities

TYPE OF GRANT Usually one-off for a specific project or part of a project. Core funding and/or salaries rarely considered

TYPE OF BENEFICIARY Registered charities working in areas outlined under Policy

RESTRICTIONS Registered charities only. Applications from individuals are not supported. No grants made in response to general appeals from large, national organisations nor to smaller bodies working in areas other than those set out above. Organisations which have other Members of The Royal Family as Patrons are not normally supported

FINANCES
- Year 1995
- Grants £21,940
- Income £11,776

TRUSTEES Henry Boyd-Carpenter, CVO, Captain Robert Neil Blair, Royal Navy, John Parsons, LVO

SUBMISSION OF APPLICATIONS At any time. Trustees meet twice a year, in March and September. Applications should include clear details of the need the intended project is designed to meet plus an outline budget. Only applications from eligible bodies are acknowledged, when further information about the project may be requested

CORRESPONDENT Captain Neil Blair, RN, Buckingham Palace, London SW1A 1AA

CLASSIFICATIONS
- Children and youth – general

C.C. NO 290140   ESTABLISHED 1984

■ The Princess Anne's Charities

OBJECTS General charitable purposes with which The Princess Royal has direct involvement

BENEFICIAL AREA Overseas

FINANCES
- Year 1993
- Grants £76,475
- Income £98,380

TRUSTEES Lt Col P E W Gibbs, CVO, The Hon Mark Bridges, Captain T J H Laurence, MVO, RN

CORRESPONDENT Lt Col P E W Gibbs, CVO, Buckingham Palace, London SW1A 1AA

CLASSIFICATIONS
- Homes and hostels

C.C. NO 277814   ESTABLISHED 1979

■ J C W Anstey Charitable Settlement

OBJECTS General charitable purposes; preference for the relief of mentally handicapped persons and elderly persons and organisations

TYPE OF BENEFICIARY Mentally handicapped

RESTRICTIONS No telephone canvassing

BENEFICIAL AREA South East England

FINANCES
- Year 1995
- Grants £2,015
- Income £2,095
- Assets £36,000

TRUSTEES G A Stacey, M J W Anstey

CORRESPONDENT Michael Anstey, Ground Floor, The Annexe, Grosvenor Hall, Bolnore Road, Haywards Heath, West Sussex RH16 4BX

CLASSIFICATIONS
- Children and youth – general
- Homes and hostels

C.C. NO 292799   ESTABLISHED 1985

■ The Armstrong Trust

OBJECTS General charitable purposes

POLICY OF TRUSTEES Preference to charities of which the Trust has special interest, knowledge or association. Primarily in the area of Bristol, Avon and Gloucestershire

TYPE OF BENEFICIARY Help to new local developments. Only small donations to the big National charities unless some special reason. Beneficiaries must be registered charities

RESTRICTIONS No grants to individuals including students

BENEFICIAL AREA Dorset, Avon, Gloucestershire

FINANCES
- Year 1994
- Grants £5,363
- Income £6,099
- Assets £70,000

TRUSTEES Miss F V Armstrong, JP, M F Armstrong, C D Armstrong, Mrs R Armstrong

CORRESPONDENT Mrs R Fergie-Woods, Secretary, Stinchcombe Manor, Stinchcombe Village, Gloucestershire GL11 6BQ

CLASSIFICATIONS
- Children and youth – general
- Community groups
- Development of character
- Youth organisations (eg Guides, Scouts, YWCA etc)

C.C. NO 250448   ESTABLISHED 1956

■ The Arnold Foundation

OBJECTS To help small, local, registered charities

POLICY OF TRUSTEES Only to support local (South West England) charities in which the Trustees have a personal knowledge and interest

TYPE OF GRANT Mainly annual donations

TYPE OF BENEFICIARY Small charities in SW England personally known to the Trustees

RESTRICTIONS Registered charities only. Applications from individuals, including students, are ineligible. No grants made in response to appeals from large national organisations, nor from any organisation working outside South West England

BENEFICIAL AREA South West England

SAMPLE GRANTS £500 annually to Tonbridge and District Sea Cadets
£500 annually to Children's World
£500 annually to the Avon Riding Centre for the Disabled
£250 annually to Wells and District Playgroup
£250 annually to the Ocean Youth Club

FINANCES
- Year 1994
- Grants £17,710
- Income £42,703
- Assets £293,928

TRUSTEES J L S Arnold (Chairman), Mrs M S Grantham, A J Meek, FRIBA, D F Smith, FCA,

SUBMISSION OF APPLICATIONS New applications will not be considered

CORRESPONDENT The Secretary, 37 Nightingale Rise, Portishead, Bristol BS20 8LN

CLASSIFICATIONS
- Children and youth – general

C.C. NO 277430   ESTABLISHED 1979

Artemis

Alphabetical register of grant making charitable trusts

■ The Artemis Charitable Trust

OBJECTS To fund work in the fields of counselling, psychotherapy and parenting

POLICY OF TRUSTEES The Trust makes grants only to charities concerned with counselling, psychotherapy and parent education and support

TYPE OF GRANT Grants are usually continued for several years. Grants often cover core funding. Grants are not made towards purchase of buildings

TYPE OF BENEFICIARY Registered charities in the counselling, psychotherapy and parenting fields

RESTRICTIONS Inland Revenue restrictions mean that grants can only be made to registered charities. Applications from individuals or from organisations which are not registered charities will not be entertained. No grants are made in response to general national appeals

BENEFICIAL AREA UK only

FINANCES
- Year 1993
- Grants £500,000
- Income £450,000
- Assets £4,500,000

TRUSTEES R W Evans, Mrs Evans

SUBMISSION OF APPLICATIONS At any time. Applicants should be aware that most of the Trust's funds are already committed to a number of ongoing projects

CORRESPONDENT R W Evans, 19 Park Hill, Ealing, London W5 2JS

CLASSIFICATIONS
- Counselling (inc helplines)

C.C. NO 291328   **ESTABLISHED** 1985

■ The Arts Council of Wales

OBJECTS To develop and improve the knowledge, understanding and practice of the arts; To develop and improve the accessibility of the arts to the public; To advise and co-operate with other bodies; To carry out the objects through the medium of both the Welsh and English languages.

POLICY OF TRUSTEES Activities limited to arts (including visual art, dance, drama, literature, music and craft)

TYPE OF GRANT Revenue grants, individual bursaries and grants towards capital expenditure through the National Lottery

TYPE OF BENEFICIARY Arts related organisations and professional artists

BENEFICIAL AREA Wales

NOTES The Arts Council of Wales also has four regional Arts boards who deal mainly with regional arts projects; ACW, South East Wales Office, Victoria Street, Cwmbran, Gwent, NP44 3YT Tel 01633 875075. ACW, North Wales Office, 10 Wellfield House, Bangor, Gwynedd, LL57 1ER Tel 01248 351077. ACW, West Wales Office, 3 Heol Goch, Carmarthen, Dyfed, SA31 1QL Tel 01267 234248. ACW, North East Wales Office, Daniel Owen Centre, Earl Road, Mold, Clwyd CH7 1AP Tel 01352 758403

SUBMISSION OF APPLICATIONS Contact the relevant art form officer for details. See notes

CORRESPONDENT Miss Beth Lawton, The Arts Council of Wales, 9 Museum Place, Cardiff CF1 3NX

CLASSIFICATIONS
- Centres, clubs and institutes
- Community groups

C.C. NO 1034245   **ESTABLISHED** 1994

■ The Ashby Charitable Trust

OBJECTS General charitable purposes

POLICY OF TRUSTEES Will consider applications from a wide range of charitable bodies, mainly registered charities

TYPE OF BENEFICIARY Registered charities, Institutions

FINANCES
- Year 1995
- Grants £10,578
- Income £40,065
- Assets £408,201

TRUSTEES B A Ashby, I Ashby, R Goodwin

CORRESPONDENT R Goodwin, 7 New Street, Ledbury, Herefordshire HR8 2DX

CLASSIFICATIONS
- Children and youth – general
- Youth organisations (eg Guides, Scouts, YWCA etc)

C.C. NO 276497   **ESTABLISHED** 1978

■ The Ashcroft Charitable Trust

OBJECTS General charitable purposes

POLICY OF TRUSTEES To consider applications quarterly

TYPE OF GRANT Majority of donations made on a regular basis

TYPE OF BENEFICIARY Children in need – Medical – General

FINANCES
- Year 1991
- Grants £7,050
- Income £9,493
- Assets £97,540

TRUSTEES Kleinwort Benson Trustees Ltd, Miss D Ashcroft

SUBMISSION OF APPLICATIONS Written applications to the Correspondent

CORRESPONDENT Kleinwort Benson Trustees Limited, PO Box 191, 10 Fenchurch Street, London EC3M 3LB

CLASSIFICATIONS
- Children and youth – general
- Adventure centres and playgrounds
- Holidays
- Homes and hostels

C.C. NO 278426   **ESTABLISHED** 1979

■ The Lord Ashdown Charitable Settlement

OBJECTS General charitable purposes, but preferably relief of pain and suffering

POLICY OF TRUSTEES Trustees support registered charities, small innovative projects and students with disabilities

RESTRICTIONS No grants for:- School fees. Second degrees. Postgraduate studies. Elective or intercalated courses. Sponsorships for expeditions. Dance or drama. Research. Well-known national charities

FINANCES
- Year 1993
- Grants £1,362,409
- Income £1,578,714
- Assets £20,417,872

TRUSTEES C M Marks, Dr R M E Stone, G F Renwick, J M B Silver

CORRESPONDENT C M Marks, FCA, 44a New Cavendish Street, London W1M 7LG

CLASSIFICATIONS
- Children and youth – general
- Holidays

C.C. NO 272708 **ESTABLISHED** 1968

■ The Norman C Ashton Foundation

OBJECTS The relief of poverty particularly amongst those connected with the company or their dependants. To assist over education. To support schools, colleges or other educational foundations recognised as charitable in law. To alleviate any national or local disaster

POLICY OF TRUSTEES Each application judged on its merits. Preference around Leeds

TYPE OF BENEFICIARY Local organisations for capital projects only

RESTRICTIONS Restricted generally to Yorkshire in main around Leeds

BENEFICIAL AREA Generally around Leeds

FINANCES
- Year 1991
- Grants £21,623
- Income £30,027
- Assets £431,889

TRUSTEES R S Ashton, J B Crowther, J S Wilson

CORRESPONDENT R S Ashton, The Spinney, 195 Adel Lane, Leeds L16

CLASSIFICATIONS
- Children and youth – general
- Holidays
- Homes and hostels

C.C. NO 260036 **ESTABLISHED** 1969

■ The Ian Askew Charitable Trust

OBJECTS General charitable purposes

POLICY OF TRUSTEES The emphasis is on Sussex charities: all forms of health research, mental health in particular; preservation of ancient buildings

TYPE OF BENEFICIARY Mainly headquarters organisations

RESTRICTIONS No grants to individuals

BENEFICIAL AREA Sussex mainly

SAMPLE GRANTS £500 to Youth Clubs Sussex
£500 to Ringmer and District Association of Youth Clubs
£100 to Young Disabled on Holiday

FINANCES
- Year 1994–95
- Grants £18,336
- Income £45,646
- Assets £1,606,812

TRUSTEES Cleone Pengelley, J R Rank, R A R Askew, R J Wainwright, G B Ackery

CORRESPONDENT c/o Kidsons Impey, Spectrum House, 20–26 Cursitor Street, London EC4A 1HY

CLASSIFICATIONS
- Adventure centres and playgrounds
- Centres, clubs and institutes
- Special needs housing
- Youth organisations (eg Guides, Scouts, YWCA etc)

C.C. NO 264515 **ESTABLISHED** 1972

■ The Dorothy Askew Trust

OBJECTS General charitable purposes

RESTRICTIONS Applications from individuals ineligible

BENEFICIAL AREA Sussex charities and charities which have previously been aided

FINANCES
- Year 1992
- Grants £24,748
- Income £25,618
- Assets £401,849

TRUSTEES I V Askew, Mrs C Pengelley, Mrs D M McAlpine, Mrs M Askew, Mrs P St Q Askew, R A R Askew, B A McAlpine, G B Ackery

CORRESPONDENT Mr A Mistry, c/o Kidsons Impey, Spectrum House, 20–26 Cursitor Street, London EC4A 1HY

CLASSIFICATIONS
- Children and youth – general
- Advancement in life
- Centres, clubs and institutes
- Holidays

C.C. NO 286088 **ESTABLISHED** 1982

■ The Astor Foundation

OBJECTS Medical projects, general charitable purposes, animal welfare

POLICY OF TRUSTEES Medical research and helping people who are disabled by physical and mental disease. Help new and imaginative charities in their early days

TYPE OF BENEFICIARY Mainly headquarters organisations. Innovatory projects rather than long established or well endowed ones (with some exceptions)

RESTRICTIONS Positively no grants to individuals. Normally not capital building works

BENEFICIAL AREA Mainland UK only

FINANCES
- Year 1994
- Grants £51,250

TRUSTEES Sir William Slack, KCVO, The Lord Astor of Hever, J R Astor, R H Astor, Dr H Swanton, C Money-Coutts

NOTES No grants made to post-graduates or those requiring funding for travel etc

CORRESPONDENT Mrs J E Jones, 5 Northview, Hungerford, Berkshire RG17 0DA

CLASSIFICATIONS
- Centres, clubs and institutes
- Development of character

C.C. NO 225708 **ESTABLISHED** 1963

Astor's

Alphabetical register of grant making charitable trusts

■ The Hon M L Astor's 1969 Charity

OBJECTS General charitable purposes

POLICY OF TRUSTEES The Trustees' present policy is to distribute funds to recognised charitable institutions only

TYPE OF BENEFICIARY Research into management of terminal illness, health hazards in the environment. Support for libraries, also children in need

RESTRICTIONS No grants to individuals

FINANCES
- Year 1995
- Grants £10,000
- Income £8,939
- Assets £128,647

TRUSTEES The Hon Mrs J C T Astor, J C L Astor

CORRESPONDENT The Trustees, 16 Lansdowne Road, Holland Park, London W11 3LL

CLASSIFICATIONS
- Day centres and nurseries
- Development of character
- Counselling (inc helplines)
- Holidays

C.C. NO 258601   **ESTABLISHED** 1969

■ Athlone Trust

OBJECTS (a) Relief of needy adopted children under the age of 18 who are in necessitous circumstances (b) Advancement of the education of adopted children under the age of 18

TYPE OF GRANT Annual or single payment

TYPE OF BENEFICIARY As above under Objects

RESTRICTIONS Restricted to adopted children under 18. At present, funds are not fully committed. Will not consider any request from non-adoptive parents for their children

FINANCES
- Year 1994
- Grants £11,914
- Income £10,451

TRUSTEES Lord Wardington, J J Tobin, Lady Sandilands, Mrs I Manning, Mrs H Halpin, P J C Canney, Mrs A Loring

SUBMISSION OF APPLICATIONS To correspondent before May and before November. Two meetings a year, and all applications for the previous six months are then considered together

CORRESPONDENT J J Tobin, 14 New Street, London EC2M 4TR

CLASSIFICATIONS
- Adoption/fostering

C.C. NO 277065   **ESTABLISHED** 1978

■ Lawrence Atwell's Charity (Skinner's Company)

OBJECTS Grants, and under certain circumstances loans, to young poor people preparing for, entering upon or engaged in any profession, apprenticeship or other occupation

POLICY OF TRUSTEES Grants which in the opinion of the Trustees will advance the beneficiaries' efforts towards earning their own living. The following applications ineligible: (a) participating in any expedition, (b) study abroad, (c) intercalated degrees

TYPE OF BENEFICIARY Individuals within prescribed age limits and terms of Trust

RESTRICTIONS Restricted to British citizens between 18–24 years of age, and 16 for artisans

BENEFICIAL AREA Great Britain and Northern Ireland

FINANCES
- Year 1995
- Grants £458,829
- Income £791,192
- Assets £10,006,247

TRUSTEES The Master and Wardens of the Worshipful Company of Skinners

CORRESPONDENT The Clerk to the Lawrence Atwell's Charity, Skinners' Hall, 8 Dowgate Hill, London EC4R 2SP

CLASSIFICATIONS
- Advancement in life

C.C. NO 210773   **ESTABLISHED** 1588

■ The Rt Hon Herbert, Baron Austin of Longbridge Will Trust

OBJECTS Charitable institutions or objects in England with main emphasis on the welfare of children and the care of old people

POLICY OF TRUSTEES The Trustees stress that new awards are now severely limited

RESTRICTIONS Organisations and projects in England only and limited to: (a) Local charities based in Birmingham and West Midlands. (b) National organisations (but not their provincial branches). The Trustees are unable to consider appeals from, or on behalf of, individual applicants

BENEFICIAL AREA England

FINANCES
- Year 1993
- Grants £146,800
- Income £146,800

TRUSTEES J M G Fea, R S Kettel

CORRESPONDENT David L Turfrey, Secretary, Lord Austin Trust, St Philips House, St Philips Place, Birmingham B3 2PP

CLASSIFICATIONS
- Adoption/fostering
- Centres, clubs and institutes
- Development of character
- Homes and hostels
- Youth organisations (eg Guides, Scouts, YWCA etc)

C.C. NO 208394   **ESTABLISHED** 1937

■ Charles and Edith Aveling Bounty

OBJECTS General charitable purposes

POLICY OF TRUSTEES Grants/gifts not made to individuals

TYPE OF BENEFICIARY Local charitable bodies

RESTRICTIONS Only as to locality

BENEFICIAL AREA Metropolitan District of Sefton, Merseyside

FINANCES
- Year 1993
- Grants £7,250
- Income £7,259
- Assets £147,564

TRUSTEES R S Irving, B G Cox, D H Hobley, D T Bushell

CORRESPONDENT Brown, Turner, Compton Carr & Co, Solicitors, 11 St George's Place, Southport, Merseyside PR9 0AL

CLASSIFICATIONS
● Homes and hostels
● Youth organisations (eg Guides, Scouts, YWCA etc)

C.C. NO 235820   **ESTABLISHED** 1959

■ The Avon Trust

OBJECTS General charitable purposes connected with the Methodist Church

---

TYPE OF BENEFICIARY Methodist Churches

BENEFICIAL AREA UK

FINANCES
● Year 1994   ● Income £12,500
● Grants £13,500   ● Assets £111,000

TRUSTEES G Field, M A Cashmore, B Cashmore, R Shaw, R A Jones, Mrs H Shaw

CORRESPONDENT R A Jones, 9 Wannerton Road, Blakedown, Kidderminster DY10 3NG

CLASSIFICATIONS
● Homes and hostels

C.C. NO 219050   **ESTABLISHED** 1959

■ The BBC Children in Need Appeal

OBJECTS The relief of need, hardship, sickness, handicap and distress among children and young persons

---

POLICY OF TRUSTEES Grants to individual children in need are made only in response to applications from groups and organisations. Children are defined as those up to and including 18 years of age. Other policy guidelines reviewed annually and detailed on information sheet sent out with application form

TYPE OF GRANT Flexible. Both capital and revenue costs considered. Up to three years, in the case of registered charities, for projects which show real evidence of strategic thinking. No lower or upper limits on amount which can be applied for but the sheer volume of applications imposes constraints

TYPE OF BENEFICIARY Disadvantaged children only via non profit-making groups and organisations in the UK. The Trustees appreciate the good works which go on for 'average' children in 'average' circumstances but they are unable to make a financial contribution

RESTRICTIONS Grants not provided for large on-going general appeals, for children to travel abroad, for private medical treatment or to finance deficits or loans

BENEFICIAL AREA UK

SAMPLE GRANTS £36,000 to Ratcliffe Trust, who run a support team for young people in Cheltenham. Grant will allow expansion throughout Gloucestershire
£33,000 over two years to fund a development officer for CHAIR, a care organisation run by and for young people with disabilities
£10,300 to Anglesey Crossroads Care Attendant Scheme for additional out of school care hours to relieve young carers
£10,000 to Rydall Bankhall Youth Centre towards salaries of three youth workers who will help develop contacts and offer information and advice locally
£5,200 to Platform, which provides music courses to homeless or ex-offending youngsters in London. Grant helped towards rent and new instruments

FINANCES
● Year 1995   ● Income £15,424,712
● Grants £16,067,429   ● Assets £10,615,825

TRUSTEES Sir Kenneth Bloomfield, M Stevenson, Elaine Ross, J Clarke, M Byford, C Browne, Jane Asher, D Carrington, Sir Robert Andrew, Alison Reed

PUBLICATIONS Annual Report. Send A4 sae to Correspondent

NOTES Changes to the existing list of beneficiaries occur infrequently

SUBMISSION OF APPLICATIONS Applications should be submitted to one of two closing dates per Trust year. The first closing date is 30th November each year and the second is the following 30th March.

Notification of outcome within 5 months of each closing date

CORRESPONDENT Julia Kaufmann, BBC Children in Need, c/o PO Box 7, London W5 2GQ

CLASSIFICATIONS
- Children and youth – general

C.C. NO 802052   **ESTABLISHED** 1989

■ BCH 1971 Charitable Trust

OBJECTS General charitable purposes

TYPE OF BENEFICIARY Registered charities only

RESTRICTIONS No grants to individuals

BENEFICIAL AREA Cornwall and Devon

FINANCES
- Year 1995
- Grants £32,000
- Income £38,000
- Assets £450,000

TRUSTEES R C Holman, M A Hayes, Miss J M Holman

CORRESPONDENT Macfarlanes, 10 Norwich Street, London EC4A 1BD

CLASSIFICATIONS
- Children and youth – general

C.C. NO 263241   **ESTABLISHED** 1971

■ The Bacta Charitable Trust

OBJECTS Welfare charitable purposes

POLICY OF TRUSTEES Generally to supporrt causes recommended to it by members of The Amusement Machine Industry

FINANCES
- Year 1992
- Grants £41,000
- Income £77,000

TRUSTEES R Withers (President), Sonia Meadon, C Henry, J Bollom, R Higgins

SUBMISSION OF APPLICATIONS In writing to the Correspondent. The Trustees do not accept any requests for a donation unless they have first been supported by a Bacta member

CORRESPONDENT J S White, Bacta House, Regents Wharf, 6 All Saints Street, London N1 9RG

CLASSIFICATIONS
- Children and youth – general
- Youth organisations (eg Guides, Scouts, YWCA etc)

C.C. NO 328668   **ESTABLISHED** 1990

■ The Nancy Balfour Trust

OBJECTS General charitable purposes

POLICY OF TRUSTEES Generally art, education and housing nationally

FINANCES
- Year 1994
- Grants £11,000
- Income £18,000
- Assets £480,000

TRUSTEES S G Kemp, Miss K Ashbrook, Miss K Evans

CORRESPONDENT S G Kemp, Messrs Sayers Butterworth, 18 Bentinck Street, London W1M 5RL

CLASSIFICATIONS
- Children and youth – general

C.C. NO 259296   **ESTABLISHED** 1969

■ Paul Balint Charitable Trust

OBJECTS General charitable purposes

POLICY OF TRUSTEES We aim to support voluntary self-help groups in the areas of: residential and day care for disabled young; temporary shelter accommodation for the young; training for gainful employment. We are also prepared to support medical research into rare chronic illnesses of children

TYPE OF BENEFICIARY Registered charities

RESTRICTIONS Grants are not given for religious purposes. Grants are not given to individuals

BENEFICIAL AREA England

FINANCES
- Year 1993
- Grants £683,200
- Income £398,108
- Assets £4,307,519

TRUSTEES Mrs M Garay, Dr A Balint, Dr G Balint-Kurti

CORRESPONDENT c/o 26 Church Crescent, London N20 0JP

CLASSIFICATIONS
- Special classes

C.C. NO 273690   **ESTABLISHED** 1977

■ The Bamford Charitable Trust

OBJECTS General charitable purposes

TYPE OF BENEFICIARY Mainly local organisations

RESTRICTIONS No grants to individuals

BENEFICIAL AREA Rocester area only

FINANCES
- Year 1992
- Grants £155,000
- Income £80,000

TRUSTEES Sir Anthony Bamford, Lady Bamford, E T D Leadbeater

SUBMISSION OF APPLICATIONS By letter only

CORRESPONDENT L Mitchell, c/o J C Bamford Excavators Ltd, Rocester, Uttoxeter, Staffordshire ST14 5JP

CLASSIFICATIONS
- Homes and hostels

C.C. NO 279848   **ESTABLISHED** 1979

■ The Barbour Trust

OBJECTS (a) Relief of patients suffering from any form of illness or disease, promotion of research into causes of such illnesses. (b) Furtherance of education. (c) Preservation of buildings and countryside of environmental, historical or architectural interest. (d) Relief of persons in need

POLICY OF TRUSTEES To provide grants to organisations in the categories stated (a), (b), (c), (d). Applications from organisations based in the North East of England are looked at favourably, particularly those based in Tyne and Wear and County Durham. Northumberland and Cleveland are considered

TYPE OF GRANT None of the categories mentioned are excluded by the Trust

TYPE OF BENEFICIARY The Trust likes to support local activities. The Trust also supports local branches of national charities

RESTRICTIONS Grants are made to registered charities only and not to individuals

BENEFICIAL AREA North East England (Tyne & Wear, Northumberland, Co Durham & Cleveland)

FINANCES
- Year 1993
- Grants £137,522
- Income £114,660
- Assets £199,282

TRUSTEES Mrs M Barbour, CBE, DL (Chairman), H J Tavroges, A A E Clenton, Helen M Barbour, BA

PUBLICATIONS A statement of the accounts of the Trust is published annually

SUBMISSION OF APPLICATIONS The Trust meets every two months to consider the applications

CORRESPONDENT Mrs M Barbour – Chairman of the Trustees, The Barbour Trust, J Barbour & Sons Ltd, Simonside, South Shields NE34 9PD

CLASSIFICATIONS
- Adventure centres and playgrounds
- Centres, clubs and institutes
- Community groups
- Day centres and nurseries
- Development of character
- Counselling (inc helplines)
- Holidays
- Homes and hostels
- Special needs housing
- Youth organisations (eg Guides, Scouts, YWCA etc)

C.C. NO 328081 **ESTABLISHED** 1988

■ The Baring Foundation

OBJECTS General charitable purposes

POLICY OF TRUSTEES To restrict its donations to (a) local projects in London, Merseyside and the North East of England (applications from local projects in other areas will not be considered); (b) national voluntary organisations (including organisations that serve only one country within the UK as well as UK-wide organisations); (c) UK charities with partners in developing countries. Applicants who are within these geographical priority areas should write to the Correspondent for more information

TYPE OF BENEFICIARY National, international and London, Merseyside and the North East

RESTRICTIONS Local appeals from outside the areas mentioned, individuals, research and expeditions will not be considered or acknowledged

BENEFICIAL AREA National, overseas, Merseyside, North East England and London

FINANCES
- Year 1994
- Grants £14,006,693
- Income £13,894,787
- Assets £34,824,406

TRUSTEES Council of Management

CORRESPONDENT Mary Scotland, Secretary to the Foundation, The Baring Foundation, 60 London Wall, London EC2M 5TQ

CLASSIFICATIONS
- Children and youth – general

C.C. NO 258583 **ESTABLISHED** 1969

■ The Barleycorn Trust (formerly The Oasis Trust)

OBJECTS Advancement of Christian faith, furtherance of religious and secular education, sick and aged, poor and needy, Christian missionary work

POLICY OF TRUSTEES National charities only. Preference given to Christian organisations

TYPE OF BENEFICIARY Registered charities, institutions with a Christian outlook

BENEFICIAL AREA UK

FINANCES
- Year 1993
- Grants £19,870
- Income £10,187

TRUSTEES H L Barlow, M M L Barlow, R I Corteen, H M Corteen

CORRESPONDENT R I Corteen, 32 Arundel Road, Cheam, Sutton, Surrey SM1 6EU

CLASSIFICATIONS
- Children and youth – general

C.C. NO 296386 **ESTABLISHED** 1986

■ The Elaine Barratt Charitable Trust

OBJECTS General charitable purposes

POLICY OF TRUSTEES Preference is given to local charities

TYPE OF BENEFICIARY Local charity organisations

RESTRICTIONS The Trustees do not respond to applications from individuals, eg students and expeditions

BENEFICIAL AREA Northampton and the local area

SAMPLE GRANTS £450 to Arthritis Care
£300 to Crisis
£300 to Barnardos
£300 to Sea Cadets
£200 to NSPCC

FINANCES
- Year 1995
- Grants £12,000
- Income £12,176
- Assets £124,744

TRUSTEES R G Chandler, Mrs J E Lee, R Barratt, A N S Jones

SUBMISSION OF APPLICATIONS The Trustees meet annually (during July/August). Trustees do not acknowledge all applications received. There is no application form and applicants should write to the Trustees c/o the correspondents address

CORRESPONDENT Mrs J E Lee, The Garden House, 36a Ash Lane, Collingtree, Northampton NN4 0ND

CLASSIFICATIONS
- Children and youth – general

C.C. NO 283286 **ESTABLISHED** 1981

■ Eleanor Barton Trust

OBJECTS General charitable purposes

POLICY OF TRUSTEES The Trustees' particular interest is in the use of the arts as therapy to enable the disadvantaged to find a new dimension to their lives. The disadvantage can be social, mental, physical and includes the elderly, those facing the

Bassham

challenge of AIDS and disaffected or mentally/physically disabled youth

TYPE OF GRANT Usually one-off grants towards specific projects

TYPE OF BENEFICIARY Usually registered charities

RESTRICTIONS No grants given for medical matters

BENEFICIAL AREA UK

SAMPLE GRANTS £250–£2,500 to arts therapy projects

FINANCES
- Year 1995
- Grants £15,000
- Income £21,000
- Assets £410,000

TRUSTEES R D Creed, C B Moynihan

SUBMISSION OF APPLICATIONS The Trustees are willing to receive but do not promise to respond to unsolicited applications

CORRESPONDENT Richard D Creed, Ouvry Creed & Co, Solicitors, Foresters House, Sherston, Malmesbury, Wiltshire SN16 0LQ

CLASSIFICATIONS
- Day centres and nurseries

C.C. NO 293212   **ESTABLISHED** 1985

■ The Paul Bassham Charitable Trust

OBJECTS General charitable purposes

POLICY OF TRUSTEES Preference given to Norfolk charitable causes; if funds permit, other charities with national coverage will be considered

TYPE OF BENEFICIARY Wide range of charitable causes within the geographical and policy areas referred to above

RESTRICTIONS Restricted to UK registered charities/charitable causes; grant payments will not be made directly to individuals

BENEFICIAL AREA Norfolk, national

FINANCES
- Year 1994
- Grants £68,850
- Income £19,224
- Assets £493,097

TRUSTEES R Lovett, R J Jacob

NOTES Applications considered quarterly by Trustees (May, August, November, February)

CORRESPONDENT R Lovett, KPMG, Holland Court, The Close, Norwich NR1 4DY

CLASSIFICATIONS
- Children and youth – general

C.C. NO 266842   **ESTABLISHED** 1973

■ The Batchworth Trust

OBJECTS General charitable purposes

TYPE OF BENEFICIARY Objects worldwide which under the law of England shall be recognised as exclusively charitable (individuals cannot be considered)

RESTRICTIONS Registered charities only; not individuals

FINANCES
- Year 1990
- Grants £160,000
- Income £260,176
- Assets £1,964,013

TRUSTEES Lockwell Trustees Ltd

CORRESPONDENT The Administrative Executive, The Batchworth Trust, 33–35 Bell Street, Reigate, Surrey RH2 7AW

CLASSIFICATIONS
- Children and youth – general
- Development of character

C.C. NO 245061   **ESTABLISHED** 1965

■ The Philip Baxendale Charitable Trust

OBJECTS General charitable purposes

POLICY OF TRUSTEES Funds already fully committed for charities selected by Trustees

RESTRICTIONS No grants to individuals

FINANCES
- Year 1995
- Grants £19,000
- Income £19,000

TRUSTEES P S Baxendale, T C Campbell, Miss O Watson

CORRESPONDENT Miss O Watson, Administrator, 34 Margaret Road, Penwortham, Preston PR1 9QT

CLASSIFICATIONS
- Children and youth – general

C.C. NO 264960   **ESTABLISHED** 1972

■ The Richard Baxendale Charitable Trust

OBJECTS General charitable purposes

POLICY OF TRUSTEES Funds already fully committed for charities selected by Trustees

RESTRICTIONS No grants to individuals. Funds fully committed

FINANCES
- Year 1995
- Grants £17,000
- Income £17,000

TRUSTEES P S Baxendale, O Watson

CORRESPONDENT Miss O Watson, 34 Margaret Road, Penwortham, Preston, Lancashire PR1 9QT

CLASSIFICATIONS
- Homes and hostels

C.C. NO 255251   **ESTABLISHED** 1967

■ The Beaverbrook Foundation

OBJECTS General charitable purposes

POLICY OF TRUSTEES Scholarship schemes are now discontinued

TYPE OF BENEFICIARY Mainly headquarters organisations or registered charities

RESTRICTIONS No grants to individuals

BENEFICIAL AREA UK, New Brunswick and Nova Scotia, Canada

FINANCES
- Year 1993
- Grants £332,212
- Income £477,332

TRUSTEES T M Aitken (Chairman), Lady Aitken (Deputy Chairman), J E A Kidd, Hon Laura Levi, Lady Beaverbrook

CORRESPONDENT Miss J Ford, General Secretary & Administrator, The Beaverbrook Foundation, 11 Old Queen Street, London SW1H 9JA

CLASSIFICATIONS
- Children and youth – general
- Adventure centres and playgrounds
- Development of character

C.C. NO 310003   **ESTABLISHED** 1954

■ The Heather Beckwith Charitable Settlement

OBJECTS General charitable purposes, usually medically oriented

POLICY OF TRUSTEES Usually in the UK

TYPE OF GRANT Depends on request

TYPE OF BENEFICIARY Nothing usually from overseas or from individuals needing financial help

RESTRICTIONS No grants to individuals or people in further education unless personally known to the Trustees

BENEFICIAL AREA UK

SAMPLE GRANTS £2,300 to Teenage Cancer Trust
£500 to National Asthma Campaign
£100 to NSPCC
£100 to Anthony Nolen Bone Marrow Trust

FINANCES
- Year 1993
- Grants £15,935
- Income £19,791

TRUSTEES Mrs H M Beckwith, J L Beckwith, M R MacFadyen

SUBMISSION OF APPLICATIONS No regular dates

CORRESPONDENT Mrs H M Beckwith, 6 Lichfield Road, Kew, Surrey TW9 3JR

CLASSIFICATIONS
- Children and youth – general

C.C. NO 1000952   **ESTABLISHED** 1990

■ John Bell Charitable Trust

OBJECTS General charitable purposes

POLICY OF TRUSTEES Restricted to Tyne and Wear. Preference to youth work and aged

TYPE OF BENEFICIARY Local organisations in Tyne and Wear, Northumberland and Durham only

RESTRICTIONS Applications are restricted to special projects in beneficial area

BENEFICIAL AREA Tyne & Wear, Northumberland & Durham

FINANCES
- Year 1995
- Grants £12,269
- Income £17,075
- Assets £170,964

TRUSTEES R I Stewart, N Sherlock, H Straker

CORRESPONDENT R I Stewart, CBE, DL, Brockenhurst, 2 The Broadway, Tynemouth, Tyne and Wear NE30 2LD

CLASSIFICATIONS
- Youth organisations (eg Guides, Scouts, YWCA etc)

C.C. NO 272631   **ESTABLISHED** 1974

■ The Sylvia Bell Charity

OBJECTS General charitable purposes, under direction of Settlor

POLICY OF TRUSTEES The Trustees favour charities based in Nottinghamshire

TYPE OF BENEFICIARY Registered charities only – where possible local branches of national charities – in areas outlined under Policy

RESTRICTIONS No grants to individuals

BENEFICIAL AREA Nottinghamshire, UK

FINANCES
- Year 1994
- Grants £6,600
- Income £7,040
- Assets £54,836

TRUSTEES M J Stacey, Mrs J G Bostock

CORRESPONDENT The Trustees, The Sylvia Bell Charity, PO Box 33 King Edward Court, Nottingham, Nottinghamshire NG1 6HB

CLASSIFICATIONS
- Children and youth – general
- Centres, clubs and institutes
- Youth organisations (eg Guides, Scouts, YWCA etc)

C.C. NO 266896   **ESTABLISHED** 1973

■ Benham Charitable Settlement

OBJECTS General charitable purposes

POLICY OF TRUSTEES Established by the late Cedric and Hilda Benham, the Trust's policy is to make a large number of relatively small grants to groups working in many charitable fields — including charities involved in medical research, disability and handicap, children, young people, churches, the disadvantaged, wild life, the environment, education, the arts and the elderly. The emphasis is very much on activities within Northamptonshire

TYPE OF BENEFICIARY Most good causes considered, including national appeals, or branches of the same in Northamptonshire. National cathedrals supported but only local churches

RESTRICTIONS Registered charities only. No individuals

BENEFICIAL AREA National, but with special interest in Northamptonshire

FINANCES
- Year 1994
- Grants £126,885
- Income £137,085
- Assets £1,819,242

TRUSTEES Mrs M M Tittle, Mrs R A Nickols, E D D'Alton, FCA, P Schofield, LLB, E N Langley

CORRESPONDENT Mrs M M Tittle, Hurstbourne, Portnall Drive, Virginia Water, Surrey GU25 4NR

CLASSIFICATIONS
- Children and youth – general

C.C. NO 239371   **ESTABLISHED** 1964

Benham

Alphabetical register of grant making charitable trusts

■ Hervey Benham Charitable Trust

OBJECTS To foster exceptional talent or endeavour in the field of artistic development (particularly musical) and maritime traditions

POLICY OF TRUSTEES To support, via grants, young people whose potential may otherwise be diminished due to physical, environmental or financial disability

TYPE OF GRANT Grants range from £100–£1,500 and may be allocated over two to three years

TYPE OF BENEFICIARY Individuals and self-help groups who require support to meet tuition/training costs

RESTRICTIONS Beneficiaries must reside in North East Essex

BENEFICIAL AREA Colchester and North East Essex

SAMPLE GRANTS Music, ballet, drama and dance students (training/tuition)
Maritime support for skipper training
Acquisition and maintenance of sail-training facilities

FINANCES
- Year 1995
- Grants £39,441
- Income £32,896
- Assets £555,301

TRUSTEES G W Bone, M R Carr, M Ellis, K E Mirams, A B Phillips

NOTES The Trustees meet quarterly to consider suitable applications from the Beneficial Area

SUBMISSION OF APPLICATIONS In writing to the Correspondent by the normal quarter days

CORRESPONDENT J Woodman, The Chase House, The Chase, Irvine Road, Colchester, Essex CO3 3TP

CLASSIFICATIONS
- Youth organisations (eg Guides, Scouts, YWCA etc)

C.C. NO 277578   **ESTABLISHED** 1978

■ The Gerald Bentall Charitable Trust

OBJECTS General charitable purposes

POLICY OF TRUSTEES Donations to charities engaged in the care of the sick and handicapped, the education and care of children, environmental resources and the old. Activities outside Southern England not supported unless their work is of national importance

RESTRICTIONS Grants are not made to individuals, students or expeditions

BENEFICIAL AREA Mainly Southern England; also South West England and Channel Islands

FINANCES
- Year 1995
- Grants £6,750
- Income £8,500
- Assets £94,000

TRUSTEES A J D Anstee, Mrs J Digby-Smith, Miss S E Digby-Smith

SUBMISSION OF APPLICATIONS All applicants are acknowledged. The Trustees usually require a copy of the applicants annual accounts

CORRESPONDENT A J D Anstee, The Gerald Bentall Charitable Trust, Anstee House, Wood Street, Kingston upon Thames, Surrey KT1 1TS

CLASSIFICATIONS
- Development of character
- Homes and hostels

C.C. NO 271993   **ESTABLISHED** 1974

■ Rowan Bentall Charity Trust

OBJECTS General charitable purposes

POLICY OF TRUSTEES To support charities in Southern England, assisting hospitals, churches, youth organisations, care of the elderly, handicapped, the armed forces, education and preservation of the environment. Donations range from £25 to £1,500. The most common donation is £100

RESTRICTIONS Grants are not made to individuals

BENEFICIAL AREA Southern England

FINANCES
- Year 1995
- Grants £15,280
- Income £17,800
- Assets £349,135

TRUSTEES L Edward Bentall, FCA, Alastair R Bentall, Kate C Bentall

CORRESPONDENT L Edward Bentall, Chairman's Office, Bentalls plc, Anstee House, Wood Street, Kingston Upon Thames, Surrey KT1 1TS

CLASSIFICATIONS
- Children and youth – general
- Homes and hostels
- Youth organisations (eg Guides, Scouts, YWCA etc)

C.C. NO 232172   **ESTABLISHED** 1960

■ Berkshire Community Trust

OBJECTS The foundation raises new funds from a broad section of corporate and individual donors to support charitable organisations serving the people of Berkshire

POLICY OF TRUSTEES The Trust seeks to provide innovative leadership on community issues through thoughtful grant making in support of those in need. A grants committee, who have recently carried out a local needs survey, have identified particular social needs including children under five, young people, families with a member with long-term disability or illness, carers, certain ethnic minority groups, families on a low income, elderly people and homeless people

TYPE OF GRANT Three categories: Grants up to £300, grants from £300–£2,000 and large grants of a maximum £15,000 annually for five years

TYPE OF BENEFICIARY Any organisation set up for charitable purposes can apply, especially for projects providing community care, counselling services and those tackling crime, poverty, discrimination and addiction. Initiatives to support voluntary sector activity in general will be welcomed as well as projects to promote voluntarism and community leadership

RESTRICTIONS The Trust does not make grants to individuals or to statutory or public bodies. Grants are not made to education, sports, the arts or environment (unless in the context of tackling wider social need). The Trust does not make grants to political or religious groups. The grants are not intended to support major capital appeals. Groups with more than one year's unrestricted reserves will not receive a grant and groups outside Berkshire need not apply

BENEFICIAL AREA Berkshire only

SAMPLE GRANTS St John Ambulance – to fund services of countywide training courses to support carers by a voucher scheme
Slough Furniture Project – towards the purchase of essential items to establish the project
Octopus Toy Lending Library – towards the purchase of a lorry body container for storage of toys
Berkshire MS Therapy Centre – to purchase two items of physiotherapy equipment to help with the lifting and turning of patients
CRUSE Bereavement Care, Reading – to set up and run a group to help children who have suffered a bereavement
Compton Village Hall – towards the refurbishment of the hall, including a disabled toilet and access

FINANCES
- Year 1994–95
- Grants £21,457
- Income £25,465
- Assets £531,147

TRUSTEES Drawn from the local community, includes representatives of local development agencies

PUBLICATIONS Newsletters. Annual Report, 'Community Needs Survey', Grants Policy and Guidelines

SUBMISSION OF APPLICATIONS Grants of up to £300 – year round application. Grants of between £300 and £2,000 – deadline March 1st and October 1st. Large grants, maximum of £15,000 annually for five years – 'Expressions of Interest' to be received by March 1st and October 1st

CORRESPONDENT Grants Administrator, Berkshire Community Trust, Arlington Business Park, Theale, Reading RG7 4SA

CLASSIFICATIONS
- Children and youth – general
- Adventure centres and playgrounds
- Centres, clubs and institutes
- Community groups
- Day centres and nurseries
- Development of character
- Counselling (inc helplines)
- Youth organisations (eg Guides, Scouts, YWCA etc)

C.C. NO 294220   **ESTABLISHED** 1985

■ The Bewley Charitable Trust

OBJECTS Fairly general, as per classification below

TYPE OF GRANT One-off. Prefer to fund running costs etc rather than building up capital endowments. Grant size £25–£100. Will consider less popular causes. Grants not normally given to any group more than once in any 12 month period

TYPE OF BENEFICIARY Community groups, self-help groups, local groups of national organisations, some international welfare groups but would prefer not to widen range of groups supported

RESTRICTIONS Funding will not be provided to individuals (including students) or to local charities outside the West Midlands. Funding will not be provided towards the cost of minibuses, expeditions or PCs. Nothing connected with the armed services will be considered

BENEFICIAL AREA Mainly West Midlands. May consider Midlands projects of larger charities

FINANCES
- Year 1993
- Grants £13,000
- Income £11,200
- Assets £130,000

TRUSTEES J E Payne (Chairman), R I Payne, D A Payne (Secretary), Mrs M J Rawcliffe, Mrs M Payne

NOTES The Bewley Charitable Trust was established by a Trust Deed in 1960

SUBMISSION OF APPLICATIONS Written. A clear letter setting out the purposes of the application, backed up with accounts, or a budget if the project is completely new. Photocopies of building society savings book entries or bank statements will not do. Piles of glossy literature are not wanted. Meetings are held quarterly in June, September, December and March. Applications should be received by the middle of the preceding month and preferably earlier. All applications acknowledged and refusals notified

CORRESPONDENT D A Payne, Secretary, Bewley Charitable Trust, 69 Dudley Road, Tipton, West Midlands DY4 8EE

CLASSIFICATIONS
- Children and youth – general
- Adventure centres and playgrounds
- Centres, clubs and institutes
- Community groups
- Day centres and nurseries
- Development of character
- Counselling (inc helplines)
- Holidays
- Homes and hostels
- Special needs housing
- Special classes
- Youth organisations (eg Guides, Scouts, YWCA etc)
- Children and violence (inc abuse)

C.C. NO 1003164   **ESTABLISHED** 1991

■ The Billmeir Charitable Trust

OBJECTS General charitable purposes

POLICY OF TRUSTEES General charitable purposes with a preference for the Elstead and Farnham areas of Surrey

BENEFICIAL AREA Surrey

FINANCES
- Year 1993
- Grants £83,000
- Income £72,011
- Assets £1,400,000

TRUSTEES B C Whitaker, F C E Telfer, M R Macfadyen

SUBMISSION OF APPLICATIONS The Trustees meet annually to consider applications although the income is virtually fully committed

CORRESPONDENT Timothy T Cripps, Secretary to the Trustees, The Billmeir Charitable Trust, Moore Stephens, 1 Snow Hill, London EC1A 2EN

CLASSIFICATIONS
- Community groups

C.C. NO 208561   **ESTABLISHED** 1956

Bilton

■ The Percy Bilton Charity

OBJECTS Youth work: to provide assistance to alleviate problems facing educationally underpriviledged, delinquent or at risk young people. To encourage young people and children to become more involved in the community in which they live. To provide facilities for recreational activities and outdoor pursuits. Initiatives to prevent educational disadvantage

POLICY OF TRUSTEES To support organisations dealing preferably with new or innovatory work within the Charity's present policy areas

TYPE OF GRANT (a) Grants up to £500 for furniture/fixtures or equipment (b) single donations in excess of £2,000

TYPE OF BENEFICIARY All youth organisations that come within the policy areas of the Charity

RESTRICTIONS What the Charity will not consider: donations for general funding; 'The Arts' (theatre, dance groups, etc); unemployment projects; general 'circularised' appeals; mini-buses and vehicles of any nature; general running expenses; bursaries; expeditions; overseas projects; salaries; research of any kind; organised playschemes; minor building/conversion works

BENEFICIAL AREA UK

SAMPLE GRANTS £20,000 to North Kensington Canalside Trust to assist in the construction of a multi-purpose sports development principally for disabled children
£20,000 to MCVS to assist in the development of an accommodation project for young people in Merseyside
£15,000 to Community Links Centre for the conversion of a public house into alcohol-free bar and social venue in Canning Town, London
£325 to Hockley Flyover Birmingham towards sports equipment
£300 to the Streetlife Trust in Blackpool for their after-school study group

FINANCES
- Year 1995
- Grants £691,401
- Income £813,580
- Assets £3,547,217

TRUSTEES Information regarding the present Trustees will be given upon request

NOTES Total grants £691,401 of which: small grants to youth organisations £36,000; general youth grants £125,000

SUBMISSION OF APPLICATIONS It is advisable to request Guidance Notes before applying to the charity. Telephone 0181 579 2829

CORRESPONDENT The Charity Administrator, Percy Bilton Charity, Bilton House, 54–58 Uxbridge Road, London W5 2TL

CLASSIFICATIONS
- Advancement in life
- Centres, clubs and institutes
- Community groups
- Development of character

C.C. NO 212474   **ESTABLISHED** 1962

■ The Bingham Trust

OBJECTS General charitable purposes

RESTRICTIONS Generally, limited to the town of Buxton and district. Grants are not made towards further education

BENEFICIAL AREA Buxton, Derbyshire

FINANCES
- Year 1994
- Grants £49,803
- Income £44,050
- Assets £498,389

CORRESPONDENT Bennett Brooke-Taylor & Wright, 4 The Quadrant, Buxton, Derbyshire SK17 6AW

CLASSIFICATIONS
- Children and youth – general

C.C. NO 287636   **ESTABLISHED** 1977

■ The Birchwood Trust

OBJECTS General charitable purposes

POLICY OF TRUSTEES To local Evangelical Christian sources. Charities, mainly connected with the church

TYPE OF BENEFICIARY Missionary societies, etc

RESTRICTIONS Only local charities. No applications will be considered as funds are already allocated

BENEFICIAL AREA Mainly within Tunbridge Wells area

FINANCES
- Year 1994
- Grants £9,115
- Income £8,622

TRUSTEES E M R Ward, D G Ward

CORRESPONDENT Messrs Cooke Matheson & Co, Solicitors, 9 Gray's Inn Square, London WC1R 5JQ

CLASSIFICATIONS
- Youth organisations (eg Guides, Scouts, YWCA etc)

C.C. NO 252252   **ESTABLISHED** 1966

■ The Birmingham Amenities and Welfare Trust

OBJECTS Assistance to medical and nursing organisations – hospital amenities – charity to sick or aged poor

POLICY OF TRUSTEES To consider any applications received, but not on annual basis. No individual cases – organised bodies only

TYPE OF BENEFICIARY Not national appeals or multiple charities unless relating specifically to Birmingham

RESTRICTIONS See Policy of Trustees

BENEFICIAL AREA Birmingham area only

FINANCES
- Year 1993
- Grants £4,800
- Income £5,161
- Assets £41,165

TRUSTEES The Council of Management

CORRESPONDENT The Trustees, The Birmingham Amenities and Welfare Trust, C P King, Amika, Broad Lane, Tanworth-in-Arden, Warwick B94 5DY

CLASSIFICATIONS
- Homes and hostels
- Special needs housing

C.C. NO 220778 **ESTABLISHED** 1950

■ The Cyril W Black Charitable Trust

OBJECTS Welfare and relief of the needy – advancement of religion

POLICY OF TRUSTEES Grants to particular projects for evangelical Christian Work and for benefit of youth and aged

RESTRICTIONS No grants to individuals – students or others

FINANCES
- Year 1994
- Grants £79,802
- Income £56,487
- Assets £1,257,703

TRUSTEES Lady Black, A W Black, K R Crabtree, Mrs J D Crabtree

CORRESPONDENT The Secretary, The Cyril W Black Charitable Trust, 6 Leopold Road, Wimbledon, London SW19 7BD

CLASSIFICATIONS
- Holidays
- Youth organisations (eg Guides, Scouts, YWCA etc)

C.C. NO 219857 **ESTABLISHED** 1949

■ Isabel Blackman Foundation

OBJECTS To assist education, social welfare, health, the furtherance of the Christian Religion, the care of old people and all such purposes as shall from time to time be charitable according to the law of England

POLICY OF TRUSTEES Grants are restricted to applicants from Hastings and District

TYPE OF BENEFICIARY Youth organisations, schools, voluntary charitable bodies, hospitals, the blind, the disabled, and old people

RESTRICTIONS Please note only applications from Hastings and District are considered

BENEFICIAL AREA Hastings and District only

FINANCES
- Year 1994–95
- Grants £179,987
- Income £164,731
- Assets £3,301,929

TRUSTEES Mrs W M Mabbett, R A Vint, R T Mennell, D J Jukes, Mrs M Haley

CORRESPONDENT R A Vint, Secretary to the Managing Trustees, Isabel Blackman Foundation, 13 Laton Road, Hastings, East Sussex TN34 2ES

CLASSIFICATIONS
- Centres, clubs and institutes
- Community groups
- Youth organisations (eg Guides, Scouts, YWCA etc)

C.C. NO 313577 **ESTABLISHED** 1966

■ The Herbert And Peter Blagrave Charitable Trust

OBJECTS This Trust supports disabled children and children with special needs

POLICY OF TRUSTEES Applications accepted from charities concerned with children with learning difficulties, disadvantaged children generally, sick children and related medical research

TYPE OF GRANT Usually one-off for a specific project or part of a project. Core funding and/or salaries rarely considered

TYPE OF BENEFICIARY Registered charities working in the areas outlined above

RESTRICTIONS Applications are only considered from registered charities. Individuals, including students, are ineligible. Normally grants are not made in response to general appeals from large national organisations

BENEFICIAL AREA Restricted to the counties of Hampshire, Berkshire and Wiltshire

SAMPLE GRANTS £10,000 to Children's Hospice Appeal towards building hospice in Winchester
£5,000 to Leukaemia Busters towards cost of flow cytometer at University of Southampton
£5,000 to National Library for the Handicapped Child towards Reach Resource Centre
£1,000 to Riding for the Disabled, Newbury, towards new minibus
£1,000 to Charity for Children with Special Needs

FINANCES
- Year 1994–95
- Grants £370,000
- Income £305,000
- Assets £6,500,000

TRUSTEES J R Whately, T W A Jackson-Stops, Sir A Birkmyre, Bt

PUBLICATIONS Annual report

SUBMISSION OF APPLICATIONS At any time. Trustees meet quarterly. Applications should include clear details of the need the intended project is designed to meet, an outline budget and where appropriate a copy of the last annual accounts. Only applications from eligible bodies are acknowledged, when further information about the project may be requested

CORRESPONDENT J R Whately, 45 Pont Street, London SW1X 0BX

CLASSIFICATIONS
- Advancement in life
- Adventure centres and playgrounds
- Centres, clubs and institutes
- Development of character
- Holidays
- Homes and hostels
- Special needs housing
- Youth organisations (eg Guides, Scouts, YWCA etc)
- Children and violence (inc abuse)

C.C. NO 277074 **ESTABLISHED** 1978

■ The Hubert Blake Charitable Trust

OBJECTS General charitable purposes

POLICY OF TRUSTEES The main areas of interest are: children and youth, nursing homes and hospices, medical and health conditions, disaster and disaster funds, refugees, holidays, outings and treats

Blanchminster

TYPE OF GRANT Grants are anything from £250–£1,000 – although Mrs Blake tends to prefer to spread the money about and make smaller contributions to more charities

TYPE OF BENEFICIARY See Policy of Trustees

BENEFICIAL AREA General cross section (UK and overseas)

SAMPLE GRANTS £750 to St Lukes Hospital
£250 to Opportunity Trust
£250 to Family Holiday Association
£250 to Youth Allyah
£100 to Royal London Society for the Blind

FINANCES
- Year 1995
- Assets £190,000
- Income £12,500

TRUSTEES Hambros Trust Company Limited

PUBLICATIONS Annual accounts

CORRESPONDENT The Trustees of the Hubert Blake Charitable Trust, Hambros Trust Company Limited, 41 Tower Hill, London EC3N 4HA

CLASSIFICATIONS
- Children and youth – general

C.C. NO 248959 **ESTABLISHED** 1965

■ The Blanchminster Trust (formerly the Blanchminster Charity)

OBJECTS (a) Relief in need. (b) Promotion of education

POLICY OF TRUSTEES Applicants must reside within the area of benefit and give proof of financial need

TYPE OF GRANT Cash or equipment. Cash may be grant or loan, equipment normally 'permanent loan'

TYPE OF BENEFICIARY Individuals or organisations having residential qualifications as above and showing proof of financial need

RESTRICTIONS Applications from Bude/Stratton only will be considered

BENEFICIAL AREA The former Urban District of Bude-Stratton as constituted on 31.3.74

FINANCES
- Year 1994
- Grants £73,863
- Income £130,133
- Assets £824,934

TRUSTEES A N Benney, C B Cornish, Miss M H Clowes, J E Gardiner, L G Harris, W J Keat, JP, Mrs P A Newman, J Richardson, R S Thorn, L M J Tozer, P Truscott, Mrs J Wonnacott, Mrs J M Shepherd

SUBMISSION OF APPLICATIONS To Clerk by letter. Applications considered at monthly meetings. All applications acknowledged

CORRESPONDENT Mr O A May, Clerk to the Trustees, Blanchminster Building, 38 Lansdown Road, Bude, Cornwall EX23 8EE

CLASSIFICATIONS
- Children and youth – general

C.C. NO 202118 **ESTABLISHED** 1421

■ The Boltons Trust

OBJECTS General charitable purposes

POLICY OF TRUSTEES Relief of suffering, medical

RESTRICTIONS No grants to individuals

FINANCES
- Year 1993
- Grants £36,000
- Income £113,352
- Assets £3,081,091

TRUSTEES C M Marks, Mrs C Albuquerque, H B Levin

CORRESPONDENT C M Marks, FCA, 44a New Cavendish Street, London W1M 7LG

CLASSIFICATIONS
- Centres, clubs and institutes

C.C. NO 257951 **ESTABLISHED** 1954

■ The Oliver Borthwick Memorial Trust

OBJECTS General charitable purposes

POLICY OF TRUSTEES Currently the main areas of interest are young people who are homeless, counselling, the disabled, the elderly, housing for homeless and help for almshouses

RESTRICTIONS Registered charities only. Applications from individuals, including students, are ineligible. All such applications will be discarded

BENEFICIAL AREA UK

FINANCES
- Year 1993
- Grants £21,000
- Income £23,000
- Assets £480,000

TRUSTEES Earl Bathurst, R Marriott, H de Quetteville, M H R Bretherton, R Graham, J Macdonald

CORRESPONDENT J A Arnold, FCA, Thorburn, Saddlers Scarp, Grayshott, Hindhead, Surrey GU26 6DZ

CLASSIFICATIONS
- Day centres and nurseries
- Special needs housing

C.C. NO 256206 **ESTABLISHED** 1968

■ The M Bourne Charitable Trust

OBJECTS General charitable purposes

POLICY OF TRUSTEES Trustees favour Jewish causes

TYPE OF BENEFICIARY Institutions and individuals

BENEFICIAL AREA UK

SAMPLE GRANTS £5,000 to Jewish Care
£950 to Ravenswood
£50 to Teenage Cancer Trust

FINANCES
- Year 1993
- Grants £17,350
- Income £49,272
- Assets £532,575

TRUSTEES C J Bourne, Mrs J H Bourne, D M Morein

CORRESPONDENT D M Morein, Seabourne Express, Purlieu House, 11 Station Road, Epping CM16 4HA

CLASSIFICATIONS
- Children and youth – general

C.C. NO 290620 **ESTABLISHED** 1984

Brighton

■ C T Bowring (Charities Fund) Ltd

OBJECTS General charitable purposes

POLICY OF TRUSTEES Registered charities only

TYPE OF BENEFICIARY National organisations and special appeals

RESTRICTIONS No grants to individuals or individual schools, churches or local scout groups, expeditions, etc

FINANCES
- Year 1995
- Grants £150,000
- Income £150,000

TRUSTEES The Directors

CORRESPONDENT F R Rutter, Director, C T Bowring (Charities Fund) Ltd, The Bowring Building, Tower Place, London EC3P 3BE

CLASSIFICATIONS
- Children and youth – general
- Adoption/fostering
- Advancement in life
- Adventure centres and playgrounds
- Centres, clubs and institutes
- Community groups
- Day centres and nurseries
- Development of character
- Counselling (inc helplines)
- Homes and hostels
- Youth organisations (eg Guides, Scouts, YWCA etc)

C.C. NO 261955   **ESTABLISHED** 1970

■ The Brand Trust

OBJECTS General charitable purposes

POLICY OF TRUSTEES To make charitable distributions in accordance with the wishes of the settlor

TYPE OF BENEFICIARY Health, welfare and the arts

RESTRICTIONS Contributions are made to registered charities only, no individuals

SAMPLE GRANTS £100 to Streatham Youth Centre
£100 to Holiday Projects West Kids
£100 to Pendyffrin Trust
£100 to Children's Family Trust

FINANCES
- Year 1995
- Grants £16,492
- Income £16,967
- Assets £123,790

TRUSTEES M L Meyer, N Meyer, I Dunlop

CORRESPONDENT M L Meyer, 4 Montagu Square, London W1H 1RA

CLASSIFICATIONS
- Children and youth – general
- Adventure centres and playgrounds
- Homes and hostels
- Special classes

C.C. NO 274704   **ESTABLISHED** 1977

■ The Bridon Group Charitable Trust

OBJECTS General charitable purposes

POLICY OF TRUSTEES Response to written applications for assistance

TYPE OF BENEFICIARY Medical/research, child/youth support, elderly/handicapped, disabled/welfare

RESTRICTIONS Constitution of Trust precludes financial support for individuals or political/religious denominations

BENEFICIAL AREA National and local (mainly North of England)

FINANCES
- Year 1991
- Grants £50,000

TRUSTEES D J Alloay, G E Armitage, A C Boydell

CORRESPONDENT I S Doig, Assistant Company Secretary, Bridon plc Carr Hill, Doncaster, South Yorkshire DN4 8DG

CLASSIFICATIONS
- Children and youth – general
- Adoption/fostering
- Centres, clubs and institutes
- Development of character
- Homes and hostels
- Youth organisations (eg Guides, Scouts, YWCA etc)

C.C. NO 258165   **ESTABLISHED** 1969

■ Brighton & Hove Charitable Youth Trust

OBJECTS (a) The provision of facilities for recreation or leisure time occupation in the interests of social welfare with the object of improving the conditions of life for persons having need of such facilities by reason of their youth (b) Such other charitable purposes as the governors may from time to time determine

TYPE OF GRANT Usually to groups, not often to individuals

TYPE OF BENEFICIARY Youth organisations, handicapped children. Maximum age 26

RESTRICTIONS Confined to Sussex, not national appeals. Confined to youth activities

BENEFICIAL AREA Sussex only

SAMPLE GRANTS £157 to Martlets Motor-cycle Club, Hastings for safety equipment
£150 to Hastings and Rother X-roads (Carers) for holiday help
£140 to Goldstone Junior School, Hove towards holiday/trip
£100 to City Gate Centre Youth Club, Brighton for indoor equipment
£50 to Brighton Unemployed Centre towards Christmas party

FINANCES
- Year 1987
- Grants £6,900
- Income £7,300
- Assets £66,000

TRUSTEES L Goldberg, Mrs J Jackson, R J G Dyson, J Conn

SUBMISSION OF APPLICATIONS Include latest balance sheet

CORRESPONDENT Mrs J I Goldberg, Hon Secretary, B & H Charitable Youth Trust, 16 Henley Road, Brighton, East Sussex BN2 5NA

CLASSIFICATIONS
- Holidays
- Youth organisations (eg Guides, Scouts, YWCA etc)

C.C. NO 268268   **ESTABLISHED** 1974

British

■ British Humane Association

OBJECTS Promotion of Humaneness for benefit of the community

POLICY OF TRUSTEES To operate Individual Grant Scheme for relief of personal and family distress with co-operation of: The Order of St John, Professional Classes Aid Council, Artists' General Benevolent Institution, Church Lads and Girls Brigade, Guild of Aid for Gentlepeople, St Luke's Hospital for Clergy

TYPE OF BENEFICIARY As recommended by above charitable bodies

RESTRICTIONS No grants to individuals

BENEFICIAL AREA UK and overseas

SAMPLE GRANTS £22,000 to Professional Classes Aid Council
£1,500 to Church Lads and Church Girls Brigade
£1,000 to Greater London Central Scout County

FINANCES
- Year 1995
- Grants £82,467
- Income £111,891
- Assets £2,123,110

TRUSTEES Board or Council of Management

SUBMISSION OF APPLICATIONS Through registered charities

CORRESPONDENT C A E Butler, FCA, British Humane Association, 24 Craddocks Avenue, Ashstead, Surrey KT21 1PB

CLASSIFICATIONS
- Advancement in life

C.C. NO 207120   **ESTABLISHED** 1922

■ The J & M Britton Charitable Trust

OBJECTS General charitable purposes with preference given to organisations in the Bristol and Avon area

POLICY OF TRUSTEES Decisions are subjective and made in the light of the Trustees opinion as to deserts

RESTRICTIONS Registered charities only, never to individuals

BENEFICIAL AREA Bristol and Avon

FINANCES
- Year 1994
- Grants £53,730
- Income £66,747

TRUSTEES R E J Bernays, R O Bernays, Lady M Merrison, J E D Wilcox, Mrs S Morgan, Secretary

CORRESPONDENT R E J Bernays, Old Down House, Tockington, Bristol, Avon BS12 4PG

CLASSIFICATIONS
- Adventure centres and playgrounds
- Community groups
- Youth organisations (eg Guides, Scouts, YWCA etc)

C.C. NO 12175   **ESTABLISHED** 1961

■ The Brocton Trust

OBJECTS For the relief of poverty, the support of Christian missions, general charitable purposes

TYPE OF GRANT Will not exceed £200

TYPE OF BENEFICIARY Not necessarily only registered charities. Smaller organisations more likely to be successful

RESTRICTIONS No large (over £30,000) appeals or general appeals from large national organisations will be considered. Small appeals identifying a specific need are preferred. Appeals from individual students for help towards cost of study will not normally be considered

BENEFICIAL AREA Usually West Midlands only

FINANCES
- Year 1991
- Grants £4,100
- Income £4,093

TRUSTEES G Botteley, J H G Botteley, S Botteley, D R Bradburn, G M Wheeler

SUBMISSION OF APPLICATIONS Trustees meet twice a year. Applications will not usually be acknowledged unless successful

CORRESPONDENT G Botteley, 53 Irnham Road, Four Oaks, Sutton Coldfield, West Midlands B74 2TQ

CLASSIFICATIONS
- Youth organisations (eg Guides, Scouts, YWCA etc)

C.C. NO 327190   **ESTABLISHED** 1986

■ R E Brook Charitable Settlement

OBJECTS General charitable purposes

POLICY OF TRUSTEES Preference to charities of which the Trustees have special interest, knowledge or association, eg health, social, population, arts, including churches and architecture, young people, including sport where appropriate

TYPE OF BENEFICIARY Appeals and institutions rather than individuals

RESTRICTIONS No grants to individuals (including students) or to large national organisations

FINANCES
- Year 1994
- Grants £4,500
- Income £4,500
- Assets £75,000

TRUSTEES The Worshipful Company of Haberdashers

CORRESPONDENT The Clerk, The Haberdashers Company, Haberdashers Hall, Staining Lane, London EC2V 7BB

CLASSIFICATIONS
- Centres, clubs and institutes
- Development of character
- Holidays
- Homes and hostels

C.C. NO 263199   **ESTABLISHED** 1971

■ The Charles Brotherton Trust

OBJECTS Advancement of education including the establishment and maintenance of scholarships and the recreational training and education of young persons – furtherance of medical and surgical research – support of medical or surgical charities

POLICY OF TRUSTEES As shown in paragraph headed Objects

TYPE OF BENEFICIARY Applications for student grants and scholarships should be made to the Bursar at the Universities of Leeds and Liverpool, the Registrar at York University and the Students Welfare Adviser at Birmingham University

RESTRICTIONS No grants to individuals – only to registered charities and recognised bodies

BENEFICIAL AREA Birmingham, Liverpool, Wakefield, York, Leeds, Borough of Bebington (Cheshire)

FINANCES
- Year 1993
- Grants £75,000
- Income £81,000
- Assets £781,600

TRUSTEES Custodian: D R Brotherton, S B Turner, C M Brotherton-Ratcliffe, J S Riches, Management: D R Brotherton, Mrs A Henson, Mrs P L M H Seeley, C M Brotherton-Ratcliffe, S B Turner

CORRESPONDENT C Brotherton-Ratcliffe, Secretary, The Charles Brotherton Trust, 41 Park Square, Leeds, West Yorkshire LS1 2NS

CLASSIFICATIONS
- Adventure centres and playgrounds
- Centres, clubs and institutes
- Development of character
- Homes and hostels
- Special needs housing
- Youth organisations (eg Guides, Scouts, YWCA etc)

C.C. NO 227067   **ESTABLISHED** 1940

■ Joseph Brough Charitable Trust

OBJECTS General charitable purposes in the historic counties of Northumberland and Durham (ie South of the Tweed and North of the Tees).

POLICY OF TRUSTEES There is a regular donation of £24,000 to the Brough Benevolent Association which helps individuals in need. Other grants are for a wide range of charitable purposes in the area of benefit. Grants are rarely for more than £1,000 and usually for a specific purpose where a contribution of up to £1,000 will make a difference

TYPE OF BENEFICIARY Voluntary organisations

RESTRICTIONS Applications outside the beneficial area. National appeals and major appeals are unlikely to be successful

BENEFICIAL AREA The historic counties of Northumberland, Durham and Newcastle upon Tyne

SAMPLE GRANTS £1,000 to the Berwick Family Centre towards the activities and group work planned through the new Berwick Family Centre on the Prior Park Estate in Berwick. Parenting skills and general work with families and children are part of the new provision
£1,000 to the Hartlepool Special Needs Support Group, an active group run by parents of mentally and physically handicapped children and young people. Providing support through information and advice, the group also organises an extensive programme of activities during the school holidays and this grant is a contribution to the costs of the summer playscheme
£500 to the Haydon Bridge Methodist Church, a contribution towards the cost of a substantial new project in the village. Whilst it is a church-based innitiative it will offer a variety of new community facilities for local residents
£500 to Abuse Counselling Training towards the training and counselling work of this volunteer run project which helps survivors and families of victims of abuse. The Brough support will purchase equipment to produce important training materials and publicity
£500 to the Hurworth Methodist Church towards the costs of extensive repair work to the church and will enable the premises to continue to be used by many groups and projects working with the local community

FINANCES
- Year 1994
- Grants £42,575
- Income £39,553
- Assets £702,475

TRUSTEES Tyne & Wear Foundation

SUBMISSION OF APPLICATIONS Telephone enquiries are welcomed. Applicants should send a letter outlining their request for support

CORRESPONDENT Carol Meredith, Assistant Director, Tyne & Wear Foundation, MEA House, Ellison Place, Newcastle upon Tyne NE1 8XS

CLASSIFICATIONS
- Children and youth – general
- Adventure centres and playgrounds
- Centres, clubs and institutes
- Community groups
- Day centres and nurseries
- Counselling (inc helplines)

C.C. NO 227332   **ESTABLISHED** 1940

■ Peter Brough Trust

POLICY OF TRUSTEES Trust set up in Paisley mainly for charitable purposes for Paisley residents

RESTRICTIONS Specific in terms of Trust Deed

BENEFICIAL AREA Mainly Paisley

CORRESPONDENT Mrs M Lindsay, Messrs MacRoberts, 152 Bath Street, Glasgow G2 4TB

CLASSIFICATIONS
- Children and youth – general

C.C. NO IR03958

■ The Jack Brunton Charitable Trust

OBJECTS General charitable purposes

POLICY OF TRUSTEES All applications are considered

TYPE OF BENEFICIARY Registered charities

RESTRICTIONS Grants are made to individuals only in very rare and exceptional circumstances

BENEFICIAL AREA Old North Riding area of Yorkshire only

SAMPLE GRANTS Watson Scout Centre
Church Youth Club, Castleton Kirby
Great Broughton Guides

Buckets

Alphabetical register of grant making charitable trusts

FINANCES
- Year 1994–95
- Grants £30,050
- Income £45,977
- Assets £767,379

TRUSTEES Lady Diana Brittan, Mrs A J Brunton, J G Brunton, B E M Jones, E Marquis, D W Noble, P Reed

CORRESPONDENT D A Swallow, FCA, Administrator, 10 Bridge Road, Stokesley, North Yorkshire TS9 5AA

CLASSIFICATIONS
- Children and youth – general
- Development of character

C.C. NO 518407 **ESTABLISHED** 1986

■ Buckets and Spades Charitable Trust

OBJECTS To assist mentally and physically handicapped children

POLICY OF TRUSTEES Wherever possible to help individual cases rather than large organisations

TYPE OF GRANT No exclusions, each case taken on its own merit

TYPE OF BENEFICIARY Wherever possible individual cases

RESTRICTIONS Applicant must be a child, although due allowance is made for older children

BENEFICIAL AREA London, Home Counties, although consideration will be given to other parts of the country

SAMPLE GRANTS £1,000 towards adapting a vehicle for a severely physically and mentally handicapped child
£500 towards a specialised computer
£134 towards the purchase of a buggy

FINANCES
- Year 1992
- Grants £70,000
- Income £30,000
- Assets £350,000

TRUSTEES Gregory Lander, Stephanie Marks, Robert John

SUBMISSION OF APPLICATIONS In writing only

CORRESPONDENT Buckets and Spades Charitable Trust, c/o Robert John Specterman, 315 Oxford Street, London W1R 1LA

CLASSIFICATIONS
- Children and youth – general

C.C. NO 269633 **ESTABLISHED** 1975

■ Buckingham Trust

OBJECTS Advancement of religion (including missionary activities) – relief of the poor, sick and aged

POLICY OF TRUSTEES Preference to charities of which the Trustees have personal interest, knowledge, or association

TYPE OF BENEFICIARY Per policy above – strictly applied

BENEFICIAL AREA UK

FINANCES
- Year 1994
- Grants £107,281
- Income £125,723
- Assets £473,726

TRUSTEES D J Hanes, D H Benson, R W D Foot, P R Edwards

CORRESPONDENT Messrs Foot Davson & Co, 17 Church Road, Tunbridge Wells, Kent TN1 1HT

CLASSIFICATIONS
- Children and youth – general

C.C. NO 237350 **ESTABLISHED** 1962

■ The Burden Trust

OBJECTS Medical research; hospitals; schools and training institutions; homes for and care of the infirm, aged and necessitous persons; children's homes and care

POLICY OF TRUSTEES Distribute annual net income under terms of the Trust Deeds

TYPE OF BENEFICIARY As set out under Objects but with a bias towards the Anglican Church (as laid down in the Trust Deeds)

BENEFICIAL AREA International

SAMPLE GRANTS Bristol Crusader's Union
Dean Close School
Discipleship Training College
Trinity College, Bristol

FINANCES
- Year 1995
- Grants £186,000
- Income £207,000
- Assets £3,800,000

TRUSTEES R D Spear (Chairman), R E J Bernays (Deputy Chairman), C A Orton, Dr M G Barker, A C Miles, Prof G M Stirrat, Lady Elizabeth White, P R B Barkworth, M C Tosh

NOTES All applications sent to Trust office are acknowledged provided an sae is enclosed

CORRESPONDENT M C Tosh, CA, Hon Secretary, Little Clandon, West Clandon, Surrey GU4 7ST

CLASSIFICATIONS
- Homes and hostels

C.C. NO 235859 **ESTABLISHED** 1913

■ Burges Salmon Charitable Trust

OBJECTS General charitable purposes

RESTRICTIONS Not individuals

BENEFICIAL AREA Priority given to Bristol area

SAMPLE GRANTS Greater Bristol Foundation
Avon Outward Bound Association
133rd Bristol Scout Group

FINANCES
- Year 1995
- Grants £6,600

TRUSTEES R S Battersby, H A C Densham

SUBMISSION OF APPLICATIONS Applications are not sought

CORRESPONDENT R S Battersby, c/o Burges, Salmon, Narrow Quay House, Prince Street, Bristol, Avon BS1 4AH

CLASSIFICATIONS
- Children and youth – general
- Youth organisations (eg Guides, Scouts, YWCA etc)

C.C. NO 272522 **ESTABLISHED** 1976

■ The J H Burn Charity Trust

OBJECTS General charitable purposes

POLICY OF TRUSTEES Fields of interest include: youth organisations, medical research, hospitals, nursing, assistance to sailors and seamen, boys' clubs, art galleries

TYPE OF BENEFICIARY Registered charities

RESTRICTIONS Will not fund individuals

BENEFICIAL AREA Funds mainly distributed in Northumberland, Newcastle-upon-Tyne and Durham

FINANCES
- Year 1994
- Grants £4,000
- Income £4,000

TRUSTEES D R B Burn, S D Burn

CORRESPONDENT D R B Burn, Carrycoats Hall, Wark, Hexham, Northumberland NE48 3JG

CLASSIFICATIONS
- Centres, clubs and institutes
- Youth organisations (eg Guides, Scouts, YWCA etc)

C.C. NO 226320   **ESTABLISHED** 1910

■ The Reg Burns Foundation

OBJECTS General charitable purposes in furtherance of the advancement of education in the beneficial area

POLICY OF TRUSTEES Advancement of education with particular reference to youth excluding theatre and arts

TYPE OF BENEFICIARY Individuals

RESTRICTIONS Applications from individuals only, not national or large scale appeals

BENEFICIAL AREA UK

FINANCES
- Year 1993
- Grants £18,143
- Income £23,625
- Assets £260,222

TRUSTEES A L C Gibbings, R P Long, P A Laird

CORRESPONDENT The Reg Burns Foundation, 81 Twyford Road, Eastleigh, Hampshire SO50 4HH

CLASSIFICATIONS
- Children and youth – general

C.C. NO 314177   **ESTABLISHED** 1968

■ The Burton Breweries Charitable Trust

OBJECTS General charitable purposes

POLICY OF TRUSTEES Only to support youth organisations which are able to satisfy the Trustees of their ability to run efficiently and sustain membership and individual young people involved in character building activities

TYPE OF GRANT Cash and pledge

TYPE OF BENEFICIARY Registered charities, youth clubs, youth organisations and individuals

RESTRICTIONS See above

BENEFICIAL AREA Burton-on-Trent and East Staffordshire

SAMPLE GRANTS £1,350 to Duke of Edinburgh Award Scheme
£1,000 to Burton Scout Council
£1,000 to Burton Venture Trust
£1,000 to St Chades Church, Burton Youth Club
£650 to Sea Cadet Corps

FINANCES
- Year 1995
- Grants £10,000
- Income £10,000
- Assets £500,000

TRUSTEES Sir Ivan Lawrence, QC, M T Southwell, (Bass), M Hubbard, (Carlsberg Tetley), M W F Hurdle, (Martens)

NOTES Telephone 01283 740600

SUBMISSION OF APPLICATIONS To Secretary

CORRESPONDENT B E Keates, FCA, Secretary to the Trustees, 181 Horninglow Street, Burton-on-Trent, Staffs DE14 1NJ

CLASSIFICATIONS
- Centres, clubs and institutes
- Community groups
- Youth organisations (eg Guides, Scouts, YWCA etc)

C.C. NO 326097   **ESTABLISHED** 1982

■ J J & M Burton Charitable Trust

OBJECTS General charitable purposes

POLICY OF TRUSTEES The Trustees do not normally respond favourably to unsolicited requests for support

RESTRICTIONS The trustees do not consider appeals from individuals or from local charities based outside Yorkshire

FINANCES
- Year 1994
- Grants £3,940
- Income £4,170
- Assets £54,347

TRUSTEES J J Burton, M J R Burton, A J Burton

CORRESPONDENT J J Burton, Castlegarth, Scott Lane, Wetherby, West Yorkshire LS22 6LH

CLASSIFICATIONS
- Community groups

C.C. NO 326865   **ESTABLISHED** 1985

■ Lucilla Butler's Trust

OBJECTS General charitable purposes

POLICY OF TRUSTEES Support youth work and young offenders

TYPE OF GRANT Usually one-off

TYPE OF BENEFICIARY Registered charities working in area outlined under Policy

RESTRICTIONS Registered charities only. Applications from individuals, including students, are ineligible

BENEFICIAL AREA Currently with strong bias towards North Yorkshire

FINANCES
- Year 1994
- Grants £1,153
- Income £1,085
- Assets £21,363

TRUSTEES Lloyd's Bank plc, Mrs L Butler, M Butler

SUBMISSION OF APPLICATIONS At any time. No acknowledgements sent. No application forms provided

Buttle

Alphabetical register of grant making charitable trusts

CORRESPONDENT Lloyd's Private Banking Limited, (A/C 97774), UK Trust Centre, The Clock House, 22–26 Ock Street, Abingdon, Oxon OX14 5SW

CLASSIFICATIONS
- Children and youth – general
- Centres, clubs and institutes

C.C. NO 265448   **ESTABLISHED** 1972

■ The Buttle Trust

OBJECTS To provide for the needs of children and young people who are adopted and facing some special problem which has arisen subsequent to adoption; who are de facto adopted (ie privately fostered); or who are estranged from their parents through no fault of their own and are living solo; also to assist other children and young people who are not only deprived of family life but also suffering from the effects of some exceptional misfortune. (Single-parenthood coupled with financial hardship cannot be regarded as a 'sufficient' misfortune)

POLICY OF TRUSTEES The Trustees' priority is to provide help within the family home at a time of crisis. School fee grants are only made in order to provide for an acute boarding need or to see a child through a phase of schooling after some disaster has struck the family. There are also restricted funds for the support of students who satisfy the criteria set out above. Grants are not made as a substitute for public benefits

TYPE OF BENEFICIARY Children and young people only

RESTRICTIONS Grants cannot be made for those over 21 (or, exceptionally, 25 in the case of students or trainees who had started their course by the time they were 21). The Trustees require that, to be eligible for assistance, beneficiaries must be of the Christian Religion; they must also be ordinarily resident in the UK

BENEFICIAL AREA United Kingdom

FINANCES
- Year 1995
- Grants £1,420,391
- Income £1,208,423
- Assets £27,400,000

TRUSTEES Mrs O K Staughton (Chairman), R Marriott (Deputy Chairman) and 15 other Trustees

CORRESPONDENT Mrs J F Marshall, MA, Director, The Buttle Trust, Audley House, 13 Palace Street, London SW1E 5HS

CLASSIFICATIONS
- Children and youth – general
- Adoption/fostering

C.C. NO 313007   **ESTABLISHED** 1953

■ Edward Cadbury Charitable Trust

OBJECTS General charitable purposes

POLICY OF TRUSTEES To continue to support, where appropriate, the interests of the Founder and the particular interests of the Trustees. The voluntary sector in the West Midlands Christian mission, the ecumenical movement and inter-faith relations. The oppressed and disadvantaged in this country and the developing world, education, the arts and the environment. The Trustees prefer to support small or new organisations and projects rather than large national organisations

TYPE OF BENEFICIARY Registered charities working in the areas outlined under Policy. Preference to the newly established

RESTRICTIONS Registered charities only, no student grants or support for individuals. The Trust is unlikely to fund projects which have popular appeal or fund things which are normally publicly funded

BENEFICIAL AREA West Midlands but in some instances National and Overseas in line with Trust policy

FINANCES
- Year 1994
- Grants £708,647
- Income £816,323
- Assets £8,851,705

TRUSTEES C E Gillett (Chairman), C S Littleboy, C R Gillett, A S Littleboy, N R Cadbury

CORRESPONDENT Mrs M Walton, Elmfield, College Walk, Selly Oak, Birmingham B29 6LE

CLASSIFICATIONS
- Centres, clubs and institutes
- Community groups
- Youth organisations (eg Guides, Scouts, YWCA etc)

C.C. NO 227384   **ESTABLISHED** 1945

■ J & L A Cadbury Charitable Trust

OBJECTS General charitable purposes

POLICY OF TRUSTEES Main areas of interest are social welfare; environment; the arts; education (Quaker and local schools only); local or historic churches; conservation

TYPE OF GRANT Not annual. Not usually for salaries

TYPE OF BENEFICIARY Registered charities working in areas outlined under Policy

RESTRICTIONS Registered charities only. No grants to individuals or London (local) charities. Not overseas

BENEFICIAL AREA Preference towards activities in the West Midlands

SAMPLE GRANTS £200 to Friends of Birmingham Schools Orchestra
£100 to Breakout Childrens' Holidays
£100 to Birmingham Young Volunteers Adventure Camps
£100 to Bath Place Community Venture
£55 to YHA

FINANCES
- Year 1995
- Grants £21,000
- Income £44,000

TRUSTEES Mrs L A Cadbury, W J B Taylor, Mrs S M Gale

SUBMISSION OF APPLICATIONS By letter with details. No official form

CORRESPONDENT The Secretary, J & L A Cadbury Charitable Trust, 2 College Walk, Birmingham, West Midlands B29 6LQ

CLASSIFICATIONS
- Children and youth – general
- Centres, clubs and institutes
- Community groups
- Development of character
- Holidays
- Youth organisations (eg Guides, Scouts, YWCA etc)

C.C. NO 241895　　**ESTABLISHED** 1965

■ Richard Cadbury Charitable Trust

OBJECTS General charitable purposes

POLICY OF TRUSTEES Personal concern. Main interest: local organisations to Birmingham and Worcester especially

TYPE OF BENEFICIARY Disadvantaged youth, handicapped and disabled, Christian-based appeals (as well as elderly and environment-based appeals)

RESTRICTIONS Registered charities only. No student grants or support of individuals

BENEFICIAL AREA Mainly local

FINANCES
- Year 1994
- Grants £35,000
- Income £35,600
- Assets £500,000

TRUSTEES R B Cadbury, Mrs M M Slora, D G Slora, Miss J Slora

NOTES Restricted from small unregistered groups. However, help can be offered through recognised religious or educational bodies in exceptional circumstances

CORRESPONDENT Mrs M M Slora, Administrator, Richard Cadbury Charitable Trust, 6 Middleborough Road, Coventry, West Midlands CV1 4DE

CLASSIFICATIONS
- Children and youth – general

C.C. NO 224348　　**ESTABLISHED** 1948

■ William Adlington Cadbury Charitable Trust

OBJECTS General charitable purposes (including projects for children and young people in the West Midlands, or where the project will have a national impact)

POLICY OF TRUSTEES (a) The West Midlands: the Society of Friends and other Churches; health; social welfare; education and training; the environment and conservation; preservation; the arts; penal affairs (b) UK: the Society of Friends; medical research; UK environmental education programmes; preservation; education projects which have national significance; penal affairs; cross-community health and social welfare projects in Northern Ireland (c) International: UK charities working overseas on long-term development projects

TYPE OF GRANT Specific grant applications are favoured. Grants between £100 and £5,000 are made to registered charities only. Major appeals are considered by Trustees at meetings in May and November. Small grants up to £500 are made on a continuing basis under the Trust's small grants programme

TYPE OF BENEFICIARY (a) Charities in the West Midlands working on projects for children and young people (b) charities whose work with young people will have national impact

RESTRICTIONS Individuals (whether for research, expeditions, educational purposes); local projects or groups outside the West Midlands; or projects concerned with travel or adventure

BENEFICIAL AREA See Policy of Trustees

SAMPLE GRANTS £2,000 to NSPCC Coventry Centenary Appeal
£2,000 to Barnardos – West Midlands
£500 to National Childrens Bureau
£250 to Whitley Junior Football Club, Coventry
£250 to Birmingham – Parkistan Scout Project

FINANCES
- Year 1995
- Grants £386,530
- Income £659,520

TRUSTEES Brandon Cadbury, Mrs Hannah H Taylor, Mrs Sarah Stafford, W James B Taylor, Rupert A Cadbury, Mrs Katherine M Hampton, Adrian D M Thomas, John C Penny

PUBLICATIONS Annual Report; Policy Statement and Guidelines

NOTES No application form needed

CORRESPONDENT Mrs C M Stober, The Secretary, W A Cadbury Charitable Trust, 2 College Walk, Birmingham, West Midlands B29 6LQ

CLASSIFICATIONS
- Children and youth – general
- Adoption/fostering
- Adventure centres and playgrounds
- Centres, clubs and institutes
- Community groups
- Day centres and nurseries
- Development of character
- Holidays
- Homes and hostels
- Special needs housing
- Youth organisations (eg Guides, Scouts, YWCA etc)

C.C. NO 213629　　**ESTABLISHED** 1923

■ The Edward & Dorothy Cadbury Trust (1928)

OBJECTS General charitable purposes

POLICY OF TRUSTEES To continue to support, where appropriate, the interests of the Founders and the particular charitable interests of the Trustees. A special preference for West Midlands appeals and health, education and the Arts

TYPE OF GRANT The size of grant varies but most are within the range of £50–£500. On-going funding commitments rarely considered

TYPE OF BENEFICIARY Registered charities working in the areas outlined under Policy

Cadell-Samworth

Alphabetical register of grant making charitable trusts

RESTRICTIONS Registered charities only. Grants not made to individuals

BENEFICIAL AREA West Midlands. In some cases National and overseas in line with Trust Policy

FINANCES
- Year 1994
- Grants £88,431
- Income £81,460
- Assets £513,511

TRUSTEES Mrs P A Gillett, Dr C M Elliott, Mrs P S Ward

SUBMISSION OF APPLICATIONS To the correspondent in writing, clearly giving relevant information concerning the projects aims and its benefits. Up to date accounts and Annual Reports where available could be helpful. The Trust does not issue application forms

CORRESPONDENT Mrs M Walton, Elmfield, 2 College Walk, Selly Oak, Birmingham B29 6LE

CLASSIFICATIONS
- Children and youth – general
- Advancement in life
- Adventure centres and playgrounds
- Centres, clubs and institutes
- Community groups
- Day centres and nurseries
- Development of character
- Counselling (inc helplines)
- Holidays
- Youth organisations (eg Guides, Scouts, YWCA etc)

C.C. NO 221441   **ESTABLISHED** 1928

■ The Cadell-Samworth Foundation
(otherwise known as Chetwode Samworth Charitable Trust)

OBJECTS General charitable purposes

TYPE OF BENEFICIARY Generally local or Midlands activities

RESTRICTIONS Preference to charities located in Notts, Derby, Leicestershire areas – registered charities only

FINANCES
- Year 1992
- Grants £31,019
- Income £61,954
- Assets £1,040,348

TRUSTEES F C Samworth, J C Samworth

CORRESPONDENT J G Ellis, Samworth Brothers Limited, Fields Farm, Cropwell Butler, Nottingham NG12 3AP

CLASSIFICATIONS
- Children and youth – general

C.C. NO 265647   **ESTABLISHED** 1973

■ CAF (Charities Aid Foundation)

OBJECTS To enable applicant charities to achieve their purposes more effectively

POLICY OF TRUSTEES Funding is offered to enable a charity to improve its management and effectiveness, for example, to improve its effectiveness in meeting its objectives, to improve its use of financial resources, facilities, members, staff or volunteers, to improve its stability or effectiveness, or to move into new areas of need. Emergency grants may be given to meet an exceptional, unforeseen financial setback, or where a single injection of funds is required to restore the viability of the charity. An increasingly important element in the amount distributed is money given directly to CAF by individuals and companies who have indicated the areas in which they would like their donation to be used. In addition to the General Fund and the disaster relief fund, set up in conjunction with the Disasters Emergency Committee, there are twelve funds to which donations may be made

TYPE OF BENEFICIARY Registered charities or those excepted under 1960 Charities Act. Grants are normally made to small and medium-sized charities with a proven track record

RESTRICTIONS No grants are made to individuals. Applications are not considered for retrospective funding, to clear debts or repay loans, towards the regular core and administrative expenditure of the charity, for training which is part of a charity's core activity, to purchase or repair buildings, to provide office equipment or furniture, for start up costs of new charities, for scientific, medical or educational research or to assist lottery bids. Grants are not provided in response to general appeals, no matter how worthwhile the cause

SAMPLE GRANTS £10,000 to National Council for Voluntary Youth Services to look at future provision of youth work by voluntary organisations
£2,400 to Tower Hamlets Youth Counselling Service

FINANCES
- Year 1994
- Grants £507,000
- Income £519,000
- Assets £8,757,000

TRUSTEES Sir John Read, FCA (President), Sir Peter Baldwin, KCB (Chairman), John A Brooks, CBE, Ian D R Campbell, FCA, Sir Geoffrey Chandler, CBE, The Lord Dahrendorf, KBE, FBA, Charles F Green, Sir Harold Haywood, KCVO, OBE, DL, William U Jackson, CBE, DL, Sir Brian Jenkins, GBE, FCA, MA, Barrie C Johnston, OBE, FPMI, Roger Lyons, Prof Naomi Sargant, Stuart Etherington, Kenneth G Faircloth, OBE, BSc (Econ), FIMI

CORRESPONDENT Mrs Judith McQuillan, Grants Administrator, Charities Aid Foundation, Kings Hill, West Malling, Kent ME19 4TA

CLASSIFICATIONS
- Children and youth – general

C.C. NO 268369   **ESTABLISHED** 1974

■ The Ellis Campbell Charitable Foundation

OBJECTS (a) Education and training for able, disabled and disadvantaged persons up to the age of 25. (b) Preservation/protection/improvement of items within the artistic/structural and mechanical heritage of the UK

POLICY OF TRUSTEES To build Trust fund to £1,000,000 plus before distributing all income

TYPE OF GRANT Usually one-off but sometimes over a period up to five years

TYPE OF BENEFICIARY Usually organisations with a proven record

RESTRICTIONS No individuals unless known to Trustees

BENEFICIAL AREA Hampshire and Perthshire preferred

SAMPLE GRANTS £500–£10,000

Alphabetical register of grant making charitable trusts **Carnegie**

FINANCES
- **Year** 1995
- **Grants** £46,931
- **Income** £33,650
- **Assets** £878,130

TRUSTEES M D C Campbell, Mrs L F Campbell, Mrs D Campbell, J Campbell, Mrs A Andrew, T M Aldridge

PUBLICATIONS Annual Report

SUBMISSION OF APPLICATIONS To Correspondent at address below. Trustees meet March, July and October. Applications by first of preceding month

CORRESPONDENT Michael Dee Campbell, Esq, DL, Shalden Park Steading, Shalden, Alton, Hants GU34 4DS

CLASSIFICATIONS
- Advancement in life
- Development of character

C.C. NO 802717   **ESTABLISHED** 1989

■ The Campden Charities

OBJECTS The Campden Charities seek to relieve poverty, hardship and distress among the residents of the former Parish of Kensington and to promote the education and training of children and young persons in the former Parish in order that they achieve their full potential. They aim to meet the needs of individuals and organisations serving those suffering deprivation without replacing funding which statutory authorities are obliged to provide. The Charities act largely as a provider of funds and believe in acting openly without discrimination

POLICY OF TRUSTEES Each application treated on merit

TYPE OF GRANT Pensions to the elderly; grants in cash or in kind to relieve need; assistance with education; all types of grants to Kensington-based organisations

TYPE OF BENEFICIARY Community-based groups

RESTRICTIONS All grants must aim to benefit bona-fide residents of the former Royal Borough of Kensington (now defined as that part of the Royal Borough of Kensington and Chelsea which lies north of Fulham Road). Applications from elsewhere will not be acknowledged

BENEFICIAL AREA See Restrictions

SAMPLE GRANTS £8,725 to Air Training Corps towards core funding and replacement of minibus
£6,500 to Westway Motor Project towards core funding and countering crime
£6,000 to RKBC Training Skills towards training costs for young people with learning difficulties
£5,000 to Inner London Probation Service Youth Enterprise towards Youth at Risk (purchase of computers)
£4,000 to London Youth Games Kensington and Chelsea Team towards transport and coaching costs

FINANCES
- **Year** 1995
- **Grants** £1,201,887
- **Income** £1,447,410
- **Assets** £28,577,148

PUBLICATIONS Annual Report and Accounts. Grant leaflet

NOTES In 1990 the Campden (Non-Educational) Charities CC No 212281 and the Campden Educational Trust CC No 312797 were amalgamated to form The Campden Charities

SUBMISSION OF APPLICATIONS Pensions — direct by letter; individual relief in need through social work agencies only; educational grants individually by letter; organisations by telephone or letter. Meetings of Trustees monthly

CORRESPONDENT Clerk to the Trustees, The Campden Charities, 27A Pembridge Villas, London W11 3EP

CLASSIFICATIONS
- Children and youth – general
- Advancement in life
- Adventure centres and playgrounds
- Centres, clubs and institutes
- Community groups
- Day centres and nurseries
- Development of character
- Holidays
- Special needs housing
- Special classes
- Youth organisations (eg Guides, Scouts, YWCA etc)

C.C. NO 1003641   **ESTABLISHED** 1629

■ The Cardy Beaver Foundation

OBJECTS General charitable purposes

POLICY OF TRUSTEES Trustees are interested in applications from smaller charities

TYPE OF GRANT Small grants over two years, large ones decided biannually

TYPE OF BENEFICIARY Small charities

FINANCES
- **Year** 1990
- **Income** £50,000

TRUSTEES J L Cardy, D J Hare, G R Coia

CORRESPONDENT G R Coia, Brannan's, 63 Stowe Road, London W12 8BE

CLASSIFICATIONS
- Children and youth – general

C.C. NO 265763   **ESTABLISHED** 1973

■ Carnegie Dunfermline Trust

OBJECTS Social, educational, cultural and recreational purposes in Dunfermline and its immediate environs

POLICY OF TRUSTEES Grants rarely given to individuals

TYPE OF BENEFICIARY Local clubs and societies; special projects

RESTRICTIONS Operates only within Dunfermline and its immediate environs

BENEFICIAL AREA Dunfermline and its immediate environs only

FINANCES
- **Year** 1995
- **Grants** £67,000
- **Income** £329,000
- **Assets** £4,963,000

TRUSTEES Appointed in terms of Royal Charter

CORRESPONDENT The Secretary, Carnegie Dunfermline Trust, Abbey Park House, Dunfermline, Fife KY12 7PB

CLASSIFICATIONS
- Centres, clubs and institutes

S.C. NO SCO 00729   **ESTABLISHED** 1903

Carr-Ellison

■ The Carr-Ellison Charitable Trust

OBJECTS In or towards charitable purposes or the relief of poverty or the advancement of education at Trustees' discretion

POLICY OF TRUSTEES Funds are fully committed and no further appeals can be considered

TYPE OF BENEFICIARY At the discretion of the Trustees

RESTRICTIONS Applications for grant aid of whatever nature from individual students are not considered

BENEFICIAL AREA Primarily Northumberland and Tyne & Wear

FINANCES
- Year 1994
- Grants £7,022
- Income £4,651

TRUSTEES J M Carr-Ellison, R H Dickinson

CORRESPONDENT The Secretary, The Carr-Ellison Charitable Trust, Hedgeley Hall, Powburn, Alnwick, Northumberland NE66 4HZ

CLASSIFICATIONS
- Children and youth – general
- Centres, clubs and institutes
- Development of character
- Youth organisations (eg Guides, Scouts, YWCA etc)

C.C. NO 206624   **ESTABLISHED** 1962

■ Sir John Cass's Foundation

OBJECTS Support for needy individuals following courses of study or training; for groups, organisations and schools serving them; aid to Church of England Schools; support for Foundation Schools and London Guildhall University

POLICY OF TRUSTEES Policy guidelines available on application

TYPE OF GRANT To individuals, recurrent or one-off support for groups, organisations and schools

TYPE OF BENEFICIARY Please see Objects and Restrictions. Preference is given to pupils and former pupils of the Foundation Schools and London Guildhall University

RESTRICTIONS Under 25s only. Individual beneficiaries must have lived within beneficial area for at least three years

BENEFICIAL AREA City of London, Boroughs of Camden, Greenwich, Hackney, Hammersmith and Fulham, Islington, Kensington and Chelsea, Lambeth, Lewisham, Newham, Southwark, Tower Hamlets, Wandsworth, Westminster

SAMPLE GRANTS £23,442 to Sir John Cass's Foundation School
£20,000 to SOVA for the continuation of a literary and numeracy project at Feltham Young Offenders Institution
£8,500 to Springboard Educational Trust towards the cost of specialist teacher for dyslexic children and computer equipment
£8,441 to Guildhall University for mathematics masterclasses

FINANCES
- Year 1994–95
- Grants £758,898
- Income £1,634,955
- Assets £14,298,399

TRUSTEES 18 Trustees: two ex-officio, eight nominated by various bodies and eight co-opted

PUBLICATIONS Annual Report, information brochure

SUBMISSION OF APPLICATIONS By application form returnable at any time; decisions made quarterly. It is advisable to ascertain the Foundation's current policies by writing in the first instance, outlining your need or proposals

CORRESPONDENT Michael Sparks, Sir John Cass's Foundation, 31 Jewry Street, London EC3N 2EY

CLASSIFICATIONS
- Children and youth – general
- Advancement in life
- Adventure centres and playgrounds
- Centres, clubs and institutes
- Youth organisations (eg Guides, Scouts, YWCA etc)

C.C. NO 312425   **ESTABLISHED** 1748

■ The Challice Trust

OBJECTS Relief of poverty – advancement of religion and education – general charitable purposes

POLICY OF TRUSTEES Help for local needs has priority

TYPE OF BENEFICIARY Local organisations and individuals

RESTRICTIONS Only local students helped

BENEFICIAL AREA Surrey

FINANCES
- Year 1994
- Grants £5,967
- Income £10,434
- Assets £252,122

TRUSTEES P W Smith, Mrs B Munro Thomson, R W Edmondson, B E Farley

CORRESPONDENT P W Smith, 29 Poltimore Road, Guildford, Surrey GU2 5PR

CLASSIFICATIONS
- Children and youth – general

C.C. NO 222360   **ESTABLISHED** 1962

■ The Chandaria Foundation

OBJECTS General charitable purposes

POLICY OF TRUSTEES Generally supporting purposes of wide application

TRUSTEES M A Croft Baker, R G Thom, S N Gibbs

CORRESPONDENT The Secretary, Chandaria Foundation, 49 Queens Gardens, London W2 3AA

CLASSIFICATIONS
- Advancement in life

C.C. NO 252669   **ESTABLISHED** 1967

■ Chapman Charitable Trust

OBJECTS General charitable purposes

POLICY OF TRUSTEES Grants are normally made only to recognised charities, mainly those in which the late Settlor and/or the Trustees have a personal interest or concern

TYPE OF BENEFICIARY At Trustees' discretion. No grants to individuals

RESTRICTIONS No grants to individuals

BENEFICIAL AREA UK

SAMPLE GRANTS £5,000 to NCH Action for Children
£1,000 to Drive for Youth
£1,000 to Friends of Rees Thomas School Pool
£500 to Land and City Families Trust
£500 to National Youth Orchestra of Great Britain

FINANCES
- **Year** 1995
- **Income** £148,000
- **Grants** £146,700
- **Assets** £3,542,000

TRUSTEES Roger S Chapman, W John Chapman, Richard J Chapman, Bruce D Chapman

CORRESPONDENT R S Chapman, Messrs Crouch Chapman, 62 Wilson Street, London EC2A 2BU

CLASSIFICATIONS
- Children and youth – general

C.C. NO 232791   **ESTABLISHED** 1963

■ Chapman Foundation

OBJECTS Provision of facilities for recreation or other leisure-time occupation for the purpose of improving the conditions of life

POLICY OF TRUSTEES Community provision normally in the Newcastle upon Tyne area

TYPE OF BENEFICIARY Charitable bodies providing social and recreational facilities

RESTRICTIONS Newcastle upon Tyne and other towns in England with 100,000+ population. But, in practice, we can rarely help organisations outside the primary area of Newcastle upon Tyne – which we interpret geographically rather than in boundary terms. Individuals never. Minibuses very rarely. Rarely to headquarter organisations

BENEFICIAL AREA UK, especially Tyne and Wear

SAMPLE GRANTS £2,000 to Wallsend Middle School Community Association for building alterations
£1,000 to Stoneygate Play Project for equipment
£250 to Gateshead Sea Cadets for equipment
£250 to Mobex North East for expedition equipment

FINANCES
- **Year** 1995
- **Income** £18,000
- **Grants** £15,500
- **Assets** £175,500

TRUSTEES J A Trotter, P J May, G Cawthorn

SUBMISSION OF APPLICATIONS By letter

CORRESPONDENT Alec Trotter, OBE, 3 Lyndhurst Road, Benton, Newcastle upon Tyne NE12 9NT

CLASSIFICATIONS
- Children and youth – general
- Adventure centres and playgrounds
- Centres, clubs and institutes
- Community groups
- Holidays
- Youth organisations (eg Guides, Scouts, YWCA etc)

C.C. NO 305984   **ESTABLISHED** 1923

■ Charipot Trust

OBJECTS General charitable purposes

POLICY OF TRUSTEES The assistance of established institutions

TYPE OF GRANT Usually one-off for part of a project; seldom in excess of £100

TYPE OF BENEFICIARY Institutions

FINANCES
- **Year** 1992
- **Income** £3,840
- **Grants** £3,840

TRUSTEES J S Bennett, Mrs M de V Bennett

NOTES The income is largely pre-committed

SUBMISSION OF APPLICATIONS In writing but will not normally be acknowledged

CORRESPONDENT Major J S Bennett, 19 The Meadow, Chislehurst, Kent BR7 6AA

CLASSIFICATIONS
- Special classes

C.C. NO 262276   **ESTABLISHED** 1971

■ Charity Projects

OBJECTS General charitable purposes

POLICY OF TRUSTEES Present policy to assist organisations working with young people (14–30) facing problems of homelessness, disability, drug and alcohol misuse and older people. In addition grants are given for development projects throughout Africa focused on addressing conflict; people in towns and cities; women; disabled people and pastoralists

TYPE OF GRANT Each application assessed on its own merit

TYPE OF BENEFICIARY Particular interest in small groups without the capacity to hire fundraisers, within our categories of beneficiary

RESTRICTIONS No grants to individuals. No grants to statutory bodies. No grants for foreign holidays

BENEFICIAL AREA United Kingdom, Africa

SAMPLE GRANTS £15,000 over two years to the Alcohol Counselling and Prevention Service, London to assist in development of services to lesbians and gay men
£15,000 over two years to Homeless Action Group in Exeter, Devon towards the cost of an accommodation worker
£7,500 to the Organisation of Blind African Caribbeans, London to provide a range of Equipment for its new resource centre
£750 to the Wales Council for the Deaf, Pontypridd, Mid Glamorgan for costs of a weekend course 'Bridge to Work' for hearing-impaired students aged 16–18

FINANCES
- **Year** 1994–95
- **Income** £21,951,197
- **Grants** £8,235,175
- **Assets** £29,763,624

TRUSTEES Paul Jackson (Chair), Paddy Coulter, Richard Curtis, Emma Freud, Mike Harris, Lenny Henry, Colin Howes, John Makinson, Alan Parker, June McKerrow, Firoze Manji

PUBLICATIONS Annual Report and Accounts, general information leaflet

SUBMISSION OF APPLICATIONS Year round: send summary of project and sae – application form will be sent if appropriate

CORRESPONDENT Jane Tewson, Chief Executive, Charity Projects, 74 New Oxford Street, London WC1A 1EF

Charterhouse

Alphabetical register of grant making charitable trusts

CLASSIFICATIONS
- Advancement in life
- Community groups
- Youth organisations (eg Guides, Scouts, YWCA etc)

C.C. NO 326568   ESTABLISHED 1984

■ The Charterhouse Charitable Trust

OBJECTS General charitable purposes

POLICY OF TRUSTEES Donations to registered charities only

TYPE OF GRANT Exclude 'starter financing'

RESTRICTIONS No donations to individuals. No sponsorships or advertising

BENEFICIAL AREA London and national charities

FINANCES
- Year 1995
- Grants £87,555
- Income £123,959
- Assets £502,427

TRUSTEES M V Blank, E G Cox

SUBMISSION OF APPLICATIONS To the Secretary, in writing, for the quarterly meeting of the Trustees

CORRESPONDENT The Secretary, The Charterhouse Charitable Trust, 1 Paternoster Row, St Paul's, London EC4M 7DH

CLASSIFICATIONS
- Children and youth – general
- Youth organisations (eg Guides, Scouts, YWCA etc)

C.C. NO 210894   ESTABLISHED 1954

■ The Chase Charity

OBJECTS General charitable purposes

POLICY OF TRUSTEES The Trustees take an interest in supporting young people in trouble or at risk. Youth homelessness is a high priority, but the Trustees are also interested in immediate treatment schemes and 'alternatives to custody' projects, in combating drug and alcohol abuse, and in a variety of activities for the young and unemployed. The Trustees are placing an increasing emphasis upon the provision of social welfare services and community development in rural areas (but not to the exclusion of urban areas). They support community ventures which tackle the need for local services and welcome applications which reflect the needs of all sections of the community. Other areas of interest include: 'The Arts', for example dance, theatre and opera groups, theatre buildings and community arts centres; and the restoration of almshouses and other historic buildings

TYPE OF GRANT Grants are generally on a one-off basis within a range of £500 to £5,000 to meet specific needs or to make a substantial impact

TYPE OF BENEFICIARY Priority is given to small agencies or projects with particular emphasis on rural areas

RESTRICTIONS Grants are limited to registered charities in the UK, individuals are ineligible for funding. Grants are not made to replace funds which have been withdrawn from other sources and the Trustees do not expect to provide funds which, in their opinion, it is the responsibility of the State to provide. The following are ineligible for funding: individual youth groups or clubs; formal education; holidays, travel or expeitions; sport; the advancement of religion; contributions to large or widely circulated appeals; contributions to general salaries or running costs; conferences, seminars or festivals; social or medical research projects; publications or films; animal welfare; endowment funds and other grant making trusts, hospital trusts

BENEFICIAL AREA UK

SAMPLE GRANTS £4,000 to Rural Youth Project, Market Rasen, Lincolnshire towards purchasing and equipping a bus to create a mobile youth centre
£2,000 to Detached Youth Project towards setting up young people in a home for the first time

FINANCES
- Year 1994–95
- Grants £199,058
- Income £237,981
- Assets £3,517,005

TRUSTEES The Council of Management: A Ramsay Hack (Chairman), Claudia Flanders, Keith Grant, Gordon Halcrow, Richard Mills, Elizabeth Moore, Ann Stannard

CORRESPONDENT Peter Kilgarriff, Secretary, The Chase Charity, 2 The Court, High Street, Harwell, Didcot, Oxon OX11 0EY

CLASSIFICATIONS
- Children and youth – general
- Advancement in life
- Community groups
- Development of character
- Counselling (inc helplines)
- Homes and hostels
- Special classes

C.C. NO 207108   ESTABLISHED 1962

■ Cherry Tree Foundation

OBJECTS General charitable purposes

POLICY OF TRUSTEES The purpose of the Trust is, in cases of financial hardship, to assist children no older than sixteen in developing their talents in the fields of music, drama and dance

TYPE OF GRANT £100–£500

BENEFICIAL AREA UK

FINANCES
- Year 1994
- Grants £3,120
- Income £2,533
- Assets £44,280

TRUSTEES P Chody, D Rawstron

SUBMISSION OF APPLICATIONS Applications are considered in June each year but are not acknowledged unless successful

CORRESPONDENT Goodman Derrick, 90 Fetter Lane, London EC4A 1EQ

CLASSIFICATIONS
- Advancement in life

C.C. NO 258842   ESTABLISHED 1966

■ The Chetwode Foundation

OBJECTS General charitable purposes

TYPE OF BENEFICIARY Generally local or Midlands activities

RESTRICTIONS Preference to Notts, Derby and Leicestershire areas

FINANCES
- Year 1992
- Grants £16,594
- Income £55,388
- Assets £644,281

TRUSTEES Mrs R G Samworth, D C Samworth, J G Ellis

CORRESPONDENT J G Ellis, Samworth Brothers Limited, Fields Farm, Cropwell Butler, Nottingham NG12 3AP

CLASSIFICATIONS
- Development of character

C.C. NO 265950   **ESTABLISHED** 1973

■ Child Growth Foundation

OBJECTS (a) The Foundation seeks to ensure that the growth of every UK child is regularly assessed and that any child growing excessively slowly or fast is referred for medical attention as soon as possible (b) The Foundation seeks to ensure that no child will be denied the drugs they need to correct their stature. (c) The Foundation supports individuals or institutions researching the cause/cures of growth conditions. (d) The Foundation maintains a network of families to offer support/advice for any family concerned/diagnosed with a growth problem

POLICY OF TRUSTEES See Objects

TYPE OF BENEFICIARY Individuals and institutions researching child/adult growth disorders

RESTRICTIONS Only applications related to growth disorders, or their causes, will be considered

BENEFICIAL AREA UK

FINANCES
- Year 1994
- Grants £201,720
- Income £429,236
- Assets £173,232

TRUSTEES Management Committee

PUBLICATIONS Patient information booklets, newsletters

CORRESPONDENT Tam Fry, Chairman, Child Growth Foundation, 2 Mayfield Avenue, Chiswick, London W4 1PW

CLASSIFICATIONS
- Children and youth – general

C.C. NO 274325   **ESTABLISHED** 1977

■ The Chrimes Family Charitable Trust

OBJECTS General charitable purposes

POLICY OF TRUSTEES The Trustees give preference to support of community welfare and work of originality or outstanding excellence

TYPE OF GRANT Discretionary

TYPE OF BENEFICIARY See Restrictions

RESTRICTIONS No grants to individuals for educational purposes

BENEFICIAL AREA Priority to Merseyside, Strathclyde and North Wales

FINANCES
- Year 1995
- Grants £10,257
- Income £15,187
- Assets £373,000

TRUSTEES Mrs Anne Williams, Mrs H Kirkham Prosser

CORRESPONDENT Mrs Anne Williams, Northfield, Upper Raby Road, Neston, South Wirral, Merseyside L64 7TZ

CLASSIFICATIONS
- Children and youth – general
- Community groups

C.C. NO 210199   **ESTABLISHED** 1955

■ Christabella Charitable Trust

OBJECTS General charitable purposes

POLICY OF TRUSTEES To support smaller local charities

TYPE OF GRANT Single donations or projects supported over a period

TYPE OF BENEFICIARY Any

RESTRICTIONS Not national appeals

BENEFICIAL AREA Essex and East London

FINANCES
- Year 1993
- Income £83,000

TRUSTEES S M Holmes, R F Folwell, Rev C F Wells

CORRESPONDENT R F Folwell, The Christabella Charitable Trust, 8 Holgate Court, 4–10 Western Road, Romford, Essex RM1 3JS

CLASSIFICATIONS
- Children and youth – general

C.C. NO 800610   **ESTABLISHED** 1988

■ The John & Celia Bonham Christie Charitable Trust

OBJECTS General charitable purposes. To promote medical research and education

POLICY OF TRUSTEES Applications are considered on merit or need. Assistance is given to special causes and charitable bodies of special interest to the Trustees. Appeals of the 'expensive glossy brochure' variety are neither welcomed nor considered

TYPE OF GRANT Yearly, usually for 3 years only

TYPE OF BENEFICIARY Small, rather than large National bodies, but at the discretion of the Settlor

RESTRICTIONS No applications from individuals directly. No new beneficiaries will be accepted until 1996

FINANCES
- Year 1992
- Grants £68,000
- Income £58,000
- Assets £921,000

TRUSTEES Mrs J R Bonham Christie, R Bonham Christie, Mrs Roger Ker, P R Fitzgerald, N R Brown, R J Bonham Christie

SUBMISSION OF APPLICATIONS No form required but a succinct Report and Accounts should be sent To correspondent

CORRESPONDENT Charitable Trust No 326296, c/o PO Box 6 Bath, Avon BA1 2YH

CLASSIFICATIONS
- Development of character
- Homes and hostels

C.C. NO 326296   **ESTABLISHED** 1983

Church

■ Church Urban Fund

OBJECTS To support those in urban areas who are poor, disadvantaged and excluded from national and Church life

POLICY OF TRUSTEES Main emphasis is on places which suffer from social disintegration. The projects supported in these areas arise directly from local needs. Both innovative and proven ideas are supported

TYPE OF GRANT Donations for capital projects and/or income requirements. Mainly revenue grants over two to three years

TYPE OF BENEFICIARY Projects should be based in an urban priority area and demonstrate, if possible, ecumenical working. They help the church be local, outward looking and participative

RESTRICTIONS No grants to individuals

BENEFICIAL AREA Urban priority areas in England

FINANCES
- Year 1994
- Grants £2,758,000
- Income £2,373,000
- Assets £23,224,000

TRUSTEES The Archbishop of Canterbury (Chairman), Stephen O'Brien (Vice Chairman), Ruth McCurry, Canon John Stanley, Margaret Swinson, Alan McLintock, Ven Stephen Lowe, Ven Granville Gibson, Rev Eileen Lake, Richard Farnell

SUBMISSION OF APPLICATIONS Through the relevant diocesan office

CORRESPONDENT Chief Executive, Church Urban Fund, 2 Great Peter Street, London SW1P 3LX

CLASSIFICATIONS
- Children and youth – general
- Community groups
- Day centres and nurseries

C.C. NO 297483   **ESTABLISHED** 1988

■ The City and Metropolitan Welfare Charity

OBJECTS To assist deserving persons who by reason of age, ill-health, accident, infirmity or straitened financial circumstances are in need of assistance. Grants are made to institutions or organisations providing welfare services established for the care and relief of such persons, with a preference for institutions or organisations which are administered in or in connection with the City of London, or are located in Greater London

POLICY OF TRUSTEES Funds fully allocated or committed

RESTRICTIONS No grants to individuals or for research purposes

BENEFICIAL AREA UK

FINANCES
- Year 1994
- Grants £26,200
- Income £29,600
- Assets £479,000

TRUSTEES As appointed by The Lord Mayor Commonalty and Citizens of the City of London, The Mercers' Co, The Leathersellers' Co, The Grocers' Co, The Haberdashers' Co, The Ironmongers' Co

SUBMISSION OF APPLICATIONS By letter

CORRESPONDENT The Clerk to the Trustees, Mercers' Hall, Ironmonger Lane, London EC2V 8HE

CLASSIFICATIONS
- Homes and hostels

C.C. NO 205943   **ESTABLISHED** 1961

■ The City of London School Charitable Trust

OBJECTS General charitable purposes

TYPE OF GRANT Single donations

TYPE OF BENEFICIARY Registered charities only

RESTRICTIONS No grants to individuals. Only one charity supported a year. Usually to charities associated with children

SAMPLE GRANTS £30,000 to Hearing Dogs for the Deaf
£29,000 to Whizz Kidz

FINANCES
- Year 1993
- Grants £23,300
- Income £23,300

TRUSTEES Committee of Staff/Governors

SUBMISSION OF APPLICATIONS In writing to correspondent by 30th April

CORRESPONDENT Dr C Pearce, Queen Victoria Street, London EC4V 3AL

CLASSIFICATIONS
- Children and youth – general

C.C. NO 1020824   **ESTABLISHED** 1993

■ City Parochial Foundation

OBJECTS To benefit directly the poor people normally resident within the Foundation's area of benefit; to administer the endowments of the City Church Fund. In addition: all grants must benefit the poor inhabitants of London. All applicants must show how in practice they are developing services for all sections of the community. Grants made should have an impact on a particular need or problem. Applicants must show that they can tackle the problem. The users of the services should be part of the designing, planning and delivery of services. Partnerships with other funds are welcome; applications involving joint funding are encouraged. Monitoring of work funded is important for both the beneficiary and the funder; the Foundation will monitor grants made, and will require the cooperation of the beneficiaries

POLICY OF TRUSTEES Priorities: There are four main elements in the strategy for 1992–96.
(a) Programme Funding: the Trustees have highlighted three areas of concern for programme funding. (i) Carers (1992–95). (ii) Mental Health (1993–96). (iii) Penal Work (1993–96). These funds have now all been allocated. (b) Strategic Funding: the Foundation will take initiatives to help maintain and develop the necessary support services for voluntary organisations. Applications are invited which focus upon: (i) Training opportunities for staff and committees, especially in new areas such as community care developments, or providing services under contract (ii) Implementation of equal opportunities policies. (iii) Support structures for

refugee communities. (iv) Proposals to help a group of organisations come together to develop a more coherent strategy in one borough, or to meet a particular need of one client group across several boroughs. (v) Proposals to address London-wide issues. (c) General Funding: There are three elements. (i) Major concerns; (ii) Sustaining organisations recently funded by the Foundation; (iii) Small grants. (i) Major concerns (1992–1994). Disability with emphasis on organisations led by people with disabilities. Education and training – services tackling under-achievement, supplementary education, English as a second language especially for women, and post-school education. Elderly and frail people living in the community. Young people – after school care, holiday care, young people with special needs, day care for young children. Welfare rights work with emphasis on money advice and debt counselling. (ii) Sustaining organisations recently funded by the Foundation. Further grants will not be given automatically, but staff will discuss with organisations what is required to continue the organisations works. (iii) Small Grants: see Notes below. 4. Exceptional Needs and Interests: the Trustees will always be ready to consider exceptionally interesting proposals in any area of work helping the poor of London. A strong case would have to be made, supported by relevant experts. Any such application should be submitted in the usual way. Black and ethnic minority organisations: the Foundation wishes to encourage applications from charitable organisations working within and managed by the black and ethnic minority communities, and is particularly aware of the opportunities to assist

TYPE OF GRANT Capital and recurrent. Interest free loans

TYPE OF BENEFICIARY Projects benefitting the poor residents of London

RESTRICTIONS Total exclusion of: community business initiatives; medical research and equipment; individuals; fee paying schools; trips abroad; general holiday playschemes; one-off events; publications; sports; major capital appeals; the direct replacement of public funds; endowment appeals. Registered charities only, except: (a) organisations in the process of obtaining registration; grants for a second year will be conditional upon registration. (b) the applicant is exempt from registration. (c) the applicant is registered as a Friendly Society

BENEFICIAL AREA The Metropolitan Police District of London and City of London; which includes all the London Boroughs

SAMPLE GRANTS £33,000 over three years to Action Group for Irish Youth towards running costs
£25,000 over two years to Teenage Information Network for advice worker
£15,000 to Newham Docklands Motorcycle Project for training worker
£15,000 over one year to Handicapped Adventure Playground Association for fieldwork service
£2,000 to Bowles Rock Trust for residential adventure centre for young disabled people

FINANCES
- **Year** 1994
- **Income** £5,328,632
- **Grants** £5,774,280

TRUSTEES Trustees of the City Parochial Foundation (address as above)

PUBLICATIONS Quinquennial Policy Report 1992–96. Explanatory leaflet

NOTES General Funding – 3 (iii) Small Grants: A small grants programme is to be introduced, so that any charitable organisation can apply for grants of up to £10,000 (normally one-off). For this there will be an application form, available on request

SUBMISSION OF APPLICATIONS Initially in writing to the Clerk. There is frequently a subsequent meeting with the Clerk to discuss any potential application. Required format of an application – statement about the organisation: legal status, aims, brief history, staffing and management committee details, current activities; reference to any previous grants from the Foundation or Trust for London should be made. Detailed financial position of organisation listing main sources of income. Statement on the particular need for which funding is being sought. Full costing of sources, especially applications to other Trusts. Details of the monitoring to be carried out on the scheme for which funding is being requested. Required accompanying documents: constitution, annual report, audited accounts, budget, job description (for a post), equal opportunities policy, names/addresses of office holders. Trustees meet quarterly: Jan, April, Oct, and Dec

CORRESPONDENT Timothy Cook, Clerk, 6 Middle Street, London EC1A 7PH

CLASSIFICATIONS
- Children and youth – general
- Adoption/fostering
- Advancement in life
- Adventure centres and playgrounds
- Centres, clubs and institutes
- Community groups
- Day centres and nurseries
- Development of character
- Counselling (inc helplines)
- Holidays
- Youth organisations (eg Guides, Scouts, YWCA etc)

C.C. NO 205629   **ESTABLISHED** 1891

■ J Anthony Clark Charitable Trust

OBJECTS General charitable purposes

POLICY OF TRUSTEES Projects oriented towards social change in areas of health, education, peace, preservation of the earth and the arts. Preference to the work of small, new or innovative projects

TYPE OF BENEFICIARY See Trustees defined policy

RESTRICTIONS No single person appeals can be considered. No grants will be made to independent schools unless they are for special needs; nor will the Trustees fund projects that are entirely based on the conservation of buildings

FINANCES
- **Year** 1993
- **Income** £133,453
- **Grants** £153,290
- **Assets** £3,585,222

TRUSTEES L P Clark, J C Clark, T A Clark, C Pym, A J R Pelly

CORRESPONDENT The Secretary, J A Clark Charitable Trust, PO Box 1704, Glastonbury, Somerset BA16 0YB

CLASSIFICATIONS
- Children and youth – general

C.C. NO 261723   **ESTABLISHED** 1995

Clark Foundation II

OBJECTS Advancement of higher education for those in financial need – Promotion of education – Provision of facilities for public benefit for social welfare and recreation

POLICY OF TRUSTEES It is not the policy of the Trustees to give grants to individual students or National charities unless there is a strong local connection

TYPE OF BENEFICIARY Normally a charitable Trust

BENEFICIAL AREA Somerset and the West of England

FINANCES
- Year 1985
- Grants £80,000
- Income £165,000
- Assets £1,406,000

TRUSTEES W Bancroft-Clark, J Daniel Clark, J Anthony Clark, JP, Anthony T Clothier

CORRESPONDENT Richard Clark, Secretary, The Clark Foundation, C & J Clark Ltd, Street, Somerset

CLASSIFICATIONS
- Centres, clubs and institutes
- Community groups
- Day centres and nurseries
- Youth organisations (eg Guides, Scouts, YWCA etc)

C.C. NO 313143   **ESTABLISHED** 1959

The Thomas Edward Clarke Trust

OBJECTS Maintenance, support and furtherance of charitable organisations for the benefit of young people in the City of Nottingham (especially for sports)

POLICY OF TRUSTEES To encourage small sports clubs, scouts, guides, boys' brigade, young people's clubs and similar organisations for the benefit of young people

TYPE OF BENEFICIARY In particular small sporting and social clubs recently formed and struggling to find their feet or those operating in poor districts

BENEFICIAL AREA Within Nottingham City Boundaries

FINANCES
- Year 1995
- Grants £7,830
- Income £8,527
- Assets £97,827

TRUSTEES A M N Rodgers, A H Browne

CORRESPONDENT Eversheds, 14 Fletcher Gate, Nottingham, Nottinghamshire NG1 2FX

CLASSIFICATIONS
- Centres, clubs and institutes
- Youth organisations (eg Guides, Scouts, YWCA etc)

C.C. NO 215217   **ESTABLISHED** 1956

Clergy Orphan Corporation

OBJECTS To educate and maintain fatherless children of the clergy until their education and training has been completed and their careers are established

POLICY OF TRUSTEES To help all needy qualified candidates until their training for a career has been completed which, for some, can mean until they are in their mid twenties

TYPE OF BENEFICIARY The fatherless sons and daughters of the clergy of the Church of England and the Church in Wales

RESTRICTIONS Must have been elected to the Foundation before the age of 18 years

FINANCES
- Year 1993
- Grants £276,957
- Income £286,271

TRUSTEES By Committee under Act of Parliament 1809

CORRESPONDENT The Secretary, Clergy Orphan Corporation, 57b Tufton Street, Westminster, London SW1P 3QL

CLASSIFICATIONS
- Special needs housing

C.C. NO 310028   **ESTABLISHED** 1749

Cleveland Community Foundation

OBJECTS To improve the quality of life of the people of Cleveland by supporting a wide range of charitable organisations working to benefit the community, particularly in support of those deprived by social, environmental and economic factors

POLICY OF TRUSTEES We seek to support locally based groups

TYPE OF GRANT For running expenses only. Capital or revenue for one year only

TYPE OF BENEFICIARY All registered charities or bonafide voluntary/community groups, provided the purpose of the grant is wholly charitable and for the benefit of people in Cleveland

RESTRICTIONS Applications are not usually considered for major appeals, sponsored events, holidays and social outings, or for individuals

BENEFICIAL AREA County of Cleveland

SAMPLE GRANTS £6,000 to Middlesbrough Youth Festival towards the cost of holding a month-long festival of activities during summer holidays
£5,000 to Durham Street Studios towards the cost of running a free music studio facility for unwaged young people
£5,000 to Community Campus towards the cost of providing housing and advice to young homeless people
£3,500 to West View Challenge for Youth to bring together disadvantaged young people in Hartlepool and provide leisure activities in town and away
£2,896 to Mohawks Basketball Club (part of a £7,000 grant) to provide training for disadvantaged young people in Stockton in the sport of basketball

FINANCES
- Year 1995
- Grants £115,279
- Income £125,126
- Assets £1,943,563

TRUSTEES Sir Roland Norman, J Bloom, J Kirton, A Kitching, R Sale, M Stewart, S Still, B Storey, H Thornton, J Foster, J Calvert, J Ord, P Sole, K Taylor

PUBLICATIONS Annual report and accounts in July and periodic newsletter

SUBMISSION OF APPLICATIONS Yearly application. Apply to the Foundation for an application form and guidelines for applicants. Applications accepted at any time and considered in February, June and October each year

CORRESPONDENT Sylvia Noddings, Director, Cleveland Community Foundation, Cleveland Business Centre, Middlesborough TS1 2RQ

CLASSIFICATIONS
- Children and youth – general
- Advancement in life
- Adventure centres and playgrounds
- Centres, clubs and institutes
- Community groups
- Day centres and nurseries
- Development of character
- Counselling (inc helplines)
- Homes and hostels
- Special needs housing
- Youth organisations (eg Guides, Scouts, YWCA etc)

C.C. NO 700568   **ESTABLISHED** 1988

■ The Clifford Charity Oxford

OBJECTS See Policy of Trustees

POLICY OF TRUSTEES To support the provision and/or maintenance of whatever facilities or arrangements will enable young people of promise to realise fully their potentialities: ie to promote excellence

TYPE OF GRANT Grants are mainly 'once and for all' and do not exceed £50

TYPE OF BENEFICIARY Mainly educational bodies and others concerned with training and welfare of young people. Preference given to small or specialised bodies

RESTRICTIONS Registered charities only. Applications from individuals, including students, are ineligible

BENEFICIAL AREA UK

SAMPLE GRANTS The Hamilton and East Kilbride Befriending Project – helping and supporting vulnerable young people in our community
St Basil's Centre, Birmingham – work with homeless young people in the West Midlands
Essex Young Jazz Musicians Support Group – encouraging the bright young jazz musicians of Essex
The Weston Spirit (Cardiff) – work with 16–17 year old inner city people
Discovery Dockland Trust (London E14) – to assist with the maintenance of the Lady Amory (a training ship)

FINANCES
- Year 1994–95
- Grants £2,760
- Income £2,670
- Assets £22,060

TRUSTEES C A Rodewald, V C Sayer

NOTES Bodies considering applications should note that policy differs from that of Mr C A Rodewald's Charitable Settlement

SUBMISSION OF APPLICATIONS Applications, which are reviewed approximately every three months, may be submitted through the correspondent at any time. No application form is required. Applications will be acknowledged after review if an sae is enclosed

CORRESPONDENT C A Rodewald, 66 Platt Lane, Manchester M14 5NE

CLASSIFICATIONS
- Children and youth – general
- Advancement in life
- Centres, clubs and institutes
- Community groups
- Development of character
- Counselling (inc helplines)
- Homes and hostels
- Special needs housing
- Special classes
- Youth organisations (eg Guides, Scouts, YWCA etc)
- Children and violence (inc abuse)

C.C. NO 278587   **ESTABLISHED** 1979

■ Lord Clinton's Charitable Trust

OBJECTS General charitable purposes in Devon only

POLICY OF TRUSTEES Young people and the encouragement of youth activities, physically handicapped and disabled people, support for the elderly, medical aid and research, maritime charities

TYPE OF BENEFICIARY Registered charities working in the areas outlined under Policy

RESTRICTIONS Registered charities only. No grants made in response to general appeals from large national organisations nor to smaller bodies working in areas other than those set out above

BENEFICIAL AREA County of Devon only

FINANCES
- Year 1993
- Assets £22,000
- Grants £14,300

TRUSTEES The Hon Charles Fane Trefusis, R A L Waller, FRICS

CORRESPONDENT R A L Waller, FRICS, Rolle Estate Office, East Budleigh, Budleigh Salterton, Devon EX9 7DP

CLASSIFICATIONS
- Children and youth – general
- Adoption/fostering
- Advancement in life
- Adventure centres and playgrounds
- Centres, clubs and institutes
- Day centres and nurseries
- Youth organisations (eg Guides, Scouts, YWCA etc)

C.C. NO 268061   **ESTABLISHED** 1974

■ Cobb Charity

OBJECTS Primarily educational, a green holistic and sustainable vision, promoting an awareness of the potential and particular value of each individual through therapy, rehabilitation and adventure, and encouragement of self-help

POLICY OF TRUSTEES See Objects

TYPE OF BENEFICIARY Small registered charities

RESTRICTIONS Registered charities only, no individuals, no student expeditions, no building restorations

BENEFICIAL AREA International, but only smaller charities need apply

SAMPLE GRANTS £750 to Inverclyde Child Support Volunteers – a voluntary service for children experiencing difficulties at home, school or in the community
£750 to Whitby Resource Centre to provide advice, self-help and support for people in need
£750 to Shaftsbury Crosses Trust towards training

Collier

Alphabetical register of grant making charitable trusts

bursaries for school leavers for apprenticeship in stone masonary

FINANCES
- Year 1995
- Grants £32,000
- Income £35,000
- Assets £449,971

TRUSTEES E Allitt, F Appelbe, C Cochran

SUBMISSION OF APPLICATIONS Preferably August or January

CORRESPONDENT Eleanor Allitt, 108 Leamington Road, Kenilworth, Warwickshire CV8 2AA

CLASSIFICATIONS
- Adventure centres and playgrounds
- Day centres and nurseries
- Development of character

C.C. NO 248030   **ESTABLISHED** 1964

■ The Collier Charitable Trust

OBJECTS General charitable purposes

POLICY OF TRUSTEES To support voluntary welfare, medical and social services

TYPE OF BENEFICIARY Preference for South East England and London

RESTRICTIONS No grants to individuals – payments only to registered charities

FINANCES
- Year 1994
- Grants £7,025
- Income £9,992
- Assets £129,513

TRUSTEES Mrs M N Collier, A J Collier

CORRESPONDENT Mrs M N Collier, 2 Coleshill House, Coleshill, Amersham, Buckinghamshire

CLASSIFICATIONS
- Children and youth – general

C.C. NO 247940   **ESTABLISHED** 1966

■ The Norman Collinson Charitable Trust

OBJECTS General charitable purposes

POLICY OF TRUSTEES Applications from individuals should be through recognised agencies. Applications from organisations should give details of their officers and recent accounts and/or budget

TYPE OF GRANT No upper or lower limit. We do not enter into on-going commitments. Grants are reconsidered each year

TYPE OF BENEFICIARY We generally restrict grants to young people, the aged, infirm and the handicapped or to individuals or organisations who provide help for such people

RESTRICTIONS The Trustees have found it necessary to place a geographical restriction and confine grants to helping people in York and district. We do however make a limited number of grants to national charities

BENEFICIAL AREA York area

SAMPLE GRANTS £5,000 to Copmanthorpe Youth Club for a new hall
£2,750 to One Parent Families, York – shoe grants
£2,000 to Galtres School, York for multi-sensory room
£1,200 to Detached Youth Work, York

£600 to Community Action Project for holidays for children

FINANCES
- Year 1994
- Grants £110,811
- Income £141,976
- Assets £1,226,066

TRUSTEES K Denham, F E Dennis, D B Holman, J M Saville, D C Fotheringham

SUBMISSION OF APPLICATIONS The Trustees meet monthly to consider applications, normally on the second Tuesday in the month

CORRESPONDENT D B Holman, Secretary, 13 Sandstock Road, Stockton Lane, York YO3 0HB

CLASSIFICATIONS
- Children and youth – general

C.C. NO 277325   **ESTABLISHED** 1979

■ The Timothy Colman Charitable Trust

OBJECTS General charitable purposes

POLICY OF TRUSTEES To further community life, especially in Norfolk

TYPE OF BENEFICIARY Primarily projects within Norfolk area. Conservation and nautical projects favoured

RESTRICTIONS No grants to individuals

BENEFICIAL AREA Norfolk

FINANCES
- Year 1994
- Grants £13,406
- Income £9,730
- Assets £223,013

TRUSTEES Coutts & Co, T J A Colman, J Colman

CORRESPONDENT The Administrator, The Timothy Colman Charitable Trust, Coutts & Co, Trustee Dept, 440 Strand, London WC2R 0QS

CLASSIFICATIONS
- Day centres and nurseries
- Youth organisations (eg Guides, Scouts, YWCA etc)

C.C. NO 206129   **ESTABLISHED** 1962

■ The Construction Industry Trust for Youth (formerly The Building Industry Youth Trust)

OBJECTS To provide individual support for the education and training of construction industry youth and assistance for youth building projects

POLICY OF TRUSTEES Grants will only be given to organisations which have no restrictions as to colour, class, creed or sect and only for the provision of permanent buildings for the use of youth between the ages of 8 and 25 years, or prospective construction industry students

TYPE OF BENEFICIARY Disadvantaged young people wishing to train in the construction industry (sponsorship) or any youth organisation (for building projects)

RESTRICTIONS Not for equipment, furniture, maintenance, repairs, decorating, transport or running costs

FINANCES
- Year 1995
- Grants £24,000
- Income £40,000
- Assets £102,000

Alphabetical register of grant making charitable trusts **Cork**

TRUSTEES Nineteen senior representatives of the building and construction industries

CORRESPONDENT The Hon Secretary, The Construction Industry Trust for Youth, 11 Upper Belgrave Street, London SW1

CLASSIFICATIONS
● Children and youth – general

C.C. NO 305977   ESTABLISHED 1961

■ The Ernest Cook Trust

OBJECTS Charitable activities of an educational nature

POLICY OF TRUSTEES To support educational work in the countryside, promoting its conservation and meeting rural needs. To assist research of a rural or environmental nature. To support organisations providing training in practical conservation and in rural skills. Limited support is given to organisations arranging educational student travel. In cases where awards are made dependent upon conditions being met, these offers are generally held open for a maximum of 12 months

TYPE OF BENEFICIARY Registered charitable organisations

RESTRICTIONS Never:- Individuals. Building or renovation. Medical related projects. Community arts programmes. Concerts, festivals, theatre, dance and sculpture projects. Expeditions, overseas study and exchange programmes. Housing. Core funding

BENEFICIAL AREA Great Britain with special consideration to Gloucestershire, Dorset, Leicestershire and Buckinghamshire

FINANCES
● Year 1993   ● Income £400,000
● Grants £407,937

TRUSTEES Sir William Benyon (Chairman), Sir Jack Boles, MBE, C F Badcock, MA, M C Tuely, A W M Christie-Miller

CORRESPONDENT The Secretary, The Ernest Cook Trust, Fairford Park, Fairford, Gloucestershire GL7 4JH

CLASSIFICATIONS
● Development of character
● Youth organisations (eg Guides, Scouts, YWCA etc)

C.C. NO 313497   ESTABLISHED 1952

■ Cooper Charitable Trust

OBJECTS General charitable purposes

POLICY OF TRUSTEES The physically handicapped and the deprived. Medical research projects. No grants to individuals. Grantees chosen by Trustees from personal knowledge

TYPE OF BENEFICIARY National charities

RESTRICTIONS No individuals

BENEFICIAL AREA EEC, Israel

FINANCES
● Year 1995   ● Income £133,989
● Grants £126,127   ● Assets £1,786,594

TRUSTEES H C Cooper, Sally Roter, Judith Portrait

CORRESPONDENT Fraser Russell, 4 London Wall Buildings, Blomfield Street, London EC2M 5NT

CLASSIFICATIONS
● Children and youth – general

C.C. NO 206772   ESTABLISHED 1962

■ Cooper Charitable Trust

OBJECTS General charitable purposes

POLICY OF TRUSTEES Preference given to the Oxford area

TYPE OF BENEFICIARY Mainly well organised local causes and institutions

RESTRICTIONS Rarely to individuals

FINANCES
● Year 1995   ● Income £17,481
● Grants £38,274   ● Assets £275,242

TRUSTEES G R Cooper, A R Cooper

CORRESPONDENT G R Cooper, Shepherd's Close, Hinksey Hill, Oxford, Oxfordshire OX1 5BQ

CLASSIFICATIONS
● Children and youth – general

C.C. NO 249879   ESTABLISHED 1966

■ J Reginald Corah Foundation Fund

OBJECTS General charitable purposes

RESTRICTIONS No educational/professional applications from individuals

BENEFICIAL AREA City and County of Leicester

FINANCES
● Year 1994   ● Income £94,433
● Grants £66,966   ● Assets £2,407,320

TRUSTEES H P Corah, R Wade, R Bowder

CORRESPONDENT Miss L A Atterbury, Harvey Ingram, Solicitors, 20 New Walk, Leicester, Leicestershire LE1 6TX

CLASSIFICATIONS
● Children and youth – general
● Centres, clubs and institutes
● Development of character
● Youth organisations (eg Guides, Scouts, YWCA etc)

C.C. NO 220792   ESTABLISHED 1953

■ Sir Kenneth Cork Charitable Trust

OBJECTS Relief of poverty and general charitable purposes

POLICY OF TRUSTEES The Trust rarely gives to organisations that it does not already support on a regular basis or who have a close connection with the City of London

BENEFICIAL AREA City of London

FINANCES
● Year 1993   ● Income £16,952
● Grants £10,005   ● Assets £85,434

TRUSTEES R Cork, S J Jeffree, N Cork

CORRESPONDENT R Cork, Moore Stephens, Chartered Accountants, 1 Snowhill, London EC1A 2EN

Does the trust you have chosen match your needs? Haphazard applications waste postage and time

CLASSIFICATIONS
- Centres, clubs and institutes
- Counselling (inc helplines)

C.C. NO 291340   ESTABLISHED 1985

■ Ruth and Charles Corman Charitable Trust

OBJECTS General charitable purposes

POLICY OF TRUSTEES The Trustees have a number of outstanding commitments which will absorb the income of the Trust for the foreseeable future

FINANCES
- Year 1994–95
- Grants £14,798
- Income £12,726
- Assets £2,146

TRUSTEES C L Corman, Mrs R Corman

CORRESPONDENT C L Corman, 24 Daleham Gardens, London NW3 5DA

CLASSIFICATIONS
- Homes and hostels

C.C. NO 277492   ESTABLISHED 1979

■ The Cotton Trust

OBJECTS General charitable purposes

POLICY OF TRUSTEES To assist, through grants, the relief of suffering and elimination and control of disease; handicapped and disabled and disadvantaged people of all ages

TYPE OF GRANT Mainly one-off grants for defined capital projects. Running costs and salaries only considered in exceptional cases

TYPE OF BENEFICIARY Generally restricted to defined capital projects

RESTRICTIONS No telephone calls. Registered charities only. No support to individuals, students, postgraduates expeditions or travelling costs. No local community applications except in Leicestershire, Hertfordshire and Buckinghamshire. No support for the construction of new buildings. No general 'circular' appeals. Maximum of 1 application per year

BENEFICIAL AREA Local (generally Leicestershire, but also Hertfordshire and Buckinghamshire). Overseas

FINANCES
- Year 1993
- Grants £249,705
- Income £240,405

TRUSTEES C B Cotton, J Cotton, L E Stilwell, A R Weston

PUBLICATIONS Annual Report

SUBMISSION OF APPLICATIONS No guidelines or application form. Essential that all applications include proof of registered charity status, a copy of the latest audited accounts, a detailed budget and funds raised. Meeting in August, December and March. Applications must be received at least one month in advance of a meeting to be considered. It is regretted that only successful applications can be answered

CORRESPONDENT I C Stilwell, PO Box 728, Tring, Hertfordshire HP23 6PS

CLASSIFICATIONS
- Children and youth – general
- Counselling (inc helplines)
- Holidays
- Special needs housing

C.C. NO 222995   ESTABLISHED 1956

■ The Coulthurst Trust

OBJECTS General charitable purposes

POLICY OF TRUSTEES Principally to make recurring donations to specific charities with surplus funds being used towards the support of specific charitable objects in the North Yorkshire Area and then, at discretion, occasionally funding will be provided towards National Appeals

RESTRICTIONS No grants to individuals

BENEFICIAL AREA Yorkshire

FINANCES
- Year 1994
- Grants £36,096
- Income £25,449

TRUSTEES Coutts & Co, Mrs S H Fenwick, M J Fenwick

CORRESPONDENT The Coulthurst Trust, Coutts & Co, Trustee Dept, 440 Strand, London WC2R 0QS

CLASSIFICATIONS
- Children and youth – general

C.C. NO 209690   ESTABLISHED 1947

■ The Peter Courtauld Charitable Trust (formerly the Petercourt Trust)

OBJECTS General charitable purposes

POLICY OF TRUSTEES Preference to charities of which the Trust has special interest, knowledge or association

RESTRICTIONS UK registered charities only. Applications from individuals, including students, are ineligible

FINANCES
- Year 1993
- Grants £16,050
- Income £16,860
- Assets £254,000

TRUSTEES W O Farrer, Mrs S M Courtauld, D A Lockhart, S P Courtauld

NOTES Applications will not necessarily be acknowledged. No telephone calls

SUBMISSION OF APPLICATIONS To the correspondent at any time

CORRESPONDENT S P Courtauld, c/o Farrer & Co, 66 Lincoln's Inn Fields, London WC2A 3LH

CLASSIFICATIONS
- Special classes

C.C. NO 258827   ESTABLISHED 1969

■ The Augustine Courtauld Trust

OBJECTS General charitable purposes

POLICY OF TRUSTEES Preference to charities in Essex of which the Trust has special interest, knowledge or association

TYPE OF BENEFICIARY Registered charities

RESTRICTIONS Applications from individuals will not be considered

BENEFICIAL AREA Mainly Essex

SAMPLE GRANTS Essex Association of Boys Clubs
Jubilee Sailing Trust
Young Concern Trust
North London Commando Rescue
The Childrens Society

FINANCES
- Year 1995
- Grants £66,800
- Income £78,543
- Assets £1,100,070

TRUSTEES The Lord Bishop of Chelmsford, The Rev A C C Courtauld, MA, The Lord Lieutenant of Essex, Col N A C Croft, DSO, OBE, MA, J Courtauld

CORRESPONDENT Birkett Long, Red House, Halstead, Essex CO9 2DZ

CLASSIFICATIONS
- Children and youth – general
- Centres, clubs and institutes
- Homes and hostels
- Youth organisations (eg Guides, Scouts, YWCA etc)

C.C. NO 226217   **ESTABLISHED** 1956

■ The Coutts Charitable Trust

OBJECTS Such charitable purposes as Coutts & Co may direct

POLICY OF TRUSTEES The Trustees do not consider personal appeals or make grants to individuals and their support is, in the main, directed towards charities involved with the homeless, disadvantaged and handicapped children and adults, those dealing with rehabilitation and teaching self-help, youth organisations and the relief of poverty. Where possible, the Trustees continue support for those charities to which they have traditionally given over a number of years and they also prefer to support organisations in areas where Coutts & Co has a physical presence

TYPE OF GRANT Regular annual grants and one-off for specific projects

RESTRICTIONS UK registered charities only. Applications from individuals, including students, are ineligible. No overseas projects considered

BENEFICIAL AREA England, in particular the London area

FINANCES
- Year 1995
- Grants £109,760
- Income £133,160

TRUSTEES Sir Ewen A J Fergusson, GCMG, GCVO, H Post, The Hon N Assheton, C M Horne, T J Lewis

SUBMISSION OF APPLICATIONS At any time. All applications should be addressed to the Correspondent and must include clear details of the purpose for which the grant is required. No guidelines or application forms issued

CORRESPONDENT T J Lewis, Assistant Secretary, Coutts & Co, 440 Strand, London WC2R 0QS

CLASSIFICATIONS
- Children and youth – general
- Advancement in life
- Centres, clubs and institutes
- Development of character
- Youth organisations (eg Guides, Scouts, YWCA etc)

C.C. NO 1000135   **ESTABLISHED** 1987

■ Cripplegate Foundation

OBJECTS (a) Providing facilities for recreation or other leisure-time occupation in the interests of social welfare with the object of improving the conditions of life for people resident or employed in the area of benefit. (b) Relieving need, hardship or distress either generally or individually for people resident or employed in the area of benefit

POLICY OF TRUSTEES To make grants as extensively as possible within the area of benefit

TYPE OF BENEFICIARY Organisations or individuals

RESTRICTIONS To area of benefit

BENEFICIAL AREA The Ancient Parish of St Giles, Cripplegate, including the former Parish of St Luke Old Street as constituted 1732 (southern Islington and the North of the City of London)

FINANCES
- Year 1994
- Grants £901,263
- Income £1,147,730
- Assets £14,916,104

TRUSTEES The Governors

CORRESPONDENT David Green, Clerk to the Governors, Cripplegate Foundation, 76 Central Street, London EC1V 8AG

CLASSIFICATIONS
- Children and youth – general
- Advancement in life
- Adventure centres and playgrounds
- Centres, clubs and institutes
- Community groups
- Day centres and nurseries
- Counselling (inc helplines)
- Holidays
- Youth organisations (eg Guides, Scouts, YWCA etc)

C.C. NO 207499   **ESTABLISHED** 1891

■ The Violet & Milo Cripps Charitable Trust

OBJECTS General charitable purposes

POLICY OF TRUSTEES Mostly prison-related

TYPE OF BENEFICIARY Mostly national charities

FINANCES
- Year 1994
- Grants £41,500
- Income £12,000
- Assets £233,000

TRUSTEES Lord Parmoor, H Curran, A Newhouse, R Liventhal

CORRESPONDENT Messrs Slaughter & May, 35 Basinghall Street, London EC2V 5DB

CLASSIFICATIONS
- Centres, clubs and institutes

C.C. NO 289404   **ESTABLISHED** 1984

■ Cripps Foundation

OBJECTS General charitable purposes

POLICY OF TRUSTEES Charity to provide support for the construction of new buildings and the maintenance of ancient buildings connected with education, religion and health and care. No grants are made to individual applicants or to organisations based outside the beneficial area

BENEFICIAL AREA Northamptonshire

FINANCES
- Year 1994
- Grants £890,200
- Income £893,000
- Assets £490,200

TRUSTEES The Council of Management

CORRESPONDENT Mellors Basden & Co, Chartered Accountants, 8th Floor, Aldwych House, 79–91 Aldwych, London WC2B 4HN

CLASSIFICATIONS
- Children and youth – general
- Centres, clubs and institutes
- Youth organisations (eg Guides, Scouts, YWCA etc)

C.C. NO 212285   **ESTABLISHED** 1955

■ The Harry Crook Charitable Trust

OBJECTS General charitable purposes

POLICY OF TRUSTEES The Trustees will generally only consider applications from registered charities within the beneficial area referred to below

TYPE OF BENEFICIARY Registered charities in the Bristol area only

RESTRICTIONS Registered charities only

BENEFICIAL AREA Bristol and District only

FINANCES
- Year 1992
- Grants £630,480
- Income £138,000
- Assets £3,208,006

TRUSTEES T G Bickle, J O Gough, R G West, Mrs I Wollen, D J Bellew

CORRESPONDENT D J Bellew, Veale Wasbrough, Solicitors, Orchard Court, Orchard Lane, Bristol BS1 5DS

CLASSIFICATIONS
- Centres, clubs and institutes
- Community groups
- Homes and hostels
- Youth organisations (eg Guides, Scouts, YWCA etc)

C.C. NO 231470   **ESTABLISHED** 1963

■ Crossfield Charitable Fund

OBJECTS General charitable purposes. Registered charitable organisations only

POLICY OF TRUSTEES Payments for charitable purposes to registered charitable organisations – national and local

TYPE OF BENEFICIARY Charitable organisations only – not individuals

FINANCES
- Year 1993
- Grants £14,424
- Income £18,727
- Assets £352,200

TRUSTEES Mrs M Crossfield, J Hargreaves

CORRESPONDENT The Manager, Barclays Bank Trust Co Ltd, Executorship & Trustee Service Osborne Court, Gadbrook Park, Rudheath, Northwich, Cheshire CW9 7UE

CLASSIFICATIONS
- Children and youth – general
- Development of character
- Homes and hostels
- Youth organisations (eg Guides, Scouts, YWCA etc)

C.C. NO 219399   **ESTABLISHED** 1959

■ D A Curry's Charitable Trust

OBJECTS General charitable purposes

POLICY OF TRUSTEES Adherence of Settlor's wishes

TYPE OF BENEFICIARY Registered charities

RESTRICTIONS No personal grants

FINANCES
- Year 1994
- Grants £20,000
- Income £20,000
- Assets £330,000

TRUSTEES Mrs L E Curry, A Curry, N J Armstrong

SUBMISSION OF APPLICATIONS In writing

CORRESPONDENT N J Armstrong, FCA, Messrs Alliotts, 5th Floor, 9 Kingsway, London WC2B 6XF

CLASSIFICATIONS
- Homes and hostels

C.C. NO 214751   **ESTABLISHED** 1962

■ The Thomas Curtis Charitable Trust

OBJECTS Relief, support and welfare of mentally and/or physically handicapped children

POLICY OF TRUSTEES Preference given to applicants from High Wycombe and the surrounding area

TYPE OF GRANT One-off lump sum for a specific project or part of a project

TYPE OF BENEFICIARY Preference given to local persons and organisations for special projects, particularly in the area of special needs

RESTRICTIONS Applications not related to above objects, and for assistance with university education are not considered

BENEFICIAL AREA High Wycombe area

SAMPLE GRANTS £414 to fund 1:1 support for special needs child at pre-school group
£300 towards cost of concert at special needs school in High Wycombe
£250 to enable special needs child to attend holiday centre while parents and siblings took a holiday
£200 towards purchase of special buggy for special needs child

FINANCES
- Year 1993
- Grants £7,300
- Income £8,000
- Assets £101,000

TRUSTEES J R Curtis, Mrs M A Curtis, Mrs Taylor-Rose

SUBMISSION OF APPLICATIONS At any time. Trustees meet three or four times a year. Applications should include clear details of the project and how funds are to be applied

CORRESPONDENT J R Curtis, Hartlands, 28 Amersham Hill Drive, High Wycombe, Buckinghamshire HP13 6QY

CLASSIFICATIONS
- Holidays
- Special needs housing

C.C. NO 293065   **ESTABLISHED** 1985

■ The Wallace Curzon Charitable Trust

OBJECTS The relief of poverty and sickness and the education of children in any country or countries, place or places, without differentiation on the ground of race, colour, nationality, creed or sex

POLICY OF TRUSTEES The overriding emphasis is on children, ie relief of poverty and sickness of children, as well as their education

TYPE OF BENEFICIARY Other charitable institutions either nationally known or of which Trustees' have direct personal knowledge

RESTRICTIONS Appeals from individuals are not accepted

BENEFICIAL AREA Worldwide, but smaller grants made with some preference for Trustees' more local schemes in Hants, Wilts and the South West

SAMPLE GRANTS £5,000 to Nepalese Orphanage
£2,000 to Save the Children
£1,500 to NSPCC
£1,500 to Barnardos
£1,000 to Hope and Homes for Children

FINANCES
- Year 1995
- Grants £16,750
- Income £24,494
- Assets £348,066

TRUSTEES R Spooner, P G D Curzon, F G D Curzon

NOTES A small percentage of grants go to musical/educational connections, eg for allocation to specific pupils with a need or to help enable productions involving school children. The 1995 figures above reflect an artificially low amount (as 1994 was artificially high) depending on the dates grants were made and the financial year. (The Income figure is the best guide, as apart from accounting expenses it is all distributed eventually)

SUBMISSION OF APPLICATIONS In order to reduce outgoings to a minimum (and to maximise grants) we only respond to applications including an sae

CORRESPONDENT Fritz Curzon, Secretary, Homanton House, Shrewton, Salisbury, Wiltshire SP3 4ER

CLASSIFICATIONS
- Children and youth – general

C.C. NO 294508   **ESTABLISHED** 1986

■ Cystic Fibrosis Trust

OBJECTS Research into Cystic Fibrosis, support for people with Cystic Fibrosis and their families; public education

POLICY OF TRUSTEES To finance research to find a complete cure whilst improving current methods of treatment. To assist by formation of branches for the purpose of advising parents about the disease. Publicising facts about Cystic Fibrosis

TYPE OF BENEFICIARY Research departments of hospitals and universities and clinical fellowships, Cystic Fibrosis centres and science studentships

RESTRICTIONS Restricted to research establishments (hospitals and universities) and Cystic Fibrosis Centres in hospitals

BENEFICIAL AREA UK

FINANCES
- Year 1995
- Grants £2,200,000
- Income £3,607,000
- Assets £4,600,532

TRUSTEES P Levy, BSc, OBE, FRICS (Chairman), Sir Robert Johnson, R Luff, OStJ Hon FRCP,CBE, N Benson, FCA (Treasurer)

CORRESPONDENT J Edkins, FCA, Executive Director, Cystic Fibrosis Trust, Alexandra House, 5 Blyth Road, Bromley, Kent BR1 3RS

CLASSIFICATIONS
- Children and youth – general

C.C. NO 229975   **ESTABLISHED** 1963

The DLM Charitable Trust

OBJECTS General charitable purposes

POLICY OF TRUSTEES To support charities operating in Oxford and the surrounding areas

RESTRICTIONS No grants to individuals

FINANCES
- Year 1990
- Grants £3,000
- Income £63,000
- Assets £1,163,000

TRUSTEES Dr E A de la Mare, Mrs P Sawyer, J A Cloke

CORRESPONDENT J A Cloke Messrs Cloke & Co, Warnford Court, Throgmorton Street, London EC2N 2AT

CLASSIFICATIONS
- Children and youth – general
- Youth organisations (eg Guides, Scouts, YWCA etc)

C.C. NO 328520   **ESTABLISHED** 1990

DM Charitable Trust

OBJECTS General charitable purposes

POLICY OF TRUSTEES To distribute income each year but no grants made from capital or to individual applicants. Currently the main areas of interest are young people (with emphasis on employment and education); the elderly; the handicapped (mentally or physically); medical research, particularly that directed towards the needs of the foregoing people. Preference is given to smaller charities which have connections with the Trustees

TYPE OF GRANT Cash grant, usually £50

TYPE OF BENEFICIARY Registered charities working in the areas mentioned

RESTRICTIONS Registered charities only. Applications from or for the benefit of individuals, including students, are ineligible. No grants made to general appeals from large national organisations nor to smaller bodies working in areas other than the Beneficial Area

BENEFICIAL AREA Preference to Essex and Hertfordshire

SAMPLE GRANTS £50 to Hertfordshire Charity for Children
£50 to Essex Scouts

FINANCES
- Year 1993
- Grants £3,940
- Income £4,990
- Assets £42,162

TRUSTEES D D Morgan, Mrs E D Moore, Mrs M H Morgan, Mrs A M D Andrews

NOTES Most grants made are renewable, and few funds are available for new beneficiaries

SUBMISSION OF APPLICATIONS In writing

CORRESPONDENT D Dudley Morgan, St Leonards House, St Leonards Road, Nazeing, Waltham Abbey, Essex EN9 2HG

CLASSIFICATIONS
- Children and youth – general
- Advancement in life

C.C. NO 232843   **ESTABLISHED** 1963

Dacorum Community Trust

OBJECTS Local charity for local needs

POLICY OF TRUSTEES Within the Dacorum area applications open to all

TYPE OF GRANT Pump priming, recurring, capital, single

TYPE OF BENEFICIARY Local groups, individuals, organisations

RESTRICTIONS No restrictions within the area

BENEFICIAL AREA Borough of Dacorum

FINANCES
- Year 1995
- Grants £7,300
- Income £15,500
- Assets £75,000

TRUSTEES G Hitchcock, M Phillips, G Wyton, L Kent, B Edwards, Mrs M Flint, A Brown, Mrs S Pesch, M Parr, Mrs A Graham-Norgan, B Bland, J Richardson

PUBLICATIONS Annual Report

SUBMISSION OF APPLICATIONS Quarterly: June, September, January, March

CORRESPONDENT G Wilkins, Development Officer, 3 St Mary's Road, Hemel Hempstead, Herts HP2 5HL

CLASSIFICATIONS
- Advancement in life
- Centres, clubs and institutes
- Community groups
- Counselling (inc helplines)
- Holidays
- Youth organisations (eg Guides, Scouts, YWCA etc)

C.C. NO 272759   **ESTABLISHED** 1976

The Damont Charitable Trust

OBJECTS General charitable purposes but primarily for The Association for Jewish Youth Inc

POLICY OF TRUSTEES Normally only for The Association for Jewish Youth. No capital can be applied so long as The Association for Jewish Youth remains in existence and recognised as a charity

RESTRICTIONS At present exclusively for the Association for Jewish Youth Inc

FINANCES
- Year 1993
- Grants £85,000
- Income £44,000
- Assets £877,000

TRUSTEES The Rt Hon Baron Swaythling, M R Nathan, M Bojam, M Taylor

CORRESPONDENT Mrs Linda Davis, Norwood House, Harmony Way, Victoria Road, London NW4 2BZ

CLASSIFICATIONS
- Children and youth – general

C.C. NO 232018   **ESTABLISHED** 1963

■ The Sir Peter Daniell Charitable Trust

OBJECTS General charitable purposes

POLICY OF TRUSTEES Funds fully committed or allocated

RESTRICTIONS Registered charities only. Applications from individuals are ineligible

FINANCES
- Year 1995
- Grants £4,000
- Income £4,000
- Assets £60,000

TRUSTEES R A Daniell, J A Daniell

SUBMISSION OF APPLICATIONS By letter

CORRESPONDENT R A Daniell, The Sir Peter Daniell Charitable Trust, 47 Flood Street, London SW3

CLASSIFICATIONS
- Centres, clubs and institutes

C.C. NO 263987   **ESTABLISHED** 1972

■ Baron Davenport's Charity Trust

OBJECTS 30% to children's organisations in Birmingham and the Midland Counties for the benefit of persons under 21 years – 30% to charitable organisations in or near Birmingham concerned with the erection and maintenance of almshouses or homes for the aged poor – 40% to necessitous elderly widows, spinsters and fatherless children who through no fault of their own are in reduced circumstances

POLICY OF TRUSTEES To distribute Trust income to organisations or individuals within terms of Trust Deed

TYPE OF BENEFICIARY Grants to individuals limited to beneficial areas above

RESTRICTIONS Restricted to the beneficiaries set out under Objects within the stated geographical area

BENEFICIAL AREA Birmingham and Midland Counties – Warwickshire, Worcestershire and Staffordshire

FINANCES
- Year 1993
- Grants £742,550
- Income £781,727
- Assets £19,643,301

TRUSTEES Ex-officio – Lord Mayor, Chief Executive, City Treasurer (City of Birmingham). Non-official Trustees – G R Willcox, A C S Hordern, T D Morris, P A Gough

CORRESPONDENT E J Rough, Secretary, 43 Temple Row, Birmingham B2 5JT

CLASSIFICATIONS
- Children and youth – general
- Holidays
- Homes and hostels
- Special needs housing
- Youth organisations (eg Guides, Scouts, YWCA etc)

C.C. NO 217307   **ESTABLISHED** 1931

■ J Davies Charities Limited

OBJECTS General charitable purposes

POLICY OF TRUSTEES Mainly Jewish charities

TYPE OF BENEFICIARY No grants given to individuals

FINANCES
- Year 1991
- Grants £33,800
- Income £36,386
- Assets £197,098

TRUSTEES Governors: F Davies, M Kayne, G Munitz, S L Orenstein, M Rabin

CORRESPONDENT M Rabin, FCA, 22 Hillcrest Avenue, Edgware, Middlesex HA8 8PA

CLASSIFICATIONS
- Homes and hostels

C.C. NO 248270   **ESTABLISHED** 1966

■ The Sarah D'Avigdor Goldsmid Charitable Trust

OBJECTS General charitable purposes

POLICY OF TRUSTEES No specific policy but see Restrictions below

TYPE OF BENEFICIARY Registered charities only

RESTRICTIONS Registered charities only. Applications by individuals not considered. Unsuccessful applications not acknowledged. Needs of the County of Kent favoured

BENEFICIAL AREA Kent

SAMPLE GRANTS £600 to Kent Association of Boys Clubs
£100 to Kent Kids Miles of Smiles
£100 to Christ Church (Oxford) United Clubs
£100 to Barnardos
£50 to Youth Clubs UK

FINANCES
- Year 1994
- Grants £18,000
- Income £28,000
- Assets £400,000

TRUSTEES Lady d'Avigdor Goldsmid, Mrs R C Teacher, A J M Teacher

PUBLICATIONS Accounts

CORRESPONDENT Mrs R C Teacher, Hadlow Place, Tonbridge, Kent TN11 0BW

CLASSIFICATIONS
- Children and youth – general

C.C. NO 233083   **ESTABLISHED** 1963

■ Lily & Henry Davis Charitable Foundation

OBJECTS General charitable purposes

POLICY OF TRUSTEES Only make grants to registered charities. Not individuals. Follow policy established by the founder – new charities rarely considered

TYPE OF BENEFICIARY Preference for National and Jewish

RESTRICTIONS No grants to individuals – grants only to registered charities

BENEFICIAL AREA UK

FINANCES
- Year 1995
- Grants £18,000
- Income £18,011
- Assets £347,604

TRUSTEES Mrs E B Rubens, J A Clemence

CORRESPONDENT BDO Stoy Hayward, 8 Baker Street, London W1M 1DA

CLASSIFICATIONS
- Children and youth – general
- Youth organisations (eg Guides, Scouts, YWCA etc)

C.C. NO 263662 **ESTABLISHED** 1971

■ Wilfrid Bruce Davis Charitable Trust

OBJECTS Improving the life of those physically disadvantaged

POLICY OF TRUSTEES The support of cancer, kidney dialysis patients and others with improved nursing care, counselling and provision of holidays are the main aims

TYPE OF BENEFICIARY Registered charities only, for work in Cornwall working towards stated Policy above

RESTRICTIONS Registered charities only. No applications from individuals considered

BENEFICIAL AREA Mainly Cornwall

FINANCES
- Year 1994
- Grants £61,688
- Income £48,361
- Assets £706,243

TRUSTEES W B Davis, MBE, Mrs D F Davis, Mrs D S Dickens

PUBLICATIONS Annual Report

SUBMISSION OF APPLICATIONS The budget for grants is filled for several years ahead and, therefore, there is little point in making applications

CORRESPONDENT W Bruce Davis, MBE, La Feock Grange, Feock, Truro, Cornwall TR3 6RG

CLASSIFICATIONS
- Children and youth – general

C.C. NO 265421 **ESTABLISHED** 1967

■ The De Clermont Charitable Company Limited

OBJECTS To help homeless children – to give them a pupose in living and to encourage Christian virtues. Self-help programmes supported. Medical research

POLICY OF TRUSTEES The aid and support of those charities that are of special interest to the Founders of this Company

TYPE OF BENEFICIARY Both headquarters organisations and local organisations but with regard to the latter we do not have funds available for areas outside the North East and Scotland

RESTRICTIONS No grants to individuals

BENEFICIAL AREA Great Britain and Northern Ireland

SAMPLE GRANTS £120 to Romanian Orphanage Trust
£100 to Royal Blind Asylum School
£100 to NCH Action for Children
£100 to National Deaf Children's Society
£50 to Adventure Holidays

FINANCES
- Year 1993
- Grants £27,613
- Income £32,494
- Assets £488,498

TRUSTEES The Directors: Mrs E K de Clermont, H S Orpwood

CORRESPONDENT Mrs E K de Clermont, Morris Hall, Norham, Berwick-upon-Tweed, Northumberland

CLASSIFICATIONS
- Children and youth – general
- Adoption/fostering
- Advancement in life
- Adventure centres and playgrounds
- Centres, clubs and institutes
- Community groups
- Development of character
- Counselling (inc helplines)
- Holidays
- Youth organisations (eg Guides, Scouts, YWCA etc)

C.C. NO 274191 **ESTABLISHED** 1977

■ De La Rue Charitable Trust (formerly The De La Rue Jubilee Trust)

OBJECTS General charitable purposes

POLICY OF TRUSTEES To allocate funds, in line with the Per Cent Club, to charitable and good causes that fall within policy categories ie, education, international understanding, relief of extreme suffering for elderly, very young and disadvantaged. Hospices and special community projects and institutions close to De La Rue locations and its international markets

TYPE OF GRANT Cash donations – usually one-off for a specific project or three-year covenants

TYPE OF BENEFICIARY Registered charities

RESTRICTIONS No requests from individuals. No small local charities or interests which are not in the vicinity of De La Rue industrial and business locations

BENEFICIAL AREA Local and international within given categories

FINANCES
- Year 1994
- Grants £171,000

TRUSTEES The Rt Hon The Earl of Limerick, David Hosie, Terry McWilliams, Liam Christie, Sarah Stroyan, (De La Rue Charitable Donations Committee)

CORRESPONDENT Appeals Secretary, De La Rue Charitable Trust, 6 Agar Street, London WC2N 4DE

CLASSIFICATIONS
- Advancement in life
- Development of character
- Holidays

C.C. NO 274052 **ESTABLISHED** 1977

■ Edmund De Rothschild Charitable Trust

OBJECTS General charitable purposes

POLICY OF TRUSTEES To support only those charities which are of special interest to the Trustees

RESTRICTIONS No grants to individuals

FINANCES
- Year 1994
- Grants £15,566
- Income £13,848
- Assets £442,054

TRUSTEES E L de Rothschild, N de Rothschild, Rothschild Trust Co Ltd

CORRESPONDENT The Trustees, Edmund de Rothschild Charitable Trust, PO Box 185, New Court, St Swithins Lane, London EC4P 4DU

CLASSIFICATIONS
- Children and youth – general

C.C. NO 247815　　　**ESTABLISHED** 1966

■ The Leopold De Rothschild Charitable Trust

OBJECTS General charitable purposes

RESTRICTIONS Registered charities only

FINANCES
- Year 1993
- Grants £33,295
- Income £41,063

TRUSTEES Rothschild Trust Corporation Ltd,

CORRESPONDENT Rothschild Trust Corporation Ltd, New Court, St Swithin's Lane, London EC4P 4DU

CLASSIFICATIONS
- Children and youth – general
- Centres, clubs and institutes
- Development of character
- Holidays
- Youth organisations (eg Guides, Scouts, YWCA etc)

C.C. NO 212611　　　**ESTABLISHED** 1959

■ The Emma de Yong Charitable Trust

OBJECTS General charitable purposes

POLICY OF TRUSTEES Children's charities, Third World relief and disaster relief

BENEFICIAL AREA International

FINANCES
- Year 1994
- Grants £8,715
- Income £7,787
- Assets £169,352

TRUSTEES Mrs E Gomme, W Gomme, R S Parker

CORRESPONDENT R S Parker, Messrs Chantrey Vellacott, 23–25 Castle Street, Reading, Berkshire RG1 7SB

CLASSIFICATIONS
- Children and youth – general

C.C. NO 290742　　　**ESTABLISHED** 1985

■ Nicholas De Yong's Charitable Trust 1984

OBJECTS General charitable purposes

POLICY OF TRUSTEES Children's charities, Third World relief and disaster relief

TYPE OF GRANT Unrestricted

TYPE OF BENEFICIARY Unrestricted

RESTRICTIONS No capital or income payments to any contributor to the Charity (or to the Settlor or his spouse)

BENEFICIAL AREA International

FINANCES
- Year 1993
- Grants £300
- Income £7,484
- Assets £153,515

TRUSTEES N J J de Yong, Mrs C A De Yong, R S Parker

NOTES Grants: excess income to be fully distributed in following year

SUBMISSION OF APPLICATIONS No fixed timetable for applications

CORRESPONDENT R S Parker, Messrs Chantrey Vellacott, 23–25 Castle Street, Reading, Berks RG1 7SB

CLASSIFICATIONS
- Children and youth – general

C.C. NO 289481　　　**ESTABLISHED** 1984

■ The Delfont Foundation

OBJECTS General charitable purposes

TYPE OF GRANT Usually one-off for specific purposes

FINANCES
- Year 1994
- Grants £49,275
- Income £23,435

TRUSTEES Lady Delfont, D Delfont, Miss J Delfont, Miss S Delfont, P Ohrenstein, G Parsons

SUBMISSION OF APPLICATIONS At any time

CORRESPONDENT The Delfont Foundation, 14 Lewes Road, Haywards Heath, West Sussex RH17 7SB

CLASSIFICATIONS
- Children and youth – general

C.C. NO 298047　　　**ESTABLISHED** 1988

■ Delmar Charitable Trust

OBJECTS General charitable purposes

POLICY OF TRUSTEES Medical treatment and research. Mental or physical rehabilitation. Children and youthwork. Social welfare. Religion

TYPE OF BENEFICIARY As listed above

RESTRICTIONS Grants can only be made to institutions not to individuals

BENEFICIAL AREA London or the neighbourhood of London

FINANCES
- Year 1995
- Grants £11,000
- Income £12,500
- Assets £200,000

TRUSTEES M J Read, D W Read

CORRESPONDENT The Secretary, Delmar Charitable Trust, 9 Bridle Close, Surbiton Road, Kingston upon Thames KT1 2JW

CLASSIFICATIONS
- Children and youth – general
- Youth organisations (eg Guides, Scouts, YWCA etc)

C.C. NO 205832　　　**ESTABLISHED** 1895

■ The Denby Charitable Foundation

OBJECTS General charitable purposes

POLICY OF TRUSTEES Currently the main areas of interest are community welfare and the assistance of disadvantaged and less fortunate members of society. The Trustees review their policy every few years

TYPE OF GRANT Usually under £500 but larger grants may be considered. Maximum grant so far £1,350 but this was exceptional. Usually grants are on-off.

Denby

Alphabetical register of grant making charitable trusts

The Trustees favour smaller grants rather than paying out the whole income for one applicant's needs.

TYPE OF BENEFICIARY Handicapped, disabled, unemployed or disadvantaged members of society. Grants have been made for youth projects, social welfare projects, community care, church restoration appeals, environmental appeals and 'disaster' appeals, eg Hungerford, Bosnia, Rwanda

RESTRICTIONS No student grants

BENEFICIAL AREA UK

SAMPLE GRANTS £300 to The Children's Society
£300 to Southwark Youth Project
£150 to Handicapped Children Special Needs
£75 to Student Community Action

FINANCES
- Year 1995
- Grants £6,500
- Income £8,379
- Assets £97,000

TRUSTEES Richard C Kirby

SUBMISSION OF APPLICATIONS At any time. The Trustees review applications once every four months. No application form is necessary. Only successful applications are acknowledged. Please do not send stamped addressed envelopes

CORRESPONDENT Richard C Kirby, Messrs Speechly Bircham, Bouverie House, 154 Fleet Street, London EC4A 2HX

CLASSIFICATIONS
- Children and youth – general

C.C. NO 326745   **ESTABLISHED** 1984

■ Denby Charitable Trust

OBJECTS General charitable purposes

TYPE OF BENEFICIARY Non selective

RESTRICTIONS Definitely no individuals except through charities

BENEFICIAL AREA UK

FINANCES
- Year 1993
- Grants £2,205
- Income £4,220
- Assets £17,563

TRUSTEES A T Denby, Mrs P N Fullerton

CORRESPONDENT Mrs P N Fullerton, Cwmirfon Lodge, Llantwrtyd Wells, Powys LD5 4TN

CLASSIFICATIONS
- Children and youth – general
- Development of character

C.C. NO 235626   **ESTABLISHED** 1964

■ J N Derbyshire Trust

OBJECTS Promotion of health. Development of physical improvement. Advancement of education. Relief of poverty, distress and sickness. The Trust supports associations which cater for the needs of young adults in their development, health and education

POLICY OF TRUSTEES Local charities receive preferential consideration

TYPE OF GRANT Cash

TYPE OF BENEFICIARY Organisations with charitable status

RESTRICTIONS No grants to individuals

BENEFICIAL AREA Nottinghamshire

SAMPLE GRANTS £1,900 to Notts Association of Boys and Keystone Clubs for general welfare
£1,000 to 6th Newark Sea Scout Group for refurbishment of showers and changing areas
£500 to 100th Nottingham (1st Notes) Sea Scouts for boat equipment
£500 to The Prince's Trust Volunteers towards the cost of educational activity week for pupils with special needs
£500 to the Duke of Edinburgh's Award for expedition equipment

FINANCES
- Year 1995
- Grants £112,202
- Income £133,095
- Assets £2,500,000

TRUSTEES The Council

CORRESPONDENT P R Moore, FCA, Foxhall Lodge, Gregory Boulevard, Nottingham, Nottinghamshire NG7 6LH

CLASSIFICATIONS
- Children and youth – general
- Adoption/fostering
- Advancement in life
- Adventure centres and playgrounds
- Centres, clubs and institutes
- Community groups
- Day centres and nurseries
- Development of character
- Counselling (inc helplines)
- Holidays
- Homes and hostels
- Special needs housing
- Special classes
- Youth organisations (eg Guides, Scouts, YWCA etc)
- Children and violence (inc abuse)

C.C. NO 231907   **ESTABLISHED** 1944

■ The Duke of Devonshire's Charitable Trust

OBJECTS General charitable purposes

POLICY OF TRUSTEES Grants made to bodies accustomed to receiving the Trustees' support

FINANCES
- Year 1992
- Grants £120,451
- Income £299,013
- Assets £4,715,185

TRUSTEES The Marquess of Hartington, R G Beckett, N W Smith

CORRESPONDENT The Comptroller, Chatsworth, Bakewell, Derbyshire DE4 1PP

CLASSIFICATIONS
- Children and youth – general
- Adventure centres and playgrounds
- Homes and hostels
- Youth organisations (eg Guides, Scouts, YWCA etc)

C.C. NO 213519   **ESTABLISHED** 1949

■ The Dibs Charitable Trust

OBJECTS General charitable purposes but specifically the relief of distress

POLICY OF TRUSTEES Grants are made for the benefit of individuals for the relief of distress caused by poverty, sickness or misfortune but applications must be made on their behalf by Social Workers in official or quasi official organisations

TYPE OF BENEFICIARY Individuals, via social workers

RESTRICTIONS The Trustees will not, in any circumstances, commit the Charitable Trust funds for payment of pensions or annuities of any description or for any other type of ongoing payments. Additionally, the Trustees will not commit funds for educational purposes or to meet the cost of travel abroad

BENEFICIAL AREA UK

FINANCES
- **Year** 1992
- **Grants** £34,589
- **Income** £27,484
- **Assets** £262,319

TRUSTEES National Westminster Bank plc, D H Isaacs, Mrs L Bloch, K Davis

CORRESPONDENT Gavin Cansdale, The DIBS Charitable Trust, National Westminster Bank plc, 62 Green Street, London W1Y 4BA

CLASSIFICATIONS
- Children and youth – general

C.C. NO 257709   **ESTABLISHED** 1968

■ The Albert Dicken Charitable Trust

OBJECTS General charitable purposes

POLICY OF TRUSTEES To support evangelical Christian work in the North East of England

TYPE OF GRANT One-off

TYPE OF BENEFICIARY All types considered, within parameters above

RESTRICTIONS Any work or person who is not involved in the extension of God's Kingdom

BENEFICIAL AREA North East of England

FINANCES
- **Year** 1993
- **Grants** £72,118
- **Income** £185,000
- **Assets** £789,244

TRUSTEES A G Dicken, P B Dicken, R Oliver

NOTES Charity is currently involved in 2 large scale projects and only minor grants will be considered during next 3 years

SUBMISSION OF APPLICATIONS Applications considered quarterly in March, June, September and December. Sae required if applicants need a reply. Only minimum information required initially, further information will be requested as considered necessary. No telephone calls

CORRESPONDENT R Oliver, c/o 7 The Avenue, Eaglescliffe, Stockton-on-Tees, Cleveland TS16 9AS

CLASSIFICATIONS
- Homes and hostels

C.C. NO 274910   **ESTABLISHED** 1977

■ Dinam Charity

OBJECTS General charitable purposes

POLICY OF TRUSTEES Support for organisations dealing with international understanding, famine relief, child welfare, environmental protection, animal welfare

TYPE OF BENEFICIARY Charitable organisations.

RESTRICTIONS Trustees are unable to award grants to individuals

BENEFICIAL AREA Wales

FINANCES
- **Year** 1993
- **Grants** £109,640
- **Income** £133,059
- **Assets** £2,466,150

TRUSTEES The Hon Mrs Mary M Noble, the Hon Mrs G R Jean Cormack, the Hon Edward D G Davies, J S Tyres

CORRESPONDENT The Hon J H Davies, Dinam Charity, 8 Southampton Place, London WC1A 2EA

CLASSIFICATIONS
- Children and youth – general

C.C. NO 231295   **ESTABLISHED** 1926

■ Elsie Doidge Fund

POLICY OF TRUSTEES No laid down policy – considered annually when applications received

TYPE OF BENEFICIARY Mainly charities located in Exeter/Torbay area of Devon and specified charities

RESTRICTIONS Specified charities

BENEFICIAL AREA Exeter/Torbay area of Devon

FINANCES
- **Year** 1995
- **Grants** £8,440
- **Income** £11,600
- **Assets** £107,057

TRUSTEES Lloyds Bank plc, 71 Lombard Street, London

CORRESPONDENT The Manager, Lloyds Private Banking Ltd, The Clock House, 22–26 Ock Street, Abingdon, Oxon OX14 5SW

CLASSIFICATIONS
- Children and youth – general
- Homes and hostels

C.C. NO 258032   **ESTABLISHED** 1966

■ The Dolphin Charitable Trust

OBJECTS General charitable purposes

POLICY OF TRUSTEES The Trustees prefer to give to charitable bodies already known to them

TYPE OF GRANT Outright donations either on a once only or an annual basis

TYPE OF BENEFICIARY Usually only registered charities

FINANCES
- **Year** 1991
- **Grants** £12,100
- **Income** £17,597
- **Assets** £186,243

TRUSTEES Kleinwort Benson Trustees Limited

NOTES Applications will not normally be acknowledged

CORRESPONDENT Kleinwort Benson Trustees Limited, PO Box 191, 10 Fenchurch Street, London EC3M 3LB

CLASSIFICATIONS
- Children and youth – general
- Homes and hostels

C.C. NO 267720   **ESTABLISHED** 1974

■ R M Douglas Charitable Trust

OBJECTS Specific objectives in Staffordshire and general charitable purposes at Trustees' discretion

TYPE OF BENEFICIARY Headquarters and local

RESTRICTIONS Any person in service of Settlor

BENEFICIAL AREA UK; mainly Staffordshire

FINANCES
- Year 1995
- Grants £76,650
- Income £71,638
- Assets £746,310

TRUSTEES Sir Robert Douglas, OBE, J R T Douglas, OBE, F W Carder

CORRESPONDENT Sir Robert Douglas, OBE, Dunstall Hall, Barton under Needwood, Staffordshire DE13 8BE

CLASSIFICATIONS
- Centres, clubs and institutes
- Community groups
- Holidays
- Homes and hostels
- Youth organisations (eg Guides, Scouts, YWCA etc)

C.C. NO 248775   **ESTABLISHED** 1966

■ The D'Oyly Carte Charitable Trust

OBJECTS General charitable purposes

POLICY OF TRUSTEES Mainly to support the arts, medical/welfare charities and the environment

TYPE OF GRANT Specific charities in which Dame Bridget D'Oyly Carte took a special interest during her lifetime are supported annually; other grants are one-off. Five major arts scholarships are given annually to Colleges; these are awarded at the discretion of the Principals of the Colleges, not the Trust

RESTRICTIONS No grants are made to individuals

BENEFICIAL AREA UK

SAMPLE GRANTS Youth Clubs UK
British Youth Opera
National Youth Music Theatre
Music for Youth
Association of Wheelchair Children

FINANCES
- Year 1993
- Grants £130,968
- Income £121,741
- Assets £6,522,933

TRUSTEES J McCracken, Sir John Batten, Sir Martyn Beckett, J Elliott, Mrs J Sibley, Mrs F Radcliffe

NOTES The majority of grants are made to national charities. Regional appeals are not considered

SUBMISSION OF APPLICATIONS In writing to the correspondent. The Trustees meet twice a year, in June and December and applications for consideration should be submitted one month in advance

CORRESPONDENT Mrs Jane Thorne, 1 Savoy Hill, London WC2R 0BP

CLASSIFICATIONS
- Children and youth – general

C.C. NO 265057   **ESTABLISHED** 1972

■ Drapers' Charitable Fund

OBJECTS General charitable purposes

POLICY OF TRUSTEES At the time of writing the criteria of eligibility and the availability of income for new projects is uncertain. Enquirers should write to the correspondent for details enclosing an sae if possible

TYPE OF GRANT £250–£5,000 usually one-off

TYPE OF BENEFICIARY Organisations, especially registered charities, not individuals

RESTRICTIONS In previous years consideration was restricted to the following categories of appeal (a) those where the area of benefit is national rather than local, (b) those where the area of benefit is in the City of London, (c) disasters and emergencies, (d) those where there is some connection, eg with textiles

BENEFICIAL AREA Great Britain and Northern Ireland, with a particular interest in the City of London

SAMPLE GRANTS £9,000 to Voluntary Service Overseas for volunteer sponsorship (exceptional grant)
£5,000 to Raleigh International's Youth Development Programme
£5,000 to Whizz Kidz for the provision of mobility aids for disabled children and young people
£5,000 to the Family Welfare Association's Advisory Service for students seeking grants
£1,000 to the London Federation of Youth Clubs for running costs
£1,000 to Discovery Dockland Trust towards the water activities centre and training ship for youth organisations

FINANCES
- Year 1995
- Grants £179,629
- Income £1,032,478

TRUSTEES Dr W B G Simmonds, A E Woodall, Rev P Taylor

PUBLICATIONS 'Guidelines for grant-seekers'

SUBMISSION OF APPLICATIONS Throughout the year but allow three to four months for a decision

CORRESPONDENT The Secretary, Drapers' Charitable Fund, Drapers' Hall, Throgmorton Avenue, London EC2N 2DQ

CLASSIFICATIONS
- Children and youth – general

C.C. NO 251403   **ESTABLISHED** 1959

■ The George Drexler Foundation

OBJECTS For charitable purposes in connection with the relief of poverty of persons formerly employed in commerce. Also to charities requiring financial support

TYPE OF BENEFICIARY Applicants should be British subjects

TRUSTEES L M Dresher, H P Hartley, C A Phillips

CORRESPONDENT The George Drexler Foundation, PO Box 338, Aylesbury, Bucks HP20 2YZ

CLASSIFICATIONS
- Counselling (inc helplines)
- Children and violence (inc abuse)

C.C. NO 313278   **ESTABLISHED** 1959

The Dulverton Trust

OBJECTS General charitable purposes

POLICY OF TRUSTEES Training, development and care of young people (especially the disadvantaged and at risk) has long been one of the two main tenets of Trust work (the other being the achievement of good conservation practice)

TYPE OF GRANT Usually one-off, not revenue or recurring

TYPE OF BENEFICIARY For national projects, not usually at local or county level

RESTRICTIONS Grants are only made to officially registered or exempt charities; not to individuals or for expeditions or to territories overseas (except for long-established projects in Africa). In addition, the Trust does not operate in the field of medicine, including drug addiction or projects concerning the mentally or physically handicapped; or museums or the preservation and repair of cathedrals, churches, historic buildings; or the whole field of the arts; or projects concerned with the care and resettlement of offenders; or for public or private schools or colleges and universities

BENEFICIAL AREA UK: not within London. Foreign: East Africa and very occasionally Central and Southern Africa. A limited number of scholarships granted to postgraduates, first degree students and sixth formers from Russia, Eastern and Central Europe

SAMPLE GRANTS £30,000 to VSO
£22,000 to Fairbridge
£18,000 to Duke of Edinburgh's Award

FINANCES
- **Year** 1995
- **Grants** £2,152,179
- **Income** £2,637,046
- **Assets** £55,542,268

TRUSTEES Hon Robert Wills, Sir David Wills, Col S J Watson, The Lord Dulverton, Dr Catherine Wills, J W Watson, C A H Wills, Sir Ashley Ponsonby, The Lord Taylor of Gryfe, The Earl of Gowrie, The Lord Carrington, Col D V Fanshawe, J Kemp-Welch

PUBLICATIONS 'An Act of Faith, The Dulverton Trust 1949–1989', Michael Tomlinson

NOTES Trust meetings four times every year ie May, July, October, January

SUBMISSION OF APPLICATIONS Maximum three sides typed A4 to Secretary, Dulverton Trust

CORRESPONDENT Major General Sir Robert Corbett, KCVO, CB, Secretary, The Dulverton Trust, 5 St James's Place, London SW1A 1NP

CLASSIFICATIONS
- Children and youth – general
- Youth organisations (eg Guides, Scouts, YWCA etc)

C.C. NO 206426   **ESTABLISHED** 1949

The Duveen Trust

OBJECTS To develop the individual potential of young people by means of encouragement of initiative

POLICY OF TRUSTEES To support projects of individual initiative by young people where self help on its own has proved insufficient

TYPE OF BENEFICIARY Individual young people and registered charities

RESTRICTIONS Grants made for young people only (up to 26 years generally)

FINANCES
- **Year** 1994
- **Grants** £15,717
- **Income** £20,389
- **Assets** £227,576

TRUSTEES Mrs L Barden, S Cotsen, A Greenbat (Chairman), G Matthews, P Shaw, P Sollosi

CORRESPONDENT Peter Shaw, Fifth Floor, 707 High Road, North Finchley, London N12 0BT

CLASSIFICATIONS
- Centres, clubs and institutes
- Community groups

C.C. NO 326823   **ESTABLISHED** 1985

■ E D B Memorial Charitable Trust

OBJECTS General charitable purposes

POLICY OF TRUSTEES Grants are made to charities with which the Trustees have personal connections

TYPE OF BENEFICIARY Registered charities only. Applications from individuals cannot be entertained

RESTRICTIONS Registered charities only

BENEFICIAL AREA London and South East England

FINANCES
- Year 1995
- Grants £6,700
- Income £5,500
- Assets £110,000

TRUSTEES Eileen M Basden, B E Basden, R D E Basden

CORRESPONDENT B E Basden, c/o Cooper Lancaster Brewers, Aldwych House, 71–91 Aldwych, London WC2B 4HP

CLASSIFICATIONS
- Children and youth – general
- Holidays

C.C. NO 229225 **ESTABLISHED** 1960

■ The Earley Charity

OBJECTS The relief of need in the area of benefit by: (a) Providing residential accommodation for the elderly; (b) Making grants and bursaries

POLICY OF TRUSTEES To give aid to: the disabled; those with housing need; those caring for elderly parents or relatives; widows/widowers; single elderly and single parents with families; those undertaking vocational training or apprenticeships; appropriate local charities and community organisations

TYPE OF GRANT One-off, normally limited range £30–£2,500 (individuals) and £250–£40,000 (organisations)

TYPE OF BENEFICIARY Individuals in need; charitable and community organisations

RESTRICTIONS Educational grants are for vocational courses only. No grants to university undergraduates. Persons aided should normally be resident within the area of benefit. No national or international appeals are considered

BENEFICIAL AREA Earley and East Reading and the immediate neighbourhood

FINANCES
- Year 1994
- Grants £183,729
- Income £338,227
- Assets £9,835,661

TRUSTEES R E Ames, D J Chilvers, R Hadfield, Dr D G Jenkins, C A Nichols, I M Robertson, Mrs M Eastwell, D C Sutton

PUBLICATIONS Annual Report

SUBMISSION OF APPLICATIONS In writing only, at any time, to the Correspondent

CORRESPONDENT L G Norton, Clerk to the Trustees, The Liberty of Earley House, Strand Way, Earley, Reading RG6 4EA

CLASSIFICATIONS
- Children and youth – general
- Adventure centres and playgrounds
- Centres, clubs and institutes
- Community groups
- Day centres and nurseries
- Holidays
- Special needs housing
- Youth organisations (eg Guides, Scouts, YWCA etc)

C.C. NO 244823 **ESTABLISHED** 1820

■ Richard Early's Charitable Settlement

OBJECTS General charitable purposes

POLICY OF TRUSTEES To review applications quarterly

TYPE OF BENEFICIARY Local charities known personally to the Early family

RESTRICTIONS The Trustees like to have personal knowledge of good causes concerned. Will not respond to applications on behalf of individuals, students or expeditions

BENEFICIAL AREA Mainly the Witney area

SAMPLE GRANTS £1,000 to 1st Witney Boys Brigade
£1,000 to Wenhelpton Boys Choir
£250 to St Felix School

FINANCES
- Year 1994
- Grants £10,550
- Income £9,312

TRUSTEES C A Early, S J Early, A I Edwards, H V Edwards

CORRESPONDENT C A Early, Grays, Far End, Sheepscombe, Gloucestershire GL6 7RL

CLASSIFICATIONS
- Children and youth – general
- Homes and hostels
- Youth organisations (eg Guides, Scouts, YWCA etc)

C.C. NO 234347 **ESTABLISHED** 1963

■ Earwicker Trust

OBJECTS General charitable purposes

TYPE OF GRANT Single donations

TYPE OF BENEFICIARY Registered charities

FINANCES
- Year 1993
- Grants £30,200
- Income £25,913
- Assets £12,913

TRUSTEES S C Earwicker, H M Earwicker, J H Pankin

CORRESPONDENT Dr H M Earwicker, 3 Normanby Road, Wollaton, Nottinghamshire NG8 2TA

CLASSIFICATIONS
- Children and youth – general

C.C. NO 1015667 **ESTABLISHED** 1990

Alphabetical register of grant making charitable trusts — **Edinburgh**

■ Sir John Eastwood Foundation

OBJECTS General charitable purposes

POLICY OF TRUSTEES At sole discretion of Trustees

TYPE OF BENEFICIARY Local organisations

RESTRICTIONS No grants to individuals

BENEFICIAL AREA Mainly Nottinghamshire

FINANCES
- Year 1993
- Grants £370,731
- Income £355,666
- Assets £7,538,249

TRUSTEES Mrs C B Mudford, Mrs D M Cottingham, G Raymond, Mrs V Hardingham, P Spencer

CORRESPONDENT G Raymond, Burns Lane, Warsop, Mansfield, Nottinghamshire NG20 0QG

CLASSIFICATIONS
- Children and youth – general
- Adoption/fostering
- Centres, clubs and institutes
- Community groups
- Holidays
- Homes and hostels
- Youth organisations (eg Guides, Scouts, YWCA etc)

C.C. NO 235389   **ESTABLISHED** 1964

■ Ebenezer Trust

OBJECTS Advancement of Protestant and Evangelical tenets of the Christian faith

POLICY OF TRUSTEES Grants mainly made where the Trustees have a personal interest

RESTRICTIONS Registered charities only

BENEFICIAL AREA Essex, London and Greater London

FINANCES
- Year 1994
- Grants £57,000
- Income £69,000
- Assets £74,000

TRUSTEES N T Davey, FCA, R M Davey

CORRESPONDENT N T Davey, 31 Middleton Road, Brentwood, Essex CM15 8DJ

CLASSIFICATIONS
- Children and youth – general
- Homes and hostels

C.C. NO 272574   **ESTABLISHED** 1976

■ The Gilbert and Eileen Edgar Foundation

OBJECTS General charitable purposes. Preference for promotion of Medical and Surgical Science, aid to young and old, encouragement of artistic taste of the public in cultural activities and preservation of the countryside and heritage

POLICY OF TRUSTEES Only causes in which the Trustees are personally interested will be supported

TYPE OF BENEFICIARY Not-for-profit organisations in the main and some individuals

RESTRICTIONS Primarily to registered charities, educational or cultural bodies

BENEFICIAL AREA Occasionally international

FINANCES
- Year 1995
- Grants £70,031
- Income £69,795
- Assets £1,508,680

TRUSTEES A E Gentilli, J G Matthews, Trustee emeritus Mrs M R Lloyd-Johnes

CORRESPONDENT Mrs A Hallam, Messrs Chantrey Vellacott, 23–25 Castle Street, Reading, Berks RG1 7SB

CLASSIFICATIONS
- Adventure centres and playgrounds
- Centres, clubs and institutes
- Community groups
- Counselling (inc helplines)
- Homes and hostels
- Youth organisations (eg Guides, Scouts, YWCA etc)
- Children and violence (inc abuse)

C.C. NO 241736   **ESTABLISHED** 1965

■ The Gilbert Edgar Trust

OBJECTS General charitable purposes

POLICY OF TRUSTEES Only charities which the Trustees find worthwhile will be supported. Support of detailed medical research, children, UK hospices, surgical aids and mental health. We rely on brochures, sent in before November, each year. We do not particularly like the large glossy expensive brochures. We like to know when targets have been achieved

TYPE OF BENEFICIARY No individuals

RESTRICTIONS No grants will be made to individual applicants — they will only be made to registered charities or educational or cultural bodies

BENEFICIAL AREA Predominately National, limited Foreign

FINANCES
- Year 1990
- Grants £50,820
- Income £46,137
- Assets £690,147

TRUSTEES Mrs G R Sinclair Hogg, S C E Gentilli, A E Gentilli, Dr R E B Solomons

CORRESPONDENT S C E Gentilli, Huttons Farm, Hambleden, Henley-on-Thames, Oxon RG9 6NE

CLASSIFICATIONS
- Children and youth – general
- Adventure centres and playgrounds
- Counselling (inc helplines)
- Holidays
- Homes and hostels

C.C. NO 213630   **ESTABLISHED** 1955

■ The Edinburgh Medical Missionary Society – Hawthornbrae Trust

OBJECTS The object of the Trust is to provide holidays for residents of Edinburgh who require convalescence on medical advice and are unable to afford such a holiday

POLICY OF TRUSTEES In accordance with the wishes of the donor

TYPE OF GRANT Grants are given to those requiring convalescence on medical advice

TYPE OF BENEFICIARY Residents of Edinburgh

RESTRICTIONS Each application requires to be completed by a sponsor such as family doctor, health visitor, social worker or minister, and be endorsed by the family doctor who may also be the sponsor. Grants can only be awarded once to each individual or family unless there are exceptional circumstances. Payments will normally be made to guest houses, travel agencies, etc, and not to individuals

BENEFICIAL AREA City of Edinburgh

FINANCES
- Year 1993
- Grants £3,092
- Income £10,063
- Assets £54,061

TRUSTEES J G Gray, SSC, R J Mackenzie, SSC, A C Robertson, AIB(Scot), A B Young, MB, ChB, FRCP, I D Gill, CA, ATII

PUBLICATIONS The Healing Hand – thrice yearly

SUBMISSION OF APPLICATIONS Application form and further information from the Executive Secretary

CORRESPONDENT F M Aitken CEng, FIEE, Executive Secretary, Edinburgh Medical Missionary Society, 7 Washington Lane, Edinburgh EH11 2HA

CLASSIFICATIONS
- Children and youth – general
- Holidays

S.C. NO SC015000   **ESTABLISHED** 1841

■ E V Elias Charitable Settlement

OBJECTS General charitable purposes

POLICY OF TRUSTEES Grants made mainly to Jewish charitable organisations

TYPE OF BENEFICIARY Registered charities

RESTRICTIONS Time charity for sixty years from 27th February 1968. Registered charities only

FINANCES
- Year 1995
- Grants £4,228
- Income £14,548
- Assets £42,178

TRUSTEES The Royal Bank of Scotland plc and others

CORRESPONDENT The Royal Bank of Scotland plc, Private Trust & Taxation, 45 Mosley Street, Manchester M60 2BE

CLASSIFICATIONS
- Children and youth – general

C.C. NO 255735   **ESTABLISHED** 1968

■ Eling Trust

OBJECTS (a) The advancement of the Christian religion more particularly according to the teaching and usage of the Orthodox Churches of the East. (b) The advancement of medical research and the study of medicine. (c) The relief of sickness and/or poverty. General charitable purposes

POLICY OF TRUSTEES To devote the whole of the income to purposes which are already laid down for some years to come. It is not the policy of the Trustees to make grants to individuals for medical education or training

TYPE OF BENEFICIARY Primarily religious and medical charities

RESTRICTIONS No grants to individuals

BENEFICIAL AREA Berkshire

FINANCES
- Year 1993
- Grants £8,000
- Income £8,268
- Assets £234,191

TRUSTEES D A W Gardiner, C J Pratt, The Rev C T Scott-Dempster

CORRESPONDENT C J Pratt, FRICS, Eling Estate Office, Hermitage, Newbury, Berkshire RG16 9UF

CLASSIFICATIONS
- Counselling (inc helplines)
- Special needs housing

C.C. NO 255072   **ESTABLISHED** 1968

■ The Maud Elkington Charitable Trust

OBJECTS General charitable purposes mainly, but not exclusively, in Desborough and the County of Northamptonshire

RESTRICTIONS No educational/professional applications from individuals

BENEFICIAL AREA Desborough and the County of Northamptonshire (but not exclusively)

FINANCES
- Year 1995
- Grants £229,090
- Income £270,158
- Assets £4,055,421

TRUSTEES R Bowder, A A Veasey, C A Macpherson

CORRESPONDENT Miss L Atterbury, Harvey Ingram, Solicitors, 20 New Walk, Leicester LE1 6TX

CLASSIFICATIONS
- Children and youth – general
- Adventure centres and playgrounds
- Centres, clubs and institutes
- Holidays
- Youth organisations (eg Guides, Scouts, YWCA etc)

C.C. NO 263929   **ESTABLISHED** 1972

■ The Ellbridge Trust

OBJECTS General charitable purposes

POLICY OF TRUSTEES Generally the smaller charities, the arts and retarded children

TYPE OF BENEFICIARY Registered charities working in the areas specified under Policy

RESTRICTIONS Registered charities only. Applications from individuals, including students, are ineligible. No donations made in response to general appeals from large national organisations nor to smaller bodies working outside the areas mentioned above

BENEFICIAL AREA UK

FINANCES
- Year 1991
- Grants £2,550
- Income £1,298
- Assets £23,702

TRUSTEES J F Child, K J Thompson

CORRESPONDENT Colin Clive, Thompson Clive & Partners Ltd, 24 Old Bond Street, London W1X 4JD

CLASSIFICATIONS
- Children and youth – general
- Special classes

C.C. NO 202705   **ESTABLISHED** 1960

Alphabetical register of grant making charitable trusts **Emmandjay**

■ The John Ellerman Foundation
(formed by the merging of the New Moorgate Trust Fund and the Moorgate Trust Fund)

OBJECTS General charitable purposes

POLICY OF TRUSTEES To consider all appeals received and grant donations based on merit and worthiness. This Foundation supports work both to assist the protection of children and to assist in the expansion of their horizons

TYPE OF GRANT Either in the form of an annual donation, subject to periodic reviews, or in the form of a 'once only' donation

TYPE OF BENEFICIARY eg medical research and care, the blind, special education, physically disabled, the deaf, the arts, hospitals, environment

RESTRICTIONS The Americas South of the United States of America are excluded. Applications from individuals not considered. Applications on behalf of religious causes, churches, general education and branches of national organisations are not considered

BENEFICIAL AREA UK, Commonwealth, foreign

SAMPLE GRANTS £15,000 to Youth Clubs UK
£10,000 to YMCA National Council
£10,000 to Youth Hostels Association
£10,000 to YWCA of Great Britain
£10,000 to the Royal Society for the Prevention of Cruelty to Children

FINANCES
- Year 1995
- Grants £3,338,000
- Income £3,959,000
- Assets £77,338,000

TRUSTEES D G Parry, Sir D A Scott, GCMG, R A LLoyd, Miss A Boschi, The Hon P Strutt, MC, D D Martin-Jenkins. Director and Secretary: P C Pratt, BSc, FCIS

SUBMISSION OF APPLICATIONS By letter only to the Director and Secretary for periodic submission to all Trustees at regular meetings. Letters to give concise details of the funding requirements

CORRESPONDENT The Director and Secretary, The John Ellerman Foundation, Suite 10, Aria House, 23 Craven Street, London WC2N 5NT

CLASSIFICATIONS
- Children and youth – general
- Adoption/fostering
- Counselling (inc helplines)
- Youth organisations (eg Guides, Scouts, YWCA etc)
- Children and violence (inc abuse)

C.C. NO 263207   **ESTABLISHED** 1971

■ Elmgrant Trust

OBJECTS General charitable purposes

POLICY OF TRUSTEES Encouragement of local life through education, the arts and the social sciences, and support for individuals wanting to make a change of direction in their lives

TYPE OF BENEFICIARY Individual and organisation

RESTRICTIONS Post-graduate study and expedition/travel grants not considered. Applications for 'change of direction' only applicable to Devon and Cornwall and in response to annual local advertisement in March

BENEFICIAL AREA Primarily local

FINANCES
- Year 1995
- Grants £138,000
- Income £140,000
- Assets £2,007,222

TRUSTEES Maurice Ash (Chairman), Michael Young, Claire Ash Wheeler, Sophie Young

CORRESPONDENT Mrs M B Nicholson, Secretary, The Elmgrant Trust, Elmhirst Centre, Dartington Hall, Totnes, Devon TQ9 6EL

CLASSIFICATIONS
- Adventure centres and playgrounds
- Centres, clubs and institutes
- Community groups
- Counselling (inc helplines)
- Holidays
- Children and violence (inc abuse)

C.C. NO 313398   **ESTABLISHED** 1936

■ The Vernon N Ely Charitable Trust

OBJECTS General charitable purposes

POLICY OF TRUSTEES No further appeals can be considered as all available funds are earmarked for distribution to charities well known to the Trustees

TYPE OF BENEFICIARY Community-based

RESTRICTIONS No grants to individuals. Income is fully committed and appeals cannot be considered

BENEFICIAL AREA Local

SAMPLE GRANTS £2,200 to London Playing Fields Society (Wilton Junior Tennis Tournament)
£600 to First Leatherhead Guides
£600 to Pouxa Children's Theatre
£600 to YMCA Wimbledon
£500 to Streatham Youth Centre
£250 to 2nd Hook Scouts
£200 to Association of Combined Youth Clubs
£100 to Training Ship Trafalgar (Cadet Corps)

FINANCES
- Year 1992
- Grants £46,598
- Income £47,902
- Assets £1,623,044

TRUSTEES J S Moyle, D P Howorth, R S Main

CORRESPONDENT Secretary to Trustees, 16 St George's Road, Wimbledon, London SW19 4DP

CLASSIFICATIONS
- Children and youth – general
- Youth organisations (eg Guides, Scouts, YWCA etc)

C.C. NO 230033   **ESTABLISHED** 1962

■ Emmandjay Charitable Trust

OBJECTS General charitable purposes

POLICY OF TRUSTEES Most particularly to help disadvantaged people, but many different projects are supported – for example, caring for the disabled, physically and mentally handicapped and terminally ill, work with young people and medical research. The Trust likes projects which reach a lot of people

RESTRICTIONS The Trust will not pay debts, does not make grants to individual students and does not respond to circulars

BENEFICIAL AREA Local to West Yorkshire when possible but not essential

Enkalon

FINANCES
- Year 1992
- Grants £140,000

TRUSTEES Mrs S Clegg, J A Clegg, Mrs S L Worthington, Mrs E A Riddell

CORRESPONDENT C T P Horne, PO Box 31, Bradford, West Yorkshire BD1 5NH

CLASSIFICATIONS
- Homes and hostels
- Special needs housing
- Youth organisations (eg Guides, Scouts, YWCA etc)

C.C. NO 212279   **ESTABLISHED** 1962

■ Enkalon Foundation

OBJECTS To improve the quality of life in Northern Ireland

TYPE OF GRANT Up to £6,000 maximum. Mainly for starter finance, single projects or capital projects. Average grant size £500

TYPE OF BENEFICIARY Cross-community groups, self-help, assistance to the unemployed, groups helping the disadvantaged

RESTRICTIONS No grants made to projects outside Northern Ireland. No grants can be made to individuals except possibly ex-employees of British Enkalon Ltd. Normally grants are not made to sporting groups and playgroups outside the Antrim Borough area or for travel outside Northern Ireland

BENEFICIAL AREA Grants made only to organisations for projects inside Northern Ireland

SAMPLE GRANTS £2,000 to Prince's Trust Northern Ireland towards various projects
£1,000 to Belfast Activity Centre towards expansion of Duke of Edinburgh Award Scheme to inner city group in Belfast
£800 to Greystone Youth and Community Group, Antrim towards leadership training and youth development work
£500 to Cinemagic (Northern Ireland) towards festival for young people of films and opportunity for young people to make short cartoon films

FINANCES
- Year 1994–95
- Grants £94,500
- Income £98,000
- Assets £1,043,008

TRUSTEES R L Schierbeek, CBE, J A Freeman, D H Templeton, OBE

PUBLICATIONS Guidelines for applicants available on request. Report and Statement of Accounts produced

SUBMISSION OF APPLICATIONS Four monthly meetings for grant applications. To follow the headings set out in guidelines

CORRESPONDENT J W Wallace, Secretary, Enkalon Foundation, 25 Randalstown Road, Antrim, Northern Ireland BT41 4LJ

CLASSIFICATIONS
- Children and youth – general

C.C. NO XN62210A   **ESTABLISHED** 1985

■ The Everard Foundation

OBJECTS General charitable purposes

POLICY OF TRUSTEES To help local charities of all sizes

TYPE OF GRANT One-off

TYPE OF BENEFICIARY If National organisation, donation must go to something tangible, locally

RESTRICTIONS Grants to individuals unlikely; local charities only

BENEFICIAL AREA East Midlands, with particular emphasis on Leicestershire

FINANCES
- Year 1994
- Grants £40,000

TRUSTEES R A S Everard, N W Smith, Mrs A C Richards

SUBMISSION OF APPLICATIONS Applications by post

CORRESPONDENT The Everard Foundation, Castle Acres, Narborough, Leicester LE9 5BY

CLASSIFICATIONS
- Youth organisations (eg Guides, Scouts, YWCA etc)

C.C. NO 272248   **ESTABLISHED** 1976

■ The Eveson Charitable Trust

OBJECTS Support or relief of the physically handicapped (including blind and deaf), the mentally handicapped, hospitals and hospices, children in need whether disadvantaged or physically or mentally handicapped, the elderly, the homeless, and for medical research into problems associated with any of the foregoing

POLICY OF TRUSTEES In view of Mrs Eveson's lifetime gifts to charities in her own area and her choice of Trustees from the same area, the thrust of giving is currently for the benefit of residents in Herefordshire, Worcestershire and the West Midlands, including Birmingham and Coventry. The Trustees do not give grants to individuals, even if the application is submitted by a charitable institution on behalf of the individual

TYPE OF GRANT Applications are considered for capital and recurrent expenditure

TYPE OF BENEFICIARY Applications considered from local charities, local branches of national charities, and national charities with a specific activity or project in the specified geographical area

RESTRICTIONS Restricted to donations to charitable institutions whose activities are confined to or primarily undertaken in the UK

BENEFICIAL AREA Hereford, Worcestershire and the county of West Midlands, including Birmingham and Coventry

SAMPLE GRANTS £15,000 to KIDS towards the purchase of a new Birmingham centre for this charity which works with pre-school children with special needs
£11,750 to NSPCC towards the running costs of projects in Hereford and Worcester, and Birmingham
£10,000 to NCH Action for Children towards the running costs of a project in Walsall for children with disabilities
£3,000 to Friends of the Hearing and Speech Centre, Hereford, towards specialised diagnostic equipment
£2,000 to Manor Park School Parents, Teachers

and Friends Association towards a minibus for this Worcester school for children with learning disabilities

FINANCES
- **Year** 1995
- **Grants** £1,570,000
- **Income** £1,791,000
- **Assets** £40,203,000

TRUSTEES The Right Rev John Oliver (Bishop of Hereford), Peter Temple-Morris, MP, Bruce R Maughling, David P Pearson, J Martin Davis

PUBLICATIONS Annual Report and Accounts submitted to the Charity Commissioners

SUBMISSION OF APPLICATIONS Applications can only be considered if they are on the Trust's standard Application for Support form which can be obtained from the Administrator at the offices of the Trust. The Trustees meet quarterly, usually at the end of March and the beginning of July, October and January. The Application for Support form must be completed and returned (together with a copy of the latest Accounts of the applying organisation) to the Trust's offices at least six weeks before the meeting at which the application is to be considered in order to give time for necessary assessment procedures, which include many visits to see applicants

CORRESPONDENT Alex Gray, Administrator, The Eveson Charitable Trust, 45 Park Road, Gloucester GL1 1LP

CLASSIFICATIONS
- Adventure centres and playgrounds
- Holidays
- Homes and hostels
- Special needs housing
- Youth organisations (eg Guides, Scouts, YWCA etc)

C.C. NO 1032204   **ESTABLISHED** 1994

■ **The FR 1978 Charitable Trust**

OBJECTS General charitable purposes

RESTRICTIONS No grants to individuals

BENEFICIAL AREA UK

FINANCES
- **Year** 1995
- **Grants** £4,618
- **Income** £5,127
- **Assets** £56,287

TRUSTEES The Rt Hon The Lady Saltoun, M A Hayes

NOTES This is a private Charitable Trust with no uncommitted funds

CORRESPONDENT Messrs Macfarlanes, l0 Norwich Street, London EC4A 1BD

CLASSIFICATIONS
- Children and youth – general

C.C. NO 277270   **ESTABLISHED** 1978

■ **The Esmee Fairbairn Charitable Trust**

OBJECTS (a) Education, (b) The Arts and Heritage. (c) Social Welfare. (d) The Environment. (e) Economic and Social Research. Applicants should obtain a copy of the Trust's policy guidelines, which explain the Trust's priorities in each of the above areas

POLICY OF TRUSTEES The Trust is committed to the preservation and development of a free society and to free market principles. It seeks to encourage the pursuit of excellence and innovation. In the social welfare field the Trust supports practical initiatives to encourage self-help and independence. The emphasis generally is on prevention and self-help rather than the alleviation of suffering

TYPE OF BENEFICIARY Registered charities working in the areas outlined under Objects

RESTRICTIONS Registered charities only. Applications on behalf of individuals and student expeditions are not supported. Medical causes (especially research) are not usually supported; nor are individual schools

BENEFICIAL AREA UK. With few exceptions the Trust does not support bodies which operate overseas or are international in character

SAMPLE GRANTS £110,000 to Greater Bristol Foundation towards Lawrence Weston programme to support local self-help initiatives £10,000 to Glasgow Council for Single Homeless towards Project Officer

FINANCES
- **Year** 1994
- **Grants** £9,141,935
- **Income** £10,216,348
- **Assets** £258,299,188

TRUSTEES J S Fairbairn (Chairman), A G Down (Treasurer), Sir Antony Acland, Gen Sir John Hackett, C J M Hardie, Mrs P Hughes-Hallett, Martin Lane Fox, Mrs V Linklater, Lord Rees-Mogg, Andrew Tuckey

Faringdon

Alphabetical register of grant making charitable trusts

PUBLICATIONS Annual Report and Accounts submitted to Charity Commissioners, Policy Guidelines

SUBMISSION OF APPLICATIONS Applicants should request a copy of the Trust's policy guidelines before submitting an application

CORRESPONDENT The Director, (Margaret Hyde), The Esmee Fairbairn Charitable Trust, 1 Birdcage Walk, London SW1H 9JJ

CLASSIFICATIONS
- Children and youth – general
- Advancement in life
- Adventure centres and playgrounds
- Centres, clubs and institutes
- Community groups
- Development of character
- Homes and hostels
- Special needs housing
- Special classes
- Youth organisations (eg Guides, Scouts, YWCA etc)

C.C. NO 200051   **ESTABLISHED** 1961

■ Lord Faringdon Charitable Trust

OBJECTS General charitable purposes, including help in education, aid in sickness, help in poverty and old age, gifts to museums

TYPE OF BENEFICIARY Registered charitable institutions

RESTRICTIONS Registered charities only at the discretion of the Trustees. Not individuals

FINANCES
- Year 1992
- Grants £76,414
- Income £83,256
- Assets £1,319,157

TRUSTEES H S S Trotter, A D A W Forbes

CORRESPONDENT Trustees of the Lord Faringdon Charitable Trust, c/o William Sturges & Co, 12 Caxton Street, London SW1H 0QY

CLASSIFICATIONS
- Youth organisations (eg Guides, Scouts, YWCA etc)

C.C. NO 206878   **ESTABLISHED** 1962

■ Lord Faringdon Second Charitable Trust

OBJECTS General charitable purposes including help in education, aid in sickness, help in poverty and old age and gifts to museums

TYPE OF BENEFICIARY Registered charitable institutions

RESTRICTIONS Registered charities only at the discretion of the Trustees. Not individuals

FINANCES
- Year 1992
- Grants £48,150
- Income £51,745
- Assets £911,764

TRUSTEES H S S Trotter, A D A W Forbes

CORRESPONDENT Trustees of Lord Faringdon Second Charitable Trust, c/o William Sturges & Co, 12 Caxton Street, London SW1H 0QY

CLASSIFICATIONS
- Homes and hostels

C.C. NO 237974   **ESTABLISHED** 1964

■ The Farne Trust

OBJECTS General charitable purposes

POLICY OF TRUSTEES Preference to charities of which the Trust has special interest, knowledge or association

TYPE OF BENEFICIARY Registered charities

RESTRICTIONS Registered charities only. Applications from individuals including students are ineligible

BENEFICIAL AREA UK and overseas

FINANCES
- Year 1995
- Grants £5,600
- Income £3,850
- Assets £123,000

TRUSTEES M J Musgrave, R C Kirby

SUBMISSION OF APPLICATIONS The Trustees do not respond to direct appeals

CORRESPONDENT M Reynolds, Messrs Speechly Bircham, Bouverie House, 154 Fleet Street, London EC4A 2HX

CLASSIFICATIONS
- Holidays
- Homes and hostels
- Special classes
- Youth organisations (eg Guides, Scouts, YWCA etc)

C.C. NO 255008   **ESTABLISHED** 1968

■ The Thomas Farr Charitable Trust

OBJECTS General charitable purposes

RESTRICTIONS Registered charities only

BENEFICIAL AREA Mainly Nottinghamshire

FINANCES
- Year 1992
- Grants £216,047
- Income £150,000
- Assets £2,393,825

TRUSTEES B H Farr, E M Astley-Arlington, P K Farr, Kleinwort Benson Trustees Ltd

CORRESPONDENT B Davys, Kleinwort Benson Trustees Ltd, PO Box 191, 10 Fenchurch Street, London EC3M 3LB

CLASSIFICATIONS
- Youth organisations (eg Guides, Scouts, YWCA etc)

C.C. NO 328394   **ESTABLISHED** 1989

■ Walter Farthing (Trust) Limited

OBJECTS To commemorate the work of the Founder of the Charity by the furtherance of suitable charitable projects

POLICY OF TRUSTEES To initiate or assist the development of projects by undertaking or grant aiding the acquisition, erection or adaptation of buildings and the provision of initial equipment

TYPE OF BENEFICIARY Organisations enlarging the range (including innovative projects) and/or volume of charitable services provided in the locality

RESTRICTIONS The Council does not ordinarily grant aid headquarters organisations of national charities, services, which public authorities are empowered to provide, individuals or current expenditure of any nature or description

BENEFICIAL AREA Chelmsford, Essex

FINANCES
- Year 1994
- Assets £636,745
- Income £37,505

TRUSTEES The Council of Management

CORRESPONDENT The Secretary, Walter Farthing (Trust) Limited, Coval Hall, Chelmsford, Essex CM1 2QF

CLASSIFICATIONS
- Children and youth – general
- Youth organisations (eg Guides, Scouts, YWCA etc)

C.C. NO 220114   **ESTABLISHED** 1957

■ The John Feeney Charitable Bequest

OBJECTS Benefit of public charities in Birmingham only. Promotion of Art in Birmingham only. Acquisition and maintenance of open spaces near Birmingham

POLICY OF TRUSTEES Capital projects preferred

TYPE OF BENEFICIARY See above

RESTRICTIONS Nothing political or denominational

BENEFICIAL AREA Birmingham

FINANCES
- Year 1993
- Grants £31,800
- Income £33,539
- Assets £878,348

TRUSTEES H Kenrick, Mrs M Smith, Rev Canon R S Stevens

CORRESPONDENT M J Woodward, Messrs Lee Crowder, 24 Harborne Road, Birmingham, West Midlands B15 3AD

CLASSIFICATIONS
- Children and youth – general
- Youth organisations (eg Guides, Scouts, YWCA etc)

C.C. NO 214486   **ESTABLISHED** 1906

■ The A M Fenton Trust

OBJECTS General charitable purposes

POLICY OF TRUSTEES To support mainly one-off national appeals, and local appeals, unlikely to assist those wishing to take higher degrees

RESTRICTIONS None but emphasis on local support

FINANCES
- Year 1991
- Grants £82,804
- Income £85,680
- Assets £440,386

TRUSTEES J L Fenton, C M Fenton

CORRESPONDENT J L Fenton, 14 Beech Grove, Harrogate, Yorkshire HG2 0EX

CLASSIFICATIONS
- Centres, clubs and institutes

C.C. NO 270353   **ESTABLISHED** 1975

■ Ferguson Benevolent Fund Limited

OBJECTS General charitable purposes including support of the Methodist Church

POLICY OF TRUSTEES To give grants for such charitable purposes as they deem worthy of their support and, in particular, are connected with the Methodist Church. Preference to charities of which the Trust has special interest, knowledge or association

TYPE OF GRANT Variable

TYPE OF BENEFICIARY Mainly to cases of social, medical and educational need, usually through charitable bodies working in those areas

RESTRICTIONS No support for trade unions and like bodies. No individual support for medical electives, private schooling, undergraduate/postgraduate study and expeditions

BENEFICIAL AREA North West England, Jersey, Overseas

FINANCES
- Year 1993
- Grants £78,000
- Income £34,000
- Assets £618,000

TRUSTEES Mrs E Higginbottom (Chairman), Mrs C M A Metcalfe, Ms S Ferguson (Secretary), Mrs P Dobson, P A L Holt, S M Higginbottom

SUBMISSION OF APPLICATIONS By letter only

CORRESPONDENT Mrs E Higginbottom, Rawfell, Gt Langdale, Nr Ambleside, Cumbria LA22 9JS

CLASSIFICATIONS
- Children and youth – general
- Centres, clubs and institutes
- Holidays

C.C. NO 228746   **ESTABLISHED** 1963

■ The Fidelity UK Foundation

OBJECTS General charitable purposes

POLICY OF TRUSTEES Trustees review all applications received

TYPE OF BENEFICIARY Projects for disabled and disadvantaged children are favoured

BENEFICIAL AREA London, Greater London, Kent and Surrey (charities which are local to our offices)

SAMPLE GRANTS £5,000 to Scotts Project, Hildenborough (home for disabled children)
£1,000 to One Small Step Richard House Appeal, London (hospice for children with terminal illness)
£500 to Barnados Trust, Tonbridge (youth centre)
£250 to Children's Trust, Tadworth (home for disabled children)
£250 to Kingswood Village's Young People's Project (youth centre)

FINANCES
- Year 1992
- Grants £30,378
- Income £30,000
- Assets £36,421

TRUSTEES Fidelity Investment Services Ltd, E C Johnson III, M P Cambridge, A J Bolton, B R J Bateman

CORRESPONDENT J Martin, Oakhill House, 130 Tonbridge Road, Hildenborough, Kent TN11 9DZ

CLASSIFICATIONS
- Children and youth – general

C.C. NO 327899   **ESTABLISHED** 1988

Fishmongers'

■ Fishmongers' Company's Charitable Trust

OBJECTS General charitable purposes

POLICY OF TRUSTEES (a) In general, the Company's charitable funds will be used for the relief of hardship and disability, education, the environment, heritage and fishery related charities. Applications will normally only be accepted from national bodies (with the exception of (b)). (b) Charities in the City of London and adjacent boroughs will also be eligible to apply. (c) Preference will be given to charities seeking to raise funds for a specific project or for research rather than for administration or general purposes. (d) In the case of requests for help for cathedrals, abbeys, churches and old buildings, priority will be given to St Paul's Cathedral and Westminster Abbey

TYPE OF BENEFICIARY Registered charities and individuals in education

RESTRICTIONS Grants are usually made once only. Educational grants are not available to people over 19 years of age

BENEFICIAL AREA City of London and adjacent boroughs

FINANCES
- Year 1994
- Grants £1,210,757
- Income £1,280,757
- Assets £1,484,978

TRUSTEES The Wardens & Commonalty

CORRESPONDENT The Clerk of The Fishmongers' Company, Fishmongers' Hall, London Bridge, London EC4R 9EL

CLASSIFICATIONS
- Children and youth – general
- Counselling (inc helplines)
- Homes and hostels
- Youth organisations (eg Guides, Scouts, YWCA etc)
- Children and violence (inc abuse)

C.C. NO 263690   **ESTABLISHED** 1972

■ The Fitton Trust

OBJECTS General charitable purposes

POLICY OF TRUSTEES No grants are made to individuals. No replies will be sent to unsolicited applications whether from individuals, charities or other bodies

TYPE OF BENEFICIARY Not individuals – charities

RESTRICTIONS No grants to individuals

BENEFICIAL AREA UK

FINANCES
- Year 1994
- Grants £52,150
- Income £89,598
- Assets £1,372,231

TRUSTEES Dr R P A Rivers, MA, MRCP, D M Lumsden, D V Brand, MA, ACA

NOTES Address for applications: The Secretary, Fitton Trust, PO Box 649, London SW3 4LA

SUBMISSION OF APPLICATIONS No formal application required; no application considered unless accompanied by fully audited accounts

CORRESPONDENT Messrs Walker Martineau, 64 Queen Street, London EC4R 1AD

CLASSIFICATIONS
- Children and youth – general
- Adoption/fostering
- Advancement in life
- Adventure centres and playgrounds
- Centres, clubs and institutes
- Holidays
- Homes and hostels
- Special classes
- Youth organisations (eg Guides, Scouts, YWCA etc)

C.C. NO 208758   **ESTABLISHED** 1928

■ The Ian Fleming Charitable Trust

OBJECTS General charitable purposes

POLICY OF TRUSTEES Income is allocated equally between: (a) Donations to national charities actively operating for the support, relief and welfare of men, women and children who are disabled or handicapped or otherwise in need of help, care and attention, and charities actively engaged in research on human diseases; (b) Music Education Awards under a scheme administered by the Musicians Benevolent Fund and advised by a committee of experts in the field of music

TYPE OF BENEFICIARY Registered charities and students of music

RESTRICTIONS Registered charities only. No grants to individuals except under Music Education Award Scheme or to purely local charities

FINANCES
- Year 1993
- Grants £58,000
- Income £58,333
- Assets £1,646,890

TRUSTEES A A I Fleming, N A M McDonald, A W N Baldwin, A H Isaacs

CORRESPONDENT A A I Fleming, Messrs Hays Allan, Southampton House, 317 High Holborn, London WC1V 7NL

CLASSIFICATIONS
- Children and youth – general

C.C. NO 263327   **ESTABLISHED** 1971

■ The Joyce Fletcher Charitable Trust

OBJECTS To support music, education, children's welfare and young adults

POLICY OF TRUSTEES Currently main areas of interest are institutions and organisations specialising in music education training, special needs education involving music, and national and local charities for children's welfare

TYPE OF GRANT Recurrent expenses or new projects. £250–£1,000

TYPE OF BENEFICIARY National and local charities

RESTRICTIONS Preference for charities with whom links already exist. No grants to individual students

BENEFICIAL AREA UK with a preference for the South West

SAMPLE GRANTS £1,000 to Off the Record (youth conselling)
£750 to Bath Area Play Project
£500 to NSPCC
£500 to English Touring Opera (education)
£250 to Youth Clubs UK

FINANCES
- Year 1995
- Grants £16,100
- Income £16,800
- Assets £200,000

TRUSTEES R A Fletcher, W D R Fletcher, A V Fretwell

SUBMISSION OF APPLICATIONS By November 1st annually. Preliminary telephone call advisable. Application by letter. Acknowledgements only if being considered

CORRESPONDENT R A Fletcher, 17 Westmead Gardens, Upper Weston, Bath BA1 4EZ

CLASSIFICATIONS
- Adventure centres and playgrounds
- Centres, clubs and institutes
- Community groups
- Day centres and nurseries
- Counselling (inc helplines)
- Holidays
- Homes and hostels
- Children and violence (inc abuse)

C.C. NO 297901   **ESTABLISHED** 1987

■ Roy Fletcher Trust

OBJECTS General charitable purposes

POLICY OF TRUSTEES Preference for youth, elderly and disadvantaged organisations

TYPE OF GRANT Preference for single payments

TYPE OF BENEFICIARY Dependent on Trustees' assessment of merit

RESTRICTIONS Unlikely to fund projects eligible for statutory funding

BENEFICIAL AREA Shropshire

FINANCES
- Year 1995
- Grants £141,000

TRUSTEES D N Fletcher, Mrs G M Mathias, Mrs R A Coles, Mrs E F Cooper

NOTES Grants stated are average for the last three years

SUBMISSION OF APPLICATIONS In writing to the Secretary – Trustees meet quarterly

CORRESPONDENT The Secretary, 95 Mount Pleasant Road, Shrewsbury, Shropshire SY1 3EL

CLASSIFICATIONS
- Children and youth – general

C.C. NO 276498   **ESTABLISHED** 1978

■ The Fleurus Trust

OBJECTS General charitable purposes

POLICY OF TRUSTEES Young people: provision for socially deprived. Addiction: drug and alcohol rehabilitation. Disabled/Handicapped: equipment and opportunities. Offenders: care and resettlement of. Prison reform: working for better conditions, provision of educational opportunities

TYPE OF GRANT One-off and recurrent

TYPE OF BENEFICIARY Small registered charities preferred, innovatory or long-established

RESTRICTIONS No grants for buildings or renovation: no large national organisations, no general appeals, no expeditions

BENEFICIAL AREA Not too specific but Essex and East Anglia favoured

SAMPLE GRANTS £200–£500 annually to Children's Family Trust
£100–£500 as individual grants for educational purposes

FINANCES
- Year 1993
- Grants £2,600
- Income £3,500
- Assets £43,000

TRUSTEES S Rose, P Rose

NOTES Applications for funding of individuals not considered until 75% of cost raised or promised

SUBMISSION OF APPLICATIONS Considered once yearly in the Autumn, require copy of applicants annual report and accounts; unsuccessful applications not acknowledged

CORRESPONDENT Mrs P Rose, 5 Writtle Green, Chelmsford, Essex CM1 3DT

CLASSIFICATIONS
- Advancement in life

C.C. NO 280047   **ESTABLISHED** 1980

■ The Gerald Fogel Charitable Trust
(supercedes the J G Fogel Charitable Trust)

OBJECTS General charitable purposes

POLICY OF TRUSTEES Deserving charities or appeal funds

TYPE OF GRANT Some recurrent, some one-off

TYPE OF BENEFICIARY Mainly headquarter organisations

RESTRICTIONS No grants to individuals or non registered charities

BENEFICIAL AREA London

FINANCES
- Year 1992
- Grants £30,000
- Income £29,000
- Assets £350,000

TRUSTEES J G Fogel, B Fogel, S Fogel, D Fogel

CORRESPONDENT J G Fogel, JP, 23 West Hill Park, Highgate, London N6 6ND

CLASSIFICATIONS
- Homes and hostels

C.C. NO 1004451   **ESTABLISHED** 1992

■ Ford of Britain Trust

OBJECTS Advancement of education and other charitable purposes beneficial to the community, with preference to those organisations located in areas in which the Ford Motor Company Limited's plants are established

POLICY OF TRUSTEES Currently the main areas of interest are children and young people (with emphasis on education, special needs children, youth organisations, counselling); community service, the disabled, social welfare. Major building projects and research projects (including medical) are rarely assisted

TYPE OF BENEFICIARY Registered charities working in the areas outlined under Policy

RESTRICTIONS Organisations outside the beneficial areas and national charities are rarely assisted, except for specific projects in Ford areas. Applications in respect of individuals (including students), charities requiring funds for overseas projects, and wholly religious or politically orientated projects are ineligible

BENEFICIAL AREA Charities located in close proximity to Ford Motor Company Limited plants in the United Kingdom

FINANCES
- Year 1995
- Grants £378,420
- Income £129,170
- Assets £1,054,702

TRUSTEES I G McAllister, CBE (Chairman), R A Hill, W G F Brooks, M J Callaghan, Prof Ann P Dowling, J H M Norris, CBE, VL, T J Belton

CORRESPONDENT R M Metcalf, Director, Ford of Britain Trust, c/o Ford Motor Co Ltd, 1–661 Eagle Way, Brentwood, Essex CM13 3BW

CLASSIFICATIONS
- Children and youth – general
- Adoption/fostering
- Adventure centres and playgrounds
- Centres, clubs and institutes
- Community groups
- Day centres and nurseries
- Development of character
- Counselling (inc helplines)
- Holidays
- Special needs housing
- Youth organisations (eg Guides, Scouts, YWCA etc)

C.C. NO 269410   **ESTABLISHED** 1975

■ The Russell and Mary Foreman 1980 Charitable Trust

OBJECTS The relief of need, hardship and physical and mental distress among persons in any part of the world – the care and protection of animals

POLICY OF TRUSTEES Distributions are made in March each year to a number of registered charities. Special areas of interest are ecology, famine relief, children and animals

TYPE OF GRANT Cash donations only. Yearly donations

TYPE OF BENEFICIARY Registered charities only

RESTRICTIONS Grants to registered charities only. No grants to individuals

BENEFICIAL AREA Worldwide

FINANCES
- Year 1992
- Grants £8,500
- Income £9,000
- Assets £170,000

TRUSTEES Royal Bank of Scotland plc

SUBMISSION OF APPLICATIONS In writing to the correspondent at any time. No acknowledgements will be sent

CORRESPONDENT The Senior Trust Officer (Ref 7980), Royal Bank of Scotland plc, Private Trust & Taxation, 45 Mosley Street, Manchester M60 2BE

CLASSIFICATIONS
- Children and youth – general
- Holidays
- Children and violence (inc abuse)

C.C. NO 281543   **ESTABLISHED** 1980

■ The Fortune Trust

OBJECTS General charitable purposes

POLICY OF TRUSTEES Mainly to support children's charities

TYPE OF BENEFICIARY Registered charities

FINANCES
- Year 1995
- Grants £8,500
- Income £12,700
- Assets £232,000

TRUSTEES Coutts & Co, Mrs A Druckman

NOTES Appeal letters will not be acknowledged

CORRESPONDENT The Correspondent, Coutts & Co, Trustee Department, 440 Strand, London WC2R 0QS

CLASSIFICATIONS
- Children and youth – general

C.C. NO 284025   **ESTABLISHED** 1981

■ The Four Lanes Trust

OBJECTS (a) Advancing education (including education in the Arts) amongst the inhabitants. (b) Promoting the social welfare and conditions of life of the said inhabitants

POLICY OF TRUSTEES Small initiatives are particularly welcomed (see Type of Grant)

TYPE OF GRANT No grants made to individuals for their personal benefit

TYPE OF BENEFICIARY The Trust does not exclude helping any person or institution whose application is within the parameter of the Trust

RESTRICTIONS Restricted to stated beneficial area

BENEFICIAL AREA Basingstoke and Deane District Council

FINANCES
- Year 1993
- Grants £30,000
- Income £34,000
- Assets £750,000

TRUSTEES The Hon Dwight Makins, The Hon Virginia Shapiro, D Roberts, Mrs G Evans

CORRESPONDENT The Hon Dwight Makins, Beaurepaire House, Sherborne St John, Basingstoke, Hampshire

CLASSIFICATIONS
- Centres, clubs and institutes
- Youth organisations (eg Guides, Scouts, YWCA etc)

C.C. NO 267608   **ESTABLISHED** 1974

■ Fourth Settlement Charity

OBJECTS General charitable purposes

POLICY OF TRUSTEES The Trustees meet annually to decide on donations to be made. In general, only certain charities in which the Trustees are personally interested are supported, thus leaving no surplus available for general grant applications

TYPE OF BENEFICIARY Mainly medical

RESTRICTIONS Individuals

FINANCES
- Year 1994
- Grants £6,000
- Income £7,500
- Assets £117,000

TRUSTEES H B Carslake, T R Kershaw, Mrs P J Collington, D R Kershaw

NOTES General applications are not considered

CORRESPONDENT H B Carslake, Messrs Martineau Johnson, St Philips House, St Philips Place, Birmingham, West Midlands B3 2PP

CLASSIFICATIONS
- Homes and hostels

C.C. NO 257352   **ESTABLISHED** 1968

■ Charles Henry Foyle Trust

OBJECTS General charitable purposes and particularly to encourage new forms of social work, research into social conditions and education, improvement of educational facilities

POLICY OF TRUSTEES Preference given to projects in and for Birmingham and NE Worcestershire

TYPE OF BENEFICIARY Registered charities – new projects

RESTRICTIONS Not to established bodies; mainly for particular projects, ie not running costs

SAMPLE GRANTS £2,000 to CBSO for the music education project for partial hearing children £1,200 to Birmingham Conservatoire for the Bursary Fund for talented needy children

FINANCES
- Year 1994–95
- Grants £62,000
- Income £76,000
- Assets £500,000

TRUSTEES Chairman of Trust – Dr B Foyle

CORRESPONDENT Trust Administrator, Charles Henry Foyle Trust, c/o Boxfoldia Ltd, Merse Road, Redditch, Worcs B98 9HB

CLASSIFICATIONS
- Adventure centres and playgrounds
- Day centres and nurseries
- Counselling (inc helplines)
- Holidays
- Youth organisations (eg Guides, Scouts, YWCA etc)

C.C. NO 220446   **ESTABLISHED** 1940

■ Sydney E Franklin Deceased's New Second Charity

OBJECTS (a) General charitable purposes (b) Subject to the trusts aforesaid of the Trust Fund the income thereof from date hereof shall be held upon trusts in equal shares for such of the purposes of the National Council of Social Service Benevolent Fund and of the United Charities Fund of the Liberal Jewish Synagogue as are charitable under the law of England

POLICY OF TRUSTEES Donations mainly given for Jewish welfare, covering hospitals, youth organisations, education and poverty

TYPE OF BENEFICIARY Charities dealing mainly with Jewish welfare

RESTRICTIONS No grants to individuals

FINANCES
- Year 1991
- Grants £20,000
- Income £23,000
- Assets £414,000

TRUSTEES A J Franklin, A Franklin

SUBMISSION OF APPLICATIONS Donations may be requested by letter, and these are placed before the Trustees at their meeting which is normally held at the end of each year

CORRESPONDENT Edwin Coe, 2 Stone Buildings, Lincoln's Inn, London WC2A 3TH

CLASSIFICATIONS
- Centres, clubs and institutes

C.C. NO 272047   **ESTABLISHED** 1973

■ Jill Franklin Trust

OBJECTS To fund: (a) The relief of poverty, disablement and distress. (b) Overseas relief and development. (c) Culture and the environment

POLICY OF TRUSTEES Concerns are delinquency, and its avoidance, respite for carers (by holidays, etc) and voluntary work

TYPE OF GRANT Particularly seed-corn money and for development

TYPE OF BENEFICIARY Charitable organisations, not individuals

RESTRICTIONS The Trust does not fund building, endowment funds, heritage schemes, religious organisations, animals, students, travel and exploration, nor any work which should be done by Government, local Government or Health Authorities and NHS Trusts

BENEFICIAL AREA Worldwide

FINANCES
- Year 1994
- Grants £55,295
- Income £31,535
- Assets £552,053

TRUSTEES N Franklin, S P Franklin, A C Franklin, T N Franklin, S A Franklin

PUBLICATIONS Annual Report

SUBMISSION OF APPLICATIONS Separate submissions should not be made both to Norman Franklin Trust and Jill Franklin Trust. The Trustees tend to look more favourably on an appeal which is simply and economically prepared, enclosing, if possible, budget and accounts and a clear statement of purpose. No acknowledgement is given of unsolicited enquiries, except where an sae is enclosed

CORRESPONDENT N Franklin, 78 Lawn Road, London NW3 2XB

CLASSIFICATIONS
- Development of character

C.C. NO 259774   **ESTABLISHED** 1988

■ The Gordon Fraser Charitable Trust

OBJECTS General charitable purposes

POLICY OF TRUSTEES At present the Trustees are particularly interested in help for children or young people in need, the environment and in assisting organisations associated with the visual arts

TYPE OF BENEFICIARY The Trustees have absolute discretion as to the charities or organisations to be assisted

RESTRICTIONS Excluded are organisations which are not registered as charities in England and Wales or registered with the Inland Revenue in Scotland. Applications from individuals are ineligible

BENEFICIAL AREA National, applications from Scotland will receive favourable consideration, but not to the exclusion of applications from elsewhere

SAMPLE GRANTS £3,000 to the London Children's Flower Society
£750 to the Stepney Children's Fund (Toynbee)
£500 to the Glasgow Children's Holiday Scheme
£400 to the Scottish Youth Dance Festival
£200 to the Jura Playgroup Association
£200 to Venture Scotland

FINANCES
- Year 1994
- Grants £86,900
- Income £89,002
- Assets £1,518,425

TRUSTEES Mrs M A Moss, W F T Anderson

SUBMISSION OF APPLICATIONS For consideration in January, April, July and October

CORRESPONDENT Mrs M A Moss, Holmhurst, Westerton Drive, Bridge of Allan, Scotland FK9 4QL

CLASSIFICATIONS
- Children and youth – general

C.C. NO 260869   **ESTABLISHED** 1966

■ Joseph Strong Frazer Trust

OBJECTS General charitable purposes

POLICY OF TRUSTEES Support of registered charities in England and Wales

TYPE OF BENEFICIARY Registered charities only in England and Wales

RESTRICTIONS No grants to individuals

BENEFICIAL AREA England and Wales

FINANCES
- Year 1995
- Grants £228,250
- Income £354,340
- Assets £5,773,384

TRUSTEES W A J Reardon Smith, Mrs R M Gibson, D A Cook, R M H Read

CORRESPONDENT W I Waites, Scottish Provident House, 31 Mosley Street, Newcastle upon Tyne, Tyne and Wear NE1 1HX

CLASSIFICATIONS
- Children and youth – general

C.C. NO 235311   **ESTABLISHED** 1940

■ A J Freeman Charitable Trust

OBJECTS General charitable purposes

TYPE OF GRANT Single donations towards specific objects

TYPE OF BENEFICIARY Registered charities

BENEFICIAL AREA Mainly Manchester

FINANCES
- Year 1993
- Grants £13,500
- Income £37,249
- Assets £91,535

TRUSTEES A J Freeman, J M Levy

CORRESPONDENT J M Levy, Kuit Steinart Levy & Co, 3 St Mary's Parsonage, Manchester M3 2RD

CLASSIFICATIONS
- Children and youth – general

C.C. NO 279522   **ESTABLISHED** 1979

■ Charles S French Charitable Trust

OBJECTS General charitable purposes

POLICY OF TRUSTEES No grants to individuals. Only very occasional grants for educational purposes and only when first approached by a school or college, not by a student

TYPE OF BENEFICIARY Charities, especially children's charities

RESTRICTIONS Strong preference for Essex, East Anglia, and North East London area. Very few grants made for purposes outside these areas

BENEFICIAL AREA NE London, East Anglia and Essex

FINANCES
- Year 1995
- Grants £117,000
- Income £137,000
- Assets £3,600,000

TRUSTEES W F Noble, R L Thomas, D B Shepperd

CORRESPONDENT R L Thomas, 169 High Road, Loughton, Essex IG10 4LF

CLASSIFICATIONS
- Children and youth – general
- Centres, clubs and institutes
- Development of character
- Homes and hostels
- Youth organisations (eg Guides, Scouts, YWCA etc)

C.C. NO 206476   **ESTABLISHED** 1959

■ The Freshgate Trust Foundation

OBJECTS General charitable purposes including educational travel, relief of the sick and poor, etc

POLICY OF TRUSTEES Favours local appeals, does not support individuals or national appeals

TYPE OF BENEFICIARY Mainly charitable organisations in South Yorkshire. Both innovatory and established bodies may be considered

RESTRICTIONS The Trust restricts its grants to charitable organisations and does not deal with applications from individuals or for church fabric unless used for a wider community purpose

BENEFICIAL AREA Mainly Sheffield and South Yorkshire

FINANCES
- Year 1993
- Grants £80,825
- Income £93,518
- Assets £1,191,718

TRUSTEES Council of Management Governing Body

CORRESPONDENT J H Robinson, Secretary, The Freshgate Trust Foundation, 346 Glossop Road, Sheffield, South Yorkshire S10 2HW

CLASSIFICATIONS
- Children and youth – general
- Adventure centres and playgrounds
- Centres, clubs and institutes
- Community groups
- Day centres and nurseries
- Development of character
- Counselling (inc helplines)

- Holidays
- Homes and hostels
- Youth organisations (eg Guides, Scouts, YWCA etc)

C.C. NO 221467 **ESTABLISHED** 1962

■ Friarsgate Trust

OBJECTS General charitable purposes contributing to welfare of children and young persons, care of the aged and of the needy and sick

POLICY OF TRUSTEES To continue support of existing beneficiaries rather than sponsoring new causes

TYPE OF BENEFICIARY Local organisations mainly

RESTRICTIONS Emphasis on West Sussex

FINANCES
- Year 1994
- Grants £58,379
- Income £53,344
- Assets £1,079,816

TRUSTEES R F Oates, H R Whittle, G N M Scoular

CORRESPONDENT Messrs Thomas Eggar & Son, Sussex House, North Street, Horsham RH12 1BJ

CLASSIFICATIONS
- Advancement in life
- Youth organisations (eg Guides, Scouts, YWCA etc)

C.C. NO 220762 **ESTABLISHED** 1955

■ The Friends of the Clergy Corporation

OBJECTS To provide financial and other assistance to: (a) The clergy of the Anglican Communion. (b) Any widow, child or other dependant of such persons who may be in financial necessity or distress

POLICY OF TRUSTEES To give help quickly, tactfully and with understanding to the clergy of the Anglican Communion and their dependants

TYPE OF GRANT Cash grants to individuals. £350 average grant for child/student

TYPE OF BENEFICIARY Anglican Communion clergy, widows and dependants

RESTRICTIONS No assistance towards the maintenance or purchase of motor vehicles, or towards the costs of education

BENEFICIAL AREA UK and overseas

FINANCES
- Year 1996
- Grants £769,322
- Income £776,482
- Assets £11,744,148

TRUSTEES The Committee of Management

PUBLICATIONS Annual Report

SUBMISSION OF APPLICATIONS Monthly

CORRESPONDENT J M Greany, Secretary, Friends of the Clergy Corporation, 27 Medway Street, Westminster, London SW1P 2BD

CLASSIFICATIONS
- Children and youth – general
- Advancement in life
- Development of character
- Holidays

C.C. NO 264724 **ESTABLISHED** 1972

■ Fritillary Trust

OBJECTS General charitable purposes

POLICY OF TRUSTEES To distribute income for the relief of poverty in the area around Binfield, Berkshire

TYPE OF BENEFICIARY See policy of trustees

BENEFICIAL AREA Binfield, Berkshire

FINANCES
- Year 1995
- Assets £127,000
- Income £7,000

TRUSTEES Hambros Trust Company Limited

PUBLICATIONS Annual accounts

CORRESPONDENT The Trustees of the Fritillary Trust, Hambros Trust Company Limited, 41 Tower Hill, London EC3N 4HA

CLASSIFICATIONS
- Youth organisations (eg Guides, Scouts, YWCA etc)

C.C. NO 255372 **ESTABLISHED** 1968

■ Frognal Trust

OBJECTS General charitable purposes – particularly UK charities for the benefit of children, the blind and otherwise handicapped, medical research, environmental heritage and old people

POLICY OF TRUSTEES The Trustees grantmaking policy is to make relatively small grants to as many qualifying charities as possible

TYPE OF BENEFICIARY Registered charities only

RESTRICTIONS No grants to charities for the benefit of animals, people living outside the UK or for the propagation of religious beliefs. The Trustees do not make grants for educational/research trips overseas

BENEFICIAL AREA UK only

FINANCES
- Year 1994
- Grants £79,500
- Income £76,000
- Assets £1,100,000

TRUSTEES Mrs P Blake-Roberts, J P van Montagu, P Fraser

SUBMISSION OF APPLICATIONS Grants Administrator, CAF, Kings Hill, West Malling, Kent ME19 4TA

CORRESPONDENT Mrs Philippa Blake-Roberts, Taylor Joynson Garrett, 50 Victoria Embankment, London EC4Y 0DX

CLASSIFICATIONS
- Children and youth – general
- Adventure centres and playgrounds
- Centres, clubs and institutes
- Counselling (inc helplines)
- Homes and hostels

C.C. NO 244444 **ESTABLISHED** 1964

■ The Patrick Frost Foundation

OBJECTS General charitable purposes

TYPE OF BENEFICIARY Registered charities

FINANCES
- Year 1993
- Income £50,852

TRUSTEES Mrs H Frost-Parkway, D Jones, L Valner, J Chedzoy

CORRESPONDENT Mrs H M Frost, c/o Trowers & Hamlins, 6 New Square, Lincoln's Inn, London WC2A 3RP

CLASSIFICATIONS
- Community groups

C.C. NO 1005505   **ESTABLISHED** 1991

■ GNC Trust

OBJECTS General charitable purposes – particulary medical, educational

POLICY OF TRUSTEES To support those charities of which the Trustees have special interest, knowledge or association

TYPE OF BENEFICIARY Charitable bodies

RESTRICTIONS No grants can be made to individuals

BENEFICIAL AREA Midlands, Hampshire and Cornwall

FINANCES
- Year 1993
- Grants £39,643
- Income £39,643
- Assets £592,267

TRUSTEES R N Cadbury, Mrs J E B Yelloly, G T E Cadbury

CORRESPONDENT Messrs Price Waterhouse, Cornwall Court, 19 Cornwall Street, Birmingham B3 2DT

CLASSIFICATIONS
- Day centres and nurseries
- Youth organisations (eg Guides, Scouts, YWCA etc)

C.C. NO 211533   **ESTABLISHED** 1960

■ Angela Gallagher Memorial Fund

OBJECTS General charitable purposes

POLICY OF TRUSTEES Grants will be made primarily to registered charities. The aim of the fund is to help children and young people within the UK. The fund will also consider Christian humanitarian and educational projects worldwide

TYPE OF GRANT Individual approved research; scholarships; block grants to Scottish universities for staff travel; university fees. Sums of £500–£5,000 annually

TYPE OF BENEFICIARY Registered charities whose Annual Accounts indicate need for assistance and a successful track record in their chosen field. Preference is given to individual projects rather than general purposes

RESTRICTIONS Donations will not be made to the following: the elderly; scientific research; hospitals and hospices; artistic and cultural appeals; animal welfare or building and equipment appeals

BENEFICIAL AREA National and international organisations based in the UK

SAMPLE GRANTS £1,000 to Children's Society £1,000 towards Peckham Project

FINANCES
- Year 1994
- Grants £31,715
- Income £41,701
- Assets £495,793

TRUSTEES Miss M E Northcote, N A Maxwell-Lawford, P A Wolrige Gordon

SUBMISSION OF APPLICATIONS In writing with supporting Accounts where possible. Applications will not be acknowledged

CORRESPONDENT Mrs D R Moss, Church Cott, The Green, Mirey Lane, Woodbury, Devon EX5 1LT

CLASSIFICATIONS
- Children and youth – general
- Development of character

C.C. NO 800739 **ESTABLISHED** 1989

■ The Gannochy Trust

OBJECTS To assist a variety of charitable organisations with a preference for youth and recreation. There is an obligation to show preference for Perth and its environs

RESTRICTIONS Applicants must be recognised as charitable by the Inland Revenue. Applications from individuals are not considered. Grants confined to Scotland

BENEFICIAL AREA Confined to Scotland

FINANCES
- Year 1993
- Grants £3,440,000
- Income £3,560,000
- Assets £76,000,000

TRUSTEES Russell A Leather (Chairman), Mark Webster, James A McCowan, Stewart Montgomery

SUBMISSION OF APPLICATIONS Meetings of Trustees are on a monthly basis

CORRESPONDENT Mrs Jean Gandhi, Kincarrathie House Drive, Pitcullen Crescent, Perth PH2 7HX

CLASSIFICATIONS
- Children and youth – general

S.C. NO SC003133 **ESTABLISHED** 1937

■ The Gatsby Charitable Foundation

OBJECTS The trustees fund major programmes to enhance education in schools, and to enhance the quality of life of the people in their categories of interest

POLICY OF TRUSTEES The trustees have identified areas of primary interest and have developed programmes which account for most of their funds. It is therefore unlikely that unsolicited proposals will be funded

TYPE OF GRANT Revenue grants

TYPE OF BENEFICIARY Registered charities

RESTRICTIONS No grants to individuals and no applications for building grants will be considered

BENEFICIAL AREA UK and Africa

FINANCES
- Year 1994
- Grants £12,068,458
- Income £15,115,385
- Assets £254,088,468

TRUSTEES Miss J S Portrait, C T S Stone

SUBMISSION OF APPLICATIONS No application forms are provided. Appeals can be submitted at any time in writing with the latest report and accounts. The appeal should be concise (one to two pages) identifying aim, approach, justification and timeliness, amount sought. Appeals will be acknowledged and further communication will only take place if the appeal is being seriously considered

CORRESPONDENT M A Pattison, 9 Red Lion Court, London EC4A 3EB

CLASSIFICATIONS
- Advancement in life
- Development of character

C.C. NO 251988 **ESTABLISHED** 1967

■ The General Charity Fund

OBJECTS General charitable purposes

POLICY OF TRUSTEES Absolute discretion of Trustees

TYPE OF GRANT Cash depending on needs of charity

TYPE OF BENEFICIARY Registered charities operating principally in the St Helens and Merseyside area

RESTRICTIONS This Trust does not give grants or financial assistance of any kind to individuals

BENEFICIAL AREA St Helens and Merseyside

SAMPLE GRANTS £500 to Weston Spirit to cover cost of one-year Weston Spirit programme for one person
£300 to Brunswick Youth Club to continue refurbishment of new building
£300 to Gordon Youth Centre for latchkey provision for younger members
£300 to NSPCC, St Helens towards Centenary Appeal

FINANCES
- Year 1995
- Grants £40,000
- Income £45,000
- Assets £1,000,000

TRUSTEES Dr L H A Pilkington, A P Pilkington, D D Mason, The Hon Mrs J M Jones

SUBMISSION OF APPLICATIONS Any time

CORRESPONDENT The General Charity Fund, PO Box 8162, London W2 1GF

CLASSIFICATIONS
- Adventure centres and playgrounds
- Centres, clubs and institutes
- Community groups
- Youth organisations (eg Guides, Scouts, YWCA etc)

C.C. NO 234710 **ESTABLISHED** 1950

■ J Paul Getty Jr General Charitable Trust

OBJECTS General charitable purposes

POLICY OF TRUSTEES Grants made in 1991 included those to charities involved with the homeless, with offenders and ex-offenders, including sex offenders, with the mentally ill, those addicted to drugs and alcohol, to community groups, self-help groups and those working with young people, and ethnic minority groups in all these categories. In addition, some grants were made for the preservation of buildings, gardens, manuscripts, etc, or to help to buy particularly important objects. Preference is given to projects not in the South-East

TYPE OF GRANT Capital or recurrent, core funding and salaries sometimes considered

TYPE OF BENEFICIARY Long-term practical projects aiming to help young adults (16+) to make something of their lives. Not activity breaks unless part of long-term plan. Not young children or educational projects. Support is given to young offenders and young homeless

RESTRICTIONS To registered charities only. Applications from individuals, including students,

Gibbins

are ineligible. No grants are made in response to general appeals from large national organisations or grant-making Trusts. Other exclusions include animals, research, medical care including hospices and any form of medical equipment, work with the blind, for cancer, for holidays or expeditions, for young children, the elderly, music, churches and cathedrals. Residential projects are unlikely to be considered

BENEFICIAL AREA No projects overseas. Preference given to areas of deprivation, particularly in the North

SAMPLE GRANTS £8,500 x3 to Project 6, Keighley for mixed-race youth group
£5,000 x3 to Churches Acting Together in Whitley
£5,000 x3 to Norris Green Youth Centre in Liverpool to complete alterations
£5,000 to Feltham YOI to set up radio service to be managed by young offenders
£5,000 to Safeground to develop drama therapy work with young people in prison

FINANCES
- **Year** 1993
- **Grants** £1,242,065
- **Income** £1,382,449
- **Assets** £33,870,568

TRUSTEES J Paul Getty Jr KBE, James Ramsden, PC, Christopher Gibbs, Vanni Treves

PUBLICATIONS Five Year Report 1986 to 1990 (while stocks last)

SUBMISSION OF APPLICATIONS The Trustees meet four times a year. Applications may be made at any time. A full letter with details of the project and its needs of not more than two pages is sufficient in the first instance. Visits are normally made to projects to be considered by the Trustees and therefore delays should be expected

CORRESPONDENT Bridget O'Brien Twohig, Administrator, J Paul Getty Jr Charitable Trust, 149 Harley Street, London W1N 2DH

CLASSIFICATIONS
- Children and youth – general
- Adoption/fostering
- Community groups
- Development of character
- Counselling (inc helplines)
- Homes and hostels

C.C. NO 292360   **ESTABLISHED** 1985

■ The Gibbins Trust

OBJECTS General charitable purposes

POLICY OF TRUSTEES Grants to organisations principally in the County of Sussex but also at national level, within England and Wales. Not overseas, international or foreign

TYPE OF BENEFICIARY Medicine and health in general including handicapped. Welfare in general including children and aged

RESTRICTIONS Time Charity. No grants to individuals

BENEFICIAL AREA Mainly Sussex but also England and Wales

FINANCES
- **Year** 1995
- **Grants** £54,235
- **Income** £43,279
- **Assets** £739,926

TRUSTEES R F Ash, R S Archer, P M Archer

CORRESPONDENT R F Ash, 5 East Pallant, Chichester, West Sussex PO19 1TS

CLASSIFICATIONS
- Children and youth – general
- Adoption/fostering
- Advancement in life
- Adventure centres and playgrounds
- Centres, clubs and institutes
- Community groups
- Day centres and nurseries
- Development of character
- Counselling (inc helplines)
- Holidays
- Homes and hostels
- Special needs housing
- Special classes
- Youth organisations (eg Guides, Scouts, YWCA etc)
- Children and violence (inc abuse)

C.C. NO 244632   **ESTABLISHED** 1965

■ The G C Gibson Charitable Trust

OBJECTS General charitable purposes

TYPE OF BENEFICIARY Registered charities only

RESTRICTIONS The Trust does not make grants to individuals

FINANCES
- **Year** 1992
- **Grants** £352,500
- **Income** £480,038
- **Assets** £4,392,607

TRUSTEES W D Gibson, G S C Gibson

CORRESPONDENT R D Taylor, Touche Ross and Co, Blenheim House, Fitzalan Court, Newport Road, Cardiff CF2 1TS

CLASSIFICATIONS
- Children and youth – general
- Adoption/fostering
- Centres, clubs and institutes
- Homes and hostels
- Special needs housing
- Youth organisations (eg Guides, Scouts, YWCA etc)

C.C. NO 258710   **ESTABLISHED** 1969

■ The Simon Gibson Charitable Trust

OBJECTS General charitable purposes

POLICY OF TRUSTEES Mainly UK charities. Most grants of £2,000

TYPE OF BENEFICIARY At Trustees' discretion

RESTRICTIONS Only give to registered charities. No individuals

BENEFICIAL AREA UK

FINANCES
- **Year** 1993
- **Grants** £227,000
- **Income** £224,650
- **Assets** £4,605,000

TRUSTEES B Marsh, Mrs A M Homfray, G D Gibson

CORRESPONDENT B Marsh, Hill House, 1 Little New Street, London EC4A 3TR

CLASSIFICATIONS
- Children and youth – general
- Adoption/fostering
- Advancement in life
- Adventure centres and playgrounds
- Centres, clubs and institutes
- Community groups
- Day centres and nurseries
- Development of character
- Holidays

- Homes and hostels
- Special needs housing
- Special classes
- Youth organisations (eg Guides, Scouts, YWCA etc)
- Children and violence (inc abuse)

C.C. NO 269501   **ESTABLISHED** 1975

■ The Hon Mr & Mrs Clive Gibson's Charity Trust

OBJECTS General charitable purposes

POLICY OF TRUSTEES Accent on children's and medical charities in the London area

TYPE OF GRANT Single grants

TYPE OF BENEFICIARY See Policy of Trustees, beneficiaries include the NSPCC London branch and young homeless housing projects

BENEFICIAL AREA London and Greater London

FINANCES
- Year 1994
- Grants £11,479
- Income £13,838
- Assets £80,000

TRUSTEES Hon Clive Gibson, Hon Mrs Clive Gibson

SUBMISSION OF APPLICATIONS To Correspondent

CORRESPONDENT The Hon Mr & Mrs Clive Gibson's Charity Trust, 27 St James' Place, London SW1A 1NR

CLASSIFICATIONS
- Children and youth – general
- Youth organisations (eg Guides, Scouts, YWCA etc)
- Children and violence (inc abuse)

C.C. NO 265768   **ESTABLISHED** 1973

■ The Hon H M T Gibson's Charity Trust

OBJECTS General charitable purposes

POLICY OF TRUSTEES No applications can be considered as funds are fully allocated

TYPE OF BENEFICIARY Registered charities only

RESTRICTIONS No applications from individuals will be considered. Registered charities only

BENEFICIAL AREA Great Britain, Northern Ireland and overseas

FINANCES
- Year 1992
- Grants £36,291
- Income £23,866
- Assets £328,604

TRUSTEES The Cowdray Trust Limited

SUBMISSION OF APPLICATIONS No applications can be considered as funds are fully allocated

CORRESPONDENT The Secretary, The Cowdray Trust Limited, Pollen House, 10–12 Cork Street, London W1X 1PD

CLASSIFICATIONS
- Children and youth – general
- Centres, clubs and institutes
- Day centres and nurseries
- Youth organisations (eg Guides, Scouts, YWCA etc)

C.C. NO 264327   **ESTABLISHED** 1972

■ The Hon P N Gibson's Charity Trust

OBJECTS General charitable purposes

POLICY OF TRUSTEES Applications for grants will only be acknowledged if a donation is to be sent

TYPE OF BENEFICIARY Registered charities only

RESTRICTIONS No applications from individuals will be considered. Registered charities only

BENEFICIAL AREA Great Britain and Northern Ireland

FINANCES
- Year 1992
- Grants £5,637
- Income £11,754
- Assets £168,187

TRUSTEES Cowdray Trust Limited

SUBMISSION OF APPLICATIONS Appeal letters should be sent to the correspondent

CORRESPONDENT The Secretary, The Cowdray Trust Limited, Pollen House, 10–12 Cork Street, London W1X 1PD

CLASSIFICATIONS
- Children and youth – general
- Centres, clubs and institutes
- Day centres and nurseries

C.C. NO 275510   **ESTABLISHED** 1977

■ The John Gilpin Trust

OBJECTS General charitable purposes

POLICY OF TRUSTEES Preference is given to charities carrying out work in the Cumbria and Merseyside areas

TYPE OF GRANT Both recurrent and one-off

TYPE OF BENEFICIARY Charities in Cumbria and Merseyside

RESTRICTIONS Unsolicited applications will usually not be considered as funds are normally committed to projects known to the trustees. The trustees regret that they are not able to reply to unsuccessful applications. No saes please. No applications are entertained from individuals

BENEFICIAL AREA Merseyside, Cumbria, Suffolk

SAMPLE GRANTS £500 to 12th Fairfield Scout Group, Liverpool

FINANCES
- Year 1992
- Grants £8,600
- Income £21,000
- Assets £350,000

TRUSTEES D J Gaffney, A T Powley

NOTES Assistance to Service and museum appeals are of interest

SUBMISSION OF APPLICATIONS Trustees will not normally consider unsolicited applications

CORRESPONDENT Cooper & Harrisson Solicitors, 1 Market Place, Southwold, Suffolk IP18 6DY

CLASSIFICATIONS
- Children and youth – general
- Adventure centres and playgrounds
- Centres, clubs and institutes
- Community groups
- Holidays
- Homes and hostels
- Youth organisations (eg Guides, Scouts, YWCA etc)

C.C. NO 276710   **ESTABLISHED** 1959

Gladstone

Alphabetical register of grant making charitable trusts

■ The E W Gladstone Charitable Trust

OBJECTS General charitable purposes

TYPE OF BENEFICIARY Registered charities

RESTRICTIONS Not individuals

BENEFICIAL AREA Mainly Flintshire and Kincardineshire

FINANCES
- Year 1995
- Grants £14,950
- Income £14,933

TRUSTEES Sir Erskine Gladstone, R A Gladstone

CORRESPONDENT Sir Erskine Gladstone, Hawarden Castle, Hawarden, Deeside, Clwyd CH5 3PB

CLASSIFICATIONS
- Youth organisations (eg Guides, Scouts, YWCA etc)

C.C. NO 260417   **ESTABLISHED** 1969

■ Glebe Charitable Trust

OBJECTS Education and provision of leisure facilities for disadvantaged young people

POLICY OF TRUSTEES The Trustees favour small underfunded projects over those charities with substantial assets and patronage however deserving

TYPE OF GRANT Preference for single one-off grants

TYPE OF BENEFICIARY Grant seeking charities and individual children and young people in need

RESTRICTIONS No school or hospital buildings and no research projects

BENEFICIAL AREA Principally national

FINANCES
- Year 1995
- Grants £20,000
- Income £26,000
- Assets £320,000

TRUSTEES Mrs H D Ewart, Mrs T C Webb, T K H Robertson

SUBMISSION OF APPLICATIONS Applications should be submitted one month before the Trustees' meetings in January and July each year. No application will be considered without annual accounts or appropriate financial information

CORRESPONDENT T K H Robertson, Manches & Co, Solicitors, Aldwych House, 81 Aldwych, London WC2 4RP

CLASSIFICATIONS
- Children and youth – general

C.C. NO 803495   **ESTABLISHED** 1989

■ The Penelope Gluckstein Charitable Settlement

OBJECTS General charitable purposes

POLICY OF TRUSTEES Mainly to assist children's charities

TYPE OF GRANT One-off donation. Virtually all donations are £100, a few are larger

TYPE OF BENEFICIARY Local or national offices of children's aid organisations

RESTRICTIONS Will definitely not fund individuals

SAMPLE GRANTS £100 to National Association of Toy Libraries
£100 to to UK Forum on Young People and Gambling
£100 to National Deaf Children's Society
£100 to Brainwave
£100 to Caring and Sharing Trust

FINANCES
- Year 1994
- Grants £12,000
- Income £12,000
- Assets £140,000

TRUSTEES P Gluckstein, R Gluckstein, S J Gluckstein

CORRESPONDENT R J Gluckstein, Highwood Ash, Highwood Hill, London NW7 4EX

CLASSIFICATIONS
- Children and youth – general
- Adventure centres and playgrounds
- Holidays
- Homes and hostels

C.C. NO 255282   **ESTABLISHED** 1968

■ The Glyn Charitable Trust

OBJECTS General charitable purposes in Great Britain

POLICY OF TRUSTEES To carry out the wishes of the Founders of the Trust to support certain specified charities

TYPE OF BENEFICIARY Registered charities only

RESTRICTIONS There will be no grants to individuals, only recognised charitable bodies

FINANCES
- Year 1993
- Grants £1,978
- Income £4,494

TRUSTEES The Royal Bank of Scotland plc

CORRESPONDENT The Royal Bank of Scotland plc, Private Trust & Taxation, PO Box 356, 45 Mosley Street, Manchester M60 2BE

CLASSIFICATIONS
- Children and youth – general

C.C. NO 245917   **ESTABLISHED** 1965

■ The Isaac Goldberg Charity Trust

OBJECTS General charitable purposes

TYPE OF GRANT Recurrent and one-off

TYPE OF BENEFICIARY Any requests considered but not those for personal benefit

RESTRICTIONS No grants to individuals

BENEFICIAL AREA UK

FINANCES
- Year 1995
- Grants £10,000
- Income £15,000
- Assets £85,000

TRUSTEES C Solomons, W Rose, D Goldberg, R Colover, Dr J MacRae

SUBMISSION OF APPLICATIONS To the correspondent prior to April of each year when Trustees meet

CORRESPONDENT C Solomons, 37 Chester Close North, Regents Park, London NW1 4JE

CLASSIFICATIONS
- Children and youth – general
- Adventure centres and playgrounds
- Day centres and nurseries
- Holidays

C.C. NO 801869   **ESTABLISHED** 1989

■ The Goldsmiths' Company's Charities

OBJECTS (a) General support of goldsmiths, silversmiths and jewellers, their trade, craft and dependants. (b) The support of London charities and of individual residents in the Greater London area. (c) General charitable purposes

POLICY OF TRUSTEES Reactive, but see Notes

TYPE OF GRANT One-off or once a year for three years

TYPE OF BENEFICIARY Charity Commission registered national (UK) or London charities; individuals connected with the trade of goldsmithing, silversmithing and jewellery; or Londoners in need

RESTRICTIONS See Type of Beneficiary and Notes

BENEFICIAL AREA UK national charities or Greater London

SAMPLE GRANTS £2,000 a year for three years to Stopover, Lewisham for the counselling programme
£2,000 to Oasis Children's Venture, Lambeth for equipment
£1,500 a year for three years to Balham and Tooting Youth Outreach Centre for core funding
£750 a year for three years to St Mary le Bow Church for the Young Single Homeless Project
£500 to Caxton House Settlement, Islington for summer playscheme

FINANCES
- Year 1994–95
- Grants £1,290,068
- Income £1,671,904

TRUSTEES The Worshipful Company of Goldsmiths

NOTES Appeals may be restricted to governing bodies or their nominated associate only. Applications from any organisation, successful or not, are considered not more frequently than once every three years. Overseas projects are not normally considered. Expeditions only funded through the Royal Geographical Society and for London colleges only. Student grants not normally considered. Students studying medicine as a second degree funded through the British Medical Association Trust. Only one application a year for Adventure Playgrounds in London considered, and that on a first-come, first-served basis. A block grant is made to the London Federation of Clubs for Young People and no appeals will be considered from individual youth clubs

SUBMISSION OF APPLICATIONS In writing to the Clerk, and to include: (a) Registered charity number; (b) Latest annual report and full audited accounts; (c) Names and addresses of two independent referees (for a first appeal only); (d) Aims and objectives of the appellant; (e) Oject of the appeal; (f) Appeal target and amount needed to meet it; (g) Major grant-giving organisations appealed to and results to date; (h) Preference for a single grant or for annual grants for up to three years; (i) Sum asked for and for what specific purpose

CORRESPONDENT The Clerk, The Goldsmiths' Company, Goldsmiths' Hall, Foster Lane, Cheapside, London EC2V 6BN

CLASSIFICATIONS
- Children and youth – general

C.C. NO 210513   **ESTABLISHED** 1961

■ The Good Neighbours Trust

OBJECTS Grants only to charitable bodies in the UK and for use in the UK in respect of the mentally and physically handicapped

POLICY OF TRUSTEES Principally in respect of specific projects for the relief of the mentally and physically handicapped. No grants to religious or environmental projects except for those aimed at benefitting the mentally and physically handicapped. No grants to individuals and in respect of overseas projects. No grants to general community projects

TYPE OF BENEFICIARY Registered charities only

RESTRICTIONS Registered charities only

BENEFICIAL AREA Great Britain and Northern Ireland, Local

FINANCES
- Year 1994
- Grants £95,700
- Income £82,319
- Assets £1,667,097

TRUSTEES K G Long (Chairman), G V Arter, R J Laver, DPA, R T Sheppard

SUBMISSION OF APPLICATIONS By letter with accounts and support information

CORRESPONDENT Peter S Broderick, Secretary, 16 Westway, Nailsea, Bristol BS19 1EE

CLASSIFICATIONS
- Adventure centres and playgrounds
- Centres, clubs and institutes
- Holidays

C.C. NO 201794   **ESTABLISHED** 1960

■ The Everard and Mina Goodman Charitable Foundation

OBJECTS General charitable purposes

POLICY OF TRUSTEES The relief of poverty; the advancement of education; the advancement of religion; attention to needs of children and youth; medicine; health; rehabilitation and training

TYPE OF BENEFICIARY Welfare organisations, children and youth, religion, medicine and health, rehabilitation and training

RESTRICTIONS It is not the policy of the Trustees to make grants to individuals

FINANCES
- Year 1995
- Grants £73,095
- Income £18,643
- Assets £75,953

TRUSTEES E N Goodman, FCA, M Goodman, M P Goodman, S J Goodman

CORRESPONDENT E N Goodman, FCA, 5 Bryanston Court, George Street, London W1H 7HA

CLASSIFICATIONS
- Advancement in life

C.C. NO 220474   **ESTABLISHED** 1962

Goodman

■ The Goodman Trust

OBJECTS Promotion, support and advancement of charitable purposes of all kinds and in particular the advancement of education and religion, the preservation and protection of health and the environment

POLICY OF TRUSTEES The Trust is introduced to charitable organisations, principally Norfolk based charities and local branches of National charities, by employees of the Florida Group Ltd

TYPE OF GRANT Normally single payments of a capital nature

RESTRICTIONS It is the Trustees' policy not to make grants to individuals to cover course fees or living expenses

BENEFICIAL AREA Mainly Norfolk

FINANCES
- Year 1991
- Grants £2,855
- Income £24,235
- Assets £56,002

TRUSTEES S J Goodman, M T Martin, B D Saull

SUBMISSION OF APPLICATIONS May and November each year

CORRESPONDENT S J Goodman, Florida Group Ltd, Dibden Road, Norwich NR3 4RR

CLASSIFICATIONS
- Youth organisations (eg Guides, Scouts, YWCA etc)

C.C. NO 298583 **ESTABLISHED** 1987

■ The S & F Goodman Trust

OBJECTS Charitable work carried on anywhere in the world by or under the direction of any person or persons or any school, hospital, clinic, home, hostel or other organisation or institution for the care, maintenance, education, welfare of persons (children and adults) suffering from any physical or mental disability, handicap or disorder

POLICY OF TRUSTEES Preference to charities of which the Trustees have special interest, knowledge or association; the Trustees respond to applications

RESTRICTIONS No grants to individuals

FINANCES
- Year 1994
- Grants £46,050
- Income £38,532
- Assets £469,436

TRUSTEES C Goodman, Mrs D Talalay

CORRESPONDENT C Goodman, 42 Shirehall Lane, London NW4 2PS

CLASSIFICATIONS
- Children and youth – general

C.C. NO 260908 **ESTABLISHED** 1969

■ The Gough Charitable Trust

OBJECTS General charitable purposes

POLICY OF TRUSTEES Youth projects; Episcopal or Church of England projects; preservation of countryside. Applications considered on merit

TYPE OF GRANT Usually one-off but some ongoing

TYPE OF BENEFICIARY Registered charities usually working in areas outlined under Policy selected by Settlor and Trustees

RESTRICTIONS Registered charities only. Applications from individuals, including students, are ineligible

BENEFICIAL AREA Preference for Scotland

FINANCES
- Year 1994
- Grants £3,785
- Income £28,900
- Assets £702,362

TRUSTEES Lloyds Bank plc, Nigel Guy de Laval Harvie

SUBMISSION OF APPLICATIONS At any time. Awards are considered quarterly. No application forms provided. No acknowledgements sent

CORRESPONDENT Mrs E D Osborn-King, Thames Valley Area Office, The Clock House, 22–26 Ock Street, Abingdon, Oxfordshire OX14 5SW

CLASSIFICATIONS
- Children and youth – general

C.C. NO 262355 **ESTABLISHED** 1961

■ The Mrs D M Graham Charity

OBJECTS General charitable purposes

POLICY OF TRUSTEES Generally donations given to 7 or 10 organisations each year

TYPE OF GRANT One-off

TYPE OF BENEFICIARY Mainly HQ organisations but occasionally some local

RESTRICTIONS No grants to individuals

BENEFICIAL AREA West Midlands

FINANCES
- Year 1994
- Grants £19,000
- Income £6,229
- Assets £94,808

TRUSTEES R A Crowdy, M Williams, Mrs A Dunford

SUBMISSION OF APPLICATIONS No specific forms. Reviewed June/July each year

CORRESPONDENT c/o Messrs Bloomer Heaven, 33 Lionel Street, Birmingham B3 1AB

CLASSIFICATIONS
- Children and youth – general

C.C. NO 278848 **ESTABLISHED** 1978

■ The Grand Metropolitan Charitable Trust

OBJECTS The Trust's focus is upon supporting UK charitable organisations that are principally concerned with helping individuals, particularly young people, to achieve self-sufficiency and priority is given to charities associated with the Group's trades and businesses

POLICY OF TRUSTEES Preference given to requests supported by group operating companies

BENEFICIAL AREA UK

FINANCES
- Year 1995
- Grants £1,050,000
- Income £1,085,000

TRUSTEES D E Tagg, G T Bush, T J Coleman, A G Eadie, C D Hitchcock

SUBMISSION OF APPLICATIONS In writing to T J Coleman, Trustee

CORRESPONDENT T J Coleman, Grand Metropolitan Charitable Trust, 64–65 North Road, Brighton, East Sussex BN1 1YD

CLASSIFICATIONS
- Children and youth – general
- Advancement in life
- Development of character
- Youth organisations (eg Guides, Scouts, YWCA etc)

C.C. NO 283129   **ESTABLISHED** 1981

■ Grange Farm Centre Trust

OBJECTS The provision or the assistance in the provision of facilities for recreation and leisure-time occupation of the inhabitants of the area of benefit and the public generally

POLICY OF TRUSTEES Achievements of the objectives of the Trust – preference given to youth, the aged and the disadvantaged

TYPE OF GRANT Donations out of income of charity only and normally for single specific projects

TYPE OF BENEFICIARY Mainly registered charities or organisations known to the Trustees

RESTRICTIONS No general purposes grants. No grants to private clubs or individuals

BENEFICIAL AREA London metropolitan police district and the Epping Forest district council area

FINANCES
- Year 1992   • Assets £1,250,000

TRUSTEES A T J Bryant (Chairman), B H Gunby, R J Pocock, B M Cox, A Pelican, R C O'Malley, A T Twynham

SUBMISSION OF APPLICATIONS To correspondent for consideration at Trustees meetings in September and March, accompanied by latest report and accounts and description and cost of project

CORRESPONDENT N E Gadsby, Clerk to the Trust, Foskett Marr Gadsby & Head, 181 High Street, Epping, Essex CM16 4BQ

CLASSIFICATIONS
- Children and youth – general

C.C. NO 285162   **ESTABLISHED** 1984

■ J G Graves Charitable Trust

OBJECTS Provision of parks and open spaces, libraries and art galleries – advancement of education – general benefit of sick and poor – such other charitable purposes as the Trustees see fit

POLICY OF TRUSTEES It is not the practice of the Trustees to make grants for the benefit of individuals. The income is mainly applied to local (Sheffield) charities for capital purposes rather than running costs

TYPE OF GRANT See Policy of Trustees

TYPE OF BENEFICIARY Charities who have similar objectives

RESTRICTIONS See Policy of Trustees

BENEFICIAL AREA Mainly Sheffield

FINANCES
- Year 1994   • Income £132,672
- Grants £67,775   • Assets £1,757,702

TRUSTEES G Young, CBE, JP, LLD, Mrs A C Womack, G W Bridge, R S Sanderson, FCA, Mrs A H Tonge, T H Reed, R T Graves, Mrs D E Hoyland, JP, S McK Hamilton, D S W Lee, Councillor P Price

NOTES 76 grants made in 1994

SUBMISSION OF APPLICATIONS In writing to reach Secretary by March 31st, June 30th, September 30th, December 31st

CORRESPONDENT R H M Plews, FCA, Secretary, J G Graves Charitable Trust, Knowle House, 4 Norfolk Park Road, Sheffield S2 3QE

CLASSIFICATIONS
- Children and youth – general

C.C. NO 207481   **ESTABLISHED** 1930

■ The Gordon Gray Trust

OBJECTS General charitable purposes

POLICY OF TRUSTEES Consideration is given to the support of national and local charities at the discretion of the Trustees

TYPE OF BENEFICIARY Concerns showing a sympathetic and up-to-date approach to youth problems with minimal administration costs

RESTRICTIONS The Trust does not support appeals on behalf of individuals

FINANCES
- Year 1994–95   • Income £33,391
- Grants £12,000   • Assets £286,830

TRUSTEES G Gray, Dr B Gray, J Urry, M M Gray

CORRESPONDENT The Clerk to the Trustees, The Gordon Gray Trust, Grange Farm, Bredon, Nr Tewkesbury, Gloucestershire

CLASSIFICATIONS
- Children and youth – general

C.C. NO 213935   **ESTABLISHED** 1960

■ Greater Bristol Foundation

OBJECTS General charitable purposes with a particular emphasis on projects focusing on youth, disablement, isolation and homelessness and safer community environment

POLICY OF TRUSTEES To fund projects of direct benefit to the community

TYPE OF GRANT General grant up to £6,000. Small grants up to £500 in emergency or start-up situations

TYPE OF BENEFICIARY Any charity aimed at increasing opportunities and enhancing the quality of life in the area, particularly smaller, low profile community groups and those at a particular disadvantage through discrimination

RESTRICTIONS Individuals will not be given grants

BENEFICIAL AREA Greater Bristol (a ten mile radius of the City centre)

FINANCES
- Year 1994   • Income £211,258
- Grants £114,421   • Assets £2,055,522

TRUSTEES J Burke, (Chairman), J Avery, A Brown, D Claisse, Stella Clark JP, C Curling, G Ferguson, Marion Jackson, D Kenworthy, Lady Merrison, D S Norton FCA, J Pontin, H Pye, A Thornhill, QC, The Right Rev B Rogerson, Bishop of Bristol, J Tidmarsh, MBE, JP, D Wood

Green

Alphabetical register of grant making charitable trusts

PUBLICATIONS Annual Report, two newsletters per year

SUBMISSION OF APPLICATIONS Application forms and guidelines on request. Applications considered in January, April, July, October; applicants will be informed of deadlines. An initial telephone enquiry recommended and welcome

CORRESPONDENT Penny Johnstone, Director, Greater Bristol Foundation, Bank of England Chambers, Wine Street, Bristol BS1 2AH

CLASSIFICATIONS
- Children and youth – general
- Adventure centres and playgrounds
- Centres, clubs and institutes
- Community groups
- Development of character
- Special needs housing
- Special classes

C.C. NO 295797   **ESTABLISHED** 1987

■ The Charles Green Foundation

OBJECTS General charitable purposes – communal benefit – relief of poverty – advancement of religion and education

POLICY OF TRUSTEES To support those charities of which the Trustees have special interest, knowledge or association

TYPE OF GRANT Cheque donations

TYPE OF BENEFICIARY Registered charities only, no individuals

RESTRICTIONS No grants to individuals or non-registered charities

BENEFICIAL AREA UK and overseas

SAMPLE GRANTS £100 to the Project Trust
£70 to the Manchester Maccabi JLB Club
£26 to the Youth and Community Trust
£26 to the Macclesfield Boys' Club
£10 to the National Council of YMCAs

FINANCES
- Year 1995
- Grants £4,163
- Income £4,437
- Assets £68,617

TRUSTEES Mrs R Green, G C Wardle, FCA

CORRESPONDENT The Trustees, The Charles Green Foundation, Hilton Chambers, 15 Hilton Street, Manchester, Greater Manchester M1 1JL

CLASSIFICATIONS
- Children and youth – general

C.C. NO 207368   **ESTABLISHED** 1962

■ Constance Green Foundation

OBJECTS General charitable purposes

POLICY OF TRUSTEES Some preference is given to Yorkshire charities. In previous years grants have been made mainly, but not exclusively, to national organisations in the fields of medicine and social welfare, with special emphasis on support of young people in need and both mentally and physically disabled persons

TYPE OF GRANT One-off

TYPE OF BENEFICIARY Community-based

RESTRICTIONS Trustee will not respond to individuals (including students)

BENEFICIAL AREA Not restricted

SAMPLE GRANTS £30,000 to Childline Yorkshire Tyne Tees Project
£5,000 to Cystic Fibrosis Holiday Fund for Children
£5,000 to Whizz Kidz for Non-mobile Children
£4,000 to Raleigh International's Youth Development Programme for Young People at Risk in Yorkshire
£2,000 to Surrey Association of Youth Clubs and Surrey PHAB
£1,000 to Huddersfield Scout Sailing

FINANCES
- Year 1995
- Grants £364,000
- Income £306,000
- Assets £5,572,000

TRUSTEES M Collinson MA (Cantab), Col H R Hall, OBE, TD, DL, N Hall, A G Collinson

NOTES Grants can only be made to trusts, associations, institutions, and organisations recognised as charitable by the laws of England

CORRESPONDENT M Collinson, Corner Cottage, 1 Trimmingham Lane, Halifax, West Yorkshire HX2 7PT

CLASSIFICATIONS
- Adventure centres and playgrounds
- Holidays
- Youth organisations (eg Guides, Scouts, YWCA etc)

C.C. NO 270775   **ESTABLISHED** 1976

■ The D W Greenwood Charitable Settlement

OBJECTS General charitable purposes

POLICY OF TRUSTEES Grants are made within the guidelines of the Charity Commission

TYPE OF GRANT One-off and short term. Recurrent up to five years

TYPE OF BENEFICIARY General

RESTRICTIONS No grants made to individual students. No foreign grants are made; community/church projects limited to Leeds and Bradford area

FINANCES
- Year 1990
- Grants £35,419
- Income £39,968
- Assets £103,368

TRUSTEES S C Rawson, J A J Hanson

NOTES All applications in writing, apart from those stated in Restrictions, are considered by the Trustees

SUBMISSION OF APPLICATIONS Apply to the Trustees at address below in writing only

CORRESPONDENT S C Rawson, East End, Norwood, Harrogate, North Yorkshire HG3 1TA

CLASSIFICATIONS
- Children and youth – general
- Development of character
- Holidays
- Homes and hostels
- Youth organisations (eg Guides, Scouts, YWCA etc)

C.C. NO 274705   **ESTABLISHED** 1977

■ Naomi & Jeffrey Greenwood Charitable Trust

OBJECTS General charitable purposes

POLICY OF TRUSTEES Trustees favour mainly Jewish charities

TYPE OF BENEFICIARY Registered charities

FINANCES
- Year 1993
- Income £26,000

TRUSTEES J M Greenwood, Mrs N Greenwood

CORRESPONDENT J M Greenwood, 50 Stratton Street, London W1X 5FL

CLASSIFICATIONS
- Counselling (inc helplines)

C.C. NO 275633   **ESTABLISHED** 1978

■ The Gresham Charitable Trust

OBJECTS General charitable purposes including charities as scheduled in Deed of Settlement

POLICY OF TRUSTEES To apportion income amongst charities named in Deed of Settlement and/or similar registered (or otherwise officially recognised) charities

TYPE OF GRANT Capital and/or revenue support

TYPE OF BENEFICIARY Established trusts

RESTRICTIONS Grants made to registered (or otherwise officially recognised) charities only

BENEFICIAL AREA UK

SAMPLE GRANTS £2,700 to Barnardos
£2,700 to National Childrens Home
£2,700 to NSPCC
£2,700 to Save the Children
£2,700 to Scope

FINANCES
- Year 1995
- Income £115,116
- Grants £112,900
- Assets £240,793

TRUSTEES R Taylor, FCA, P S Vaines, FCA

CORRESPONDENT Brebner, Allen & Trapp, Chartered Accountants, The Quadrangle, 180 Wardour Street, London W1E 6JZ

CLASSIFICATIONS
- Children and youth – general

C.C. NO 257036   **ESTABLISHED** 1965

■ Grocers' Charity

OBJECTS General charitable purposes, with particular emphasis on the improvement of the quality of life

POLICY OF TRUSTEES Within broad aims which are reflected in the wide pattern of grants, the Trustees currently have a special interest in the relief of poverty (including youth) and the disabled

TYPE OF BENEFICIARY Registered charities working in the areas outlined under 'Policy'

RESTRICTIONS Registered charities only. Applications from individuals (including students), expeditions, hospices and research projects are ineligible. Support for churches and independent schools is restricted to those having specific close and long standing connections with The Grocers' Company

BENEFICIAL AREA UK

SAMPLE GRANTS £1,000 to Raleigh International for the Youth Development Programme which enables disadvantaged young people to participate in expeditions
£250 to Adventure Unlimited. This Brighton-based charity works with disadvantaged young people in the Sussex area. It creates opportunities and provides encouragement through a series of activity programmes. The grant was for equipment
£250 to Neighbours in Poplar. This organisation works in the East End of London. The grant was made towards the provision of summer outings and activities orangised for local young people

FINANCES
- Year 1994/5
- Income £264,000
- Grants £221,000
- Assets £5,100,000

TRUSTEES The Grocers' Trust Company Ltd

SUBMISSION OF APPLICATIONS In writing to the Correspondent. Trustees meet four times a year in January, April, June and November.

CORRESPONDENT Miss Anne Blanchard, Charity Administrator, Grocers' Charity, Grocers' Hall, Princes Street, London EC2R 8AD

CLASSIFICATIONS
- Children and youth – general
- Advancement in life
- Centres, clubs and institutes
- Holidays
- Homes and hostels
- Special needs housing

C.C. NO 255230   **ESTABLISHED** 1968

■ The Guardian Royal Exchange Charitable Trust

OBJECTS General charitable purposes

POLICY OF TRUSTEES Each application on its merits but to people rather than animals or buildings

TYPE OF GRANT One-off or recurrent

TYPE OF BENEFICIARY Medical, welfare, arts, environmental

RESTRICTIONS Registered and established charities only, local charities only considered if GRE have a major presence in the local area. Individuals including students are ineligible

BENEFICIAL AREA UK

FINANCES
- Year 1995
- Income £226,096
- Grants £225,537

TRUSTEES The Hon G E Adeane, CVO, J M Menzies, J Sinclair, J R W Clayton

SUBMISSION OF APPLICATIONS By post. Reviewed continuously. Include latest accounts

CORRESPONDENT A Wilkins Esq, Appeals Secretary, Guardian Royal Exchange Assurance plc, Royal Exchange, London EC3V 3LS

CLASSIFICATIONS
- Children and youth – general
- Advancement in life
- Centres, clubs and institutes
- Development of character

Gunnell

- Homes and hostels
- Youth organisations (eg Guides, Scouts, YWCA etc)
- Children and violence (inc abuse)

C.C. NO 326003 **ESTABLISHED** 1981

■ The Gunnell Charitable Trust

OBJECTS General charitable objects at discretion of Trustees

POLICY OF TRUSTEES Grants relating to needs of (a) children (b) handicapped people

TYPE OF GRANT Excluding starter finances. Each grant considered annually on its own merit

TYPE OF BENEFICIARY Preference for established United Kingdom charitable objects

RESTRICTIONS Grants to individuals not considered

BENEFICIAL AREA UK

FINANCES
- **Year** 1995
- **Grants** £7,300
- **Income** £6,377
- **Assets** £113,000

TRUSTEES Mrs D J Tribe, Mrs A M Shawcross

SUBMISSION OF APPLICATIONS Grant allocations made annually in July/August; only written applications considered, but not acknowledged

CORRESPONDENT Mrs D J Tribe, Old Barn, Kingwood Common, Henley-on-Thames, Oxon RG9 5NS

CLASSIFICATIONS
- Adoption/fostering
- Youth organisations (eg Guides, Scouts, YWCA etc)

C.C. NO 271529 **ESTABLISHED** 1976

■ The Gunter Charitable Trust

OBJECTS General charitable purposes

POLICY OF TRUSTEES To support organisations known to the Trust

TYPE OF BENEFICIARY All types considered

FINANCES
- **Year** 1994
- **Grants** £57,114
- **Income** £55,338
- **Assets** £1,023,589

TRUSTEES J de C E Findlay, H R D Billson

CORRESPONDENT H R D Billson, 28 Lincoln's Inn Fields, London WC2A 3HH

CLASSIFICATIONS
- Counselling (inc helplines)

C.C. NO 268346 **ESTABLISHED** 1974

■ Gwynedd County Council Welsh Church Fund

OBJECTS General charitable purposes

POLICY OF TRUSTEES Applications which are of direct benefit to the County and inhabitants of Gwynedd only considered

TYPE OF BENEFICIARY Local organisations, local branches of national organisations, or specific local projects run by national organisations

RESTRICTIONS (a) Personal applications are not entertained. (b) Only registered charities can receive financial assistance

BENEFICIAL AREA The County of Gwynedd

FINANCES
- **Year** 1995
- **Grants** £71,590
- **Income** £72,546
- **Assets** £942,275

TRUSTEES Gwynedd County Council

CORRESPONDENT County Secretary, Gwynedd County Council, County Offices, Caernarfon, Gwynedd LL55 1SH

CLASSIFICATIONS
- Children and youth – general

C.C. NO 221004 **ESTABLISHED** 1974

■ HACT (The Housing Associations Charitable Trust)

OBJECTS The Housing Associations Charitable Trust (HACT) is a specialist grantmaking charity working throughout the UK to support voluntary housing organisations. HACT aims to help these organisations to provide good quality housing and related services for: (a) single homeless people with support needs (b) people with special needs (c) refugee led groups (d) black and minority ethnic communities (e) older people. HACT achieves these aims by: (a) providing grants and loans (b) giving fundraising information and advice (c) promoting housing issues to other charitable donors (d) assisting other charitable donors with ways in which they can fund housing projects most effectively

POLICY OF TRUSTEES Grants or loans will be considered for organisations helping meet the housing needs of disabled people, people with learning difficulties, people with mental health problems, people with drug or alcohol problems, people who have been in prison or are at risk of offending, people with HIV or AIDS, and young single homeless people with support needs

TYPE OF GRANT To meet 'setting up costs' of new organisations, training grants, development worker costs, work to promote good practice, loans towards capital costs

TYPE OF BENEFICIARY Voluntary organisations meeting the housing or housing related needs of groups listed above and also targeting one of the following: (a) user participation (b) rural areas (c) people with mental health problems, black, minority ethnic or refugee communities or women with additional needs

RESTRICTIONS HACT will not generally fund projects which are eligible for statutory funding and does not consider requests for on-going revenue funding or consider applications from individuals.

BENEFICIAL AREA UK

SAMPLE GRANTS £10,000 to OSCAR, London to fund supported housing for young people with Sickle Cell Disease
£5,000 to Good Practice in Mental Health, UK-wide to promote good practice in development of services for young homeless people with mental health problems
£4,000 to St Helen's Accommodation Project, North West for a worker to develop accommodation and support for young homeless women

FINANCES
- Year 1995
- Grants £1,116,369
- Income £1,212,675
- Assets £2,859,599

TRUSTEES Twenty Trustees appointed by The Council of The National Federation of Housing Associations

PUBLICATIONS Annual Review and Accounts, bi-annual newsletter

SUBMISSION OF APPLICATIONS Please call Ginny Castle, Special Needs Housing Adviser on 0171 336 7877 to discuss any possible application. Applications can only be made on HACT's application form

CORRESPONDENT Vivien Knibbs, Director, HACT, Yeoman House, 168–172 Old Street, London EC1V 9BP

CLASSIFICATIONS
- Homes and hostels
- Special needs housing

C.C. NO 256160   ESTABLISHED 1960

■ The Hadrian Trust

OBJECTS General charitable purposes

POLICY OF TRUSTEES To help social welfare and environmental organisations within the boundaries of the old counties of Northumberland and Durham (this includes Tyne and Wear). The main heading under which applications are considered are: social welfare, youth, women, the elderly, the disabled, ethnic minorities, the arts, the environment, education and churches

TYPE OF GRANT Usually one-off. Average grant is £1,000

TYPE OF BENEFICIARY Typical grants in 1991 were to: councils for voluntary service, advice projects, women's projects, youth clubs and schools, counselling services, charities for disabled, church restoration appeals

RESTRICTIONS General applications from large national organisations are not considered nor from smaller bodies working outside the beneficial area. Applications from individuals are considered if the circumstances are exceptional and the applicant resides or is working within the beneficial area. Grants to individuals are usually made through a social service or welfare organisation

BENEFICIAL AREA Northumberland, Tyne and Wear, Durham and Cleveland (North of the Tees)

SAMPLE GRANTS £1,000 to Youth Clubs Association
£1,000 to Detached Youth Project

FINANCES
- Year 1995
- Grants £169,740
- Income £191,051
- Assets £2,395,336

TRUSTEES P R M Harbottle, B J Gillespie, J B Parker

CORRESPONDENT John Parker, 36 Rectory Road, Gosforth, Newcastle upon Tyne NE3 1XP

CLASSIFICATIONS
- Centres, clubs and institutes
- Community groups
- Day centres and nurseries
- Development of character
- Counselling (inc helplines)
- Special needs housing
- Youth organisations (eg Guides, Scouts, YWCA etc)

C.C. NO 272161   ESTABLISHED 1976

Hall

■ E F & M G Hall Charitable Trust

OBJECTS General charitable purposes

POLICY OF TRUSTEES Annual and occasional donations

TYPE OF BENEFICIARY Children's and old people's charities, disabled, medical, church and others

RESTRICTIONS No grants to individuals

FINANCES
- Year 1992
- Grants £15,000
- Income £17,000
- Assets £400,000

TRUSTEES E F Hall, Mrs M G Hall, P E Webster

CORRESPONDENT E Finden Hall, Holmsley House, Holtye Common, Cowden, Edenbridge, Kent TN8 7ED

CLASSIFICATIONS
- Holidays

C.C. NO 256453   **ESTABLISHED** 1968

■ The Hame Trust

OBJECTS General charitable purposes

POLICY OF TRUSTEES To support Christian motivated charities

TYPE OF BENEFICIARY Mainly Evangelical Christian Missions

SAMPLE GRANTS £1,300 to Crusader Union
£800 to Scripture Union
£200 to Haslemere Crusader
£200 to Project Trust
£100 to King's World Trust for Children

FINANCES
- Year 1995
- Grants £8,430
- Income £8,350
- Assets £39,957

TRUSTEES Mrs M I E Rogers, N H Rogers, P D Warren

SUBMISSION OF APPLICATIONS Applications are not invited as funds are fully committed

CORRESPONDENT Mr & Mrs N H Rogers, Kingsley Edge, Kingsley Green, Haslemere, Surrey GU27 3LR

CLASSIFICATIONS
- Youth organisations (eg Guides, Scouts, YWCA etc)

C.C. NO 261070   **ESTABLISHED** 1970

■ Hampstead Wells and Campden Trust

OBJECTS To relieve in cases of need persons who are sick, convalescent, disabled, handicapped or infirm; to relieve either generally or individually persons in conditions of need, hardship or distress; to assist institutions providing services or facilities which afford relief of need or distress

POLICY OF TRUSTEES The Trustees consider all bona fide applications but do not enter into any commitments to repeat or renew any particular grant. (Once recurrent grants have been awarded they are in practice normally continued)

TYPE OF GRANT Mainly once-off to individuals and organisations; but recurrent grants of small amounts are made to elderly and handicapped people

TYPE OF BENEFICIARY Organisations and institutions in Hampstead and Camden, as well as individuals

RESTRICTIONS Grants may not be made towards the payment of rates or taxes, or in principle, where statutory agencies have the liability to help. Any recurrent grants made to elderly or disabled people are kept within amounts which do not affect their entitlement to social security benefits

BENEFICIAL AREA The former Metropolitan Borough of Hampstead, now situated within the London Borough of Camden. Organisations in Camden with beneficiaries in Hampstead are considered

FINANCES
- Year 1994–95
- Grants £571,439
- Income £675,844
- Assets £10,140,274

TRUSTEES Fourteen Co-optative Trustees appointed for five years, five Nominative Trustees appointed by the London Borough of Camden for four years, the Vicar of Hampstead, ex-officio

PUBLICATIONS Annual Accounts & Report, explanatory leaflet

NOTES About 1,000 grants were made in the period concerned. The basic policy of the Trustees is to respond to need, within the restrictions outlined above, as and when it is brought to their attention

SUBMISSION OF APPLICATIONS No restriction as to dates. Most applications received through statutory or voluntary social service organisations. Some investigations are carried out by the Trusts's own part-time social worker

CORRESPONDENT Mrs Sheila A Taylor, Director & Clerk to the Trustees, 62 Rosslyn Hill, London NW3 1ND

CLASSIFICATIONS
- Adventure centres and playgrounds
- Centres, clubs and institutes
- Community groups
- Day centres and nurseries
- Holidays

C.C. NO 208787   **ESTABLISHED** 1971

■ Hampton Fuel Allotment Charity

OBJECTS The relief in need and relief in sickness of persons resident in the area of benefit; the advancement of education of children and young persons resident in the said area and in the interests of social welfare, the provision of recreation facilities for the inhabitants of the area

BENEFICIAL AREA The ancient town of Hampton, the former Borough of Twickenham, the Borough of Richmond-upon-Thames

FINANCES
- Year 1995
- Grants £1,278,912
- Income £1,653,968
- Assets £29,239,228

TRUSTEES J A Webb, Cllr Mrs M J M Woodriff, A G Cavan, A H Wood, J M Stone, H E Severn, Dr D Lister, Mrs M T Martin, P W Simon, A D Smith, Rev W D Vanstone

CORRESPONDENT A Goode, Clerk to the Trustees, 15 Hurst Mount, High Street, Hampton, Middlesex TW12 2SA

CLASSIFICATIONS
- Children and youth – general
- Special classes

C.C. NO 211756   **ESTABLISHED** 1811

■ Handicapped Children's Aid Committee

OBJECTS To assist organisations concerned with handicapped or underprivileged children (or any other suitable charity) irrespective of colour, race or creed

POLICY OF TRUSTEES To assist handicapped children by means of equipment and services

TYPE OF BENEFICIARY Individual children, families, hospitals. Individual up to a maximum of £2,000

RESTRICTIONS No bequests of money are made

FINANCES
- Year 1995
- Grants £221,050
- Income £201,132
- Assets £300,000

TRUSTEES The Committee

CORRESPONDENT Mrs B Erndon, 11 Fairholme Gardens, Finchley, London N3 3ZD

CLASSIFICATIONS
- Children and youth – general
- Homes and hostels
- Special needs housing

C.C. NO 200050   **ESTABLISHED** 1961

■ The Kenneth Hargreaves Trust

OBJECTS See classification

POLICY OF TRUSTEES Currently the main areas of interest are medical research, education, environmental resources, arts and community projects, particularly organisations in which people help voluntarily

TYPE OF BENEFICIARY Registered charities working in the areas outlined under 'policy'

RESTRICTIONS Registered charities only. Applications from individuals are ineligible

BENEFICIAL AREA Great Britain, but preference given to local charities

FINANCES
- Year 1994
- Grants £30,000
- Income £35,000
- Assets £500,000

TRUSTEES Dr Ingrid Roscoe, Mrs Sheila Holbrook, P Chadwick, Mrs Margret Hargreaves-Allen

PUBLICATIONS Annual report

CORRESPONDENT Mrs Sheila Holbrook, (Hon Treasurer), Bridge End Cottage, Linton, Wetherby, West Yorkshire LS22 4JB

CLASSIFICATIONS
- Community groups
- Development of character

C.C. NO 223800   **ESTABLISHED** 1957

■ R J Harris Charitable Settlement

OBJECTS General charitable purposes

POLICY OF TRUSTEES To make grants of a general charitable nature to registered charities or for charitable purposes in the UK as the Trustees in their discretion think fit

TYPE OF BENEFICIARY Local organisations within beneficial area given precedence

BENEFICIAL AREA precedence to West Wilts, Avon, North Somerset, and South Gloucestershire areas

FINANCES
- Year 1993
- Grants £139,262
- Income £67,625
- Assets £1,057,622

TRUSTEES T C M Stock, H M Newton-Clare, J L Rogers, A Pitt

CORRESPONDENT J Thring, Messrs Thrings and Long, Solicitors, Midland Bridge Road, Bath, Avon BA1 2HQ

CLASSIFICATIONS
- Community groups
- Youth organisations (eg Guides, Scouts, YWCA etc)

C.C. NO 258973   **ESTABLISHED** 1969

■ The Philip & Pauline Harris Charitable Trust (formerly Settlement)

OBJECTS General charitable purposes

TYPE OF BENEFICIARY Registered charities only, main interests medical research and education

FINANCES
- Year 1994
- Grants £348,604
- Income £27,633
- Assets £1,352,430

TRUSTEES Lord Harris of Peckham, M P S Barton, H R Sykes

SUBMISSION OF APPLICATIONS Funds are fuly committed and the Trust is unable to respond to further appeals

CORRESPONDENT D G Bompas, CMG, Managing Executive, 187–189 Sevenoaks Way, Orpington, Kent BR5 3AQ

CLASSIFICATIONS
- Children and youth – general
- Development of character

C.C. NO 283735   **ESTABLISHED** 1981

■ The Harris Charity

OBJECTS Young persons charitable purposes, under 25

TYPE OF GRANT Prefer capital projects and provision of equipment

TYPE OF BENEFICIARY Prefer local applications

BENEFICIAL AREA Lancashire preference to Preston area

FINANCES
- Year 1994
- Grants £96,305
- Income £105,306
- Assets £1,856,785

TRUSTEES Mrs C Marshall, Mrs S Jackson, W S Huck, E J Booth, J Cotterall, T W S Croft, E C Dickson, S R Fisher, Mrs A Scott, Mrs R Jolly, S Huck, S B R Smith

SUBMISSION OF APPLICATIONS Half yearly by 30th September and 31st March

CORRESPONDENT P R Metcalf, FCA, Richard House, 9 Winckley Square, Preston, Lancashire PR1 3HP

CLASSIFICATIONS
- Children and youth – general

C.C. NO 526206   **ESTABLISHED** 1883

Harrisons

Alphabetical register of grant making charitable trusts

■ Harrisons & Crosfield Charitable Fund

OBJECTS General charitable purposes

POLICY OF TRUSTEES To support charities assisting disadvantaged people

TYPE OF GRANT Mostly one-off or recurrent for up to four years and some annual donations

TYPE OF BENEFICIARY Headquarters of organisations

RESTRICTIONS Applications are not invited from charities and are not considered from individuals. Requests for advertising in souvenir brochures are never considered. Telephone or written requests from professional fund raisers are discouraged

BENEFICIAL AREA UK

SAMPLE GRANTS £2,500 annually over four years to Princes Youth Business Trust
£1,000 to Rural and Urban Training Scheme
£500 annually over four years to Suffolk Clubs for Young People
£500 annually over four years to Streatham Youth Centre
£500 annually over four years to Royal Philanthropic Society
£500 annually over four years to Boys' and Girls' Clubs of Scotland

FINANCES
- Year 1993
- Grants £95,507

TRUSTEES G W Paul, W J Turcan, P D Brown

NOTES Our existing list is constantly under review and rather than add new charities we are more inclined to increase the donations to those already listed. During the last few years we have added some local charities

CORRESPONDENT The Secretary, H & C Charitable Fund, One Great Tower Street, London EC3R 5AH

CLASSIFICATIONS
- Youth organisations (eg Guides, Scouts, YWCA etc)

C.C. NO 277899   **ESTABLISHED** 1979

■ Haslemere Estates Charitable Trust

OBJECTS General charitable purposes

POLICY OF TRUSTEES To restrict grants solely to youth activities in London and the London environment

RESTRICTIONS No grants to individuals

BENEFICIAL AREA Mainly London area

FINANCES
- Year 1993
- Grants £12,000
- Income £13,000

TRUSTEES P R Van Romunde, P D Webster, J S Winpenny

CORRESPONDENT Miss G Webber, Haslemere Estates plc, 4 Carlos Place, Mayfair, London W1Y 5AE

CLASSIFICATIONS
- Children and youth – general
- Centres, clubs and institutes
- Homes and hostels
- Youth organisations (eg Guides, Scouts, YWCA etc)

C.C. NO 262931   **ESTABLISHED** 1971

■ The Howard Hatton Charitable Trust

OBJECTS General charitable purposes

POLICY OF TRUSTEES The income of the Trust is small and is used by the Trustees for the charities in which they have a particular interest. It is unlikely that new applications for grants will be considered

TYPE OF BENEFICIARY Local charities

RESTRICTIONS In view of the small income enjoyed by this Trust it is most unlikely that the Trustees will give any consideration to applications for grants other than from local charities

BENEFICIAL AREA Worcestershire

FINANCES
- Year 1990
- Grants £1,671
- Income £2,552
- Assets £25,286

TRUSTEES Lady Suzanne Rollo & Dunning, Mrs A C Collis, J J Forbes

CORRESPONDENT Mrs A C Collis, Dernhills, Kinlet, Nr Bewdley, Worcs DY12 3BY

CLASSIFICATIONS
- Children and youth – general

C.C. NO 214325   **ESTABLISHED** 1959

■ The Hawthorne Charitable Trust

OBJECTS General charitable purposes

POLICY OF TRUSTEES The Trustees make donations, generally on an annual basis, to a large number of charities mainly concerned with the environment, the care of the young and the elderly, the relief of pain, sickness and poverty, and the advancement of medical research, particularly into the various forms of cancer

TYPE OF BENEFICIARY See Policy of Trustees

RESTRICTIONS It is not the Trustees' policy to make grants to individuals

BENEFICIAL AREA The Trustees' policy is to give to national organisations or to local organisations in the Hereford and Worcester area

FINANCES
- Year 1995
- Grants £126,928
- Income £87,610
- Assets £3,617,542

TRUSTEES Mrs A Berington, R J Clark

CORRESPONDENT Messrs Baker Tilly, Chartered Accountants, 2 Bloomsbury Street, London WC1B 3ST

CLASSIFICATIONS
- Children and youth – general
- Centres, clubs and institutes
- Counselling (inc helplines)
- Homes and hostels
- Youth organisations (eg Guides, Scouts, YWCA etc)

C.C. NO 233921   **ESTABLISHED** 1964

■ Haymills Charitable Trust

OBJECTS Youth charitable purposes

POLICY OF TRUSTEES The Trustees regularly review their policy to make the best use of the funds available by donating varying amounts to projects which they believe will offer maximum benefit. In particular they seek to support projects which they believe are not widely known and thus likely to be inadequately supported. Their main support is to registered charities operating in areas known to them, especially those lying in and to the West of London and in Suffolk, where Haymills Group have their main works or offices

TYPE OF GRANT Trustees meet at least twice a year, usually in March and October, to determine the extent of individual grants which are to be made. These fall into four main categories; Education: grants for tuition of individuals of any age – to schools, colleges and Universities. Medicine: grants to hospitals and associated institutions and those concerned with less widely publicised medical research. Welfare: primarily to include former Haymills' Staff, and to others who are considered to be 'in necessitous circumstances' or who are otherwise distressed or disadvantaged. Youth: support for schemes to assist in education, welfare and training of young people

TYPE OF BENEFICIARY Any personal applications for support will not be considered unless supported by a letter from a University, a College or other appropriate authority. Each year, a limited number of applicants will be considered under Haymills Young People Employment Initiative, who can show that they are committed to further education and training preferably for employment in the construction industry

RESTRICTIONS At the moment, no further major grants can be considered as our funds are already committed

BENEFICIAL AREA West London, Berkshire, Oxfordshire, Buckinghamshire, Bedfordshire, Hertfordshire, Essex, Wiltshire,Dorset, Gloucestershire, East Anglia

FINANCES
- **Year** 1995
- **Grants** £59,000
- **Income** £76,000
- **Assets** £1,258,000

TRUSTEES G A Cox, E F C Drake, A M H Jackson, K C Perryman, J A Sharpe, J L Wosner, I W Ferres

SUBMISSION OF APPLICATIONS The Trustees are unable to acknowlegde applications made to them

CORRESPONDENT I W Ferres, c/o Haymills, Empire House, Hanger Green, London W5 3BD

CLASSIFICATIONS
- Children and youth – general

C.C. NO 277761 **ESTABLISHED** 1979

■ The Hayward Foundation

OBJECTS General charitable purposes for those of any age with special needs; medical research, voluntary special education, preservation and the environment

TYPE OF BENEFICIARY Registered charities only, no grants through third parties

RESTRICTIONS No grants to individuals, nor for revenue, holidays, travel, expeditions, vehicles, general appeals, deficit funding and what is properly the responsibility of a statutory body

BENEFICIAL AREA British Isles

FINANCES
- **Year** 1994
- **Grants** £855,611
- **Income** £3,032,147
- **Assets** £23,084,860

TRUSTEES E G Sykes (President), I F Donald (Chairman), Sir Jack Hayward, OBE, Dr J C Houston, CBE, FRCP, Mrs S J Heath, G J Hearne, CBE, C W Taylor, FCA, J N van Leuven

CORRESPONDENT M T Schnebli, The Hayward Foundation, 45 Harrington Gardens, London SW7 4JU

CLASSIFICATIONS
- Children and youth – general
- Adoption/fostering
- Community groups
- Development of character
- Special needs housing
- Special classes

C.C. NO 201034 **ESTABLISHED** 1961

■ The Charles Hayward Trust

OBJECTS General charitable purposes

POLICY OF TRUSTEES Support for community based local organisations, urban and rural, responsible for their own management and finances. Priority given to schemes benefitting those (of any age) with special needs

TYPE OF GRANT Usually one-off capital expenditure. Vehicles rarely considered

TYPE OF BENEFICIARY Registered charities only. No grants through third parties

RESTRICTIONS No grants made in response to general appeals from large national bodies. No grants made for general medical purposes. No grants to individuals, nor for holidays, expeditions or educational visits. Revenue or revenue related expenditure rarely considered. Applications for any of the above purposes are unlikely to be acknowledged, nor are obvious 'mail shot' applications

BENEFICIAL AREA UK

FINANCES
- **Year** 1993
- **Grants** £609,100
- **Income** £784,500
- **Assets** £7,000,000

TRUSTEES I F Donald (Chairman), Miss A T Rogers, A D Owen, A H McIlreath

SUBMISSION OF APPLICATIONS Applications should be personally signed by a Trustee or some other person with similar responsibility for the affairs of the applicant organisation. Applications may be submitted at any time but are unlikely to be considered in the quarter in which they are received. Trustees meet quarterly. NB Connected charity: Please also refer to the Hayward Foundation; applications may be suited to the policy of one or the other – never both. Duplicated applications will not be acknowledged

CORRESPONDENT M T Schnebli, The Charles Hayward Trust, 45 Harrington Gardens, London SW7 4JU

CLASSIFICATIONS
- Advancement in life
- Adventure centres and playgrounds
- Development of character
- Homes and hostels

C.C. NO 281781 **ESTABLISHED** 1983

Heath

■ Heath Charitable Trust

OBJECTS General charitable purposes

TYPE OF GRANT Annually to selected charities

RESTRICTIONS Donations generally to areas of great need. Not to individuals for education, etc

BENEFICIAL AREA Essex

TRUSTEES D I E Heath, Mrs V Heath, M R MacFadyen, I S M Robertson

PUBLICATIONS Annual Report and Accounts

SUBMISSION OF APPLICATIONS Fully committed. No new appeals please

CORRESPONDENT D I E Heath, Heath Charitable Trust, 18 Woodside, Leigh-on-Sea, Essex SS9 4QU

CLASSIFICATIONS
- Children and youth – general

C.C. NO 1031484   **ESTABLISHED** 1995

■ Hedgcock Bequest

OBJECTS General charitable purposes

POLICY OF TRUSTEES Only for the benefit of Brighton people

TYPE OF BENEFICIARY Local organisations and charities

RESTRICTIONS No grants to individuals

BENEFICIAL AREA Brighton

FINANCES
- Year 1988
- Grants £10,425
- Income £9,856
- Assets £180,790

TRUSTEES Borough of Brighton

CORRESPONDENT The Borough Secretary, Hedgcock Bequest, Town Hall, Brighton, East Sussex BN1 1JA

CLASSIFICATIONS
- Centres, clubs and institutes
- Day centres and nurseries
- Youth organisations (eg Guides, Scouts, YWCA etc)

C.C. NO 230147   **ESTABLISHED** 1903

■ The Hedley Foundation

OBJECTS General charitable purposes

POLICY OF TRUSTEES The Foundation considers appeals from registered charities in the United Kingdom relating to new hospices, special equipment for the disabled and for hospitals, the Macmillan Nurses scheme, youth activities and some school improvement projects, some community and welfare schemes and support for medical research programmes. A few (usually local) conservation projects are also helped each year. The work of the Christian Church – particularly in deprived areas – is supported when possible

TYPE OF BENEFICIARY Registered charities within the United Kingdom, never individuals

RESTRICTIONS The Foundation does not normally make donations to large National appeals or to assistance overseas; museum appeals and housing associations' applications cannot usually be considered

BENEFICIAL AREA UK

SAMPLE GRANTS £25,000 to Drive for Youth (building)
£12,500 to Teenage Cancer Trust (equipping ward)
£10,000 to Ethan Wilkinson School, Manchester (equipment)
£6,000 to Voices Foundation (training conference)
£5,000 to Jibcraft (start-up)

FINANCES
- Year 1995
- Grants £857,350
- Income £1,077,400
- Assets £19,434,150

TRUSTEES C H W Parish (Chairman), P H Byam-Cook, D V Fanshawe, P H Holcroft, J F M Rodwell, Sir Christopher Airy

SUBMISSION OF APPLICATIONS No special form, but should include latest accounts: trustees meet monthly

CORRESPONDENT The Secretary, The Hedley Foundation, 9 Dowgate Hill, London EC4R 2SU

CLASSIFICATIONS
- Children and youth – general

C.C. NO 262933   **ESTABLISHED** 1971

■ J R Henderson's Settlement

OBJECTS General charitable purposes

POLICY OF TRUSTEES General charities. Not educational

TYPE OF BENEFICIARY Charities in which the Settlor is personally interested

RESTRICTIONS Time Charity

BENEFICIAL AREA Berkshire

FINANCES
- Year 1994
- Grants £4,558
- Income £12,861
- Assets £73,834

TRUSTEES H M Henderson, N J Henderson

CORRESPONDENT Henderson Administration Ltd, 3 Finsbury Avenue, London EC2M 2PA

CLASSIFICATIONS
- Children and youth – general
- Youth organisations (eg Guides, Scouts, YWCA etc)

C.C. NO 226645   **ESTABLISHED** 1960

■ The Hertfordshire Community Trust

OBJECTS General charitable purposes

POLICY OF TRUSTEES To support the work of local charities and voluntary groups for the benefit of the community

TYPE OF GRANT Cash grant for specific projects or developments. Mainly £100–£1,500. Most at this stage are on a one-off basis. Available for equipment, training, publicity and start-up/development costs, ie any purpose that will help a local group to expand or develop its service to the community

TYPE OF BENEFICIARY Any locally based charity or voluntary group benefiting local people. Many are smaller, less well known groups or less 'popular' causes that often find it extremely difficult to obtain funds elsewhere

RESTRICTIONS No major appeals, endowment funds, research, sponsored events, promotion of religion.

Grants will not normally be made to individuals. Arts, sport and the environment are normally supported only when there is a benefit to the disadvantaged

BENEFICIAL AREA Hertfordshire

SAMPLE GRANTS £1,500 to Wheels! in Stevenage and North Herts for tools and equipment to kit out a workshop, where young people can get involved in building and maintaining cars. This is part of an initiative to reduce car crime
£800 to Harpenden Lions Club for materials for the Skills for the Primary School Child/Skills for Life programmes
£600 to London Colney Youth Project to purchase cooker and microwave for this new drop-in centre, which provides information and counselling services plus opportunites to develop personal and social skills
£400 to Thunderidge Youth Club for a music centre and games equipment

FINANCES
- **Year** 1995
- **Grants** £67,000
- **Income** £173,000
- **Assets** £438,000

TRUSTEES P Burgin, Prof N Buxton, Mrs B Goble, P Groves, M Le Fleming, Miss C McCaffrey, P Norcross, M Osbaldeston, V Paige, R Richardson, N Rossiter, D Thomson, A Tucker

PUBLICATIONS Annual report, leaflets, newsletter

SUBMISSION OF APPLICATIONS An informal discussion, often by telephone, is encouraged first. An application form and guidelines may then be issued. Deadlines for return are the end of February, May, August and November. All applicants are advised within six to eight weeks of these dates

CORRESPONDENT Tony Gilbert, Director, 2 Townsend Avenue, St Albans, Herts AL1 3SG

CLASSIFICATIONS
- Children and youth – general
- Community groups
- Day centres and nurseries
- Development of character

C.C. NO 299438   **ESTABLISHED** 1988

■ The Highland Children's Trust

OBJECTS (a) Maintenance in suitable accommodation (b) education (c) obtaining employment (d) setting up in business (e) finding suitable homes (f) providing holidays

POLICY OF TRUSTEES Highland region only. Children and young people up to 25 years. Educational purposes – student hardship, holidays, equipment for disabled to help education, expenses in obtaining work. Maintaining in accommodation whilst in need of care. Setting up in business

TYPE OF GRANT Small one-off grants for specific purposes or occasionally spread over several months

TYPE OF BENEFICIARY Only local individuals, or those who are in further education outwith Highland region but whose home is in Highland region

RESTRICTIONS Only to individuals. No grants for consumables (eg food, clothing)

BENEFICIAL AREA Highland region (present local government area)

FINANCES
- **Year** 1995
- **Grants** £16,000
- **Income** £35,000
- **Assets** £550,000

TRUSTEES Rev C A Fraser, J O Waddell, Cllr T MacKenzie, A W Currie, J I Ross Martin

SUBMISSION OF APPLICATIONS Governors meet every two months approximately

CORRESPONDENT Mrs S A Grant, Administrator, Highland Children's Trust, 105 Castle Street, Inverness IV2 3EA

CLASSIFICATIONS
- Advancement in life
- Holidays

S.C. NO SC006008   **ESTABLISHED** 1983

■ Joseph and Mary Hiley Trust

OBJECTS General charitable purposes. Principally local medical, religious and educational purposes

POLICY OF TRUSTEES Grants are made to a wide variety of charitable organisations operating in the areas of medicine, youth work, religion and the caring agencies.

TYPE OF BENEFICIARY Local needs receive preference

RESTRICTIONS No individuals

BENEFICIAL AREA Yorkshire (West Riding)

FINANCES
- **Year** 1991
- **Grants** £22,018
- **Income** £31,503
- **Assets** £325,888

TRUSTEES Mary Hiley, E M Hjort, Mrs M B Kitchen, Mrs A B Palmer

CORRESPONDENT Mrs J Hiley, 3 Greenhills, Rawdon, Leeds LS19 6NP

CLASSIFICATIONS
- Children and youth – general

C.C. NO 248301   **ESTABLISHED** 1966

■ Gay & Peter Hartley's Hillards Charitable Trust

OBJECTS General charitable purposes

POLICY OF TRUSTEES To give aid to those poor, needy and sick who live in the areas which were served by a Hillards store. Churches, community centres and schools within those areas may also be beneficiaries but it is preferable if they have charitable status themselves

RESTRICTIONS Personal applications are not usually granted unless they come through another charity. As a body, the Trustees do not give to national charities but the individual Trustees have some discretion in that respect

BENEFICIAL AREA Areas which were served by a Hillards store

SAMPLE GRANTS £10,000 to Westminster Pastoral Fund, Leeds branch
£500 to Skipton Youth and Community Centre
£250 to St Anne's Shelter and Housing Association
£250 to Leeds Drug Project

FINANCES
- **Year** 1994
- **Grants** £48,165
- **Income** £70,577

TRUSTEES P A H Hartley, Mrs G Hartley, MBE, S R H Hartley, Miss S Hartley, BA, MBA, A C H Hartley, MA, Miss A Hartley

NOTES Full accounts are on file at the Charity Commision

SUBMISSION OF APPLICATIONS The Trustees meet at the end of each year and all applications should be in the hands of the Secretary before November 1st. There is no formal application nor is there any particular policy on re-application at the moment. Applicants are told if they have not been successful

CORRESPONDENT Mrs G Hartley, MBE, Secretary, 400 Shadwell Lane, Leeds LS17 8AW

CLASSIFICATIONS
● Community groups

C.C. NO 327879 **ESTABLISHED** 1988

■ Lady Hind Trust

OBJECTS General charitable purposes

TYPE OF BENEFICIARY Grants to individuals are only considered in most exceptional cases and preference is give to applications relating to projects and activities in Nottinghamshire and Norfolk

RESTRICTIONS Grants are rarely made for the repair of Parish Churches outside Nottinghamshire and Norfolk

BENEFICIAL AREA England and Wales only

FINANCES
● **Year** 1995   ● **Income** £235,598
● **Grants** £274,407   ● **Assets** £5,961,965

TRUSTEES W D Crane, J A L Barratt, C W L Barratt, W F Whysall

CORRESPONDENT Eversheds, 14 Fletcher Gate, Nottingham, Nottinghamshire NG1 2FX

CLASSIFICATIONS
● Children and youth – general
● Centres, clubs and institutes

C.C. NO 208877 **ESTABLISHED** 1951

■ Mrs F E Hinton Charitable Trust

OBJECTS General charitable pruposes

TYPE OF GRANT Small one-off cash grants Recurrent

TYPE OF BENEFICIARY Registered charities, institutions

SAMPLE GRANTS £500 to Friends for the Young Deaf

FINANCES
● **Year** 1995   ● **Income** £8,733
● **Grants** £3,500   ● **Assets** £208,722

TRUSTEES D T Matheson, D J Knight

CORRESPONDENT D T Matheson, 4 Wood Street, London EC2V 7JB

CLASSIFICATIONS
● Children and youth – general

C.C. NO 299799 **ESTABLISHED** 1988

■ The Hobson Charitable Trust

OBJECTS General charitable purposes — Assistance to the needy — Advancement of Roman Catholic Religion — Advancement of education

POLICY OF TRUSTEES The Trust income is usually fully committed

TYPE OF BENEFICIARY General

FINANCES
● **Year** 1993   ● **Income** £5,000
● **Grants** £5,000   ● **Assets** £100,000

TRUSTEES P R Noble, J C Vernor Miles, L A Ellison

CORRESPONDENT J C Vernor Miles, Messrs Vernor Miles & Noble, 5 Raymond Buildings, Gray's Inn, London WC1R 5DD

CLASSIFICATIONS
● Children and youth – general

C.C. NO 247437 **ESTABLISHED** 1966

■ Bill & May Hodgson Charitable Trust

OBJECTS General charitable purposes

TYPE OF BENEFICIARY Registered Charities only

BENEFICIAL AREA Tyne & Wear

FINANCES
● **Year** 1992   ● **Income** £21,700
● **Grants** £15,400   ● **Assets** £223,083

TRUSTEES R M Wilson, H Straker, Col G S May

CORRESPONDENT Dickinson Dees, Solicitors, Cross Hours, Westgate Road, Newcastle upon Tyne NE99 1SB

CLASSIFICATIONS
● Counselling (inc helplines)

C.C. NO 295313 **ESTABLISHED** 1986

■ The C B and A B Holinsworth Fund of Help

OBJECTS Furtherance of the work of the voluntary hospital or hospitals, whether by means of direct contributions to the funds or otherwise; the relief of sick persons; the benefit of poor persons requiring convalescence

POLICY OF TRUSTEES With their limited resources, the Trustees prefer to assist individuals rather than charitable bodies, but not with the clearance of debts

TYPE OF BENEFICIARY Private individuals, the majority of whom are referred by hospitals, social workers and general practitioners in the Birmingham area

RESTRICTIONS The Trustees cannot apply any income in relief of public funds

BENEFICIAL AREA In or near the City of Birmingham

FINANCES
● **Year** 1990   ● **Income** £5,965
● **Grants** £4,393   ● **Assets** £61,217

TRUSTEES Three Representative Trustees appointed by the Council of the City of Birmingham and three Co-opted Trustees

CORRESPONDENT The Secretary, The C B and A B Holinsworth Fund of Help, The Council House, Birmingham, West Midlands B1 1BB

CLASSIFICATIONS
- Homes and hostels

C.C. NO 217792   **ESTABLISHED** 1938

■ The Dorothy Holmes Charitable Trust

OBJECTS General charitable purposes

POLICY OF TRUSTEES The Beneficial Area is national, with preference for charities in the area of Poole and District (Dorset)

TYPE OF BENEFICIARY UK registered charities only

RESTRICTIONS UK Registered charities only

BENEFICIAL AREA UK, with preference for Poole and District (Dorset)

FINANCES
- Year 1994
- Grants £28,000
- Income £44,500
- Assets £577,800

TRUSTEES D S Roberts, B M Cody, M E A Cody, S C Roberts

SUBMISSION OF APPLICATIONS By letter to the Correspondent

CORRESPONDENT The Dorothy Holmes Charitable Trust, c/o Smallfield, Cody & Co, 5 Harley Place, Harley Street, London W1N 1HB

CLASSIFICATIONS
- Children and youth – general

C.C. NO 237213   **ESTABLISHED** 1964

■ Homelands Charitable Trust

OBJECTS General charitable purposes

POLICY OF TRUSTEES Adherence with Settlor's wishes

TYPE OF BENEFICIARY Registered charities for religious, medical, childcare and animal welfare purposes

RESTRICTIONS No personal grants

FINANCES
- Year 1990
- Grants £120,000
- Income £160,000
- Assets £1,501,000

TRUSTEES D G W Ballard, Rev C Curry, N J Armstrong

SUBMISSION OF APPLICATIONS In writing

CORRESPONDENT L D F Casbolt, FCA, Messrs Alliotts, 5th Floor, 9 Kingsway, London WC2B 6XF

CLASSIFICATIONS
- Adoption/fostering
- Centres, clubs and institutes
- Holidays
- Homes and hostels

C.C. NO 214322   **ESTABLISHED** 1962

■ The Homfray Trust

OBJECTS General charitable purposes

POLICY OF TRUSTEES To assist the families of former or retired employees of Homfray & Co Ltd in financial difficulty. To help certain charitable and other organisations who assist children and the aged, usually in West Yorkshire and particularly in Halifax and Sowerby Bridge

TYPE OF BENEFICIARY No assistance is given to individual students

FINANCES
- Year 1994
- Grants £13,074
- Income £14,030
- Assets £222,653

TRUSTEES H J H Gillam, G S Haigh, D Murray Wells

CORRESPONDENT G S Haigh, Newlands House, Warley, Halifax, West Yorkshire HX2 7SW

CLASSIFICATIONS
- Children and youth – general

C.C. NO 214503   **ESTABLISHED** 1928

■ The Hoover Foundation

OBJECTS General charitable purposes

POLICY OF TRUSTEES Wide range of charities including education (mainly supported through grants to universities, normally for research in the engineering subjects), welfare, medical research and small local charities

TYPE OF BENEFICIARY National registered charities, universities and small local charities working in the areas outlined in Beneficial Area

RESTRICTIONS The Trustees do not make grants to individuals, including students

BENEFICIAL AREA National, but biased towards South Wales, Glasgow, Bolton and West London

FINANCES
- Year 1991
- Grants £113,430
- Income £177,856
- Assets £2,144,618

TRUSTEES G J Kumman, D J Lint, S J West

CORRESPONDENT Mrs Marion Heeffey, The Hoover Foundation, Hoover European Appliance Group, Pentrebach, Merthyr Tydfil, Mid Glamorgan UB4 0JN

CLASSIFICATIONS
- Day centres and nurseries
- Homes and hostels
- Youth organisations (eg Guides, Scouts, YWCA etc)

C.C. NO 200274   **ESTABLISHED** 1961

■ The Charity of Joseph Hopkins

OBJECTS Relief of persons resident in the City of Birmingham who are in conditions of need, hardship or distress

POLICY OF TRUSTEES To support small local charities

TYPE OF BENEFICIARY Organisations relieving need particularly for children and the elderly

RESTRICTIONS Birmingham residents and Trusts

BENEFICIAL AREA City of Birmingham

FINANCES
- Year 1993
- Grants £65,130
- Income £76,904
- Assets £460,916

TRUSTEES A C S Hordern, A V Blakemore, R H Vernon, M N W Wilcox, Mrs P B Hodder, A Cook, Mrs J R Jaffa, Miss K Baldwin, A T Argyle, R J Sargeant, Miss A M Grove

Hornby

CORRESPONDENT The Clerks to the Trustees, The Joseph Hopkins Charity, Martineau Johnson, St Philip's House, St Philip's Place Birmingham B3 2PP

CLASSIFICATIONS
- Children and youth – general
- Adventure centres and playgrounds
- Centres, clubs and institutes
- Community groups
- Day centres and nurseries
- Holidays
- Homes and hostels
- Youth organisations (eg Guides, Scouts, YWCA etc)

C.C. NO 217303   **ESTABLISHED** 1681

■ The Edward Hornby Charitable Trust

OBJECTS General charitable purposes

POLICY OF TRUSTEES Deprived children, the elderly, the ill, the blind, the deaf. Not animals. Crafts only when connected with youth or therapeutic treatment. Prefer the innovatory and less long-established

TYPE OF GRANT Now cutting down on recurrent and increasing one-off

TYPE OF BENEFICIARY The Trustees tend to help small hospices, small schools for deaf children, boys' clubs, children's holidays, etc

RESTRICTIONS Registered charities only but not large National ones. No museums nor the Arts

FINANCES
- Year 1992
- Assets £26,000
- Income £2,500

TRUSTEES E M Hornby, Mrs E Cobb, Mrs A Hornby

PUBLICATIONS Annual Report

NOTES The Trust is small and the recurrent beneficiary list is full

SUBMISSION OF APPLICATIONS No telephone calls. No application form. Applications reviewed at any time. No sae required. Unsuccessful applicants are seldom acknowledged unless something constructive can be suggested

CORRESPONDENT Mrs A Hornby, Hodges Barn, Shipton Moyne, Tetbury, Glos GL8 8PR

CLASSIFICATIONS
- Advancement in life
- Development of character

C.C. NO 278232   **ESTABLISHED** 1979

■ The Horne Foundation

OBJECTS General charitable purposes. Education and youth-orientated organisations in the Northampton area

POLICY OF TRUSTEES Predominantly large grants towards building projects (education, welfare). Main interests: education, youth, young homeless, arts in Northampton area

TYPE OF GRANT Lump sum

TYPE OF BENEFICIARY Local start-up projects mainly involving new buildings

RESTRICTIONS Prefer organisations with no religious affiliation. Do not support private education

BENEFICIAL AREA Mainly Northamptonshire

SAMPLE GRANTS £100,000 to North Borough Council for athletics track and club house
£96,000 to young people's hostel, Kettering
£10,000 to NAYC Octopus Project
£8,600 to Dengate concert tickets for sixth forms
£8,000 to Barn Theatre, Moulton

FINANCES
- Year 1993
- Grants £360,000
- Income £400,000
- Assets £6,000,000

TRUSTEES K E Horne, E J Davenport, R M Harwood, C A Horne

SUBMISSION OF APPLICATIONS At any time

CORRESPONDENT Mrs R M Harwood, The Gnomes, Church Street, Boughton, Northampton NN2 8FG

CLASSIFICATIONS
- Children and youth – general
- Centres, clubs and institutes

C.C. NO 283751   **ESTABLISHED** 1981

■ The Hornsey Parochial Charities
(Educational and Vocational Foundation)

OBJECTS The benefit of persons under the age of 25 years who are permanently resident in the Ancient Parish of Hornsey, North London who, in the opinion of the Trustees, are in need of financial assistance for further education or to assist their entry in a trade, calling or profession or the promotion of their education, including social or physical training

POLICY OF TRUSTEES Applicants must have been residing permanently in the Ancient Parish

TYPE OF BENEFICIARY Individuals and organisations in need

RESTRICTIONS Residential qualification, no commitment to continuing grants

BENEFICIAL AREA The Ancient Parish of Hornsey (North London)

FINANCES
- Year 1995
- Grants £47,300
- Income £61,400
- Assets £384,000

TRUSTEES Chairman and 12 other Trustees

CORRESPONDENT Clerk to the Trustees, 47 The Chine, London N10 3PX

CLASSIFICATIONS
- Adventure centres and playgrounds
- Centres, clubs and institutes
- Community groups
- Youth organisations (eg Guides, Scouts, YWCA etc)

C.C. NO 312810   **ESTABLISHED** 1955

■ The Thomas Hudson Benevolent Trust

OBJECTS General charitable purposes

POLICY OF TRUSTEES For groups (not individuals) particularly disabled

TYPE OF BENEFICIARY Registered charities only

RESTRICTIONS Time charity — to be terminated on 4/11/2000

BENEFICIAL AREA UK but with preference for Humberside and East Riding

SAMPLE GRANTS Handicapped
Cancer Research
Local youth centres

FINANCES
- Year 1990
- Grants £3,000
- Income £3,476
- Assets £97,908

TRUSTEES T D Hudson, M H Hudson

CORRESPONDENT T D Hudson, Wauldby Manor, Welton, Humberside HU15 1QR

CLASSIFICATIONS
- Centres, clubs and institutes
- Holidays
- Youth organisations (eg Guides, Scouts, YWCA etc)

C.C. NO 239339　　　ESTABLISHED 1964

■ The Charles Hughesdon Foundation

OBJECTS General charitable purposes

POLICY OF TRUSTEES To consider each application on its merits

TYPE OF GRANT Mainly one-off

RESTRICTIONS No grants to individuals

FINANCES
- Year 1994
- Grants £720
- Income £856
- Assets £26,588

TRUSTEES Coutts & Co, C F Hughesdon

SUBMISSION OF APPLICATIONS Applications should be submitted in writing; they will not be acknowledged but if successful a cheque will be issued

CORRESPONDENT Messrs Coutts & Co, Financial Services Division, Trustee Department, 440 Strand, London WC2R 0QS

CLASSIFICATIONS
- Children and youth – general

C.C. NO 277962　　　ESTABLISHED 1979

■ The Hull & East Riding Charitable Trust

OBJECTS General charitable purposes

POLICY OF TRUSTEES Each application judged on its own merits

TYPE OF GRANT Prefer to fund capital costs of a project but will consider funding revenue costs over a limited period of time

TYPE OF BENEFICIARY Charitable purposes in the Hull and former East Riding area of Yorkshire

RESTRICTIONS No organisations/causes of political nature nor for religious purposes; unlikely to support individuals

BENEFICIAL AREA Hull and East Riding area of Yorkshire

SAMPLE GRANTS £130,000 to Humberside Youth Association
£100,000 to Lifestyle
£22,250 to Hull Boys' Club
£16,400 to Youth Action

FINANCES
- Year 1994
- Grants £149,439
- Income £253,783
- Assets £3,389,555

TRUSTEES M J Hollingbery, Mrs M R Barker, A M Horsley

PUBLICATIONS Annual accounts. Trust guidelines

SUBMISSION OF APPLICATIONS Donations considered at meetings in May and November. Applications must be received by 30 April and 31 October

CORRESPONDENT H C Palmer, Queen Victoria House, Guildhall Road, Hull, Humberside HU1 1HH

CLASSIFICATIONS
- Centres, clubs and institutes
- Youth organisations (eg Guides, Scouts, YWCA etc)

C.C. NO 516866　　　ESTABLISHED 1985

■ The Patrick Mitchell Hunter Fund

OBJECTS General charitable purposes within the city of Aberdeen

POLICY OF TRUSTEES To support local charities in Aberdeen

TYPE OF BENEFICIARY All types of deserving charities based in Aberdeen

RESTRICTIONS Only applications from charities or philanthropic institutions based in Aberdeen considered

BENEFICIAL AREA Aberdeen only

FINANCES
- Year 1993
- Grants £12,000
- Income £12,700
- Assets £250,000

TRUSTEES J T C Gillan, W Howie

CORRESPONDENT Wilsone & Duffus, PO Box No 81, 7 Golden Square, Aberdeen, Scotland AB9 8EP

CLASSIFICATIONS
- Children and youth – general
- Homes and hostels
- Youth organisations (eg Guides, Scouts, YWCA etc)

C.C. NO CR 3825　　　ESTABLISHED 1954

■ William Hunt's Trust

OBJECTS General charitable purposes

POLICY OF TRUSTEES Established national charities and local charities of which the Trust has special interest, knowledge or association, no grants are made to individuals

TYPE OF BENEFICIARY Mainly local

FINANCES
- Year 1995
- Grants £1,000
- Income £3,400
- Assets £67,073

TRUSTEES G E Rushmore, R R Long

CORRESPONDENT Birkett Long, Red House, Halstead, Essex CO9 2DZ

CLASSIFICATIONS
- Adventure centres and playgrounds
- Homes and hostels

C.C. NO 245178　　　ESTABLISHED 1965

David Hyman Charitable Trust

OBJECTS General charitable purposes

POLICY OF TRUSTEES The Trust will support the disabled and handicapped including the blind and deaf with particular emphasis on children (and old people). It will also help, in certain cases, the homeless. It will help students who are disabled to the extent of being confined to a wheelchair. It will also help in the realm of, for example, holidays for deprived children

BENEFICIAL AREA UK

FINANCES
- Year 1990
- Grants £44,765
- Income £29,059

TRUSTEES D Hyman, B A Hyman, J D Hyman

CORRESPONDENT David Hyman Charitable Trust, 16 Mulberry Walk, London SW3 6DY

CLASSIFICATIONS
- Children and youth – general
- Holidays
- Homes and hostels

C.C. NO 274072   **ESTABLISHED** 1977

The International Nickel Donations Fund

OBJECTS General charitable purposes

POLICY OF TRUSTEES Preference given to those charities in which the Trust has special interest, knowledge or association in the fields of medicine, community culture and education. Youth causes is not a special priority, but if a particular youth charity falls within our guidelines it will be considered by the Trustees

TYPE OF BENEFICIARY Charities operating near to Company plants and offices, operating as local rather than national organisations

RESTRICTIONS No grants are made to individuals nor in response to circular-type appeals

FINANCES
- Year 1993
- Grants £15,870
- Income £10,000

TRUSTEES I Kirman, A H Kamdar, A J L Glover, G B Nairn, M R Nicholas

CORRESPONDENT Miss S A James, Secretary, International Nickel Donations Fund, 5th Floor, Windsor House, 50 Victoria Street, London SW1H 0XB

CLASSIFICATIONS
- Children and youth – general

C.C. NO 267453   **ESTABLISHED** 1974

The Inverforth Charitable Trust

OBJECTS General charitable purposes

POLICY OF TRUSTEES To support smaller national charities, with emphasis on care, in the areas of physical and mental health, hospices, youth and education, handicapped and aged, or specialist caring charities; music and the arts; heritage. Happier with running costs than with projects

TYPE OF GRANT Willing to support administrative costs. Gifts are made in units of £500–1,000–1,500 with a few larger gifts deriving from long standing connections, from a list which is reviewed annually. Repeat donations are more common than to new applicants. £19,000 to 'youth' and 'education' in 1995

RESTRICTIONS No localised charities: no churches, village halls, schools, etc. No animal charities. No branches, affiliates or subsidiary charities. Charities only, no individuals. No repeat applications at less than annual intervals. These guidelines are strictly enforced, and non-qualifying applications are not reported to the Trustees

BENEFICIAL AREA UK

SAMPLE GRANTS £1,500 to NCH – Action for Children
£1,500 to Treloan Trust
£1,500 to Youth Clubs UK
£1,000 to Ocean Youth Club
£500 to GAP Activity Projects

FINANCES
- Year 1995
- Grants £215,500
- Income £170,000
- Assets £2,808,000

TRUSTEES Elizabeth, The Lady Inverforth, Lord Inverforth, The Hon Mrs Jonathan Kane, Michael Gee

PUBLICATIONS Annual Report, to Charity Commission

SUBMISSION OF APPLICATIONS In writing to the correspondent. Initial telephone calls are discouraged. No special forms are necessary, although accounts are desirable. A summary is prepared for the Trustees, who meet quarterly. Replies are normally sent to all applicants; allow up to four months for answer or grant. The correspondent receives well over 1,000 applications a year, and advises of a very high failure rate for new applicants. No need for an sae

CORRESPONDENT E A M Lee, FCIB, Barrister-at-Law, Secretary and Treasurer, The Farm, Northington, Alresford, Hampshire SO24 9TH

CLASSIFICATIONS
- Children and youth – general
- Development of character

C.C. NO 274132   **ESTABLISHED** 1977

■ The Ireland Fund of Great Britain

OBJECTS Irish charitable purposes

POLICY OF TRUSTEES Peace, reconciliation, cultural activity and the alleviation of poverty among Irish communities north and south of the border and in Great Britain

TYPE OF GRANT Annual disbursement

TYPE OF BENEFICIARY Projects concerned with Policy of Trustees

RESTRICTIONS No grants to individuals

BENEFICIAL AREA Ireland and Great Britain

FINANCES
- Year 1994
- Grants £82,450
- Income £112,306

TRUSTEES Ms J Saatchi, B Hayes, K Pakenham, Dr A O'Reilly, J Riordan, G O'Reilly

SUBMISSION OF APPLICATIONS British-based applications to be sumitted in October, Irish-based applications to be submitted in February

CORRESPONDENT Mrs Jacqueline Dutton, 8–10 Greyfriars Road, Reading, Berkshire RG1 1QE

CLASSIFICATIONS
- Community groups
- Youth organisations (eg Guides, Scouts, YWCA etc)

C.C. NO 327889   **ESTABLISHED** 1988

■ Isle of Dogs Community Foundation

OBJECTS To promote relief of poverty and sickness. To promote advancement of education and learning. To advance public education and learning. To advance public education in the arts. To provide or assist in provision of facilities for recreation or leisure-time occupation

TYPE OF GRANT The Trustees will consider:
(a) Applications for 'small' grants, normally up to £400. (b) Applications for 'standard' grants, which may be up to £5,000 pa over a three-year period. Applications on a 'challenge' basis, where grant aid is used to lever other support, are welcomed

TYPE OF BENEFICIARY Community organisations directly benefiting the residents of the beneficial area

RESTRICTIONS No grants to individuals or for travel

BENEFICIAL AREA Blackwall and Millwall wards of the London Borough of Tower Hamlets

FINANCES
- Year 1995
- Grants £91,294
- Income £109,267
- Assets £704,578

TRUSTEES NCC Property Ltd, Port of London Properties Ltd, The Telegraph plc, Island House Church & Community Centre, Poplar Play, AICVC, Alpha Grove Community Centre, LDDC (3), London Borough of Tower Hamlets. Individual member: David Chesterton

PUBLICATIONS Annual Report, publicity leaflet

SUBMISSION OF APPLICATIONS There are normally two grant rounds each year, in Spring and Autumn. Please enquire for further details of current policy and for an application form (sae appreciated)

CORRESPONDENT The Administrator, Isle of Dogs Community Foundation, 20 Mastmaker Road, London E14 9UB

CLASSIFICATIONS
- Children and youth – general
- Community groups
- Day centres and nurseries
- Special classes
- Youth organisations (eg Guides, Scouts, YWCA etc)

C.C. NO 802942   **ESTABLISHED** 1990

■ J and A Charitable Trust

OBJECTS General charitable purposes

POLICY OF TRUSTEES To pay or apply the income to such charitable institutions or for such charitable purposes as the Trustees from time to time decide

FINANCES
- Year 1994
- Grants £3,400
- Income £8,245
- Assets £137,290

TRUSTEES J Sieff, A J Bernstein

CORRESPONDENT Messrs H W Fisher & Company, Acre House, 11–15 William Road, London NW1 3ER

CLASSIFICATIONS
- Children and youth – general
- Centres, clubs and institutes

C.C. NO 277368   **ESTABLISHED** 1979

■ The Yvette and Hermione Jacobson Charitable Trust

OBJECTS General charitable purposes

POLICY OF TRUSTEES For young people, disabled, elderly

TYPE OF BENEFICIARY Registered charities working in areas outlined under Policy

RESTRICTIONS Under terms of Trust donations are only made to registered charities not to individuals

BENEFICIAL AREA London, North Yorkshire

FINANCES
- Year 1993
- Grants £24,846
- Income £27,329
- Assets £389,130

TRUSTEES Mrs H Allen, Miles Allen

SUBMISSION OF APPLICATIONS At any time to the address below by letter. Trust income required to meet our present commitments

CORRESPONDENT Mrs J L Allen, JP, 43 Acacia Road, London NW8 6AP

CLASSIFICATIONS
- Children and youth – general

C.C. NO 264491   **ESTABLISHED** 1972

■ John James Bristol Foundation

OBJECTS General charitable purposes

BENEFICIAL AREA Bristol

FINANCES
- Year 1992
- Income £2,913,942

TRUSTEES J James, Ms J Y Johnson, Ms P M Owens, Mrs E Pennington, T R Webley, Mrs J James

SUBMISSION OF APPLICATIONS To Secretary any time – grants normally made in March and September

CORRESPONDENT Mrs G Powney, Secretary to the Trustees, 7 Clyde Road, Redland, Bristol BS6 6RG

CLASSIFICATIONS
- Day centres and nurseries

C.C. NO 288417   **ESTABLISHED** 1983

■ The James Trust

OBJECTS General charitable purposes

POLICY OF TRUSTEES To direct the giving of a limited number of donors to the churches, Christian organisations and individuals of their choice. Support is primarily to Christian causes

TYPE OF GRANT One-off payments

TYPE OF BENEFICIARY Principally Christian organisations

RESTRICTIONS No grants to individuals not known personally to the Trustees

BENEFICIAL AREA UK and overseas

FINANCES
- Year 1994
- Grants £50,925
- Income £28,208
- Assets £8,649

TRUSTEES R J Todd, P Smith

SUBMISSION OF APPLICATIONS To Correspondent

CORRESPONDENT R J Todd, 27 Radway Road, Upper Shirley, Southampton, Hampshire SO15 7PL

CLASSIFICATIONS
- Children and youth – general
- Community groups

C.C. NO 800774   **ESTABLISHED** 1989

■ The Jarman Charitable Trust

OBJECTS General charitable purposes. Youth work, youth clubs, schools

POLICY OF TRUSTEES To support youth and child welfare work – church building extension schemes and general social services in Birmingham District

TYPE OF GRANT Annual donations and one-off payments

TYPE OF BENEFICIARY Youth and child welfare, aged and adult welfare, hospitals, churches

RESTRICTIONS The Trust does not give grants to individuals. Holders of Charity Number prefered

BENEFICIAL AREA Birmingham and District

SAMPLE GRANTS £250 to Birmingham Association of Youth Clubs
£200 to Birmingham Children's Camp
£200 to Stonehouse Gang
£130 to Small Heath School
£130 to St Paul's Community Project Ltd

FINANCES
- Year 1993
- Grants £32,560
- Income £31,155
- Assets £170,000

TRUSTEES G M Jarman, B J Jarman, I J Jarman, S Chilton

SUBMISSION OF APPLICATIONS February and September – telephone calls and sae not required. Application forms not used. Applications not acknowledged. Statement of account if possible. Applications reviewed – April and November

CORRESPONDENT Mrs B J Jarman, 50 Shakespeare Drive, Shirley, Solihull, West Midlands B90 2AN

CLASSIFICATIONS
- Centres, clubs and institutes
- Day centres and nurseries
- Homes and hostels
- Youth organisations (eg Guides, Scouts, YWCA etc)

C.C. NO 239198 **ESTABLISHED** 1964

■ John Jarrold Trust Ltd

OBJECTS General charitable purposes of all kinds and in particular of education and research in all or any of the natural sciences

POLICY OF TRUSTEES Funds fully committed for a long time ahead

TYPE OF GRANT One-off

TYPE OF BENEFICIARY Charities – not individuals

RESTRICTIONS No grants to individuals

BENEFICIAL AREA Norwich and East Anglia

FINANCES
- Year 1995
- Grants £181,831
- Income £174,749
- Assets £95,321

TRUSTEES Council of Management

SUBMISSION OF APPLICATIONS Applications are reviewed at six monthly intervals. No application form is used

CORRESPONDENT B Thompson, Messrs Jarrold & Sons Ltd, Whitefriars, Norwich, Norfolk NR3 1SH

CLASSIFICATIONS
- Children and youth – general
- Adventure centres and playgrounds
- Centres, clubs and institutes
- Community groups
- Day centres and nurseries
- Development of character
- Youth organisations (eg Guides, Scouts, YWCA etc)

C.C. NO 242029 **ESTABLISHED** 1965

■ The Jenour Foundation

OBJECTS General charitable purposes

POLICY OF TRUSTEES Preference to local charities

TYPE OF GRANT At Trustees' discretion

TYPE OF BENEFICIARY Registered charities only

RESTRICTIONS Donations to registered charities only

FINANCES
- Year 1993
- Grants £47,500
- Income £56,000
- Assets £728,176

TRUSTEES P J Phillips, MA, G R Camfield, FCA

CORRESPONDENT R D Taylor, Blenheim House, Fitzalan Court, Newport Road, Cardiff CF2 1TS

CLASSIFICATIONS
- Children and youth – general
- Community groups
- Day centres and nurseries
- Youth organisations (eg Guides, Scouts, YWCA etc)
- Children and violence (inc abuse)

C.C. NO 256637 **ESTABLISHED** 1968

■ Jewish Child's Day

OBJECTS To aid necessitous Jewish children, in making grants to other organisations for such purpose

POLICY OF TRUSTEES To consider applications from organisations in Great Britain and elsewhere for grants for specific purposes of direct benefit to Jewish children. Accounts for the past year must be furnished

TYPE OF GRANT For medical or scientific equipment, educational material, playthings, clothing, medical supplies etc of direct benefit to Jewish children with special needs. Grants are not made towards salaries or capital costs

TYPE OF BENEFICIARY Organisations caring for Jewish children

RESTRICTIONS Grants are made to registered charities only. Applications from individuals, including students, are not normally supported. No grants are made in response to general appeals from large national organisations nor to smaller bodies working in areas other than those set out above

FINANCES
- Year 1993
- Grants £183,185
- Income £240,162

TRUSTEES The National Council

PUBLICATIONS Newsletter published 2 or 3 times per annum

SUBMISSION OF APPLICATIONS Applications need to be received by January and July for consideration at Allocations Meetings in March and September

CORRESPONDENT P Shaw, Executive Director, Jewish Child's Day, 6th floor, 707 High Road, London N12 0BT

CLASSIFICATIONS
- Children and youth – general
- Advancement in life
- Adventure centres and playgrounds
- Centres, clubs and institutes
- Community groups
- Day centres and nurseries
- Counselling (inc helplines)
- Holidays
- Homes and hostels
- Special needs housing
- Special classes
- Children and violence (inc abuse)

C.C. NO 209266 **ESTABLISHED** 1947

■ The Nicholas Joels Charitable Trust

OBJECTS General charitable purposes

TYPE OF BENEFICIARY Registered charities only

FINANCES
- Year 1993
- Grants £16,230
- Income £13,343
- Assets £84,910

TRUSTEES N E Joels, J J Joels, H Joels

SUBMISSION OF APPLICATIONS In writing only

CORRESPONDENT Messrs M S Zatman & Co, Refuge House, 9–10 River Front, Enfield, Middlesex EN1 3SZ

CLASSIFICATIONS
- Children and youth – general

C.C. NO 278409 **ESTABLISHED** 1978

Joicey

■ The Joicey Trust

OBJECTS General charitable purposes

POLICY OF TRUSTEES The Trustees support both Capital and Revenue projects but tend to favour discrete projects over the support of general running costs. Start-up finance is sometimes available, always providing that the Trustees believe that the project can become viable without the Trusts assistance in a small number of years. National appeals are not normally supported unless there is specific evidence of activity benefitting the local area. Unsuccessful applications are not acknowledged unless an sae is provided with the original application

TYPE OF BENEFICIARY Preferably charities in North East

RESTRICTIONS Excluded from consideration are (a) bodies not having registered charitable status, (b) personal applications, and (c) applications on behalf of individuals. Applications from groups that do not have an identifiable project within the beneficial area will not be considered

BENEFICIAL AREA The County of Northumberland and that area of the old metropolitan County of Tyne and Wear

FINANCES
- Year 1995
- Grants £151,000
- Income £151,000
- Assets £3,185,992

TRUSTEES Lord Joicey, Lady Joicey, Elizabeth, Lady Joicey, R H Dickinson, Hon A H Joicey

SUBMISSION OF APPLICATIONS Twice yearly – by end of May and November, in writing to the Appeals Secretary N A Furness at the above address. Applications should include a brief description of the project, together with a copy of the previous years audited accounts and where possible a copy of the current years projected income and expenditure. Large projects should give an indication from where the major sources of funding are likely to come. There are no formal application forms

CORRESPONDENT N A Furness, FCA, Appeals Secretary, Joicey Trust, Messrs Dickinson Dees, Cross House, Westgate Road, Newcastle upon Tyne NE99 1SB

CLASSIFICATIONS
- Children and youth – general
- Adventure centres and playgrounds
- Centres, clubs and institutes
- Community groups
- Day centres and nurseries
- Counselling (inc helplines)
- Special needs housing
- Children and violence (inc abuse)

C.C. NO 244679   ESTABLISHED 1965

■ Edward Cecil Jones Settlement

OBJECTS General charitable purposes

POLICY OF TRUSTEES Local registered charities only considered

TYPE OF GRANT Recurrent and occasional one-off

TYPE OF BENEFICIARY Local registered charities

RESTRICTIONS No grants to individuals

BENEFICIAL AREA County Borough of Southend-on-Sea only

FINANCES
- Year 1993
- Grants £240,920
- Income £211,833
- Assets £374,846

TRUSTEES J E Tolhurst, J S Cue, W J Tolhurst

SUBMISSION OF APPLICATIONS December. No application form used

CORRESPONDENT The Secretary, Edward Cecil Jones Settlement, Messrs Tolhurst & Fisher, Trafalgar House, Nelson Street, Southend-on-Sea, Essex SS1 1EF

CLASSIFICATIONS
- Children and youth – general
- Adoption/fostering
- Homes and hostels
- Youth organisations (eg Guides, Scouts, YWCA etc)

C.C. NO 216166   ESTABLISHED 1957

■ The Anton Jurgens Charitable Trust

OBJECTS General charitable purposes

POLICY OF TRUSTEES To make grants only to those charities which benefit people

TYPE OF GRANT Single cash payments of an appropriate amount

TYPE OF BENEFICIARY Registered charities

FINANCES
- Year 1994
- Grants £285,500
- Income £270,608
- Assets £4,350,356

TRUSTEES C V M Jurgens (Chairman and Secretary), A H M Jurgens (Treasurer), M J Jurgens, M B W M Jurgens, E Deckers, F A V Jurgens

SUBMISSION OF APPLICATIONS To correspondent in August each year

CORRESPONDENT E W Jowett, Messrs Allen & Overy, 9 Cheapside, London EC2V 6AD

CLASSIFICATIONS
- Children and youth – general
- Centres, clubs and institutes
- Community groups
- Day centres and nurseries
- Development of character
- Youth organisations (eg Guides, Scouts, YWCA etc)

C.C. NO 259885   ESTABLISHED 1969

■ The KC Charitable Trust

OBJECTS General charitable purposes

POLICY OF TRUSTEES Principally small local charities preferably concerned with drug abuse, medical research, children/youth (especially the unemployed with special emphasis on re-training schemes and workshops), and aged

TYPE OF GRANT The Trustees will consider regular and once-and-for-all donations

TYPE OF BENEFICIARY Small local charities concerned with drug abuse, medical research, children/youth (especially the unemployed with special emphasis on re-training schemes and workshops) and aged

RESTRICTIONS No grants to individuals

BENEFICIAL AREA Principally Scotland – special emphasis placed on those charities concerned with the Edinburgh area

FINANCES
- Year 1991
- Grants £3,450
- Income £21,330
- Assets £145,878

TRUSTEES Kleinwort Benson Trustees Limited

NOTES It is not the Trustees' policy to acknowledge appeals and applicants will only receive a communication if their appeal has been successful

SUBMISSION OF APPLICATIONS Applications in writing to the correspondent and considered half yearly by the Trustees

CORRESPONDENT Kleinwort Benson Trustees Limited, PO Box 191, 10 Fenchurch Street, London EC3M 3LB

CLASSIFICATIONS
- Counselling (inc helplines)

C.C. NO 268413   **ESTABLISHED** 1974

■ Sheila Kay Fund

OBJECTS To advance public education in the field of social work and to encourage men and women to undertake work in social welfare and similar charitable activities for the benefit of the community in the Metropolitan County of Merseyside

POLICY OF TRUSTEES Trustees' priority, within the broad frame of reference of the Fund, is to local people (a) helping or hoping to help in their local communities, (b) who have limited educational backgrounds, not graduates

TYPE OF GRANT Priority is given to part-time social & community work education, courses, conferences and education visits. The grants are for small amounts to cover fares, fees, babysitting or other incidental expenses. Advice and information is also given

TYPE OF BENEFICIARY Individuals not graduates

RESTRICTIONS Metropolitan County of Merseyside only. Not graduates

BENEFICIAL AREA Merseyside only

FINANCES
- Year 1994
- Grants £22,500
- Income £30,850
- Assets £15,000

TRUSTEES S Bradley, L Dodds, S Ferguson, A Gegg, S Jones, J Lansley, J Moores, M Simpson, V Roberts, L Ward, L White, P Cox

PUBLICATIONS Information leaflet, annual reports

NOTES Company Limited by Guarantee no 2818044

SUBMISSION OF APPLICATIONS If possible minimum of 6 weeks before decision required by applicant. Longer for full-time students

CORRESPONDENT Sheila Kay Fund, 44 Duke Street, Liverpool, Merseyside L1 5AS

CLASSIFICATIONS
- Advancement in life
- Counselling (inc helplines)

C.C. NO 1021378   **ESTABLISHED** 1976

■ The Nancy Kenyon Charitable Trust

OBJECTS General charitable purposes

POLICY OF TRUSTEES Primarily for people and causes known to the Trustees

TYPE OF GRANT Lump sum

TYPE OF BENEFICIARY See Policy of Trustees

RESTRICTIONS No grants to individuals

FINANCES
- Year 1991
- Grants £35,950
- Income £28,146
- Assets £403,714

TRUSTEES C M Kenyon, R B Kenyon, R G Brown

NOTES Applications for causes not known to the Trustees are considered annually in December

SUBMISSION OF APPLICATIONS To correspondent

CORRESPONDENT R B Brown, c/o BDO Binder Hamlyn, Victoria Square, Victoria Street, St Albans AL1 5BB

CLASSIFICATIONS
- Centres, clubs and institutes

C.C. NO 265359   **ESTABLISHED** 1972

■ C M Keyser Charitable Trust (formerly Mr C M Keyser's 1973 Settlement)

OBJECTS General charitable purposes

POLICY OF TRUSTEES Preference to charities of which the Trust has special interest, knowledge or association

TYPE OF GRANT Reviewed annually

TYPE OF BENEFICIARY Registered charities

RESTRICTIONS No grants to individuals

FINANCES
- Year 1995
- Grants £12,121
- Income £13,063

TRUSTEES Mrs M I Keyser, A C Keyser, Miss A M Keyser

SUBMISSION OF APPLICATIONS To the Trustees at any time

CORRESPONDENT Mrs C M Keyser, West Riddens, Ansty, Near Haywards Heath, West Sussex RH17 5AJ

CLASSIFICATIONS
- Children and youth – general

C.C. NO 265716   **ESTABLISHED** 1973

■ The Lorna King Charitable Trust

OBJECTS General charitable purposes

POLICY OF TRUSTEES Generally to support charities providing relief and comfort for those suffering from incapacity, need and infirmities

TYPE OF GRANT £25–£100

TYPE OF BENEFICIARY Both headquarters and local organisations

RESTRICTIONS Registered charities only. Applications from individuals, including students, are ineligible

BENEFICIAL AREA East Midlands

FINANCES
- Year 1994
- Grants £1,000
- Income £1,200

TRUSTEES The Hon Mrs R Marckus, R J R King, A C E Musk, P J S King, J R C King

SUBMISSION OF APPLICATIONS Applications are reviewed in January

CORRESPONDENT Mrs J Barrick, Inglenook, Knottingley, West Yorkshire

CLASSIFICATIONS
- Children and youth – general

C.C. NO 250041   **ESTABLISHED** 1966

■ The King's Fund (formerly King Edward's Hospital Fund for London)

OBJECTS Health care in London. Projects outside London are only supported under specific grant programmes which are initiated by the Fund, usually on an annual basis

POLICY OF TRUSTEES The Grants Committee's priority areas for funding from 1994–1997 are: (a) Projects that encourage equal access to health care. (b) Projects in primary and community care. (c) Projects that will improve the quality of London's acute health services. (d) Projects that will strengthen the voice of the user. (e) Projects that link the arts and health. When considering an application the Trustees look for the following: Will it improve London's health care? Is it promoting fairness in health care? Will it involve health service users? Will it be clear whether it works? Does it support equal opportunities?

TYPE OF GRANT The maximum length of funding is three years

TYPE OF BENEFICIARY Voluntary or statutory health care services in or serving Greater London

RESTRICTIONS Does not support: medical or clinical research; medical equipment; general appeals; long-term funding; vehicles; capital projects (buildings and equipment); holidays and outings; individuals; work outside London

BENEFICIAL AREA London

SAMPLE GRANTS £40,000 to Place to Be towards the Carlton Emotional Support project, which provides a range of therapeutic services for children at Carlton Primary School who may be suffering from emotional, learning or behavioural problems
£14,382 to the Anna Freud Centre towards research to design and standardise measures of child development and adjustments, in order to facilitate evaluation of the effectiveness of child psychotherapy and psychoanalysis
£10,000 to National Association for the Education of Sick Children towards the start-up costs of the organisation, and to a national fact finding survey to establish facts about the education provision for sick children nationwide
£7,500 to Progressive Youth Organisation, a Bengali youth group in Tower Hamlets which works with young people at risk, to fund a part-time HIV/drugs worker to work with young people on local housing estates, to try and prevent the spread of drug abuse and its associated problems amongst the Bengali youth
£1,500 to Young People First to produce a book and tape on a conference run by and for people with Down's Syndrome

FINANCES
- Year 1993
- Grants £1,833,000
- Income £12,757,000
- Assets £131,026,000

TRUSTEES The Management Committee (Chairman: S M Gray) under the authority of the President and General Council

PUBLICATIONS Detailed guidelines for applicants and annual reports

NOTES The figure for Income comprises £5,719,000 investment income and £7,038,000 earned income and grants from other charitable/statutory bodies. Besides grant-giving, the Fund also supports the King's Fund College which aims to raise management standards in the health care fields through seminars, courses and field-based consultancy; the King's Fund Centre which aims to support innovations in the NHS and related organisations, to learn from them, and to encourage the use of good new ideas and practices. The Centre also provides conference facilities and a library service for those interested in health care; the King's Fund Institute which seeks to improve the quality of public debate about health policy through impartial analysis; and the King's Fund Organisational Audit which works to improve the quality of health by the application of organisational standards to hospital and primary care services

SUBMISSION OF APPLICATIONS Potential applicants are advised to contact the Grants Department and obtain a copy of the grant guidelines before making an application. The guidelines are in two parts: Part 1 offers a summary of the various grant programmes and outlines priority themes for the Main Grants Programme. Part 2 gives guidance on submitting an application. The guidelines are also available on tape

CORRESPONDENT Susan Elizabeth, Grants Director, The King's Fund, 11–13 Cavendish Square, London W1M 0AN

CLASSIFICATIONS
- Children and youth – general
- Counselling (inc helplines)

C.C. NO 207401   **ESTABLISHED** 1897

■ The Kirby & West Charitable Trust

OBJECTS General charitable purposes

TYPE OF BENEFICIARY Registered charities

BENEFICIAL AREA mainly Leicester

FINANCES
- Year 1993
- Grants £26,000
- Income £47,657
- Assets £249,768

TRUSTEES B A F Smith, J C Smith, S M Watson

CORRESPONDENT B A F Smith, Kirby & West Ltd, Richard III Road, Leicester LE3 5QU

CLASSIFICATIONS
- Youth organisations (eg Guides, Scouts, YWCA etc)

C.C. NO 700119   **ESTABLISHED** 1988

■ Richard Kirkman Charitable Trust

OBJECTS General charitable purposes

TYPE OF BENEFICIARY Registered charities

BENEFICIAL AREA Southampton

FINANCES
- Year 1993
- Grants £9,250
- Income £49,736
- Assets £32,803

TRUSTEES M Howson-Green, Mrs F O Kirkman

CORRESPONDENT M Howson Green, Charter Court, Third Avenue, Southampton SO9 1QS

CLASSIFICATIONS
- Children and youth – general

C.C. NO 327972   **ESTABLISHED** 1988

■ Kleinwort Benson Charitable Trust

OBJECTS General charitable purposes

POLICY OF TRUSTEES To respond to national appeals only

TYPE OF GRANT Financial donations of £250–£1,000

TYPE OF BENEFICIARY Registered national charities

RESTRICTIONS Local appeals and individuals will not be considered

BENEFICIAL AREA UK

SAMPLE GRANTS £1,000 to Drive for Youth
£1,000 to Youth Clubs UK
£1,000 to YMCA
£5,000 to British Youth Opera

FINANCES
- Year 1994
- Grants £310,000

TRUSTEES Kleinwort Benson Trustees Limited, P J M Prain

SUBMISSION OF APPLICATIONS In writing only to Correspondent for consideration at quarterly meetings

CORRESPONDENT Philip J M Prain, Kleinwort Benson Limited, 20 Fenchurch Street, London EC3P 3DB

CLASSIFICATIONS
- Children and youth – general
- Centres, clubs and institutes
- Holidays
- Homes and hostels
- Youth organisations (eg Guides, Scouts, YWCA etc)

C.C. NO 278180   **ESTABLISHED** 1979

■ The Sir Cyril Kleinwort Charitable Settlement

OBJECTS The Trustees are particularly interested in the fields of education, job-creation, conservation, arts, medical research and care, population control and youth development

POLICY OF TRUSTEES In approved cases, the Trustees will provide assistance towards start-up or capital costs and, with lower priority, towards ongoing expenses. They will normally contribute for say three to five years and then withdraw to devote their resources to other projects

TYPE OF GRANT Regular grants together with a number of once and for all donations

TYPE OF BENEFICIARY Charities known or local to the Trustees and substantial national charitable bodies (but not the local branches or offshoots of these)

RESTRICTIONS The Trustees will not respond favourably to appeals from individuals, nor to those from small local charities, eg individual churches, Village Halls, etc, where there is no special connection

BENEFICIAL AREA Gloucestershire

FINANCES
- Year 1992
- Grants £499,728
- Income £566,258
- Assets £7,582,078

TRUSTEES Kleinwort Benson Trustees Limited

NOTES The Trustees meet twice a year, usually in May and November to consider the appeals that have been received

SUBMISSION OF APPLICATIONS In writing to the correspondent

CORRESPONDENT Kleinwort Benson Trustees Limited, PO Box 191, 10 Fenchurch Street, London EC3M 3LB

CLASSIFICATIONS
- Children and youth – general
- Centres, clubs and institutes
- Homes and hostels
- Youth organisations (eg Guides, Scouts, YWCA etc)

C.C. NO 229915   **ESTABLISHED** 1963

■ Sir James Knott Trust

OBJECTS General charitable purposes

POLICY OF TRUSTEES To make grants to registered charities only

TYPE OF GRANT From £100 to over £10,000

TYPE OF BENEFICIARY For the benefit and well-being of the community

RESTRICTIONS Registered charities only

BENEFICIAL AREA Northumberland, Durham and Tyne & Wear only

FINANCES
- Year 1993
- Grants £991,000
- Income £1,023,000
- Assets £18,541,944

Kroch

TRUSTEES The Rt Hon The Viscount Ridley, KG, DL, Prof the Hon O F W James, M R Cornwall Jones, C A F Baker-Cresswell

NOTES This Trust supercedes the Sir James Knott Settlement (No 227333) which was removed from the Charity Commission Register in June 1991

SUBMISSION OF APPLICATIONS In writing, quoting the applicant's registered charity number and providing full back up information, including details of the connection with the North East of England, steps taken to raise funds and the amount already raised, etc: The trustees meet three times a year

CORRESPONDENT Brigadier (Retd) J F F Sharland, Secretary, Sir James Knott Trust, 16–18 Hood Street, Newcastle-upon-Tyne NE1 6JQ

CLASSIFICATIONS
- Children and youth – general
- Adventure centres and playgrounds
- Centres, clubs and institutes
- Day centres and nurseries
- Development of character
- Counselling (inc helplines)
- Homes and hostels
- Youth organisations (eg Guides, Scouts, YWCA etc)

C.C. NO 1001363 **ESTABLISHED** 1990

■ The Heinz & Anna Kroch Foundation

OBJECTS This Foundation exists to further medical research and to assist individuals suffering severe poverty and financial hardship. Applications must be through a recognised agency eg Social Services, Citizens Advice Bureau etc

POLICY OF TRUSTEES The trustees are most interested in making grants which relate to individuals, not for specific projects. We have made grants to young people, (through the Social Services or housing associations) but these have been for reasons of hardship

TYPE OF GRANT Grants do not exceed £20,000

TYPE OF BENEFICIARY Medical research, humanitarian causes and individual rights, social services

RESTRICTIONS No grants are made to students or for holidays

BENEFICIAL AREA All countries

FINANCES
- Year 1995
- Grants £79,000
- Income £115,000
- Assets £2,000,000

TRUSTEES Mrs A C Kroch-Rhodes, B Rhodes, H J Kroch, P A English, C T Richardson

SUBMISSION OF APPLICATIONS Throughout the year

CORRESPONDENT Mrs H Astle, Administrator, The Heinz & Anna Kroch Foundation, PO Box 17, Worsley, Manchester M28 2SB

CLASSIFICATIONS
- Children and youth – general

C.C. NO 207622 **ESTABLISHED** 1962

■ The Kirby Laing Foundation

OBJECTS General charitable purposes

TYPE OF GRANT Donations – no loans

TYPE OF BENEFICIARY Registered charities only, no gifts to individuals

RESTRICTIONS Does not give to individuals for educational or travel purposes

BENEFICIAL AREA UK

FINANCES
- Year 1993
- Grants £1,209,210
- Income £1,365,803
- Assets £18,636,476

TRUSTEES Sir Kirby Laing, Lady Laing, S Webley, D E Laing

NOTES Giving is coordinated with that of the Beatrice and J W Laing Trusts and with the Maurice Laing Foundation. A separate approach to these Trusts is, therefore, not necessary. To save administration expenses letters of refusal are not sent unless applicants have enclosed a stamped addressed envelope. If no reply is received it can be assumed that the Trusts are unable to give

SUBMISSION OF APPLICATIONS By letter at any time – meetings approximately quarterly, please do not telephone

CORRESPONDENT R M Harley, Box 1, 133 Page Street, Mill Hill, London NW7 2ER

CLASSIFICATIONS
- Development of character
- Youth organisations (eg Guides, Scouts, YWCA etc)

C.C. NO 264299 **ESTABLISHED** 1972

■ The Maurice Laing Foundation

OBJECTS General charitable purposes

POLICY OF TRUSTEES This Trust supprts youth work/ initatives aimed at developing character and good citizenship and promoting Christian faith and values

TYPE OF GRANT Donations – no loans

TYPE OF BENEFICIARY Registered charities only – preferably Headquarters organisation. No gifts to individuals

RESTRICTIONS Does not give grants to individuals for travel or educational purposes. No gifts to playschemes or to schools, except where there has been a personal connection with the Trustees. In general the Trust seldom gives to unsolicited appeals

BENEFICIAL AREA UK

FINANCES
- Year 1994
- Grants £1,399,037
- Income £2,717,864
- Assets £40,824,882

TRUSTEES Sir Maurice Laing, D Edwards, T D Parr, J H Laing, Mrs L Saad, A Gavazzi

NOTES Giving is coordinated with that of the Beatrice, Kirby and J W Laing Trusts. A separate approach to these Trusts is, therefore, not necessary. To save administration expenses, letters of refusal are not sent unless applicant has enclosed a stamped addressed envelope. If no reply is received it may be assumed that the Trusts are unable to give

SUBMISSION OF APPLICATIONS By letter at any time – meetings approximately quarterly. Telephone calls are discouraged and may well provoke adverse reaction

CORRESPONDENT R M Harley, Box 1, 133 Page Street, Mill Hill, London NW7 2ER

CLASSIFICATIONS
- Development of character
- Youth organisations (eg Guides, Scouts, YWCA etc)

C.C. NO 264301   **ESTABLISHED** 1972

■ Beatrice Laing Trust

OBJECTS The relief of poverty, the advancement of the evangelical faith at home and abroad

POLICY OF TRUSTEES Small (three-figure) annual grants to a wide range of charities. Some special gifts for particular projects of a larger nature

TYPE OF GRANT Cash. No loans

TYPE OF BENEFICIARY National and local charities serving deprived sections of the community, home and foreign missionary societies, a few grants to individuals working in the mission field to assist their work

RESTRICTIONS No grants to individuals for education or travel

BENEFICIAL AREA UK and overseas

FINANCES
- **Year** 1995
- **Grants** £625,203
- **Income** £738,402
- **Assets** £10,779,117

TRUSTEES Sir Kirby Laing, Sir Maurice Laing, J M K Laing, D E Laing, C M Laing, J H Laing

NOTES Trust is run in co-ordination with the Kirby Laing and Maurice Laing Foundations and the J W Laing Trust. It is seldom that gifts are duplicated by these Trusts. In order to save administration expenses letters of refusal are not sent unless there is strong reason (such as a stamped addressed envelope) to suppose such a letter to be necessary. Applicants may assume that if they receive no reply the Trusts are unable to give

SUBMISSION OF APPLICATIONS By letter at any time. Telephone calls are discouraged and may have an adverse effect. Appeals considered monthly

CORRESPONDENT The Administrator, Beatrice Laing Trust, Box 1, 133 Page Street, London NW7 2ER

CLASSIFICATIONS
- Children and youth – general
- Community groups
- Homes and hostels
- Special needs housing
- Special classes

C.C. NO 211884   **ESTABLISHED** 1952

■ Laing's Charitable Trust

OBJECTS The relief of poverty, incapacity or sickness or the advancement of education or religion or such other charitable purposes generally as the Trustees shall in their absolute discretion think fit, having special regard to the provision of gratuities or allowances for employees of John Laing plc or their dependants who are in special need of financial assistance on account of any illness or on account of old age or from other causes

POLICY OF TRUSTEES To consider applications from applicants as shown below under Type of Beneficiary

TYPE OF GRANT Mainly one-off and are £50–£100

TYPE OF BENEFICIARY Employees of John Laing plc and their dependants or charitable (registered or exempt) organisations

RESTRICTIONS No grants to individuals (other than to Laing Group employees and/or their dependants). Written applications only

FINANCES
- **Year** 1994
- **Grants** £1,023,408
- **Income** £1,375,052
- **Assets** £22,939,964

TRUSTEES Sir Kirby Laing, Sir Maurice Laing, R A Wood, J M K Laing, D C Madden

SUBMISSION OF APPLICATIONS In writing to the Secretary. No particular form of application is required. The Trust asks applicants, in the interest of reducing costs, to accept a non-response as a negative reply; if more is sought, a reply-paid envelope must be sent with the application. The Trust does not encourage exploratory telephone calls on 'how best to approach the Trust'

CORRESPONDENT D W Featherstone, Secretary, Laing's Charitable Trust, 133 Page Street, London NW7 2ER

CLASSIFICATIONS
- Children and youth – general
- Advancement in life
- Adventure centres and playgrounds
- Centres, clubs and institutes
- Community groups
- Development of character
- Counselling (inc helplines)
- Holidays
- Homes and hostels
- Special needs housing
- Special classes
- Youth organisations (eg Guides, Scouts, YWCA etc)
- Children and violence (inc abuse)

C.C. NO 236852   **ESTABLISHED** 1962

■ Lalonde Charitable Trust

OBJECTS General charitable purposes

POLICY OF TRUSTEES To favour children's charities

TYPE OF BENEFICIARY Community-based voluntary groups

BENEFICIAL AREA Mainly Bristol

SAMPLE GRANTS £1,000 to Woodside Family Centre
£250 to Fairbridge, Avon

FINANCES
- **Year** 1995
- **Grants** £12,000
- **Income** £12,000
- **Assets** £250,000

Lancaster's

Alphabetical register of grant making charitable trusts

TRUSTEES R A Lalonde, B M Lalonde

CORRESPONDENT R A Lalonde, 2 Norland Road, Clifton, Bristol, Avon BS8 3LP

CLASSIFICATIONS
- Children and youth – general

C.C. NO 802863   **ESTABLISHED** 1989

■ Bryan Lancaster's Trust

OBJECTS General charitable purposes

POLICY OF TRUSTEES Help towards setting up rather than running costs, generally for community and welfare projects. We have a preference for small and newer charities, working in the North West

TYPE OF GRANT Usually one-off grants towards a specific object

TYPE OF BENEFICIARY See Policy of Trustees

RESTRICTIONS Applications from individuals and students are not usually considered

BENEFICIAL AREA UK

FINANCES
- Year 1993
- Grants £29,000
- Income £27,500

TRUSTEES D M Butler, A LeMare, C Cathrow

SUBMISSION OF APPLICATIONS At any time. Trustees meet about every two months. No telephone calls. Please enclose sae; no acknowledgement without. By letter, no application form

CORRESPONDENT David M Butler, 9 Greenside, Kendal, Cumbria LA9 5DU

CLASSIFICATIONS
- Children and youth – general

C.C. NO 222902   **ESTABLISHED** 1719

■ The Allen Lane Foundation

OBJECTS General charitable purposes

POLICY OF TRUSTEES Principally to give help to projects throughout the United Kingdom concerned with the problems of social disadvantage, mental handicap and the environment. The Trustees have also started a limited funding programme for women's groups in the Republic of Ireland. They are concerned, for instance, with the needs of groups which help young people at risk, deprived children, ethnic minority groups, refugees, victims of violence, single parent families and ex-offenders as well as the handicapped. They give especially sympathetic consideration to pioneering causes and to those which may have less popular appeal. They also offer support where they can to organisations in the community which encourage self-help

TYPE OF GRANT Grants are normally made for one year only although longer-term funding may sometimes be offered for a maximum of three consecutive years. Most grants are in the range of £500–£5,000

TYPE OF BENEFICIARY Registered charities only in the UK

RESTRICTIONS The Trustees do not respond to large national appeals, to requests for funding for private education, individual study, overseas travel, arts projects or any project of a sectarian or religious nature. They do not make grants for cases of personal need, building costs, the capital purchase costs of property, the restoration of historic buildings, medical research or the costs of publications. The Trustees regret that they are no longer able to consider help with the costs of holidays or holiday playschemes or with projects concerned with addiction

FINANCES
- Year 1994
- Grants £344,996
- Income £458,086
- Assets £6,228,378

TRUSTEES Mrs Christine Teale, Mrs Clare Morpurgo, B C G Whitaker, Charles Medewar, Sebastian Morpurgo, Zoe Teale

PUBLICATIONS Fact sheet. Summary of evaluation of Irish funding programme

NOTES The Trustees regret that applications far outstrip the funds available and not all good or appropriate projects can be offered funding even though they may fall well within current policy. A rejection is no reflection on the merit of the appeal

SUBMISSION OF APPLICATIONS Applications may be sent to the Secretary at the address below at any time. These should include full information about the aims and structure of the organisation applying for a grant together with details of the funding required for the specific aspect of their work which the applicants would like the Trustees to consider. Other sources of funding should be identified and plans for the future should be outlined where these are known. An indication of how projects are to be monitored should be included. Grants, which can be made only for charitable purposes, are allocated at meetings of Trustees which are held three times a year. Applications cannot be considered between meetings nor can any group apply for funding more than once in a calendar year

CORRESPONDENT Heather Swailes, The Allen Lane Foundation, Room 6A, Winchester House, 11 Cranmer Road, London SW9 6EJ

CLASSIFICATIONS
- Adoption/fostering
- Adventure centres and playgrounds
- Community groups
- Day centres and nurseries
- Counselling (inc helplines)
- Children and violence (inc abuse)

C.C. NO 248031   **ESTABLISHED** 1966

■ Langdale Trust

OBJECTS General charitable purposes

POLICY OF TRUSTEES To assist the infirm, youth organisations, the poor and needy of all ages

TYPE OF GRANT Annual for general and specific use

TYPE OF BENEFICIARY Other charitable organisations

BENEFICIAL AREA Grants given to Oxfam, Save the Children etc. Funds to be used for overseas projects

FINANCES
- Year 1991
- Grants £80,000
- Income £93,000
- Assets £493,000

TRUSTEES T R Wilson, M J Woodward, Mrs T M Elvin

SUBMISSION OF APPLICATIONS March

CORRESPONDENT M J Woodward, Messrs Lee Crowder, 24 Harborne Road, Birmingham, West Midlands B15 3AD

CLASSIFICATIONS
- Centres, clubs and institutes
- Day centres and nurseries
- Holidays
- Youth organisations (eg Guides, Scouts, YWCA etc)

C.C. NO 215317   **ESTABLISHED** 1960

■ The Langtree Trust

OBJECTS General charitable purposes

POLICY OF TRUSTEES Trustees' policy is to consider requests only from within the County of Gloucestershire

TYPE OF GRANT Usually one-off for a specific project

TYPE OF BENEFICIARY The local community

RESTRICTIONS No grants to individuals for training for higher qualifications. Occasional grants to students on, eg Outward Bound, Operation Raleigh. No grants in response to general appeals from large national organisations

BENEFICIAL AREA Gloucestershire only

FINANCES
- Year 1993
- Grants £42,321
- Income £45,266
- Assets £911,822

TRUSTEES R H Mann, Col P Haslam, Mrs J Humpidge, G J Yates, Mrs A M Shepherd

SUBMISSION OF APPLICATIONS To the correspondent at any time for consideration at meetings held about every three months. No form is used: application is by simple letter. National appeals are not acknowledged unless there is a specific relevance to Gloucestershire. Relevant details of the sums required and annual finances will assist judgement of grants

CORRESPONDENT The Secretary, The Langtree Trust, c/o Randall & Payne, Rodborough Court, Stroud, Gloucestershire GL5 3LR

CLASSIFICATIONS
- Centres, clubs and institutes
- Day centres and nurseries
- Holidays

C.C. NO 232924   **ESTABLISHED** 1963

■ The Lankelly Foundation

OBJECTS General charitable purposes

POLICY OF TRUSTEES Currently the Trust's main priorities are to help: communities/families to create an environment in which they can flourish; groups marginalised because of poverty, unemployment or crime; and the mentally or physically handicapped. Broad priority areas include young people, homelessness, penal affairs, alcohol and drugs, ethnic minorities and the elderly. (Heritage and 'The Arts' are lower priority, but in these areas, preference will be given to groups isolated by place, culture, or disadvantaged by poverty or disability)

TYPE OF GRANT Grants are rarely less than £5,000 and are always for specific purposes but may cover capital or revenue costs

TYPE OF BENEFICIARY Registered charities working in the areas outlined under Policy of Trustees with a focus on smaller charities with a local or regional remit

RESTRICTIONS Registered charities only. Applications from individuals, including students, are ineligible. No grants made in response to general appeals from large, national organisations, nor to circular appeals of any kind. No grants are made in support of the advancement of religion, individual youth clubs and children under five (other than summer holiday schemes)

BENEFICIAL AREA UK but not Greater London area

SAMPLE GRANTS £40,000 to Raleigh Trust London towards the Youth Development Programme on Merseyside. (Spread over two years)
£11,000 to Learning Through Action Trust towards developing new teaching resource pack for secondary schools. (One-off)
£10,000 to Young Person's Advisory Service, Liverpool towards cost of major new refurbishment programme. (One-off)

FINANCES
- Year 1994–95
- Grants £2,606,490
- Income £2,236,703
- Assets £7,097,073

TRUSTEES A Ramsey Hack, C Heather, W J Mackenzie, Shirley Turner, L Fraser-McKenzie, Mrs G Linton, Lady Meslyn-Rees

PUBLICATIONS Annual Report. Guidelines for applicants

NOTES In September 1993 the assets of the Hambland Foundation were transferred to its sister Trust the Lankelly Foundation. The Hambland Foundation has ceased to operate as a grantmaking trust

SUBMISSION OF APPLICATIONS At any time. Trustees meet quarterly. Applications should include clear details of the need the project is designed to meet plus an outline budget, annual report and accounts

CORRESPONDENT Peter Kilgarriff, Secretary, The Lankelly Foundation, 2 The Court, High Street, Harwell, Didcot, Oxon OX11 0EY

CLASSIFICATIONS
- Children and youth – general
- Community groups
- Development of character
- Holidays
- Special needs housing

C.C. NO 256987   **ESTABLISHED** 1968

■ Laspen Trust (formerly the Penrhyn Charitable Trust)

OBJECTS General charitable purposes

POLICY OF TRUSTEES Youth, arts, handicapped, health, welfare, environmental. Applications are considered on their relative merits, preference being given to those associated with the beneficial area, particularly the locality of the Trust

TYPE OF GRANT Usually one-off donations

TYPE OF BENEFICIARY Mainly registered charities

RESTRICTIONS No grants to individuals

BENEFICIAL AREA UK with preference for North Wales, Merseyside, Northern Ireland

SAMPLE GRANTS £375 to Harvest Trust
£250 to Childline Wales

Laurence's

£250 to The Weston Spirit, Liverpool
£100 to British Schools Exploring Society
£100 to Brownlow Play Association

FINANCES
● Year 1995
● Grants £6,875
● Income £8,033
● Assets £126,355

TRUSTEES The Lady Janet Douglas Pennant, R C H Douglas Pennant, J C Douglas Pennant (Secretary)

SUBMISSION OF APPLICATIONS June or December. In the interest of economy unsuccessful applications or inquiries are not acknowledged or answered

CORRESPONDENT J C Douglas Pennant, Penrhyn, Bangor, Gwynedd LL57 4HN

CLASSIFICATIONS
● Children and youth – general
● Adventure centres and playgrounds
● Centres, clubs and institutes
● Day centres and nurseries
● Development of character
● Holidays
● Homes and hostels
● Youth organisations (eg Guides, Scouts, YWCA etc)

C.C. NO 276043   **ESTABLISHED** 1978

■ Kathleen Laurence's Trust

OBJECTS General charitable purposes

TYPE OF GRANT General

RESTRICTIONS No grants to individuals

BENEFICIAL AREA UK

FINANCES
● Year 1993
● Income £117,000

TRUSTEES Coutts and Company Trustees

SUBMISSION OF APPLICATIONS Quarterly in February, May, August, November

CORRESPONDENT The Manager, Trustee Department, Coutts & Co, 440 The Strand, London WC2R 0QS

CLASSIFICATIONS
● Children and youth – general

C.C. NO 296461   **ESTABLISHED** 1987

■ The Lavender Trust

OBJECTS General charitable purposes

POLICY OF TRUSTEES Principally support of evangelical christianity and relief of sickness

RESTRICTIONS No individuals

BENEFICIAL AREA Surrey

FINANCES
● Year 1993
● Grants £14,995
● Income £16,000
● Assets £4,006

TRUSTEES C D Leck, E J Leck

SUBMISSION OF APPLICATIONS In writing, Trustees consider applications throughout the year

CORRESPONDENT C D Leck, 50 Hartley Down, Purley, Surrey CR8 4EA

CLASSIFICATIONS
● Children and youth – general

C.C. NO 290935   **ESTABLISHED** 1984

■ The Lawlor Foundation

OBJECTS The principal objective of this Foundation is the relief of poverty and advancement of education in Northern Ireland and the Republic of Ireland. Funding is also given to projects aiming to treat and prevent drug abuse and alcohol abuse. The Foundation is permitted to support 'general charitable purposes', and a number of donations reflect the Trustees' personal interests

POLICY OF TRUSTEES The Trustees have a particular interest in promoting co-operation and mutual understanding between the peoples of Ireland, North and South. Currently, the emphasis is on education

TYPE OF GRANT Grants are made on a one-off or recurring basis and can include core funding and salaries. A substantial proportion of the Foundation's income is committed on a long-term basis, which restricts disposable income. Grants made to individuals are between £100 and £1,500; grants made to organisations are between £250 and £10,000. The maximum length of support is normally three years, but schools are invited to reapply at the end of this period

TYPE OF BENEFICIARY The principal beneficiaries of the Foundation include British-based organisations which support Irish immigrants and vulnerable young people, and a number of Northern Irish educational establishments and individual students

RESTRICTIONS No grants are made in response to general appeals from large national organisations outside the geographical areas of Ireland, London and the Home Counties

BENEFICIAL AREA Mainly Northern Ireland. Also Republic of Ireland and Britain

SAMPLE GRANTS £10,000 to Jesus College, Cambridge to enable the College to help financially disadvantaged undergraduates from Northern Ireland. (This is the third annual grant)
£10,000 to Brent Adolescent Centre, London to support the organisation's treatment of and research into adolescent breakdown. (This is a continuation of recurrent annual grants)
£2,500 to Irish Youth Foundation towards the support of a large number of Irish youth groups throughout Britain. (This was the second of two annual grants)
£1,200 to O'Casey Theatre Training Project, Derry to fund a bursary for a student to take part in a six-week professional training course in Derry. (This was a one-off grant)

FINANCES
● Year 1994–95
● Grants £133,520
● Income £160,876
● Assets £2,190,169

TRUSTEES E L Lawlor, V K Lawlor, K K Lawlor, F M Baker, S D Morris, M Spiro

PUBLICATIONS Annual Report

NOTES Fax number: 01992 578727

SUBMISSION OF APPLICATIONS At any time by letter to the Secretary, with description of project and latest accounts. Preliminary telephone enquires are also welcomed. The Trustees meet in March, June, September and December

CORRESPONDENT Mrs Carley Brown, Secretary to the Lawlor Foundation, 117 High Street, Epping, Essex CM16 4BD

CLASSIFICATIONS
- Advancement in life
- Centres, clubs and institutes
- Community groups
- Development of character

C.C. NO 297219   ESTABLISHED 1987

■ Raymond and Blanche Lawson Charitable Trust

OBJECTS General charitable purposes

POLICY OF TRUSTEES The Trustees support local charities. They discourage applications from outside the area

TYPE OF GRANT The charity normally makes annual grants to registered charities

TYPE OF BENEFICIARY Registered charities working in the area. Preference is often given to newly established charities

RESTRICTIONS Registered charities only. Applications from individuals, including students, are not entertained

BENEFICIAL AREA Whilst national charities are considered, local charities are favoured

FINANCES
- Year 1995
- Grants £64,602
- Income £90,251
- Assets £725,379

TRUSTEES J V Banks, J A Bertram, Mrs P E V Banks

SUBMISSION OF APPLICATIONS At any time. The Trustees are in regular contact. Applications should include clear details of the need for which assistance is sought

CORRESPONDENT Mrs P E V Banks, 28 Barden Road, Tonbridge, Kent TN9 1TX

CLASSIFICATIONS
- Development of character
- Homes and hostels

C.C. NO 281269   ESTABLISHED 1980

■ The Julian Layton Charity Trust

OBJECTS General charitable purposes

POLICY OF TRUSTEES Primarily to support Jewish charities

TYPE OF GRANT One-off

TYPE OF BENEFICIARY Jewish charities

RESTRICTIONS No individuals

FINANCES
- Year 1994
- Grants £6,000
- Income £9,477
- Assets £181,843

TRUSTEES A H Woolf, K H L Layton, R A Barsham

SUBMISSION OF APPLICATIONS Applications not normally considered

CORRESPONDENT R A Barsham, Messrs Barsham, Bradford & Hamilton, 1 Lincoln's Inn Fields, London WC2A 3AA

CLASSIFICATIONS
- Centres, clubs and institutes

C.C. NO 239268   ESTABLISHED 1964

■ The Leach Fourteenth Trust

OBJECTS General charitable purposes

POLICY OF TRUSTEES Trustees mainly seek out their own ventures to support

TYPE OF BENEFICIARY Grants to registered charities only

RESTRICTIONS Grants to registered charities only

BENEFICIAL AREA UK

FINANCES
- Year 1994
- Grants £70,000
- Income £110,150
- Assets £1,800,000

TRUSTEES W J Henderson, M A Hayes, Mrs J M M Nash, R Murray-Leach

SUBMISSION OF APPLICATIONS No application forms. Not all applications acknowledged

CORRESPONDENT Mr and Mrs R Murray-Leach, Nettleton Mill, Castle Combe, Nr Chippenham, Wiltshire SN14 7HJ

CLASSIFICATIONS
- Children and youth – general

C.C. NO 204844   ESTABLISHED 1961

■ The Alfred Leadbeater Trust

OBJECTS Medical institutions or charities and children's homes

TYPE OF GRANT Donations

RESTRICTIONS Restricted to the benefit of medical institutions and children's orphanages and homes within the City of Birmingham

BENEFICIAL AREA Birmingham

FINANCES
- Year 1991
- Grants £8,050
- Income £8,246
- Assets £53,550

TRUSTEES Mrs P Henderson, Mrs L C Ludgate, W A Ludgate, D R Henderson and two representatives of Birmingham City Council

SUBMISSION OF APPLICATIONS By 1st June in each year and considered at Annual Meeting in July

CORRESPONDENT Cartwright & Lewis, 5 Oak Tree Lane, Selly Oak, Birmingham B29 6JE

CLASSIFICATIONS
- Homes and hostels

C.C. NO 215238   ESTABLISHED 1923

■ The League of the Helping Hand

OBJECTS To help and alleviate individual cases of suffering in mind or body among persons who, in the opinion of the General Committee of the League, are of gentle birth and in reduced circumstances

POLICY OF TRUSTEES The Objects have been extended to include everyone of good character who find themselves in financial difficulties through serious physical or mental illness

TYPE OF GRANT Over half the beneficiaries receive regular quarterly grants designed to cover essential costs for as long as their circumstances remain unchanged, up to £10 weekly given towards nursing home fees, but waiting list here.

Single grants for replacement of household furnishings and appliances, convalescence and respite care

TYPE OF BENEFICIARY Individuals in financial need as result of physical or mental illness

RESTRICTIONS Grants to individuals only. Must be referred by professionals in writing. No telephone calls

BENEFICIAL AREA Throughout UK

FINANCES
- Year 1994
- Grants £70,331
- Income £78,036
- Assets £951,591

TRUSTEES Rev R D Beal, Mrs S A Ram, Rev D Staple, T R Darvall, N W Roskill, Mrs G Lavelle, Mrs B Slater, J S Korn, W A Angelo-Sparling

PUBLICATIONS Report and Accounts annually in August

SUBMISSION OF APPLICATIONS Applications for regular ongoing grants considered quarterly. Those for single payment grants every 6 weeks. For nursing home fees when they reach top of waiting list. Please send sae

CORRESPONDENT Mrs I Goodlad, Secretary, 226 Petersham Road, Petersham, Richmond, Surrey TW10 7AL

CLASSIFICATIONS
- Children and youth – general
- Special needs housing

C.C. NO 208792   ESTABLISHED 1908

■ The William Leech Charity

OBJECTS General charitable purposes

POLICY OF TRUSTEES Grants are only rarely made outside Northumberland, Tyne and Wear, Co Durham

RESTRICTIONS No grants to individuals, students, expeditions

BENEFICIAL AREA North East of England only

SAMPLE GRANTS £2,500 to Dockray House West End Boys' Club
£1,000 for three years to Berwick Youth Project
£500 to County of Durham School Benevolent Fund for coats and shoes for needy children
£500 to Fairbridge for youth work in Tyne and Wear

FINANCES
- Year 1994
- Grants £434,358
- Income £501,953
- Assets £5,507,069

TRUSTEES R E Leech (Chairman), K G M M Alberti, C J Davies, J E Miller, A Reed, N Sherlock, B W Spark

SUBMISSION OF APPLICATIONS In writing only. Trustees meet six times a year. At the end of January, March, May, July, September and November

CORRESPONDENT Mrs K M Smith, The William Leech Charity, 4 St James' Street, Newcastle upon Tyne, Tyne and Wear NE1 4NG

CLASSIFICATIONS
- Adoption/fostering
- Centres, clubs and institutes
- Community groups
- Homes and hostels
- Special needs housing

- Special classes
- Youth organisations (eg Guides, Scouts, YWCA etc)
- Children and violence (inc abuse)

C.C. NO 265491   ESTABLISHED 1972

■ The Lester Trust Fund

OBJECTS Religious, educational or social work

RESTRICTIONS Trustees limit support to organisations based in London

BENEFICIAL AREA London

FINANCES
- Year 1991
- Assets £139,165
- Income £19,361

TRUSTEES C Snelling

CORRESPONDENT C Snelling, Midgley, Snelling & Co, 61–65 Baker Street, Weybridge, Surrey KT13 8AH

CLASSIFICATIONS
- Advancement in life

C.C. NO 292583   ESTABLISHED 1929

■ Lord Leverhulme's Charitable Trust

OBJECTS General charitable purposes

POLICY OF TRUSTEES Priority given to certain Trusts and charitable organisations in Cheshire and to major general appeals

TYPE OF GRANT Cash grants

TYPE OF BENEFICIARY Registered charities only

RESTRICTIONS Preference for the County of Cheshire

BENEFICIAL AREA In particular Cheshire

FINANCES
- Year 1995
- Grants £759,272
- Income £499,728

TRUSTEES A H S Hannay, A E J Heber-Percy

SUBMISSION OF APPLICATIONS By post to Joint Secretary

CORRESPONDENT The Trustees of The Lord Leverhulme Charitable Trust, 1 Embankment Place, London WC2N 6NN

CLASSIFICATIONS
- Centres, clubs and institutes
- Community groups
- Youth organisations (eg Guides, Scouts, YWCA etc)

C.C. NO 212431   ESTABLISHED 1957

■ Joseph Levy Charitable Foundation

OBJECTS General charitable purposes

POLICY OF TRUSTEES Primarily preference given to projects concerned with medicine and health and children and youth

TYPE OF GRANT Recurrent and one-off

TYPE OF BENEFICIARY Registered charities only

RESTRICTIONS No individuals considered

BENEFICIAL AREA UK

FINANCES
- Year 1995
- Grants £800,000
- Income £785,000
- Assets £8,990,000

TRUSTEES Mrs N F Levy, P L Levy, OBE, S Krendel, LL B, Mrs J Jason, N W Benson, FCA

SUBMISSION OF APPLICATIONS At any time to the Director by letter

CORRESPONDENT Dr Sidney Brichto, Joseph Levy Charitable Foundation, Pegasus House, 37–43 Sackville Street, London W1X 2DL

CLASSIFICATIONS
- Children and youth – general
- Advancement in life
- Centres, clubs and institutes

C.C. NO 245592   **ESTABLISHED** 1965

■ Lewis Family Charitable Trust

OBJECTS General charitable purposes

POLICY OF TRUSTEES Special preference to disabled

TYPE OF GRANT Grants are normally made only once a year

TYPE OF BENEFICIARY Charitable and medical institutions

RESTRICTIONS Grants are not made to individuals

BENEFICIAL AREA International

FINANCES
- Year 1975
- Grants £180,151
- Income £202,540
- Assets £55,177

TRUSTEES D Lewis, B Lewis

SUBMISSION OF APPLICATIONS January, each year. Grants are not made to individuals

CORRESPONDENT The Secretary, Lewis Family Charitable Trust, Chelsea House, West Gate, London W5 1DR

CLASSIFICATIONS
- Children and youth – general
- Homes and hostels

C.C. NO 259892   **ESTABLISHED** 1969

■ The Lewis Family Charitable Trust

OBJECTS General charitable purposes

POLICY OF TRUSTEES Relief of poverty and help to handicapped and sick

TYPE OF GRANT Cash donations one-off and recurrent – some for indefinite periods

TYPE OF BENEFICIARY Registered charities only, normally national Headquarters organisations and mainly those concerned with the elderly and handicapped (long established)

RESTRICTIONS No grants to individuals

FINANCES
- Year 1992
- Grants £9,039
- Income £9,039
- Assets £150,000

TRUSTEES T Lewis, D Lewis, R K Lewis

SUBMISSION OF APPLICATIONS Mainly March, September. No application form. No telephone calls. We request sae's from recurrent beneficiaries. Applications cannot be acknowledged and must state registered charity number

CORRESPONDENT D Lewis, 22 York Terrace West, Regent's Park, London NW1 4QA

CLASSIFICATIONS
- Children and youth – general

C.C. NO 262872   **ESTABLISHED** 1971

■ The John Spedan Lewis Foundation

OBJECTS General charitable purposes

POLICY OF TRUSTEES To serve charitable purposes, particularly those that reflect the interest of John Spedan Lewis in education, the arts, the natural sciences — horticulture, ornithology, entomology and the encouragement of potential talent, particularly among the young

TYPE OF GRANT Mostly straight donations which may be repeated. Salaries not normally funded

TYPE OF BENEFICIARY Preference given to smaller, more imaginative appeals. The Trustees do not make donations to local branches of national organisations, individual students or expeditions

RESTRICTIONS Objects must be exclusively charitable according to the law

BENEFICIAL AREA Great Britain and Northern Ireland

FINANCES
- Year 1995
- Grants £31,800
- Income £27,400
- Assets £664,000

TRUSTEES S Hampson, M K J Miller, W L R E Gilchrist, H M J King, Miss C Walton

SUBMISSION OF APPLICATIONS Write to Secretary giving details and enclosing, where applicable, latest report and accounts

CORRESPONDENT N Waldemar Brown, Secretary, The John Spedan Lewis Foundation, 171 Victoria Street, London SW1E 5NN

CLASSIFICATIONS
- Children and youth – general
- Advancement in life
- Development of character
- Special classes

C.C. NO 240473   **ESTABLISHED** 1964

■ Lilley Benevolent Trust

OBJECTS General charitable purposes

POLICY OF TRUSTEES The Trustees consider annually the charities to be supported. Preference is given to registered charities of which they have special interest or association, in particular those with connections with Sussex

TYPE OF GRANT Mainly recurrent

TYPE OF BENEFICIARY Registered charities

RESTRICTIONS No grants to individuals – Registered charities only

BENEFICIAL AREA mainly Sussex

FINANCES
- Year 1993
- Grants £17,850
- Income £19,988
- Assets £158,871

TRUSTEES T J R Lilley, N T Neal, A Osmond, Carole Lilley, J P Merricks, JP

SUBMISSION OF APPLICATIONS In writing – before October in any one year

CORRESPONDENT D W J O'Brien, The Grey House, Hooe Common, Battle, East Sussex TN33 9EN

Linder

Alphabetical register of grant making charitable trusts

CLASSIFICATIONS
- Adoption/fostering
- Counselling (inc helplines)
- Children and violence (inc abuse)

C.C. NO 232174   **ESTABLISHED** 1961

■ The Enid Linder Foundation

OBJECTS General charitable purposes with a bias towards the relief of poverty

POLICY OF TRUSTEES To support a limited number of charities on an ongoing basis rather than to make ad hoc contributions. This policy is reviewed from time to time and when possible, additional charities are supported. Also try to support a small number of students each year with a bias towards medicine and research

TYPE OF GRANT Ongoing normally twice-yearly. Students receive one-off payments

TYPE OF BENEFICIARY Authorised charities and qualifying individuals

RESTRICTIONS The funds of the Trust are limited and consequently donations or grants to individuals are rare. No grants are given for specifically religious purposes and the Trustees rarely respond to ad hoc or crisis appeals

BENEFICIAL AREA International

FINANCES
- Year 1994
- Grants £250,000

TRUSTEES J E Ladeveze, Mrs A A Ladeveze, G S K Huntly, J S Stubbings, M Butler

SUBMISSION OF APPLICATIONS The Trustees consider applications from charities annually (Feb/March). Student applications should be made April/May for following academic year all applications are acknowledged

CORRESPONDENT Mrs A A Ladeveze, Secretary to the Trustees, 1 North Court, Great Peter Street, Westminster, London SW1P 3LL

CLASSIFICATIONS
- Homes and hostels

C.C. NO 267509   **ESTABLISHED** 1974

■ The Fred Linford Charitable Trust

OBJECTS General charitable purposes

POLICY OF TRUSTEES Giving strictly limited to the area of South Staffordshire

RESTRICTIONS Those outside the beneficial area are ineligible for funding

BENEFICIAL AREA South Staffordshire only

FINANCES
- Year 1995
- Assets £155,000
- Income £10,000

TRUSTEES D Linford, J K Linford

CORRESPONDENT D Linford, The Kennels, Upper Longdon, Rugeley, Staffordshire WS15 1QF

CLASSIFICATIONS
- Children and youth – general

C.C. NO 1012203   **ESTABLISHED** 1966

■ The Lister Charitable Trust

OBJECTS General charitable purposes

POLICY OF TRUSTEES To advance the educational and physical, mental and spiritual development of children (or young persons under the age of 25) by providing or assisting in providing facilities for training in sailing and seamanship of children and young persons who have need of such facilities by reason of poverty or social or economic circumstances (so that they may grow to full maturity as individuals and members of society) and to provide or assist in the provision of facilities for recreation and other leisure time occupation of the general public with the object of improving their conditions of life

TYPE OF GRANT Usually one-off for specific project or part of a project. Core funding and/or salaries rarely considered

TYPE OF BENEFICIARY Registered charities working in the areas outlined under Policy ie sailing/seamanship

RESTRICTIONS Registered charities only. Applications from individuals, including students, are ineligible. No grants made in response to general appeals from large, national organisations nor to smaller bodies working in areas other than those set out above

BENEFICIAL AREA UK

FINANCES
- Year 1995
- Grants £100,000
- Income £355,000
- Assets £5,164,000

TRUSTEES J C Douglas-Withers, N A V Lister, B J C Hall, D J Lister, D A Collingwood

PUBLICATIONS Annual report

SUBMISSION OF APPLICATIONS At any time. Applications should include clear details of the need the intended project is designed to meet plus an outline budget. Only applications from eligible bodies are acknowledged, when further information may be requested

CORRESPONDENT N A V Lister, Windyridge, The Close, Totteridge, London N20 8PT

CLASSIFICATIONS
- Advancement in life
- Development of character

C.C. NO 288730   **ESTABLISHED** 1981

■ Liverpool Children's Welfare Trust

OBJECTS Provision of material needs, cots, prams, bedding, clothing and footwear, etc. Holidays for mothers and children. Fares for visiting sick children in hospital

POLICY OF TRUSTEES Grants allocated to individual cases of need. Deprived, sick and disabled children as recommended by social workers, health visitors, and others

TYPE OF GRANT For material needs — cots, beds, bedding, clothing, footwear, etc, also holidays

TYPE OF BENEFICIARY Any child in need under the age of 16 years

RESTRICTIONS No foreign holidays, expeditions, general appeals, or medical equipment

BENEFICIAL AREA Grants only allocated to individual cases of need on Merseyside

FINANCES
- Year 1992
- Income £7,000

TRUSTEES The Committee of the Trust

SUBMISSION OF APPLICATIONS Application forms obtainable from the Committee Secretary. Committee meets on the third Tuesday every month except August. All applications acknowledged

CORRESPONDENT R Currie, Director, Liverpool Children's Welfare Trust, 18 Seel Street, Liverpool, Merseyside L1 4BE

CLASSIFICATIONS
- Holidays

C.C. NO 208604   **ESTABLISHED** 1974

■ Lloyds Bank Charitable Trust

OBJECTS General charitable purposes

POLICY OF TRUSTEES Wide ranging but focused on education, environment, employment, health and social welfare

TYPE OF GRANT Variable

TYPE OF BENEFICIARY Registered charities or those with charitable status accorded by the Inland Revenue

RESTRICTIONS No grants to individuals, nor to denominational or political appeals. Will not provide support to projects which could be seen as relieving the Government of its responsibilities. No response to wholly printed or circular letters

BENEFICIAL AREA UK

FINANCES
- Year 1994
- Grants £1,183,000
- Income £1,109,000
- Assets £87,000

TRUSTEES Lloyds Bank Charitable Trust Ltd

PUBLICATIONS 'More than Money'

SUBMISSION OF APPLICATIONS To the Correspondent

CORRESPONDENT A M Finch, Community Affairs Manager, Corporate Communications, Lloyds Bank plc, 71 Lombard Street, London EC3P 3BS

CLASSIFICATIONS
- Children and youth – general

C.C. NO 298327   **ESTABLISHED** 1987

■ Lloyd's Charities Trust

OBJECTS General charitable purposes

POLICY OF TRUSTEES Donations given to registered national and international charities only. Appeals received from individuals, provincial branches of national charities and charities of a purely 'local' nature are not considered

TYPE OF GRANT Single donations, no covenants

RESTRICTIONS No grants to individuals or associations not registered as charities. No sponsorship

BENEFICIAL AREA UK and International

FINANCES
- Year 1994
- Grants £310,140
- Income £340,871
- Assets £368,694

TRUSTEES The members of Lloyd's Charitable Committee for the time being

PUBLICATIONS Annual Report

SUBMISSION OF APPLICATIONS Application by letter with copy of current Report and Accounts of charity concerned and confirmation of registration as a charity for tax purposes. Limited number of applications considered

CORRESPONDENT Mrs L Harper, Secretary, Lloyd's Charities Trust, Lloyd's of London, One Lime Street, London EC3M 7HA

CLASSIFICATIONS
- Children and youth – general
- Adoption/fostering
- Advancement in life
- Adventure centres and playgrounds
- Centres, clubs and institutes
- Day centres and nurseries
- Development of character
- Counselling (inc helplines)
- Homes and hostels
- Special needs housing

C.C. NO 207232   **ESTABLISHED** 1953

■ London Law Trust

OBJECTS General charitable purposes

POLICY OF TRUSTEES The prevention and cure of illness and disability in children and young people; the alleviation of illness and disability in children and young people; and the encouragement in young people of the qualities of leadership and service to the community

TYPE OF GRANT Usually one-off grants for or towards specific projects. Short-term on-going support may also be considered

TYPE OF BENEFICIARY Registered charities only, or bodies with charitable status working in the areas outlined under Policy. In the case of research projects, preference is given to seed corn or small projects, and in other cases to new ventures

RESTRICTIONS Registered charities only, or bodies with charitable status. Applications from individuals, including students, are ineligible. No grants made in response to local appeals from branches of national organisations

BENEFICIAL AREA UK

SAMPLE GRANTS £5,000 to Down's Syndrome Association for research into the syndrome
£2,500 to Alder Hey Children's Hospital for research into epilepsy
£2,500 to Kintyre Tall Ships Youth Challenge to assist young people on sail training ships
£1,500 (x two years) to the Cammomile Centre to support training of disabled young people
£1,000 to the Fluency Trust to assist in the running of speech training course for children
£1,000 to Hawks, a small adventurous exploits training club in St Ives for the under-16s

FINANCES
- Year 1993
- Grants £103,000
- Income £138,391
- Assets £2,601,368

TRUSTEES Prof A R Mellows, TD, PhD, LLD, Brigadier Sir Jeffrey Darell, Bart, MC, R A Pellant, FCA, ATII

PUBLICATIONS Annual Report & Accounts

SUBMISSION OF APPLICATIONS By September 1st each year. Further information will be requested

London

from shortlisted applicants. Grant Adviser (Mrs B M Crabbe) may visit applicants

CORRESPONDENT G D Ogilvie, Secretary, London Law Trust, c/o Alexanders Easton Kinch, 203 Temple Chambers, Temple Avenue, London EC4Y 0DB

CLASSIFICATIONS
- Children and youth – general
- Advancement in life
- Development of character

C.C. NO 255924   **ESTABLISHED** 1968

■ The London Taxi Drivers' Fund for Underprivileged Children

OBJECTS Disadvantaged children in Greater London

TYPE OF BENEFICIARY Under 18 years – individuals and small groups

RESTRICTIONS General appeals for reserves and circular letters generally not entertained

BENEFICIAL AREA Greater London

FINANCES
- Year 1993
- Grants £25,000
- Income £30,000

TRUSTEES The Commitee of working London Taxi-drivers

SUBMISSION OF APPLICATIONS Appeals considered at monthly intervals

CORRESPONDENT G Down, MBE, 14 Langdon Drive, Kingsbury, London NW9 8NR

CLASSIFICATIONS
- Children and youth – general
- Adventure centres and playgrounds
- Centres, clubs and institutes
- Community groups
- Day centres and nurseries
- Development of character
- Homes and hostels
- Youth organisations (eg Guides, Scouts, YWCA etc)

C.C. NO 249562   **ESTABLISHED** 1928

■ The Lord's Taverners

OBJECTS The policy of the Lord's Taverners is to provide aid:- (a) To enable youngsters to keep physically fit and mentally alert through the playing of team games, especially cricket. (b) To provide financial support for charities which specialise in sport for the disabled. (c) To provide New Horizons Minibuses for handicapped children, to enable them to get away from the confines of Homes and Institutions. (d) To encourage handicapped people to participate in sport

POLICY OF TRUSTEES To raise money for the Lord's Taverners Foundation. The Trustees are represented by the Council of Management who are the governing body of the Charity. The Foundation grant aids the National Cricket Association and the English Schools' Cricket Association. Some help for Playgrounds is given to the National Playing Fields Association

TYPE OF GRANT Capital expenditure only

TYPE OF BENEFICIARY (a) Cricket clubs who run Colts sides. (b) Homes, Hospitals, Institutions etc who have need of Minibuses for transporting children with a mental or physical handicap. (c) Organisations helping children and young people with mental or physical handicap to participate in sport

FINANCES
- Year 1991
- Grants £1,039,126
- Income £1,219,264

TRUSTEES The Council of Management

PUBLICATIONS Literature on the aims and objects of the club as well as films on loan can be supplied on application to the Director

SUBMISSION OF APPLICATIONS To be made via parent body, ie NCA or ESCA in connection with cricket. All other charitable objectives apply to the Director, Lord's Taverners

CORRESPONDENT The Director, The Lord's Taverners, 22 Queen Anne's Gate, London SW1H 9AA

CLASSIFICATIONS
- Adventure centres and playgrounds

C.C. NO 306054   **ESTABLISHED** 1950

■ The Low & Bonar Charitable Fund

OBJECTS The principal object of the Fund is the betterment of the human condition and, in particular, the relief of human suffering

POLICY OF TRUSTEES The Trustees give priority to charities falling into the following categories :- (a) medical, encompassing research, treatment and the general welfare of patients including those physically and mentally handicapped (b) the welfare of the old and infirm (c) the protection and welfare of children and young people (d) the relief of human suffering where not otherwise covered under (a) to (c) above. The Trustees also give consideration to charities meeting social, cultural and environmental needs and such other charities whose work they judge to be of value

TYPE OF GRANT One-off cash grants. A number of charities do receive recurring annual grants, but these are re-considered each year and there is no commitment to repeat

TYPE OF BENEFICIARY Bodies recognised as having charitable status by the Inland Revenue under the Income Tax Acts. In the case of National or International charities grants may be either to the Headquarters' organisation or, if there is a Scottish or local branch, to such branch. Donations are principally to established charities but innovatory projects are also considered

RESTRICTIONS The Trustees are precluded by the Trust Deed from making donations for any purpose other than that which is recognised as a charitable purpose within the meaning of the Income Tax Acts in force from time to time. They do not give grants to individuals nor do they help out with debt, festivals, church restoration

BENEFICIAL AREA Principally the UK

FINANCES
- Year 1995
- Grants £50,900
- Income £50,685
- Assets £217,503

TRUSTEES G C Bonar, H W Laughland, J L Heilig, N D McLeod, P A Bartlett, R D Clegg

SUBMISSION OF APPLICATIONS Meetings held at three-monthly intervals with a principal annual review in March each year. Appeals should be in writing and appellants should provide evidence of charitable status and their latest audited Report and Accounts

CORRESPONDENT M G Long, Secretary, PO Box 51, Dundee, Scotland DD1 9JA

CLASSIFICATIONS
- Children and youth – general
- Adoption/fostering
- Advancement in life
- Adventure centres and playgrounds
- Centres, clubs and institutes
- Day centres and nurseries
- Development of character
- Homes and hostels
- Special needs housing
- Special classes
- Youth organisations (eg Guides, Scouts, YWCA etc)

S.C. NO SC010837   **ESTABLISHED** 1963

■ Lower Hall Charitable Trust

OBJECTS General charitable purposes. No grants to general national appeals

POLICY OF TRUSTEES Preference to Salop and Wolverhampton charities

TYPE OF BENEFICIARY Charities personally known to the Trust

RESTRICTIONS Must be registered charities not students

BENEFICIAL AREA Salop and Wolverhampton area only

FINANCES
- Year 1995
- Grants £3,000
- Income £3,300
- Assets £63,000

TRUSTEES C F Dumbell, Mrs D C Dumbell

SUBMISSION OF APPLICATIONS On anniversary of previous payments. At any time by post with sae

CORRESPONDENT C F Dumbell, Lower Hall, Worfield, Nr Bridgnorth, Salop WV15 5LH

CLASSIFICATIONS
- Children and youth – general
- Homes and hostels

C.C. NO 256663   **ESTABLISHED** 1968

■ The Vanessa Lowndes Charitable Trust

OBJECTS Aid to handicapped children and selected charitable purposes

POLICY OF TRUSTEES The Trustees prefer to support charities which support the blind and handicapped with some restrictions causing priority to be given to national charities in which New Zealand has an interest

TYPE OF GRANT Donations £100–£300

TYPE OF BENEFICIARY Handicapped children's charities NZ and selected UK

RESTRICTIONS No grants to individuals. Restricted to certain IR approved registered charities plus those in which New Zealand is particularly interested

BENEFICIAL AREA New Zealand

FINANCES
- Year 1995
- Grants £17,000
- Income £19,100
- Assets £240,000

TRUSTEES Miss V Lowndes, A N Hay, M H Wadsworth, P E Rood, M J Calder

NOTES Restricted to named UK charities by deed

SUBMISSION OF APPLICATIONS By letter with descriptive pamphlet

CORRESPONDENT W J Calder Sons & Co, 1 Regent Street, London SW1Y 4NW

CLASSIFICATIONS
- Children and youth – general
- Adoption/fostering
- Centres, clubs and institutes
- Day centres and nurseries
- Development of character
- Holidays
- Homes and hostels

C.C. NO 262166   **ESTABLISHED** 1971

■ The Lubricators Charitable Trust
(known informally as XIX Charitable Foundation)

OBJECTS General charitable purposes

TYPE OF BENEFICIARY The Guild will normally only assist children and old people and such assistance will invariably only be given in cases where there is no public or quasi public assistance

FINANCES
- Year 1992
- Grants £30,000
- Income £30,000
- Assets £65,000

TRUSTEES J Graham, P D Smithson

CORRESPONDENT The Guild of the Nineteen Lubricators, Amhurst Brown Colombotti, 2 Duke Street, St James's, London SW1Y 6BJ

CLASSIFICATIONS
- Children and youth – general

C.C. NO 272237   **ESTABLISHED** 1976

■ The Luke Trust

OBJECTS Charitable purposes connected with Christian religion

TYPE OF BENEFICIARY Registered charities and institutions

BENEFICIAL AREA Mainly Bedfordshire

FINANCES
- Year 1993
- Grants £17,500
- Income £19,235
- Assets £192,897

TRUSTEES Rt Hon Lord Luke of Pavenham, Hon H de B Lawson Johnson, J A P Whinney, D G Ward,

CORRESPONDENT R H C Heptinstall, c/o Historic Churches, Preservation Trust, Fulham Palace, London SW6 6EA

CLASSIFICATIONS
- Children and youth – general

C.C. NO 1000550   **ESTABLISHED** 1943

Lyon's

Alphabetical register of grant making charitable trusts

■ John Lyon's Charity

OBJECTS General charitable purposes for the inhabitants of the Beneficial Area

POLICY OF TRUSTEES Priority to be given to the education and welfare of children and young people

RESTRICTIONS Registered charities only

BENEFICIAL AREA London Boroughs of Barnet, Brent, Camden, Ealing, Hammersmith and Fulham, Harrow, Kensington and Chelsea and the Cities of London and Westminster

FINANCES
- **Year** 1995
- **Grants** £1,013,905
- **Income** £1,040,712
- **Assets** £20,915,967

TRUSTEES The Keepers and Governors of Possessions Revenues and Goods of the Free Grammar School of John Lyon (a Charter Corporation)

NOTES The figure for Income is approximate

SUBMISSION OF APPLICATIONS 10 October 1996, 16 January 1997, 18 April 1997, 6 October 1997

CORRESPONDENT A J F Stebbings, Clerk to the Trustee, 45 Pont Street, London SW1X 0BX

CLASSIFICATIONS
- Children and youth – general

C.C. NO 237725 **ESTABLISHED** 1578

■ MKR Charitable Trust (formerly Rose Charitable Settlement)

OBJECTS General charitable purposes

POLICY OF TRUSTEES To assist Israel, support Jewish and other genuine local charities

TYPE OF GRANT One-off

TYPE OF BENEFICIARY Both headquarters and local organisations

RESTRICTIONS Private schemes not normally sponsored

BENEFICIAL AREA Local (West Midlands)

FINANCES
- **Year** 1991
- **Grants** £25,180
- **Income** £30,762

TRUSTEES M K Rose, Mrs I W Rose, H Aron, C Mullen, S Gould

SUBMISSION OF APPLICATIONS By written application to the correspondent

CORRESPONDENT M K Rose, 20 Coppice Close, Dovehouse Lane, Solihull, West Midlands B91 2ED

CLASSIFICATIONS
- Homes and hostels

C.C. NO 256336 **ESTABLISHED** 1968

■ The B V MacAndrew Trust

OBJECTS General charitable purposes, with preference to help for the aged and for youth

POLICY OF TRUSTEES To assist private individuals with very small amounts (in the region of £25–£50 on a one-off basis)

TYPE OF GRANT Primarily for domestic assistance

TYPE OF BENEFICIARY Those recommended by local contacts

RESTRICTIONS Restricted to local individuals

BENEFICIAL AREA East and West Sussex

FINANCES
- **Year** 1992
- **Grants** £51,153

TRUSTEES D J E Diplock, E S Diplock

NOTES Applications from the existing local contacts exceed the funds available

SUBMISSION OF APPLICATIONS By letter

CORRESPONDENT D J E Diplock, 79 Church Road, Hove, East Sussex BN3 2BB

CLASSIFICATIONS
- Children and youth – general

C.C. NO 206900 **ESTABLISHED** 1950

The E M MacAndrew Trust

OBJECTS General charitable purposes

POLICY OF TRUSTEES General charitable interests

TYPE OF GRANT Discretionary

TYPE OF BENEFICIARY Other charitable organisations

BENEFICIAL AREA UK

FINANCES
- Year 1995
- Grants £29,046
- Income £33,029
- Assets £587,566

TRUSTEES A R Nicholson, P Colquhoun

SUBMISSION OF APPLICATIONS In writing. Trustees meet quarterly

CORRESPONDENT J P Thornton, Administrator, J P Thornton & Co, Chartered Accountants, Inglewood, Aylesbury, Buckinghamshire HP22 4HD

CLASSIFICATIONS
- Children and youth – general

C.C. NO 290736 **ESTABLISHED** 1984

Macdonald-Buchanan Charitable Trust

OBJECTS General charitable purposes

POLICY OF TRUSTEES Preference to charities of which the Trust has special interest, knowledge or association

RESTRICTIONS The Trustees will not normally make grants to individuals and in order to contain costs appeals will not be acknowledged

FINANCES
- Year 1991
- Grants £57,003
- Income £160,849
- Assets £1,773,726

TRUSTEES All correspondence to be via Kleinwort Benson Trustees Ltd

SUBMISSION OF APPLICATIONS In writing to the correspondent

CORRESPONDENT The Secretary, The Macdonald-Buchanan Charitable Trust, c/o Kleinwort Benson Trustees Ltd, PO Box 191, 10 Fenchurch Street, London EC3M 3LB

CLASSIFICATIONS
- Adventure centres and playgrounds
- Centres, clubs and institutes
- Development of character

C.C. NO 209994 **ESTABLISHED** 1952

Macfarlane Walker Trust

OBJECTS General charitable purposes

POLICY OF TRUSTEES Grants to former employees and their families of Macfarlane Walker

TYPE OF GRANT Recurrent and single donations

TYPE OF BENEFICIARY Registered charities, individuals and institutions

BENEFICIAL AREA Gloucester

FINANCES
- Year 1993
- Grants £26,407
- Income £32,118
- Assets £265,972

TRUSTEES R F Walker, D F Walker, A L Hancock, D A Launchbury,

SUBMISSION OF APPLICATIONS For educational grants only through the Principal of an educational institution already supported. Grants will not be made to individual applicants

CORRESPONDENT D A Launchbury, Secretary to the Trustees, Heather Brae, Ryeworth Drive, Charlton Kings, Cheltenham GL52 6LU

CLASSIFICATIONS
- Children and youth – general

C.C. NO 227890 **ESTABLISHED** 1963

MacGregor's Bequest

OBJECTS Charities for the benefit of the poor of the City of Glasgow

POLICY OF TRUSTEES To distribute the free annual income of the Bequest for the benefit of the poor as the Director of Finance may deem expedient

TYPE OF GRANT Annual lump sums

TYPE OF BENEFICIARY Payments made under this Trust are to be used for the benefit of the poor

RESTRICTIONS Any religious body or society excluded

BENEFICIAL AREA Must benefit Glasgow residents

SAMPLE GRANTS £1,000 to NCH Action for Children towards Ruchill Child and Family Centre and Glasgow Children and Families Counselling Poject
£700 to Glasgow Children's Holiday Scheme
£600 to Dunsyre Holiday Camp Trust towards countryside holidays for underprivileged children
£500 to Fairbridge in Scotland for general financial assistance
£500 to Venture Scotland towards residential and social development courses for young disadvantaged people

FINANCES
- Year 1992
- Grants £8,550
- Income £9,500
- Assets £110,500

TRUSTEES The Glasgow District Council Finance Committee

PUBLICATIONS Annual Accounts of Glasgow District Council

SUBMISSION OF APPLICATIONS The Director of Finance, Glasgow District Council, Glasgow G2 1DU

CORRESPONDENT The Director of Finance, City Chambers, PO Box 19, 285 George Street, Glasgow, Scotland G2 1DU

CLASSIFICATIONS
- Children and youth – general
- Centres, clubs and institutes

C.C. NO CR 10597 **ESTABLISHED** 1928

The Mackintosh Foundation

OBJECTS To promote dramatic art; other causes include: children and education, AIDS, the homeless, SE Asian refugees and other charitable objects

POLICY OF TRUSTEES Flexible

TYPE OF GRANT All types

TYPE OF BENEFICIARY Charities, students

Macpherson

RESTRICTIONS Political or religious causes are not supported

BENEFICIAL AREA International (principally UK, USA, SE Asia)

SAMPLE GRANTS £20,000 to Children's Trust
£12,500 to Farms for City Children
£11,000 to Youth Music

FINANCES
- Year 1994–95
- Grants £1,182,950
- Income £1,170,002
- Assets £4,818,800

TRUSTEES Sir Cameron Mackintosh, Martin J McCallum, Nicholas D Allott, D Michael Rose, Ms P MacNaughton, Alain Boüblil

SUBMISSION OF APPLICATIONS Appeals to Miss S Dennehy, (Appeals Secretary), The Mackintosh Foundation, 1 Bedford Square, London WC1B 3RA

CORRESPONDENT D Michael Rose, The Mackintosh Foundation, Watchmaker Court, 33 St John's Lane, London EC1M 4DB

CLASSIFICATIONS
- Advancement in life
- Development of character
- Homes and hostels

C.C. NO 327751   **ESTABLISHED** 1988

■ Macpherson Memorial Trust

OBJECTS To award a limited number of scholarships for educational courses or travel projects of an educational nature, which, in the opinion of the Trustees, will help develop the character and skills of the applicant

---

TYPE OF GRANT Of varying value, but usually not in excess of £1,000

TYPE OF BENEFICIARY Only open to persons, normally under the age of 25 years, who are involved in the brewing, distilling, malting or grain associated industries

RESTRICTIONS See Type of Beneficiary

BENEFICIAL AREA UK

SAMPLE GRANTS £1,000 to three students towards an educational tour of Belgium

FINANCES
- Year 1994–95
- Grants £2,176
- Income £3,911
- Assets £75,642

TRUSTEES S B Simpson, Miss L Macpherson, R B Pirie, D W Ringrose, P Bentley, P Ellis

SUBMISSION OF APPLICATIONS Applications are considered by the Trustees throughout the year

CORRESPONDENT The Clerk to the Trustees, Macpherson Memorial Trust, 31b Castlegate, Newark, Nottinghamshire NG24 1AZ

CLASSIFICATIONS
- Development of character

C.C. NO 327576   **ESTABLISHED** 1987

■ The MacRobert Trusts

OBJECTS General charitable purposes

POLICY OF TRUSTEES Currently, the major categories under which Trustees consider support are:- Science and technology, Ex-Servicemen's hospitals and homes, Youth, Education, Services and sea, Community welfare, Disabled and handicapped. The minor categories are:- Agriculture and horticulture, Medical care, Arts and music, Tarland and Deeside

TYPE OF GRANT The Trustees are prepared to make core/revenue grants where appropriate but favour projects. They recognise that, at present, experiment and innovation are much more difficult to fund and the Trust's role in funding them the more significant. Grants vary but most lie between £100 and £5,000. Occasionally, Trustees make a recurring grant for up to three years

RESTRICTIONS Trustees do not support: religious organisations (but not including youth/community services provided by them, or local churches), overseas organisations, individuals, endowment funds, general appeals, political organisations, student bodies, fee-paying schools, expeditions, retrospective grants, departments within a university (unless the appeal gains the support of, and is channelled through, the Principal)

BENEFICIAL AREA United Kingdom but preference is given to organisations in Scotland. 75% of all grants made in Scotland

SAMPLE GRANTS £5,000 to the Bowles Rocks Trust Ltd – Bowles Outdoor Centre, Kent towards the Lodge project
£2,500 to the Roses Charitable Trust, Argyll towards provision of bursaries for young people taking part in 1995 multi-activity and sail training courses
£1,500 to Flower of Scotland Campaign – Lifestyle Video for Teenagers, Inverness towards the Lifestyle Video
£1,500 to Sea Cadet Corps – Stonehaven and District Unit No. 475 towards the provision of a fast rescue craft

FINANCES
- Year 1995
- Grants £686,427

TRUSTEES Air Vice-Marshall G A Chesworth, CB, OBE, DFC, I G Booth, FCA, D M Heughan, MSc, CEng, FIMgt, FRSA, Dr June Paterson-Brown, CBE, DL, MB, ChB, A M Scrimgeour, R M Sherriff, CBE, DL (Chairman), A M Summers, BA(Cantab)

NOTES The name 'The MacRobert Trusts' denotes a number of charitable Trusts originating from the late Lady MacRobert. Although each Trust is a separate legal entity with different Trustees, they share a common Administrator. Currently, there are four Trusts: The MacRobert Trust – SCO13507, The Douneside Trust – SCO06668, The Lady MacRobert Special Trust – SCO07587 and The Sir Alexander MacRobert Memorial Trust – SCO00178

SUBMISSION OF APPLICATIONS There is no application form. Applications should include: charity title and a description of its activities, registered charity number, list of the charity's key people, details of the project for which a grant is sought including costings, funds raised in relation to the target and funds promised (if any), latest full audited accounts and annual report. The Trustees look for clear, realistic and attainable aims. All applications are acknowledged. The Trustees meet twice a year, in March and October. Applications for the March meeting need to reach the Trust by late October and for the October meeting by early June. Applicants are informed of Trustees' decision within one week of the meeting

CORRESPONDENT The Administrator, The MacRobert Trusts, Balmuir, Tarland, Aboyne, Aberdeenshire AB34 4UA

CLASSIFICATIONS
- Children and youth – general
- Community groups

C.C. NO 231193   **ESTABLISHED** 1954

■ Man of the People Fund

OBJECTS Welfare and care of handicapped children, grossly deprived children, disabled adults, frail elderly, the deaf and the blind, cancer research

TYPE OF GRANT Mainly one-off sums for capital projects

TYPE OF BENEFICIARY Registered charities concerned with welfare of deprived children, the blind and the deaf, disabled adults and handicapped children (mainly hereditary disorders), the frail elderly. Charities promoting medical research into disorders encountered in UK special schools for the handicapped child

RESTRICTIONS No grants made to individuals or to charities on behalf of individuals. No part of Trust funds to be applied to or for benefit of Mirror Group Newspapers Ltd

BENEFICIAL AREA UK only

FINANCES
- Year 1990
- Grants £142,000
- Income £142,000

TRUSTEES The Editor; Chairman; Finance Director; Company Secretary of 'The People'

NOTES Disbursements made only in March when total collected is distributed. No grants made to individuals

SUBMISSION OF APPLICATIONS Applications must be from registered charities and in writing, accompanied by supporting literature, etc. Applications can be made at any time but grants are given only in March of each year when the entire proceeds of the annual appeal to 'The People' readers is distributed, leaving no residue

CORRESPONDENT The Administrator, Man of the People Fund, The People, 1 Canada Square, Canary Wharf, London E14 5AP

CLASSIFICATIONS
- Children and youth – general

C.C. NO 258111   **ESTABLISHED** 1959

■ The Manchester Guardian Society Charitable Trust

OBJECTS General charitable purposes

POLICY OF TRUSTEES The emphasis is very much on helping the Greater Manchester area

TYPE OF GRANT Primarily small single capital projects not exceeding £5,000

TYPE OF BENEFICIARY Preference is usually shown to the smaller charity operating within Greater Manchester

RESTRICTIONS The Trustees do not give grants to individuals. They very much prefer the applicant to be a registered charity although this is not mandatory

BENEFICIAL AREA Greater Manchester

FINANCES
- Year 1993
- Grants £69,207
- Income £68,689
- Assets £1,250,000

TRUSTEES P R Green, G D Thomas, D A Sutherland, W R Lees-Jones, Mrs J Powell, D G Wilson, Mrs J Harrison, Mrs O Haig, W Smith, P Goddard, D Wainwright

PUBLICATIONS An annual report and accounts is prepared and the annual general meeting is held either at the September meeting or the November meeting of the Trustees

SUBMISSION OF APPLICATIONS Applications are considered at quarterly meetings of the Trustees which take place on the first Monday in March, June and September and the last Monday in November. Applications should be received at least 14 days before these dates

CORRESPONDENT J A H Fielden, Cobbett Leak Almond, Ship Canal House, King Street, Manchester M2 4WB

CLASSIFICATIONS
- Children and youth – general
- Centres, clubs and institutes

C.C. NO 515341   **ESTABLISHED** 1987

■ R W Mann Trustees Limited

OBJECTS Relief of poor aged or infirm – advancement of education and public religion – social charitable welfare

POLICY OF TRUSTEES Fixed grants out of income: Councils of Social Service – £3,000, St Mary's Church, Monkseaton – £1,200, Newcastle University – £3,000

TYPE OF GRANT Recurrent expenditure, capital or single expenditure

TYPE OF BENEFICIARY Local activities or local branches of national charities

RESTRICTIONS No grants to individuals

BENEFICIAL AREA Usually Tyne & Wear, occasionally beyond with a preference for North Tyneside

FINANCES
- Year 1994
- Grants £158,849
- Income £184,224
- Assets £2,010,327

TRUSTEES The Directors, ie Mrs J Hamilton, J L Hamilton, Mrs A M Heath, G Javens

SUBMISSION OF APPLICATIONS At any time in the year subject to funds being available, written applications with sae required. Trustees meetings are held approximately at intervals of three months. There are no application forms

CORRESPONDENT R W Mann Trustees Limited, 56 Leazes Park Road, Newcastle upon Tyne, Tyne and Wear NE1 4PG

CLASSIFICATIONS
- Children and youth – general
- Advancement in life
- Centres, clubs and institutes
- Community groups
- Day centres and nurseries
- Development of character
- Counselling (inc helplines)
- Holidays
- Youth organisations (eg Guides, Scouts, YWCA etc)

C.C. NO 259006   **ESTABLISHED** 1959

Manning

Alphabetical register of grant making charitable trusts

■ Leslie & Lilian Manning Trust

OBJECTS General charitable purposes

POLICY OF TRUSTEES To assist mainly charities in the North-East – principally those in the field of medicine and health and welfare. Not educational or for individuals

TYPE OF GRANT Annual – but not necessarily recurrent

TYPE OF BENEFICIARY Charities or organisations working in the areas outlined under Policy. Principally those with local affinities

RESTRICTIONS Applications from individuals including students are ineligible

BENEFICIAL AREA Principally the North East

FINANCES
- Year 1991
- Grants £24,650
- Income £27,340
- Assets £246,888

TRUSTEES D J M Wilson, N Sherlock, P Jones, D Jones

SUBMISSION OF APPLICATIONS Once a year in January. Trustees meet in March

CORRESPONDENT D Wilson, Messrs Eversheds, Milburn House, Dean Street, Newcastle upon Tyne, Tyne and Wear NE1 1NP

CLASSIFICATIONS
- Homes and hostels
- Youth organisations (eg Guides, Scouts, YWCA etc)

C.C. NO 219846   **ESTABLISHED** 1960

■ The Marchday Charitable Fund

OBJECTS General charitable purposes

POLICY OF TRUSTEES To help those less fortunate than ourselves to improve their living conditions, education and quality of life

TYPE OF GRANT Monetary, between £1000 to £7000 per annum

RESTRICTIONS Smaller charities prefered where the trustees can establish an on-going contact. The trustees cannot reply to all requests

BENEFICIAL AREA London and South East region

SAMPLE GRANTS Anne Frank Educational Trust – support over three years towards the cost of the Anne Frank in the World Exhibition, which presents the moral issues of Anne Frank's story and promotes tolerance and care
Creative Writing Journal, Huntercentre YOI – assisting with the costs of educating young offenders to produce a prison journal and distribute it
Centrepoint – supporting the Resettlement Officer at the Delancey Street hostel for homeless young women with emotional and other problems

FINANCES
- Year 1995
- Grants £53,000
- Income £50,000

TRUSTEES D Goldstein, A Kleiner, Mrs L Kleiner, D Leigh, Mrs R Leigh, Ms M Quinn

SUBMISSION OF APPLICATIONS In writting, preferably with budget

CORRESPONDENT Mrs R Leigh, The Marchday Group plc, 48 Portland Place, London W1N 3AG

CLASSIFICATIONS
- Counselling (inc helplines)
- Homes and hostels

C.C. NO 328438   **ESTABLISHED** 1989

■ The Margaret Foundation

OBJECTS General charitable purposes

POLICY OF TRUSTEES Medical research, welfare of elderly and children and the general relief of suffering

TYPE OF GRANT One-off payments

TYPE OF BENEFICIARY Registered charities

RESTRICTIONS No personal applications please

BENEFICIAL AREA UK

SAMPLE GRANTS £6,500 to NSPCC
£6,000 to St Christopher's Fellowship

FINANCES
- Year 1993
- Grants £16,000
- Income £19,500
- Assets £256,000

TRUSTEES Royal Bank of Canada Trust Corporation Limited, 71 Queen Victoria Street, London EC4V 4DE

SUBMISSION OF APPLICATIONS May and November

CORRESPONDENT Ms Pat Moody, Royal Bank of Canada Trust Corporation Limited, 71 Queen Victoria Street, London EC4V 4DE

CLASSIFICATIONS
- Children and youth – general
- Children and violence (inc abuse)

C.C. NO 1001583   **ESTABLISHED** 1990

■ The Erich Markus Charitable Foundation

OBJECTS General charitable purposes

POLICY OF TRUSTEES Trustees are primarily interested in social welfare causes

TYPE OF BENEFICIARY Registered charities and institutions

RESTRICTIONS Do not consider individuals or salaries

FINANCES
- Year 1993
- Income £59,000

TRUSTEES Erich Markus Charity Trustees

CORRESPONDENT A Walker, Trust Manager, Paynes Hicks Beach, Solicitors, 10 New Square, Lincoln's Inn, London WC2A 3QG

CLASSIFICATIONS
- Children and youth – general

C.C. NO 283128   **ESTABLISHED** 1981

■ The Betty Martin Charity

OBJECTS Educational

POLICY OF TRUSTEES To provide financial help to young people to enable them to acquire (marketable) skills

TYPE OF GRANT Top-up grants to pay fees, travel expenses, maintenance in apprenticeships, purchase of books, tools, etc

TYPE OF BENEFICIARY Young people living within the preferred beneficial area

BENEFICIAL AREA Preference to a radius of 15 miles from Midhurst Parish Church

SAMPLE GRANTS £1,700 to student towards the fees of a Postgraduate Diploma in Counselling in Primary Health Care
£575 to student (attending course in health and social care) towards cost of books and travel

FINANCES
- Year 1994
- Income £20,000
- Assets £500,000

TRUSTEES Mrs Joanna Whitmore-Jones, D J McCahearty, Mrs Joan Manning, Dr B J Marien, Dr H W Martin

SUBMISSION OF APPLICATIONS Application forms from the correspondent. Trustees meet about once a month. All applications will be acknowledged

CORRESPONDENT Dr H W Martin, MD, MRCS, Eversheds, Carron Lane, Midhurst, West Sussex GU29 9LD

CLASSIFICATIONS
- Advancement in life

C.C. NO 1029337   **ESTABLISHED** 1993

■ The Sir George Martin Trust

OBJECTS Education, social welfare, general charitable purposes, especially in Yorkshire

POLICY OF TRUSTEES The Trust assists a very wide range of charitable causes with a number of awards to schools and groups working with young people. Although emphasis is placed on projects located in the County of Yorkshire and in particular Leeds and Bradford, some grants are made in other parts of the North of England and occasionally national appeals are considered

TYPE OF GRANT Grants for capital rather than revenue projects; reluctant to support general running costs. Grants are not repeated to any charity in any one year; the maximum number of consecutive grants is three, though a one-off approach to grant applications is preferred. Average donation is just over £1,175

TYPE OF BENEFICIARY Wide ranging, within the Trust's geographical priorities

RESTRICTIONS The Trust is unable to consider applications from organisations without charitable status. No support for individuals or for post-graduate courses. No support for publishing books or articles or for seminars. The Trust does not like to fund projects that were formerly statutorily funded

BENEFICIAL AREA Mainly Yorkshire, in particular Leeds and Bradford, occasionally national

FINANCES
- Year 1994
- Grants £267,000

TRUSTEES Sir George Martin Trust Company Ltd

NOTES The Trust also supports The United Kingdom Charitable Trusts Initiative, a move to persuade wealthy people in the United Kingdom to create their own charitable Foundations

SUBMISSION OF APPLICATIONS The Trust meets in December and June each year to consider applications. These should be made in writing to the Secretary. Due to the increase in costs of postage unsuccessful applications outside the area of the Trust giving will not now be acknowledged. Relevant applications will be considered at the Trustees meetings but only those successful will be informed. No final response to an application means that the application has been unsuccessful. Telephone calls are not encouraged

CORRESPONDENT P J D Marshall, Secretary, Sir George Martin Trust, Netherwood House, Ilkley, Yorkshire LS29 9RP

CLASSIFICATIONS
- Children and youth – general
- Development of character

C.C. NO 223554   **ESTABLISHED** 1956

■ The Catherine Martineau Charitable Trust

OBJECTS General charitable purposes

POLICY OF TRUSTEES Relief of poverty and distress. Conservation of National Heritage and the Arts

TYPE OF GRANT Usually one-off

TYPE OF BENEFICIARY Registered charities working in area outlined under Policy

RESTRICTIONS Applications from individuals, including students will not be considered

FINANCES
- Year 1991
- Income £8,000
- Grants £8,000

TRUSTEES C E M Martineau, Miss J T Martineau, Mrs S G Martineau

SUBMISSION OF APPLICATIONS Trustees meet once a year in December. Applications should include clear details of need

CORRESPONDENT C E M Martineau, Jock Farm, Little Henham, Saffron Walden, Essex CB11 3XR

CLASSIFICATIONS
- Children and youth – general

C.C. NO 297993   **ESTABLISHED** 1987

■ The Nancie Massey Charitable Trust

OBJECTS General charitable purposes

POLICY OF TRUSTEES Income split between five areas per Fields of Interest

TYPE OF GRANT Cash only

TYPE OF BENEFICIARY Charitable groups only

RESTRICTIONS No grants to individuals

BENEFICIAL AREA Edinburgh

FINANCES
- Year 1995
- Income £167,000
- Grants £150,000

TRUSTEES J G Morton, C A Crole, A P Trothman

SUBMISSION OF APPLICATIONS In writing to the correspondent

CORRESPONDENT J G Morton, 3 Albyn Place, Edinburgh EH2 4NQ

CLASSIFICATIONS
- Children and youth – general

ESTABLISHED 1989

Matchan

■ The Leonard Matchan Fund Limited

OBJECTS General charitable purposes

POLICY OF TRUSTEES Grants only to other registered charities

TYPE OF BENEFICIARY Social and medical welfare charities

RESTRICTIONS No grants to individuals

BENEFICIAL AREA UK

FINANCES
- Year 1995
- Grants £64,000
- Income £60,775
- Assets £622,571

TRUSTEES The Council of Management

SUBMISSION OF APPLICATIONS By letter to the Secretary

CORRESPONDENT Ms J Sutherland, (Secretary), 16 The Towers, Lower Mortlake Road, Richmond, Surrey TW9 2JR

CLASSIFICATIONS
- Community groups

C.C. NO 257682   **ESTABLISHED** 1968

■ The Material World Charitable Foundation Limited

OBJECTS General charitable purposes

TYPE OF GRANT Donations from £250 to £10,000

TYPE OF BENEFICIARY Environmental organisations, charities benefitting children

RESTRICTIONS Donations given only to registered charities in areas shown under Type of Beneficiary

FINANCES
- Year 1993
- Grants £3,400
- Income £12,321

TRUSTEES The Directors

SUBMISSION OF APPLICATIONS To correspondent – letter only in first instance

CORRESPONDENT The Secretary, The Material World Charitable Foundation Ltd, 26 Cadogan Square, London SW1X 0JP

CLASSIFICATIONS
- Advancement in life

C.C. NO 266746   **ESTABLISHED** 1973

■ Matthews Wrightson Charity Trust (formerly Stewart Wrightson Charity Trust)

OBJECTS General charitable purposes

POLICY OF TRUSTEES The Trustees favour smaller charities seeking to raise under £250,000 and particularly under £250, with a bias towards Christian work and organisations helping the disadvantaged re-integrate into the community. Unusual ideas within the guidelines often catch the Trustees' eye

TYPE OF GRANT Cash grants, on annual basis

TYPE OF BENEFICIARY See policy of Trustees

RESTRICTIONS Are excluded: Unconnected local churches, schools and village halls, etc. No animal charities. Individuals, eg going abroad to work under charitable auspices might receive funding

BENEFICIAL AREA UK

SAMPLE GRANTS £250 to Children's Family Trust
£250 to Franklin Youth Trust
£250 to GAP Activity Projects
£250 to Whizz Kidz

FINANCES
- Year 1995
- Grants £66,500
- Income £66,500
- Assets £916,000

TRUSTEES Miss P W Wrightson, A H Isaacs, G D G Wrightson

PUBLICATIONS Annual Report

NOTES Gifts are made in small units, normally £250, with a few larger gifts deriving specifically from old connections

SUBMISSION OF APPLICATIONS In writing to the correspondent. Initial telephone calls are discouraged. No special forms: accounts desirable. The Trustees are sent covering letters only (1–2 pages) monthly, and meet six-monthly for policy and administrative decisions. No reply to unsuccessful applicants; expect a two month delay if successful. The correspondent receives about 1,000 applications a year, and repeat donations are more common than to new charities

CORRESPONDENT Adam Lee, Secretary and Administrator, The Farm, Northington, Alresford, Hampshire SO24 9TH

CLASSIFICATIONS
- Children and youth – general
- Development of character
- Holidays
- Homes and hostels
- Youth organisations (eg Guides, Scouts, YWCA etc)
- Children and violence (inc abuse)

C.C. NO 262109   **ESTABLISHED** 1970

■ The Amela and Jack Maxwell Foundation (formerly Joseph Collier Charitable Trust)

OBJECTS General charitable purposes

POLICY OF TRUSTEES Donations made purely at the discretion of Trustees

RESTRICTIONS No grants to individuals or expeditions. Only successful applications will be replied to

FINANCES
- Year 1994
- Grants £23,474
- Income £22,425
- Assets £286,711

TRUSTEES Mrs P H Maxwell, J A C Bentall

CORRESPONDENT Mrs P H Maxwell, 20 Old Bailey, London EC4M 7BH

CLASSIFICATIONS
- Children and youth – general

C.C. NO 209618   **ESTABLISHED** 1957

■ Anthony Mayhew Charitable Trust (formerly the R & A Mayhew Charitable Trust)

OBJECTS General charitable purposes

POLICY OF TRUSTEES No individuals, registered charities only

RESTRICTIONS Not able to help individuals or students, must be registered charities

BENEFICIAL AREA Mainly Sussex

FINANCES
- Year 1993
- Grants £3,500
- Income £3,279

TRUSTEES A D Mayhew, Mrs C A Mayhew

CORRESPONDENT A D Mayhew, Broomham Farm, Chiddingly, East Sussex BN8 6JG

CLASSIFICATIONS
- Holidays
- Homes and hostels
- Youth organisations (eg Guides, Scouts, YWCA etc)

C.C. NO 277348 **ESTABLISHED** 1978

■ The Ivona Mays-Smith Charitable Trust

OBJECTS General charitable purposes

POLICY OF TRUSTEES To implement the charitable intentions of Mrs Mays-Smith

TYPE OF GRANT Discretionary

TYPE OF BENEFICIARY Various

RESTRICTIONS None

BENEFICIAL AREA England and Wales

SAMPLE GRANTS £1,500 per annum to Roedean School Bursary

FINANCES
- Year 1994
- Grants £3,500
- Income £3,700
- Assets £53,000

TRUSTEES J A H West, L H Judd

SUBMISSION OF APPLICATIONS Funds are fully committed for the foreseeable future

CORRESPONDENT Cumberland Ellis Peirs, Columbia House, 69 Aldwych, London WC2B 4RW

CLASSIFICATIONS
- Children and youth – general

C.C. NO 326177 **ESTABLISHED** 1981

■ The Robert McAlpine Foundation

OBJECTS General charitable purposes

POLICY OF TRUSTEES Continuing support to registered charities personally known to the Trustees. Few outside applications are countenanced

TYPE OF BENEFICIARY Registered charities only who work to help disadvantaged youngsters in inner-city areas

RESTRICTIONS No individuals

BENEFICIAL AREA UK

FINANCES
- Year 1987
- Grants £138,376
- Income £188,253
- Assets £2,169,901

TRUSTEES The Hon David M McAlpine, M H D McAlpine, Kenneth McAlpine, Cullum McAlpine, Adrian McAlpine

SUBMISSION OF APPLICATIONS Considered annually, normally in November

CORRESPONDENT The Secretary to the Trustees, The Robert McAlpine Foundation, 40 Bernard Street, London WC1N 1LG

CLASSIFICATIONS
- Advancement in life

C.C. NO 226646 **ESTABLISHED** 1963

■ A N McKechnie Foundation

OBJECTS General charitable purposes

POLICY OF TRUSTEES Areas of interest include those specified under Classification as well as medical research and invalid aid, ex-servicemen's and police charities

TYPE OF GRANT Recurrent operational expenses

TYPE OF BENEFICIARY National bodies

RESTRICTIONS No grants to individuals

FINANCES
- Year 1994
- Grants £5,225
- Income £6,421
- Assets £100,289

TRUSTEES R F Beard, B R P Yates

SUBMISSION OF APPLICATIONS Annually

CORRESPONDENT R F Beard, FCA, Beard & Company, Burleigh, Old Church Road, Colwall, Malvern, Worcestershire WR13 6EZ

CLASSIFICATIONS
- Adventure centres and playgrounds
- Centres, clubs and institutes
- Counselling (inc helplines)
- Holidays

C.C. NO 264569 **ESTABLISHED** 1971

■ The McKenna & Co Foundation

OBJECTS General charitable purposes, in particular charitable purposes connected with children, the mentally or physically handicapped or disabled, the aged, the deaf and medical research

RESTRICTIONS No grants to organisations that are not registered charities

FINANCES
- Year 1994
- Grants £61,122
- Income £49,616

TRUSTEES C B Powell-Smith, Mrs C F Woolf, R S Derry-Evans

SUBMISSION OF APPLICATIONS In writing to the correspondent

CORRESPONDENT McKenna & Co, Mitre House, 160 Aldersgate Street, London EC1A 4DD

CLASSIFICATIONS
- Advancement in life

C.C. NO 268859 **ESTABLISHED** 1981

■ The Robert McKenzie Trust

OBJECTS General charitable purposes

POLICY OF TRUSTEES To promote education and the relief of poverty

TYPE OF BENEFICIARY Registered charities

FINANCES
- Year 1993
- Income £24,000

TRUSTEES D Sherborn, M R Le Garst, A W Metherell, G W Phillips, D K Wilson

Measures

Alphabetical register of grant making charitable trusts

CORRESPONDENT P D Donald, Messrs Underwood & Co, 40 Welbeck Street, London W1M 8LN

CLASSIFICATIONS
- Counselling (inc helplines)

C.C. NO 285586   **ESTABLISHED** 1982

■ The James Frederick and Ethel Anne Measures Charity

OBJECTS General charitable purposes

POLICY OF TRUSTEES Applicants must usually originate in the West Midlands. Applicants must show evidence of self-help in their application. Trustees have a preference for disadvantaged people. Trustees favour grants towards the cost of equipment. Applications by individuals in cases of hardship will not usually be considered unless sponsored by a local authority, health professional or other welfare agency.

TYPE OF GRANT Grants (occasionally repeats) of £50 to £500

TYPE OF BENEFICIARY All categories within the West Midlands Area

RESTRICTIONS Trustees have a dislike for students who have a full local authority grant and want finance for a different course or study

BENEFICIAL AREA West Midlands or West Midlands branches of national organisations

SAMPLE GRANTS £250 to Raleigh International

FINANCES
- Year 1995   • Grants £42,000

TRUSTEES D J K Nichols, C H Lees, Dr I D Kerr, R S Watkins

SUBMISSION OF APPLICATIONS By letter to correspondent. No reply to unsuccessful applicants unless sae is enclosed – Trustees meetings every three months

CORRESPONDENT D J K Nichols, c/o Messrs Tyndallwoods, Solicitors, 5 Greenfield Crescent, Edgbaston, Birmingham B15 3BE

CLASSIFICATIONS
- Children and youth – general
- Adventure centres and playgrounds
- Centres, clubs and institutes
- Holidays
- Youth organisations (eg Guides, Scouts, YWCA etc)

C.C. NO 266054   **ESTABLISHED** 1973

■ K S Mehta Charitable Trust (also known as Mahavir Trust)

OBJECTS General charitable purposes

POLICY OF TRUSTEES Trustees give to further religious causes; help the handicapped; help the poor and needy; medical expenses for the poor and needy; scholarships; animal welfare

TYPE OF BENEFICIARY Registered charities

FINANCES
- Year 1992   • Income £49,577
- Grants £25,572

TRUSTEES H S Mehta, P S Mehta, J S Mehta

CORRESPONDENT K S Mehta, Technomatic Ltd, Techno House, 468 Church Lane, London NW9 8UF

CLASSIFICATIONS
- Youth organisations (eg Guides, Scouts, YWCA etc)

C.C. NO 298551   **ESTABLISHED** 1987

■ The Violet Melchett Children's Trust

OBJECTS The provision of assistance and treatment (both ante-natal and post-natal) for poor mothers and young children in any part of London

POLICY OF TRUSTEES The Trustees are currently supporting major projects initiated by national charities. No funds are available for other applications at present. No grants given in response to general or large scale appeals, and such applications will not be acknowledged

TYPE OF GRANT Preferably non-recurring, although requests for regular annual support are occasionally considered. Annual, as a proportion of income

TYPE OF BENEFICIARY Groups, institutions or registered charities. No applications from individuals are considered

RESTRICTIONS Only projects benefitting mothers or children in what was the GLC area can be supported; no applications can be considered at present

BENEFICIAL AREA London only

FINANCES
- Year 1994   • Income £11,000
- Grants £5,250   • Assets £250,000

TRUSTEES Peter Mond, Cassandra Wedd

PUBLICATIONS A statement of income and expenditure for the last year showing brief details of grants made will be supplied on receipt of an sae

NOTES Please note Restrictions on Trust (London area only) and Policy of Trustees; no applications can be considered at present

SUBMISSION OF APPLICATIONS At any time

CORRESPONDENT Peter Mond, 14 Falkland Road, London NW5 2PT

CLASSIFICATIONS
- Adventure centres and playgrounds
- Day centres and nurseries

C.C. NO 228197   **ESTABLISHED** 1931

■ The Anthony and Elizabeth Mellows Charitable Settlement

OBJECTS General charitable purposes

POLICY OF TRUSTEES (a) The training and development of children and young people (b) the encouragement of hospices and medical research (c) support of 'The Arts' and (d) the acquisition of objects to be used or displayed in houses of the National Trust or Churches of the Church of England. The Trustees can only consider projects recommended to them by those national institutions with whom they are in close co-operation

TYPE OF GRANT Generally single projects

TYPE OF BENEFICIARY National bodies only

RESTRICTIONS Applications from individuals, including students, are ineligible

Alphabetical register of grant making charitable trusts

Metropolitan

FINANCES
- Year 1995
- Grants £40,000
- Income £39,000
- Assets £522,000

TRUSTEES Prof A R Mellows, Mrs E A Mellows

SUBMISSION OF APPLICATIONS Applications are considered when received, but only from National Institutions. No specific date. No applications forms are used. Grants will be made three times a year when the Trustees meet to consider applications

CORRESPONDENT Prof A R Mellows, TD, 22 Devereux Court, Temple Bar, London WC2R 3JJ

CLASSIFICATIONS
- Advancement in life

C.C. NO 281229   **ESTABLISHED** 1980

■ The Mental Health Foundation

OBJECTS As the UK's only charity concerned with both mental illness and learning disabilities, the Mental Health Foundation plays a vital role in pioneering new approaches to prevention treatment and care. The Foundation's work includes: allocating grants for research and community projects, contributing to public debate, educating and influencing policy makers and healthcare professionals and striving to reduce the stigma attached to mental illness and learning disabilities

POLICY OF TRUSTEES To spend all monies raised voluntarily to aid research and to support pioneer projects in the field of mental health

TYPE OF GRANT Grants to innovative projects in mental health. Research fellowships also given

TYPE OF BENEFICIARY There are three grant-making Committees: (a) Community Services Development; (b) Learning Disabilities; (c) Scientific Research. For details on each of the Committees and guidelines for applicants, please write to the Grants Administrator

RESTRICTIONS See Objects above. Work must be carried out in UK. Individual grants are not made for students to complete their studies or to obtain a higher degree

BENEFICIAL AREA UK

FINANCES
- Year 1995
- Grants £2,113,000
- Income £3,089,000

TRUSTEES Prof Sir Raymond Hoffenberg, KBE (President), Sir Nevil Macready, Bt, CBE (Chairman), C Richard Plummer (Hon Treasurer), David Backhouse, Tessa Baring, Neil Crichton Miller, David Faulkner, CB, John Henderson, TD, DL, The Lady Kingsdown, Prof Malcolm Lader, Rodney Leach, The Hon Robert Loder, CBE, Major-General Robert Loudon, CB, OBE, Michael Mockridge, Prof Eugene Paykel, Sir Humphrey Potts, Lady Runciman, OBE, Jocelyn Stevens, CVO, Sir William Utting, CB, Mike Wilson

PUBLICATIONS List available from Mental Health Foundation, information department

SUBMISSION OF APPLICATIONS For details on each of the grant-making committees and guidelines for applicants, please write to the Grants Administrator

CORRESPONDENT June McKerrow, The Mental Health Foundation, 37 Mortimer Street, London W1N 7RJ

CLASSIFICATIONS
- Advancement in life
- Counselling (inc helplines)
- Children and violence (inc abuse)

C.C. NO 801130   **ESTABLISHED** 1949

■ Mercers' Charitable Foundation

OBJECTS General charitable purposes

POLICY OF TRUSTEES Grants to registered charities only, no grants to individuals. The Company does not respond to circular (mail-shot) appeals. Unsolicited general appeals are considered but not encouraged. Medical research appeals are normally only entertained from hospitals with which the Company has a connection

FINANCES
- Year 1994
- Grants £1,100,000

TRUSTEES Mercers' Company

CORRESPONDENT The Charities Administrator, Mercers' Charitable Foundation, Mercers' Hall, Ironmonger Lane, London EC2V 8HE

CLASSIFICATIONS
- Children and youth – general
- Adoption/fostering

C.C. NO 326340   **ESTABLISHED** 1982

■ The Metropolitan Hospital-Sunday Fund

OBJECTS To maintain, improve and stimulate the care provided for sick and disabled people of London by the award of Specific Purpose grants to hospitals, homes and medical charities, who are themselves registered charities and outside the NHS. To provide NHS hospitals throughout London with Samaritan Funds, Special Reserve Fund and long-stay holiday grants for their social workers to use in helping both current in-patients and out-patients

POLICY OF TRUSTEES To provide grants to improve the standard of care provided for sick and disabled people of London

TYPE OF GRANT Specific Purpose grants awarded to hospitals, homes and medical charities outside the NHS. Samaritan Fund grants to NHS hospitals to enable social workers to assist current in-patients and out-patients with small, day to day expenditures not available from statutory sources. Special Reserve Fund grants to NHS hospitals to enable social workers to assist current in-patients and out-patients with expenditure of £50 and above and long stay holiday grants for patients in long-stay or geriatric wards to have a holiday away from the hospital. Funds fully committed for charities selected by Trustees

TYPE OF BENEFICIARY Hospitals, homes and medical charities outside the NHS who are themselves registered charities. NHS hospitals throughout London

RESTRICTIONS No grants awarded for research, new capital building work or where the care is not mainly for London residents

BENEFICIAL AREA Greater London (within the parameter of the M25 London orbital motor way)

FINANCES
- Year 1994
- Grants £323,143
- Income £396,912

TRUSTEES Council of the Fund. Chairman: R G Holland-Martin

PUBLICATIONS Annual Report and Accounts. Appeal leaflet. Short history of the Fund.

SUBMISSION OF APPLICATIONS NHS hospitals at any time. Others in January of each year. All subject to the submission of application forms available upon request together with guidelines

CORRESPONDENT Howard F Doe (Secretary), 45 Westminster Bridge Road, London SE1 7JB

CLASSIFICATIONS
- Children and youth – general

C.C. NO 206784   **ESTABLISHED** 1872

■ Mickel Fund

OBJECTS General charitable purposes

TYPE OF BENEFICIARY Registered charities mainly

BENEFICIAL AREA Prefer local but give to national charities

NOTES Applications from individuals will not be acknowledged

CORRESPONDENT J R C Wark, McTaggart & Mickel Ltd, 126 West Regent Street, Glasgow G2 2BH

CLASSIFICATIONS
- Children and youth – general
- Adventure centres and playgrounds
- Centres, clubs and institutes
- Homes and hostels
- Youth organisations (eg Guides, Scouts, YWCA etc)

C.C. NO IR03266

■ Middlesex County Rugby Football Union Memorial Fund

OBJECTS Poor relief – sick relief – physical education of handicapped children and young persons

TYPE OF GRANT Mainly one-off sums for capital projects. The grants are normally modest having regard to the resources of the fund

TYPE OF BENEFICIARY The elderly, disadvantaged youth, the handicapped and disabled

RESTRICTIONS Preference given to participants or former participants in sport

FINANCES
- Year 1995
- Grants £93,100
- Income £132,980
- Assets £671,462

TRUSTEES A E Agar, M J Christie, C D L Hogbin, R Storry Deans, Sir Peter Yarranton

SUBMISSION OF APPLICATIONS To the Trust correspondent

CORRESPONDENT C D L Hogbin, Chestnut Cottage, 20a Stubbs Wood, Chesham Bois, Bucks HP6 6EY

CLASSIFICATIONS
- Adventure centres and playgrounds
- Centres, clubs and institutes

C.C. NO 209175   **ESTABLISHED** 1947

■ Frederick Milburn Charitable Trust

OBJECTS General charitable purposes, but mainly to help the elderly, disadvantaged youth and the disabled

POLICY OF TRUSTEES To help and encourage local charities and like institutions on a regular income basis and occasionally to assist with capital projects out of income on a non-recurring basis

TYPE OF GRANT Recurrent

TYPE OF BENEFICIARY Local charities – not individuals

RESTRICTIONS Charities which cover Tyneside and Northumberland

BENEFICIAL AREA Tyneside and Northumberland

FINANCES
- Year 1994
- Grants £4,575
- Income £4,924
- Assets £40,805

TRUSTEES R L Allison, Sir Richard E Renwick, Bt, Lady Caroline Renwick

SUBMISSION OF APPLICATIONS Once a year in October. In writing please

CORRESPONDENT R L Allison, Secretary, Frederick Milburn Charitable Trust, c/o Eversheds Ingledew Wright, B Floor, Milburn House, Newcastle upon Tyne NE1 1NP

CLASSIFICATIONS
- Children and youth – general
- Advancement in life
- Centres, clubs and institutes
- Homes and hostels
- Youth organisations (eg Guides, Scouts, YWCA etc)

C.C. NO 219848   **ESTABLISHED** 1929

■ Millfield House Foundation

OBJECTS Social change in Tyne & Wear

POLICY OF TRUSTEES To consider only proposals which seek: (a) to contribute to public debate and the policy-making process at national or local level, the lessons of first-hand experience of social need, or the implications of research in Tyne and Wear; or (b) to elucidate and tackle the fundamental causes of deprivation in Tyne and Wear, rather than simply alleviating it; or (c) to develop activities which have been proven elsewhere but have not been developed in Tyne and Wear, particularly those which empower people and communities to overcome their difficulties and exploit their own resources

TYPE OF GRANT Significant and medium-term support to a relatively few selected projects or organisations – alone, or in partnership with other funders. Since Millfield House Foundation (MHF) can only afford to have six to eight such grants in payment at the same time, it will be able to approve only one or two new applications a year. Possibly, in some cases, a small grant to support work needed in preparation for an application for a major grant

TYPE OF BENEFICIARY Voluntary agencies, or policy research groups, working with or in the interests of the socially and economically disadvantaged

RESTRICTIONS The following are ineligible for funding. Any proposal: (a) not relating to the people in Tyne and Wear; (b) from well-established national charity or general appeal;

(c) for work in the arts, medicine, conservation; (d) for buildings, or for purely academic research; (e) to make up a deficit already incurred, to replace withdrawn, expired or reducing statutory funding, or to provide what should be the responsibility of statutory agencies; (f) to meet the needs of particular individuals; (g) for travel or an educational bursary; (h) for a project likely to qualify for statutory, EU or National Lottery funding, or likely to appeal to most local or national charitable trusts or similar sources; (i) for the delivery of a service, however great the need, unless it contributes to any of the aims listed under Policy of the Trustees

BENEFICIAL AREA Tyne and Wear and proximity

FINANCES
- Year 1994–95
- Grants £118,943
- Income £84,575
- Assets £2,083,480

TRUSTEES D A McClelland, J McClelland, R Chubb, S McClelland, W G McClelland

PUBLICATIONS Information leaflet giving guidelines for applicants; report on grantmaking 1984–89 (report for 1989–96 forthcoming)

NOTES Since the present policy was introduced only in 1996, recent grants are not relevant. Earlier MHF funding has led to publications on poverty and social conditions in Tyne and Wear, eg the Child Poverty Action Group

SUBMISSION OF APPLICATIONS To the correspondent in writing by end-March or end-September. Not acknowledged if obviously ruled out by MHF published restrictions (see above)

CORRESPONDENT MHF, 66 Elmfield Road, Newcastle upon Tyne NE3 4BD

CLASSIFICATIONS
- Children and youth – general

C.C. NO 271180   **ESTABLISHED** 1976

■ The Millichope Foundation

OBJECTS General charitable purposes

POLICY OF TRUSTEES Social and health funding which is not covered by government programmes. The arts and conservation

TYPE OF GRANT Straight donation. Normally an annual commitment for a period of 5 years

TYPE OF BENEFICIARY Registered charities only

RESTRICTIONS Registered charities only. Applications from individuals, including students, are ineligible

BENEFICIAL AREA Some grants to national and international organisations. Local applications limited to the West Midlands and Shropshire only

FINANCES
- Year 1993
- Grants £129,738
- Income £135,165

TRUSTEES M L Ingall, L C N Bury, Mrs S A Bury, Mrs B Marshall

SUBMISSION OF APPLICATIONS In writing. In order to keep costs to a minimum we do not enter into correspondence with applicants unless an sae is enclosed

CORRESPONDENT Mrs S A Bury, Millichope Park, Munslow, Craven Arms, Shropshire SY7 9HA

CLASSIFICATIONS
- Children and youth – general
- Centres, clubs and institutes
- Development of character
- Homes and hostels
- Youth organisations (eg Guides, Scouts, YWCA etc)

C.C. NO 282357   **ESTABLISHED** 1981

■ The Peter Minet Trust

OBJECTS General charitable purposes

POLICY OF TRUSTEES Priority to registered charities within the Boroughs of Lambeth and Southwark chiefly supporting youth, sick and disabled, disadvantaged, the elderly, the arts and the environment. Occasional support to capital appeals from national charities with similar aims

TYPE OF GRANT Usually one-off for a specific project or part of a project

TYPE OF BENEFICIARY Registered charities working in the areas outlined under Policy. Exclusions:- (a) Appeals from organisations whose sole, or main purpose, is to make grants to other charities. (b) Parochial appeals, other than those within the Trust's immediate locality. In this context, parochial means that all, or most of, the beneficiaries reside within the applicant's immediate locality. (c) Appeals for deficit funding. (d) Appeals received within twelve calendar months of a previous grant

RESTRICTIONS Registered charities only. Applications from individuals are ineligible. No grants made in response to general appeals from large, national organisations

BENEFICIAL AREA But very predominantly Lambeth and Southwark

FINANCES
- Year 1994–5
- Grants £119,445
- Income £156,318
- Assets £1,567,885

TRUSTEES President: Mrs P B Minet, J C B South (Chairman), Mrs S P Dunn, N McGregor-Wood, Ms P Jones, H J Parratt, Mrs R L C Rowan

NOTES Trustees regret it is impossible to acknowledge all applications because of the number and expense involved

SUBMISSION OF APPLICATIONS At any time. Trustees meet quarterly. Applications should include clear details of the need the project is designed to meet plus an outline budget and latest audited accounts. Unsuccessful applications will not be acknowledged unless an sae is enclosed

CORRESPONDENT Ms Lyn Roberts, Administrator, The Peter Minet Trust, 54–56 Knatchbull Road, London SE5 9QY

CLASSIFICATIONS
- Children and youth – general
- Adoption/fostering
- Adventure centres and playgrounds
- Centres, clubs and institutes
- Community groups
- Day centres and nurseries
- Counselling (inc helplines)
- Holidays
- Homes and hostels
- Special needs housing
- Youth organisations (eg Guides, Scouts, YWCA etc)

C.C. NO 259963   **ESTABLISHED** 1969

Mishcon

■ Victor Mishcon Trust

OBJECTS General charitable purposes

POLICY OF TRUSTEES Within the limited funds available each application is considered on its merits with preference given to applications for the relief of poverty from recognised organisations

TYPE OF GRANT One-off as a rule

TYPE OF BENEFICIARY as above

FINANCES
- Year 1992
- Grants £59,789
- Income £61,828
- Assets £935,873

TRUSTEES Lord Mishcon, The Lady Mishcon, P A Cohen

CORRESPONDENT Messrs Mishcon DeReya & Co, 21, Southampton Row, London WC1B 5HS

CLASSIFICATIONS
- Children and youth – general
- Centres, clubs and institutes
- Homes and hostels
- Youth organisations (eg Guides, Scouts, YWCA etc)

C.C. NO 213165   **ESTABLISHED** 1961

■ The Montagu Family Charitable Trust

OBJECTS General charitable purposes

POLICY OF TRUSTEES Donations are restricted to charities personally known to the Trustees

FINANCES
- Year 1993
- Grants £10,000
- Income £10,784
- Assets £186,682

TRUSTEES The Rt Hon Lord Swaythling, The Hon Charles Montagu, The Hon Nicole Campbell

CORRESPONDENT The Rt Hon Lord Swaythling, c/o Wedlake Bell, 16 Bedford Street, Covent Garden, London WC2E 9HF

CLASSIFICATIONS
- Children and youth – general

C.C. NO 277466   **ESTABLISHED** 1979

■ The George A Moore Foundation

OBJECTS General charitable purposes, especially for youth in Yorkshire

POLICY OF TRUSTEES The Trustees choose from a wide selection of applications received during the year. Since it is not generally their practice to support a charity or organisation on a regular basis, the type of grants made can vary quite widely from one year to another and care is taken to avoid duplicating grant assistance in a general field of interest, even if the specific objectives and requirements of several charities within such a field vary. In addition to responding to appeals received, the Trustees also research and select specific areas where they wish to direct assistance. Areas which are not or cannot be covered by official sources are favoured

TYPE OF GRANT Grants are generally non-recurrent and the Foundation is reluctant to contribute to revenue appeals. Roughly 50% of the grants made are £500 or below

TYPE OF BENEFICIARY See Policy and Restrictions

RESTRICTIONS No assistance will be given to individuals, courses of study, expeditions, overseas travel, holidays or for purposes outside the UK. Local appeals for national charities will only be considered if in Yorkshire. Because of present long-term commitments, the Foundation is not prepared to consider appeals for religious property or institutions, or for further medical research work

BENEFICIAL AREA Principally Yorkshire but consideration given to some major national charities under certain circumstances

FINANCES
- Year 1993
- Grants £290,640
- Income £444,280
- Assets £4,675,260

TRUSTEES George A Moore, CBE, KStJ, Mrs E Moore, J R Moore, Mrs A L James

SUBMISSION OF APPLICATIONS In writing to the correspondent. No guidelines or application forms are issued. The trustees meet approximately four times a year and an appropriate response is sent out after the relevent meeting

CORRESPONDENT Miss L P Oldham, The George A Moore Foundation, Follifoot Hall, Pannal Road, Follifoot, Harrogate, North Yorkshire HG3 1DP

CLASSIFICATIONS
- Youth organisations (eg Guides, Scouts, YWCA etc)

C.C. NO 262107   **ESTABLISHED** 1970

■ The Moores Family Charity Foundation

OBJECTS General charitable purposes

POLICY OF TRUSTEES To concentrate support in Merseyside. The main areas of interest are charitable groups concerned with senior citizens; youth/children; mentally/physically disabled; women; community organisations; black/ethnic minorities

TYPE OF GRANT Most of the income is apportioned between individual Family Trusts. A limited amount is available for small single payment grants made directly by the Foundation. Grants between £25 and £1,000 are given towards small equipment/furniture/utensils; minor running costs; holidays/trips; advice/counselling, eg leaflets, cassettes, etc; volunteers expenses/training; transport costs

TYPE OF BENEFICIARY The main areas of interest include young people and children (including pre-school); senior citizens; mentally and physically disabled; self-help health groups; homeless; women; community education (not academic); black/ethnic groups; community organisations; family welfare organisations

RESTRICTIONS No grants for individuals, salaries, purchase or repair of vehicles, organ restoration, research, medical equipment, animal charities, statutory projects, conservation. Buildings and building work have a very low priority

BENEFICIAL AREA The Foundation gives preference to applications from Merseyside. Currently (1996) it is not inviting applications from organisations working in any other geographical areas although applications from organisations who have received grants in the past will be considered

SAMPLE GRANTS £400 to Brunswick Youth Club, Bootle, Liverpool towards the cost of kitchen/

coffee bar equipment for this mixed youth club
£300 to Newton le Willows Family and Community Association towards the cost of 1994 summer play scheme
£200 to Lilliputs Playgroup, Warrington towards the purchase of a sand playtray on wheels and construct-a-frame indoor playhouse for playgroup
£125 to Children's Association for Respite from Emotional Distress (CARED), Liverpool towards the food costs for the 1994 summer respite holiday programme for children from Merseyside with emotional problems
£100 to Litherland Boys' Club, Liverpool towards the costs of an integrated summer camp for a group of young people with disabilities

FINANCES
- Year 1993
- Income £880,867
- Grants £919,905

TRUSTEES John Moores, Peter Moores, Lady Grantchester, James Suenson-Taylor

SUBMISSION OF APPLICATIONS In writing to the correspondent, you should include accounts, a budget and details of funding raised or for which you have applied and your charitable status. Applications are considered on a continuing basis. All applications are acknowledged. Four meetings per year. Guidelines issued on request

CORRESPONDENT Mrs Patricia Caton, The Moores Family Charity Foundation, PO Box 28, Crosby, Liverpool L23 0XJ

CLASSIFICATIONS
- Adventure centres and playgrounds
- Centres, clubs and institutes
- Community groups
- Day centres and nurseries
- Development of character
- Counselling (inc helplines)
- Holidays

C.C. NO 282964   **ESTABLISHED** 1968

■ The Morgan Crucible Company Charitable Trust

OBJECTS General charitable purposes

POLICY OF TRUSTEES Small, specialist charities preferred in fields: health care, medical research, children, support for disabled or ill. Donations made direct, not through intermediate charities. Tend to exclude overseas, armed forces, restoration of buildings, private persons, travel, wild-life, countryside

TYPE OF GRANT Donations made to same charities for a period of years. One payment per annum

TYPE OF BENEFICIARY Physically or mentally handicapped people, young people in deprived or undesirable circumstances, local (Windsor area) good causes

RESTRICTIONS No donations are made to individuals, parish churches

BENEFICIAL AREA Primarily Wirral, Leeds, South Wales, Worcester, Thames Valley, South London

FINANCES
- Year 1994
- Income £99,566
- Grants £99,566

TRUSTEES Sir James Spooner, Dr E B Farmer

SUBMISSION OF APPLICATIONS Written only

CORRESPONDENT D J Coker, The Morgan Crucible Company plc, Morgan House, Madeira Walk, Windsor, Berkshire SL4 1EP

CLASSIFICATIONS
- Advancement in life
- Community groups
- Development of character
- Counselling (inc helplines)
- Holidays

C.C. NO 273507   **ESTABLISHED** 1977

■ S C and M E Morland's Charitable Trust

OBJECTS General charitable purposes

POLICY OF TRUSTEES Support to Quaker charities and others of which the Trustees have special interest, knowledge or association

TYPE OF BENEFICIARY Registered charities

RESTRICTIONS To registered charities only, not to individuals

FINANCES
- Year 1994
- Income £6,205
- Grants £6,122
- Assets £28,238

TRUSTEES J C Morland, J E Morland

NOTES Assets are held in trust

SUBMISSION OF APPLICATIONS Applications will only be acknowledged if an sae is enclosed

CORRESPONDENT J C Morland, The Gables, Parbrook, Glastonbury, Somerset BA6 8PB

CLASSIFICATIONS
- Counselling (inc helplines)

C.C. NO 201645   **ESTABLISHED** 1957

■ Arthur Morphy Memorial Fund

OBJECTS General charitable purposes

POLICY OF TRUSTEES The Trustees future policy will be to support charities which support the population of South West London and Surrey. Those charities are likely to be based in South West London and Surrey, have branches within that area, or be national charities which operate in that area

TYPE OF GRANT No limitation (as at present)

TYPE OF BENEFICIARY Charitable organisations

RESTRICTIONS No applications from individuals can be considered

BENEFICIAL AREA South West London and Surrey

FINANCES
- Year 1994
- Income £9,500
- Grants £9,500
- Assets £231,000

TRUSTEES E E Chapman, L H Chapman

SUBMISSION OF APPLICATIONS Applications are considered annually. Applicants are encouraged to send full details of the charitable work undertaken

CORRESPONDENT Messrs Russell-Cooke, Potter & Chapman, 11 Old Square, Lincoln's Inn, London WC2A 3TS

CLASSIFICATIONS
- Counselling (inc helplines)
- Homes and hostels
- Special needs housing

C.C. NO 270056 **ESTABLISHED** 1964

■ The Peter Morrison Charitable Foundation

OBJECTS General charitable purposes

POLICY OF TRUSTEES To support a wide range of social welfare causes

TYPE OF BENEFICIARY Registered charities

FINANCES
- Year 1993
- Income £56,390

TRUSTEES M J Morrison, I R Morrison

CORRESPONDENT J Payne, Hope Agar, Chartered Accountants, Epworth House, 25 City Road, London EC1Y 1AR

CLASSIFICATIONS
- Children and youth – general

C.C. NO 277202 **ESTABLISHED** 1978

■ Mount 'A' Charitable Trust

OBJECTS General charitable purposes

POLICY OF TRUSTEES Grants made at the request of the Settlor and her family; acknowledgements should be addressed to the Trustee

TYPE OF BENEFICIARY Registered charities only

BENEFICIAL AREA International

FINANCES
- Year 1995
- Grants £66,955
- Income £39,754
- Assets £210,616

TRUSTEES The Barbinder Trust

CORRESPONDENT The Director, The Barbinder Trust, 9 Greyfriars Road, Reading, Berks RG1 1JG

CLASSIFICATIONS
- Children and youth – general
- Centres, clubs and institutes
- Community groups
- Holidays
- Youth organisations (eg Guides, Scouts, YWCA etc)

C.C. NO 264127 **ESTABLISHED** 1971

■ Mount 'B' Charitable Trust

OBJECTS General charitable purposes

POLICY OF TRUSTEES Grants made at the request of the Settlor and her family, acknowledgements should be addressed to the Trustee

TYPE OF BENEFICIARY Registered charities only

BENEFICIAL AREA International

FINANCES
- Year 1995
- Grants £67,405
- Income £39,754
- Assets £213,668

TRUSTEES The Barbinder Trust

CORRESPONDENT The Director, The Barbinder Trust, 9 Greyfriars Road, Reading, Berks RG1 1JG

CLASSIFICATIONS
- Children and youth – general
- Centres, clubs and institutes
- Holidays
- Youth organisations (eg Guides, Scouts, YWCA etc)

C.C. NO 264129 **ESTABLISHED** 1971

■ Gweneth Moxon Charitable Trust

OBJECTS General charitable purposes

RESTRICTIONS No grants to individuals

FINANCES
- Year 1993
- Grants £40,619
- Income £44,875

CORRESPONDENT National Westminster Bank, Keble House, Southernhay Gardens, Exeter, Devon EX1 1NP

CLASSIFICATIONS
- Youth organisations (eg Guides, Scouts, YWCA etc)

C.C. NO 266672 **ESTABLISHED** 1970

■ The Munro Charitable Trust

OBJECTS General charitable purposes

POLICY OF TRUSTEES To support smaller charities which enable people of all age groups to enjoy activities not otherwise available to them for reasons of disability or deprivation

TYPE OF GRANT Single grant

TYPE OF BENEFICIARY Smaller charities favoured

BENEFICIAL AREA Charities operating in or benefiting residents of West Sussex, west and south-west London are favoured; however, where possible, charities operating nationally in the field covered by the policy may be supported

SAMPLE GRANTS £500 to Association of Wheelchair Children
£250 to Sussex Youth Clubs
£250 to Streatham Youth Project

FINANCES
- Year 1995
- Grants £8,000
- Income £9,296
- Assets £206,600

TRUSTEES Sir Alan Munro, N G Munro

SUBMISSION OF APPLICATIONS To save postage, applications will not be acknowledged. Successful applicants will hear within a week of Trustees' meetings which usually take place in the spring and autumn. In writing to correspondent. Reference: MAH 222521

CORRESPONDENT The Secretary, The Munro Charitable Trust, c/o Royal Bank of Scotland plc, 49 Charing Cross, London SW1A 2DX

CLASSIFICATIONS
- Advancement in life
- Development of character
- Holidays

C.C. NO 251649 **ESTABLISHED** 1966

■ Natwest Staff Samaritan Fund

OBJECTS Donations to hospitals, institutions and other charitable bodies for such amounts as the Trustees direct

POLICY OF TRUSTEES To provide financial resources for the purchase of equipment and facilities which will save lives, enhance recovery or give a greater quality of life to the dying or disabled

TYPE OF GRANT Cash payments for the purchase of specific items of equipment which will be of direct benefit to those in need

TYPE OF BENEFICIARY Hospitals, hospices and other charities associated with the welfare of the physically and mentally handicapped and able bodied

RESTRICTIONS No grants to individuals or for research/general appeals

BENEFICIAL AREA Great Britain

FINANCES
- Year 1991
- Grants £126,000
- Income £93,000

TRUSTEES J M Spurr, W T Butterworth, I R Farnsworth, J W Goodswen, F P Hencken, D W Hewson, Miss J A Musson, W J C Rouse, G J Wise

PUBLICATIONS Helping Hand

SUBMISSION OF APPLICATIONS Recommendations from members of staff of National Westminster Group have priority but other written requests will be considered

CORRESPONDENT The Secretary, NatWest Staff Samaritan Fund, 8th Floor, Wettern House, 56 Dingwall Road, Croydon, Surrey CR9 3HB

CLASSIFICATIONS
- Homes and hostels

C.C. NO 253694   **ESTABLISHED** 1924

■ The Needham Cooper Charitable Trust

OBJECTS General charitable purposes

TYPE OF GRANT At discretion of Trustees

TYPE OF BENEFICIARY Registered charities in beneficial area above

RESTRICTIONS Registered charities only. Applications from individuals, including students, are ineligible. No grants made to large national organisations except those with a branch locally

BENEFICIAL AREA Bristol and District

SAMPLE GRANTS £5,000 to 'Splash' Bristol police summer scheme
£2,000 to Bristol Children's Help Society
£500 to County of Avon Schools' Orchestra

FINANCES
- Year 1994–95
- Grants £222,620
- Income £217,487
- Assets £2,513,642

TRUSTEES Mrs E J B Cooper, S F T Cox, Mrs J L V Penson, R C Baxter

PUBLICATIONS Annual report and accounts to Charity Commission

SUBMISSION OF APPLICATIONS At any time. Trustees meet half-yearly. Applications should include details of the need the intended project is designed to meet, plus an outline budget and current balance sheet. We acknowledge all applications

CORRESPONDENT Mrs E J B Cooper, The Needham Cooper Charitable Trust, Home Farm, Yate Rocks, Yate, Bristol BS17 5BS

CLASSIFICATIONS
- Adventure centres and playgrounds
- Centres, clubs and institutes
- Counselling (inc helplines)
- Homes and hostels
- Youth organisations (eg Guides, Scouts, YWCA etc)

C.C. NO 327865   **ESTABLISHED** 1988

■ The Neighbourly Charitable Trust

OBJECTS General charitable purposes

POLICY OF TRUSTEES Trustees tend to support the same charities consistently over the years

TYPE OF GRANT Recurrent

TYPE OF BENEFICIARY Registered charities, institutions

BENEFICIAL AREA Mainly Bedfordshire

FINANCES
- Year 1995
- Grants £8,250
- Income £39,074
- Assets £579,899

TRUSTEES B A Allen, J R Sell, D Watts

CORRESPONDENT D Watts, 8 Upper Marlborough Road, St Albans, Hertfordshire AL1 3UR

CLASSIFICATIONS
- Children and youth – general

C.C. NO 258488   **ESTABLISHED** 1969

■ New Court Charitable Trust

OBJECTS General charitable purposes

POLICY OF TRUSTEES (a) To maintain existing commitments. (b) Provide limited finance to help small nationally orientated charities to become established. (c) Encourage co-ordination between charities working in related fields. (d) To support projects in which Trustees have a special interest and within policy laid down by the Deed

TYPE OF GRANT Usually single donation

TYPE OF BENEFICIARY Grants are seldom made to regional branches of national charities, local activities or towards building projects.

RESTRICTIONS Donations can only be made to registered charities

BENEFICIAL AREA UK

FINANCES
- Year 1994
- Grants £25,081
- Income £18,786

TRUSTEES E L de Rothschild, Sir Evelyn de Rothschild, L D de Rothschild, CBE, Hon Amschel Rothschild

Newby

Alphabetical register of grant making charitable trusts

SUBMISSION OF APPLICATIONS In writing only to correspondent

CORRESPONDENT The Secretary, New Court Charitable Trust, New Court, St Swithin's Lane, London EC4P 4DU

CLASSIFICATIONS
- Children and youth – general
- Centres, clubs and institutes
- Development of character

C.C. NO 209790   **ESTABLISHED** 1947

■ Newby Trust Ltd

OBJECTS The Trust has no easily definable objects, it responds to appeals

POLICY OF TRUSTEES Within the general objects of the Trust, one category for special support is selected each year. In 1994–95 community welfare. In 1995–96 mentally disabled. The policy of the Trustees is to help with running costs and specific objectives, not salaries

TYPE OF GRANT Usually one-off for part of a project. Core funding and salaries rarely considered

TYPE OF BENEFICIARY No preference

RESTRICTIONS For medical welfare and relief of poverty, grants are made only to health authorities, the NHS, social services or registered charities; applications from individuals are not considered. For training and education, grants are not normally considered except for students undertaking second degrees, for training in manual skills, and for help towards the completion of professional qualifications, and payments are invariably made to the educational body concerned, not to the individual

BENEFICIAL AREA UK

SAMPLE GRANTS £5,000 to the Child Psychotherapy Trust
£3,000 to Second Chance Foundation
£2,000 to Centre for Adolescent Studies
£100 to Lindsay Park Nursery, Kilmarnock for general expenses
£85 to Sheffield Social Services towards holiday for family suffering effects of abuse

FINANCES
- Year 1994
- Grants £228,286
- Income £245,189
- Assets £4,946,000

TRUSTEES The Directors

PUBLICATIONS Annual Report

SUBMISSION OF APPLICATIONS At any time. First applications should be made in writing. Applications from students and trainees should include clear details of the course being undertaken, personal circumstances and financial need. They should be accompanied by a CV, the names and addresses of two appropriate referees, and an sae. Decisions about relief of poverty and most medical welfare applications are made within one month; students should expect to wait about two months; decisions on larger institutional grants are made twice yearly at meetings of the Trustees. Foreign students are considered if circumstances beyond their control have led to a breakdown in funding during their course

CORRESPONDENT Mrs M Batstone, Secretary, Hill Farm, Froxfield, Nr Petersfield, Hampshire GU32 1BQ

CLASSIFICATIONS
- Children and youth – general
- Adventure centres and playgrounds
- Day centres and nurseries
- Holidays
- Children and violence (inc abuse)

C.C. NO 227151   **ESTABLISHED** 1938

■ Newcastle Children's Mission & Institute

OBJECTS Benefit of children and adults in the City and County of Newcastle upon Tyne

POLICY OF TRUSTEES To assist youth work in the City of Newcastle upon Tyne

TYPE OF GRANT Normally £100

TYPE OF BENEFICIARY Youth organisations in Newcastle upon Tyne

RESTRICTIONS No grants to individuals. No grants outside Newcastle upon Tyne

BENEFICIAL AREA The City of Newcastle upon Tyne only

SAMPLE GRANTS Newcastle Youth Chamber Orchestra
Scout and Ranger Guide Groups
South Benwell Playgroup

FINANCES
- Year 1995
- Grants £3,050
- Income £2,502
- Assets £46,240

TRUSTEES C H Morton, J K Kilner, L Ramsay, W Collins, Mrs E Morton

NOTES Grants have been made regularly to three church-based organisations and the amounts paid to them have exceeded the normal grants referred to above. Organisations operating outside the Newcastle upon Tyne area are asked not to apply

SUBMISSION OF APPLICATIONS To J K Kilner (as below). Trustees meet half yearly. No application form

CORRESPONDENT J K Kilner, 30 Cloth Market, Newcastle upon Tyne NE1 1EE

CLASSIFICATIONS
- Children and youth – general
- Centres, clubs and institutes
- Homes and hostels
- Youth organisations (eg Guides, Scouts, YWCA etc)

C.C. NO 230905   **ESTABLISHED** 1963

■ The Newman Charitable Trust

OBJECTS General charitable purposes

POLICY OF TRUSTEES Only to support charities known personally to the Trustees

TYPE OF GRANT A great majority of the anticipated income from this Trust is committed for some years ahead

TYPE OF BENEFICIARY Other registered charities only

RESTRICTIONS No grants to individuals

BENEFICIAL AREA Worldwide

FINANCES
- Year 1991
- Assets £400,000

TRUSTEES Newman Trustees Ltd

SUBMISSION OF APPLICATIONS Grants are not made to individuals, but to charities only

CORRESPONDENT Newman Trustees Ltd, Irwin House, 118 Southwark Street, London SE1 0SW

CLASSIFICATIONS
- Children and youth – general
- Youth organisations (eg Guides, Scouts, YWCA etc)
- Children and violence (inc abuse)

C.C. NO 264032   **ESTABLISHED** 1972

■ Nichol-Young Foundation

OBJECTS Relief of poverty – advancement of education – advancement of religion – general charitable purposes

POLICY OF TRUSTEES Grants to organisations in East Anglia especially considered. Present income fully committed

TYPE OF GRANT Grants are either one-off or for a limited period only

TYPE OF BENEFICIARY Mainly local but not exclusively so

BENEFICIAL AREA East Anglia especially

FINANCES
- **Year** 1995
- **Grants** £22,862
- **Income** £39,703
- **Assets** £691,155

TRUSTEES Rev J D Mitson, Rev Carole M Mitson

SUBMISSION OF APPLICATIONS To The Trustees, Nichol-Young Foundation, c/o 24–26 Museum Street, Ipswich IP1 1HZ. Applications may be made at any time but will only be considered periodically. Unsuccessful applications will generally not be acknowledged

CORRESPONDENT J D Mitson, Messrs Birketts, 24–26 Museum Street, Ipswich, Suffolk IP1 1HZ

CLASSIFICATIONS
- Youth organisations (eg Guides, Scouts, YWCA etc)

C.C. NO 259994   **ESTABLISHED** 1969

■ The Educational Foundation of Alderman John Norman

OBJECTS Educational charitable purposes

TYPE OF BENEFICIARY Children and young persons who are descendants of Alderman John Norman; children and young people residing in the parish of Catton, Norwich; other charitable educational institutions in Norwich and the immediate suburbs

BENEFICIAL AREA Local – Norwich

FINANCES
- **Year** 1992
- **Grants** £193,000

CORRESPONDENT N F Saffell, Old Bank of England Court, Queen Street, Norwich, Norfolk NR2 4TA

CLASSIFICATIONS
- Centres, clubs and institutes
- Community groups
- Development of character

C.C. NO 313105   **ESTABLISHED** 1973

■ The Norman Family Charitable Trust

OBJECTS General charitable purposes

POLICY OF TRUSTEES Not to make grants to individuals but to support the relief of suffering and the provision of a better way of life for those needing help (both humans and animals)

TYPE OF GRANT At the discretion of the Trustees

TYPE OF BENEFICIARY At the discretion of the Trustees

RESTRICTIONS No support will be given to projects involving experiments on live animals or the maintenance of churches, ancient monuments etc or to overseas projects

BENEFICIAL AREA Devon, Cornwall, Somerset

FINANCES
- **Year** 1995
- **Grants** £177,414
- **Income** £241,248
- **Assets** £3,000,000

TRUSTEES W K Norman, P M Norman, R J Dawe, Mrs M H Evans

SUBMISSION OF APPLICATIONS In writing to the address below stating the registration number of the applicant with the Charity Commissioners

CORRESPONDENT W K Norman, Rosemerrin, 5 Coastguard Road, Budleigh Salterton, Devon EX9 6NU

CLASSIFICATIONS
- Adoption/fostering
- Advancement in life
- Adventure centres and playgrounds
- Centres, clubs and institutes
- Day centres and nurseries
- Development of character
- Homes and hostels

C.C. NO 277616   **ESTABLISHED** 1979

■ Normanby Charitable Trust

OBJECTS General charitable purposes

POLICY OF TRUSTEES It is the normal policy of the Trustees only to make grants to recognised charities

RESTRICTIONS No specific restrictions

BENEFICIAL AREA Special interest in Yorkshire

SAMPLE GRANTS £20,000 to Yorkshire and Humberside Cadet Trust
£5,000 to Children's Country Holidays Fund

FINANCES
- **Year** 1995
- **Grants** £375,000
- **Income** £249,000
- **Assets** £5,975,000

TRUSTEES The Dowager Marchioness of Normanby, The Marquis of Normanby, Lady Lepel Kornicka, Lady Evelyn Buchan, Lady Peronel Phipps de Cruz, Lady Henrietta Sedgwick

SUBMISSION OF APPLICATIONS Applications are considered periodically but may be submitted at any time. Applications should be addressed to the correspondent, they will not be acknowledged, telephone calls are not encouraged. In writing to the correspondent

CORRESPONDENT Deloitte and Touche, 10–12 East Parade, Leeds, West Yorkshire LS1 2AJ

Northcott

CLASSIFICATIONS
- Children and youth – general
- Holidays
- Youth organisations (eg Guides, Scouts, YWCA etc)

C.C. NO 252102   ESTABLISHED 1966

■ Northcott Charitable Trust

OBJECTS General charitable purposes

POLICY OF TRUSTEES Grants made chiefly to charities in Exeter and district

TYPE OF GRANT No particular type, but mainly non-recurrent

TYPE OF BENEFICIARY Mainly headquarters of organisations and local organisations

RESTRICTIONS No grants to individuals

BENEFICIAL AREA Mainly Exeter and district

FINANCES
- Year 1993
- Grants £2,340
- Income £2,442
- Assets £20,166

TRUSTEES T E Grimes, D P Cody

SUBMISSION OF APPLICATIONS Direct at any time. No application form

CORRESPONDENT T E Grimes, Smallfield & Co, 18–22 Disney Place, London SE1 1HS

CLASSIFICATIONS
- Children and youth – general

C.C. NO 211770   ESTABLISHED 1956

■ The Northumberland Village Homes Trust

OBJECTS 1. The relief of poverty, distress and sickness among children and young persons under the age of 18 years. 2. To promote the education and training of young persons under the age of 18 years

POLICY OF TRUSTEES As stated in Objects

TYPE OF GRANT As stated in Objects

TYPE OF BENEFICIARY Children and young persons under the age of 18 years only

RESTRICTIONS As stated in Objects. No personal applications will be considered by the Trustees unless supported by a letter from a registered charity, local authority or unless the applicant is personally known to one of the Trustees who has actual personal knowledge of that applicant's circumstances

BENEFICIAL AREA All areas, however applications from the United Kingdom and in particular from the North East of England are given priority

FINANCES
- Year 1991
- Grants £107,300
- Income £175,953
- Assets £932,353

TRUSTEES D Welch, Mrs J M Paley, B Porter, Mrs L I Lawrence, Richard Baron Gisborough, Mrs E P Savage, K Hunt, J M O'Neill

NOTES The Trustees meet twice yearly in May and November. Applications to be considered at the Trustees' meeting should be made on or before 31st March and on or before 30th September respectively. Applications for grants should state:- (a) Whether or not the applicant is a private person, private charity or registered charity. (b) If the applicant is a private person, the application must be supported by a letter from a registered charity, local authority or a Trustee who has actual personal knowledge of that applicant's circumstances. (c) If a private or registered charity the objects should be clearly stated. (d) In all cases, the amount of grant required and the purpose for which it will be applied must be clearly stated. (e) In all cases, it should be stated whether or not the applicant receives funding from any other charity, local or government body or would qualify for such funding

SUBMISSION OF APPLICATIONS Applications should be made to the Trustees in March and September each year

CORRESPONDENT Mrs Savage, c/o Gibson Pybus Reay-Smith & Bellwood, 42 Mosley Street, Newcastle upon Tyne NE1 1DF

CLASSIFICATIONS
- Children and youth – general
- Adoption/fostering
- Advancement in life
- Adventure centres and playgrounds
- Centres, clubs and institutes
- Community groups
- Day centres and nurseries
- Development of character
- Counselling (inc helplines)
- Holidays
- Homes and hostels
- Special needs housing
- Special classes
- Youth organisations (eg Guides, Scouts, YWCA etc)

C.C. NO 225429   ESTABLISHED 1888

■ The Norton Foundation

OBJECTS To help children and young persons under the age of 25 years who are in need of care or rehabilitation or aid of any kind, particularly as a result of delinquency, deprivation, maltreatment or neglect or who are in danger of lapsing or relapsing into delinquency

POLICY OF TRUSTEES The Trustees will consider applications from individuals in need and from organisations working with young persons in need — only in their primary beneficial area of Birmingham and the County of Warwick

TYPE OF GRANT Grants to individuals for specific needs. Grants to suitable organisations for any capital or revenue purpose

TYPE OF BENEFICIARY Children and young persons in need due to any cause. Organisations which help such young persons

BENEFICIAL AREA The UK and in particular the Birmingham area and the county of Warwick

SAMPLE GRANTS £10,000 to Saint Basil's Centre Ltd
£10,000 to Swalcliffe Park School Trust
£5,000 to Break Out Children's Holidays
£5,000 to South Birmingham Young Homeless Project
£5,000 to Coventry city farm

FINANCES
- Year 1995
- Grants £171,000
- Income £126,000
- Assets £2,558,000

TRUSTEES D P J Monk, Mrs E Corney, Mrs S V Henderson, Mrs P Francis, H Antrobus, J R

Kendrick, B W Lewis, A Newland, D F Perkins, R H G Suggett

SUBMISSION OF APPLICATIONS To clerk from whom application forms can be obtained. Applications from individuals dealt with when received. Applications from organisations dealt with in May of each year

CORRESPONDENT Mrs Jane M Emms, Clerk to the Trustees, PO Box 040, Kenilworth, Warkwickshire CV8 2ZR

CLASSIFICATIONS
- Children and youth – general
- Advancement in life
- Adventure centres and playgrounds
- Centres, clubs and institutes
- Community groups
- Day centres and nurseries
- Development of character
- Counselling (inc helplines)
- Holidays
- Homes and hostels
- Special needs housing
- Youth organisations (eg Guides, Scouts, YWCA etc)
- Children and violence (inc abuse)

C.C. NO 702638   **ESTABLISHED** 1990

■ Norwich Church of England Young Men's Society

OBJECTS To promote the welfare of members spiritually, socially, intellectually and physically and to aid missionary work at home or abroad

POLICY OF TRUSTEES No fixed policies. Financial restraints on own activities necessitates mainly local grants

TYPE OF GRANT One-off

TYPE OF BENEFICIARY Mainly local

RESTRICTIONS No grants to individuals

BENEFICIAL AREA Mainly local

FINANCES
- Year 1994
- Grants £4,514
- Income £133,000

TRUSTEES J Pidgen, D Pilch, J Copeman, Rev Canon D Sharp

PUBLICATIONS Annual report

NOTES Grant restriction to Church allied activities only

SUBMISSION OF APPLICATIONS All applications discussed by General Committee and Finance Committee quarterly. Only successful applications acknowledged

CORRESPONDENT C J Free, 3 Brigg Street, Norwich, Norfolk NR2 1QN

CLASSIFICATIONS
- Centres, clubs and institutes
- Community groups
- Day centres and nurseries
- Special classes
- Youth organisations (eg Guides, Scouts, YWCA etc)

C.C. NO 206425   **ESTABLISHED** 1847

■ The Oak Trust

OBJECTS General charitable purposes

POLICY OF TRUSTEES Preference to charities of which the Trust has special interest, knowledge or association

TYPE OF GRANT Donations rather than subscriptions

TYPE OF BENEFICIARY Registered charities

RESTRICTIONS Applications from individuals will not be considered

FINANCES
- Year 1995
- Grants £31,708
- Income £41,697
- Assets £566,314

TRUSTEES The Rev A C C Courtauld, MA, J Courtauld, Dr E Courtauld

NOTES No telephone applications please. Please apply in writing giving details of your appeal

SUBMISSION OF APPLICATIONS To R R Long

CORRESPONDENT Birkett Long, Red House, Colchester Road, Halstead, Essex CO9 2DZ

CLASSIFICATIONS
- Centres, clubs and institutes

C.C. NO 231456   **ESTABLISHED** 1963

■ The Oakdale Trust

OBJECTS General charitable purposes

POLICY OF TRUSTEES Preference to charities of which the Trust has special interest, knowledge or association. Youth projects, medical and arts, conservation organisations

TYPE OF GRANT Single outright grants

TYPE OF BENEFICIARY Preference for charities in Wales. No grants to individuals

RESTRICTIONS No grants to individuals

BENEFICIAL AREA UK, and Wales in particular

FINANCES
- Year 1994
- Grants £94,500
- Income £88,000

TRUSTEES B Cadbury, Mrs F F Cadbury, R A Cadbury, F B Cadbury, Dr R C Cadbury, Mrs O H Tatton-Brown

SUBMISSION OF APPLICATIONS Any time. No form required but applications should be concise, quoting Charity Registration Number, a summary of their achievements, plans, needs and a copy or summary of their most recent annual accounts. All applications are carefully considered but owing to lack of secretarial help, no acknowledgement can be expected

CORRESPONDENT B Cadbury, Tan y Coed, Pantydwr, Rhayader, Powys LD6 5LR

Ogilvie

CLASSIFICATIONS
- Adventure centres and playgrounds
- Community groups
- Youth organisations (eg Guides, Scouts, YWCA etc)

C.C. NO 218827 **ESTABLISHED** 1950

■ Ogilvie Charities (Deed No 2)

OBJECTS Specific philanthropic work. Assistance to present or former governesses or female teachers in straitened circumstances. Country holidays for London children. Support of Charity's own Homes and Almshouses and residents living in them. Aid to other charitable institutions in Metropolitan London, Essex and Suffolk or, if situated beyond, serving the needs of people living in those areas

POLICY OF TRUSTEES Grants made through medical and other social workers who are already aware of what is available. No payment of debts a policy of Trustees

TYPE OF GRANT One-off usually

TYPE OF BENEFICIARY Individuals or organisations meeting criteria defined by objects of Trust

BENEFICIAL AREA Great Britain, but primarily London, Essex and Suffolk

SAMPLE GRANTS £100–£250 to charities providing holidays for London children

FINANCES
- Year 1992
- Grants £13,500

SUBMISSION OF APPLICATIONS Applications received through social worker or other official sources, not by personal application. Preliminary telephone enquiries acceptable and may prevent abortive correspondence

CORRESPONDENT The General Manager, The Ogilvie Charities, The Gate House, 9 Burkitt Road, Woodbridge, Suffolk IP12 4JJ

CLASSIFICATIONS
- Holidays

C.C. NO 211778 **ESTABLISHED** 1890

■ William Older's School Charity

OBJECTS To promote the education of children residing in the beneficial area

POLICY OF TRUSTEES To provide financial assistance for educational purposes to applicants residing in the beneficial area

TYPE OF GRANT For educational purposes

TYPE OF BENEFICIARY Local schools, playgroups and other educational establishments in academic or specialised courses of study, plus individuals

RESTRICTIONS Restricted to applicants residing in the beneficial area of the Parish of Angmering

BENEFICIAL AREA Parish of Angmering, West Sussex. Applicants must be resident in the Beneficial Area

FINANCES
- Year 1991
- Grants £8,131
- Income £10,456
- Assets £61,049

TRUSTEES Rev A Wells, L A Baker, N Hare, Mrs J Hawke, R Hale

SUBMISSION OF APPLICATIONS Trustees meetings are held quarterly. Applications to be submitted in writing to the correspondent giving clear details of financial need plus an outline budget

CORRESPONDENT Mrs A C Wood, JP, Secretary, Larks Rise, Rectory Lane, Angmering Village, West Sussex BN16 4JU

CLASSIFICATIONS
- Children and youth – general
- Advancement in life
- Adventure centres and playgrounds
- Day centres and nurseries
- Holidays
- Special classes
- Youth organisations (eg Guides, Scouts, YWCA etc)

C.C. NO 306424 **ESTABLISHED** 1976

■ Oldham Foundation

OBJECTS General charitable purposes

POLICY OF TRUSTEES Main donations to former employees of Oldham Batteries (employed before 1971) and charitable activities where Trustees give personal service or where they know people who do so

TYPE OF GRANT Annual grant to former employees. Grants usually one-off. Does not provide core funding

RESTRICTIONS Applications from individuals, including students, are ineligible with the exception of those already selected for schemes like Operation Raleigh. No grants to general appeals from national bodies. Inappropriate appeals are not acknowledged

BENEFICIAL AREA North West and South West of England. Charities aided in the area may have objectives overseas

SAMPLE GRANTS £500 to Operation Raleigh
£250 to Outward Bound
£250 to Oban Youth

FINANCES
- Year 1992
- Grants £160,000
- Income £180,000
- Assets £750,000

TRUSTEES O Oldham (Chairman), J Bodden, Mrs D Oldham, J Oldham, S Roberts, Prof R Thomas

SUBMISSION OF APPLICATIONS Any time. Trustees meet twice a year. Applications should include clear details of projects, budgets, and/or accounts where appropriate. Telephone submissions not accepted

CORRESPONDENT Mrs D Oldham, King's Well, Douro Road, Cheltenham, Gloucestershire GL50 2PF

CLASSIFICATIONS
- Children and youth – general
- Adventure centres and playgrounds
- Centres, clubs and institutes
- Community groups
- Day centres and nurseries
- Development of character
- Holidays
- Youth organisations (eg Guides, Scouts, YWCA etc)

C.C. NO 269263 **ESTABLISHED** 1974

■ K A Oppenheim Charitable Settlement

OBJECTS General charitable purposes

POLICY OF TRUSTEES To consider all worthwhile causes

TYPE OF GRANT Grants do not normally exceed £150

TYPE OF BENEFICIARY Great variety, from national to local charitable causes

FINANCES
- Year 1990
- Grants £4,021
- Income £2,842
- Assets £29,255

TRUSTEES K A Oppenheim, Mrs L Oppenheim, R O Goldstein

SUBMISSION OF APPLICATIONS Personal research grants on quarterly basis, closing dates for applications end September, November, February, April. Major research grants on annual basis, closing date for archaeological fieldwork applications end December, for other projects end April

CORRESPONDENT K A Oppenheim, 13 Belsize Lane, Hampstead, London NW3 5AD

CLASSIFICATIONS
- Children and youth – general

C.C. NO 272608 **ESTABLISHED** 1976

■ Ormiston Trust

OBJECTS General charitable purposes, particularly children and youth

TYPE OF GRANT Capital and recurrent grants for Trust managed projects

TYPE OF BENEFICIARY Registered charities, not individuals

RESTRICTIONS Grants only made to projects managed by the Ormiston Charitable Trust

BENEFICIAL AREA East Anglia

FINANCES
- Year 1995
- Assets £4,289,695
- Income £600,986

TRUSTEES P G Murray, E G Murray, P D Taylor

SUBMISSION OF APPLICATIONS Detailed appeals may be submitted at any time through the correspondent and should be accompanied by supporting financial statements and audited accounts

CORRESPONDENT P G Murray, 10 Abercorn Place, London NW8 9XP

CLASSIFICATIONS
- Children and youth – general

C.C. NO 259334 **ESTABLISHED** 1969

■ The Owen Family Trust (formerly New Hall Charity Trust)

OBJECTS General charitable purposes

POLICY OF TRUSTEES Mainly support for projects known personally by Trustees. Education, young people, Christian projects, conservation, medical, music

TYPE OF BENEFICIARY Schools, Christian youth centres, Churches, community associations, national schemes and organisations

RESTRICTIONS Grants to individuals are unlikely

BENEFICIAL AREA National, but mainly West Midlands and North Wales

SAMPLE GRANTS £5,000 to YMCA
£1,000 to Scripture Union

FINANCES
- Year 1994
- Grants £26,628
- Income £39,312
- Assets £455,604

TRUSTEES Mrs H G Jenkins, A D Owen

NOTES The Trust is only able to consider about five new projects each year. Due to cost it is regretted not all applications will be acknowledged

SUBMISSION OF APPLICATIONS Send brochures with explanatory letter

CORRESPONDENT A D Owen, Mill Dam House, Mill Lane, Aldridge, Walsall WS9 0NB

CLASSIFICATIONS
- Centres, clubs and institutes
- Youth organisations (eg Guides, Scouts, YWCA etc)

C.C. NO 251975 **ESTABLISHED** 1967

■ PB Charitable Trust

OBJECTS General charitable purposes

RESTRICTIONS Appeals restricted to charitable institutions only. No mail shots and telephone appeals

FINANCES
- Year 1993
- Grants £33,050
- Income £45,754

TRUSTEES Mrs J M Pritchard-Barrett, A Pritchard-Barrett, Mrs A D Marks, Miss M A Falk

CORRESPONDENT Messrs Farrer and Company, 66 Lincoln's Inn Fields, London WC2A 3LH

CLASSIFICATIONS
- Homes and hostels

C.C. NO 802328   **ESTABLISHED** 1991

■ The PDC Trust

OBJECTS General charitable purposes

POLICY OF TRUSTEES National organisations, children (including handicapped children), Third World, especially under-nourishment and lack of medical facilities, charities connected with the Armed Forces, charitable institutions in the field of art

RESTRICTIONS No appeals from individuals. No appeals for repairs or improvements to Churches and other buildings except in Hampshire and possibly in London

BENEFICIAL AREA UK and overseas

FINANCES
- Year 1994
- Grants £9,446
- Income £9,764
- Assets £159,428

TRUSTEES Mrs J C S Paravicini, S T Gray, Smith & Williamson Trust Corporation, J Paravicini, N Paravicini

SUBMISSION OF APPLICATIONS Applications in writing, with supporting evidence, to the Trustees at any time. Only successful applications will be acknowledged – usually within three months of receipt

CORRESPONDENT S T Gray, Smith & Williamson, Chartered Accountants, No I Riding House Street, London W1A 3AS

CLASSIFICATIONS
- Children and youth – general
- Centres, clubs and institutes
- Development of character
- Holidays

C.C. NO 266255   **ESTABLISHED** 1973

■ PF Charitable Trust

OBJECTS To support religious, educational and other charities

POLICY OF TRUSTEES To make contributions to medical research, welfare, religious and educational bodies and other legal charities

TYPE OF GRANT Various

TYPE OF BENEFICIARY Appeals that essentially concern a local community and local branches of national charities are not normally supported. No grants to individuals

RESTRICTIONS No grants to individuals, unregistered bodies or individual churches

FINANCES
- Year 1994
- Grants £727,875

TRUSTEES R Fleming, V P Fleming, P Fleming, R D Fleming

NOTES Hospices are now covered by a large donation to Help the Hospices

SUBMISSION OF APPLICATIONS To the Correspondent at any time, in writing with full information. Replies will be sent to unsuccessful applications only if an sae is enclosed

CORRESPONDENT The Secretary, PF Charitable Trust, 25 Copthall Avenue, London EC2R 7DR

CLASSIFICATIONS
- Children and youth – general
- Youth organisations (eg Guides, Scouts, YWCA etc)

C.C. NO 220124   **ESTABLISHED** 1951

■ PJD Charitable Trust

OBJECTS General charitable purposes and in particular the RNLI, Church of England Children's Society, National Trust and British Red Cross Society

POLICY OF TRUSTEES It is the Trustees policy to benefit principally charities to alleviate disease and human suffering, charities for the old, charities for former serving officers and charities connected with the sea. Individual applications are not encouraged and will not, it is regretted, be acknowledged

FINANCES
- Year 1993
- Grants £2,700
- Income £2,423
- Assets £25,656

TRUSTEES B N A Weatherill, P D Dixon

CORRESPONDENT B N A Weatherill, Wedlake Bell, 16 Bedford Street, Covent Garden, London WC2E 9HF

CLASSIFICATIONS
- Children and youth – general

C.C. NO 261158   **ESTABLISHED** 1970

■ The Gerald Palmer Trust

OBJECTS (a) The advancement of the Christian religion more particularly according to the teaching and usage of the Orthodox Churches of the East. (b) The advancement of medical research and the study of medicine. (c) The relief of sickness and/or poverty. General charitable purposes

POLICY OF TRUSTEES It is not the policy of the Trustees to grant-aid small local charities geographically remote from the Trust's estate in Berkshire

RESTRICTIONS No grants to individuals

BENEFICIAL AREA Berkshire

FINANCES
- Year 1994
- Grants £47,375
- Income £148,860
- Assets £6,339,412

TRUSTEES J M Clutterbuck, D R W Harrison, C J Pratt, FRICS, J N Abell

SUBMISSION OF APPLICATIONS To the Correspondent

CORRESPONDENT C J Pratt, FRICS, Eling Estate Office, Hermitage, Newbury, Berkshire RG16 9UF

CLASSIFICATIONS
- Counselling (inc helplines)
- Special needs housing

C.C. NO 271327   **ESTABLISHED** 1968

■ The Constance Paterson Charitable Foundation

OBJECTS General charitable purposes

POLICY OF TRUSTEES Medical research, welfare of elderly and children

TYPE OF GRANT One-off payments

TYPE OF BENEFICIARY Registered charities

RESTRICTIONS No personal applications please

BENEFICIAL AREA UK

SAMPLE GRANTS £2,000 to Evelina Childrens' Hospital Appeal
£1,500 to NSPCC
£1,000 to The Lady Hoare Trust

FINANCES
- Year 1993
- Grants £37,400
- Income £41,000
- Assets £583,000

TRUSTEES Royal Bank of Canada Trust Corporation Limited

SUBMISSION OF APPLICATIONS May and November

CORRESPONDENT Ms Pat Moody, Royal Bank of Canada Trust Corporation Limited, 71 Queen Victoria Street, London EC4V 4DE

CLASSIFICATIONS
- Children and youth – general

C.C. NO 249556   **ESTABLISHED** 1966

■ Arthur James Paterson Charitable Trust

OBJECTS General charitable purposes

POLICY OF TRUSTEES Medical research, welfare of elderly and children

TYPE OF GRANT One-off payments

TYPE OF BENEFICIARY Registered charities

RESTRICTIONS No personal applications, please

BENEFICIAL AREA UK

SAMPLE GRANTS £2,000 to Royal Scottish Society for Prevention of Cruelty to Children
£2,000 to Child Psychotherapy Trust

FINANCES
- Year 1993
- Grants £30,000
- Income £50,000
- Assets £680,000

TRUSTEES Royal Bank of Canada Trust Corporation Ltd

SUBMISSION OF APPLICATIONS February and August

CORRESPONDENT Ms Pat Moody, Royal Bank of Canada Trust Corporation Ltd, 71 Queen Victoria Street, London EC4V 4DE

CLASSIFICATIONS
- Children and youth – general

C.C. NO 278569   **ESTABLISHED** 1979

■ R J Paul's Charitable Trust

OBJECTS General charitable purposes

POLICY OF TRUSTEES Grants to Housing, Hospital, and Youth Associations

TYPE OF GRANT Housing, Hospital, and Youth Associations

TYPE OF BENEFICIARY Mainly local organisations

RESTRICTIONS Time limit

BENEFICIAL AREA County of Suffolk (mainly) East Anglia

FINANCES
- Year 1993
- Grants £16,950
- Income £15,788
- Assets £55,000

TRUSTEES Miss M J Paul, J M Paul

SUBMISSION OF APPLICATIONS To correspondent, as above

CORRESPONDENT Miss M J Paul, Woodside, Constitution Hill, Ipswich, Suffolk IP1 3RH

CLASSIFICATIONS
- Holidays
- Youth organisations (eg Guides, Scouts, YWCA etc)

C.C. NO 213660   **ESTABLISHED** 1949

■ The Harry Payne Trust

OBJECTS General charitable purposes

POLICY OF TRUSTEES To give priority to charitable work in Birmingham, where the trust was founded, in response to appeals

TYPE OF GRANT Some once only, some annually

Pedmore

TYPE OF BENEFICIARY Various, but main areas are the elderly, the disadvantaged generally and youth related projects

RESTRICTIONS No grants made to individuals or to any political party or to projects outside geographical area of support. Applications from individuals or outside geographical area will not be acknowledged

BENEFICIAL AREA Birmingham and the West Midlands

FINANCES
- Year 1995
- Income £38,264
- Grants £38,100
- Assets £755,713

TRUSTEES Mrs A K Burnett, J E Payne, R King, BEM (Chairman), D F Dodd, R C King (Secretary), R I Payne, Mrs B J Major, OBE, D J Cadbury

NOTES Applications must be accompanied by an up-to-date copy of audited accounts and should aim to arrive, at latest, by end of May or end of October to be considered at the next meeting

SUBMISSION OF APPLICATIONS By application form available from the Secretary. The Trustees meet twice a year in June and November

CORRESPONDENT R C King, Secretary, The Harry Payne Trust, 25 Bury Green, Wheathampstead, St Albans, Herts AL4 8DB

CLASSIFICATIONS
- Centres, clubs and institutes
- Community groups
- Day centres and nurseries
- Counselling (inc helplines)
- Holidays
- Special needs housing
- Youth organisations (eg Guides, Scouts, YWCA etc)

C.C. NO 231063   ESTABLISHED 1939

■ **Pedmore Sporting Club Trust Fund**

OBJECTS General charitable purposes

POLICY OF TRUSTEES In response to applications only

TYPE OF GRANT Capital projects not general funding

BENEFICIAL AREA Local West Midlands causes as general rule

FINANCES
- Year 1995
- Income £37,000
- Grants £21,000
- Assets £224,731

TRUSTEES P Pioli, N A Hickman, C Cooper, R Herman-Smith

SUBMISSION OF APPLICATIONS Written applications to the Secretary

CORRESPONDENT P J E Harley, Pedmore House, Ham Lane, Pedmore, Stourbridge, West Midlands

CLASSIFICATIONS
- Children and youth – general
- Adventure centres and playgrounds
- Centres, clubs and institutes
- Holidays
- Homes and hostels
- Youth organisations (eg Guides, Scouts, YWCA etc)

C.C. NO 263907   ESTABLISHED 1973

■ **The Philip & Judith Petley Charitable Trust**

OBJECTS General charitable purposes

POLICY OF TRUSTEES To favour Christian causes and give support to human welfare causes

TYPE OF BENEFICIARY Registered charities

FINANCES
- Year 1993
- Income £15,372

TRUSTEES P T Petley, R H Neville

SUBMISSION OF APPLICATIONS No unsolicited or individual applications will be considered

CORRESPONDENT Ms A L Calder, Monro Penne Father & Co, 8 Great James Street, London WC1N 3DA

CLASSIFICATIONS
- Children and youth – general

C.C. NO 277991   ESTABLISHED 1979

■ **Pettit Charitable Trust**

OBJECTS General charitable purposes

TYPE OF GRANT Grants made for the furtherance of Christianity, youth work, physical and mental health and other charitable objects. Grants are in the region of £100

TYPE OF BENEFICIARY General grants to registered charities only

FINANCES
- Year 1994
- Income £7,479
- Grants £7,975
- Assets £15,094

TRUSTEES K J Pettit, Mrs H J Lipman, C H Pettit, J F Warren, P J Pettit, Mrs S J Sutcliffe

SUBMISSION OF APPLICATIONS Small grants approved at annual Trustees' meeting in November to small registered charities for payment at Christmas. Replies will only be made to successful applicants

CORRESPONDENT K J Pettit, 11 Church Street, Rickmansworth, Hertfordshire WD3 1DB

CLASSIFICATIONS
- Centres, clubs and institutes
- Homes and hostels
- Youth organisations (eg Guides, Scouts, YWCA etc)

C.C. NO 242223   ESTABLISHED 1963

■ **The John Phillimore Charitable Trust**

OBJECTS General charitable purposes

POLICY OF TRUSTEES The main areas of concern are physical and mental disabilities, eg asthma, the blind and the deaf; youth education and preservation of heritage, eg cathedrals

TYPE OF GRANT Normally grants are made on a single payment basis

TYPE OF BENEFICIARY Registered charities only

RESTRICTIONS Applications from individuals, including students, are ineligible

BENEFICIAL AREA Counties of Kent and Hampshire

SAMPLE GRANTS £250 to Crown and Manor Boys Club

£100 to Farlington School Trust
£100 to Hampshire Playing Fields Association

FINANCES
- Year 1995
- Grants £13,900
- Income £8,000
- Assets £145,000

TRUSTEES Baring Trust Co, Limited

SUBMISSION OF APPLICATIONS Applications should be made to the correspondents. No preliminary telephone call required

CORRESPONDENT Baring Trust Co, Limited, 155 Bishopsgate, London EC2M 3XY

CLASSIFICATIONS
- Advancement in life

C.C. NO 264788 **ESTABLISHED** 1972

■ The Phillips Family Charitable Trust

OBJECTS General charitable purposes

TYPE OF BENEFICIARY Registered charities

RESTRICTIONS No grants to individuals

FINANCES
- Year 1993
- Grants £36,546
- Income £42,216
- Assets £190,610

TRUSTEES M D Paisner, M L Phillips, Mrs R Phillips, P S Phillips, G M Philips

CORRESPONDENT M D Paisner, Paisner & Co, Solicitors, Bouverie House, 154 Fleet Street, London EC4A 2DQ

CLASSIFICATIONS
- Children and youth – general

C.C. NO 279120 **ESTABLISHED** 1979

■ The David Pickford Charitable Foundation

OBJECTS General charitable purposes with preference to Christian youth work

POLICY OF TRUSTEES Support a residential Christian youth centre in Kent for those in the 15 to 25 age group and other similar activities

TYPE OF GRANT Mainly for Christian youth work

TYPE OF BENEFICIARY Mainly, but not solely, youths and christian evangelism

RESTRICTIONS No grants to individuals. No building projects

FINANCES
- Year 1995
- Grants £40,000
- Income £52,828
- Assets £761,490

TRUSTEES D M Pickford, Mrs E G Pickford

NOTES Applications will not be acknowledged. Those falling outside the Type of Beneficiary mentioned above will be ignored

SUBMISSION OF APPLICATIONS In writing any time

CORRESPONDENT D M Pickford, Elm Tree Farm, Mersham, Ashford, Kent TN25 7HS

CLASSIFICATIONS
- Adoption/fostering
- Youth organisations (eg Guides, Scouts, YWCA etc)

C.C. NO 243437 **ESTABLISHED** 1965

■ Pike Charity Settlement

OBJECTS General charitable purposes

POLICY OF TRUSTEES To support charitable work in Devon

TYPE OF GRANT One-off sums

TYPE OF BENEFICIARY Entirely confined to Devon: educational, youth, ecclesiastical, medical

RESTRICTIONS Appeals from outside Devon are ineligible

BENEFICIAL AREA Devon only

FINANCES
- Year 1991
- Grants £11,955
- Income £13,002

TRUSTEES C D Pike, Mrs M Pike, J D Pike, Dr P A D Holland, JP

SUBMISSION OF APPLICATIONS No appeals from outside Devon will be considered

CORRESPONDENT C D Pike, OBE, DL, Dunderdale Lawn, Penshurst Road, Newton Abbot, Devon TQ12 1EN

CLASSIFICATIONS
- Children and youth – general
- Development of character
- Homes and hostels

C.C. NO 247657 **ESTABLISHED** 1965

■ The Pilgrim Trust

OBJECTS The preservation of the national heritage and the promotion of the future well-being of the country

POLICY OF TRUSTEES The Trustees revise their guidelines annually. Their 1995–96 policy includes supporting: 'Social Welfare' issues such as: schemes for the prevention of crime particularly among juveniles; bail hostels, prison visitor facilities and prison education; unemployment, with special reference to young people who have never been employed; accommodation for the homeless; rehabilitation of drink and drug addicts. Other areas of support cover 'Art and Learning' and the 'Preservation of buildings of outstanding architectural interest'

TYPE OF GRANT Normally once only grants for specific purposes (may be spread over a few years), or for capital expenditure

TYPE OF BENEFICIARY Local and national but not normally local branches of national charities

RESTRICTIONS Only charitable bodies in the UK are eligible for funding, not individuals. The Trust does not fund: education, youth centres, childrens' playgrounds, community centres and clubs, 'mega-appeals' from national or non-national museums, revenue funding, activities which are the responsibility of central of local government, medical research

BENEFICIAL AREA UK

FINANCES
- Year 1993
- Grants £1,347,397
- Income £1,640,756
- Assets £32,685,756

TRUSTEES Mrs M Moore (Chairman), The Rt Hon Lord Jenkins of Hillhead, The Rt Hon The Lord Thomson of Monifieth, KT, PC, N Barker, The Marchioness of Anglesey, DBE, Sir Claus Moser, KCB, CBE, FBA, The

Pilkington's

Alphabetical register of grant making charitable trusts

Rt Hon Lord Armstrong of Ilminster, GCB, CVO, N MacGregor, The Rt Hon Lord Justice Bingham, Lord Cobbold, Miss E Turton

PUBLICATIONS Annual Report

SUBMISSION OF APPLICATIONS By correspondence at any time — Trustees meet four times a year

CORRESPONDENT The Secretary, The Pilgrim Trust, Fielden House, Little College Street, London SW1P 3SH

CLASSIFICATIONS
- Advancement in life
- Development of character

C.C. NO 206602   **ESTABLISHED** 1930

■ Dr L H A Pilkington's Charitable Trust

OBJECTS General charitable purposes

POLICY OF TRUSTEES To grant donations to applicants who they consider suitable, but normally to organisations within the British Isles and not to individuals

TYPE OF GRANT Cash

TYPE OF BENEFICIARY Charities and other beneficial organisations

RESTRICTIONS Registered charities only. No individual grants

BENEFICIAL AREA Worldwide

FINANCES
- **Year** 1991
- **Grants** £48,950
- **Income** £44,303
- **Assets** £302,513

TRUSTEES Mrs Eunice Henniger, P Henniger, Mrs Eleanor Bankes, T A Bankes

SUBMISSION OF APPLICATIONS Applications in writing to the Trustees at any time outlining the purposes for which the donation is requested and any supporting literature. No formal application forms

CORRESPONDENT Dr L H A Pilkington's Charitable Trust, PO Box 428, Guernsey, CI

CLASSIFICATIONS
- Children and youth – general
- Centres, clubs and institutes
- Development of character
- Homes and hostels
- Youth organisations (eg Guides, Scouts, YWCA etc)

C.C. NO 241296   **ESTABLISHED** 1966

■ The John Pitman Charitable Trust

OBJECTS General charitable purposes

POLICY OF TRUSTEES Grants to charities which provide services to individuals, to enable the individuals to live their life more fully

TYPE OF GRANT No restriction – either capital or revenue

TYPE OF BENEFICIARY No restriction

RESTRICTIONS Registered charities only. No grants to individuals, research bodies or education

BENEFICIAL AREA South East England

SAMPLE GRANTS £1,000 to the Family Holiday Association

FINANCES
- **Year** 1993
- **Grants** £8,250
- **Income** £41,650
- **Assets** £362,416

TRUSTEES J M Pitman, N A R Winckless, B Hong Tan, V N C S Browne, J L L McKenzie

SUBMISSION OF APPLICATIONS Periodically, but no set dates

CORRESPONDENT J M Pitman, Messrs Pitman Power & Co, Parkgate House, 27 High Street, Hampton Hill, Middlesex TW12 1NB

CLASSIFICATIONS
- Children and youth – general
- Development of character
- Holidays

C.C. NO 803018   **ESTABLISHED** 1989

■ The Sir Richard Carew Pole 1973 Charitable Trust

OBJECTS General charitable purposes

POLICY OF TRUSTEES Principally to assist charities and charitable purposes in Cornwall and Devon

TYPE OF GRANT The Trustees have no particular policy

TYPE OF BENEFICIARY Donations normally made only to registered charities, but applications will be considered from individuals for non-full time education purposes

BENEFICIAL AREA National, but mainly Cornwall and Devon

FINANCES
- **Year** 1993
- **Grants** £36,800
- **Income** £52,169
- **Assets** £580,431

TRUSTEES J C Richardson, J R Cooke-Hurle

SUBMISSION OF APPLICATIONS Applications are considered six monthly in March and September

CORRESPONDENT J C Richardson, Messrs Dawson & Co, 2 New Square, Lincoln's Inn, London WC2A 3RZ

CLASSIFICATIONS
- Children and youth – general
- Youth organisations (eg Guides, Scouts, YWCA etc)

C.C. NO 266291   **ESTABLISHED** 1973

■ Carew Pole Charitable Trust

OBJECTS General charitable purposes

POLICY OF TRUSTEES Principally to assist charities and charitable purposes in Cornwall and Devon

TYPE OF GRANT The Trustees have no particular policy

TYPE OF BENEFICIARY Donations normally made only to registered charities, but applications will be considered from individuals for non-full time education purposes

BENEFICIAL AREA National, but mainly Cornwall and Devon

FINANCES
- **Year** 1993
- **Grants** £35,216
- **Income** £30,277
- **Assets** £642,441

TRUSTEES J R Cooke-Hurle, J C Richardson

NOTES This Charitable Trust was founded by Sir John Gawen Carew Pole, Bt, DSO, whose family has both lived in and been connected with Cornwall for many years

SUBMISSION OF APPLICATIONS Applications are considered six monthly in March and September

CORRESPONDENT J C Richardson, Messrs Dawson & Co, 2 New Square, Lincoln's Inn, London WC2A 3RZ

CLASSIFICATIONS
- Adventure centres and playgrounds
- Development of character

C.C. NO 255375   **ESTABLISHED** 1968

■ The Portrack Charitable Trust

OBJECTS General charitable purposes

POLICY OF TRUSTEES Grants are only made to charities or individuals known to the Trustees

FINANCES
- Year 1994
- Grants £27,748
- Income £26,028
- Assets £185,457

TRUSTEES Clare, Lady Keswick, Mrs M Keswick Jencks, C A Jencks

CORRESPONDENT Matheson Bank Ltd, Jardine House, 6 Crutched Friars, London EC3N 2HT

CLASSIFICATIONS
- Children and youth – general

C.C. NO 266120   **ESTABLISHED** 1973

■ S H and E C Priestman Trust

OBJECTS General charitable purposes

POLICY OF TRUSTEES Preference given to East Riding of Yorkshire area

TYPE OF GRANT For specific needs rather than regular income support

TYPE OF BENEFICIARY Children, aged, medical care, overseas and home missions

RESTRICTIONS No grants to individuals, National Societies (except for work in East Riding of Yorkshire area) or professional 'Appeals' (where agents and appeal staff are employed or paid)

BENEFICIAL AREA East Riding of Yorkshire

FINANCES
- Year 1994
- Grants £15,500
- Income £14,595
- Assets £139,635

TRUSTEES P A Robins, Mrs J A Collier

SUBMISSION OF APPLICATIONS To the secretary at any time by post. Grants are normally made in March and September

CORRESPONDENT Mrs J A Collier, 40 Braids Walk, Kirkella, Hull HU10 7PD

CLASSIFICATIONS
- Centres, clubs and institutes

C.C. NO 224581   **ESTABLISHED** 1960

■ The Primrose Trust

OBJECTS General charitable purposes

POLICY OF TRUSTEES The Trustees make their own decisions regarding donations

TYPE OF GRANT At Trustees' discretion. Range £500 to £10,000

TYPE OF BENEFICIARY Registered charities

RESTRICTIONS Donations only to registered charities

FINANCES
- Year 1988
- Grants £11,500
- Income £18,309
- Assets £260,491

TRUSTEES M G Clark, G E G Daniels, C Clark

SUBMISSION OF APPLICATIONS Unsolicited applications will not be acknowledged

CORRESPONDENT G E G Daniels, Greig Middleton & Co Ltd, Westgate House, Womanby Street, Cardiff CF1 2UD

CLASSIFICATIONS
- Children and youth – general

C.C. NO 800049   **ESTABLISHED** 1988

■ The Project Charitable Trust

OBJECTS Advancing the education of young people by providing opportunities for service in partnership with people overseas, or general charitable purposes

POLICY OF TRUSTEES Funds available are solely used for the benefit of Project Trust's own volunteers. Young people are sent overseas for 12 months as volunteers

TYPE OF GRANT The Trust provides a minimum grant of £510 per volunteer

TYPE OF BENEFICIARY Restricted to Project volunteers

RESTRICTIONS Grants restricted to part-sponsorship of young people selected by and sent overseas by the Trust. Grants are solely for the benefit of Project Trust's own volunteers, outsiders need not apply for grants

BENEFICIAL AREA Overseas

FINANCES
- Year 1995
- Grants £687,039
- Income £701,461
- Assets £842,969

TRUSTEES P L H Bristol, Lt Col the Hon P H Lewis, I G Fallon

PUBLICATIONS Annual report and quarterly newsletter, Project Post

NOTES In the 1995–96 programme there are 210 volunteers going to 22 countries all outside Europe. Volunteers spend a year overseas learning about their host community and helping, particularly with teaching

SUBMISSION OF APPLICATIONS Applications to become a volunteer should be made up to December 31st of the year previous to the year the volunteer wishes to go abroad. Applicants should be aged between 17 and 19 and should still be in full-time secondary education when applying

CORRESPONDENT The Director, The Hebridean Centre, Ballyhough, Isle of Coll, Argyll, Scotland PA78 6TE

Provincial

CLASSIFICATIONS
- Development of character

C.C. NO 306088   ESTABLISHED 1969

■ The Provincial Trust for Kendal

OBJECTS General charitable purposes

POLICY OF TRUSTEES Normally specific appeals by local registered charities or other bodies formed for charitable purposes, whose income is used directly to benefit the people of Cumbria, in particular those in Kendal and district. Local branches of national bodies also if income is used to benefit local people

TYPE OF GRANT One-off

TYPE OF BENEFICIARY Only local organisations

RESTRICTIONS Donations confined to County of Cumbria

BENEFICIAL AREA County of Cumbria, mainly Kendal and district

FINANCES
- Year 1995
- Grants £12,207
- Income £9,285
- Assets £59,228

TRUSTEES D Alexander (Chairman), P S Duff, W Stewart, Miss E Howe, A R Vince

PUBLICATIONS Annual Digest of Trustees' Report and Accounts

SUBMISSION OF APPLICATIONS In writing giving full details to Secretary

CORRESPONDENT H F Lowe, Secretary, Sand Aire House, Kendal, Cumbria LA9 4BE

CLASSIFICATIONS
- Adventure centres and playgrounds
- Centres, clubs and institutes
- Development of character
- Homes and hostels

C.C. NO 509209   ESTABLISHED 1979

■ The Ronald & Kathleen Pryor Charity

OBJECTS General charitable purposes

POLICY OF TRUSTEES Gifts to registered charities only

TYPE OF BENEFICIARY Registered charities

RESTRICTIONS No individuals

BENEFICIAL AREA Sheffield and South Yorkshire

SAMPLE GRANTS £1,000 to Sheffield MENCAP
£1,000 to South Yorkshire Police Lifestyle Appeal

FINANCES
- Year 1994
- Grants £24,500
- Income £22,000

TRUSTEES P W Lee, CBE, Miss M Upton, J D Grayson

CORRESPONDENT Miss M Upton, Edward Pryor & Son Ltd, Egerton Street, Sheffield S1 4JX

CLASSIFICATIONS
- Youth organisations (eg Guides, Scouts, YWCA etc)

C.C. NO 276868   ESTABLISHED 1978

■ The Pye Christian Trust

OBJECTS General charitable purposes. Mainly Christian-based

POLICY OF TRUSTEES To support methodist and baptist based projects. To support Christian churches and organisations involved in outreach and relief in the Lancaster district, nationally and overseas. Also other relief organisations

TYPE OF GRANT Direct

TYPE OF BENEFICIARY Registered charities

BENEFICIAL AREA Lancaster District, National and overseas according to organisation

SAMPLE GRANTS £1,000 to NCH Action for Children
£500 to Torchbearer Trust
£300 to NORLISCU – schools outreach
£200 to NSPCC

FINANCES
- Year 1993
- Income £34,000

TRUSTEES J A Pye, Mrs M Pye

NOTES While the Methodist Church is a significant beneficiary locally (Lancaster District) and nationally, we are not in a position to assist church building projects in other towns or areas (we have been receiving many requests for these)

CORRESPONDENT J A Pye, W & J Pye Ltd, Fleet Square, Lancaster, Lancashire LA1 1HA

CLASSIFICATIONS
- Children and youth – general

C.C. NO 501654   ESTABLISHED 1972

■ The Pye Foundation

OBJECTS To promote, maintain, improve and advance education in all its branches to promote the welfare of and to relieve the aged, impotent and poor and the relief of distress and to carry out such other charitable objects as the Trustees may from time to time in their absolute discretion think fit

POLICY OF TRUSTEES Elderly, young people, disabled. No applications from individuals or students considered

TYPE OF GRANT Recurrent and one-off

TYPE OF BENEFICIARY Registered charities with a beneficial erea of Cambridge only

RESTRICTIONS Will not respond to individuals, students, expeditions, national appeals, overseas

BENEFICIAL AREA Cambridgeshire only

FINANCES
- Year 1995
- Grants £68,000
- Income £69,000
- Assets £1,313,678

TRUSTEES P M Threlfall, F Keys, J A House, Ven R S Dell, A B Dasguptia, D M J Ball, R R Pascoe

SUBMISSION OF APPLICATIONS Eligible applications considered at quarterly meetings of Trustees. Applications from individuals not considered. No application form used; no application acknowledgements issued

CORRESPONDENT M R Hensby, Secretary, The Pye Foundation, Botanic House, 100 Hills Road, Cambridge CB2 1LQ

CLASSIFICATIONS
- Children and youth – general
- Centres, clubs and institutes
- Community groups
- Homes and hostels
- Youth organisations (eg Guides, Scouts, YWCA etc)

C.C. NO 267851　　　　**ESTABLISHED** 1974

■ Mr and Mrs J A Pye's No 1 Charitable Settlement

OBJECTS General charitable purposes

TYPE OF BENEFICIARY Recognised

RESTRICTIONS Payments are not made to individuals, the Trustees only support recognised charities

SAMPLE GRANTS £500 to Oxfordshire Association of Young People
£500 to Operation Raleigh
£500 to Young Persons Concert Foundation

FINANCES
- Year 1994–95
- Grants £298,050
- Income £343,462
- Assets £5,513,456

TRUSTEES G W F Archer, R H Langdon-Davies, G C Pye

CORRESPONDENT Messrs Darby & Son, 50 New Inn Hall Street, Oxford, Oxfordshire

CLASSIFICATIONS
- Centres, clubs and institutes
- Homes and hostels
- Youth organisations (eg Guides, Scouts, YWCA etc)

C.C. NO 242677　　　　**ESTABLISHED** 1965

■ Pyke Charity Trust

OBJECTS General charitable purposes

POLICY OF TRUSTEES The Foundation operates in four general areas to which it allocates funds: education and training, disabled welfare, social and community needs, medical welfare but not research. The Trustees give grants only to recognised charities. Overall the policy of the Trustees is to support underfunded voluntary organisations to enable the disabled and those who are disadvantaged through social or economic circumstances to make a contribution to the community. Education and Training. Projects for disabled which offer employment training, life skills and independent living. Projects which enhance educational opportunities for children up to secondary school level. (No adult or tertiary education). Projects to enhance the wider education, understanding and promotion of life skills for young people. In very few, very exceptional cases help may be given to stabilize the education and home life of children. Only the most exceptional cases of need are investigated. Full disclosure of all the circumstances leading to the application is required and a home visit will be necessary. Disabled Welfare. Projects for all types of disabled welfare are considered, preference is given to physical disabilities. Social and Community Needs. Projects which assist the disabled and disadvantaged to play a part in the community. Community centres for all ages – family centres, youth clubs, elderly people's clubs, child care provision and drop in clubs. Any project that will enhance the quality of life for disabled people. Promotion of health, home nursing schemes, day care centres for the disabled and elderly. The Trustees support projects which encourage respect for the local community and environment, crime prevention. The Trust does not fund medical research. It may support medical welfare schemes where equipment can enhance the lives of individual disabled people or families

TYPE OF GRANT One-off only. Usually for a specific project. Core funding, running costs and salaries are not considered. Grants usually in the range £500 to £5,000

TYPE OF BENEFICIARY Help only given to registered charities

RESTRICTIONS The following lie outside our current guidelines: medical research, postgraduate studies, individual sponsorship, drug or alcohol related charities, HQ's of national charities, holiday groups, national and local government responsibilities, organisations which are not recognised charities, activities which collect funds for subsequent redistribution, expeditions or overseas travel, animal charities, promotion of religion, fabric appeals for places of worship, loans and business finance

BENEFICIAL AREA UK

FINANCES
- Year 1994
- Income £120,000

TRUSTEES J M van Zwanenberg, R J van Zwanenberg, N J van Zwanenberg, J Macpherson

SUBMISSION OF APPLICATIONS These should be made in good time for the Trustees' meetings in February, June and October. Guidelines for applicants can be sent on request. Applications must include: (a) Full up to date accounts (to the year ending not more than 15 months before the application). (b) Details of what the charity is and does. (c) What the appeal is for. (d) Details of amounts required and raised so far. (e) Who else they have applied to. (f) How much they expect to receive from other sources. (g) Any other information that will help the Trustees. (h) Details of any application that is likely to fund all or most of the requirements in the application, eg Lottery, etc

CORRESPONDENT N van Zwanenberg, Barlocco Farm, Auchencairn, Castle Douglas, Dumfries Scotland DG7 1RQ

CLASSIFICATIONS
- Children and youth – general

C.C. NO 296418　　　　**ESTABLISHED** 1960

Racal

■ Racal Charitable Trust

OBJECTS General charitable purposes

POLICY OF TRUSTEES Preference given to national charities, or those local to group companies, concerned with disease, deprived children and the aged

TYPE OF GRANT Both recurrent and one-off

TYPE OF BENEFICIARY National and local charities

RESTRICTIONS No grants for educational scholarships, historic buildings, expeditions, individuals. No response to circular letters

BENEFICIAL AREA UK

FINANCES
- **Year** 1992
- **Grants** £100,000
- **Income** £100,000

TRUSTEES W K G Ward, I Melrose, Sir Clive Whitmore

NOTES The Trust has no assets of its own. Income for donations is as decided by Racal Electronics plc and varies from year to year

SUBMISSION OF APPLICATIONS In writing to the Correspondent. Acknowledgement is not given

CORRESPONDENT Mrs S Butler, Secretary, Racal Charitable Trust, Western Road, Bracknell, Berkshire RG12 1RG

CLASSIFICATIONS
- Children and youth – general
- Advancement in life

C.C. NO 289457 **ESTABLISHED** 1984

■ Radley Charitable Trust

OBJECTS Support for individual students in special need, organisations encouraging student exchange or voluntary service, and those assisting disadvantaged youth

POLICY OF TRUSTEES To help individuals or small bodies which are unlikely to have a wide appeal or support

TYPE OF GRANT Normally one-off grants of up to £500

TYPE OF BENEFICIARY Preference given to organisations encouraging inter-racial self-help projects, community youth work, and assistance to schools in poor areas of the Third World

RESTRICTIONS Limited to the type of beneficiaries listed below

BENEFICIAL AREA International, and throughout the UK, but with special concern for East Anglia, since based there

SAMPLE GRANTS £1,000 to assist in the expansion of the work of the Daneford Trust which organises work exchanges between young people from inner-city areas of the UK and those of Africa, Asia and the Caribbean
£250 to the Lighthouse Community Project to help purchase a house for at-risk homeless in Ballymena, County Antrim
£250 to Brighton University to help pay for a mature student's research project on the rehabilitation and care of juvenile arthritis sufferers

FINANCES
- **Year** 1995
- **Grants** £13,000
- **Income** £19,000

TRUSTEES C F Doubleday, I R Menzies, P F Radley, J J Wheatley

SUBMISSION OF APPLICATIONS Letters with details, enclosing sae, to the Correspondent. The name of a referee who is in a position to support the application must be included. Priority will normally be given to individual applications

CORRESPONDENT P F Radley, 12 Jesus Lane, Cambridge CB5 8BA

CLASSIFICATIONS
- Children and youth – general

C.C. NO 208313 **ESTABLISHED** 1951

■ Raeth Charity

OBJECTS General charitable purposes, and in particular the relief of persons within the beneficial area who are suffering from mental illness, arrested or incomplete development of mind, psychopathic disorder or other disorder or disability of mind by providing accommodation and care, whether temporary or permanent for such persons, or by making grants of money, clothing or otherwise to or for the benefit of such persons or by arranging for them to be visited in hospitals or other places where they are from time to time residing or undergoing treatment or by paying for research or special treatment or by paying for or arranging holidays or recreation for them

BENEFICIAL AREA West and East Sussex, Gloucestershire and Avon

FINANCES
- **Year** 1982
- **Grants** £190
- **Income** £3,487
- **Assets** £29,412

TRUSTEES R Etherton, E Carew-Shaw, Mrs J P Etherton, Miss M O'Brien, P J G Etherton

CORRESPONDENT Secretary to the Trustees, Raeth Charity, Greentrees Estate, Balcombe, Haywards Heath, West Sussex RH17 6JZ

CLASSIFICATIONS
- Homes and hostels

C.C. NO 272091 **ESTABLISHED** 1976

■ ZVM Rangoonwala Foundation

OBJECTS General charitable purposes

POLICY OF TRUSTEES Donations to recognised charities mainly in connection with children and old people

TYPE OF GRANT No grants for salaries and administrative expenses

TYPE OF BENEFICIARY Community services

RESTRICTIONS Must be a registered charity

BENEFICIAL AREA Great Britain and Northern Ireland

FINANCES
- Year 1994
- Assets £75,000

TRUSTEES R H Angus, Mrs E M Fane-Saunders, MBE, A Rangoonwala

CORRESPONDENT Asif Rangoonwala, Honorary Secretary, 123 George Street, London W1H 5TB

CLASSIFICATIONS
- Children and youth – general
- Community groups

C.C. NO 271513 **ESTABLISHED** 1976

■ The Rank Xerox Trust

OBJECTS The advancement of equality of opportunity, the cause of the disabled and disadvantaged youth (under 16)

POLICY OF TRUSTEES Preference for making one-off grants only

TYPE OF GRANT Cash only – min £5,000, max £10,000 – for specfic projects

TYPE OF BENEFICIARY Usually local mid-sized organisations – not national bodies

RESTRICTIONS No grants – only to charities

BENEFICIAL AREA United Kingdom

FINANCES
- Year 1994
- Grants £45,000
- Income £40,000

TRUSTEES S Dillon, S C Cronin, S W Pantling, C J Pinney

SUBMISSION OF APPLICATIONS Applications are reviewed half yearly

CORRESPONDENT Tracy Young, The Rank Xerox Trust, Bridge House, Oxford Road, Uxbridge UB8 1HS

CLASSIFICATIONS
- Advancement in life
- Counselling (inc helplines)
- Special needs housing
- Children and violence (inc abuse)

C.C. NO 284698 **ESTABLISHED** 1982

■ The Eleanor Rathbone Charitable Trust (formerly Miss E F Rathbone Charitable Trust)

OBJECTS General charitable purposes

POLICY OF TRUSTEES Preference to charities of which the Trust has special interest, knowledge or association. Interest in charities benefiting women and neglected causes

TYPE OF GRANT Mainly donations

TYPE OF BENEFICIARY Mainly Merseyside. Social work charities, arts and education (not individuals)

RESTRICTIONS No grants to individuals

BENEFICIAL AREA UK with preference for Merseyside

FINANCES
- Year 1992
- Grants £158,365
- Income £172,000
- Assets £3,300,000

TRUSTEES Dr B L Rathbone, W Rathbone Jnr, Miss J A Rathbone, P W Rathbone, Mrs B Pedersen

SUBMISSION OF APPLICATIONS By letter

CORRESPONDENT Rathbone Bros & Co, Port of Liverpool Building, 4th Floor, Pier Head, Liverpool L3 1NW

CLASSIFICATIONS
- Children and youth – general
- Centres, clubs and institutes
- Holidays
- Youth organisations (eg Guides, Scouts, YWCA etc)

C.C. NO 233241 **ESTABLISHED** 1947

■ The Ravenscroft Foundation

OBJECTS General charitable purposes

POLICY OF TRUSTEES To assist any cause or project which the Trustees consider to be charitable and deserving

TYPE OF GRANT Lump sum payment

TYPE OF BENEFICIARY Limited to local causes

BENEFICIAL AREA Now limited entirely to local causes

FINANCES
- Year 1994
- Grants £11,695
- Income £6,061
- Assets £132,772

TRUSTEES J E Ravenscroft, MA (Cantab), S E Ravenscroft, MA, LLM (Cantab), Mrs K Ravenscroft

SUBMISSION OF APPLICATIONS In writing in first instance to the correspondent

CORRESPONDENT J E Ravenscroft, Solicitor, 763 Durham Road, Gateshead, Tyne and Wear NE9 6PD

CLASSIFICATIONS
- Adventure centres and playgrounds
- Centres, clubs and institutes
- Day centres and nurseries
- Holidays
- Youth organisations (eg Guides, Scouts, YWCA etc)

C.C. NO 282359 **ESTABLISHED** 1981

■ The Ravensdale Trust

OBJECTS General charitable purposes

POLICY OF TRUSTEES No grants to individuals

TYPE OF BENEFICIARY Registered charities

BENEFICIAL AREA Merseyside

FINANCES
- Year 1995
- Grants £24,350
- Income £62,583
- Assets £1,636,600

TRUSTEES Dr L H A Pilkington, Mrs E Bankes, D D Mason

SUBMISSION OF APPLICATIONS By letter. No application form. No acknowledgement of applications. Donations are made in June and October of each year

CORRESPONDENT Messrs Alsop Wilkinson, India Buildings, Liverpool, Merseyside L2 0NH

CLASSIFICATIONS
- Children and youth – general

C.C. NO 265165 **ESTABLISHED** 1973

Raymond

Alphabetical register of grant making charitable trusts

■ Roger Raymond Charitable Trust No 2

OBJECTS General charitable purposes

POLICY OF TRUSTEES Funds already allocated

TYPE OF GRANT Educational type of grant

TYPE OF BENEFICIARY Chosen by Trustees

RESTRICTIONS Grants fully allocated each year in advance

BENEFICIAL AREA UK

FINANCES
- Year 1993
- Assets £1,700,000
- Income £100,000

TRUSTEES R W Pullen, P F Raymond, M Raymond,

CORRESPONDENT R W Pullen, Sayers Butterworth, 18 Bentinck Street, London W1M 5RL

CLASSIFICATIONS
- Centres, clubs and institutes
- Homes and hostels
- Youth organisations (eg Guides, Scouts, YWCA etc)

C.C. NO 267029   **ESTABLISHED** 1974

■ The Rayne Foundation

OBJECTS General charitable purposes

POLICY OF TRUSTEES To sponsor developments in medicine, education, social welfare and the Arts. To relieve distress and to promote the welfare of the young and the aged

TYPE OF GRANT Capital expenditure and recurrent expenses

TYPE OF BENEFICIARY National headquarters of multiple charities only

RESTRICTIONS Grants to registered charities only – no grants to individuals

FINANCES
- Year 1995
- Grants £1,643,437
- Income £1,669,290
- Assets £26,682,478

TRUSTEES The Lord Rayne, Lady Rayne, The Lord Greenhill of Harrow, GCMG, OBE, E L George, FCA, R A Rayne, Air Commodore F M Milligan, CBE, AFC, Sir Claus Moser, KCB, CBE, FBA

NOTES Re: Foreign Beneficial Area – for specific projects only as decided by Trustees

SUBMISSION OF APPLICATIONS To correspondent at any time. Trustees meet quarterly

CORRESPONDENT R D Lindsay-Rea, MA, Carlton House, 33 Robert Adam Street, London W1M 5AH

CLASSIFICATIONS
- Children and youth – general

C.C. NO 216291   **ESTABLISHED** 1962

■ The Rayne Trust (formerly the Rayne Charitable Trust)

OBJECTS General charitable purposes

POLICY OF TRUSTEES Relief of distress, welfare of the aged and young

TYPE OF GRANT Capital expenditure and recurrent expenses

TYPE OF BENEFICIARY National headquarters of multiple charities only

RESTRICTIONS Grants to registered charities only – no grants to individuals

FINANCES
- Year 1995
- Grants £169,440
- Income £161,003
- Assets £462,481

TRUSTEES The Lord Rayne (Director), Lady Rayne (Director), R A Rayne (Director)

SUBMISSION OF APPLICATIONS At any time

CORRESPONDENT R D Lindsay-Rea, MA, Carlton House, 33 Robert Adam Street, London W1M 5AH

CLASSIFICATIONS
- Children and youth – general
- Centres, clubs and institutes
- Holidays
- Homes and hostels

C.C. NO 207392   **ESTABLISHED** 1958

■ The John Rayner Charitable Trust

OBJECTS General charitable purposes, and to improve the well-being of children and young people

POLICY OF TRUSTEES Preference given to smaller, established charities

TYPE OF GRANT Single donations, occasionally given over a period of years

TYPE OF BENEFICIARY Charities helping the homeless, addiction, medical research, etc

RESTRICTIONS Applications from individuals not usually considered

BENEFICIAL AREA UK, Merseyside and Yorkshire

SAMPLE GRANTS £10,000 to Wessex Children's Hospice
£10,000 to Aler Hey Children's Hospital, Liverpool
£2,000 to Shaftesbury Homes and Arethusa
£1,000 to National Playing Fields Association
£1,000 to Make-a-Wish Foundation

FINANCES
- Year 1995
- Grants £18,000
- Income £27,000
- Assets £550,000

TRUSTEES Mrs J Rayner and others

CORRESPONDENT Mrs J Rayner, 42 Radnor Walk, London SW3 4BN

CLASSIFICATIONS
- Homes and hostels

C.C. NO 802363   **ESTABLISHED** 1989

■ The Albert Reckitt Charitable Trust

OBJECTS General charitable purposes (excluding political or sectarian) including charities connected with the Society of Friends

POLICY OF TRUSTEES Support of national organisations

TYPE OF GRANT Donations or yearly subscriptions, to registered charities

TYPE OF BENEFICIARY National organisations, as distinct from local bodies

RESTRICTIONS Registered charities only. Applications from individuals are ineligible

BENEFICIAL AREA Great Britain

FINANCES
- Year 1995
- Grants £58,000
- Income £57,000
- Assets £1,390,000

TRUSTEES Sir Michael Colman, Bt, B N Reckitt, Mrs M Reckitt, Mrs G M Atherton, Mrs S C Bradley, D F Reckitt, J Hughes-Reckitt, P C Knee

SUBMISSION OF APPLICATIONS By 31st March

CORRESPONDENT J Barrett, Secretary, The Albert Reckitt Charitable Trust, Southwark Towers, 32 London Bridge Street, London SE1 9SY

CLASSIFICATIONS
- Children and youth – general

C.C. NO 209974   ESTABLISHED 1946

■ Reeve's Foundation

OBJECTS Education of young people (aged 25 or under in exceptional cases up to aged 40) who are in need of financial assistance

POLICY OF TRUSTEES Priority given to cases of acute need and special educational requirements; there is a long standing connection with Christ's Hospital

TYPE OF GRANT Bursaries, maintenance allowances, assistance with school fees, grants for school clothing, equipment

TYPE OF BENEFICIARY Principally individuals. Applicants or their parent(s) must have lived or worked for the last 12 months, or for at least two of the last ten years, in the area of benefit. Occasionally schools substantially serving the area

BENEFICIAL AREA The City of London and the London Boroughs of Camden and Islington

FINANCES
- Year 1995
- Grants £270,000
- Income £336,000

TRUSTEES Rector of St Sepulchre's, 12 others appointed by various bodies

SUBMISSION OF APPLICATIONS Meetings normally in February, May, July, September and December

CORRESPONDENT The Clerk to the Governors, Reeve's Foundation, 90 Central Street, London EC1V 8AQ

CLASSIFICATIONS
- Advancement in life
- Development of character

C.C. NO 312504   ESTABLISHED 1702

■ The Rhondda Cynon Taff Welsh Church Acts Fund (formerly known as The Mid Glamorgan Welsh Church Acts Fund)

OBJECTS General charitable purposes

POLICY OF TRUSTEES Grants distributed locally to Rhondda, Cynon, Taff, Bridgend and Merthyr. No contribution given towards running expenses (capital only)

TYPE OF GRANT Capital expenditure (vast amount of grants devoted to maintenance of church buildings)

TYPE OF BENEFICIARY Local activities. (Applications will be considered from organisations outside Rhondda Cynon Taff provided that the work of the organisation is of local significance)

RESTRICTIONS No grants to other local authorities' projects, clubs with a liquor licence, individuals, students

BENEFICIAL AREA Rhondda Cynon Taff

FINANCES
- Year 1994–95
- Grants £290,000
- Income £386,000
- Assets £5,108,000

TRUSTEES Rhondda Cynon Taff County Borough Council

PUBLICATIONS Annual statement of accounts

SUBMISSION OF APPLICATIONS New grants distributed annually. Application forms must be received at the correspondent's address by 31 July

CORRESPONDENT The Treasurer's Dept, Rhondda Cynon Taff County Borough Council, County Hall, Cardiff CF1 3NE

CLASSIFICATIONS
- Children and youth – general

C.C. NO 506658   ESTABLISHED 1961

■ Richmond Parish Lands Charity

OBJECTS The relief of the poor (and aged) inhabitants of the benefit area. Provision of educational facilities and improving conditions of life of said inhabitants

POLICY OF TRUSTEES To consider grant applications as received

TYPE OF GRANT Any in conformity with Objects

TYPE OF BENEFICIARY see Restrictions

RESTRICTIONS Strict adherence to defined benefit area. Grant aid to organisations only except for education and small grants to individuals referred by nominated agencies

BENEFICIAL AREA Richmond, Kew and North Sheen

FINANCES
- Year 1995
- Grants £481,000
- Income £623,000
- Assets £22,724,000

TRUSTEES Five nominations by local organisations, four by London Borough of Richmond (including the Mayor ex officio) plus four co-opted

PUBLICATIONS Annual Report and Accounts

NOTES Individual grants for education but restricted to benefit area residents

SUBMISSION OF APPLICATIONS To the Clerk at any time. Trustees meet 10 times a year

CORRESPONDENT The Clerk to the Trustees, The Vestry House, 21 Paradise Road, Richmond, Surrey TW9 1SA

CLASSIFICATIONS
- Children and youth – general
- Community groups

C.C. NO 200069   ESTABLISHED 1786

Riddleston

Alphabetical register of grant making charitable trusts

■ The Harry James Riddleston Charity of Leicester

OBJECTS Interest free loans to or for the benefit of such deserving and necessitous persons or for such charitable educational purposes as the Trustees may in their absolute discretion select. Preference given to applicants of British birth and of the Christian faith and in particular who are sons or daughters of Free Masons who have been assisted by Free Masons in their education

POLICY OF TRUSTEES Preference given to applicants furthering their education or setting up in business. No loans made to other charities only to individuals. Loans not made for house purchase or improvements

TYPE OF GRANT Interest free loan repayable 10 years from date thereof (maximum £4,000)

TYPE OF BENEFICIARY Limited to persons resident in Counties of Leicestershire and Rutland under 35 years of age

RESTRICTIONS At present restricted under the terms of the scheme by the Trust to the counties of Leicestershire and Rutland

BENEFICIAL AREA Leicestershire and Rutland

FINANCES
- Year 1990
- Assets £411,287
- Income £20,668

TRUSTEES G Moore, G R Buckingham and 13 others

PUBLICATIONS Advertisements in local press

SUBMISSION OF APPLICATIONS On application form obtainable from correspondent

CORRESPONDENT Mrs M E Bass, Clerk to the Charity, The Harry James Riddleston Charity of Leicester, 10 New Street, Leicester LE1 5ND

CLASSIFICATIONS
- Advancement in life

C.C. NO 262787 **ESTABLISHED** 1970

■ The Ridgmount Foundation (formerly The Leslie and Margaret Jones Trust)

OBJECTS General charitable purposes

TYPE OF GRANT One-off

TYPE OF BENEFICIARY Registered charities

FINANCES
- Year 1993
- Grants £5,000
- Income £61,102
- Assets £516,587

TRUSTEES S Cox, L Jones, Mrs M H Jones, J J Jones, W P Jones, R D Walley

CORRESPONDENT R D Walley, Mundays, Solicitors, Crown House, Church Road, Claygate, Surrey KT10 0LP

CLASSIFICATIONS
- Centres, clubs and institutes

C.C. NO 1016703 **ESTABLISHED** 1992

■ The F A Riley-Smith Charitable Trust

OBJECTS To support Christian and developing world projects, community schemes in the Trust's locality, environmental work

RESTRICTIONS Grants to registered chrities only. No grants will be made to individuals

SAMPLE GRANTS £1,025 to CAFOD
£150 to Barnardos
£150 to Church of England Children's Society
£150 to NSPCC
£100 to Save the Children

FINANCES
- Year 1995
- Grants £3,575
- Income £2,884
- Assets £50,748

TRUSTEES Mrs A J Riley-Smith, A W A Riley-Smith

SUBMISSION OF APPLICATIONS Applications in writing to be made to the correspondent

CORRESPONDENT A W A Riley-Smith, PO Box 27, Ripon, North Yorkshire HG4 5XB

CLASSIFICATIONS
- Children and youth – general

C.C. NO 266203 **ESTABLISHED** 1973

■ The Rind Foundation

OBJECTS General charitable purposes

POLICY OF TRUSTEES Examination of applications from wide range of proposals

TYPE OF GRANT Contributions to funding of projects

TYPE OF BENEFICIARY Youth, elderly, handicapped/disabled

RESTRICTIONS Restricted to registered charities

FINANCES
- Year 1992
- Grants £20,000
- Income £15,000
- Assets £140,000

TRUSTEES Mrs S Rind, C Fenton, FCA, A M Rind

PUBLICATIONS Annual report and audited accounts internally circulated

NOTES Full distribution of Annual Income

SUBMISSION OF APPLICATIONS By letter. Quarterly meetings

CORRESPONDENT A M Rind, 37 Upper Brook Street, London W1Y 2PR

CLASSIFICATIONS
- Adventure centres and playgrounds

C.C. NO 276311 **ESTABLISHED** 1978

■ The Rivendell Trust

OBJECTS General charitable purposes

POLICY OF TRUSTEES To assist small charities that benefit people, particularly children, the sick disabled, the handicapped and mentally ill and those with family problems. Consideration will also be given to applications from individuals for educational purposes – particularly music

TYPE OF GRANT Usually single cash payments

TYPE OF BENEFICIARY As above

RESTRICTIONS (a) Applications for the construction, restoration or purchase of buildings are not normally considered and (b) Grants to individuals are limited to (i) those in the above catagories (ii) children and bona fide students within the UK in connection with education in music. (c) Further grants to charities or individuals will normally be considered once every three years

BENEFICIAL AREA Worldwide

SAMPLE GRANTS £400 to Birmingham Conservatoire Junior School
£300 to Disability Aid Foundation
£200 to the Fourth Fulwood Scouts
£150 to Children's Country Holiday Fund
£100 to Peter Pan Playgroup

FINANCES
- **Year** 1995
- **Grants** £33,400
- **Income** £44,000
- **Assets** £800,000

TRUSTEES Mrs S D Caird, G Caird, Miss M J Verney, E R Verney, A Layton, J W Dolman, Dr I Laing

NOTES All applications from individuals should include: (a) their Curriculum Vitae/purpose of grant, (b) an analysis of costs, (c) details of any other grants or funding they may have received, (d) a brief summary of their own and/or parents' financial position, (e) sae. Because of the number of grants received, failure to supply the above could result in an application failing

SUBMISSION OF APPLICATIONS Charities: Comprehensive details should be with a statement of the previous two years' accounts. Individuals apply in writing to Mrs T Burrell, 1 Dean Farrar Street, London SW1H 0DY for application form

CORRESPONDENT M J Day, 1 Dean Farrar Street, Westminster, London SW1H 0DY

CLASSIFICATIONS
- Children and youth – general

C.C. NO 271375   **ESTABLISHED** 1975

■ The River Trust

OBJECTS Christian causes

POLICY OF TRUSTEES To make donations only to national Christian charities and Christian charities local to Sussex

BENEFICIAL AREA Sussex

FINANCES
- **Year** 1991
- **Grants** £122,400
- **Income** £146,055
- **Assets** £280,849

TRUSTEES Kleinwort Benson Trustees Limited

SUBMISSION OF APPLICATIONS To the correspondent

CORRESPONDENT Kleinwort Benson Trustees Ltd, PO Box 191, 10 Fenchurch Street, London EC3M 3LB

CLASSIFICATIONS
- Holidays

C.C. NO 275843   **ESTABLISHED** 1977

■ The Cheshire Robbins Trust

OBJECTS To promote any charitable purposes for the benefit of the community in the Counties of Hampshire and Dorset and in particular the advancement of Christian work and witness the advancement of education and the relief of poverty, disease and sickness either at home or overseas

TYPE OF BENEFICIARY Christian organisations/ lifeboat institution

BENEFICIAL AREA Hampshire and Dorset

FINANCES
- **Year** 1994
- **Grants** £4,700
- **Income** £6,500

TRUSTEES G L Robbins, Mrs D A Robbins, A M Robbins, Mrs T J Tarrant

SUBMISSION OF APPLICATIONS Personal letter

CORRESPONDENT G L Robbins, Avonbank, Waterloo Bridge, Christchurch, Dorset

CLASSIFICATIONS
- Children and youth – general
- Advancement in life
- Development of character
- Counselling (inc helplines)

C.C. NO 273040   **ESTABLISHED** 1976

■ Sir Edward Robinson Charitable Trust

OBJECTS The chief object of the Trust is to support Numismatics

POLICY OF TRUSTEES In addition to the above Object, the Trust makes grants to a number of organisations for which the Trustees have special concern. It is unlikely that they can add new bodies to this list

TYPE OF GRANT Small to moderate donations. Applications from from young individuals if under charitable auspices

TYPE OF BENEFICIARY Registered charities only

RESTRICTIONS Registered charities only

FINANCES
- **Year** 1995
- **Grants** £26,000
- **Income** £26,000

TRUSTEES G G M Hughes, V H Robinson, O H Robinson, Fay Gordon Hill, Gillian Maude, Sophia Heseltine

SUBMISSION OF APPLICATIONS By letter only. Regret no acknowledgement

CORRESPONDENT Miss F Gordon Hill, Keeper's Cottage, Fontmell Parva, Blandford Forum, Dorset DT11 8QZ

CLASSIFICATIONS
- Children and youth – general

C.C. NO 211848   **ESTABLISHED** 1956

The J C Robinson Trust No 3

OBJECTS Youth organisations, training, the disabled and individuals in special need

POLICY OF TRUSTEES To help people to develop their maximum potential

TYPE OF GRANT Recurrent or one-off

TYPE OF BENEFICIARY Individuals in need and registered charities

RESTRICTIONS No grants made for historic buildings or village halls except very local. No grants made for foreign travel

BENEFICIAL AREA Sussex, Bristol and South Gloucester

SAMPLE GRANTS £1,000 to Crawley Scouts for new hut
£500 to Bristol Mediation to help community relations
£500 to Southmead Youth Centre for equipment
£500 to handicapped person towards cost of new transport
£500 to Refugee Council to help resettlement

FINANCES
- Year 1991
- Grants £18,000

TRUSTEES Miss C M Howe, Mrs E M Howe, Dr C J Burns-Cox

SUBMISSION OF APPLICATIONS By post – no special form; telephone in emergencies

CORRESPONDENT Dr C J Burns-Cox, Southend Farm, Wotton under Edge, Gloucester GL12 7PB

CLASSIFICATIONS
- Centres, clubs and institutes
- Community groups
- Day centres and nurseries

C.C. NO 207294 **ESTABLISHED** 1931

Roedean School Mission Fund

OBJECTS For the relief of disadvantaged children. Equipment bought for playgroups

POLICY OF TRUSTEES To choose low cost holidays, run by small registered charities (this does not include social services), where some form of learning experience is incorporated into the holiday

TYPE OF GRANT One-off cash grants ranging from £50 to £500, occasionally recurrent but subject to review

TYPE OF BENEFICIARY Needy children in Greater London and Sussex under 16

RESTRICTIONS Children under 16 in the United Kingdom only. No grants made to individuals on direct application

BENEFICIAL AREA Greater London and Sussex

FINANCES
- Year 1993
- Grants £6,209
- Income £6,079

TRUSTEES Managing Committee

NOTES We endeavour to make our limited funds stretch as far as possible, so most successful applications come from those who provide low cost holidays, or who will put a small sum to good use in the purchase of equipment etc

SUBMISSION OF APPLICATIONS Grants made in March, June and November. No expenses are claimed, so applications cannot be acknowledged unless successful

CORRESPONDENT Mrs J V Edwards, 7 Beaumont Mews, London W1N 3LP

CLASSIFICATIONS
- Development of character
- Holidays

C.C. NO 244996 **ESTABLISHED** 1968

Rokeby Charitable Trust

OBJECTS General charitable purposes

POLICY OF TRUSTEES A special intent with a modest balance distributable to local charities only

TYPE OF BENEFICIARY Local charities and local voluntary agencies (eg Relate, CAB, etc)

BENEFICIAL AREA Rugby area and Rugby School in particular

FINANCES
- Year 1995
- Grants £11,600
- Income £14,500
- Assets £186,000

TRUSTEES P A Batt (Chairman), A Lee, J C Marshall, R M Furber, J R Frankton

SUBMISSION OF APPLICATIONS By letter to correspondent throughout the year, only from local charities

CORRESPONDENT Mrs M Sherman, 283 Alwyn Road, Bilton, Rugby, Warwickshire CV22 7RP

CLASSIFICATIONS
- Children and youth – general
- Youth organisations (eg Guides, Scouts, YWCA etc)

C.C. NO 257600 **ESTABLISHED** 1968

Rosca Trust

OBJECTS General charitable purposes. Interested in new projects

POLICY OF TRUSTEES The Rosca Trust can only make donations to registered charities and it is the fixed policy of the Trustees only to make donations to charities operating within the Borough of Southend-on-Sea, and immediately adjoining districts. Applications from outside this area will not receive any response. Preference is given to charities catering for the needs of those under the age of 20, or over the age of 65 or to medical (in the widest sense) charities, or religious charities

TYPE OF GRANT Special consideration is given to one-off donations for capital projects. Regular donations are also given to other local charities

TYPE OF BENEFICIARY Registered charities only

RESTRICTIONS No grants to individuals, Trustees only make donations to charities operating within the Borough of Southend-on-Sea, and immediately adjoining districts

BENEFICIAL AREA Southend-on-Sea & District only

SAMPLE GRANTS Sea Cadets – refurbishment of headquarters
Venture Scout Unit – help with new minibus
Women's Aid Refuge – play group room extension
Bar-n-Bus Youth Project – mobile bus for sea front, schools and rural area youth work

FINANCES
- **Year** 1993
- **Grants** £17,000
- **Income** £24,865
- **Assets** £66,673

TRUSTEES K J Crowe, T T Ray, Mrs D A Powell, Mrs M Golding

NOTES Applications reviewed in April – no application form. Sae appreciated but not necessary. Preliminary telephone calls considered unnecessary. Local branches preferred, both innovatory or long established

SUBMISSION OF APPLICATIONS To correspondent

CORRESPONDENT K J Crowe, 19 Avenue Terrace, Westcliff-on-Sea, Essex SS0 7PL

CLASSIFICATIONS
- Centres, clubs and institutes

C.C. NO 259907   **ESTABLISHED** 1966

■ The Ross Charitable Trust

OBJECTS General charitable purposes

POLICY OF TRUSTEES No particular policy

TYPE OF BENEFICIARY Community-based local projects

RESTRICTIONS Donations are not made to individuals

BENEFICIAL AREA Donations usually to charities within the Gloucestershire area

FINANCES
- **Year** 1995
- **Grants** £1,718
- **Income** £2,422
- **Assets** £32,876

TRUSTEES J G Ross, J W Sharpe

SUBMISSION OF APPLICATIONS The Trustees do not generally consider applications from the public – no preliminary telephone calls are to be made. Applications will not be acknowledged unless successful

CORRESPONDENT J W Sharpe, c/o Osborne Clarke, 30 Queen Charlotte Street, Bristol, Avon BS99 7QQ

CLASSIFICATIONS
- Children and youth – general

C.C. NO 286196   **ESTABLISHED** 1982

■ The Rothley Trust

OBJECTS General charitable purposes

POLICY OF TRUSTEES Apart from a few charities with which the Trust has been associated for many years, its activities are now directed exclusively towards North East England (Northumberland to North Yorkshire inclusive). Third World appeals, arising from this area only, will be considered

TYPE OF GRANT Mainly donations towards specific projects and not running costs

TYPE OF BENEFICIARY Registered charities, in the categories of children, community, education, handicapped, medical, religion, Third World and youth

RESTRICTIONS No grants outside the beneficial area or for further education or for the repair of buildings used primarily for worship. Organisations for the elderly, ex-services, the arts and wildlife will not be considered

BENEFICIAL AREA North East England – Northumberland to North Yorkshire

SAMPLE GRANTS £825 to Youth Clubs Northumbria
£250 to Scouts and Guides, 1st Dipton Group, Newcastle upon Tyne
£250 to Northumbria Police towards Ovingham Youth Club
£100 to Boys Brigade, Hartlepool

FINANCES
- **Year** 1995
- **Grants** £124,000
- **Income** £148,000
- **Assets** £1,906,000

TRUSTEES Dr H A Armstrong, R P Gordon, R R V Nicholson, C J Davies, Mrs R Barkes, Mrs A Galbraith, C J Pumphrey

SUBMISSION OF APPLICATIONS No forms issued. Write to the correspondent. Applications from the beneficial area only will be acknowledged

CORRESPONDENT Peter Tennant, Secretary, The Rothley Trust, Mea House, Ellison Place, Newcastle upon Tyne NE1 8XS

CLASSIFICATIONS
- Children and youth – general

C.C. NO 219849   **ESTABLISHED** 1959

■ The Rowan Charitable Trust

OBJECTS The Trust exists to further humanitarian causes. Prior consideration will be given to agencies working for development and human rights overseas and in areas of deprivation in Britain

POLICY OF TRUSTEES The Trust exists to further humanitarian causes. Prior consideration will be given to agencies working for development and human rights overseas and in areas of deprivation in Britain. Consideration will also be given to agencies working for the protection of the environment

TYPE OF BENEFICIARY Registered charities only

BENEFICIAL AREA Overseas

FINANCES
- **Year** 1995
- **Grants** £385,875
- **Income** £259,316
- **Assets** £4,328,601

TRUSTEES D D Mason, Mrs H Russell, A Baillie

CORRESPONDENT Coopers and Lybrand, 9 Greyfriars Road, Reading, Berks RG1 1JG

CLASSIFICATIONS
- Children and youth – general
- Centres, clubs and institutes

C.C. NO 242678   **ESTABLISHED** 1964

■ The Christopher Rowbotham Charitable Trust

OBJECTS To promote the wellbeing, both mental and physical, of children and young people. To provide equipment for improving quality of life. To provide help for clubs for those who might otherwise be on the streets and, therefore, vulnerable to crime or addiction. To provide holidays. To provide sheltered employment. To provide support, advice and backup to the disadvantaged to gain further education or employment

POLICY OF TRUSTEES To support selected national charities with branches in the North West and North East, and local charities, as stated below.

Priority given to smaller charities with low overheads

TYPE OF GRANT Mostly regular grants. Salaries never considered. Cash

RESTRICTIONS Registered charities only. Applications from individuals, including students, are ineligible. No grants made in response to general appeals from large national organisations. No grants overseas. No grants for capital projects

BENEFICIAL AREA NE England, NW England

SAMPLE GRANTS £1,000 to Fairbridge (NE and NW) for two groups
£750 to Sea Cadets (NE or NW) for three groups
£500 to AIDIS (NE or NW)
£250 to Young Disabled Holidays
£200 to Northumbria Daybreak

FINANCES
- Year 1995
- Grants £30,000
- Income £35,000
- Assets £400,000

TRUSTEES Mrs C A Jackson, Mrs E J Wilkinson, J T Jessup

NOTES Appeals from the North East should be sent to Mrs Jackson at address below. Appeals from the North West should be sent to: Mrs Wilkinson, PO Box 43, Bolton, Lancs BL1 5EZ

SUBMISSION OF APPLICATIONS At any time. Trustees meet annually in May. No applications acknowledged

CORRESPONDENT Mrs C A Jackson, 18 Northumberland Square, North Shields, Tyne & Wear NE30 1PX

CLASSIFICATIONS
- Children and youth – general
- Centres, clubs and institutes
- Development of character
- Holidays
- Youth organisations (eg Guides, Scouts, YWCA etc)

C.C. NO 261991　　**ESTABLISHED** 1970

■ **The Rowley Trust**

OBJECTS The general benefit of women and girls

POLICY OF TRUSTEES Trustees are specifically interested in applications related to the benefit of women and girls

TYPE OF BENEFICIARY Individuals or women's organisattions specifically to help women in need

RESTRICTIONS Females only

BENEFICIAL AREA Staffordshire

FINANCES
- Year 1992
- Grants £33,035
- Income £51,185
- Assets £694,452

TRUSTEES R J McCormick, G W Appleyard, M Thornton, S Morgan, R P Whitehurst, J Broad, R Harris, J Forrester, K Duncan-Brown, J R Gregory, R Thys, S Martin

SUBMISSION OF APPLICATIONS Application form and guidelines can be obtained from the Clerk of the Trust, Miss P A Grocott

CORRESPONDENT P A Grocott, 313 Uttoxeter Road, Blythe Bridge, Stoke-on-Trent, Staffordshire ST11 9QA

CLASSIFICATIONS
- Advancement in life

C.C. NO 508630　　**ESTABLISHED** 1988

■ **Joseph Rowntree Foundation**
(formerly the Joseph Rowntree Memorial Trust)

OBJECTS To search out the causes of social problems and so contribute to their solutions by funding a programme of useful research and pioneering development projects in the fields of housing, social policy, social care and local/central government relations

POLICY OF TRUSTEES The Foundation is not a grant-making body in the normal sense working in partnership with projects once grants are awarded. The Foundation initiates projects as well as considering unsolicited proposals in the areas of the Foundation's interest

RESTRICTIONS The Foundation does not make grants to individuals or respond to general appeals. Capital and revenue grants to support ongoing work of existing organisations are specifically excluded

BENEFICIAL AREA UK

FINANCES
- Year 1993
- Grants £5,827,000
- Income £7,495,000
- Assets £178,254,000

TRUSTEES Sir Donald Barron (Chairman), Sir Peter M Barclay, Sir Patrick Nairne, J Nigel Naish, Sir William Utting, Erica F Vere, Dame Rachel Waterhouse, R Maxwell

PUBLICATIONS 'Findings' – short briefing papers summarising the main findings of projects in the Research and Development Programme (approx 100 issued each year in four series: Housing, Social Policy, Social Care, Local/Central Government Relations); Reports (approx 50 in a year) designed to present research results with clarity and impact; 'Search' – a quarterly magazine featuring recent work of the Foundation

NOTES NB Tel no for publications orders: 01904 654328

SUBMISSION OF APPLICATIONS Meetings of Trustees are held quarterly. There is no application form: proposals should be set out with clarity and brevity. Notes for guidance are given in a booklet describing the Foundation's Research and Development programme, available from the above address. Proposals are considered by the appropriate Research Committee, meeting quarterly, before referral to the Trustees

CORRESPONDENT Richard S Best, OBE, Director, The Homestead, 40 Water End, York YO3 6LP

CLASSIFICATIONS
- Homes and hostels
- Special needs housing

C.C. NO 210169　　**ESTABLISHED** 1904

Sainsbury

■ J B Rubens Foundation

OBJECTS General charitable purposes

POLICY OF TRUSTEES The Trustees are unable to entertain applications made by or on behalf of individuals

FINANCES
- **Year** 1993
- **Grants** £40,235
- **Income** £536,559
- **Assets** £6,261,688

TRUSTEES M L Phillips, M D Paisner, Mrs R Phillips, P R Smith

CORRESPONDENT J B Rubens Charity Trustees Ltd, Rolls House, 7 Rolls Buildings, Fetter Lane, London EC4A 1NH

CLASSIFICATIONS
- Children and youth – general
- Development of character
- Counselling (inc helplines)

C.C. NO 218366   **ESTABLISHED** 1959

■ The Frank and Enid Rubens Highgate Trust

OBJECTS General charitable purposes

POLICY OF TRUSTEES Grants only to registered charities. New charities rarely considered

TYPE OF GRANT Small cash grants

TYPE OF BENEFICIARY National, London and Jewish charities

RESTRICTIONS No grants to individuals – grants only to registered charities

BENEFICIAL AREA UK

FINANCES
- **Year** 1995
- **Grants** £4,892
- **Income** £4,696
- **Assets** £102,689

TRUSTEES Mrs E B Rubens, J A Clemace

SUBMISSION OF APPLICATIONS Direct to Trustees at 3 Bacon's Lane, London N6 6BL

CORRESPONDENT BDO Stoy Hayward, 8 Baker Street, London W1M 1DA

CLASSIFICATIONS
- Children and youth – general

C.C. NO 272139   **ESTABLISHED** 1976

■ The SMB Trust

OBJECTS General charitable purposes

POLICY OF TRUSTEES To make monetary grants

TYPE OF GRANT Most on annual basis; others non-recurring

TYPE OF BENEFICIARY Mainly to bodies for advancement of Christian religion and relief of suffering

RESTRICTIONS Grants to individuals not normally considered

FINANCES
- **Year** 1992
- **Grants** £66,400
- **Income** £118,500
- **Assets** £1,857,000

TRUSTEES N A Cox, Miss K Wood, B H Mitchell, E D Anstead

SUBMISSION OF APPLICATIONS To correspondent – Trustees meet quarterly

CORRESPONDENT N A Cox, 72 Grosvenor Road, Tunbridge Wells, Kent TN1 2AZ

CLASSIFICATIONS
- Homes and hostels
- Youth organisations (eg Guides, Scouts, YWCA etc)

C.C. NO 263814   **ESTABLISHED** 1962

■ The Alan & Babette Sainsbury Charitable Fund

OBJECTS General charitable purposes

TYPE OF BENEFICIARY Registered charities only

FINANCES
- **Year** 1993
- **Grants** £387,550
- **Income** £367,347
- **Assets** £1,550,369

TRUSTEES The Rt Hon Lord Sainsbury, the Hon Simon Sainsbury, Miss J S Portrait

CORRESPONDENT Clark Whitehill, 25 New Street Square, London EC4A 3LN

CLASSIFICATIONS
- Children and youth – general

C.C. NO 292930   **ESTABLISHED** 1953

■ The Sainsbury Charitable Fund Ltd

OBJECTS Sponsors registered charities and community groups through predominantly eduaction-based projects

POLICY OF TRUSTEES All sponsorships must be within the trading area of one or more stores to add value with staff/customer involvement

TYPE OF GRANT Sponsorship of a specific project, or part of project

TYPE OF BENEFICIARY Registered charities, community and self-help groups

RESTRICTIONS Individual sponsorship, religious and political causes, extensions/restoration of

St Hilda's

buildings, National Health schemes are outside the scope

BENEFICIAL AREA Customer base of UK trading stores

SAMPLE GRANTS £12,000 to London Federation of Clubs for Young People
£1,000 to Lambeth Summer Projects
£400 to Medway/Swale Safety in Action Scheme
£150 to Re-Solv
£100 to Torbay Children's Week

FINANCES
- Year 1995–96
- Income £802,000

TRUSTEES J R Pillipson, C J Leaver, N F Matthews, M Pattison, R Sellers

NOTES All stores have a community budget to support local fundraising with gift vouchers

SUBMISSION OF APPLICATIONS At any time. Trustees meet quarterly. Grants up to £500 considered weekly. Applications must include aims and objectives, target audience and possible links with at least one Sainsbury's store. Submissions can be made via Store Managers

CORRESPONDENT Mrs S Mercer, The Sainsbury Charitable Fund Ltd, Stamford House, Stamford Street, London SE1 9LL

CLASSIFICATIONS
- Children and youth – general
- Community groups

C.C. NO 245843   **ESTABLISHED** 1965

■ St Hilda's Trust

OBJECTS The furtherance of such legally charitable purpose in connection with the Church of England and the Diocese of Newcastle as the Managing Trustees of the Trust may think proper and in particular, but not so as to limit or restrict the furtherance of such purposes, the relief either generally or individually of persons who are in conditions of need, hardship and distress within the Diocese of Newcastle

POLICY OF TRUSTEES The Trustees are more interested in the support of projects involving the employment of staff qualified to provide care and support of those in need than in the provision of buildings, equipment or motor vehicles

TYPE OF GRANT Wide-ranging but seldom recurrent

TYPE OF BENEFICIARY The Trust's main areas of concern within its overall objects are young people generally and in particular today's equivalent of the original clientele of St Hilda's School (an Approved School and a Community Home) and those whose needs are not met by state social welfare provisions. However, the Trustees do not necessarily limit themselves to these areas

BENEFICIAL AREA Diocese of Newcastle (Newcastle upon Tyne, North Tyneside and Northumberland)

SAMPLE GRANTS £15,000 over three years to the Cedarwood Trust to provide help for Meadowell Estate
£2,000 to South Benwell Playgroup to help with start-up costs in a very deprived area
£400 to St Oswald's Church Holiday Club

FINANCES
- Year 1994
- Income £48,764
- Grants £56,332
- Assets £824,472

TRUSTEES Bishop of Newcastle, Archdeacon of Northumberland, R P Gordon, Dr R Nicholson, Dr M J Wilkinson, E Wright

SUBMISSION OF APPLICATIONS Completed application forms should be received no later than the last day of March, June, September or December for consideration at the Trustees' meeting in the following months

CORRESPONDENT Col Michael Craster, Church House, Grainger Park Road, Newcastle upon Tyne, Tyne and Wear NE4 8SX

CLASSIFICATIONS
- Children and youth – general
- Community groups
- Counselling (inc helplines)
- Homes and hostels
- Special needs housing

C.C. NO 500962   **ESTABLISHED** 1989

■ St Katharine & Shadwell Trust

OBJECTS The Trust is established for the benefit of the residents of the St Katharine and Shadwell wards of the London Borough of Tower Hamlets by: (a) Promotion of the advancement of education and learning (including training in employment skills) (b) Provision of facilities for recreation or other leisure time occupations (c) Relief of poverty and sickness (d) Advancement of public education in the Arts (e) Provision of housing accommodation for the needy

POLICY OF TRUSTEES Priority is given to education and training of children and adults. The Trust will not normally: (a) Make grants to individuals (b) Fund travel or study outside the area (c) Fund what could be paid for by statutory sources (d) Fund the purchase, repair or maintenance of buildings or vehicles (e) Support religious groups or political groups (f) Fund research (g) Sponsor fundraising (h) Make retrospective grants or pay off mortgages, deficits, etc

TYPE OF GRANT Variable

TYPE OF BENEFICIARY Organisations providing a benefit for residents of the St Katharine and Shadwell wards of the London Borough of Tower Hamlets

BENEFICIAL AREA St Katharine and Shadwell wards of the London Borough of Tower Hamlets

SAMPLE GRANTS £6,778 to Tower Hamlets pre-school Playgroups Association to fund support and development work in Wapping neighbourhood
£250 to Tower Hamlets Schools Youth Games 1994 towards the cost of games

FINANCES
- Year 1994
- Income £251,603
- Grants £139,709
- Assets £4,505,980

TRUSTEES Sir David Hancock, Mrs M Clark, Sir David Hardy, Mrs S McAtee, Mrs M Nepstad, Ms J Reed, R Roberts, E Sorensen, P Stehrenberger, Cllr Mrs Pola Uddin, Cllr Abdul Asad, The Rev Malcolm Johnson, A Whyte

PUBLICATIONS 'Artists in Residence: A Teachers' Handbook', Annual report and accounts

SUBMISSION OF APPLICATIONS Applications should be made in writing. Telephone enquiries are welcomed. Trust meets four times a year

CORRESPONDENT The Director, St Katharine & Shadwell Trust, PO Box 1779, London E1 8NL

CLASSIFICATIONS
- Advancement in life
- Centres, clubs and institutes
- Community groups
- Development of character
- Special classes

C.C. NO 1001047   ESTABLISHED 1990

■ The Basil Samuel Charitable Trust

OBJECTS General charitable purposes

RESTRICTIONS Donations to registered charities only

FINANCES
- Year 1991
- Grants £355,000
- Income £509,171
- Assets £1,337,790

TRUSTEES B Samuel, C Samuel

SUBMISSION OF APPLICATIONS In writing

CORRESPONDENT Basil Samuel, Knighton House, 52–66 Mortimer Street, London W1N 8BD

CLASSIFICATIONS
- Advancement in life
- Counselling (inc helplines)

C.C. NO 206579   ESTABLISHED 1959

■ Peter Samuel Charitable Trust

OBJECTS General charitable purposes

POLICY OF TRUSTEES As in Objects

TYPE OF GRANT Single and annual donations

TYPE OF BENEFICIARY Registered charities only

RESTRICTIONS (a) No grants to individuals. (b) No grants to charities relating to purely local interests other than in Berkshire and Hampshire

BENEFICIAL AREA Berkshire and Hampshire

FINANCES
- Year 1994
- Grants £124,545
- Income £161,142
- Assets £2,073,106

TRUSTEES The Viscount Bearsted, The Hon Nicholas Samuel, The Hon Michael Samuel

SUBMISSION OF APPLICATIONS Any time to correspondent

CORRESPONDENT Mrs Wendy Lucken, Farley Farms, Bridge Farm, Reading Road, Arborfield, Berks RG2 9HT

CLASSIFICATIONS
- Advancement in life
- Adventure centres and playgrounds
- Centres, clubs and institutes
- Community groups
- Homes and hostels
- Youth organisations (eg Guides, Scouts, YWCA etc)

C.C. NO 269065   ESTABLISHED 1975

■ The Malcolm Sargent Cancer Fund for Children

OBJECTS To alleviate the suffering and promote the relief and care of children and young people up to the of age of 21 suffering from cancer, leukaemia or Hodgkin's disease, either in hospital or at home

POLICY OF TRUSTEES To promote the welfare and care of children and young people suffering from cancer, leukaemia or Hodgkin's disease by giving immediate practical help. To appoint Malcolm Sargent social workers at leading cancer hospitals for children. To open Malcolm Sargent Holiday Houses

TYPE OF GRANT Grants given as travel expenses to enable the child to be visited in hospital or attend out-patients, holidays, expenses connected with home nursing, clothing, beds and bedding, toys or anything connected with the welfare of the child which will improve the quality of life

TYPE OF BENEFICIARY Any child or young person up to the age of 21 recommended by a consultant, hospital, GP, area health authority, district nurse or social worker

RESTRICTIONS Grants not awarded for funeral expenses or any form of tombstone or memorial tablet

BENEFICIAL AREA UK

SAMPLE GRANTS £450 to a musician afflicted by cancer for a flute
£125 to family with a two-year-old child with cancer towards the replacement of a stolen hoover

FINANCES
- Year 1995
- Grants £2,104,600
- Income £2,849,400
- Assets £8,478,100

TRUSTEES John Pendower, MBE, FRCS (Chairman), Lady Moyra Campbell, Prof O B Eden, MB, FRCPE, Peter Gerrard, CBE, Sir Andrew Hugh Smith, David Knowles, Sir David Landale, KCVO, Dr Diana Tait, MD, MRCP, FRCRC

PUBLICATIONS 25-minute video 'Not the Odd One Out' (England), 25-minute video 'Reaching Out' (Scotland) both directed by David Williams

SUBMISSION OF APPLICATIONS An Application for Grant form is required. Any application is dealt with immediately on receipt, please telephone, all applications are acknowledged

CORRESPONDENT Mrs Diane Yeo, Chief Executive, The Malcolm Sargent Cancer Fund for Children, 14 Abingdon Road, London W8 6AF

CLASSIFICATIONS
- Counselling (inc helplines)

C.C. NO 256435   ESTABLISHED 1968

■ Save & Prosper Educational Trust

OBJECTS The advancement of education in Great Britain (a) by making donations or subscriptions to charitable bodies, schools, universities, colleges or other charitable institutions which promote education in Great Britain; (b) generally by doing such things as may advance education

POLICY OF TRUSTEES (a) Support to primary and secondary schools, tertiary educational establishments such as universities as well as research bodies and museums. (b) Community projects, particularly those relating to children and young people in inner-cities. We aim to improve the education and training of these people, particularly in information technology, and to widen the opportunities open to them, giving them prospects or a more rewarding adult life. (c) Arts education with the emphasis on helping more people gain access to the arts and to appreciate them better. Support for performing, fine and decorative arts is usually directed at school-age children and students. (d) Education for the disadvantaged. This covers special needs, inner cities, ethnic minorities and, more recently, the rural disadvantaged. (e) Scholarships and bursaries to organisations for supporting educational fees and maintenance. Support is not given directly to individuals. (f) New and innovative ways of advancing education in the UK

TYPE OF GRANT Many grants in £5,000–£10,000 range; in suitable cases may be extended over two or three years

TYPE OF BENEFICIARY Educational projects in UK

RESTRICTIONS Applications from individuals cannot be considered nor general appeals from national charities

FINANCES
- Year 1995
- Grants £1,155,000
- Income £1,485,000

TRUSTEES Save & Prosper Group Limited

SUBMISSION OF APPLICATIONS In writing to the Director at any time. Applications will be acknowledged and normally reviewed, and a decision given within 3 months

CORRESPONDENT D Grant, Director, Save & Prosper Educational Trust, Finsbury Dials, 20 Finsbury Street, London EC2Y 9AY

CLASSIFICATIONS
- Children and youth – general
- Advancement in life
- Adventure centres and playgrounds
- Centres, clubs and institutes
- Community groups
- Day centres and nurseries
- Development of character
- Counselling (inc helplines)
- Youth organisations (eg Guides, Scouts, YWCA etc)

C.C. NO 325103   **ESTABLISHED** 1974

■ Save & Prosper Foundation

OBJECTS General charitable purposes

POLICY OF TRUSTEES General charitable purposes but with a strong interest in education particularly special needs education

TYPE OF GRANT Grants vary in size over a large range

TYPE OF BENEFICIARY Organisations working for children and young people, particularly in deprived areas and for disadvantaged groups

RESTRICTIONS No grants to individuals nor in response to general appeals from national charities

BENEFICIAL AREA UK

FINANCES
- Year 1994
- Grants £190,000
- Income £299,000
- Assets £2,468,000

TRUSTEES Save & Prosper Group Limited

SUBMISSION OF APPLICATIONS No application form. Initially, a fairly short letter describing the project together with basic supporting material, if appropriate. Large quantities of back-up material are not required

CORRESPONDENT D Grant, Director, Save & Prosper Foundation, Finsbury Dials, 20 Finsbury Street, London EC2Y 9AY

CLASSIFICATIONS
- Children and youth – general
- Community groups
- Development of character
- Youth organisations (eg Guides, Scouts, YWCA etc)

C.C. NO 291617   **ESTABLISHED** 1985

■ Henry James Sayer Charity

OBJECTS General charitable purposes

POLICY OF TRUSTEES To support small local charities who make application to the Trustees for financial help for specific projects

TYPE OF GRANT Cash – normally not recurrent Mainly budgetry support for Christian led homes, schools, hospitals and training centres

TYPE OF BENEFICIARY Charitable organisations and, but only in exceptional cases, individuals

RESTRICTIONS Birmingham charities only

BENEFICIAL AREA Birmingham

FINANCES
- Year 1994
- Grants £18,330
- Income £22,939
- Assets £492,400

TRUSTEES M B Shaw, T Sloan, Alderman Shepherd, Councillor M Kazi, Miss A M Grove

SUBMISSION OF APPLICATIONS In writing to the correspondent by 1st April and 1st October each year – audited accounts are required

CORRESPONDENT D J Nightingale, Martineau Johnson, Solicitors, St Philips House, St Philips Place, Birmingham B3 2PP

CLASSIFICATIONS
- Children and youth – general
- Homes and hostels

C.C. NO 222438   **ESTABLISHED** 1944

■ The R H Scholes Charitable Trust

OBJECTS General charitable purposes

POLICY OF TRUSTEES Preference is given to charities in which the Trustees have special interest, knowledge or association. Each application is considered and assessed but amount of grant depends on applicants' needs and funds available. Due to substantial reduction in income, funds available for new applicants are virtually non existent. The Trustees prefer to increase grants to existing beneficiaries when funds are available rather than take on new charities

TYPE OF GRANT Both recurrent and one-off grants are made depending upon needs of beneficiary. Average grant £175

TYPE OF BENEFICIARY See Policy of Trustees

RESTRICTIONS Grants only to registered charities. No grants to individuals. Trustees will not respond to applications from any individuals

BENEFICIAL AREA England

SAMPLE GRANTS £500 to Children's Country Holidays Fund for the provision of holidays for children from deprived homes
£500 to Manchester and Salford Family Service Unit to help with their social work
£300 to the Royal Merchant Navy School Foundation to help provide for the education of children of seamen who have suffered some misfortune
£200 to the Sail Training Association to assist disadvantaged young people to benefit from character building experiences of crewing a tall ship
£200 to Voluntary Service Overseas towards sponsoring a volunteer to work in the field overseas

FINANCES
- Year 1995
- Grants £11,500
- Income £10,894
- Assets £458,000

TRUSTEES R H C Pattison, Mrs A J Pattison

SUBMISSION OF APPLICATIONS Annually but the majority of income is already committed to support charities currently benefiting. There is little available for new appeals. All applications should include the latest annual report and audited accounts

CORRESPONDENT R H C Pattison, Fairacre, Bonfire Hill, Southwater, Horsham, West Sussex RH13 7BU

CLASSIFICATIONS
- Children and youth – general
- Advancement in life
- Centres, clubs and institutes
- Development of character
- Holidays

C.C. NO 267023   **ESTABLISHED** 1974

■ The Schuster Charitable Trust

OBJECTS General charitable purposes

TYPE OF GRANT Mainly one-off grants

TYPE OF BENEFICIARY Registered charities

RESTRICTIONS No grants to individuals, no grants for holiday trips

BENEFICIAL AREA Preference to local charities

SAMPLE GRANTS £1,000 to Oxfordshire Association for Young People
£500 to NCH
£250 to REACT

FINANCES
- Year 1995
- Grants £24,224
- Income £23,643
- Assets £93,504

TRUSTEES Mrs J V Clarke, P J Schuster, R D Schuster

SUBMISSION OF APPLICATIONS At all times, no application form used. No replies to unsuccessful applicants

CORRESPONDENT Mrs J V Clarke, Nether Worton House, Middle Barton, Chipping Norton, Oxford OX7 7AT

CLASSIFICATIONS
- Children and youth – general
- Adoption/fostering
- Youth organisations (eg Guides, Scouts, YWCA etc)

C.C. NO 234580   **ESTABLISHED** 1964

■ The Scott Bader Commonwealth Ltd

OBJECTS To assist distressed and needy of all nationalities – establish and support charitable institutions whose objects may include the advancement of education

POLICY OF TRUSTEES To look for projects, activities or charities which: respond to the needs of those who are most underprivileged, disadvantaged, poor or excluded; encourage the careful use and protection of the earth's resources (those which assist poor rural people to become self-reliant are particularly encouraged); promote peace-building and democratic participation

TYPE OF GRANT One-off usually

TYPE OF BENEFICIARY Projects, activities or charities which find difficulty raising funds; which are innovative, imaginative and pioneering; which are initiated and/or supported by local people

RESTRICTIONS The Commonwealth does not support charities concerned with the well being of animals, individuals in need or organisations sending volunteers abroad. Does not respond to general appeals or support the larger well-established national charities. Does not provide educational bursaries or grants for academic research. Does not support projects which should properly be the responsibility of the State or make grants to replace withdrawn or expired statutory funding, or to make up deficits already incurred. Does not support the arts, museums or travel/adventure

BENEFICIAL AREA UK

FINANCES
- Year 1994
- Grants £169,000
- Income £122,397
- Assets £380,140

TRUSTEES The Board of Management

SUBMISSION OF APPLICATIONS No application form. Any time. Trustees meet monthly

CORRESPONDENT The Secretary, Scott Bader Commonwealth Ltd, Wollaston, Wellingborough, Northamptonshire NN9 7RL

CLASSIFICATIONS
- Children and youth – general

C.C. NO 206391   **ESTABLISHED** 1951

■ The Francis C Scott Charitable Trust

OBJECTS General charitable purposes

POLICY OF TRUSTEES The Trust targets its funds to registered charities in Cumbria and Lancashire that assist disadvantaged people. The first priority is given to charities in Cumbria. No grants to individuals

TYPE OF GRANT Capital or revenue. Occasionally recurrent

TYPE OF BENEFICIARY Any charity working with disadvantaged people

RESTRICTIONS Restricted to organisations working with disadvantaged people. Not medical research. Not church restoration. Not expeditions. Not individuals. Not environmental. Not Arts

BENEFICIAL AREA Cumbria and Lancashire

Scott

FINANCES
- Year 1995
- Grants £812,102
- Income £847,752
- Assets £24,325,194

TRUSTEES R W Sykes, (Chairman), W A Willink, F A Scott, Dr R Hanham, W Dobie, I H Pirnie, CB, Miss M M Scott, F J R Botty

NOTES The Trust is reluctant to give grants to compensate for the withdrawal or expiry of funding previously obtained from Statutory sources

SUBMISSION OF APPLICATIONS By application form. Trustees meetings held three times per year in March, July and November

CORRESPONDENT D J Harding, Director, Francis C Scott Charitable Trust, Sand Aire House, Kendal, Cumbria LA9 4BE

CLASSIFICATIONS
- Adventure centres and playgrounds
- Centres, clubs and institutes
- Counselling (inc helplines)
- Holidays
- Homes and hostels
- Special needs housing
- Special classes

C.C. NO 232131   **ESTABLISHED** 1963

■ The Frieda Scott Charitable Trust

OBJECTS General charitable purposes

POLICY OF TRUSTEES Grants to registered charities, within the old County of Westmorland and the area covered by South Lakes District Council, in which the Trust has special interest, knowledge or association. No grants to individuals

TYPE OF BENEFICIARY Small local charities, church restoration, parish halls, youth groups

RESTRICTIONS Not individuals. No grants to charities outside the stated geographical area

BENEFICIAL AREA The old County of Westmorland and the North Lonsdale Parliamentary Constituency and the area covered by South Lakes District Council

FINANCES
- Year 1995
- Grants £139,150
- Income £172,934
- Assets £4,990,772

TRUSTEES Mrs C Brockbank (Chairman), Mrs O Clarke, MBE, O Turnbull, R A Hunter, Miss C R Scott, P R W Hensman, D Y Mitchell

SUBMISSION OF APPLICATIONS Applications by letter considered three times per year, in April, July and November

CORRESPONDENT D J Harding, Secretary, The Frieda Scott Charitable Trust, Sand Aire House, Kendal, Cumbria LA9 4BE

CLASSIFICATIONS
- Adventure centres and playgrounds
- Community groups
- Day centres and nurseries
- Counselling (inc helplines)
- Holidays
- Youth organisations (eg Guides, Scouts, YWCA etc)

C.C. NO 221593   **ESTABLISHED** 1962

■ The Storrow Scott Charitable Will Trust

OBJECTS General charitable purposes

POLICY OF TRUSTEES Trustees give to registered charities who operate mainly in the North of England with a preferred beneficial area of north of the River Tyne

TYPE OF GRANT £150 to £5000

TYPE OF BENEFICIARY Registered charities

RESTRICTIONS Not individuals

BENEFICIAL AREA The North of England, especially Northumberland and Tyne and Wear

FINANCES
- Year 1995
- Grants £15,400
- Income £18,930
- Assets £328,596

TRUSTEES G W Meikle, J S North Lewis

CORRESPONDENT G W Meikle, Dickinson Dees, Solicitors, Cross House, Westgate Road, Newcastle upon Tyne NE99 1SB

CLASSIFICATIONS
- Centres, clubs and institutes
- Youth organisations (eg Guides, Scouts, YWCA etc)

C.C. NO 328391   **ESTABLISHED** 1989

■ The Scouloudi Foundation (formerly the Twenty-Seven Foundation)

OBJECTS General charitable purposes

POLICY OF TRUSTEES The present policy is to distribute the whole of each year's income among three different categories of grants: (a) An annual donation to the Institute of Historical Research, University of London, to sponsor historical research, publications and fellowships, 'Historical Awards'. (b) Annual donations to a regular list of national charities, 'Regular Donations'. (c) Single donations in connection with capital projects and extraordinary appeals; 'Special Donations'

TYPE OF GRANT See Policy above

TYPE OF BENEFICIARY (a) Historical Awards: Graduates with Honours Degrees in History or related subject. (b) Regular Donations: Registered national (not local) charities. (c) Special Donations: Registered charities, not individuals or welfare activities of a purely local nature

RESTRICTIONS Donations restricted to charities as defined by section 45 (1) of the Charities Act 1960. No Regular or Special Donations to individuals or local organisations. Historical research awards are not available to those registered for undergraduate or postgraduate courses. Special donations are not made towards the day-to-day fundraising of charities. The Regular Donations list is fixed and no new recipients are envisaged in the near future

BENEFICIAL AREA UK

SAMPLE GRANTS £800 to Barnardos
£400 to Invalid Children's Aid Association
£400 to National Association of Boys' Clubs

FINANCES
- Year 1995
- Grants £131,400
- Income £153,292
- Assets £3,682,653

TRUSTEES M E Demetriadi, Miss B R Masters, OBE, BA, FSA, J D Marnham, FCA, Miss S E Stowell, MA

Alphabetical register of grant making charitable trusts **Securicor**

PUBLICATIONS Notes for the Guidance of Applicants for Special Donations and Historical Awards are available on request from the correspondent

SUBMISSION OF APPLICATIONS For Historical Awards, by March 20th each year to the Secretary, The Scouloudi Foundation Awards Committee, Institute of Historical Research, Senate House, University of London WC1E 7HU. For all other purposes, at anytime, to the correspondent with full but concise details of the appeal. The Trustees decide upon grants once a year in April

CORRESPONDENT The Administrators, Hays Allan Accountants, Southampton House, 317 High Holborn, London WC1V 7NL

CLASSIFICATIONS
- Children and youth – general
- Advancement in life
- Adventure centres and playgrounds
- Centres, clubs and institutes
- Development of character

C.C. NO 205685   **ESTABLISHED** 1962

■ The Seahorse Charitable Trust

OBJECTS General charitable purposes

POLICY OF TRUSTEES To support established school scholarships and a few selected charities with several thousand pounds per annum for two or more years

TYPE OF GRANT General charitable grants

TYPE OF BENEFICIARY Organisation helping disadvantaged youth, certain medical appeals, youth employment trust, and the support of carers. Donations to help with the education of the family of a Pewterer. Two bursaries at a fee-paying school

RESTRICTIONS Support for individuals is restricted to ongoing scholarships only. Note that appeals to support other individuals for education or other enterprises are not considered

BENEFICIAL AREA UK

SAMPLE GRANTS Prince's Youth Business Trust Dulwich College (A-level bursaries) Fairbridge, Tyne and Wear

FINANCES
- Year 1995
- Grants £16,500
- Income £31,300
- Assets £477,962

TRUSTEES The Worshipful Company of Pewterers

SUBMISSION OF APPLICATIONS At any time. Trustees meet half yearly in June and November. This trust passes on the bulk of claims to the Company's general charity Trustees who can disburse donations of a few hundred pounds. The Seahorse Trustees select a few charities for support for three or more years with £3,000–£4,000 per annum

CORRESPONDENT The Clerk to the Trustees, Pewterers Hall, Oat Lane, London EC2V 7DE

CLASSIFICATIONS
- Youth organisations (eg Guides, Scouts, YWCA etc)

C.C. NO 267420   **ESTABLISHED** 1974

■ Sears Foundation

OBJECTS General charitable purposes

RESTRICTIONS All income of the Foundation is fully committed

BENEFICIAL AREA UK

FINANCES
- Year 1994–95
- Grants £237,000

TRUSTEES Sears Nominees Limited

SUBMISSION OF APPLICATIONS To the Trustees

CORRESPONDENT The Secretary, The Sears Foundation, 40 Duke Street, London W1A 2HP

CLASSIFICATIONS
- Children and youth – general
- Centres, clubs and institutes
- Day centres and nurseries
- Development of character
- Youth organisations (eg Guides, Scouts, YWCA etc)

C.C. NO 283532   **ESTABLISHED** 1981

■ Second Ferndale Trust

OBJECTS General charitable purposes, acting as a grant-maker to charitable institutions only

POLICY OF TRUSTEES The Trustees have established a regular pattern of donations which absorb all the available funds and regret that they are unable to assist new applicants at the present time

BENEFICIAL AREA Tunbridge Wells

FINANCES
- Year 1994
- Grants £2,470
- Income £1,602

TRUSTEES Mrs B V Christianson, C Christianson, C A Christianson, P Christianson

CORRESPONDENT P Christianson, Old Orchard, Pennington Road, Southborough, Tunbridge Wells, Kent TN4 0SX

CLASSIFICATIONS
- Community groups

C.C. NO 277295   **ESTABLISHED** 1978

■ The Securicor Charitable Trust

OBJECTS General charitable purposes

POLICY OF TRUSTEES The Trustees prefer to support specific charitable projects rather than large general appeals

TYPE OF GRANT Maximum donation £250

TYPE OF BENEFICIARY General and medical charitable activities

RESTRICTIONS No educational grants, expeditions, wildlife. No advertising

BENEFICIAL AREA Mainly UK but also worldwide

FINANCES
- Year 1995
- Grants £52,590
- Income £55,902

TRUSTEES Mrs A Munson, (Chairman), Mrs I Cowden, A J Gribbon, R K Davies, L K Gateson

NOTES No telephone calls please

Seedfield

Alphabetical register of grant making charitable trusts

SUBMISSION OF APPLICATIONS Trustees meet monthly. They consider only written applications. No application form

CORRESPONDENT The Chairman, Securicor Charitable Trust, Sutton Park House, 15 Carshalton Road, Sutton, Surrey SM1 4LD

CLASSIFICATIONS
- Children and youth – general
- Adventure centres and playgrounds
- Centres, clubs and institutes
- Development of character
- Holidays
- Homes and hostels
- Youth organisations (eg Guides, Scouts, YWCA etc)

C.C. NO 274637   **ESTABLISHED** 1977

■ The Seedfield Trust

OBJECTS Christian charitable purposes

POLICY OF TRUSTEES To support the preaching and teaching of the Christian faith throughout the world, including publication and distribution of Scripture, Christian literature and audio-visual aids. To assist in the relief of human suffering and poverty, including retired ministers and missionaries

RESTRICTIONS Registered charities only

BENEFICIAL AREA National, overseas

FINANCES
- **Year** 1993
- **Grants** £65,000
- **Income** £70,896
- **Assets** £1,106,236

TRUSTEES J Atkins, K Buckler, D Ryan, D Heap, Mrs J Buckler, L E Osborn

SUBMISSION OF APPLICATIONS Applications should be addressed to the Correspondent for consideration by the Trustees who meet twice yearly

CORRESPONDENT K Buckler, Folly Bank Farm, Goodshaw Lane, Rossendale, Lancs BB4 8DW

CLASSIFICATIONS
- Advancement in life
- Development of character

C.C. NO 283463   **ESTABLISHED** 1981

■ Leslie Sell Charitable Trust

OBJECTS General charitable purposes

POLICY OF TRUSTEES Assistance for Scout and Guide Associations in the UK

TYPE OF GRANT Usually single cash payments for a specific project. Core funding and salaries not considered

TYPE OF BENEFICIARY See Policy

RESTRICTIONS Registered charities or individuals backed by such Associations only. No grants made in response to general appeals from large national organisations nor to smaller bodies working in areas other than those set out above

BENEFICIAL AREA UK

FINANCES
- **Year** 1995
- **Grants** £664,400
- **Income** £127,421
- **Assets** £1,300,382

TRUSTEES Mrs M R Wiltshire, P S Sell, D Watts

SUBMISSION OF APPLICATIONS Generally by letter to the correspondent at any time. Applications should include clear details of the project or purpose for which funds are required, together with estimate of total costs and total funds raised by group or individual for project

CORRESPONDENT D Watts, The Estate Office, 8 Upper Marlborough Road, St Albans, Hertfordshire AL1 1LJ

CLASSIFICATIONS
- Youth organisations (eg Guides, Scouts, YWCA etc)

C.C. NO 258699   **ESTABLISHED** 1969

■ The Sheldon Trust

OBJECTS General charitable purposes

POLICY OF TRUSTEES Preference to charities of which the Trust has special interest, knowledge or association

TYPE OF GRANT Single payments, pump-priming, recurrent grants

TYPE OF BENEFICIARY Encouragement of local voluntary groups, recreational facilities, youth, community and facilities for the deprived. Other beneficiaries include groups concerned with rehabilitation for drugs, alcohol, and solvent abuse and those concerned with mental health, the mentally handicapped, the handicapped, religious causes and the elderly

RESTRICTIONS Pump-priming, recurrent grants, one-off payments

BENEFICIAL AREA National, preference to Warwickshire and Midlands

SAMPLE GRANTS £2,500 to South Birmingham Young Homeless Project
£1,000 to Rydal Youth Club
£1,000 to Warwickshire Association of Boys Clubs
£500 to Rugby Mayday Trust

FINANCES
- **Year** 1995
- **Grants** £123,700
- **Income** £135,591
- **Assets** £1,150,184

TRUSTEES Rev R Bidnell, R V Wiglesworth, J C Barratt, R Bagshaw

PUBLICATIONS Annual Report. 'The Situation of AET Sponsored Namibians After their Return Home'

SUBMISSION OF APPLICATIONS March, July, November

CORRESPONDENT The Sheldon Trust, Box S, White Horse Court, 25c North Street, Bishop's Stortford, Herts CM23 2LD

CLASSIFICATIONS
- Children and youth – general
- Advancement in life
- Community groups

C.C. NO 242328   **ESTABLISHED** 1965

■ The Sylvia and Colin Shepherd Charitable Trust

OBJECTS General charitable purposes

POLICY OF TRUSTEES In the medium term policy is to build up the Trust's capital base. Currently the main areas of interest are community initiatives, child care, the mentally or physically handicapped, conservation, medical support and equipment, care of the elderly

TYPE OF GRANT Usually for specific projects on an enabling basis. Core funding or ongoing support will not normally be provided

TYPE OF BENEFICIARY Registered charities working in the areas outlined under Policy and Beneficial Area. Preference to newly established or small local groups

RESTRICTIONS Registered charities only. Applications from individuals, including students, and expeditions are ineligible unless sponsored by a charitable organisation or similar. Preference is given to smaller organisations in the beneficial area

BENEFICIAL AREA The Trust's priority is to assist organisations in Greater York, North Yorkshire, Yorkshire and the North East of England in that order of priority

FINANCES
- Year 1994
- Grants £26,175
- Income £43,027
- Assets £350,000

TRUSTEES C S Shepherd, Mrs S Shepherd, Mrs S C Dickson

SUBMISSION OF APPLICATIONS At any time. The Trustees meet frequently and aim to respond quickly to requests for support. Applicants should include details of the need to be met and their achievements in their field of work and enclose a copy of their annual accounts

CORRESPONDENT C S Shepherd, 15 St Edward's Close, York YO2 2QB

CLASSIFICATIONS
- Day centres and nurseries

C.C. NO 272788 **ESTABLISHED** 1973

■ Colonel J D Sherwood Charitable Trust

OBJECTS General charitable purposes

POLICY OF TRUSTEES To continue to support charities in the county of Essex which were of interest to the Settlor, the late Col J D Sherwood

TYPE OF GRANT Annual or on application, if approved by Trustees

TYPE OF BENEFICIARY Registered charities only

BENEFICIAL AREA Essex

FINANCES
- Year 1994
- Grants £12,450
- Income £20,686
- Assets £134,994

TRUSTEES Barbinder Executor & Trustees, G C Drew

SUBMISSION OF APPLICATIONS To the correspondent

CORRESPONDENT The Director, Barbinder Executors & Trustees, 9 Greyfriars Road, Reading, Berkshire RG1 1JG

CLASSIFICATIONS
- Children and youth – general
- Centres, clubs and institutes
- Youth organisations (eg Guides, Scouts, YWCA etc)

C.C. NO 213058 **ESTABLISHED** 1950

■ Thomas Stanley Shipman Charitable Trust

OBJECTS General charitable purposes, including relief of poverty by grants and otherwise and limited educational assistance to local residents

POLICY OF TRUSTEES To primarily restrict support to those charities operating for the benefit of the citizens of the City and County of Leicester

TYPE OF GRANT Unrestricted

BENEFICIAL AREA City and County of Leicester

FINANCES
- Year 1993
- Grants £69,000
- Income £46,000
- Assets £1,023,000

TRUSTEES Mrs J Cartwright, E Watts, M T Newby, H R Ellis

SUBMISSION OF APPLICATIONS Three times per year, 30th April, 31st Aug, 31st Dec

CORRESPONDENT A R York, FCA, 18 Friar Lane, Leicester LE1 5RA

CLASSIFICATIONS
- Development of character
- Homes and hostels
- Youth organisations (eg Guides, Scouts, YWCA etc)

C.C. NO 200789 **ESTABLISHED** 1961

■ Bassil Shippam Trust

OBJECTS General charitable purposes, including but not limited to the relief of poverty and advancement of education and religion

POLICY OF TRUSTEES Support is concentrated on local charities located in West Sussex rather than on national appeals, with emphasis on Christian objects

TYPE OF GRANT General but emphasis on youth

TYPE OF BENEFICIARY General, but grants to individuals are only made in exceptional cases where strong Christian links

BENEFICIAL AREA Mainly West Sussex

FINANCES
- Year 1994
- Grants £43,000
- Income £34,500
- Assets £520,000

TRUSTEES J H S Shippam, C W Doman, D S Olby, S W Young, M Hanwell, S Trayler, R Tayler

SUBMISSION OF APPLICATIONS To correspondent

CORRESPONDENT Messrs Thomas Eggar Verrall Bowles, 5 East Pallant, Chichester PO19 1TS

CLASSIFICATIONS
- Adventure centres and playgrounds
- Centres, clubs and institutes
- Homes and hostels
- Youth organisations (eg Guides, Scouts, YWCA etc)

C.C. NO 256996 **ESTABLISHED** 1967

■ Silvester Charitable Gift Trust

OBJECTS General charitable purposes

POLICY OF TRUSTEES Trustees are interested in education. Preference is given to able children who are not financially privileged

TYPE OF BENEFICIARY Small charities, individuals

Singer

BENEFICIAL AREA Richmond

FINANCES
- Year 1995
- Income £8,000

TRUSTEES G R Whittaker, M S Whittaker, K Morton

CORRESPONDENT M S Whittaker, 43 Lancaster Park, Richmond, Surrey TW10 6AD

CLASSIFICATIONS
- Children and youth – general

C.C. NO 1022224   **ESTABLISHED** 1993

■ Singer Foundation

OBJECTS General charitable purposes

POLICY OF TRUSTEES To sponsor projects that encourage individual effort and enterprise ie to encourage people of all ages, especially the young, to help themselves by helping others in any way that is acceptable to the Trustees and the Charity Division of the Inland Revenue

TYPE OF GRANT One-off – max of £250 awarded, this may be reviewed from time to time for each project

TYPE OF BENEFICIARY Local organisations – scouts, guides, youth clubs, etc. Self-help work and sponsorship for unpaid voluntary charitable work. Individual sponsorship for unpaid voluntary charitable work under-taken in the British Isles only

RESTRICTIONS Sponsorship is only awarded for approved unpaid voluntary work undertaken in the British Isles

BENEFICIAL AREA Sponsorship can only be earned in the British Isles, otherwise the beneficial area is unrestricted if politics are not involved

FINANCES
- Year 1992
- Grants £6,896
- Income £38,458
- Assets £420,867

TRUSTEES D A Day, B J Scandrett, J F Wooolgrove, J Day

NOTES Grants are only made when the projects or voluntary unpaid charitable work has been satisfactorily carried out. Written confirmation is requested from third party

SUBMISSION OF APPLICATIONS Requests for application forms and details by letter only to the correspondent

CORRESPONDENT Mrs J Day, North Farm, Cherington, Shipston on Stour, Warwickshire

CLASSIFICATIONS
- Children and youth – general
- Centres, clubs and institutes
- Youth organisations (eg Guides, Scouts, YWCA etc)

C.C. NO 277364   **ESTABLISHED** 1960

■ The Skelton Bounty

OBJECTS General charitable purposes in the county of Lancashire as it existed in 1934

POLICY OF TRUSTEES Restricted to Lancashire charities (not national ones unless operating in Lancashire from a permanent establishment within the County predominantly for the benefit of residents from that County) assisting youth, the aged and infirm

TYPE OF GRANT Capital expenditure preferred

TYPE OF BENEFICIARY See under Policy of Trustees

RESTRICTIONS Religious charities, medical and scientific research and minibus appeals are not encouraged. Grants can only be made to registered charities

BENEFICIAL AREA Lancashire – meaning the geographical County as it existed in 1934

SAMPLE GRANTS £1,000 to British Blind Sport for their 'Have-a-Go' day in Burnley
£830 to Air Training Corps (Merseyside Wing) for provision of athletics kit
£830 to Central Youth Club, Liverpool for the purchase of musical instruments
£500 to 7F (1st City of Liverpool) Squadron Air Training Corps for provision of adventure training equipment

FINANCES
- Year 1995
- Grants £57,370
- Income £58,319

TRUSTEES G P Bowring, S R Fisher, Sir W L Mather, Lord Shuttleworth, Sir K M Stoddart, Mrs A Fishwick, K A Gledhill, Lady Towneley, A W Waterworth

SUBMISSION OF APPLICATIONS Between 1st January and 31st March on form obtainable from correspondent

CORRESPONDENT Messrs Cockshott Peck Lewis, 24 Hoghton Street, Southport, Merseyside PR9 OXH

CLASSIFICATIONS
- Adventure centres and playgrounds
- Centres, clubs and institutes
- Community groups
- Day centres and nurseries
- Holidays
- Youth organisations (eg Guides, Scouts, YWCA etc)
- Children and violence (inc abuse)

C.C. NO 219370   **ESTABLISHED** 1934

■ Edward Skinner Charitable Trust

OBJECTS The maintenance, advance and promotion of the Christian Faith and support of religious and charitable societies and institutions

POLICY OF TRUSTEES Support of the West Watch Trust which provides facilities for Christian groups and organisations running house parties, camps, retreats, etc at West Watch, Chelwood Gate and other Christian organisations

TYPE OF GRANT Cash payments, no payment to individuals

TYPE OF BENEFICIARY Evangelical missions

RESTRICTIONS Not able to support individuals

BENEFICIAL AREA UK and overseas

FINANCES
- Year 1995
- Grants £24,100
- Income £37,000
- Assets £482,133

TRUSTEES E D Anstead, L W Richards, P J Stanford, Mrs B M O'Driscoll

NOTES Main object of Trust to support West Watch Trust, Chelwood Gate

SUBMISSION OF APPLICATIONS To correspondent

CORRESPONDENT L W Richards, 11 White Lodge, 33 Lansdowne Road, Tunbridge Wells, Kent TN1 2NN

CLASSIFICATIONS
- Youth organisations (eg Guides, Scouts, YWCA etc)

C.C. NO 258519   ESTABLISHED 1968

■ Skinners' Company Lady Neville Charity

OBJECTS General charitable purposes

POLICY OF TRUSTEES Primarily support of institutions which have connections with the Company thereafter generally

TYPE OF GRANT Usually single donations in the order of £100–£200

TYPE OF BENEFICIARY Registered charities only

RESTRICTIONS (a) Grants are not made to schools other than to those directly connected with the Company. (b) Grants are not made to individuals. (c) Grants are not normally made for medical or other research. (d) Grants are not normally made for purely local charities outside London

BENEFICIAL AREA UK

FINANCES
- Year 1995
- Grants £174,000
- Income £179,000
- Assets £500,000

TRUSTEES The Worshipful Company of Skinners

NOTES (a) Applications must include copy of latest accounts. (b) Applications are not acknowledged: successful applicants will be notified normally in January or July of each year. (c) Successful applicants should not apply again for at least 12 months

SUBMISSION OF APPLICATIONS In writing to the correspondent at any time

CORRESPONDENT The Clerk to the Skinners' Company, Skinners' Hall, 8 Dowgate Hill, London EC4R 2SP

CLASSIFICATIONS
- Children and youth – general

C.C. NO 277174   ESTABLISHED 1978

■ The John Slater Foundation

OBJECTS General charitable purposes

POLICY OF TRUSTEES The relief of suffering

TYPE OF GRANT Mainly to national charities

TYPE OF BENEFICIARY Registered charities

RESTRICTIONS No grants to individuals

BENEFICIAL AREA West Lancashire

FINANCES
- Year 1995
- Grants £124,500
- Income £118,067
- Assets £1,911,570

TRUSTEES Midland Bank Trust Company Limited

SUBMISSION OF APPLICATIONS Half-yearly – 1st May and 1st November by letter

CORRESPONDENT The Secretary, The John Slater Foundation, Midland Personal Asset Manager, Pearl Assurance House, 2 Derby Square, Liverpool L2 9XW

CLASSIFICATIONS
- Children and youth – general
- Community groups
- Youth organisations (eg Guides, Scouts, YWCA etc)

C.C. NO 231145   ESTABLISHED 1963

■ Slater Trust Limited

OBJECTS Children and youth work, old and infirm people, medical work, scholarships and bursaries and assistance to educational establishments

POLICY OF TRUSTEES Only local applications considered for new grants

TYPE OF GRANT Recurrent nationally and local

TYPE OF BENEFICIARY Only local organisations for new grants

RESTRICTIONS No new grants to individuals. No new grants at present

BENEFICIAL AREA Local

FINANCES
- Year 1995
- Grants £11,242
- Income £18,756
- Assets £238,163

TRUSTEES The Council

NOTES Present commitments restrict availability of new grants

SUBMISSION OF APPLICATIONS Only local

CORRESPONDENT The Secretary, Slater Trust Ltd, PO Box No2, Cockermouth, Cumbria

CLASSIFICATIONS
- Children and youth – general

C.C. NO 230099   ESTABLISHED 1963

■ The N Smith Charitable Settlement

OBJECTS General charitable purposes

POLICY OF TRUSTEES All appellants must be of registered charitable status

RESTRICTIONS No applications from individuals will be considered

FINANCES
- Year 1993
- Grants £35,900
- Income £63,324
- Assets £1,513,028

TRUSTEES J S Cochrane, T R Kendal, P R Green, J H Williams-Rigby

CORRESPONDENT Bullock, Worthington & Jackson, 1 Booth Street, Manchester M2 2HA

CLASSIFICATIONS
- Children and youth – general
- Centres, clubs and institutes
- Development of character

C.C. NO 276660   ESTABLISHED 1978

■ E H Smith Charitable Trust

OBJECTS General charitable purposes

POLICY OF TRUSTEES Each application is considered on its own merits, but we are prepared to consider children and youth causes

FINANCES
- Year 1991
- Income £130,676

TRUSTEES K H A Smith, Mrs B M Hodgskin-Brown, D P Enselle

CORRESPONDENT K H A Smith, 1 Sherbourne Road, Acocks Green, Birmingham B27 6AB

CLASSIFICATIONS
- Children and youth – general

C.C. NO 328313   **ESTABLISHED** 1989

■ The Harold Smith Charitable Trust

OBJECTS General charitable purposes

POLICY OF TRUSTEES To assist other charities

TYPE OF GRANT Principally one-off

TYPE OF BENEFICIARY Any charitable institution

RESTRICTIONS Educational grants to individuals are not undertaken

BENEFICIAL AREA UK

FINANCES
- Year 1992
- Grants £77,000
- Income £54,881
- Assets £715,858

TRUSTEES B V Norgan, Mrs S E Norgan, Mrs M L J Wallace

PUBLICATIONS Statement of Accounts

NOTES Sae must accompany every request, please

SUBMISSION OF APPLICATIONS Monthly in writing

CORRESPONDENT B V Norgan, Hunter's Moon, Brighton Road, Pease Pottage, Nr Crawley, West Sussex RH11 9AG

CLASSIFICATIONS
- Children and youth – general
- Advancement in life
- Centres, clubs and institutes
- Development of character
- Holidays
- Youth organisations (eg Guides, Scouts, YWCA etc)

C.C. NO 277172   **ESTABLISHED** 1978

■ Henry Smith (Estates Charities)

OBJECTS Donations to: hospitals, dispensaries, infirmaries, homes for incurables, convalescent homes or societies for providing the poor with surgical appliances or medical aid, charities for promotion of moral welfare or social services, charities for rehabilitation and training of disabled persons, charities for obtaining for children of the poor of Greater London the benefit of a visit to the country or other change of air

POLICY OF TRUSTEES The Trustees do not favour grants to other grant making organisations. Where possible they like to fund the whole of a moderate sized project or to provide substantial pump-priming grants. Grants may also be allocated towards a particular item within the budget of a project which the Trustees decide to support

TYPE OF GRANT One-off or ongoing

RESTRICTIONS Grants made only to organisations, not individuals

BENEFICIAL AREA UK

SAMPLE GRANTS £80,000 to De Paul Trust towards refurbishment of a hostel for young homeless
£35,000 to Osteopathic Centre for Children towards the salary and cost of the clinic director
£20,000 to Childline to enable the charity to increase the services it offers
£15,000 to Friends of the Young Deaf towards training programme for young deaf people
£7,000 to Childrens Country Holiday Fund towards the cost of providing holidays for needy London children

FINANCES
- Year 1994
- Grants £12,900,000
- Income £13,312,000
- Assets £383,708,000

TRUSTEES Lord Kindersley, Lord Ashcombe, and others

SUBMISSION OF APPLICATIONS Applications for assistance should not be addressed to the Trustees

CORRESPONDENT B T McGeough, 5 Chancery Lane, London EC4A 1BU

CLASSIFICATIONS
- Children and youth – general

C.C. NO 230102   **ESTABLISHED** 1626

■ The Leslie Smith Foundation

OBJECTS General charitable purposes

POLICY OF TRUSTEES Preference given to charities in which the Trust has special interest, knowledge or association. The Trust supports work to promote the welfare of children, including help for the disabled and disadvantaged and for schools, both specialising in this area and generally

TYPE OF GRANT For specific purposes, non-recurring

TYPE OF BENEFICIARY Small, local

RESTRICTIONS Registered charities. Applications from individuals are not normally eligible

SAMPLE GRANTS £40,000 to Castle School, Newbury to fund the construction of a playground for disabled children
£10,000 to Wessex Children's Hospice – general grant
£5,000 to Centre 35 – young people's counselling and information centre
£2,500 to Langley School Development Appeal
£1,000 to Weymouth Boy's Club – general grant

FINANCES
- Year 1995
- Grants £41,000
- Income £103,000
- Assets £1,250,000

TRUSTEES M D Willcox, Mrs E A Furtek

SUBMISSION OF APPLICATIONS At any time but as administration is kept to a minimum only successful appeals will be acknowledged

CORRESPONDENT M D Willcox, The Old Coach House, Bergh Apton, Norwich, Norfolk NR15 1DD

CLASSIFICATIONS
- Adoption/fostering
- Advancement in life
- Adventure centres and playgrounds
- Counselling (inc helplines)
- Holidays
- Homes and hostels

C.C. NO 250030   **ESTABLISHED** 1964

The Stanley Smith General Charitable Trust

OBJECTS General charitable purposes

FINANCES
- Year 1993
- Income £348,910

TRUSTEES J L Norton, J J Dilger

CORRESPONDENT J Norton, Messrs BDO Binder Hamlyn, Chartered Accountants, 20 Old Bailey, London EC4M 7BH

CLASSIFICATIONS
- Children and youth – general
- Homes and hostels

C.C. NO 326226   **ESTABLISHED** 1982

The Albert & Florence Smith Memorial Trust

OBJECTS General charitable purposes

POLICY OF TRUSTEES Essex charities only considered

TYPE OF GRANT Recurrent and occasional one-off

TYPE OF BENEFICIARY Essex registered charities

RESTRICTIONS No grants to individuals

BENEFICIAL AREA Essex

FINANCES
- Year 1993
- Grants £193,675
- Income £334,877
- Assets £1,266,330

TRUSTEES J E Tolhurst, W J Tolhurst, P J Tolhurst

SUBMISSION OF APPLICATIONS June and December. No application form used

CORRESPONDENT J E Tolhurst, Messrs Tolhurst & Fisher, Trafalgar House, Nelson Street, Southend-on-Sea, Essex SS1 1EF

CLASSIFICATIONS
- Children and youth – general
- Centres, clubs and institutes
- Homes and hostels
- Youth organisations (eg Guides, Scouts, YWCA etc)

C.C. NO 259917   **ESTABLISHED** 1969

The Sydney Smith Trust

OBJECTS General charitable purposes mainly in the fields of education and religion

POLICY OF TRUSTEES Preference is given to individuals. Assistance is only given to local charities of which the Trustees have special knowledge or association. Applications for grant-aid from charities outside the area designated will not be acknowledged

TYPE OF GRANT Single and recurring

TYPE OF BENEFICIARY Individuals and charities

BENEFICIAL AREA Humberside, mainly City of Hull

SAMPLE GRANTS £2,000 to Sydney Smith School

FINANCES
- Year 1995
- Grants £15,350
- Income £11,547
- Assets £96,428

TRUSTEES Midland Bank Trust Company Limited, Mrs D Picksley, N Moody, A G Picksley

---

SUBMISSION OF APPLICATIONS To correspondent by letter, with full details of background to application

CORRESPONDENT Trust Manager, Midland Trusts, Cumberland House, 15–17 Cumberland Place, Southampton SO15 2UY

CLASSIFICATIONS
- Homes and hostels

C.C. NO 252112   **ESTABLISHED** 1966

The Snowball Trust

OBJECTS Sick and disabled children

TYPE OF GRANT Cash

TYPE OF BENEFICIARY Either an individual or an institution for the benefit of an identified individual up to 18 years of age

RESTRICTIONS Beneficiary must live in Coventry or Warwickshire and must be 18 years of age or younger

BENEFICIAL AREA Coventry and Warwickshire

FINANCES
- Year 1993
- Grants £74,772
- Income £98,396
- Assets £193,852

TRUSTEES Celia Grew (Chairman), N Benson, S Linell, H Jones, A Rhodes

SUBMISSION OF APPLICATIONS To Mrs Pauline Blackham, Secretary to the Trustees, Coventry Evening Telegraph, Corporation Street, Coventry, CV1 1FP

CORRESPONDENT The Snowball Trustees, Daffern & Co, Queens House, 2nd Floor, Queens Road, Coventry CV1 3EG

CLASSIFICATIONS
- Children and youth – general

C.C. NO 702860   **ESTABLISHED** 1989

The Sobell Foundation

OBJECTS General charitable purposes

POLICY OF TRUSTEES Although in some cases the Trustees make donations for specific purposes which are discussed with the charities concerned, the bulk of their small donations are made in response to applications. In general, the Trustees donate on a national rather than a narrowly local basis. Although occasional donations are made locally, this is because there is a specific interest in the area in question. Very narrowly local appeals are not likely to be successful

TYPE OF GRANT With the exception of certain major projects, the bulk of the Trustees' donations are for the general purposes of the charities and not ear-marked for a special purpose

TYPE OF BENEFICIARY The Trustees have a very lively interest in the sick, aged, needy and disabled, including, in particular, disabled children

RESTRICTIONS In practice, no grants are made to individuals

FINANCES
- Year 1994
- Grants £317,000
- Income £488,477

TRUSTEES D Lewis, R K Lewis, Lord Crathorne

SUBMISSION OF APPLICATIONS The Trustees prefer to receive applications in writing. They do not wish to receive preliminary telephone calls. There are no precise dates for Trustees' meetings, but these take place frequently. No guidelines are issued

CORRESPONDENT Messrs Eversheds, Senator House, 85 Queen Victoria Street, London EC4V 4JL

CLASSIFICATIONS
- Children and youth – general
- Adoption/fostering
- Adventure centres and playgrounds
- Centres, clubs and institutes
- Community groups
- Day centres and nurseries
- Counselling (inc helplines)
- Holidays
- Homes and hostels
- Special needs housing
- Youth organisations (eg Guides, Scouts, YWCA etc)
- Children and violence (inc abuse)

C.C. NO 274369   **ESTABLISHED** 1977

■ South Yorkshire Community Foundation (formerly South Yorkshire Foundation)

OBJECTS The Foundation exists to help community groups which are trying to improve the quality of life in South Yorkshire

POLICY OF TRUSTEES Policy is reviewed annually; current priorities are:- Neighbourhood based community development initiatives. The education and training needs of voluntary community groups. Voluntary sector housing and homelessness initiatives. Community information and advice services. Community based health projects. Preference is given to projects where a grant of a few hundred pounds will make a significant difference, that means that most projects helped are small ones. Grants for both capital and revenue. Capital projects costing more than £50,000 are most unlikely to receive funding from the Foundation

TYPE OF GRANT A small number of large grants are made each year but most grants are for amounts under £1,000. Applications are encouraged from small, local groups who find it hard to raise money elsewhere

RESTRICTIONS Unlikely to receive support (unless fitting strongly with the above priority categories):- arts projects, environmental projects, bands, sports clubs, uniformed youth groups, minibuses. No grants are made for holidays, trips and excursions, repayment of debts, academic research, or to individuals

BENEFICIAL AREA South Yorkshire

FINANCES
- Year 1993
- Grants £77,587
- Income £185,000
- Assets £468,920

TRUSTEES R Darlison (Chairman), T Hale, P Lee, B Upton, J Powlett Smith, I Aiken, P Wetzel, B Willis, D Clark, I Porter, Lord Scarborough, J H Neill (President)

SUBMISSION OF APPLICATIONS Applications forms are available from the Foundation. The Trustees meet quarterly in January, April, July and September. Applications must reach the Foundation six weeks before these meetings. When your application arrives at the Foundation office, as long as it meets the stated guidelines, it goes out to one of the four District Advisory Committees (DACs). The Committees are made up of local people with an interest in the voluntary sector. A member of the committee may want to visit you before your application is discussed. The DACs meet quarterly, about two weeks before the Trustees, and send recommendations about each application to the Trustees' meeting

CORRESPONDENT Margaret Thompson, 47 Wilkinson Street, Sheffield S10 2GB

CLASSIFICATIONS
- Children and youth – general
- Community groups

C.C. NO 517714   **ESTABLISHED** 1983

■ W F Southall Trust

OBJECTS Society of Friends (Quakers), peace, education, alcohol and drug addiction, social welfare and related charities

TYPE OF GRANT Normally single payments

TYPE OF BENEFICIARY Registered charities only

RESTRICTIONS No grants are made to individuals

FINANCES
- Year 1994
- Grants £170,000
- Income £170,617

TRUSTEES Mrs Daphne Maw, C M Southall, D H D Southall, Mrs Annette Wallis, M Holtom

NOTES Gifts to registered charities only

SUBMISSION OF APPLICATIONS To correspondent

CORRESPONDENT S T Rutter, Messrs Rutters, Solicitors, 2 Bimport, Shaftesbury, Dorset SP7 8AY

CLASSIFICATIONS
- Centres, clubs and institutes
- Community groups
- Homes and hostels
- Youth organisations (eg Guides, Scouts, YWCA etc)

C.C. NO 218371   **ESTABLISHED** 1937

■ Southdown Trust

OBJECTS Advancement of education. General charitable purposes

POLICY OF TRUSTEES Support of individual ventures of general educational benefit. Response to applications

TYPE OF GRANT A small number of modest grants made each year, sometimes repeated – no grants for salaries/running costs

TYPE OF BENEFICIARY Individuals, families proposing a particular venture. Initiative, selflessness

RESTRICTIONS Grants only made to individuals (or, in rare instances, families). No grants for art, dance, medicine, sociology or theatre, law, journalism

BENEFICIAL AREA Great Britain and Northern Ireland

FINANCES
- Year 1994
- Grants £7,855
- Income £10,000
- Assets £172,000

TRUSTEES J G Wyatt, H R Wyatt, A C Pugh

SUBMISSION OF APPLICATIONS In writing to the correspondent. Full information must be sent. A stamped addressed envelope must be included with each application. No telephone calls

CORRESPONDENT The Secretary, Southdown Trust, Canbury School, Kingston Hill, Kingston-upon-Thames, Surrey KT2 7LN

CLASSIFICATIONS
- Children and youth – general
- Development of character

C.C. NO 235583 **ESTABLISHED** 1963

■ The Eric F Sparkes Charitable Trust

OBJECTS General charitable purposes

POLICY OF TRUSTEES To support other charities where Trustees are satisfied assistance is of significant benefit

TYPE OF GRANT General one off for specific projects or support of national charitable organisations

TYPE OF BENEFICIARY Local charities in Devon and special cases known to Trustees

RESTRICTIONS Generally no grants to individuals

BENEFICIAL AREA Mainly Warwickshire and Devon

FINANCES
- Year 1993
- Grants £25,850
- Income £26,950

TRUSTEES J M Davies, H M Turner, Mrs K A Davies

SUBMISSION OF APPLICATIONS Individual applications are considered but distribution normally made only in the autumn. Applications for revenue grants should enclose most recent accounts. For capital, total cost and anticipated start date. Charity registration number should be given. Regret applications cannot be acknowledged

CORRESPONDENT H M Turner, 2 Vaughan Parade, Torquay, Devon TQ2 5EF

CLASSIFICATIONS
- Children and youth – general
- Centres, clubs and institutes
- Community groups
- Homes and hostels

C.C. NO 233085 **ESTABLISHED** 1963

■ The Spencer Hart Charitable Trust

OBJECTS General charitable purposes

TYPE OF BENEFICIARY Registered charities,

FINANCES
- Year 1993
- Grants £24,900
- Income £39,600
- Assets £290,848

TRUSTEES J S Korn, I A Burman

CORRESPONDENT J S Korn, c/o Beechcroft Stanleys, 20 Furnival Street, London EC4A 1BN

CLASSIFICATIONS
- Children and youth – general
- Adoption/fostering

C.C. NO 800057 **ESTABLISHED** 1988

■ Sport Aid 88 Trust

OBJECTS Charities to do with children

POLICY OF TRUSTEES To give towards the relief of poverty, disease and malnutrition and to provide recreational and educational facilities

FINANCES
- Year 1992
- Grants £698,025
- Income £107,049
- Assets £699,830

TRUSTEES C J Lang, H R H Stinson, R Charlton, J M R Cohen, R B Brooke

CORRESPONDENT Messrs MacIntyre Hudson, Chartered Accountants, Ashley House, 18–20 George Street, Richmond, Surrey TW9 1HD

CLASSIFICATIONS
- Children and youth – general

C.C. NO 297373 **ESTABLISHED** 1988

■ The Spurgin Charitable Trust

OBJECTS To support people caring agencies

TYPE OF GRANT Both recurrent and one-off

TYPE OF BENEFICIARY Generally to people caring agencies in Scotland

RESTRICTIONS Donations made only at the discretion of the Trustees

BENEFICIAL AREA Predominantly Scotland

SAMPLE GRANTS £500 to childrens' holiday scheme

FINANCES
- Year 1995
- Grants £13,559
- Income £11,885
- Assets £136,589

TRUSTEES G G MacMillan, MA, Mrs L C Richardson

SUBMISSION OF APPLICATIONS Requests for aid considered on merit – by letter

CORRESPONDENT G G MacMillan, Finlaystone, Langbank, Renfrewshire PA14 6TJ

CLASSIFICATIONS
- Holidays

C.C. NO 210562 **ESTABLISHED** 1962

■ Stanley Foundation Limited

OBJECTS Promotion of education and science, poor relief and general charitable purposes

POLICY OF TRUSTEES The Trustees do not make grants to individuals

FINANCES
- Year 1991
- Grants £143,992
- Income £190,193
- Assets £2,880,843

TRUSTEES Council of Management

CORRESPONDENT Nicholas Stanley, 19 Holland Park, London W11 3TD

CLASSIFICATIONS
- Children and youth – general
- Centres, clubs and institutes

C.C. NO 206866 **ESTABLISHED** 1962

Star Foundation

■ The Star Foundation Trust

OBJECTS General charitable purposes

POLICY OF TRUSTEES Preference to charities of which the Trust has special interest, knowledge or association

FINANCES
- Year 1992
- Grants £34,425
- Income £44,116
- Assets £497,837

TRUSTEES A C Wilson, Dr Elizabeth Frankland Moore, OBE, LLD, J Crawford, Mrs J S McCreadie, Mrs J Cameron

CORRESPONDENT Dr Elizabeth Frankland Moore, OBE, LLD, Trustee The Star Foundation Trust, c/o Lloyds Bank, 83 Cannon Street, London EC4

CLASSIFICATIONS
- Centres, clubs and institutes

C.C. NO 257711   **ESTABLISHED** 1968

■ The June Stevens Foundation

OBJECTS General charitable purposes

POLICY OF TRUSTEES Trustees have a particular interest in animals and children

TYPE OF GRANT Cash

TYPE OF BENEFICIARY Charitable organisations only

BENEFICIAL AREA National but with a preference for Gloucestershire

SAMPLE GRANTS £500 to Scope for general purposes
£500 to Barnardos
£500 to Winston's Wish (Gloucestershire Royal Hospital) project to help grieving children
£500 to St Thomas Moore Catholic Primary School towards employment of a relief teacher
£500 to Sir Charles Playgroup

FINANCES
- Year 1995
- Grants £11,200
- Income £13,396
- Assets £309,000

TRUSTEES J D Stevens, A J Quinton, A R St C Tahourdin

CORRESPONDENT A Tahourdin, 13 Bedford Row, London WC1R 4BU

CLASSIFICATIONS
- Children and youth – general

C.C. NO 327829   **ESTABLISHED** 1988

■ The Leonard Laity Stoate Charitable Trust

OBJECTS (a) General charitable purposes.
(b) Methodism in the specified counties (see Beneficial Area)

POLICY OF TRUSTEES Some of income taken up with a pattern of donations already established. We regret that unsuccessful applications cannot be acknowledged unless sae supplied. No telephone applications please

TYPE OF GRANT Usually one-off for a specific project or part of a project. Normal range of grant; £100–£1000

TYPE OF BENEFICIARY Small local projects with a good measure of self-help are preferred

RESTRICTIONS No grants to individuals unless supported by a registered charity. Large projects (over £250,000) or general appeals mailed out by national charities are unlikely to be successful

BENEFICIAL AREA England and Wales, but preference for West of England: Avon, Cornwall, Devon, Dorset and Somerset (especially West Somerset)

SAMPLE GRANTS £500 to a Dorset youth club for refurbishment of premises
£500 to an Avon Scoutgroup for new headquarters
£300 to a Somerset village playgroup for new equipment
£250 to a Bristol special school for handicapped children's holiday

FINANCES
- Year 1994
- Grants £15,000
- Income £22,000

TRUSTEES D L Stoate, G L Stoate, S R Duckworth, Mrs S Harnden, C Stoate

SUBMISSION OF APPLICATIONS To the correspondent in writing. Grants can be considered at any time but the best time for submission is April/May. No special application form. Accounts or budget should be attached where possible, together with clear details of the need the intended project is designed to meet. No telephone applications please

CORRESPONDENT Geoffrey L Stoate, LLB, Combe House, Hill Lane, Bicknoller, Taunton, Somerset TA4 4EF

CLASSIFICATIONS
- Children and youth – general
- Community groups
- Day centres and nurseries
- Youth organisations (eg Guides, Scouts, YWCA etc)

C.C. NO 221325   **ESTABLISHED** 1950

■ F C Stokes Trust

OBJECTS General charitable purposes

BENEFICIAL AREA West Midlands

FINANCES
- Year 1993
- Grants £17,000
- Income £16,736
- Assets £120,006

TRUSTEES D Baume, R J Brown

CORRESPONDENT D Baume, Secretary and Trustee, c/o Payne Skillington, 12 Manor Road, Coventry, West Midlands CV1 2LG

CLASSIFICATIONS
- Children and youth – general

C.C. NO 289255   **ESTABLISHED** 1962

■ Eric Stonehouse Trust Ltd

OBJECTS To advance education and religion; to relieve the mentally and physically handicapped; the relief of poverty, suffering and distress; general charitable purposes

POLICY OF TRUSTEES Preference is given to charities which meet one or more of the following criteria: Those local to the Trustees and their families. (East Anglia, Yorkshire, London). Those which are small, innovatory projects of real value to the local community where they are being established, and which need help to get started. Those which promote the education and care of disadvantaged children. Those which are engaged in research into the causes and cure of serious illnesses. Those which provide support and rehabilitation for people who have been crippled. International charities based in this country which are able to supply substantial relief for problems which are particularly acute in developing countries

TYPE OF GRANT Cash £50–£200 range

RESTRICTIONS Registered charities only. Applications from individuals, including students, are ineligible. No grants made in response to appeals from large, national organisations

BENEFICIAL AREA UK, but including charities based in the UK working abroad

SAMPLE GRANTS £100 to Mexico Child Link Trust for provision of housing and care for children with mental handicap in Puebla, Mexico
£50 to Scottish Gospel Outreach for the rehabilitation of drug-dependent young people in Glasgow

FINANCES
- Year 1995
- Grants £1,850
- Income £2,545
- Assets £44,198

TRUSTEES Rev M N France, Mrs E France, Miss C S France, Miss M L France

SUBMISSION OF APPLICATIONS Applications should be sent by post to the Correspondent. They will not normally be acknowledged. They will be reviewed three times a year. No application forms. At any time

CORRESPONDENT Rev Dr M N France, The Old Rectory, Starston, Harleston, Norfolk IP20 9NG

CLASSIFICATIONS
- Children and youth – general
- Homes and hostels
- Special needs housing

C.C. NO 261197 **ESTABLISHED** 1970

■ The Samuel Storey Family Charitable Trust

OBJECTS General charitable purposes

TYPE OF BENEFICIARY Registered charities

RESTRICTIONS Not overseas

FINANCES
- Year 1993
- Grants £16,000
- Income £41,726
- Assets £305,659

TRUSTEES Sir Richard Storey, Bt, A D W Hoskyns, Hon Mrs J Cator

CORRESPONDENT G A Toffs, Buckton House, 37 Abingdon Road, London W8 6AH

CLASSIFICATIONS
- Children and youth – general
- Community groups

C.C. NO 267684 **ESTABLISHED** 1974

■ David James Streeter Charitable Settlement

OBJECTS General charitable purposes

POLICY OF TRUSTEES Income distributed as required by the Settlor

TYPE OF GRANT Cash — generally not in excess of £100

TYPE OF BENEFICIARY Mainly established charities, some extra curricular activities, eg university expeditions, self-help groups and course fees

FINANCES
- Year 1994
- Grants £3,300
- Income £3,690

TRUSTEES Barclays Bank Trust Co Ltd

SUBMISSION OF APPLICATIONS By letter

CORRESPONDENT Barclays Bank Trust Co Ltd, Executorship & Trustee Service 65/28/1497, Osborne Court, Gadbrook Park, Rudheath, Northwich, Cheshire CW9 7UE

CLASSIFICATIONS
- Children and youth – general

C.C. NO 266514 **ESTABLISHED** 1973

■ Sulgrave Charitable Trust

OBJECTS Carrying on or managing or subscribing to or assisting boys' clubs

POLICY OF TRUSTEES To assist the Sulgrave Boys' Club and other boys' clubs in the London area

TYPE OF GRANT Cash

TYPE OF BENEFICIARY Boys' clubs

RESTRICTIONS Cash grants to boys' clubs in the London area only

BENEFICIAL AREA London area

FINANCES
- Year 1993
- Grants £50,335
- Income £46,184
- Assets £414,215

TRUSTEES M B Fellingham, P J Grant, London Federation of Boys' Clubs Incorp

SUBMISSION OF APPLICATIONS Grants to Sulgrave Boys' Club and London Federation of Boys' Clubs Incorp only

CORRESPONDENT Penningtons, Solicitors, Highfield, Brighton Road, Godalming, Surrey GU7 1NS

CLASSIFICATIONS
- Centres, clubs and institutes

C.C. NO 231952 **ESTABLISHED** 1930

■ The Summerfield Charitable Trust

OBJECTS General charitable purposes

POLICY OF TRUSTEES The Trustees are particularly interested in hearing from those involved with helping the needy, the arts (and the elderly). Causes in Gloucestershire attract most attention; applicants from outside the county, where they are successful, are only likely to receive relatively small grants. Viewed especially favourably are: the needs of those living in rural areas; ventures which make a point of using volunteers (and which train volunteers); applicants who show clear indications that they have assessed the impact of their projects upon the environment and joint appeals from groups working in similar areas, who wish to develop a partnership. The Trustees particularly welcome innovative ideas from small, voluntary groups

TYPE OF GRANT One-off. The Trustees prefer to award one-off grants to help fund specific projects, rather than to make payments for revenue items

TYPE OF BENEFICIARY The elderly, charities local to Gloucestershire, the Arts. Private organisations and individuals are only very rarely supported, students being more likely to find favour than those with other needs. In any event the Trustees urge individuals to use a specialist charity to sponsor their application

RESTRICTIONS Donations are not usually given to: medical research; London-based projects; national charities, where the Trust has already supported a local branch; organisations working outside the UK; private education or animal welfare appeals

BENEFICIAL AREA Grants given are primarily based and working in Gloucestershire. However, other applicants are considered and occasionally receive a small grant

SAMPLE GRANTS £3,000 to Gloucestershire Wheels Project (runs preventative schemes for young offenders) towards cost of part-time mechanic offering his skills to the young people
£2,000 to Young Gloucestershire towards mobile drugs advice and information service
£1,500 to Cheltenham Opportunity Centre (pre-school activities and therapy to special needs children) towards soft-play room
£1,000 to Noah's Ark Children's Venture, Cotswolds (rural, residential facilities for inner-city children) towards building for children with disabilities
£500 to Warwickshire Association of Youth Clubs towards purchase of arts equipment

FINANCES
- Year 1993
- Grants £382,145

TRUSTEES The Earl Fortescue, M M Davis

PUBLICATIONS Grants report available from Administrator

SUBMISSION OF APPLICATIONS The Trustees meet quarterly, in January, April, July and October when they consider all applications received prior to the end of the preceding month. Applicants should write to the correspondent stating in their own words what is required, the purpose of the application, a brief history, a financial summary and (where relevant) registered charity number. Applicants are asked to complete a questionaire on environmental matters. Further, please say if and when you have previously applied to the Trust for a grant. Applicants are informed of the Trustees' decisions as soon as possible after their meetings. All new applications are acknowledged; stamped addressed envelopes are welcomed

CORRESPONDENT Mrs Lavinia Sidgwick, Administrator, PO Box 4, Winchcombe, Cheltenham, Gloucestershire GL54 5ZD

CLASSIFICATIONS
- Children and youth – general
- Advancement in life
- Adventure centres and playgrounds
- Centres, clubs and institutes
- Community groups
- Day centres and nurseries
- Development of character
- Counselling (inc helplines)
- Homes and hostels
- Special needs housing

C.C. NO 802493   **ESTABLISHED** 1989

■ The Late Misses A N Summer's and I May's Charitable Settlement

OBJECTS Four named ecclesiastic, children and animal societies and to institutions and societies for promoting research into and relief of cancer, rheumatism and blindness and for promoting the relief of hunger in any part of the world, institutions and societies for promoting the welfare of clergy and ex-servicemen and their families and dependants

POLICY OF TRUSTEES Funds are fully committed to the support of charities whose aims are either set out in the Trust Deed or for which the Trustees feel would have been those supported by the Settlors

TYPE OF GRANT Varying cash distributions

TYPE OF BENEFICIARY Restricted to the type of charity listed in Objects

RESTRICTIONS Restricted to the type of charity listed in Objects

FINANCES
- Year 1995
- Grants £25,250
- Income £25,250
- Assets £485,000

TRUSTEES Lloyds Bank plc and D J Bellew

SUBMISSION OF APPLICATIONS Applications received in writing are considered half yearly in March and September

CORRESPONDENT UK Trust Centre, Lloyds Private Banking Ltd, The Clock House, 22–26 Ock Street, Abingdon, Oxfordshire OX14 5SW

CLASSIFICATIONS
- Children and youth – general

C.C. NO 239980   **ESTABLISHED** 1964

■ Sir John Sumner's Trust Section 'A'

OBJECTS For works and objects of Philanthropy, Public Utility, Education (See 'Notes'), Literature, Art, Archaeology and Research (other than experiments involving animal suffering)

POLICY OF TRUSTEES Mainly (a) grants to persons in necessitous circumstances and (b) donations to charitable organisations

TYPE OF GRANT Quarterly grant and one-off donations. Grants are few and far between and are not normally more than £500

TYPE OF BENEFICIARY Students of nursing/medicine. Any organisations on behalf of youth causes

RESTRICTIONS Party politics, religion – though purely social efforts connected with religious denominations are not excluded. Research where vivisection is involved

BENEFICIAL AREA Throughout UK but preference to West Midlands

SAMPLE GRANTS £500 to Childline
£50 to local police towards holidays

FINANCES
- Year To Feb 1995
- Grants £30,485
- Income £31,812
- Assets £296,000

TRUSTEES J B Sumner, JP (Chairman), Mrs E J Wood, A B Sumner, J M G Fea, Lady Richard Wellesley

NOTES Grants for education are only made in exceptional circumstances and generally to those who are undertaking courses concerned with nursing or mental care

SUBMISSION OF APPLICATIONS Personal applications from students or organisations by letter giving details of requirements and finances. All other applications from individuals must be completed on pro-forma supplied at request and generally supported by social services departments, hospital officials or the Probation Service

CORRESPONDENT The Secretary, Sir John Sumner's Trust, 8th Floor, Union Chambers, 63 Temple Row, Birmingham B2 5LT

CLASSIFICATIONS
- Children and youth – general

C.C. NO 218620 **ESTABLISHED** 1927

■ The Bernard Sunley Charitable Foundation

OBJECTS To or for such charitable institutions or charitable objects as the Trustees in their discretion may select

TYPE OF GRANT Flexible

TYPE OF BENEFICIARY See Objects above

RESTRICTIONS Registered charities only. No grants to individuals

BENEFICIAL AREA Worldwide

FINANCES
- Year 1994–95
- Grants £3,941,000
- Income £4,462,000
- Assets £52,136,000

TRUSTEES John Sunley, Sir William Shapland, Mrs Joan Tice, Mrs B Sunley, Sir Donald Gosling

PUBLICATIONS Annual Report

NOTES Of total figure for Grants, above, £287,000 went to youth clubs, youth training and sports organisations

SUBMISSION OF APPLICATIONS No standard application form. Applications in writing may be submitted at any time with latest accounts. Regret no reply to unsuccessful applicants

CORRESPONDENT Duncan C Macdiarmid, CA, Director, The Bernard Sunley Charitable Foundation, 53 Grosvenor Street, London W1X 9FH

CLASSIFICATIONS
- Children and youth – general
- Centres, clubs and institutes
- Youth organisations (eg Guides, Scouts, YWCA etc)

C.C. NO 213362 **ESTABLISHED** 1960

■ Adrienne & Leslie Sussman Charitable Trust

OBJECTS General charitable purposes

RESTRICTIONS Registered charities only – not local branches of national charities, except with London Borough of Barnet

FINANCES
- Year 1993
- Income £33,409

TRUSTEES L Sussman, Mrs A H Sussman, M Paisner

CORRESPONDENT Mrs A H Sussman, 25 Tillingbourne Gardens, London NW3 3JJ

CLASSIFICATIONS
- Children and youth – general

C.C. NO 274955 **ESTABLISHED** 1977

■ Swale Charity Trust

OBJECTS General charitable purposes

BENEFICIAL AREA Kent

FINANCES
- Year 1992
- Grants £4,037
- Income £25,560
- Assets £74,027

TRUSTEES A Smith, Mrs V Smith

CORRESPONDENT A Smith, 30 School Lane, Bapchild, Sittingbourne, Kent ME9 9NL

CLASSIFICATIONS
- Development of character

C.C. NO 298925 **ESTABLISHED** 1988

■ The Charles Sykes Trust (known as The Charles and Elsie Sykes Trust)

OBJECTS General charitable purposes

POLICY OF TRUSTEES Support of registered charities mainly connected with the aged, young children, persons suffering from disabilities and medical research

TYPE OF GRANT Donations in cash, usually one-off for a specific project or part thereof

TYPE OF BENEFICIARY Registered charities only

RESTRICTIONS No grants to individuals or for their benefit

BENEFICIAL AREA UK and occasionally overseas

FINANCES
- Year 1993
- Grants £333,600
- Income £312,000
- Assets £7,484,000

TRUSTEES H T Bartrop, Mrs A E Barker, Mrs G M Dance, J Horrocks, Dr D M Moore, M G H Garnett, the Lord Mountgarret, G T Tate, J Ward

SUBMISSION OF APPLICATIONS To the correspondent, full details and audited accounts must be supplied. Acknowledgements given if sae supplied

CORRESPONDENT The Hon Secretary, The Charles Sykes Trust, Queensgate House, 23 North Park Road, Harrogate, North Yorkshire HG1 5PF

CLASSIFICATIONS
- Children and youth – general
- Centres, clubs and institutes
- Community groups
- Counselling (inc helplines)

Symons

- Holidays
- Homes and hostels
- Special classes
- Youth organisations (eg Guides, Scouts, YWCA etc)

C.C. NO 206926 **ESTABLISHED** 1954

■ The Stella Symons Charitable Trust

OBJECTS General charitable purposes

POLICY OF TRUSTEES To provide assistance to organisations operating in fields where specific identifiable needs can be shown and which are in the opinion of the Trustees not adequately catered for or likely to have large scale popular appeal

TYPE OF GRANT Outright gifts and larger sums on loan on beneficial terms

TYPE OF BENEFICIARY Not individuals or politically biased organisations

RESTRICTIONS The Trustees do not normally favour projects which substitute the statutory obligations of the state or projects which in their opinion should be commercially viable operations per se

BENEFICIAL AREA UK and international projects with some funds reserved for projects and organisations local to Shipston on Stour

FINANCES
- Year 1995
- Grants £37,954
- Income £49,418
- Assets £668,633

TRUSTEES M E Bosley, J S S Bosley, K A Willis

NOTES The Trustees will consider all applications submitted but regretably will not be able to support all that they might wish to

SUBMISSION OF APPLICATIONS By post to address below with no follow up please

CORRESPONDENT J S S Bosley, 20 Mill Street, Shipston on Stour, Warwickshire

CLASSIFICATIONS
- Children and youth – general
- Holidays

C.C. NO 259638 **ESTABLISHED** 1968

■ TSB Foundation for England and Wales

OBJECTS Education and training, medical and scientific research, social and community needs

POLICY OF TRUSTEES Generally: (a) Education and training: employment training for disadvantaged and disabled people, promotion of life skills among young people, and enhancing educational opportunities for all ages. (b) Scientific and medical research: underfunded fields of research, particularly related to maladies which prevent a significant percentage of the population from remaining in work. Current areas of support are mental health and ageing research projects. A pro-active approach is adopted and unsolicited appeals are unlikely to be successful.(c) Social and community needs: to assist disadvantaged and disabled people to play a full part in the community through support of community centres, crisis and advice centres, care for disabled and elderly people, health, civic responsibilities, cultural enrichment (with direct benefit to disadvantaged and disabled people). Current areas of particular focus are: employment training (in particular of disadvantaged or disabled people); crime prevention; homelessness (in particular helping homeless people back into mainstream society); carers; promotion of volunteering; parenting. Particular emphasis will be given to the needs of young people and rural communities

TYPE OF GRANT Usually one-off for a specific project

TYPE OF BENEFICIARY Registered charities

RESTRICTIONS Registered charities only. Applications from individuals, including students, are ineligible. The following are ineligible: animals, overseas, geographic/scenic, mainstream schools, colleges or universities, hospitals/medical centres (capital costs, including building appeals, running costs), sponsorship, fabric appeals for places of worship, promotion of religion, endowment funds, fundraising, general appeals, organisations redistributing funds to charities or individuals, loans or business finance, restoration of buildings, expeditions or overseas travel

BENEFICIAL AREA England and Wales

SAMPLE GRANTS £10,000 to Who Cares? towards the employment development project for young people in care (spread over two years) £2,000 to Cormet Youth and Community Club, Wigan to purchase mountain bikes for youth club £500 to Friends of Highfield House Children's Centre, Barnstaple towards purchase of outdoor equipment for the centre for disabled children

FINANCES
- Year 1995
- Grants £2,000,849
- Income £2,033,784
- Assets £367,799

TRUSTEES The Duke of Westminster (Chairman), Mrs Joanna Foster (Deputy Chairman), P D Allen, Lord Edward FitzRoy, D A Hinton, Lady Mary Holborow, J P R Holt, Dr C M Kenrick, J W Robertson, R D Wood, M W E Thompson, L E Linaker

PUBLICATIONS Annual Report and Accounts, brochure, guidelines leaflet

NOTES Restrictions: an exception is made to the restriction against mainstream educational establishments where the project is specifically to benefit disabled students

SUBMISSION OF APPLICATIONS Application forms are available from the Foundation's office and can be returned at any time. The Foundation only supports charities recognised by the Charity Commissioners or to which the Inland Revenue have accorded charitable status

CORRESPONDENT Mrs Kathleen Duncan, Director General, PO Box 140, St Mary's Court, 100 Lower Thames Street, London EC3R 6HX

CLASSIFICATIONS
- Children and youth – general
- Advancement in life
- Centres, clubs and institutes
- Community groups
- Day centres and nurseries
- Development of character
- Counselling (inc helplines)
- Youth organisations (eg Guides, Scouts, YWCA etc)

C.C. NO 327114   **ESTABLISHED** 1986

■ TSB Foundation for Scotland

OBJECTS General charitable purposes

POLICY OF TRUSTEES The Foundation has for its objects: 'General charitable purposes, but primarily to advance education and training, to advance scientific or medical research and to promote the provision of facilities in the interests of social and community welfare'

TYPE OF GRANT Grants are made to local charities in Scotland and may be either one-off or on a recurrent basis. The Trustees are reluctant to assist bodies with routine annual running costs and salary costs

TYPE OF BENEFICIARY Registered charities with an emphasis on community-based groups

RESTRICTIONS Established charities only. No grants to individuals, core funding or general appeals

BENEFICIAL AREA Scotland

SAMPLE GRANTS £46,000 to Princes Trust to fund youth crime initiative
£7,400 to Scottish National Council of YMCAs to assist with homeless project in Perth
£3,500 to St Andrews University Voluntary Service for new minibus
£2,000 to Wick Youth Club for activity equipment
£2,000 to Compass Outdoor Centre towards new minibus

FINANCES
- Year 1995
- Grants £600,000
- Income £550,000

TRUSTEES Dame Mary Corsar (Chairman), J W Cradock, P C Paisley, J D M Robertson, C Donald, A Denholm, R G E Peggie

SUBMISSION OF APPLICATIONS Application forms available on request from the Secretary. Trustees meet quarterly in January, April, July and October. Applications are required to be submitted at least six weeks in advance of these meetings

CORRESPONDENT A S Muirhead, Secretary, Henry Duncan House, 120 George Street, Edinburgh EH2 4TS

CLASSIFICATIONS
- Adoption/fostering
- Advancement in life
- Adventure centres and playgrounds
- Centres, clubs and institutes
- Community groups
- Day centres and nurseries
- Development of character
- Counselling (inc helplines)
- Holidays
- Homes and hostels
- Special needs housing
- Special classes
- Youth organisations (eg Guides, Scouts, YWCA etc)
- Children and violence (inc abuse)

C.C. NO CR 43309   **ESTABLISHED** 1986

■ Alfred Tankel Charitable Trust

OBJECTS General charitable purposes

POLICY OF TRUSTEES No grants to bodies acting in a fund raising capacity only

TYPE OF GRANT One-off

TYPE OF BENEFICIARY Welfare organisations directly involved in welfare work

RESTRICTIONS No grants to individuals

BENEFICIAL AREA Southern England only

FINANCES
- Year 1995
- Grants £50,103
- Income £38,665

TRUSTEES A Tankel, Mrs B R Tankel

SUBMISSION OF APPLICATIONS No application form. No specific dates for grants

CORRESPONDENT AMP House, 2 Cyprus Road, London N3 3LE

CLASSIFICATIONS
- Counselling (inc helplines)

C.C. NO 275747   **ESTABLISHED** 1977

■ A R Taylor Charitable Trust

OBJECTS The relief of poverty, the advancement of religion, the advancement of education and general charitable purposes

POLICY OF TRUSTEES Preference is given to charities in which the Trustees have special interest, knowledge or association. Funds are fully committed or allocated

TYPE OF GRANT Both one-off and recurrent grants are made. There is no formal limit to the length of time recurrent grants are made for

RESTRICTIONS Registered charities or similar bodies only. Applications from individuals for assistance with education or personal projects for themselves or members of their family will not be considered

BENEFICIAL AREA UK, with preference for Hampshire and Isle of Wight

FINANCES
- Year 1994
- Grants £34,070
- Income £35,593
- Assets £896,000

TRUSTEES A R Taylor, Mrs E J Taylor

Taylor

SUBMISSION OF APPLICATIONS Applications may be made at any time but will only be considered periodically. The trust does not use an application form. Unsuccessful applications will generally not be acknowledged

CORRESPONDENT J Bristol, Birketts, Solicitors, 24–26 Museum Street, Ipswich, Suffolk IP1 1HZ

CLASSIFICATIONS
- Children and youth – general
- Centres, clubs and institutes

C.C. NO 275560   **ESTABLISHED** 1978

■ A P Taylor Fund

OBJECTS For the use of the inhabitants of the Parishes of Hayes and Harlington (as they existed on 9.1.53) without distinction of political, religious or other opinion

TYPE OF BENEFICIARY Recreation and leisure

BENEFICIAL AREA Hayes and Harlington

FINANCES
- Year 1994
- Income £58,500

TRUSTEES Six various

CORRESPONDENT P King, Secretary/Treasurer, 10 Chestnut Close, Hayes, Middlesex UB3 1JF

CLASSIFICATIONS
- Youth organisations (eg Guides, Scouts, YWCA etc)

C.C. NO 260741   **ESTABLISHED** 1969

■ Tesco Charity Trust

OBJECTS General charitable purposes

POLICY OF TRUSTEES Main areas of interest are: the Arts, sporting facilities, the promotion of health and care for the disabled, education and support for work in the community

FINANCES
- Year 1991
- Assets £678,257
- Income £129,788

TRUSTEES Sir Ian MacLaurin, R S Ager, J Eastoe, P Stephens, D C Tuffin

CORRESPONDENT J A Eastoe, Tesco House, Delamare Road, Cheshunt, Herts EN8 9SL

CLASSIFICATIONS
- Community groups

C.C. NO 297126   **ESTABLISHED** 1987

■ The Margaret Thatcher Charitable Trust

OBJECTS General charitable purposes

POLICY OF TRUSTEES The Trustees' policy is to consider applications from charitable institutions and to make donations to such institutions as the Trustees think fit. Such institutions may include those concerned with youth causes

TYPE OF GRANT Charitable donations

TYPE OF BENEFICIARY Charitable organisations involved in national or local projects

BENEFICIAL AREA UK and overseas

SAMPLE GRANTS £1,000 to NSPCC
£1,000 to RSSPCC
£1,000 to NCH Action for Children
£1,000 to Wishing Well Appeal (Great Ormond Street Hospital)
£500 to Foundation for Study of Infant Deaths

FINANCES
- Year 1992
- Grants £36,300
- Income £57,887
- Assets £672,584

TRUSTEES The Baroness Thatcher, Mrs C M Crawford, P J Gee

NOTES Please note that the details given under the heading Finances do not relate solely to youth causes but represent the total level of finances of the Trust

SUBMISSION OF APPLICATIONS No specific date. No application form

CORRESPONDENT Mrs C M Crawford, 73 Chester Square, London SW1W 1DU

CLASSIFICATIONS
- Children and youth – general

C.C. NO 800225   **ESTABLISHED** 1988

■ The Thorpe Charity Trust

OBJECTS General charitable purposes

POLICY OF TRUSTEES The Trustees favour Roman Catholic projects, particularly those with minimum administration expenses and where a grant of hundreds of pounds will have a significant impact

TYPE OF GRANT Cash sums not normally exceeding £500, annual or one-off

TYPE OF BENEFICIARY See policy above

RESTRICTIONS (a) Medical research. (b) Construction or development of buildings unless for Roman Catholic purposes. (c) Individual student applications, unless vouched by Roman Catholic authority

BENEFICIAL AREA United Kingdom, Third World Countries

SAMPLE GRANTS £500 to Let the Children Live
£500 to St Omer's Handicapped Children's Trust
£300 to Hull University Chaplaincy

FINANCES
- Year 1995
- Grants £10,250
- Income £11,000
- Assets £170,000

TRUSTEES C M Thorpe, P D P Thorpe, Mrs M Legg, M P Thorpe

SUBMISSION OF APPLICATIONS In writing, preferably October/November, including clear details of the need and an outline budget. Applications with stamped addressed envelopes will be acknowledged. Grant meetings held annually December/January

CORRESPONDENT C M Thorpe, 17 Valley Bridge Parade, Scarborough, North Yorks YO11 2JX

CLASSIFICATIONS
- Counselling (inc helplines)
- Holidays

C.C. NO 282068   **ESTABLISHED** 1973

Mrs R P Tindall's Charitable Trust

OBJECTS General charitable purposes

POLICY OF TRUSTEES The charity is primarily used for local religious, welfare and educational purposes

TYPE OF GRANT Financial range £10–£1,000 (average £200)

TYPE OF BENEFICIARY Individuals in need; institutions which help them, also religious welfare and educational charities

RESTRICTIONS No personal applications

BENEFICIAL AREA Wiltshire and Dorset

SAMPLE GRANTS £1,000 to British Federation of Young Choirs Concert in Salisbury Cathedral

FINANCES
- Year 1995
- Grants £8,500
- Income £9,300
- Assets £142,000

TRUSTEES Mrs R P Tindall, Rev Canon F C Tindall, D P Herbert, M R F Newman, G Fletcher, Mrs A C Philp

CORRESPONDENT Messrs Fletcher & Partners, Crown Chambers, Bridge Street, Salisbury SP1 2LZ

CLASSIFICATIONS
- Youth organisations (eg Guides, Scouts, YWCA etc)

C.C. NO 250558   **ESTABLISHED** 1966

Tollemache (Buckminster) Charitable Trust

OBJECTS General charitable purposes

POLICY OF TRUSTEES Reviewed regularly

TYPE OF BENEFICIARY To registered charities – not to individuals

RESTRICTIONS Donations to registered charities only

BENEFICIAL AREA UK

FINANCES
- Year 1995
- Grants £18,000
- Income £18,000
- Assets £160,000

TRUSTEES Sir Lyonel Tollemache, Bt, H M Neal, W H G Wilks

SUBMISSION OF APPLICATIONS To Secretary, no acknowledgements sent

CORRESPONDENT The Secretary, Tollemache (Buckminster) Charitable Trust, Estate Office, Buckminster, Near Grantham, Lincolnshire NG33 5SD

CLASSIFICATIONS
- Children and youth – general

C.C. NO 271795   **ESTABLISHED** 1976

The Torquay Charities

OBJECTS To apply its income for or towards such charitable purpose or purposes in the (former) Borough of Torquay as the Executive Committee shall from time to time in its discretion select

POLICY OF TRUSTEES Preference given to organisations rather than individuals

TYPE OF GRANT Pecuniary

TYPE OF BENEFICIARY Charitable institution

RESTRICTIONS The Trustees cannot make grants to persons or organisations not connected with Torquay

BENEFICIAL AREA Former municipal Borough of Torquay: now part of the Borough of Torbay

FINANCES
- Year 1994
- Grants £3,020
- Income £3,577
- Assets £46,604

TRUSTEES S Adams, JP (Chairman), M Cox, JP, Mrs A D Almy, JP, P Lansdell, R D Newman (Hon Secretary)

SUBMISSION OF APPLICATIONS Application forms and further information are obtainable from the Hon Secretary, to whom applications should be submitted by the end of April for consideration by the Trustees at the beginning of June of each year. Applications should be supported if possible by recent accounts; if these are not available the Trustees will require such details as may be available regarding the applicant's finances or proposed finances

CORRESPONDENT R D Newman, Hon Secretary, The Torquay Charities, 2 Vaughan Parade, Torquay, Devon TQ2 5EF

CLASSIFICATIONS
- Children and youth – general

C.C. NO 215537   **ESTABLISHED** 1955

The Fred Towler Charity Trust

OBJECTS General charitable purposes, primarily sick relief and aged and holidays for residents in the Diocese of Bradford

POLICY OF TRUSTEES To provide holidays for aged (one-third of income). To support charities devoted to sick, youth and aged (two-thirds of income)

TYPE OF GRANT For recurrent operational expenses

TYPE OF BENEFICIARY Local charities or local branches of national societies

RESTRICTIONS Gifts are to local charities or local branches of national societies; no grants to individuals

BENEFICIAL AREA Bradford

FINANCES
- Year 1994
- Grants £35,397
- Income £34,425
- Assets £550,747

TRUSTEES Ten professional & business men in Bradford District

SUBMISSION OF APPLICATIONS April and October annually

CORRESPONDENT P G Meredith, Clark Whitehill Josolyne, Chartered Accountants, Cheapside Chambers, 43 Cheapside, Bradford BD1 4HP

CLASSIFICATIONS
- Children and youth – general

C.C. NO 225026   **ESTABLISHED** 1939

Troughton's

■ Mrs S H Troughton's Charity Trust

OBJECTS General charitable purposes

POLICY OF TRUSTEES Applications for grants will only be acknowledged if a donation is to be sent.

TYPE OF GRANT Pecuniary

TYPE OF BENEFICIARY Registered charities only

RESTRICTIONS No applications from individuals will be considered. Registered charities only

BENEFICIAL AREA Great Britain and Northern Ireland

FINANCES
- Year 1992
- Grants £5,434
- Income £8,897
- Assets £133,182

TRUSTEES The Dickinson Trust Limited

SUBMISSION OF APPLICATIONS Appeal letters should be sent to the correspondent

CORRESPONDENT The Secretary, The Dickinson Trust Limited, Pollen House, 10–12 Cork Street, London W1X 1PD

CLASSIFICATIONS
- Children and youth – general
- Advancement in life
- Adventure centres and playgrounds
- Centres, clubs and institutes
- Day centres and nurseries
- Development of character
- Youth organisations (eg Guides, Scouts, YWCA etc)

C.C. NO 265957   **ESTABLISHED** 1972

■ The Truemark Trust

OBJECTS General charitable purposes

POLICY OF TRUSTEES Small organisations more likely to be favoured. Innovatory projects preferred. Current main areas of interest are the disabled, the elderly and those otherwise disadvantaged and include counselling and community support groups in areas of unrest or deprivation, alternative health projects

TYPE OF GRANT Usually one-off for a specific project or part of a project. Core funding and/or salaries rarely considered. Average size of grant £1,000

TYPE OF BENEFICIARY Registered charities working in the areas outlined under Policy, with preference for neighbourhood-based community projects and innovatory work with less popular groups

RESTRICTIONS Registered charities only. Applications from individuals, including students, are ineligible. No grants are made in response to general appeals from large national organisations. Grants are seldom available for churches or church buildings or for scientific or medical research projects

BENEFICIAL AREA UK

SAMPLE GRANTS £1,000 to Care for Handicapped Children
£1,000 to Edge Hill youth club, Liverpool
£1,000 to Pub with no Beer, Lurgan, Northern Ireland
£500 to Camping Holidays for Inner City Kids
£500 to Larche Adventure Playground

FINANCES
- Year 1994
- Grants £92,860
- Income £140,300
- Assets £1,588,589

TRUSTEES Sir William Wood (Senior Trustee), Michael Collishaw, Michael Meakin, Sir Thomas Lucas, Alan Thompson, Richard Wolfe

SUBMISSION OF APPLICATIONS At any time. Trustees meet four times a year. Applications should include clear details of the need the intended project is designed to meet plus an outline budget and the most recent available annual accounts of the charity. Only applications from eligible bodies are acknowledged

CORRESPONDENT Mrs W A Collett, PO Box 2, Liss, Hants GU33 7YW

CLASSIFICATIONS
- Children and youth – general
- Adventure centres and playgrounds
- Centres, clubs and institutes
- Counselling (inc helplines)
- Holidays

C.C. NO 265855   **ESTABLISHED** 1973

■ Trust for London

OBJECTS The objects of the Trust are to benefit voluntary organisations with charitable purposes in London

POLICY OF TRUSTEES The trust targets small local community based organisations with charitable purposes, which are independent of larger bodies. 'Small' is defined as being entirely volunteer or membership based or with no more than the equivalent of two full-time paid staff. The trust is guided by five factors: (a) to have an initiating and pro-active role, rather than wait for applications (b) to seek to ensure that its grants have a distinctive and particular impact (c) to be accessible to small groups (d) to work to stated priorities (e) to recognise the value of practical advice and support. Priorities: (i) Continuation Grants. A major priority is to consider applications from some of the organisations previously grant aided with revenue costs by the trust. Further grants will not be given automatically, but Field Officers will discuss with organisations what is required to continue their work. The trust remains concerned to support women's groups, black and ethnic minority women's groups and black and ethnic minority organisations. (ii) New Priorities. Applications will be considered from small groups in any London borough which fall within the following categories: self-help groups with special emphasis on women's groups; supplementary schools; work with disabled people, children or adults, in the black and ethnic minority; communities; outreach work with women and children in refugee communities

TYPE OF GRANT The trust's grants will range from £250 to £10,000 for capital costs or for one year's revenue costs. Revenue grants may also be given over a two or three-year period though normally with a reducing level of grant

TYPE OF BENEFICIARY The type of beneficiary is small voluntary organisations with charitable purposes. 'Small' is defined as meaning an organisation having no more than the equivalent of two full-time paid staff

RESTRICTIONS Grants will not be given for major capital schemes, in response to general appeals, to individuals, for research, as part of a full time salary, to replace cuts by statutory authorities, or to umbrella bodies to distribute, to organisations which have received grants from the City Parochial Foundation

BENEFICIAL AREA The area of benefit is the 32 London Boroughs and the City of London

SAMPLE GRANTS £20,000, over two years, to Notting Hill Youth Project towards cost of a coordinator
£9,000 to Al-Noor Youth Association towards tutors' fees and equipment
£7,632 to Camden Young Women's Centre towards running costs and a sessional worker
£5,000 to Sutton Young People's Association towards cost of a coordinator
£5,000 to Turkish Youth and Community Association towards running costs

FINANCES
- **Year** 1994
- **Grants** £926,132
- **Income** £1,011,798
- **Assets** £11,308,016

TRUSTEES The Trustees are the same 21 Trustees as are responsible for the City Parochial Foundation which is the Trustee of the Trust for London

PUBLICATIONS Publications of the trust are the Annual Report and the leaflet giving guidelines for applicants

SUBMISSION OF APPLICATIONS All organisations are encouraged to talk with the staff of the trust before finalising any application. Applicants are required to fill in an application form and provide the documents requested on it. Staff may well have questions to ask and may usually visit the organisation. Only when the staff member responsible regards the application process as completed will it be eligible to be considered. An organisation may make only one application in any 12 month period. Deadlines are: 31st January for March meeting, 30th April for June meeting, 31st July for September meeting and 15th October for December meeting

CORRESPONDENT Timothy Cook, Secretary, 6 Middle Street, London EC1A 7PH

CLASSIFICATIONS
- Children and youth – general

C.C. NO 294708　　**ESTABLISHED** 1986

■ The Sir Mark and Lady Turner Charitable Settlement

OBJECTS General charitable purposes

POLICY OF TRUSTEES Principally small local charities preferred concerned with children/youth, aged, medical research, the under-privileged and those serving the community in the Highgate area

TYPE OF GRANT Established regular donations, although once and for all donations are considered

TYPE OF BENEFICIARY Children/youth, aged, medical research and the under-privileged

RESTRICTIONS Due to the pressure on their limited funds, the Trustees regret that they must restrict consideration of appeals to those which are concerned with the welfare of children/youth, aged, medical research and the under-privileged, together with those charities serving in the local community in the London Borough of Highgate

BENEFICIAL AREA London but some national in exceptional circumstances

FINANCES
- **Year** 1992
- **Grants** £14,450
- **Income** £11,840
- **Assets** £89,939

TRUSTEES Kleinwort Benson Trustees Limited

NOTES It is not the Trustees policy to acknowledge appeals and applicants will only receive a reply if their appeal has been successful

SUBMISSION OF APPLICATIONS In writing to correspondent and considered half-yearly by Trustees

CORRESPONDENT Kleinwort Benson Trustees Ltd, PO Box 191, 10 Fenchurch Street, London EC3M 3LB

CLASSIFICATIONS
- Children and youth – general
- Centres, clubs and institutes
- Community groups
- Day centres and nurseries

C.C. NO 264994　　**ESTABLISHED** 1972

■ The Douglas Turner Charitable Trust

OBJECTS General charitable purposes

RESTRICTIONS Registered charities only

BENEFICIAL AREA Mainly Birmingham and West Midlands

FINANCES
- **Year** 1994
- **Grants** £345,008
- **Income** £352,472
- **Assets** £8,102,028

TRUSTEES R D Turner, W S Ellis, J R Clemishaw, D P Pearson

NOTES The Trust is presently heavily committed and new applications can only be considered from the Birmingham area

CORRESPONDENT J E Dyke, 1 The Yew Trees, High Street, Henley-in-Arden, Solihull B95 5BN

CLASSIFICATIONS
- Children and youth – general
- Adoption/fostering
- Advancement in life
- Centres, clubs and institutes
- Community groups
- Development of character
- Special classes
- Youth organisations (eg Guides, Scouts, YWCA etc)

C.C. NO 227892　　**ESTABLISHED** 1964

■ The R D Turner Charitable Trust

OBJECTS General charitable purposes

BENEFICIAL AREA Birmingham

FINANCES
- **Year** 1994
- **Grants** £46,700
- **Income** £40,943
- **Assets** £926,820

TRUSTEES W S Ellis, J R Clemishaw, D P Pearson

NOTES The Trust has for many years been fully committed to existing beneficiaries

SUBMISSION OF APPLICATIONS The Trust is at present fully committed

CORRESPONDENT J E Dyke, 1 The Yew Trees, High Street, Henley-in-Arden, Solihull B95 5BN

Turner

Alphabetical register of grant making charitable trusts

CLASSIFICATIONS
- Development of character
- Youth organisations (eg Guides, Scouts, YWCA etc)

C.C. NO 263556   **ESTABLISHED** 1971

■ G J W Turner Trust

OBJECTS General charitable purposes

POLICY OF TRUSTEES To pay out the same general level of grants and accumulate the balance for major projects

TYPE OF GRANT Cash donations. Recurrent

TYPE OF BENEFICIARY UK registered charities

RESTRICTIONS No grants to individuals

BENEFICIAL AREA West Midlands, but worldwide in exceptional circumstances

FINANCES
- **Year** 1994
- **Grants** £7,300
- **Income** £8,155
- **Assets** £222,816

TRUSTEES D P Pearson, A G D Inglis, W I Jollie

SUBMISSION OF APPLICATIONS To the correspondent at the above address prior to the annual meeting in July

CORRESPONDENT W I Jollie, The G J W Turner Trust, Messrs Eversheds, 10 Newhall Street, Birmingham B3 3LX

CLASSIFICATIONS
- Children and youth – general

C.C. NO 258615   **ESTABLISHED** 1969

■ The Edwin Henry Tutty Charitable Trust

OBJECTS General charitable purposes

TYPE OF BENEFICIARY Registered charities

RESTRICTIONS Do not consider individuals

FINANCES
- **Year** 1991
- **Income** £23,478

TRUSTEES E H Tutty and two others

CORRESPONDENT E H Tutty, Richmond, West Drive, Sudbrooke, Lincoln LN2 2RA

CLASSIFICATIONS
- Youth organisations (eg Guides, Scouts, YWCA etc)

C.C. NO 253124   **ESTABLISHED** 1967

■ The 29th May 1961 Charity

OBJECTS General charitable purposes

POLICY OF TRUSTEES Preference for long term projects to which there are a number of existing commitments. No great scope at present for the inclusion of additional beneficiaries

TYPE OF GRANT Grants are made annually in March, June, September and December. The minimum grant is usually £500. Most grants are made on a recurring basis

TYPE OF BENEFICIARY Funds are mainly made available to charities involving relief of the ill; the support of youth and the underprivileged and help for the aged. Grants to individuals cannot be made

RESTRICTIONS Grants may not be made to individuals

BENEFICIAL AREA UK, with preference to West Midlands region, also Coventry area in particular

FINANCES
- **Year** 1995
- **Grants** £2,967,000
- **Income** £3,022,000
- **Assets** £57,628,000

TRUSTEES V E Treves, J R Cattell, P Varney, A J Mead

NOTES Contact name Miss Fiona Brown

SUBMISSION OF APPLICATIONS To the correspondent enclosing balance sheets or other financial information. The charity has no application forms and applications are not usually acknowledged

CORRESPONDENT Messrs Macfarlanes, 10 Norwich Street, London EC4A 1BD

CLASSIFICATIONS
- Children and youth – general
- Adoption/fostering
- Advancement in life
- Adventure centres and playgrounds
- Centres, clubs and institutes
- Community groups
- Day centres and nurseries
- Development of character
- Counselling (inc helplines)
- Holidays
- Homes and hostels
- Youth organisations (eg Guides, Scouts, YWCA etc)

C.C. NO 200198   **ESTABLISHED** 1961

■ Tyne & Wear Foundation

OBJECTS General charitable purposes in Tyne & Wear and Northumberland

POLICY OF TRUSTEES To help those in greatest need. Projects that help communities and individuals who are disadvantaged because of poverty, poor health or disability are of particular interest. To encourage ordinary people to be involved in developing and managing their own affairs. To make grants to voluntary groups for training, advice and consultancy. To foster a sense of pride and achievement through self-help and voluntary effort. Applications from groups which have the potential for first class work and which may influence others in their field will be selected. At present there is limited scope for new initiatives supported by the Foundation to go on to obtain support from statutory funders. We are therefore willing to contribute, for a limited period, to the existing work of organisations which are undertaking exceptionally valuable work. We will not replace statutory funding but recognise that there may be ways in which groups can be helped to reorganise their activities so as to operate more cost effectively. We want to use our resources to help overcome any possible discrimination against, for example, women, the disabled or ethnic minorities, in the targeting of help from charitable groups and in the way the charities themselves are run. In discussing applications, we want to make sure that proposals can be of benefit to whoever needs help and that, if appropriate, funding includes such items as creches and translations

TYPE OF GRANT Mostly single grants but some grants recurrent for up to three years

TYPE OF BENEFICIARY Voluntary organisations

RESTRICTIONS The Foundation does not make grants for capital projects – such as building work – or for equipment or purely academic research. Grants to individuals are excluded. It does not support major circular appeals, holiday projects, or to make grants for work which has already taken place. Its interests lie within the broad heading of 'social welfare'. Applications relating to the arts and the environment will be considered only if they directly benefit people in high social need

BENEFICIAL AREA Tyne & Wear and Northumberland

SAMPLE GRANTS £15,000 over two years to the Oxclose Young People's Project
£5,500 to the Commercial Road Youth and Community Project
£4,000 to the Bangladeshi Youth Project
£3,100 to the YMCA Ashington
£2,000 to the Teen Bar Project, Morpeth

FINANCES
- Year 1994
- Grants £809,500
- Income £964,828
- Assets £3,325,250

TRUSTEES Directors: Richard Harbottle (Chair), Carole Howells (Vice Chair), Alan Wardropper (Treasurer), Sir Tom Cowie, David Francis, Sylvia Murray, Pauline Nelson, John Squires, Anthony Tompkins, Mike Worthington, Brian Latham, Grigor McClelland, Alastair Balls, Pummi Mattu, Alma Caldwell, Tony Winder, Alan Share

PUBLICATIONS Annual Review. Guidance notes for applicants

SUBMISSION OF APPLICATIONS Major grants over £2,000 are awarded bi-annually in the spring and autumn. Small grants under £2,000 are considered quarterly. Informal enquires can be made to the Assistant Director, Carol Meredith

CORRESPONDENT Carol Meredith, Assistant Director, Tyne & Wear Foundation, MEA House, Ellison Place, Newcastle upon Tyne NE1 8XS

CLASSIFICATIONS
- Adoption/fostering
- Advancement in life
- Adventure centres and playgrounds
- Centres, clubs and institutes
- Community groups
- Day centres and nurseries
- Counselling (inc helplines)
- Special needs housing

C.C. NO 700510   **ESTABLISHED** 1988

■ Bernard Van Leer Foundation UK Trust

OBJECTS Charitable purposes specifically linked to experimental work in the field of education of disadvantaged children

POLICY OF TRUSTEES To enable children (aged 0–7) who are impeded through the social and cultural inadequacy of their background and/or environment nevertheless to achieve the greatest possible realisation of their innate potential

TYPE OF GRANT Donations towards recurrent support for specifically agreed experimental periods

TYPE OF BENEFICIARY Institutions such as educational authorities, universities, and private bodies clearly engaged in activities relevant to the objects of the Trust. Does not make grants to individuals or to general appeals

RESTRICTIONS No contributions are made to general appeals, the capital or recurrent costs of on-going work, nor for study or travel

BENEFICIAL AREA UK and overseas

FINANCES
- Year 1995
- Grants £5,416,268
- Income £4,618,700

TRUSTEES The Royal Bank of Scotland plc

PUBLICATIONS Newsletter of the Bernard van Leer Foundation (periodical)

SUBMISSION OF APPLICATIONS At any time

CORRESPONDENT The Manager, The Royal Bank of Scotland plc, Private Trust & Taxation, 2 Festival Square, Edinburgh EH3 9SU

CLASSIFICATIONS
- Advancement in life
- Community groups

C.C. NO 265186   **ESTABLISHED** 1972

■ The Vec Acorn Trust

OBJECTS General charitable purposes

POLICY OF TRUSTEES To help young people between the ages of 16 and 25 who are disadvantaged either medically or as a result of the environment in which they live. To assist in developing their potential in skills which otherwise they may not be able to achieve. To give support to projects which reach a number of people but with the emphasis on self help

TYPE OF GRANT The Trustees are prepared to consider applications on their merit as to whether they involve single or recurring grants

TYPE OF BENEFICIARY The Trustees prefer to support projects not attached to already well established charitable organisations and are willing to consider joint ventures

RESTRICTIONS Grants are made only to medically or environmentally disadvantaged young people

BENEFICIAL AREA South West Hampshire

Victoria

SAMPLE GRANTS £19,000 annually for three years to It's Your Choice towards salary/costs for information and advice worker providing accessible, up-to-date relevant information for young people
£10,000 annually for three years to Minstead Training Project towards salary for manager of landscape gardening and maintenance sheltered work scheme
£5,000 annually for three years to Artsway, a centre for contemporary and visual arts in the New Forest
£5,000 to Hampshire Foundation for Young Musicians to sponsor Hampshire Award Scheme for students in South West Hampshire
£1,000 to 18-year-old student due to family problems paying rent for sheltered accommodation until end of term

FINANCES
- **Year** 1993
- **Income** £60,000
- **Assets** £1,200,000

TRUSTEES Mrs V E Coates, K Newman, MBE, D A Rule, ACIB, Mrs P L Youngman

SUBMISSION OF APPLICATIONS The Trustees meet quarterly

CORRESPONDENT Mrs S Leary, Secretary to the Trustees, Pennington Chase, Lower Pennington Lane, Lymington, Hants SO41 8AN

CLASSIFICATIONS
- Children and youth – general
- Advancement in life
- Centres, clubs and institutes
- Community groups
- Development of character
- Youth organisations (eg Guides, Scouts, YWCA etc)

C.C. NO 1002997   **ESTABLISHED** 1991

■ Queen Victoria & Johnson Memorial Trust

OBJECTS Income to be applied only for the benefit of sick, poor persons resident in the City of Sheffield

POLICY OF TRUSTEES Grants are generally made to charities or groups rather than individuals

TYPE OF GRANT Grants made: (a) for capital purposes, (b) for special purposes, (c) for revenue purposes

TYPE OF BENEFICIARY Local organisations

RESTRICTIONS As for Objects

BENEFICIAL AREA City of Sheffield

FINANCES
- **Year** 1995
- **Income** £11,635
- **Grants** £9,075
- **Assets** £128,423

TRUSTEES Mrs J A Lee, Mrs J Tyzack, Mrs S E Wilson, Mrs R Viner, A E H Roberts, Mrs P Sims, Mrs P Heath, R D Cheetham, A J Riddle, Miss E Murray

NOTES 26 grants made in 1995

SUBMISSION OF APPLICATIONS In writing, to reach the Clerk by the following dates: 31 January, 30 April, 31 July and 31 October

CORRESPONDENT R H M Plews, FCA, Clerk to the Trustees, Queen Victoria & Johnson Memorial Trust, Knowle House, 4 Norfolk Park Road, Sheffield S2 3QE

CLASSIFICATIONS
- Children and youth – general
- Community groups

C.C. NO 224263   **ESTABLISHED** 1952

Wakeham

■ The Charity of Thomas Wade & Others

OBJECTS General charitable purposes

POLICY OF TRUSTEES Provision of open spaces, allotments, playing fields, facilities for recreation, amusement, entertainment, including establishment of Community and Youth Centres and for the general social intercourse of inhabitants of the City of Leeds; or grants to any authority, association or body providing such facilities

TYPE OF GRANT Non-recurring capital costs, start-ups

TYPE OF BENEFICIARY Mainly youth organisations and community centres. Tend not to support schools or medicine or health orientated bodies. Past beneficiaries include YMCA and YWCA, Age Concern, Central Yorks Scout Council, Hunslet Boys' Club, Leeds Childrens' Holiday Camps Association, South Leeds Youth Theatre

RESTRICTIONS Applications for grants to individuals, medical research, educational bursaries, sports organisations which are not registered charities, and schemes which are the financial responsibility of the local authority or statutory bodies will not be considered

BENEFICIAL AREA Leeds (pre-1974 boundary of the City). Postal districts LS1-17

SAMPLE GRANTS Leeds YMCA
Leeds YWCA
South Leeds Children's Holiday Scheme
South Leeds Youth Theatre
Leeds Sea Cadet Corps

FINANCES
- Year 1993
- Grants £150,750
- Income £147,443
- Assets £2,312,500

TRUSTEES Lord Mayor, Rector of Leeds, J Roberts, E M Arnold, R T P Peacock, J Horrocks, P J D Marshall, Dr A Cooke, M J Dodgson, I A Ziff, J Tinker (+ three representatives of Leeds City Council)

SUBMISSION OF APPLICATIONS Trustees meet April, July and November. Applications should reach them at least three weeks before the meeting because applications are checked, applicants visited and the project discussed. Essential to submit accounts and contact telephone number with application. Reports are required from all successful applicants

CORRESPONDENT W M Wrigley, Dibb Lupton Broomhead, 117 The Headrow, Leeds LS1 5JX

CLASSIFICATIONS
- Children and youth – general
- Advancement in life
- Adventure centres and playgrounds
- Centres, clubs and institutes
- Community groups
- Day centres and nurseries
- Development of character
- Holidays
- Youth organisations (eg Guides, Scouts, YWCA etc)

C.C. NO 224939   ESTABLISHED 1530

■ The Wakeham Trust

OBJECTS General charitable purposes with special attention to be paid to projects for community development and education and community service by young people

POLICY OF TRUSTEES We like to help projects which are (a) small, so that grants of up to £500 will make a real difference (b) doing something which is new (either in national terms, or in their locality) (c) run by ordinary people, not social work professionals (d) involving people – especially young people and the elderly – in helping their own communities (e) (in many cases) unconventional and unlikely to attract funding from more traditional sources (f) not on the grapevine in terms of having ready access to funding from large foundations. We are especially interested in helping projects making imaginative use of Community Service Volunteers, and in unconventional community arts projects

TYPE OF GRANT £50–£500. We normally support each project only once. We aim to provide start-up finance, not continuing support. Grants can only be made to registered charities, though we can often help new non-registered groups via grants to an umbrella charity such as a Church or CVS

TYPE OF BENEFICIARY Registered charities working in the areas outlined under Policy

RESTRICTIONS No individuals. No national appeals. No playgroups, playing fields, or boy scouts, etc unless they are doing something very unusual and are helping other people. No consciousness raising. No building appeals or vehicles

BENEFICIAL AREA Normally UK, but we will consider Third World projects meeting our normal criteria, if there is a sponsoring UK charity

FINANCES
- Year 1995
- Grants £14,000
- Income £14,000

TRUSTEES H Carter, Mrs A Knight, B Newbolt, Ms S Owen, R Salmon, Ms T Silkstone

SUBMISSION OF APPLICATIONS At any time. Trustees meet twice a year usually in October and April. Write to Julie Austin with an outline of why you need help, and how you will spend the money. You should also show what other fund raising you have done, how many people you will actually be helping, and how you will expect to become self-sufficient in terms of fund raising in the future. If you can show evidence of support and interest from your local community (such as press cuttings) this will help your application. Please do include an sae but do not include any precious original material such as photographs, in case we lose them. Please enclose the name and charity registration number of a charity which is willing to accept a grant on your behalf, if your project is not itself registered. Applications can take time to be ready for submission to the Trustees – so please apply early, so that we can tell you if we need more information

CORRESPONDENT Mrs Julie Austin, Organiser, The Wakeham Trust, Wakeham Lodge, Terwick Hill, Rogate, Nr Petersfield, Hampshire GU31 5EJ

CLASSIFICATIONS
- Advancement in life
- Adventure centres and playgrounds

Wales'

- Community groups
- Counselling (inc helplines)
- Holidays

C.C. NO 267495   **ESTABLISHED** 1974

■ The Princess of Wales' Charities Trust

OBJECTS General charitable purposes

POLICY OF TRUSTEES The Princess of Wales' Charities Trust makes donations to charitable bodies and for charitable purposes at the discretion of the Trustees. The Trustees are principally concerned to continue to support charitable bodies and purposes in which The Princess of Wales has a particular interest

TYPE OF BENEFICIARY Registered charities within areas outlined in Policy

RESTRICTIONS Registered charities only. Applications from individuals are not supported

FINANCES
- Year 1995
- Grants £112,785
- Income £94,123

TRUSTEES Sir Matthew Farrer, KCVO, Angela Hordern

SUBMISSION OF APPLICATIONS At any time, in writing to the Correspondent

CORRESPONDENT Angela Hordern, St James's Palace, London SW1A 1BS

CLASSIFICATIONS
- Children and youth – general

C.C. NO 293879   **ESTABLISHED** 1981

■ Robert & Felicity Waley-Cohen Charitable Trust

OBJECTS General charitable purposes

FINANCES
- Year 1995
- Income £17,706

TRUSTEES R B Waley-Cohen, The Hon F A Waley-Cohen

CORRESPONDENT R B Waley-Cohen, 18 Gilston Road, London SW10 9SR

CLASSIFICATIONS
- Children and youth – general

C.C. NO 272126   **ESTABLISHED** 1976

■ The Cynthia Walker Charitable Trust

OBJECTS General charitable purposes

POLICY OF TRUSTEES Grants are only made to those charities of which the Trust has special knowledge or association

TYPE OF GRANT One-off

TYPE OF BENEFICIARY Mainly headquarters organisations

RESTRICTIONS No grants to individuals

FINANCES
- Year 1995
- Grants £4,653
- Income £7,090
- Assets £62,400

TRUSTEES Mrs N Horne, M P Walker

SUBMISSION OF APPLICATIONS Grant applications are considered periodically. No acknowledgement will be made of applications other than to successful grantees

CORRESPONDENT Messrs Bury & Walkers, Solicitors, Britannic House, Regent Street, Barnsley, South Yorkshire S70 2EQ

CLASSIFICATIONS
- Youth organisations (eg Guides, Scouts, YWCA etc)

C.C. NO 264043   **ESTABLISHED** 1972

■ Thomas Wall Trust

OBJECTS Grants to charitable organisations in the field of education and social welfare

POLICY OF TRUSTEES Grants to charitable organisations in education and social welfare will preferably be made to those which are small or pioneering, and for specific purposes, not for recurrent costs

TYPE OF GRANT For non-recurring expenses. maximum grant £500

RESTRICTIONS Not for building projects nor large general appeals

BENEFICIAL AREA UK

SAMPLE GRANTS £500 to Braunstone Summer Camp, Leicester towards provision of summer camps
£500 to Polka Youth Theatre, Wimbledon towards renewal of seating
£500 to North London Rescue Commando towards climbing equipment
£500 to Cestrian Venture Unit, Runcorn towards equipment for activity centre
£500 to Streatham Youth Centre towards provision of sporting activities

FINANCES
- Year 1995
- Grants £49,155
- Income £90,170
- Assets £1,968,635

TRUSTEES P H Williams, MA, DPhil (Chairman), T Snow, MA, Miss A S Kennedy, MA, P H Bolton, MA, G Copland, MA, D Phil, C Phys, MInst P, FRSA, N H Baring, BA, C R Broomfield, MA, Mrs H E Cameron, MA, F V McClure, BA. One representative from each of Secondary Heads Association and Oxford, Cambridge and London Universities, and five co-opted

SUBMISSION OF APPLICATIONS The Trustees meet to consider applications twice a year, in July and December. Applications for consideration in July need to be received by mid-May, and in December by mid-October

CORRESPONDENT W B Cook, MA, Director, The Thomas Wall Trust, Charterford House, 75 London Road, Headington, Oxford OX3 9AA

CLASSIFICATIONS
- Adventure centres and playgrounds
- Holidays
- Youth organisations (eg Guides, Scouts, YWCA etc)

C.C. NO 206121   **ESTABLISHED** 1920

■ The A F Wallace Charity Trust

OBJECTS General charitable purposes

POLICY OF TRUSTEES The income derived from the Charity Trust is fully committed at the present time

TYPE OF GRANT Mainly one-off

RESTRICTIONS Registered charities only

FINANCES
- **Year** 1988
- **Grants** £39,328
- **Income** £42,322
- **Assets** £534,109

TRUSTEES F A Wallace, A J W F Wallace

SUBMISSION OF APPLICATIONS To the Correspondent

CORRESPONDENT Warne Investment & Financial Services Ltd, Red Lion Buildings, 12 Cock Lane, London EC1A 9BU

CLASSIFICATIONS
- Centres, clubs and institutes
- Homes and hostels
- Youth organisations (eg Guides, Scouts, YWCA etc)

C.C. NO 207110   **ESTABLISHED** 1912

■ The Francis Wallis Charitable Trust

OBJECTS General charitable purposes

POLICY OF TRUSTEES The policy is wide and could be said to be any deserving cause (excluding individuals)

TYPE OF GRANT Mostly one-off but there are some regulars

TYPE OF BENEFICIARY Can be either HQ or local branches

RESTRICTIONS No grants to individuals

BENEFICIAL AREA London area and South East England, in particular Surrey, Hampshire, Isle of Wight and Essex

FINANCES
- **Year** 1995
- **Grants** £26,000
- **Income** £54,203
- **Assets** £797,978

TRUSTEES Mrs D I Wallis, T B Hughes, F H Hughes, A J Hills

SUBMISSION OF APPLICATIONS Certainly no telephone calls. Brief written details are required with an addressed envelope. There is no application form and applications will not be acknowledged

CORRESPONDENT T B Hughes, FCA, 25 Chargate Close, Burwood Park, Walton-on-Thames, Surrey KT12 5DW

CLASSIFICATIONS
- Children and youth – general
- Advancement in life
- Centres, clubs and institutes
- Community groups
- Development of character
- Counselling (inc helplines)
- Holidays
- Homes and hostels

C.C. NO 279273   **ESTABLISHED** 1979

■ Warbeck Fund Limited

OBJECTS General charitable purposes

POLICY OF TRUSTEES Grants are not made to individuals but only to other charities

TYPE OF BENEFICIARY Both headquarters and local organisations

RESTRICTIONS No grants to individuals

BENEFICIAL AREA Payments to UK charities only, but ultimate beneficiary anywhere

FINANCES
- **Year** 1993
- **Grants** £690,592
- **income** £145,212
- **Assets** £1,136,292

TRUSTEES M B David and others

SUBMISSION OF APPLICATIONS Funds fully committed

CORRESPONDENT The Secretary, Warbeck Fund Limited, 32 Featherstone Street, London EC1Y 8QX

CLASSIFICATIONS
- Development of character
- Holidays

C.C. NO 252953   **ESTABLISHED** 1967

■ The Ward Blenkinsop Trust

OBJECTS General charitable purposes (with emphasis on support for medical research)

TYPE OF GRANT Mainly cash

TYPE OF BENEFICIARY Mainly Research Foundations and charitable organisations

RESTRICTIONS No grants to individuals

BENEFICIAL AREA A special interest in the Merseyside area

FINANCES
- **Year** 1995
- **Grants** £185,517
- **Income** £212,559
- **Assets** £2,978,667

TRUSTEES J H Awdry, A M Blenkinsop, T R Tilling

SUBMISSION OF APPLICATIONS In writing from charitable organisations, not individuals

CORRESPONDENT J H Awdry, Broxbury, Codmore Hill, Pulborough, West Sussex RH20 2HY

CLASSIFICATIONS
- Centres, clubs and institutes
- Holidays
- Homes and hostels
- Youth organisations (eg Guides, Scouts, YWCA etc)

C.C. NO 265449   **ESTABLISHED** 1972

■ John Wates Charitable Trust

OBJECTS General charitable purposes

POLICY OF TRUSTEES Emphasis on young people, musicians and advancement of religion

TYPE OF GRANT For single projects (most less than £500)

TYPE OF BENEFICIARY Charities and individuals but not to national appeals or building appeals nor for educational holidays

BENEFICIAL AREA Mainly London area and South East

SAMPLE GRANTS £225 towards cost of National Youth Orchestra course
Five grants of £200 to music students in higher education
£100 for course at Zippo Circus Arts
£75 towards cost of ordinance books

FINANCES
- **Year** 1994
- **Grants** £2,700
- **Income** £2,010
- **Assets** £39,100

TRUSTEES J N Wates, Mrs C Wates, J R F Lulham, N N J Smith

Wates

SUBMISSION OF APPLICATIONS Allocations made infrequently

CORRESPONDENT N N J Smith, Messrs Oswald Hickson Collier & Co, 1 Pemberton Row, Fetter Lane, London EC4A 3EX

CLASSIFICATIONS
- Advancement in life

C.C. NO 290555   **ESTABLISHED** 1984

■ The Wates Foundation

OBJECTS The alleviation of distress and the improvement of the quality of life, especially in the urban community

POLICY OF TRUSTEES In line with its origin, the Foundation has always had an interest in the built environment and its impact on society. There is an emphasis on the physical, mental and spiritual welfare of the young and disadvantaged aged 8–25. The problems of unemployment, homelessness, substance abuse and offending are of particular concern. Post-school education and training, particularly in good citizenship, are also supported. From 1994–97 there will be concentration on the field of addiction and criminality. Racial equality is stressed throughout. The majority of grants are made in the London area, particularly in South London and nearby. A few are made in Northern Ireland, Merseyside and the North East. Applicants outside these areas should consider carefully whether their project is exceptional enough to justify a departure from the Foundation's normal practice

TYPE OF GRANT Normal range up to £25,000. Maximum length of support three years

TYPE OF BENEFICIARY Special emphasis on groups giving help to disadvantaged young; also on those educating the young towards citizenship, against drugs

RESTRICTIONS No grants are made to individuals. Grants are not normally made to large well-established charities, umbrella bodies, large building projects, other grant-making bodies, medical appeals, sporting, social or fund-raising events, foreign travel, expeditions, schools (other than special schools), work with children under eight (unless handicapped), repair of churches or church halls. A few grants are made to UK organisations working in Eastern Europe and the Third World; no grants are made in the Republic of Ireland. Recipients must have charitable status

BENEFICIAL AREA Mainly the London area and nearby but a few grants may be made in the Merseyside region, the North East and Northern Ireland

SAMPLE GRANTS £5,000 to Apprentice Master Link (non-profit making club linking would-be apprentices with tutors or 'masters' who have a skill which can be passed on)
£3,000 to LEAP towards cost of training young unempolyed volunteers for work with small groups on resolving conflict and violence
£580 to Linacre College for a special WC/shower room in a ground-floor study bedroom adapted in every respect for occupation by a disabled student
£300 to Chatrodd Trust for English classes for young Bangladeshis in Stepney

FINANCES
- Year 1994–95
- Grants £933,666
- Income £137,810
- Assets £23,932,046

TRUSTEES The Wates Foundation Ltd (Chairman – Mrs Ann Ritchie, JP)

PUBLICATIONS Annual reports

SUBMISSION OF APPLICATIONS Any time, by letter to the Director, with description of project and latest accounts. An information sheet is available on application

CORRESPONDENT Sir Martin Berthoud, KCVO, CMG, Director, The Wates Foundation, 1260 London Road, Norbury, London SW16 4EG

CLASSIFICATIONS
- Adoption/fostering
- Advancement in life
- Adventure centres and playgrounds
- Centres, clubs and institutes
- Community groups
- Counselling (inc helplines)
- Holidays
- Homes and hostels
- Special needs housing
- Youth organisations (eg Guides, Scouts, YWCA etc)
- Children and violence (inc abuse)

C.C. NO 247941   **ESTABLISHED** 1966

■ May Watkinson Charity Trust

OBJECTS General charitable purposes

POLICY OF TRUSTEES To support musically talented pupils who require assistance due to lack of parental support because of their circumstances. To limit the sphere covered to those charities which have been supported since the inception of the Trust. Exceptions will only be made in very special circumstances, and these will be limited to particular areas which would have been of interest to the Settlor

TYPE OF GRANT Cash

TYPE OF BENEFICIARY Mainly local students and headquarters organisations

RESTRICTIONS No grants to individuals under ordinary circumstances

BENEFICIAL AREA Local to Grimsby area

SAMPLE GRANTS £397 to one student for new flute
£350 to one student for six week placement with Sydney Opera, Australia

FINANCES
- Year 1993
- Grants £10,561
- Income £11,508
- Assets £144,481

TRUSTEES J T Bootyman, B W Moore, T I Robinson

SUBMISSION OF APPLICATIONS It is desired, if possible, to avoid the receipt of numerous appeals, which have little chance of receiving a grant in view of the majority of the funds being committed to particular charities which receive annual grants, coupled with areas of local concern. This is a costly exercise for those making the appeals and disappointing to the Trustees when help cannot be given

CORRESPONDENT T I Robinson, FCA, Messrs Forrester Boyd, 26 South St Mary's Gate, Grimsby, S Humberside DN31 1LW

CLASSIFICATIONS
- Development of character

C.C. NO 263257   **ESTABLISHED** 1971

■ John Watson's Trust

OBJECTS (a) Grants to children and young persons under 21, physically or mentally handicapped or socially disadvantaged, for further education and training, equipment, travel, and educational, social, recreational and cultural activities. Grants to charitable organisations and ad hoc groups in this field and to bodies and persons for educational experiments and research. (b) Grants for boarding education to orphans, children of single-parent families (widely defined) and children subject to some other special family difficulty. See the John Watson's Trust Scheme 1984 (SI 1984 No 1480)

POLICY OF TRUSTEES For grants under Objects (a), preference is to be given to the interests of beneficiaries ordinarily resident in Lothian

TYPE OF GRANT Equipment, staff, small capital expenditure, tuition, student support, personal equipment, (eg special wheelchairs, special typewriters), projects and activities including travel. Grant one year only but can be extended. Grants for Objects (a) are likely to be in the main around the £100–£1,000 mark and are unlikely to exceed £10,000 (though some in £5,000 range)

TYPE OF BENEFICIARY Individuals, charitable organisations, ad hoc groups, research bodies or persons. Beneficiaries must be under 21 years of age

RESTRICTIONS Confined to under 21s

BENEFICIAL AREA Objects (a) essentially Scotland with preference for Lothian. Objects (b) Scotland only

FINANCES
- Year 1994
- Grants £140,000
- Income £175,000
- Assets £1,854,000

TRUSTEES Six representatives of the Society of Writers to Her Majesty's Signet, two representatives from Lothian Regional Council, one from the Merchant Company Education Board, one from the Lothian Association of Youth Clubs, and one additional member

PUBLICATIONS Background Notes and application forms available

NOTES Enquiries in writing, please

SUBMISSION OF APPLICATIONS Trustees meet eight times a year

CORRESPONDENT J Penney, Administrator, John Watson's Trust, Grants Committee, HM Signet Library, Parliament Square, Edinburgh EH1 1RF

CLASSIFICATIONS
- Children and youth – general
- Advancement in life
- Adventure centres and playgrounds
- Centres, clubs and institutes
- Counselling (inc helplines)
- Holidays
- Special classes

ESTABLISHED 1984

■ The Weavers' Company Benevolent Fund

OBJECTS General charitable purposes

POLICY OF TRUSTEES Trustees restrict their grants to projects concerned with helping young people at risk from criminal involvement, and with the rehabilitation of prisoners and ex-prisoners

TYPE OF GRANT Pump-priming grants for 1–3 years for new and innovatory projects and small donations

TYPE OF BENEFICIARY Registered charities; small, community-based groups

RESTRICTIONS Grants restricted to registered charities. No grants to individuals

BENEFICIAL AREA UK, but with emphasis on Greater London

SAMPLE GRANTS Mansfield House – establishment of project invloving recruiting young people at risk as volunteers
NACRO – advice and information centre on remand wing at HMP Brixton
Open Door – establishment of advice and information centre for young people
Chapeltown Initiative – research into truancy and the development of an alternative education programme
Barnfield Project – support for estate-based community organisation

FINANCES
- Year 1994
- Grants £160,048
- Income £165,531
- Assets £3,475,000

TRUSTEES The Worshipful Company of Weavers

PUBLICATIONS Leaflet of Guidelines

SUBMISSION OF APPLICATIONS Applications should be made by letter in the first instance and may be made at any time

CORRESPONDENT Mrs F Newcombe, Clerk to the Weavers' Company, Saddlers' House, Gutter Lane, London EC2V 6BR

CLASSIFICATIONS
- Centres, clubs and institutes
- Counselling (inc helplines)

C.C. NO 266189 **ESTABLISHED** 1973

■ William Webster Charitable Trust

OBJECTS General charitable purposes

POLICY OF TRUSTEES Generally to fund capital projects

TYPE OF GRANT Mainly one-off

TYPE OF BENEFICIARY Registered charitable organisations in the North East of England, or for the benefit of branches in the North East of England

RESTRICTIONS Grants are restricted to registered charitable organisations only from the North East of England

BENEFICIAL AREA North East of England and York

FINANCES
- Year 1995
- Grants £122,150
- Income £104,727

TRUSTEES Barclays Bank Trust Company Limited

Wedge

Alphabetical register of grant making charitable trusts

SUBMISSION OF APPLICATIONS Details required are: details of the project, the amount of funding required, the funding raised from other sources, and a copy of the last report and accounts of the organisation. Meetings of the Trustees are held in March, July and November

CORRESPONDENT Barclays Bank Trust Co Ltd, Executorship & Trustee Service 65–1735, Osborne Court, Gadbrook Park, Rudheath, Northwich, Cheshire CW9 7RE

CLASSIFICATIONS
- Children and youth – general
- Advancement in life
- Adventure centres and playgrounds
- Centres, clubs and institutes
- Community groups
- Holidays
- Homes and hostels
- Youth organisations (eg Guides, Scouts, YWCA etc)

C.C. NO 259848   **ESTABLISHED** 1969

■ The Wedge

OBJECTS General charitable purposes

POLICY OF TRUSTEES The Trust makes grants only to organisations undertaking play and youth work in Merseyside. It prefers to support small local organisations rather than large or national bodies

TYPE OF GRANT Grants to small local charities undertaking play and youth work. The Trust prefers to make a larger number of small grants rather than a few large grants. Grants are both single payment and recurrent, usually in the region of £50–£500. Grants are made towards playscheme running costs, play equipment, day trips for playschemes

RESTRICTIONS No grants are given for holidays, salaries, building costs or to religious organisations

BENEFICIAL AREA Liverpool

FINANCES
- Year 1991
- Grants £28,542
- Income £26,667
- Assets £18,255

TRUSTEES B Moores, A C McIntyre, A T Mcfarlane

SUBMISSION OF APPLICATIONS Applications should be in writing including a detailed budget and a copy of the latest available accounts. Trustees meet quarterly

CORRESPONDENT A C McIntyre, South Moss House, Pasture Lane, Formby, Merseyside L37 0AP

CLASSIFICATIONS
- Children and youth – general
- Adventure centres and playgrounds
- Community groups

C.C. NO 328382   **ESTABLISHED** 1988

■ The Weinstock Fund

OBJECTS General charitable purposes

POLICY OF TRUSTEES Nationally constituted charities mainly for children, old and handicapped people, social welfare and education

TYPE OF GRANT Cash

TYPE OF BENEFICIARY Registered charities

RESTRICTIONS Individuals and non-registered organisations

FINANCES
- Year 1991
- Grants £234,810
- Income £400,483
- Assets £2,100,996

TRUSTEES D Lewis, M Lester, S A Weinstock

SUBMISSION OF APPLICATIONS Annually

CORRESPONDENT Miss J M Elstone, MBE, 1 Stanhope Gate, London W1A 1EH

CLASSIFICATIONS
- Children and youth – general
- Adoption/fostering
- Centres, clubs and institutes
- Community groups
- Day centres and nurseries
- Development of character
- Holidays
- Homes and hostels

C.C. NO 222376   **ESTABLISHED** 1962

■ The James Weir Foundation

OBJECTS General charitable purposes

POLICY OF TRUSTEES To subscribe to national appeals and to support local Scottish appeals in the Glasgow and Ayrshire area in particular

TYPE OF GRANT Lump sum. Many annually recurrent or one-off: £250–£2,000

TYPE OF BENEFICIARY Mainly Scottish charities – educational, medical, housing, help for the aged

RESTRICTIONS No covenants. Preferably registered charities. No grants to individuals

BENEFICIAL AREA UK, Glasgow and Ayrshire

FINANCES
- Year 1993
- Grants £125,000
- Income £130,000
- Assets £3,089,436

TRUSTEES Hon G Weir, S Bonham, W Ducas

NOTES Trustees review appeals twice per year and mutually agree who benefits

SUBMISSION OF APPLICATIONS To the correspondent. No application form required. Trustees meet twice annually May and October. No acknowledgements

CORRESPONDENT Mrs L Lawson, The James Weir Foundation, 84 Cicada Road, London SW18 2NZ

CLASSIFICATIONS
- Children and youth – general
- Centres, clubs and institutes
- Holidays
- Homes and hostels

C.C. NO 251764   **ESTABLISHED** 1967

■ The Barbara Welby Trust

OBJECTS General charitable purposes

POLICY OF TRUSTEES Preference given to charities of which the Founder had special knowledge or with the objects of which she was specially associated

TYPE OF GRANT Donations

TYPE OF BENEFICIARY Normally limited to established charitable foundations and institutions

BENEFICIAL AREA England, Scotland, Wales and overseas

FINANCES
- Year 1995
- Grants £24,000
- Income £36,118
- Assets £589,025

TRUSTEES N J Barker, C W H Welby, C N Robertson

NOTES Applications for individual assistance not normally considered unless made through an established charitable organisation

SUBMISSION OF APPLICATIONS At any time, by letter to the correspondent

CORRESPONDENT Messrs Dawson & Co, 2 New Square, Lincoln's Inn, London WC2A 3RZ

CLASSIFICATIONS
- Children and youth – general
- Development of character
- Holidays

C.C. NO 252973   **ESTABLISHED** 1967

■ The Weldon UK Charitable Trust

OBJECTS General charitable purposes

POLICY OF TRUSTEES The Trustees tend to make few but relatively large commitments

FINANCES
- Year 1995
- Grants £161,000
- Income £30,000
- Assets £527,000

TRUSTEES J M St J Harris, H J Fritze

CORRESPONDENT J M St J Harris, 4 Grosvenor Place, London SW1X 7HJ

CLASSIFICATIONS
- Children and youth – general

C.C. NO 327497   **ESTABLISHED** 1987

■ Westminster Amalgamated Charity

OBJECTS Grants for the relief and for the welfare of beneficiaries (holidays, convalescent homes, remedial treatment) or provision of facilities for recreation and leisure-time occupation

POLICY OF TRUSTEES As laid down by the Charity Commission Scheme

TYPE OF GRANT Individuals – in the City of Westminster (excluding Paddington and St Marylebone). Organisations – the whole City of Westminster

TYPE OF BENEFICIARY Organisations – City of Westminster and for individuals – Old City of Westminster (excludes Paddington and St Marylebone)

RESTRICTIONS Confined to the City of Westminster

BENEFICIAL AREA City of Westminster excluding Paddington and St Marylebone

FINANCES
- Year 1993
- Grants £185,491
- Income £243,040
- Assets £2,820,161

SUBMISSION OF APPLICATIONS To the Clerk

CORRESPONDENT Clerk to the Trustees, Westminster Amalgamated Charity, 6 New Bridge Street, London EC4V 6AB

CLASSIFICATIONS
- Children and youth – general

C.C. NO 207964   **ESTABLISHED** 1961

■ Anne Duchess of Westminster's Charity

OBJECTS General charitable purposes

POLICY OF TRUSTEES Funds are fully allocated or committed

TYPE OF BENEFICIARY Children, the aged, blind, nurses, forces welfare, hospitals

RESTRICTIONS No grants to individuals

FINANCES
- Year 1993
- Grants £17,533
- Income £18,751
- Assets £200,029

TRUSTEES G K Ridley, J M Marshall

CORRESPONDENT Miss A Stubbs, Eaton Estate Office, Eccleston, Chester CH4 9ET

CLASSIFICATIONS
- Children and youth – general
- Centres, clubs and institutes

C.C. NO 245177   **ESTABLISHED** 1965

■ Garfield Weston Foundation

OBJECTS The Foundation was created with general charitable objectives. The aims of the Trustees are to support a broad range of activities in the fields of religion, education, the environment, the arts, health (including research) and other areas of general benefit to the community in the UK

POLICY OF TRUSTEES The size and scope of donation depend on the nature of the appeals under consideration. The Trustees endeavour to support appeals across the broad spectrum, including causes and projects having a substantial impact within the community or of significant national importance through to requests from small charitable funds or individuals applying on behalf of causes deemed worthy of support. All appeals under consideration are reviewed by a committee of the Trustees and the policy is to give proper consideration and a prompt response to all applicants. Grants to individuals not normally considered

TYPE OF GRANT Usually contributions to a specific project or part of a project. Core funding and/or salaries rarely considered

TYPE OF BENEFICIARY UK registered charities working in the areas outlined under Objects

RESTRICTIONS UK registered charities only although applications from churches are excepted from this restriction

BENEFICIAL AREA UK

FINANCES
- Year 1992
- Grants £7,705,150
- Income £11,189,707
- Assets £24,750,579

TRUSTEES G H Weston, W G Galen Weston, M L Burnett, B E Mitchell, R N Baron, C H W Dalglish, G H Weston, J Khayat, A C Hobhowse, G G Weston

SUBMISSION OF APPLICATIONS At any time. Written applications only which should include details of the need the intended project is designed to meet plus an outline budget

CORRESPONDENT H W Bailey, Garfield Weston Foundation, Weston Centre, Bowater House, 68 Knightsbridge, London SW1X 7LR

CLASSIFICATIONS
- Children and youth – general

C.C. NO 230260 **ESTABLISHED** 1958

■ The Hon Mrs R G A Whetherly's Charitable Trust

OBJECTS General charitable purposes

POLICY OF TRUSTEES Particular consideration given to charities in the fields of mental health, child welfare and cancer research

TYPE OF GRANT Cash grants

TYPE OF BENEFICIARY Registered charities only

FINANCES
- Year 1995
- Income £7,778

TRUSTEES The Barbinder Trust

NOTES No donations were made during 1995 due to death of Settlor

SUBMISSION OF APPLICATIONS By post to correspondent

CORRESPONDENT The Joint Secretary, The Barbinder Trust, Plumtree Court, London EC4A 4HT

CLASSIFICATIONS
- Children and youth – general
- Homes and hostels

C.C. NO 257825 **ESTABLISHED** 1968

■ Whitaker Charitable Trust

OBJECTS General charitable purposes

POLICY OF TRUSTEES The Trust's resources are heavily committed and only very limited funds are available for charities not previously supported by the Trustees

TYPE OF GRANT Cash payments

TYPE OF BENEFICIARY Registered charities only

RESTRICTIONS No grants to individuals or for the maintenance or repair of individual churches

FINANCES
- Year 1992
- Income £124,896
- Grants £111,705
- Assets £3,464,160

TRUSTEES D W J Price, E R H Perks, E J R Whitaker

SUBMISSION OF APPLICATIONS To the Correspondent at any time. Trustees meet half yearly. Applications should include clear details of the need the intended project is designed to meet plus a copy of the latest accounts available and an outline budget. If an acknowledgement of the application or notification, in the event of the application not being accepted, is required, an sae should be enclosed

CORRESPONDENT Currey & Co, Solicitors, 21 Buckingham Gate, London SW1E 6LS

CLASSIFICATIONS
- Centres, clubs and institutes
- Holidays
- Youth organisations (eg Guides, Scouts, YWCA etc)

C.C. NO 234491 **ESTABLISHED** 1964

■ Whitehall Charitable Foundation Limited

OBJECTS The company is registered as a charity; it is established for the benefit of seafaring men and women and their families and such other members of the general public as may be deemed to be deserving, such benefit being given for educational and welfare purposes

POLICY OF TRUSTEES About 20 donations per annum

TYPE OF GRANT 10 regular, remainder one-off

TYPE OF BENEFICIARY Preference for children's charities, charities assisting disabled people, local charities (Hampshire, North Yorkshire)

RESTRICTIONS No grants to individuals

BENEFICIAL AREA Hampshire, North Yorkshire

FINANCES
- Year 1995
- Income £10,500
- Grants £9,100
- Assets £140,000

TRUSTEES M T Turnbull, S M Turnbull, J M Turnbull, R M Turnbull

SUBMISSION OF APPLICATIONS These are reviewed twice a year, usually in July and December. We do not acknowledge all applications

CORRESPONDENT M T Turnbull, 5 Springlakes Estate, Deadbrook Lane, Aldershot, Hampshire GU12 4UH

CLASSIFICATIONS
- Holidays
- Homes and hostels

C.C. NO 272297 **ESTABLISHED** 1976

■ Sydney Dean Whitehead's Charitable Trust

OBJECTS Education and advancement of boys and girls whose parents cannot provide them with suitable education. General charitable purposes

POLICY OF TRUSTEES The trustees basically apply their funds towards supporting parents with the educational costs of their children and respond more readily to appeals relating to children with special talents particularly in the artistic fields and also respond more readily to appeals which show that there is an element of self-help already in operation. A stamped addressed envelope with applications would be appreciated

TYPE OF GRANT Donations. Annual grants made to approximately 25 beneficiaries for educational costs

TYPE OF BENEFICIARY The Trustees also support parents with the educational cost of their children where lack of finance could preclude those children from receiving the type of education which their particular 'gift' merits

RESTRICTIONS None, although medical applications are not considered

BENEFICIAL AREA Greater Manchester and Lancashire preferred

FINANCES
- Year 1995
- Grants £24,507
- Income £27,920
- Assets £571,352

TRUSTEES Mrs I P Pembroke, Mrs F C P Whitehead, Dr D S Whitehead, B J W Langley

NOTES The Trustees have now approved the format of a questionnaire which most applicants are required to complete to provide the basic information to enable the Trustees to assess the application

SUBMISSION OF APPLICATIONS The Trustees would like to have some sort of financial statement (as up to date as possible) with applications from charities or where individuals are applying, some sort of guide as to what amount of support is required by the applicant. To Secretary, in writing

CORRESPONDENT Ernst & Young, Lowry House, 17 Marble Street, Manchester M2 3AW

CLASSIFICATIONS
- Advancement in life

C.C. NO 207714   **ESTABLISHED** 1946

■ The Will Charitable Trust

OBJECTS General charitable purposes

POLICY OF TRUSTEES Four categories: (a) Countryside conservation. (b) Care of blind and prevention of blindness. (c) Care of cancer sufferers and their families. (d) Residential care of the mentally handicapped in communities providing family environment and maximum choice of lifestyle

TYPE OF GRANT As determined by needs of grantee or project

TYPE OF BENEFICIARY Registered charity with proven record in relevant field

RESTRICTIONS Registered charities only. Grants for academic or research projects not normally considered

FINANCES
- Year 1995
- Grants £8,150,000
- Income £910,000
- Assets £16,500,000

TRUSTEES H N Henshaw, P J Andras, A McDonald

SUBMISSION OF APPLICATIONS In writing by early February in categories (b) and (d) above and by early September in categories (a) and (c) above

CORRESPONDENT Mrs Vanessa Reburn, Messers Farrer and Co, 66 Lincolns Inn Fields, London WC2A 3LH

CLASSIFICATIONS
- Special needs housing

C.C. NO 801682   **ESTABLISHED** 1989

■ Mr Frederick Wills 1961 Charitable Trust

OBJECTS General charitable purposes, with emphasis on Christian education, care of the handicapped (and elderly)

POLICY OF TRUSTEES The main areas of interest are currently: care of handicapped children and the elderly, together with Christian education. The Trustees aim to distribute the income to its greatest advantage and they review their policy every three years

TYPE OF GRANT Usually one-off for a specific project or part of a project. Core funding and/or salaries rarely considered

TYPE OF BENEFICIARY Registered charities working in the areas outlined above under Policy with particular preference to children's charities

RESTRICTIONS Registered charities only. Applications from individuals, including students, are ineligible. No grants will be made in response to general appeals from large national organisations, nor to smaller bodies working in areas other than those set out above

BENEFICIAL AREA Charities within Gloucestershire and the North of Scotland

FINANCES
- Year 1995
- Grants £1,765
- Income £2,486
- Assets £52,600

TRUSTEES Major M T N H Wills

PUBLICATIONS Annual Accounts

SUBMISSION OF APPLICATIONS Trustees meet half yearly to consider applications which should include clear details of the need, the intended project and the outline budget. Applications should be made to the Correspondent in writing when further information about the project may be requested

CORRESPONDENT The Secretary, The Old House, Rendcomb, Cirencester Glos GL7 7EY

CLASSIFICATIONS
- Children and youth – general

C.C. NO 204303   **ESTABLISHED** 1961

■ Major Michael Thomas Wills 1961 Charitable Trust

OBJECTS General charitable purposes

POLICY OF TRUSTEES Leading national charities and smaller regional and county charities with particular emphasis on youth and moral welfare

TYPE OF GRANT £25–£300

TYPE OF BENEFICIARY As Policy of Trustees

RESTRICTIONS Registered charities only. No grants to individuals

FINANCES
- Year 1995
- Grants £5,496
- Income £5,079
- Assets £120,108

TRUSTEES Captain F H P H Wills, R J Shepherd

SUBMISSION OF APPLICATIONS Donations are normally made annually around April/May

CORRESPONDENT Messrs Coopers & Lybrand, Lennox House, Beaufort Buildings, Spa Road, Gloucester GL1 1XD

CLASSIFICATIONS
- Children and youth – general
- Advancement in life
- Adventure centres and playgrounds
- Centres, clubs and institutes
- Holidays
- Homes and hostels

C.C. NO 204302   **ESTABLISHED** 1961

Wills

Alphabetical register of grant making charitable trusts

■ P J H Wills 1962 Charitable Trust

OBJECTS General charitable purposes

POLICY OF TRUSTEES To support main charities with emphasis on human suffering, disablement and poverty. Regretfully individual trips are not supported

TYPE OF GRANT £25–£200

TYPE OF BENEFICIARY Registered charities as above, particularly those providing training or medical services in developing countries

BENEFICIAL AREA Gloucestershire

FINANCES
- Year 1993
- Grants £2,000
- Income £2,200
- Assets £38,000

TRUSTEES Major M T N H Wills, Miss G S Wills

SUBMISSION OF APPLICATIONS Donations are made around April/May. No telephone calls, and no correspondence or acknowledgement of applications

CORRESPONDENT P J H Wills, Kirkham Farm, Lower Slaughter, Cheltenham, Gloucestershire GL54 2JS

CLASSIFICATIONS
- Children and youth – general

C.C. NO 264810 **ESTABLISHED** 1962

■ The H D H Wills 1965 Charitable Trust

OBJECTS General charitable purposes

POLICY OF TRUSTEES Funds are fully committed and donations can only be made to registered charities

RESTRICTIONS No grants to individuals

BENEFICIAL AREA UK including the Channel Islands and the Irish Republic

FINANCES
- Year 1995
- Grants £74,106
- Income £308,357
- Assets £9,305,243

TRUSTEES J Kemp-Welch, Hon V M G A Lampson, J B S Carson, Lady E H Wills

SUBMISSION OF APPLICATIONS No application form in use. No specific dates for making applications but at present few new applications can be considered

CORRESPONDENT Mrs I R Wootton, 12 Tokenhouse Yard, London EC2R 7AN

CLASSIFICATIONS
- Children and youth – general
- Centres, clubs and institutes

C.C. NO 244610 **ESTABLISHED** 1965

■ Dame Violet Wills Charitable Trust

OBJECTS General charitable purposes

POLICY OF TRUSTEES Unlimited

TYPE OF GRANT One-off

TYPE OF BENEFICIARY Associations for Evangelical religious purposes

RESTRICTIONS No grants to individuals

FINANCES
- Year 1995
- Grants £86,600
- Income £98,187
- Assets £1,374,275

TRUSTEES H E Cooper, R D Speare, Dr D Cunningham, S Burton, Rev A Motyer, Prof A Linton, Miss J Guy, G Landreth, W Appleby, D Bowles, D Cleave, A Cooper

SUBMISSION OF APPLICATIONS January and July

CORRESPONDENT H E Cooper, FCA, c/o Messrs Ricketts, Cooper & Co, Thornton House, Richmond Hill, Clifton, Bristol BS8 1AT

CLASSIFICATIONS
- Youth organisations (eg Guides, Scouts, YWCA etc)

C.C. NO 219485 **ESTABLISHED** 1955

■ The Connolly Thomas Wilson Foundation

OBJECTS We aim to help disadvantaged young people living in Northamptonshire between the ages of 14 and 21 in character building exercises, eg Outward Bound, Duke of Edinburgh Award, etc

POLICY OF TRUSTEES To give a helping hand to youngsters who themselves have made an effort to succeed. Sponsorship of individual sportspeople

TYPE OF GRANT Cash contributions towards courses for individuals

TYPE OF BENEFICIARY Mainly young individuals aged between 14 and 21 years of age

RESTRICTIONS Age limit between 14 and 21 years of age

BENEFICIAL AREA Northamptonshire

FINANCES
- Year 1995
- Grants £20,000
- Income £20,000

TRUSTEES L A Wilson, S G Schanschieff, D M Auden, T O'Connor, Administrative Trustee: N C Wilson, Treasurer: C Hayward

SUBMISSION OF APPLICATIONS Firstly by letter to correspondent

CORRESPONDENT N C Wilson, 1a Kennel Terrace, Brixworth, Northampton NN6 9DL

CLASSIFICATIONS
- Advancement in life
- Development of character
- Special classes

C.C. NO 267063 **ESTABLISHED** 1973

■ Wiltshire Community Foundation

OBJECTS The promotion of any charitable purposes for the county of Wiltshire and its immediate neighbourhood to support a co-ordinated programme of charitable projects aimed at developing the potential of local urban and rural communities for the benefit of all who live and work in Wiltshire

POLICY OF TRUSTEES Main projects fund: (a) Supporting community care. (b) Tackling isolation. (c) Investing in young people. (d) Community development fund. (e) Initiatives fund

TYPE OF GRANT Grants not normally issued for capital expenditure, contribution to large appeals or for individuals

TYPE OF BENEFICIARY Voluntary and community groups in Wiltshire

RESTRICTIONS The following are ineligible for funding: projects outside Wiltshire, individuals, sponsored events, advancement of religion, medical research and equipment, animal welfare, party political activities

BENEFICIAL AREA Wiltshire

FINANCES
- Year 1994–95
- Grants £137,760
- Income £359,914
- Assets £361,082

TRUSTEES D Newbigging, OBE (Chairman), C Bartholomew, J Ainslie, OBE, Gill Prior, Moyra James, MBE, Jane MacTaggart, Marigold Treloar, Maj Gen T Jeapes, CB, OBE, MC, S Willcox, Ann Poole, Sir John Sykes, Bt, J Emmerson, Zandria Pauncefort, Col (Retd) D Rogers, OBE, Elinor Goodman

PUBLICATIONS Grants Policy Booklet. Annual Report and Accounts. 'Communities at Risk in Wiltshire' (a needs assessment report)

SUBMISSION OF APPLICATIONS On official form following discussions with Grants Manager. Decisions are made at quarterly grants meetings

CORRESPONDENT Helen Gibbs, Grants Manager, WCF, 48 New Park Street, Devizes, Wiltshire SN10 1DS

CLASSIFICATIONS
- Children and youth – general
- Community groups
- Homes and hostels

C.C. NO 298936   **ESTABLISHED** 1991

■ The Harold Hyam Wingate Foundation

OBJECTS General charitable purposes

POLICY OF TRUSTEES The Foundation makes regular donations to organisations with charitable status in the following fields: medical, educational, cultural and welfare. The balance of the Foundation's funds are reserved for special projects. (In addition, the Trustees have established a Scholarship Scheme to assist individuals – for details please send sae to Jane Reid, Administrator, Wingate Scholarships)

TYPE OF GRANT Either one-off or recurrent for a limited period. Average grant £500–£1,000

BENEFICIAL AREA UK, Israel, Ireland, present and former Commonwealth countries

FINANCES
- Year 1994
- Grants £352,998
- Income £850,589
- Assets £23,079,732

TRUSTEES Mrs M Wingate, A J Wingate, R C Wingate

NOTES In addition, £300,000 is available each year for Wingate Scholarships which are strictly for individuals. They cover a very broad spectrum of subjects. Candidates must be over 24 and resident in the British Isles. Information for applicants is obtainable, in writing only, from the Administrator of the Wingate Scholarships at the above address. Please send sae

SUBMISSION OF APPLICATIONS Applications should be submitted in writing and will generally be acknowledged only if sae is enclosed or application is successful. Individuals wishing to apply for Scholarships should request application forms

CORRESPONDENT Mrs K C Cohen, 38 Curzon Street, Mayfair, London W1Y 8EY

CLASSIFICATIONS
- Children and youth – general
- Counselling (inc helplines)

C.C. NO 264114   **ESTABLISHED** 1960

■ Mrs Wingfield's Charitable Trust

OBJECTS General charitable purposes

POLICY OF TRUSTEES Applications considered on merit and available funds

TYPE OF GRANT Single payment, no restriction on capital expenditure or revenue costs

TYPE OF BENEFICIARY Mainly established organisations in charitable or artistic fields

RESTRICTIONS Grants not normally made to individuals, unless case of exceptional merit

BENEFICIAL AREA UK

FINANCES
- Year 1995
- Grants £15,069
- Income £13,741
- Assets £174,451

TRUSTEES J M Dodds, D J Onslow

SUBMISSION OF APPLICATIONS In writing, Trustees meet as and when required. Applications reviewed February, May, August, November. Stamped self-addressed envelope, please. Absolutely no personal callers or telephone enquiries

CORRESPONDENT Messrs Dyke Yaxley & Co, Abbey House, Abbey Foregate, Shrewsbury, Salop SY2 6BH

CLASSIFICATIONS
- Children and youth – general
- Homes and hostels

C.C. NO 269524   **ESTABLISHED** 1974

■ Hyman Winstone Foundation

OBJECTS General charitable purposes

POLICY OF TRUSTEES General areas of interest – with emphasis on local charities

TYPE OF BENEFICIARY Registered charities working in the areas outlined above

RESTRICTIONS Registered charities only – no applications from individuals

FINANCES
- Year 1994
- Grants £24,200
- Income £18,500
- Assets £280,000

TRUSTEES T B Gee, M H Elliott, R J Elliott, D H Gee

SUBMISSION OF APPLICATIONS In writing to the Correspondent below

CORRESPONDENT M H Elliott, Benson Burdekin with Flint & Co, Solicitors, 32 Wilkinson Street, Sheffield S10 2GB

CLASSIFICATIONS
- Children and youth – general

C.C. NO 224442   **ESTABLISHED** 1956

Wolfe

■ The Wolfe Family's Charitable Trust

OBJECTS General charitable purposes with particular reference to the needs of handicapped children

POLICY OF TRUSTEES Considerations of need, under headings:- children and elderly (disability/hardship), special consideration for applications on behalf of youth disablement and learning difficulties

TYPE OF GRANT Cash

RESTRICTIONS Grants only made to registered charities, with preference for smaller bodies and projects linked to children's hospitals

BENEFICIAL AREA Mainly Great Britain and Northern Ireland

SAMPLE GRANTS £200 to NSPCC
£150 to Association of Brain-injured Children
£150 to Fiveways School
£150 to Guy's Hospital towards Evelina Children's Unit
£150 to Children's Country Holiday Fund

FINANCES
- Year 1994
- Grants £12,350
- Income £16,980

TRUSTEES G M Wolfe, A C Wolfe, B F Robinson

SUBMISSION OF APPLICATIONS By post. Trustees meet 4 times a year and grants usually made quarterly. No facilities exist for acknowledgment of applications

CORRESPONDENT G M Wolfe, The Heights, Berghers Hill, Wooburn Common, Nr High Wycombe, Bucks HP10 0JP

CLASSIFICATIONS
- Children and youth – general
- Centres, clubs and institutes
- Holidays
- Homes and hostels

C.C. NO 266242　　　　**ESTABLISHED** 1973

■ The Women Caring Trust

OBJECTS To give practical help to innocent families in the troubled areas of Northern Ireland; to promote integrated education and the support of groups and organisations working for peace and reconciliation among young people

POLICY OF TRUSTEES A leg-up, not a hand-out: Trustees are keen to encourage new projects, particularly cross-community, wherever possible

TYPE OF GRANT Usually one-off for specific projects

TYPE OF BENEFICIARY Integrated schools, community playgroups, play buses, youth clubs, women's groups, cross-community holiday schemes

RESTRICTIONS No grants to individuals. Holiday schemes outside the island of Ireland are not considered. Core-funding or salaries rarely considered. Applications from mentally or physically handicapped support groups are currently rarely accepted

BENEFICIAL AREA Northern Ireland

FINANCES
- Year 1995
- Grants £76,559
- Income £116,000
- Assets £184,702

TRUSTEES His Honour Judge Hubert Dunn, QC, Mrs G Darling (NI), Mrs M Garland, Mrs J Herdman (NI), Mrs E Kennedy, Mrs D Lindsay (NI), Mrs M Mackie (NI), Mrs A McKenzie-Hill, Mr S Tester, CA

PUBLICATIONS Annual Report, descriptive brochure

SUBMISSION OF APPLICATIONS Trustees meet quarterly. Grants under £500 can be approved between meetings. Applications to Women Caring Trust, c/o 70–72 Lisburn Road, Lisburn, Belfast BT9 6AF, in writing, with details of the proposed project, Statement of Accounts and an outline budget. All projects are visited and monitored by NI Trustees or their representatives. At any time in writing

CORRESPONDENT General Secretary, Women Caring Trust, 38 Ebury Street, London SW1W 0LU

CLASSIFICATIONS
- Children and youth – general
- Adventure centres and playgrounds
- Community groups
- Day centres and nurseries
- Holidays

C.C. NO 264843　　　　**ESTABLISHED** 1972

■ Edwin Woodhouse Charitable Trust

OBJECTS General benefit of charities in Leeds

POLICY OF TRUSTEES The income is applied in promoting and maintaining such charities and charitable purposes arising within pre-1974 boundary of Leeds. Specific causes eligible for assistance are: (a) education and learning, (b) hospital and convalescent treatment, (c) provision of open space, (d) general improvement of the City of Leeds. The Trustees favour those charities who provide assistance with heating, lighting, food, children and the elderly

TYPE OF GRANT Cash grant up to a normal maximum of £100

RESTRICTIONS Grants to charitable organisations only. No grants to individuals

BENEFICIAL AREA City of Leeds pre-1974 City Boundary only. Postal Districts LS1–LS17

SAMPLE GRANTS NW Leeds Scout Troop
South Leeds Children's Holiday Fund
Dragonfly Holidays

FINANCES
- Year 1994
- Grants £900
- Income £1,300
- Assets £21,000

TRUSTEES W M Wrigley, L N Roberts, Miss A S Duchart

SUBMISSION OF APPLICATIONS The Trustees meet once a year in September. Fully committed – no applications accepted

CORRESPONDENT W M Wrigley, 117 The Headrow, Leeds LS1 5JX

CLASSIFICATIONS
- Centres, clubs and institutes

C.C. NO 224936　　　　**ESTABLISHED** 1924

■ Woodlands Trust

OBJECTS General charitable purposes

POLICY OF TRUSTEES Preference to charities of which the Trust has special interest, knowledge or association

TYPE OF GRANT One-off payments, some recurrent donations

TYPE OF BENEFICIARY Youth 16–25 linked in with disablement, mental illness, community, environment, music, homelessness, counselling. Elderly, and projects personally known to Trustees

RESTRICTIONS No consideration will be given to the cost of buildings, but will consider alterations, extensions, furnishings and equipment. No individuals

BENEFICIAL AREA West Midlands, St Albans, London within the boundaries of the M25

FINANCES
- **Year** 1995
- **Grants** £48,000
- **Income** £44,000
- **Assets** £756,378

TRUSTEES J D W Field, J C Barratt, Miss J Steele, Mrs R M Bagshaw, Mrs J N Houston

NOTES NB Following a meeting of the Trustees held end of September 1994, it was resolved that the trust funds of the Acorn Trust and the Mary James Trust be applied for the general charitable purposes of the Woodlands Trust

SUBMISSION OF APPLICATIONS Six monthly. The Trust Administrator will only enter into correspondence if: (a) further information is required concerning the appeal, (b) the appeal has been placed on the Trustees' next agenda. Notification will then be given as to the Trustees' decision

CORRESPONDENT The Trust Administrator, Box W, White Horse Court, 25c North Street, Bishop's Stortford, Herts CM23 2LD

CLASSIFICATIONS
- Children and youth – general
- Adventure centres and playgrounds
- Centres, clubs and institutes
- Homes and hostels
- Special needs housing
- Youth organisations (eg Guides, Scouts, YWCA etc)

C.C. NO 259569   **ESTABLISHED** 1969

■ The Woodroffe Benton Foundation

OBJECTS (a) Financial assistance in times of disaster on behalf of individuals in need within the UK through registered charitable bodies (b) Provision of sheltered accommodation (c) Promotion of education – especially at Queen Elizabeth Grammar School in Ashbourne with scholarships, etc (d) Conservation (e) General charitable purposes

TYPE OF GRANT Starter finances, recurrent and single grants

RESTRICTIONS None, provided that the grants are made within the objects of the Foundation. Grants are not made outside the UK. Grants only made to registered national charities, not to individuals

BENEFICIAL AREA UK, Derbyshire (so far as education is concerned)

FINANCES
- **Year** 1995
- **Grants** £140,650
- **Income** £156,074
- **Assets** £3,766,384

TRUSTEES J J Hope (Chairman), C G Russell, FCA, G R Bartlett, Miss C Clout, K P W Stoneley, JP, MSc, FCIS, ATII (Secretary)

SUBMISSION OF APPLICATIONS No application form, but advice given as to how to apply on request. Trustees meet quarterly – main grants are made annually after end of financial year in December. If applications have to be handwritten – and typewritten is preferred – then black ink should be used as applications are photocopied for the Trustees. Audited Accounts and Annual Reports are invariably required. All applications are acknowledged but further letters are only sent to successful applicants

CORRESPONDENT K P W Stoneley, JP, MSc, FCIS, ATII, 11 Park Avenue, Keymer, Hassocks, West Sussex BN6 8LT

CLASSIFICATIONS
- Homes and hostels
- Youth organisations (eg Guides, Scouts, YWCA etc)

C.C. NO 328011   **ESTABLISHED** 1988

■ The Woodward Charitable Trust

OBJECTS General charitable purposes

TYPE OF GRANT Any amount considered

TYPE OF BENEFICIARY Any considered suitable. Registered charities only

RESTRICTIONS No grants to individuals

BENEFICIAL AREA UK and overseas

FINANCES
- **Year** 1993–94
- **Grants** £248,297
- **Income** £277,470

TRUSTEES S A Woodward, Mrs C Woodward, HON & V Trustee Limited

SUBMISSION OF APPLICATIONS Applications and annual reports should be sent to Corresponsent address

CORRESPONDENT PO Box 70, Chipping Norton, Oxon OX7 6RD

CLASSIFICATIONS
- Adventure centres and playgrounds
- Counselling (inc helplines)

C.C. NO 299963   **ESTABLISHED** 1988

■ The Woolmen's Company Charitable Trust

OBJECTS General charitable purposes

POLICY OF TRUSTEES To support charities concerned with the development of wool and of the City of London

TYPE OF GRANT Usually one-off

TYPE OF BENEFICIARY No particular restrictions

RESTRICTIONS In accordance with Trustees' policy

BENEFICIAL AREA London

FINANCES
- **Year** 1995
- **Grants** £10,616
- **Income** £22,477
- **Assets** £113,396

Worshipful

Alphabetical register of grant making charitable trusts

TRUSTEES The Company

SUBMISSION OF APPLICATIONS In writing

CORRESPONDENT The Worshipful Company of Woolmen, Hollands, Hedsor Road, Bourne End, Bucks SL8 5EE

CLASSIFICATIONS
- Children and youth – general
- Development of character

C.C. NO 262211   **ESTABLISHED** 1970

■ The Worshipful Company of Blacksmiths Charitable Trust

OBJECTS To assist selected registered charities

POLICY OF TRUSTEES Scholarships and bursaries for the education and training of young blacksmiths and to provide for our own pensioners, specific causes

TYPE OF GRANT Cash

TYPE OF BENEFICIARY Charitable organisations and recognised teaching establishments for blacksmiths

RESTRICTIONS To only deal with registered charities of our choice

BENEFICIAL AREA London

FINANCES
- Year 1995
- Grants £4,000
- Income £30,000

TRUSTEES The Worshipful Company of Blacksmiths Charitable Trust

SUBMISSION OF APPLICATIONS Not required. To correspondent

CORRESPONDENT The Clerk, Worshipful Company of Blacksmiths, 27 Cheyne Walk, Grange Park, London N21 1DB

CLASSIFICATIONS
- Development of character

C.C. NO 216614   **ESTABLISHED** 1957

■ The Worshipful Company of Founders Charities

OBJECTS General charitable purposes

POLICY OF TRUSTEES Connected with Foundry Industry, support for the young or the old

TYPE OF GRANT One-off

TYPE OF BENEFICIARY Needy dependants of members of the Company or in the Foundry Industry for one Trust, open for individual application for the remaining Trusts

RESTRICTIONS Dependants of members of the Company only for one Trust, open on remaining Trusts

FINANCES
- Year 1991
- Grants £16,000

TRUSTEES The Master Wardens and Commonalty of the Founders

SUBMISSION OF APPLICATIONS Before end of May in each year

CORRESPONDENT The Clerk, The Worshipful Company of Founders, Founders' Hall, 1 Cloth Fair, London EC2Y 8DL

CLASSIFICATIONS
- Homes and hostels
- Special needs housing
- Youth organisations (eg Guides, Scouts, YWCA etc)

C.C. NO 222905   **ESTABLISHED** 1941

■ The Worshipful Company of Glass Sellers' Charity Trust

OBJECTS General charitable purposes

POLICY OF TRUSTEES To support particularly those charities with some connection with the City of London or glass industry

TYPE OF GRANT Charitable donations

TYPE OF BENEFICIARY As in Policy of Trustees

FINANCES
- Year 1994
- Grants £23,235
- Income £21,175
- Assets £73,105

TRUSTEES R Long, M R Nathan, A S Miller, R L Thomas

SUBMISSION OF APPLICATIONS To above correspondent – quarterly meetings. Trustees meet at quarterly intervals to consider applications. Appeals must be accompanied by most recently published Annual Report and Accounts. All applications will be acknowledged

CORRESPONDENT B J Rawles, 43 Aragon Avenue, Thames Ditton, Surrey KT7 0PY

CLASSIFICATIONS
- Adventure centres and playgrounds
- Centres, clubs and institutes
- Holidays

C.C. NO 253943   **ESTABLISHED** 1967

■ The Worshipful Company of Shipwrights Charitable Fund

OBJECTS Support for objectives charitable at law connected with the maritime activity of the UK, including training for maritime industry

POLICY OF TRUSTEES Support confined to charities associated with maritime industry and the City of London, including youth and educational work

TYPE OF GRANT Recurrent and one-off

TYPE OF BENEFICIARY Variable, but who are citizens of the United Kingdom of Great Britian and Northern Ireland

RESTRICTIONS Donations will only be granted to activities with a waterborne element

BENEFICIAL AREA UK

SAMPLE GRANTS £3,000 to outside training in the faculty of Marine Technology, University of Newcastle Upon Tyne
£500 to Sea Cadet units

FINANCES
- Year 1994
- Grants £48,000
- Income £74,000
- Assets £462,000

TRUSTEES The Wardens of the Company

SUBMISSION OF APPLICATIONS Address to the Clerk, Shipwrights' Company

CORRESPONDENT The Clerk, The Worshipful Company of Shipwrights, Ironmonger's Hall, Barbican, London EC2Y 8AA

Yapp

CLASSIFICATIONS
- Holidays

C.C. NO 262403 **ESTABLISHED** 1948

■ John William Wright Deceased Trust

OBJECTS General charitable purposes

POLICY OF TRUSTEES A proportion of grants is usually given to Methodist charities

TYPE OF GRANT For capital expenditure of a non-recurring nature

TYPE OF BENEFICIARY Preference is given to charities operating in Lincoln and Lincolnshire, only very exceptionally are grants made outside this area

RESTRICTIONS No grants to individuals

BENEFICIAL AREA Preference to Lincoln and Lincolnshire

SAMPLE GRANTS £100 to The Eyeless Trust – general costs
£800 to Childline – telephone helpline
£700 to Lincs Rural Activities Centre – generator
£500 to local Guides and Scouts – Scout hut
£300 to Lincoln Music Festival – masterclass for brass players

FINANCES
- Year 1995
- Grants £15,200
- Income £13,634
- Assets £204,033

TRUSTEES R D Atkinson, P R Strange, Mrs G N Harrison

NOTES Recent grants include grants to churches for organ and other repairs, grants to Lincolnshire Heritage projects, Macmillan Nurse Appeal, Shelter, NCH, Woodland Trust and Help the Aged all for work based in Lincolnshire

SUBMISSION OF APPLICATIONS By letter

CORRESPONDENT Messrs Andrew & Co, (Ref JD), St Swithin's Square, Lincoln, Lincolnshire LN2 1HB

CLASSIFICATIONS
- Children and youth – general

C.C. NO 249619 **ESTABLISHED** 1964

■ The Yapp Education and Research Trust

OBJECTS To promote and assist the advancement of education and learning and of scientific and medical research

POLICY OF TRUSTEES In general, the Trustees prefer to fund capital expenditure rather than revenue expenditure. Grants for the advancement of education and learning are normally limited to schools, universities, polytechnic colleges, and similar institutions

TYPE OF GRANT Outright grants only, not loans

TYPE OF BENEFICIARY Applicants having charitable status only

RESTRICTIONS Grants are made to applicants having charitable status only. Grants are not made to: (a) Individuals (b) Applicants seeking to raise over £20,000 (c) University expeditions (d) School buildings or development funds (e) Applicants who have received a grant from the Trust within the preceding three years

BENEFICIAL AREA United Kingdom only

SAMPLE GRANTS £1,900 to Moseley Park Grant Maintained School
£1,200 to Bradshaw County Primary School
£1,000 to Kent Schools Netball Association
£1,000 to Schools Outreach
£500 to Yorkshire Youth and Music

FINANCES
- Year 1994
- Grants £78,850
- Income £78,871
- Assets £1,160,714

TRUSTEES Rev T C Brooke, Miss A J Norman, M W Rapinet, P M Williams, P G Murray

NOTES The Trustees meet three times a year, usually in March, July, and November, to allocate grants. Completed grant application forms need to be submitted at least six weeks before the date of the Meeting at which they are to be considered

SUBMISSION OF APPLICATIONS Applicants should apply in writing to the Correspondent giving brief details of the purpose for which a grant is sought. Eligible applicants are then asked to complete a short grant application form

CORRESPONDENT L V Waumsley, Messrs Kidd Rapinet, Solicitors, 14–15 Craven Street, London WC2N 5AD

CLASSIFICATIONS
- Day centres and nurseries

C.C. NO 257145 **ESTABLISHED** 1968

Yapp Welfare

■ The Yapp Welfare Trust

OBJECTS To promote and assist any charitable activity directed to:- (a) care and housing of old people, (b) youth Clubs, youth hostels, students hostels or like institutions connected with the welfare of youth, (c) care or special education of people who are mentally or physically handicapped, (d) advancement of moral welfare

POLICY OF TRUSTEES In general, the Trustees prefer to fund capital expenditure rather than revenue expenditure. The advancement of religion as such is not regarded as an eligible object of the Trust

TYPE OF GRANT Outright grants only, not loans

TYPE OF BENEFICIARY Applicants having charitable status only

RESTRICTIONS Grants are made to applicants having charitable status only. Grants are not made to:- (a) individuals, (b) applicants seeking to raise over £10,000, (c) university expeditions, (d) school building or development funds, (e) applicants who have received a grant from the Trust within the preceding three years

BENEFICIAL AREA UK only

SAMPLE GRANTS £2,000 to Lurgan YMCA
£600 to Norwich (5th) Boys' Brigade Company
£500 to Buxton Sea Cadets
£500 to City of Coventry Corps of Drums
£500 to Cumbria North and East Scouts Association

FINANCES
- Year 1994
- Grants £132,780
- Income £162,606
- Assets £2,385,737

TRUSTEES The Rev T C Brooke, Miss A J Norman, M W Rapinet, P M Williams, P G Murray

NOTES The Trustees meet three times a year, usually in March, July and November, to allocate grants. Completed Grant Application Forms need to be submitted at least six weeks before the date of the Meeting at which they are to be considered

SUBMISSION OF APPLICATIONS Applicants should apply in writing to the Correspondent giving brief details of the purpose for which a grant is sought. Eligible applicants are then asked to complete a short Grant Application Form

CORRESPONDENT L V Waumsley, Messrs Kidd Rapinet, 14–15 Craven Street, London WC2N 5AD

CLASSIFICATIONS
- Homes and hostels

C.C. NO 257144   **ESTABLISHED** 1968

■ The Yorkshire Bank Charitable Trust

OBJECTS General charitable purposes

POLICY OF TRUSTEES Charities considered for support include those engaged in youth work, facilities for the less able-bodied and mentally handicapped, counselling and community work in depressed areas, with some support also being given for education and the arts. The Trustees would be unlikely to make more than one donation within any 12-month period

TYPE OF GRANT Usually one-off for a specific project or part of a project

TYPE OF BENEFICIARY Registered charities working in the fields outlined under 'policy'

RESTRICTIONS Registered charities only. Applications from individuals, including students, are ineligible. No grants made in response to general appeals from national organisations

BENEFICIAL AREA Within the area covered by branches of the Bank, ie in England from north of the Thames Valley to Newcastle upon Tyne

FINANCES
- Year 1994
- Grants £93,365
- Income £139,628
- Assets £731,034

TRUSTEES G R Hamilton, G P Savage, D T Gallagher

SUBMISSION OF APPLICATIONS At any time. Applications should include relevant details of the need the intended project is designed to meet

CORRESPONDENT R G Kitley, Secretary, Yorkshire Bank plc, 20 Merrion Way, Leeds, West Yorkshire LS2 8NZ

CLASSIFICATIONS
- Children and youth – general

C.C. NO 326269   **ESTABLISHED** 1982

■ Young Explorers' Trust

OBJECTS To increase the opportunities for young people to take part in exploration, discovery and challenging adventure and to make these expeditions safer and more worthwhile

POLICY OF TRUSTEES To encourage activities of an enterprising and exploratory nature involving an expedition

TYPE OF GRANT Lump sum, varying from £100–£500. The Trust also administers various trade awards

TYPE OF BENEFICIARY Schools, youth group and peer group expeditions involved in expedition activities abroad. Expeditions with disadvantaged members are encouraged to apply. Groups need not be members of the Trust

RESTRICTIONS Grants are only awarded to groups going on an overseas expedition, of at least two weeks duration in the field, which have most of their members below the age of 20. Newly developed groups and expeditions with disadvantaged members are eligible. Applications from individuals will not be considered. Only those following Young Explorers' Trust 'Code of Practice'

BENEFICIAL AREA UK

FINANCES
- Year 1994–95
- Grants £650
- Income £86,000
- Assets £10,000

TRUSTEES A B Ware, A C Jermy, R Crabtree, G Derrick, R Gilbert, J Hegarty, R Putnam, J Warr

PUBLICATIONS 'Code of Practice for Youth Expeditions' 1995, 'Safe and Responsible Youth Expeditions' 1995, 'Environmental Responsiblity for Expeditions' 1995

NOTES The Trust also administers a fund, the Jim Bishop Awards, for individuals, under the age of 19, taking part in adventurous activities at home or abroad. Forms from YET to be returned by 1st February

SUBMISSION OF APPLICATIONS Apply for forms which must be completed and returned via referee to the Screening Panel Convenor by 1st December or 1st May usually at least six months in advance of the expedition

Young

CORRESPONDENT Young Explorers' Trust, 1 Kensington Gore, London SW7 2AR

CLASSIFICATIONS
- Advancement in life
- Development of character

C.C. NO 1006211   **ESTABLISHED** 1972